LEGAL REASONING
AND LEGAL WRITING

LEGAL REASONING
AND LEGAL WRITING

Structure, Strategy, and Style

Richard K. Neumann, Jr.
Associate Professor of Law
Hofstra University

Little, Brown and Company
Boston Toronto London

Library of Congress Catalog Card No. 89-063541
ISBN 0-316-60379-1

Second Printing

EB

Published simultaneously in Canada
by Little, Brown & Company (Canada) Limited

Printed in the United States of America

for

Richard K. Neumann, Sr. and
Marjorie Batter Neumann,

who taught everything
on which this book is based

Themistocles . . . beyond all others deserves our admiration. . . . [H]e had the power to reach the right conclusion in matters that have to be settled on the spur of the moment and do not admit of long discussions, and in estimating what was likely to happen, his forecasts of the future were always more reliable than those of others. He could perfectly well explain any subject with which he was familiar, and even outside his own department he was still capable of giving an excellent opinion. He was particularly remarkable at looking into the future and seeing there the hidden possibilities for good or evil. To sum him up in a few words, it may be said that [he] was supreme at doing precisely the right thing at precisely the right moment.

—Thucydides

Summary of Contents

Table of Contents

I

INTRODUCTION TO LAW AND ITS STUDY   1

1. An Introduction to American Law   3

III
CONSTRUCTING PROOF OF A CONCLUSION OF LAW   **87**

6. Working with Rules   **89**

7. Organizing Proof of a Conclusion of Law   **111**

8. Selecting Authority   **127**

Preface

This is a text both for first-year legal writing and moot court programs and for second-year appellate advocacy courses and competitions. Most students are so challenged by the writing and reasoning problems in these settings that they benefit from a unified treatment through progressively more difficult stages of instruction on closely related skills. A teacher in a first-year program can use a large number of the book's features to teach legal writing and the reasoning that goes into it. In a second-year appellate advocacy course or competition, the text shows students how to carry that instruction to a much more sophisticated level. The text has been designed so that it can be used in the first year alone, in the first and second years together, or in the second year alone.

Legal reasoning and legal writing are taught together in this text because the reasoning and writing processes are so inseparable that one cannot fully be taught without the other. For several years now, legal writing teachers have known that writing is better learned when combined with at least some instruction in legal reasoning. But it is also true that legal reasoning is learned more thoroughly when combined with legal writing. Because the act of writing forces the writer to test thought in order to express it fully and precisely, complex analysis cannot be said to be complete until it is written and written well. Every lawyer has experienced over and over again the abandonment of an idea that felt valuable when thought about, sounded valuable when spoken, but nevertheless proved faulty when — in the end — it "wouldn't write." And every lawyer has experienced the obverse as well: sitting down to write with a single idea and finding that the act of writing draws the idea out, fertilizes it, causes it to sprout limbs and roots, to germinate, and to spread into a forest of ideas.

In addition, the text focuses on the construction of proof of a conclusion of law and teaches format, style, and grammar collaterally. The goal is to help students learn how to make the kind of writing decisions that center on the need to prove analysis. Most students have enormous difficulties learning to construct proof. Where format and style receive primary emphasis, the problem is compounded because the student has been invited to mimic the customary appearance of a document, rather than to think through its content and inner logic. At the same time, format makes more sense to students who have already learned the dynamics of proof, and legal writing's heightened requirements of style and grammar may be easier to accept when they are explained as ways of clarifying proof.

Accordingly, the heart of the text weds legal writing and legal reasoning instruction together into an explanation of all the skills needed to plan and write a Discussion in an office memorandum or an Argument in a persuasive memorandum or brief. Chapters 6 through 13 show how to use the structure of rules; organize proof; select authority; integrate research with writing; work with precedent, statutes, and facts; and use citations and quotations. Chapters 14 and 15 add the skills of argument: strategic thinking, theory development, understanding the judicial audience, argumentation techniques, and argumentation ethics. And the exercises in Chapters 6, 10, 11, and 12 are designed to help students get inside the process of creation and learn something about how to make professional decisions.

The earlier chapters (1–5) are a preparation for that, introducing foundation concepts of law and its study (the origin of common law, the process of litigation, causes of action and affirmative defenses, dissecting opinions and briefing cases, and the interdependence among facts, issues, and rules), as well as the style and process of legal writing (language as a professional tool, legal writing art forms, differences between predictive and persuasive writing, planning and rewriting, clarity, conciseness, forcefulness, punctuation, and effective paragraphing).

And later chapters (16–21) show how to build the rest of the document around the Discussion or Argument (fact statements, questions presented, point headings, memo and brief writing, and appellate practice). Chapter 22 covers oral argument.

On the inside covers of the book is a list of questions that students should ask themselves while working through successive drafts of a document. Each question represents a recurring problem in student writing — the sort that a teacher marks over and over again on student papers. A page number appears in parentheses after each item on the list. Students can use the list to make sure they have attended to likely problems. And teachers can use it to ease the burden of writing so many comments on student papers. Rather than write the same or a similar comment repetitiously, a teacher can circle the problem passage on the student's paper and write the question number ("4-A," for example) in the margin. At the page indicated on the inside covers, the student will find a complete explanation of the problem, what causes it, and how to fix it.

Acknowledgments

I am grateful to many people who generously contributed their thoughts to the development of this book. Among them are Burton Agata, Lisa Aisner, Aaron Balasny, Sara Bennett, Susan Brody, Susan Bryant, Robin Charlow, Barbara Child, Alice Duecker, Deborah Ezbitski, Neal Feigenson, Eric Freedman, William Ginsburg, John Gregory, Marc Grinker, Donna Hill, Joseph Holmes, Ellen James, Martha Krisel, Eric Lane, Ed McDougal, Juliet Neisser, Stuart Rabinowitz, John Regan, Carole Shapiro, Suzanne Spector, and Aaron Twerski, as well as the anonymous reviewers who examined the manuscript for Little, Brown. Research assistance was provided by Fusae Nara, Dan Wallach, and Carolyn Weissbach. Elliott Milstein and Joseph Harbaugh had much influence on the pedagogy that has shaped this book. Richard Heuser, Richard Audet, Cate Rickard, and their colleagues at Little, Brown have enormous insight into the qualities that make a text useful; their perceptiveness and creativity ultimately caused this book to become a different and far better text than it otherwise would have been. And Deborah Ezbitski inspired in countless ways.

Copyright Acknowledgments

Permission to reprint copyrighted excerpts from the following is gratefully acknowledged:

D. Binder & P. Bergman, *Fact Investigation: From Hypothesis to Proof* 92-96 (1984). Copyright © 1984 by the West Publishing Co.

James P. Degnan, *The Ph.D. Illiterate,* The Washington Post, Sept. 12, 1976. Copyright © 1976 by the author and by The Washington Post.

Robert Heidt, *Recasting Behavior: An Essay for Beginning Law Stu-*

LEGAL REASONING
AND LEGAL WRITING

I
INTRODUCTION TO LAW AND ITS STUDY

1 An Introduction to American Law

§1.1 The Origin of Common Law

At Pevensey, on the south coast of England, a man named William, Duke of Normandy, came ashore, together with ten thousand soldiers and knights, on a morning in late September 1066. Finding the town unsatisfactory for his purpose, he destroyed it and moved his people nine miles east to a coastal village called Hastings. A few days later, the English king, Harold, arrived with an army of roughly the same size. The English had always fought on foot, rather than on horseback, and in a day-long battle they were cut down by the Norman knights. According to legend, Harold was at first disabled by a random arrow shot through his eye and then killed by William himself, who marched his army north, burning villages on the way and terrorizing London into submission.

Although in December he had himself crowned king of England, William controlled only a small part of the country, and in the following years he had to embark on what modern governments would call campaigns to pacify the countryside. In 1069, for example, his army marched to York and executed every English male of any age discovered along the way, flattened the town, and then marched on to Durham, burning every farm and killing every English-speaking person to be found—all with the result that seventeen years later the survey recorded in Domesday Book revealed almost no population in Yorkshire. In the five years after William landed at Pevensey, one-fifth of the population of England was killed by the Norman army of occupation or died of starvation after the Norman army burned the food supply. To atone for all this bloodshed, William later built a monastery at Hastings. For nine centuries, it has been known as Battle Abbey, and its altar sits on the spot where Harold is said to have died.

The picturesque Norman castles throughout England were built not to defend the island from further invasion, but to subjugate and imprison the English themselves while William expropriated nearly all the land in the country and gave it to Normans, who became a new aristocracy. With the exception of a few collaborators, everyone whose native language was English became — regardless of earlier social station — landless and impoverished. Normans quickly occupied even the most local positions of power, and suddenly the average English person knew no one in authority who understood English customs, English law, or even much of the language. William himself never learned to speak it.

Pollock and Maitland call the Norman Conquest "a catastrophe which determines the whole future history of English law."[1] Although the Conquest's influences on English law were many, for the moment let us focus only on two.

The first concerns the language of law and lawyers. Norman French was the tongue of the new rulers, and eventually it became the language of the courts as well. The sub-language called Norman Law French could still be heard in courtrooms many centuries later,[2] even after the everyday version of Norman French had merged with Middle English to produce Modern English, a language rich in nuance because it inherited two distinct families of vocabulary. As late as 1731, Parliament was compelled to enact a statute providing that all court documents "shall be in the English tongue only, and not in Latin or French."[3]

Law is filled with terms of art expressing technical and specialized meanings, and a large proportion of these terms survive from Norman Law French. Some of the more familiar examples include *appeal, arrest, assault, attorney, contract, counsel, court, crime, defendant, evidence, judge, jury, plaintiff, suit,* and *verdict.* In the next few pages, you will also encounter *allegation, cause of action, demurrer, indictment, party,* and *plead.*[4] And in the next few months you will come across *battery, chose in action, curtesy, damages, devise, easement, estoppel, felony, larceny, lien, livery of seisin, misdemeanor, replevin, slander, tenant,* and *tort.* Even the bailiff's cry that still opens many American court sessions — "Oyez, oyez, oyez!" — is the Norman French equivalent of "Listen up!"[5]

---

§1.1 1. F. Pollock & F. Maitland, *The History of English Law Before the Time of Edward I* 79 (2d ed. 1899).

2. Blackstone called Norman Law French a "badge of slavery."4 W. Blackstone, *Commentaries* *416. Before the Conquest, courts were conducted in English, and law was written in English or Latin.

3. Records in English Act, 1731, 4 Geo. II ch. 26.

4. Begin now the habit of looking up every unfamiliar term of art in a law dictionary, which you should keep close at hand while studying for each of your courses.

5. Some words entered the English language directly from the events of the Conquest itself. The English learned to call the bowels of a castle a dungeon because that is what the Normans called it, and because no such places had existed in England before Normans started chaining the English up in dungeons. And in the law school course in property, you will soon become familiar with various types of *fees: fee simple absolute, fee simple conditional, fee simple defeasible, fee tail.* These are not money paid for services. They are forms of property rights, and they are descended directly from the feudal enfeoffments that William introduced into England in order to distribute the country's land among his followers. Even today, these terms appear in the French word order, with modifiers following the noun.

The second, and more important, influence concerns the way law is created. It is a comparatively modern invention for a legislature to "pass a law." (Lawyers say "enact a statute.") The embryonic medieval parliaments of England and Scandinavia instead made more specific decisions, such as when to plunder Visby or whether to banish Hrothgar. Although in some countries law might come from royal decree, in England before the Conquest it arose more often from the custom of each locality, as known to and enforced by the local courts. What was legal in one village or shire might be illegal (because it offended local custom) in the next. "This crazyquilt of decentralized judicial administration was doomed after 1066. From the time of the Norman Conquest, . . . the steady development in England was one of increasing dominance of the royal courts of justice over the local, customary-law courts."[6] The reason was that the newly created Norman aristocracy, which now operated the local courts, got into conflict with the Norman monarch over the spoils of power, while the English, defeated in their own country, began to find more justice in the king's courts than in their local lords' capricious enforcement of what had once been reliable custom.

Because communication and travel were so primitive, the "crazyquilt" pattern of customary law had not before troubled the English. Instead, it had given them an agreeable opportunity to develop, through local habit, rules that suited each region and village relatively well. For two reasons, however, the king's courts would not enforce customary law. The practical reason was that a judge of a national court cannot know the customary law of each locality. The political reason was that the monarchy's goal was to centralize power in itself and its institutions. Out of this grew a uniform set of rules, common to every place in the country and eventually known as the common law of England. Centuries later, British colonists in North America were governed according to that common law, and, upon declaring their independence, adopted it as each state's original body of law. Although a fair proportion of the common law has since been changed through statute or judicial decision, it remains the foundation of our legal system, and common law methods of reasoning dominate the practice and study of law.

In a medieval England without a "law-passing" legislature and with a king far too busy to create a body of law by decree, where did this common law come from? The somewhat oversimplified answer is that the judges figured it out for themselves. They started from the few rules that plainly could not be missing from medieval society, and over centuries—faced with new conditions and reasoning by analogy—they discovered other rules of common law, as though each rule had been there from the beginning, but hidden. The central tool in this process has been a rule called *stare decisis,* Latin for "let stand that which has been decided," or, more loosely, "follow the rules courts have followed in the past." Although a lay person might assume that the law is made only in legislatures and that the only value to reading judicial decisions would be to see illustrations of how the law is

---

6. Jones, *Our Uncommon Common Law,* 42 Tenn. L. Rev. 443, 450 (1975).

applied, in common law countries[7] judicial opinions[8] are not mere illustrations of law at work. In a common law country, decisions — or *precedent* — are one of two sources of law, statutes and statute-like enactments being the other.

Thus, in order to discover and state the law, a lawyer must possess the skills of interpreting judicial opinions, interpreting statutes, researching in law books to find statutes and cases, and expressing analysis cogently, both orally and in writing. Each of these skills is so complex that the three years of law school are not enough to master them, and an effective attorney thus continues long after graduation to learn new techniques of interpretation, research, and expression. Before you can begin to interpret precedent, you will need to understand some of the fundamental concepts of litigation and judicial procedure.

§1.2 Causes of Action and Affirmative Defenses

Realistically, the law cannot remedy every wrong, and many problems are more effectively resolved through other means, such as the political process, mediation, bargaining, and economic and social pressure. Unless the legal system directs its resources to resolving those problems it handles best, it would collapse under the sheer weight of an unmanageable workload and would thus be prevented from attempting even the problem-solving it does well. Thus, a fundamental task in law is the definition of wrongs for which courts will provide relief.

A harm the law will remedy is called a *cause of action* (or, in some courts, a *claim* or a *claim for relief*). A cause of action is a factual formula that, when satisfied, entitles a plaintiff to a court-ordered remedy unless the defendant can prove an *affirmative defense.* An affirmative defense is another factual formula that, when satisfied, deprives a plaintiff of a right to a remedy, even if that plaintiff has been able to prove a cause of action. Lawyers call these factual formulas *tests,* and each constituent part of a test is called an *element.* A test is satisfied only where each of the elements can be identified among the facts of a case.

For example, where a plaintiff proves that a defendant intentionally confined him and that the defendant was not a law enforcement officer acting within the scope of an authority to arrest, the plaintiff has proved a cause of action called *false imprisonment.* The test is expressed as a list of elements: "False imprisonment consists of (1) a confinement (2) of the plaintiff (3) by the defendant (4) intentionally (5) where the defendant is not a sworn law enforcement officer acting within his or her authority." Proof of false im-

---

7. The doctrine of stare decisis is generally observed only in countries whose law is descended from English law. With very rare exceptions, stare decisis is not observed, for example, in continental Europe or in Latin America.

8. Lawyers call judicial opinions "cases," even though the opinions represent only a small part of what happens in litigation. A lawsuit may have begun years before and may sometimes continue for years after a particular opinion is written.

prisonment would customarily result in a court's awarding a remedy called *damages,* which obliges the defendant to compensate the plaintiff in money for the latter's injuries. But that is not always so: if the defendant can prove that she caught the plaintiff shoplifting in her store and restrained him only until the police arrived, she might have an affirmative defense that is sometimes called a *shopkeeper's privilege.* Where a defendant proves a shopkeeper's privilege, a court will not award the plaintiff damages, even if he has proved false imprisonment. Again, the test is expressed as a list of elements: "A shopkeeper's privilege exists where (1) a shopkeeper or shopkeeper's employee (2) has reasonable cause to believe that (3) the plaintiff (4) has shoplifted (5) in the shopkeeper's place of business and (6) the confinement occurs in a reasonable manner, for a reasonable time, and no more than needed to detain the plaintiff for law enforcement purposes." (Notice how the law makes its decisions through *burdens of proof:* the plaintiff has the burden of proving the facts that, added together, substantiate his cause of action, and the defendant has the burden of proving the facts that substantiate any affirmative defense she might raise.)

Notice, too, that elements fall into categories. Some elements encompass physical activity ("a confinement"); other elements specify states of mind ("intentionally"); others address status or condition ("a shopkeeper or shopkeeper's employee"); and still others require abstract qualities ("in a reasonable manner, for a reasonable time, and no more than needed to detain the plaintiff for law enforcement purposes"). State-of-mind and abstract-quality elements will probably puzzle you more than others will. The plaintiff, for example, might be able to prove a confinement through a witness who saw a door being locked. And if the shopkeeper's own testimony is not good enough to prove her status, she can probably produce a license to do business at the place where the plaintiff says he was confined, or any other of the multitude of documents or witnesses that can be used to show that one operates a store. These elements are straightforward because they are tangible.

But how will the plaintiff be able to prove that the defendant acted "intentionally," and how will the defendant be able to show that she confined the plaintiff "in a reasonable manner, for a reasonable time, and no more than needed to detain the plaintiff for law enforcement purposes"? Because thoughts and abstractions cannot be witnessed, the law is left to judge an abstraction or a party's state of mind from the actions and other events surrounding it. If, for example, the plaintiff can prove that the defendant took him by the arm, pulled him into a room, and then locked the door herself, he may be able to carry his burden of showing that she acted "intentionally." And the defendant may be able to carry her burden of proving the confinement to have been reasonably carried out if she can show that when she took the defendant by the arm, he had been trying to run from the store; that she called the police immediately; and that she turned the defendant over to the police as soon as they arrived.

Because each state can devise its own rules of law—within limits explored in the courses on constitutional law, criminal law, and criminal procedure—the elements of a given test may differ from state to state. Even though virtually all states condition a shopkeeper's privilege on proof of the shopkeeper's "reasonable cause to believe" (or similar words to the same effect), a state could require much more (such as "belief held to a moral certainty") or even much less (perhaps "mere suspicion, regardless of its basis").

In designing a lawsuit, the plaintiff's attorney will choose a provable view of the facts and a credible interpretation of the law that should combine to give the plaintiff a cause of action that will withstand affirmative defenses. That way of looking at the controversy is called a *theory of the case.* The defendant's lawyer must design a theory, too, although the defense theory will naturally be intended to accomplish the opposite of the plaintiff's theory. Theory design is one of the most difficult, challenging, and creative tasks of lawyering, and it is one that we will explore in detail in later chapters.

§1.3   An Overview of the Process of Litigation

Zoologists and botanists speak of an organism's life cycle, the span of time between conception and death during which the organism may assume a variety of different forms. At different times, for instance, the same creature might take the form of an almost immeasurably small egg, a larva, an object hidden in a cocoon, or a butterfly. A lawsuit goes through a similar life cycle.

A lawsuit typically is conceived during an interview in an attorney's office, where a person who has experienced difficulty asks the attorney for assistance. Assuming that the client and attorney decide that the most effective strategy is to sue, the life cycle, depending on the circumstances, may grow through (1) an embryonic phase of *service of process, pleadings,* and *motions* challenging the pleadings; (2) a pretrial phase of fact *discovery,* negotiation, and additional motions; (3) a trial phase in a lower court; (4) a post-trial phase of motions challenging aspects of the trial; (5) a phase of *appeal* to one or more appellate courts; and (6) in the event of *reversal,* a post-appeal phase in which the litigation is returned to the trial court for a proceeding (such as a new trial) ordered by an appellate court. The vast majority of suits, however, for one reason or another do not complete the full cycle, most often where the attorneys are able to negotiate a compromise. Once litigation begins, the person who has consulted the attorney is transformed into a *plaintiff* (or, in some cases, a *petitioner* or *claimant*), and the person who is sued becomes a *defendant* (or, in some cases, a *respondent*). Collectively, they are the *parties.*

§1.3.1   Phase 1: Pleadings and Service of Process

A lawsuit begins the first phase of its life cycle in the form of a *service of process,* which is the delivery (either literally or *constructively*) to the defendant of a document called a *summons*.[1] The summons performs the dual functions of (1) notifying the defendant that a lawsuit (also called an *action*) has been started against her, and (2) bringing the defendant under the power of the court in which the case is to be tried. The power of a court to adjudicate is called its *jurisdiction*, a subtle and complex concept that is a primary theme of the first-year course in civil procedure.

The lawsuit continues the first phase of its life cycle in the form of *pleadings*, which are documents submitted[2] by the parties to outline the most critical facts that they intend to prove at trial and thus to narrow and define the controversy between them. The plaintiff begins with a *complaint* (called a *bill* or *declaration* in some courts). There the plaintiff must allege facts that, taken together, constitute a cause of action. The complaint is usually served at the same time as the summons.

The defendant can respond to the summons and complaint with either or both of two steps:

The defendant's first option is to move to dismiss. Such a *motion*[3] can be made on any of a number of grounds. In law school textbooks, the ground you will most often encounter is the defendant's assertion that the plaintiff's complaint should be dismissed because it does not allege facts that — even if proven — would constitute a cause of action.[4] The idea behind this procedure is that the plaintiff should not be permitted to tie up the court system with a trial that he is doomed to lose even if he were to prove everything claimed in the complaint. The purpose of a trial is to determine the relevant facts, and a trial is a waste of effort if the plaintiff's claims — even if true — do not add up to a cause of action. For example, assume that the complaint alleges that the defendant accidentally closed and thus inadvertently locked a door that provided the only means of escaping a room in which the plaintiff, unknown to the defendant, was sitting. Such a complaint should be

§1.3   1. The term *service* refers to the delivery—to a party, an attorney, or a witness—of any litigation document (also called a "paper," regardless of the number of pages). Although technically the phrase *service of process* can mean service of any litigation paper, most lawyers will—unless the context suggests otherwise—understand the phrase to mean service of a summons.

2. When a lawyer "submits" a document, that document is filed with the court clerk after a copy of it is served on the opposing party (or, after the litigation has begun, on the opposing party's attorney). Actually, the word *submit* is so fuzzy that lawyers do not often use it in this sense. For precision, lawyers often say that a document has been "served and filed."

3. A motion is a request, by a party, for a court order. An order is a court's command that something be done or not be done. When a defendant moves to dismiss a complaint, he asks that the court grant an order commanding that the complaint be deemed a nullity. If the motion is granted, the result is not that the court clerk tears up the complaint and throws it away. Instead, both the complaint and the order are placed in the court's file on the case. Even years later, both documents can be read by anyone who inspects the file, but the order destroys the legal effect of the complaint.

4. These decisions are good teaching vehicles because a court must explicate the law governing a particular cause of action to determine whether a complaint states that cause of action. Depending on the procedural rules governing the court in which the suit has been brought, a defendant might also choose to make such a motion on the grounds that the court lacks jurisdiction over the defendant (an issue you will encounter often in the course on civil procedure); that the court lacks jurisdiction over the subject matter of the litigation; that venue is improper; that the issues between the parties have already been resolved in another action; that another action already pending would dispose of the same issues; and so forth.

dismissed because it lacks an allegation that the defendant intentionally confined the plaintiff and because that lack suggests that the plaintiff is unable to prove the element of intent. Depending on the state whose courts are involved, a motion to dismiss on this basis is called a *motion to dismiss for failure to state a cause of action*, a *motion to dismiss for failure to state a claim*, or a *demurrer*. In federal courts, the motion is one *to dismiss for failure to state a claim upon which relief can be granted*.[5] These motions all attack the sufficiency of the complaint. If the defendant wins such a motion, the complaint is stricken and the plaintiff loses the suit unless he is able to serve and file an amended complaint that would survive a similar motion.[6]

The defendant's alternative is to serve an *answer*. In fact, a defendant must serve and file an answer if she has not moved to dismiss the complaint or if she made such a motion and lost it. Put another way, a motion to dismiss is optional, but an answer is required unless the motion is made and granted.[7] The answer must admit or deny each of the allegations in the complaint and may also pose one or more affirmative defenses by alleging additional facts. In the answer, the defendant might also plead a *counter-claim*, in which the roles are reversed and the defendant seeks relief from the plaintiff for an alleged cause of action. If the defendant pleads a counter-claim, the plaintiff must serve a *reply*, which admits or denies the allegations in the counterclaim.

Although a motion attacking the sufficiency of the complaint calls for a ruling from the trial court, an answer, which is intended to outline the defendant's side of the case, does not. If the defendant has served and filed only an answer, the case proceeds in the general direction of trial. The reason for this distinction is that, while an answer merely responds to the allegations in the complaint so that the court and the parties can learn which allegations are disputed, a motion challenging the sufficiency of the complaint is a demand that the court dismiss the complaint and terminate the case without further proceedings.

---

5. *See* Rule 12(b)(6) of the Federal Rules of Civil Procedure. (In all likelihood, you have already purchased a copy of the Federal Rules as assigned reading for the course in civil procedure. You cannot become an effective attorney without developing procedure sense, which is an intuitive understanding of how the rules of procedure work. You can begin acquiring that sense by consulting a rule whenever you read or hear anything about it that seems new to you.)

6. A plaintiff gets another chance to plead because, in dismissing a complaint, a court decides only that the complaint does not *state* a cause of action. The plaintiff might actually *have* a cause of action but, for one reason or another, might have failed to articulate it properly in the complaint. In some courts, when a complaint is dismissed for failure to state a cause of action, the plaintiff has the right to serve and file an amended complaint intended to cure the problems exposed by the motion. In other courts, a plaintiff can do so only if the court grants permission. If the amended complaint can survive another motion to dismiss, the plaintiff's action is resuscitated and continues through its life cycle. If not, the action itself is dismissed, which is the equivalent of burying the litigation.

7. In the course on civil procedure, you will learn of the care an attorney must take in deciding whether to move before answering. Although many defenses can be raised either by motion or in an answer, some defenses are *waived* unless made by motion.

§1.3.2 Phase 2: Between Pleadings and Trial

If the action has not been dismissed in the pleading phase, the attorneys will proceed to conduct *discovery*. They might also negotiate, and they might make motions for *summary judgment*.

Discovery is a collection of formal and informal procedures in which each party obtains information and evidence from the other. The most frequently used discovery devices are *interrogatories* and *depositions*. Interrogatories are written questions that one party poses to the other; the answers must be in writing and under oath. A deposition, on the other hand, is an oral examination: either attorney can subpoena a witness or an opposing party, who must appear before a court reporter, take an oath, and answer questions posed by the attorney. If the parties negotiate, their attorneys will explore the possibility of resolving the case through an agreement between themselves, rather than asking a judge and perhaps a jury to decide. In the course on civil procedure, you will learn more about the tools of discovery, and later in clinical and simulated practice courses you will have an opportunity to learn about negotiation and trial preparation.

If a court grants a summary judgment, it decides the case without a trial because of the absence of an issue of fact. To understand summary judgment, you must appreciate the difference between issues of law and issues of fact. It is an *issue of law* (a question about the law) whether, in a given state, the shopkeeper's privilege requires that the defendant "reasonably believed" the plaintiff shoplifted, or whether local law requires instead a different state of mind (such as one of the possibilities mentioned at the top of page 8). On the other hand, it is an *issue of fact* (a question about a fact) whether a particular shopkeeper actually saw a plaintiff try to leave a shop with unpaid-for merchandise.

When one of the parties believes that the case lacks issues of fact— believes, in other words, that the evidence is not in conflict about what happened before the suit began—that party can move for summary judgment, asking a court to decide the case without a trial by resolving the issues of law alone. In a case with no issues of fact, summary judgment is both possible and efficient because a trial's sole purpose is to resolve factual questions through evaluation of evidence. A court will deny the motion if it concludes that there really are issues of fact. If a court sees no issues of fact but decides that the party who made the motion is not entitled to judgment, the court might deny the motion, or it might even grant summary judgment to the other party.

§1.3.3 Phase 3: Trial

At trial, the lawsuit undergoes a radical transformation. While the pretrial phase is prolonged and often preoccupied with the written word, trial is a confrontation within a concentrated period of time, dominated by *testi-*

mony from witnesses and by oral objections and argument from the attorneys.

At trial, the plaintiff must present evidence to prove facts that substantiate each element of the cause of action. If the plaintiff does not do so—and thus does not make out a *prima facie case*—he cannot win. On the other hand, if the plaintiff does prove a prima facie case, the defendant must then present evidence that negates the plaintiff's proof, evidence that proves additional facts constituting an affirmative defense, or evidence that does both. If the plaintiff makes out a prima facie case, the defendant will lose unless she either proves an affirmative defense or overcomes, with contradictory evidence, the plaintiff's prima facie proof of at least one element of the cause of action.

In a trial with a jury, the jury's role is to decide, in the form of a *verdict*, issues of fact, while the role of the judge is to decide issues of law, including issues of procedure and the admissibility of evidence. In a bench trial (where there is no jury), the judge decides both kinds of issues by making *findings of fact* and *conclusions of law*, which are set out in a written or oral opinion.

Aside from selection of the jury (if there is one), the first event in a trial is an *opening statement*, in which the plaintiff's attorney outlines the case he or she hopes to prove. The defendant's attorney follows with a similar statement. Then, during the evidence-taking phase of the trial, the plaintiff presents his case in the form of witnesses and exhibits, and, after the plaintiff *rests*, the defendant follows by doing the same thing. Sometimes—such as where the defendant raises an affirmative defense—the plaintiff may follow with additional evidence in *rebuttal*. After the evidence-taking phase is complete, the attorneys make oral *summations* of their cases to the jury (or to the judge if there is no jury). In the *charge*, the judge instructs the jury how to apply the law to whatever facts the jury might find. Because the jury may resolve only issues of fact, these *jury instructions* correspond to the judge's holdings of law in a trial to the bench. The judge's holdings (in a bench trial) or his instructions (in a jury trial) are his interpretations of the applicable substantive law. In accordance with the verdict in a jury trial, or with the findings of fact in a bench trial, the judge signs a *judgment* which, depending on who has won, either provides or denies the remedy asked for by the plaintiff (and, if the answer includes a counterclaim, likewise for the defendant).

Among the many types of motions attorneys may make at trial is one that tests the sufficiency of an opponent's evidence and that, if granted, results directly in judgment for the party making the motion. In jury trials, this is most often called a *motion for a directed verdict*. Generally, a party can make such a motion once the opponent has rested his or her case. These motions can be made more than once, but they will be granted only if the judge concludes that on the evidence a jury could not reasonably return a verdict against the party making the motion. In bench trials, the corresponding motion is most commonly called a *motion for judgment*.

The fourth and fifth phases in the lawsuit's life cycle revert to emphasis on the written word.

§1.3.4   Phase 4: Post-Trial Motions

The most important post-trial motions are the *motion to set aside the verdict and grant a new trial* and the *motion for judgment notwithstanding the verdict*. Both are made to the trial court, and both challenge the sufficiency of the evidence on which the verdict is based.

Depending on the local procedural rules, a motion to set aside the verdict and grant a new trial can be granted where the judge erred in a ruling that prejudiced the verdict, where new evidence that would have changed the verdict has been discovered, or where the verdict was at least in part the result of misconduct by a witness, an attorney, a juror, the judge, or a court employee.

The motion for judgment notwithstanding the verdict is commonly referred to as a "motion for judgment n.o.v.," from the Latin expression *non obstante veredicto* (meaning "notwithstanding the verdict"); it can be granted only where the judge denied but, in hindsight, ought to have granted an earlier motion for a directed verdict. Because courts generally prefer to give a jury at least a chance to come to an appropriate verdict, a trial judge might deny a motion for directed verdict but subsequently grant a motion for judgment n.o.v. made by the same party, even though both motions are to be decided according to the same reasoning.

§1.3.5   Phase 5: Appeal

An *appeal* is a request by the losing party for a higher court to reverse or alter one or more *rulings* by the trial court. The party taking the appeal becomes the *appellant* (or, in some instances, the *petitioner*), while the other party becomes the *appellee* (or the *respondent*). The appellate court does not retry the case. Instead, it examines the trial court's *record,* which might be made up of the pleadings, the motions, the trial transcript, the verdict, the judgment, and so forth. If the appellate court agrees that the complained-of rulings were in error, it reverses the judgment below and *remands* the case to the trial court with instructions to cure the error, perhaps by entering judgment for the appellant or by holding a new trial. On the other hand, if the appellate court finds no error, it *affirms* the judgment.

Jury verdicts are not usually reviewed on appeal, and findings of fact are reviewed infrequently. Rather, the appellant's attorney must point to specific rulings on the law by the trial judge and argue that those rulings were incorrect and *materially* led to the adverse judgment. Among the trial court rulings most often appealed are those on motions challenging the sufficiency of the complaint; motions for summary judgment; motions and objections challenging the admissibility of evidence offered at trial; motions for a directed verdict; requests for jury instructions; motions for new trials; and motions for judgment n.o.v.

Most opinions in law school casebooks record and explain the decisions on appeals that have grown out of these or similar motions. In order to understand what the court has done in these opinions, you must understand the case's *procedural posture,* a concept that includes the type of motion involved, the party who made it, the context in which it was made, and whether the decision was made in a trial court or in an appellate court. As you will learn, the logic used to decide the motion varies according to the procedural posture.

§1.3.6 Phase 6: Post-Appeal Proceedings

If an appellate court reverses and remands, the trial court has more work to do. That work might be much, such as holding a new trial, or it might be little, such as modifying the judgment or order appealed from so that it conforms with the decision of the appellate court. Sometimes, one of the parties concludes that the trial court has committed additional error after the remand, and yet another appeal ensues.

§1.3.7 Criminal Cases

Although the life cycle of a criminal case is generally analogous to that of civil litigation, the procedures and terminology are quite different.

In a criminal case, a *prosecuting attorney* represents the government, which alone can start the litigation. The initial allegations are in an *indictment* or *information,* which a criminal defendant might move to dismiss just as a civil defendant might move to dismiss a complaint. There are no interrogatories or depositions in a criminal case, but there may be a *preliminary hearing.* If at trial the defendant is *convicted,* the remedy will be a *sentence,* such as imprisonment, probation, or a fine. In the course on criminal procedure, you will learn about *suppression motions, grand juries,* and other matters peculiar to criminal litigation.

A case is not criminal merely because a government is a party. Governments often can sue and be sued in civil actions as well. A relatively simple example occurs where a private car collides with a truck owned by a government: generally, the government and the owner of the car can sue each other in civil proceedings to determine who pays the cost of repairs. If the police believe either driver violated the traffic laws, that driver might be prosecuted in a separate criminal or quasi-criminal proceeding.

§1.3.8 The Adversary System: An Introduction

Although the legislative and executive branches of government are accustomed to taking the initiative themselves in making decisions and solving problems, one of the distinguishing features of the judicial branch is its passivity. Judges are permitted to solve only those problems that have been presented by the parties to a lawsuit and only those problems that have been presented in the required procedural formats, largely in the motions and

14

appeals about which you have just read. Litigation is thus *"party-initiated* and *party-controlled.* The case is organized and the issues defined by exchanges between the parties. . . . The trial judge is a neutral arbiter of their interactions who decides questions of law only if they are put in issue by an appropriate move of a party."[8]

Judicial passivity is a product of the *adversary system,* which is peculiar to those countries whose legal institutions are descended from the English common law. Ramifications of the adversary system permeate every aspect of the American legal profession, determining the lawyer's role, skills, and ethical responsibilities. The adversary system survives partly because of the distrust of authority that permeates English and American history. In countries with a traditionally greater deference to government, courts operate differently. In the European inquisitorial system, for example, the judge is a far more active player. In most European countries, the judge identifies the issues, investigates the facts, selects the witnesses and questions them, and takes most of the procedural initiatives, while the attorneys sit by, interjecting now and then. In the adversary system, on the other hand, the attorneys — through their disagreements — frame the issues and dominate the litigation, and the judge is active only when the attorneys ask for a ruling.

The common law trial judge is not charged with the European trial judge's active responsibility to find the truth. Instead, when the attorneys ask a common law trial judge to make a ruling, his or her responsibility is to decide whether the party charged with a pleading or evidentiary burden has carried it. The theory of the adversary system is a theory of debate, if not combat: from the clash of two active advocates committed to differing viewpoints, the passive decision-maker should be able to separate the persuasive from the unpersuasive. The inquisitorial theory is one of semi-scientific experiment: an aggressive decision-maker should be able to find the truth by evaluating data that has not been manipulated by advocates.

Paradoxically, the common law appellate judge is considered by European legal scholars to be a figure of awesome power. What common law trial judges lack in authority to guide the progress of an individual lawsuit is more than made up for by the common law appellate judges' power to guide, through precedent, the growth of the law itself. But even common law judges cannot make law on any subject they please: with few exceptions, precedent occurs only when a court rules on issues framed by the parties. Karl Llewellyn put it this way:

> The court can decide *only* the particular dispute which is before it. When it speaks to that question, it speaks ex cathedra, with authority, . . . with an almost magical power. When it speaks to the question before it, it announces *law,* and if what it announces is new, . . . it *makes* the law. But when it speaks to any other question at all, it says mere words, which no man needs to follow. Are such words worthless? They are not. We know them as judicial *dicta;* when they are wholly off the point at issue we call them *obiter dicta —*

8. Chayes, *The Role of the Judge in Public Law Litigation,* 89 Harv. L. Rev. 1281, 1283 (1976) (emphasis in original).

words dropped along the road, wayside remarks. Yet even wayside remarks shed light on the remarker. They may be very useful in the future to him, or to us. But he will not feel bound to them, as to his ex cathedra utterance. They came not hallowed by a Delphic frenzy.[9]

§1.4   The Importance of Understanding Procedure

At this point, you are probably at least somewhat puzzled about procedure. But in law school courses, you will not be able to understand the material or explain your analysis precisely unless you understand the procedure governing the issue at hand. To gain that knowledge, do the following:

1. Read *all* of §1.3 again — and again — until the fog begins to clear away and at least the main features of the terrain become apparent.

2. Diagram the sequence of procedural events described in §1.3. It matters little what kind of diagram you make, so long as the result is complete and accurate. The act of diagramming will help you absorb the details, and you can use the diagram later to help orient yourself if you do not understand how a particular procedural event fits into the whole.

3. Throughout the year, in this course and in others, whenever you read a court's opinion, look for the procedural event that led to the decision. Refer back to §1.3 and to your legal dictionary if you have not yet learned how that procedural event operates and what its ramifications are. Courts decide different kinds of motions differently, and, unless you understand the differences, you will not be able to figure out what the court is up to.

---

9. The Bramble Bush 42 (1960).

2 An Introduction to Judicial Opinions

§2.1 The Anatomy of Opinions

In an opinion announcing a court's decision, one might find nine different kinds of pronouncement:

1. a recitation of procedural events
2. a recitation of pleaded or evidentiary events
3. a statement of the issue or issues to be decided by the court
4. a summary of the arguments made by each side
5. the court's holding on each issue
6. the rule or rules of law the court enforces through each holding
7. the court's reasoning
8. dicta
9. a statement of the relief granted or denied

Only infrequently, however, do all nine occur in the same opinion.

Opinions often begin with (1) a recitation of *procedural events* inside the litigation that have raised the issue decided by the court. Examples are motions, hearings, trial, judgment, and appeal. Although the court's description of these events may, because of unfamiliar terminology, seem at first like a fog, you must be able to understand procedural histories because the manner in which an issue is raised determines the method a court will use to decide it. A court decides a motion for a directed verdict, for example, very differently from the way it rules on a request for a jury instruction, even though both might require the court to consider the same point of law. The procedural events determine the case's *procedural posture* at the time the decision was made.

Frequently, the court will next describe (2) the *pleaded events* or the *evidentiary events* on which the ruling is based. The pleaded events and the evidentiary events are the window through which the court looks at the pre-litigation facts, the ones that preceded and caused the litigation. Ultimately, a court's knowledge about the pre-litigation facts can come only through proof offered by the parties. Therefore, the only way a court can narrate the pre-litigation facts is either by describing the evidence tending to prove them or — on a motion to dismiss a pleading — by describing the allegations in the pleading that constitute an offer to prove facts. Evidentiary events might include the testimony and exhibits at trial or at a hearing, or perhaps affidavits and exhibits submitted in connection with a motion. But if the procedural posture involved a motion challenging a pleading[1] — that is, before any evidence could be submitted — the decision would be based on the allegations in the challenged pleading (usually a complaint). (With nearly every other kind of procedural posture, the *pleaded* events would not be significant because the case would have progressed past the pleading stage.)

A court might also set out (3) a statement of the *issue or issues* before the court for decision and (4) a *summary of the arguments* made by each side, although either or both are often only implied. A court will further state (or at least imply) (5) the *holding* on each of the issues and (6) the *rule or rules* of law the court enforces in making each holding, together with (7) the *reasoning behind* — often called the *rationale for* — its decision. Somewhere in the opinion, the court might place some (8) *dicta*. (You will learn more about dicta in the next few months, but for the moment think of it as discussion unnecessary to support a holding and therefore lacking binding precedential authority.)

An opinion usually ends with (9) *a statement of the relief granted or denied.* If the opinion represents the decision of an appellate court, the relief may be an affirmance, a reversal, or a reversal combined with a direction to the trial court to proceed in a specified manner. If the opinion is from a trial court, the relief is most commonly the grant or denial of a motion.

Exercise I.   *Dissecting the Text of* Meints v. Huntington

Read *Meints v. Huntington* and determine where (if anywhere) each of these types of pronouncement occurs. Mark up the text generously and be prepared to discuss your analysis in class. Look up in a legal dictionary every unfamiliar word and every familiar word that is used in an unfamiliar way.

MEINTS v. HUNTINGTON
276 F. 245 (8th Cir. 1921)

LEWIS, District Judge. John Meints, a resident and citizen of South Dakota, brought this action against O. P. Huntington and others, residents and citizens of Rock County, Minnesota, to recover damages, on

§2.1   1. See pages 9-10.

the charge that they deported him from Minnesota to South Dakota on the night of August 19, 1918, and maltreated him on the way. After a lengthy trial, exhibited here by 1100 pages of testimony, the greater part of which relates to the loyalty of the defendants and the disloyalty of plaintiff during the late World War, there was verdict and judgment for defendants.

The plaintiff was born in Illinois, went to Rock County, Minnesota, and resided there in the town of Luverne for sixteen or seventeen years prior to the summer of 1918. In the spring of that year he was suspected of being interested in or of having contributed to the support of a Non-Partisan League newspaper printed and published in that town; on account of that, and also because it was claimed that he was disloyal, a large body of men, including some of the defendants, went to his house about midnight of June 19th, woke him up, compelled him to dress and come out, and some of them in automobiles took him across the State line into Iowa, a distance of about fifteen miles, told him not to return and left him there. He then went to St. Paul and reported the occurrence to a U.S. Government agent in the Department of Justice. That agent sent two men to Rock County to make an investigation, and on their report, Mr. Campbell of that Department advised plaintiff to return to Rock County but to go to the home of his two sons, some twelve miles out from Luverne, and remain there. He did return the latter part of July and went to his sons' home. On the night of August 3rd, men in eight or nine automobiles went out to the sons' house. Among them were the defendants Huntington, Connell, Ihlan, Miner, Turnbull and Kimmerling. They tried to enter the house by unlocking the doors with keys which they had, but were not able to do so, and finally obtained entrance by going through the cellar. They were hunting for plaintiff, but could not find him. In the late afternoon of August 19th some seventy-five to eighty men in about twenty-five automobiles, most of them from Luverne, met at a church about four miles from the sons' house, and proceeded from there in a body, arriving at the sons' house about dusk. The plaintiff and his sons saw them coming, went into the house and fastened the screen door on the inner side. The married son's wife and children were also in the house and shortly became greatly excited and alarmed, as their outcries demonstrated. Huntington and others went to the door and demanded to know where the plaintiff was, and that they be permitted to enter. The son who stood inside the door refused to open it and declined to admit them. The defendant Long at once forced the door open and a number of men immediately entered, including Long and Huntington. The son testified that he was assaulted by them and thrown out of the house. They denied that, and testified that his bloody face was caused by his own struggles while they held him to prevent violence on his part. The plaintiff stood at the head of the stairway with a gun and a fork handle. At first he refused to come down or to permit anyone to come up. The other son was induced by some of the defendants, or others with them, to go up and tell his father that they did not intend violence. The plaintiff sent back word by his son that the defendant Long might come up and he would talk with him. He then came down with Long and was taken in Huntington's automobile to Luverne. Huntington drove, and some of the other defendants were in the car with him and the plaintiff. Most of the crowd went with them, but a few turned west toward the South Dakota line before Luverne was reached. Plaintiff was held at Luverne until about eleven o'clock, and while there was refused permission to see his wife or to talk with her over the telephone. About that hour he was again put in Huntington's car. Defendants Huntington, Long, Michaelson and Smith also got in, and they started for the South Dakota line, some fifteen miles away, accompanied by another auto in which were defendants Turnbull, Connell, Kimmerling and McDermott. They reached the State line about midnight, and were stopped there by armed men whose faces were masked. They took Meints from Huntington's car, assaulted him, whipped him, threatened to shoot him, besmeared his body with tar and feathers, and told him to cross the line into South Dakota, and that if he ever returned to Minnesota he would be hanged. . . .

On the foregoing facts, . . . there can be no doubt that from the time the crowd reached the sons' house and on up to the time Meints crossed the State line, he was coerced and compelled by a show of force to submit himself to the will of others, that he was unlawfully restrained of his liberty, falsely imprisoned for the time being, . . . and that this was done . . . to drive him from the State of Minnesota. And so we say at once that the trial court erred in refusing to instruct a verdict for the plaintiff and against all defendants who took part; for it cannot be maintained that because Meints may have been, in their opinion, disloyal, and was interested in and gave support to the Non-Partisan League Newspaper, that that would put him at the mercy of defendants and invest them with the right and power to adjudge and inflict punishment, nor would the fact that the defendants were loyal men . . . have the slightest tendency to excuse or justify in the eyes of the law the acts charged against them. . . . Mr. Cooley, in his work on Torts, says [that] ". . . any restraint put by fear or force upon the actions of another is unlawful and constitutes a false imprisonment, unless a showing of justification makes it a true or legal imprisonment." . . .

The court yielded to the contention of the defendants that the plaintiff could not recover for anything that was done prior to the assaults made upon him, when the State line was reached, on the claim that he had consented to everything that had happened before that, and so instructed the jury over the objection of the plaintiff. This was prejudicial error. Can it be seriously thought that it was the wish of plaintiff to leave Rock County? His home was in Luverne, his wife was there, he had lived there for many years, all of his family and all of his interests were in Rock County; he had, to the knowledge of some, if not all, of the defendants but recently returned to remain there. He evidently knew the purpose of these men when he saw them coming, some of them had been hunting for him in the night-time a few days before. He armed himself to resist them, but they came in such numbers and invaded the home in such a ruthless and high-handed manner that resistance was obviously futile. He knew, and every rational thought convinces, that if he had not submitted he would have been more severely treated. Who would have the temerity to argue that they would have permitted him to remain, or after starting, to have alighted from Huntington's auto and return? While they held him for two or three hours in Luverne he was refused permission to see his wife or to talk with her over the 'phone. He was in a large room with a crowd about him who jeered him and asked him questions so thickly that there was no opportunity to attempt to answer, and an attempt, if it had been made, would have been without avail. No argument can blot out the fact, which stands predominant throughout the record, that he was a prisoner from the time these men reached his sons' house until he passed over the State line into South Dakota, and everyone who reads the record must know that resistance on his part to their will would not have been tolerated. In *Comer v. Knowles,* 17 Kan. 436, it is said:

> False imprisonment is necessarily a wrongful interference with the personal liberty of an individual. The wrong may be committed by words alone, or by acts alone, or by both, and by merely operating on the will of the individual, or by personal violence, or by both. It is not necessary that the individual be confined within a prison, or within walls; or that he be assaulted, or even touched. It is not necessary that there should be any injury done to the individual's person, or to his character, or reputation. Nor is it necessary that the wrongful act be committed with malice, or ill will, or even with the slightest wrongful intention. Nor is it necessary that the act be under color of any legal or judicial proceeding. All that is necessary is, that the individual be restrained of his liberty without any sufficient legal cause therefor, and by words or acts which he fears to disregard.

In *Pike v. Hanson,* 9 N.H. 491, the plaintiff did not intend to pay a tax, and the collector was so informed. He, in demanding the tax, declared to the plaintiff that he arrested her, and she paid the money under that restraint. It was held that the facts were sufficient to sustain her action for assault and false imprisonment. The court summarized the doctrine announced by Starkie on *Evidence,* thus:

> That in ordinary practice words are sufficient to constitute an imprisonment, if they impose a restraint upon the person and the plaintiff is accordingly restrained, for he is not obliged to incur risk of personal violence and insult by resisting until actual violence be used.

. . . The court, acting on its conclusion of fact that plaintiff had consented to everything before the State line was reached, instructed the jury over plaintiff's objection and exception that he could recover only against those who maltreated him at the South Dakota line, and that if the evidence was not sufficient in the judgment of the jury to satisfy them as to the identity of those men they would return a verdict for the defendants, there being no liability on the part of any of the defendants except those, if any, who assaulted him there. This we think was also error. As already said, those who took the plaintiff from the sons' home, those who participated to any extent in so doing, those who aided in his

21

deportation on the way, and those who abused him at the State line and warned him that if he ever returned to Minnesota he would be hanged, were all actively engaged in the execution of one purpose, and the transaction throughout . . . was for the accomplishment of that purpose. . . .

It is also claimed by the defendants that what was done by them was done to protect the plaintiff against others who might injure him because of his disloyalty, or his reputation for disloyalty. This presents a new doctrine unknown to us, and no authority has been cited to support it. We cannot believe that the law will ever sanction the claim, either in defense or mitigation, that the rights of one may be violated for the purpose of preventing others from doing the same thing. . . .

The judgment is reversed and the cause remanded for a new trial.

A decision's *citation* is made up of the case's name, references to the reporter or reporters in which the decision was printed, the name of the court where the decision was made, and the year of the decision. For *Meints*, all this information appears in the heading on page 18.

The case name is composed by separating the last names of the parties with a "v." If the opinion was written by a trial court, the name of the plaintiff appears first. In some appellate courts, the name of the appellant comes first, but in others the parties are listed as they were in the trial court. With multiple plaintiffs or defendants, the name of only the first listed per side appears in the case name.

Reporters are publications that print opinions, mostly from appellate courts. There are two kinds: official reporters published under the control of courts and unofficial ones published by private companies. Most opinions appear both in an official reporter and in at least one unofficial reporter. Some courts, however, publish their decisions in only one reporter, which has an official status but an unofficial format. *Meints v. Huntington* was decided by the Eighth Circuit of the United States Court of Appeals, and decisions of the United States Courts of Appeals appear only in the Federal Reporter (abbreviated "F."). The decision you have just read begins on page 245 of volume 276.

Thus, *Meints* is cited to in the following form: *Meints v. Huntington*, 276 F. 245 (8th Cir. 1921).[2]

§2.2   The Interdependence Among Facts, Issues, and Rules

Many facts are mentioned in an opinion merely to provide background, continuity, or what journalists call "human interest" to what would other-

2. In Chapter 13, you will learn more about constructing legal citations.

wise be a tedious and disjointed recitation. Of the remaining facts, some are merely related to the court's thinking, while others *caused* the court to come to its decision. This last group could be called the *determinative facts* or the *essential facts*. They are essential to the court's decision because they determined it: if they had been different, the decision would have been different. The determinative facts lead to the rule of the case—the rule of law for which the case stands as precedent—and the discovery of that rule is the most important goal of case analysis. (Of course, where several issues are raised together in a case, the court must make several rulings and an opinion may thus stand for several different rules.)

The determinative facts can be identified by asking the following question: *if a particular fact had not happened, or if it had happened differently, would the court have made a different ruling?* If so, that fact is one of the determinative facts. This can be illustrated through a nonjudicial decision of a sort with which you might recently have had some experience. Assume that a rental agent has just shown you an apartment and that the following are true:

    A.   The apartment is located half a mile from the law school.

    B.   It is a studio apartment, with one room, a kitchenette, and a bathroom.

    C.   The building appears to be well-maintained and safe.

    D.   The apartment is at the corner of the building, and windows on two sides provide ample light and ventilation.

    E.   It is on the third floor, away from the street, and the neighbors do not appear to be noisy people.

    F.   The rent is $300 per month, furnished.

    G.   The landlord will require a year's lease, and subleasing would be difficult.

    H.   You have a widowed aunt, with whom you get along well and who lives alone in a house 45 minutes by bus from the law school, and she has offered to let you use the second floor of her house during the school year. The house and neighborhood are safe and quiet, and the living arrangements would be satisfactory to you.

    I.   You have made a commitment to work next summer in El Paso.

    J.   You have taken out substantial loans to go to law school.

    K.   You neither own nor have access to a car.

    L.   Reliable local people have told you that you are unlikely to find an apartment that is better, cheaper, or more convenient than the one you have just inspected.

Which facts are essential to your decision? If the apartment had been a mile from the law school (rather than a half-mile), would your decision have been different? If not, the first listed fact could not be determinative. It might be part of the factual mosaic and might explain why you looked at the apartment in the first place, but you would not base your decision on it. (Go through the listed facts and mark in the margin whether each is determinative of your decision.)

Facts recited specifically in an opinion can sometimes be reformulated generically. In the hypothetical above, for example, a generic restatement of fact *H* might be the following: "you have a rent-free alternative to the apartment, but the alternative will require 45 minutes of travel each way and the expense of public transportation." That formulation is generic because it includes other specific possibilities that in the end have the same relevant characteristics and effect. It would include, for example, the following, seemingly different, facts: "you are a member of the clergy in a religion that has given you a leave of absence to attend law school; you may continue to live rent-free in the satisfactory quarters your religion has provided, but to get to the law school, you will have to walk 15 minutes and then ride a subway for 30 minutes more, at the same cost as a bus."

A rule of law is essentially a principle that governs how a particular type of decision is to be made — or, put another way, how certain types of facts are to be treated by the official (such as a judge) who must make a decision. Where a court does not state a rule of the case — or where it ambiguously states a rule — the reader might arrive at an arguably supportable formulation of the rule by considering the determinative facts to have caused the result. There is room for interpretive maneuver where one could reasonably interpret the determinative facts narrowly (specifically) or broadly (generically).

Notice how different formulations of a rule can be extracted from the apartment example. A narrow formulation might be the following:

> A law student who has a choice between renting an apartment and living in the second floor of an aunt's house should choose the latter where the student has had to borrow money to go to law school; where the apartment's rent is $250 per month but the aunt's second floor is free except for bus fares; where the student must work in El Paso during the summer; and where it is difficult locally to sublease an apartment.

Because this formulation is limited to the specific facts given in the hypothetical, it could directly govern only an extremely small number of future decision-makers. It would not, for example, directly govern the member of the clergy described above, even if she must spend next summer doing relief work in Somalia.

Although another decision-maker might be able to reason by analogy from the narrow rule set out above, a broader, more widely applicable formulation, stated generically, would directly govern both situations:

> A student on a tight budget should not sign a year's lease where the student cannot live in the leased property during the summer and where a nearly free alternative is available.

An even more general formulation would govern an even wider circle of applications:

24

A person with limited funds should not lease property that person cannot fully use where there is a nearly free alternative.

The following, however, is so broad as to be meaningless:

A person should not spend money in a way that would later lead to problems.

The interpretation of opinions could hardly be called easy. "Cases do not unfold their principles for the asking," wrote Cardozo. "They yield up their kernel slowly and painfully." [1] Courts often do not explicitly state the issue, the holding, or the rule for which the case is to stand as precedent, and the determinative facts are not usually labelled as such. Whenever a court gives less than a full explanation, you must use what is explicitly stated to pin down what is only implied. Fortunately, the determinative facts, the issue, the holding, and the rule are all dependent on each other. In the apartment hypothetical, for example, if the issue were different—say, "How shall I respond to an offer to join the American Automobile Association?"—the selection of determinative facts would also change. (In fact, the only determinative one would be fact K: "You neither own nor have access to a car.") You will often find yourself using what the court tells you about the issue or the holding to fill in what the court has not told you about the determinative facts—and vice versa.

For example, where the court recites the rule but does not identify the issue or specify which facts are determinative, you might discover the issue and the determinative facts by answering the following questions:

1. Who is suing whom over what series of events and to get what relief?
2. What rule does the court enforce?
3. What element of that rule appears to be the focus of the controversy?
4. How does the court decide that controversy?
5. On what facts does the court rely in making that decision?
6. What question did the court answer?

With other kinds of opinions, depending on what the court does or does not tell you, your inquiry might have to be structured differently. For example, if you have been told the issue but not the rule or determinative facts, you would need to ask a different set of questions.

1. Who is suing whom over what series of events and to get what relief?
2. What issue does the court say it intends to decide?
3. How does the court decide that issue?
4. On what facts does the court rely in making that decision?
5. What rule does the court enforce?[2]

§2.2 1. B. Cardozo, *The Nature of the Judicial Process* 29 (1921).
  2. In answering this question, use the same kind of reasoning we applied to the apartment hypothetical; develop several different phrasings of the rule (broad, narrow, middling); and identify the one the court is most likely to have had in mind.

Bear in mind one of the cardinal rules of intellectual detective work, whether done by a scientist in the laboratory, by an historian with freshly discovered but ambiguous documents, or by Miss Marple with the murder evidence: design the sequence of inquiry so that you begin with what you already know and can progress through what you do not know in a manner that helps you build on each thing you discover along the way.

Cases are hard not because judges like to make puzzles, but for more practical reasons. Even the most prescient judges cannot foresee every ramification of every decision or all of the future factual contexts to which a precedent might be applied. Sometimes, an inadvertently imprecise phrase in an opinion creates room for interpretation. And, invariably, it is not humanly possible for a court to explain all its reasoning: the effort would be so immense that many fewer cases could be decided. In any event, one of the most important skills of effective lawyering is the ability to find room for interpretive maneuver and to exploit it to advantage. The lawyer's art is in part to see meaning that is both favorable to the client and at the same time credible and persuasive to a court. Fact interpretation is a very large part of that skill.

Exercise II.   Analyzing the Meaning of Meints v. Huntington

What was the issue on appeal in *Meints*? What rule did the appellate court enforce? What were the determinative facts? Be prepared to state and argue your conclusions in class.

§2.3   Briefing Cases

In law school, the word *brief* can mean either of two things. Within a few months, you will learn the basic technique of writing an *appellate brief,* which—despite its name—is a large and complex document written to persuade a court to rule in favor of one's client. Another kind of brief is a short analytical outline of a court's opinion. Students make these outlines to prepare for class, and you are about to write one. (In law students' vernacular, you are about to *brief a case.*)

The effort of making the brief requires that you sort out the logic by which the case was decided. When an attorney wants to use a precedent as a basis for planning litigation or for advising a client, the attorney might brief the precedent to get a more precise understanding of its meaning and to make useful notes for further reference. Students use briefs not only to analyze and make notes from cases they have found through research in the library, but more often to prepare for classes in which students and teacher work together to interpret decisions.

Since no two lawyers share exactly the same thinking and working methods, no two lawyers brief in precisely the same way. Moreover, a lawyer will brief simple cases differently from complex ones, cases to be used in planning litigation differently from those to be used in drafting a contract or will, and so forth. Not only must you develop a briefing technique individualized to your patterns of preparation and thought, but you will need the versatility to vary your briefing style according to the task at hand. As in so much of law, the test for success is how well a given piece of work accomplishes what it was designed to do.

Think of the briefing method set out in the following pages as a starting point. Adapt it as needed to the different sorts of opinions you study, and, as you go along, modify it also to suit the work habits you find most effective in the different classes for which you must prepare.

A brief might include, in outline form, the following items:

1. the title of the case, its date, the name of the court, and the place where the opinion can be found
2. the identities of the parties
3. the procedural history
4. the facts
5. the issue or issues
6. a summary of the arguments made by each side
7. the holding and the rule for which the case stands
8. the court's reasoning
9. the order or judgment the court made as a result of its decision
10. any comments of your own that may be useful but that are not covered by any other category

Each of these categories bears explanation.

1. Title, date, court, location of opinion. This is the easiest part. For *Meints*, a brief might begin as follows:

Case: Meints v. Huntington
               (8th Cir. 1921)
               page 18 in text

If you were briefing a case in the library, however, you would use the citation (276 F. 245) in place of a page number in the text. The point is to note the place where the opinion can be found.[1]

2. Identities of parties. This requires some thought: how do the identities of the parties frame the controversy? In *Meints*, for example, you might write:

Parties: P = dissenter in WW I

               Ds = residents of Rock Co., Minn.

---

§2.3   1. In the example, the words *in text* are not necessarily surplusage. In many courses, you will have a paperback supplement to the text, and occasionally a professor will distribute additional material in photocopy form.

Should the briefer add that the plaintiff was a resident of South Dakota, but that he also had been a resident of Rock County before the events sued over? In the second paragraph of the opinion the court goes to considerable effort to describe a prior incident—not a part of this lawsuit—in which the plaintiff had been forcibly taken from his home into Iowa and was "told . . . not to return." The court does not specifically say that the plaintiff was afraid of what awaited him if he had gone home, but that is clearly implied. In the first paragraph of the opinion, the court uses the word *deported* to describe the events that caused the plaintiff to end up in South Dakota. What does all this tell you about whether the plaintiff's prior and current residences are determinative facts? If you believe they are mere background facts, then you would include them in your brief only if they are needed to make sense out of the story. The prior residence in Rock County does seem to be needed for that purpose, but the current residence in South Dakota does not. On the other hand, if you believe that the court's reasoning is based on the view that the law cannot permit private citizens to "deport" to other states people who hold unpopular opinions, then you should make sure that your brief records the plaintiff's residence at the time of the litigation. Because this is a matter of identity as well as an arguably determinative fact, it really does not matter much whether you add it under "Parties" or under "Facts."

3. Procedural history. Here list the litigation events that are essential to the decision the court must make. Most published opinions are from appellate courts, and an appellate procedural history includes the trial court rulings appealed from. In *Meints,* for example:

> **Proc. Hist.:**   P sued for false imprisonment and assault. (Assault holding deleted from op.) Verdict for Ds. P appealed from trial judge's instructions to jury that P could not recover for events before he was assaulted at South Dakota state line.

4. Facts. Here write a short narrative limited to the determinative facts and whatever other details are necessary to make sense out of the story. Omit facts that neither are determinative nor are needed to make the story coherent.

5. The issue. You must *define* the dispute before the court. The following attempts at stating the issue in *Meints* fail to define the dispute on appeal:

> Were Ds liable for false imprisonment?

> Had P consented to be transported to South Dakota?

> Did the trial court correctly instruct the jury?

> Did the trial court correctly instruct the jury on the law of consent in false imprisonment?

The first example is wrong because on appeal the issue is whether the trial court—which means the judge in the trial court—committed an error prejudicing the appellant. Jury verdicts, you will recall, are not in themselves appealable, but the actions of the trial judge are. It was for the jury to decide, through its verdict, whether the defendants were liable for false imprisonment, but, since the jurors were presumably all lay people, they could fulfill that function only if the trial judge correctly instructed them on the law. Of all the many types of error that could be complained of on appeal, the plaintiff-appellant in *Meints* claimed error in the jury instructions. The second example is wrong for the same reason as the first, although the second example specifies the question of consent and thus gets closer to the analytical problem posed by the case. The third example is at least premised on an understanding that the appellate court is confined to reviewing the jury instructions.[2] But the third example is faulty because it merely *describes*—and does not *define*—the dispute on appeal: the third example does not set out what the claimed error in the instructions might have been. The fourth example is better, in that it alludes to the part of the law involved, but it is still not a definition of the question before the court.

There are many adequate ways to phrase the issue in *Meints*, but one would be the following:

> **Issue:** Did the trial court err in instructing the jury that P could not recover for false imprisonment because he had consented to be taken to another state and left there?

This is a definition of the issue and not a mere description of it: it is exactly the question that the *Meints* court answered. Frame your issues with care and keep the following in mind:

First, your statement of the issue must be phrased in terms of the procedural events that have created a need for a decision. In *Meints*, those procedural events are the specified jury instructions and an appeal based on them. In law school classes, the appeal is such a routine event that it can be implied in your brief.

Second, refer to the governing rule and specify the element that is in controversy. The example on this page mentions a cause of action (a kind of rule) for false imprisonment, as well as an element of that cause of action (the plaintiff's lack of consent to the restraint).

Third, allude to enough of the determinative facts to make the issue concrete. The last example refers to the trip to South Dakota, which is the form of restraint claimed by the plaintiff. That is probably enough here. It is not necessary to pack into the issue every one of a long list of determinative facts, but if your list happens to be short to begin with, you might be able to

---

2. A jury instruction is *reversible* error only if it both incorrectly states the law and could have *caused* the verdict at issue. An instruction that incorrectly states the law might arguably be error, but if a properly instructed jury might have returned the same verdict, a reversal would be pointless. That is why the appellate court in *Meints* considered the question of whether the evidence could have led a properly instructed jury to return a verdict for the plaintiff.

formulate an artful issue incorporating them all. If your list happens to be so long that an intelligible issue cannot include every one, the most critical and central facts are those that must be included.

Finally, an issue can often be more profitably stated as a question about a rule of law: "Has a false imprisonment plaintiff been restrained without his consent where he does not object to being taken away after . . . ?" In each course, you will be able to get some indication, from the professor's evaluation of student discussion in class, of whether a rule-oriented statement of the issue is more appropriate to the material.

6. A summary of the arguments made by each side.   Do not go overboard. Record the *essential* points of each side's argument.

7. The holding and the rule.   Strictly speaking, the holding and the rule are two different things. In *Meints,* the holding is that the trial court erred by instructing the jury that the plaintiff had consented to be taken to South Dakota, but the rule for which the case stands is a principle that can be applied to decide other controversies in the future. Just as we formulated broad and narrow principles from the apartment hypothetical, the rule of the case can be stated narrowly or broadly, depending on how you conceptualize the determinative facts:

narrow:	A person is restrained without his consent where a large number of men break into his sons' house, throw one son out of the building [and so on, with a list of every fact that deprived the plaintiff of freedom of movement].
broad:	A person is restrained without his consent where his submission to the restraint is obtained "by words or acts which he fears to disregard."

As with the apartment, the narrow rule would directly govern only an exceedingly small number of future controversies, while the broader formulation will have a wider utility. Broad formulations should not, however, be taken too far. The following does not accurately represent the rule enforced in *Meints:*

A person is restrained without his consent where he did not do what he wanted because otherwise he might suffer.

Part of a lawyer's creativity is discovering deeper meaning in an opinion by devising several alternative formulations of a rule. The art is to phrase the rule broadly enough that it has a reasonably general applicability, but not so broadly that it exceeds the principle that the court thought it was following. Within these limits, many decisions will afford several different but arguable ways to phrase a particular rule.

Sometimes a court provides a succinct statement of the rule. At other times, a court merely sets out the facts and issue and then, without saying much more, decides for one party or the other. In the first kind of opinion, the court's words provide one — sometimes the only — phrasing of the rule. In the latter, you must construct the rule yourself out of the determinative facts. *Meints* is somewhere in between. The court does not state a rule in a single sentence, but it does provide wording (some of which appears in the "broad" example on page 30) that can be used to state generically the determinative facts. Even where the court provides a succinct statement of the rule, it is often possible to arrive at a different but arguable formulation of the rule by examining what the court did with the determinative facts.

Although there is a difference between the rule (which is stated so as to govern future cases) and the holding (which decides questions like whether a particular party is entitled to requested relief, whether the trial court erred, and so on), the distinction tends to blur because lawyers often use "holding" to refer to the rule for which the case is precedent. That is understandable: after all, we read these cases to learn that rule and for little else. A law school professor who asks you the "holding" of a case may want to know the holding (in the narrow sense), the rule, or both. An efficient way of briefing is to record both:

Issue:	Did the trial court err in instructing the jury that P could not recover for false imprisonment because he had consented to be taken to another state and left there?
Holding:	No.
Rule:	A person is restrained without his consent where any submission to the restraint is obtained "by words or acts which he fears to disregard."

8. The court's reasoning. Here summarize the court's thinking, noting both the steps of logic the court went through and the public policies the court thought it was advancing through its decision.

9. Judgment or order. What did the court do as a result of its holding? Usually, it will be enough for you to write "reversed," "affirmed," "motion denied," or whatever order or judgment the court made.

10. Comments. Did the court write any instructive dicta? Do you agree or disagree with the decision? Why? Does the briefed case give you a deeper understanding of other cases you have already studied in the same course? Does material in a concurring or dissenting opinion add to your understanding?

━━━━━━━━━

If an opinion resolves several issues, you will need to go through items 5 through 8 separately for each issue. For example, the middle of a brief of a two-issue decision might look something like this:

Issue #1: . . .   arguments: . . .
                    holding: . . .
                    rule: . . .
                    reasoning: . . .

Issue #2: . . .   arguments: . . .
                    holding: . . .
                    rule: . . .
                    reasoning: . . .

Read the entire opinion at least once before beginning to brief. You might work efficiently by making some temporary notes as you read, but you will waste effort if you start structuring your understanding—which is what briefing does—before you are able to see the decision *as a whole.*

A long-winded brief filled with the court's own words is far less useful than a short one in which you have boiled the opinion down to its essence. In the sample excerpts from a brief that appear on the preceding pages, you might have noticed that the court is quoted only once, but that those quoted words are perhaps the most important ones in the opinion. Briefs are a means, not an end: for you the hard work will be to understand what happened in the case and why, and the brief is only a repository for your analysis. You will waste effort if you spend too much time in writing and too little in thinking. In fact, if you do little more than edit the court's words into a brief, you have probably not understood the case. A better practice is to quote only those words that are absolutely essential to the case's meaning.

Finally, remember that each course, each professor, and each law student is unique. Your briefing technique will evolve into something different from that of the student who sits next to you because your mental habits are different, and you will need material from which you can recite quickly and efficiently. Moreover, your briefing for one course and its professor may become different from the way you brief for another course and professor because of differences in teaching style and in the subject matter.

Exercise III.   Briefing Eilers v. Coy

Using the techniques described above, write out a brief of *Eilers v. Coy.*

EILERS v. COY
582 F. Supp. 1093 (D. Minn. 1984)

MACLAUGHLIN, District Judge. The plaintiff in this case, William Eilers, has moved [for] a directed verdict against the defendants on his claims that the defendants falsely imprisoned him. . . .

. . . The plaintiff [was] abducted . . . in Winona, Minnesota in the early afternoon of Monday, August 16, 1982, by [his] parents . . . and by the defendant deprogrammers who had been hired by the parents. . . . The plaintiff was 24 years old at the time. . . .

At the time of the abduction, [the plaintiff was a member] of the religious group Disciples of the Lord Jesus Christ. There is ample evidence that this group is an authoritarian religious fellowship directed with an iron hand by Brother Rama Behera. There is also evidence that Bill Eilers' personality, and to some extent his appearance, changed substantially after he became a member of the group. These changes were clearly of great concern to members of the plaintiff's family. However, other than as they may have affected the intent of the parents . . . in the actions they took . . . , the beliefs and practices of the Disciples of the Lord Jesus Christ should not be, and are not, on trial in this case.

[In] Winona . . . on August 16, 1982, the plaintiff, who was on crutches at the time due to an earlier fall, was grabbed from behind by two or more security men, forced into a waiting van, and driven to the Tau Center in Winona, Minnesota. Forcibly resisting, he was carried by four men to a room on the top floor of the dormitory-style building. The windows of this room were boarded over with plywood, as were the windows in his bathroom and in the hallway of the floor. The telephone in the hallway had been dismantled.

The plaintiff was held at the Tau Center for five and one-half days and subjected to the defendants' attempts to deprogram him. Shortly after his arrival at the Tau Center, and after a violent struggle with his captors, the plaintiff was handcuffed to a bed. He remained handcuffed to the bed for at least the first two days of his confinement. During this initial period, he was allowed out of the room only to use the bathroom, and was heavily guarded during those times. On one occasion, the plaintiff dashed down the hall in an attempt to escape, but was forcibly restrained and taken back to the room. . . .

The defendants and the plaintiff's relatives had agreed in advance of the abduction that the plaintiff would be kept at the Tau Center for one week, regardless of whether the plaintiff consented to their actions. At no time during the week was the plaintiff free to leave the Tau Center, nor at any time were reasonable means of escape available to him. Three of the eight people hired by the parents were designated "security men." These individuals, described by witnesses as at least six feet tall and weighing over 200 pounds, guarded the exits on the floor at all times.

On the evening of Saturday, August 21, 1982, as the plaintiff was leaving the Tau Center to be transported to Iowa City, Iowa for further deprogramming, he took advantage of his first opportunity to escape and jumped from the car in which he was riding. Local residents, attracted by the plaintiff's calls for help, assisted the plaintiff in making his escape and the police were summoned.

The evidence has also shown that within three weeks before the abduction occurred, the plaintiff's relatives had contacted authorities in Trempealeau County, Wisconsin [where he was living at the time] in an attempt to have the plaintiff civilly committed. Family members have testified that they believed the plaintiff was suicidal because of a letter he had written to his grandmother before joining the Disciples of the Lord Jesus Christ in which he wrote that demons were attacking his mind and telling him to kill himself rather than go to the Lord. . . . Joyce Peterson, a psychiatric social worker, interviewed the plaintiff in person on July 26, 1982. After interviewing the plaintiff and consulting with the Trempealeau County Attorney, Peterson informed the plaintiff's relatives that no legal grounds existed in Wisconsin for confining the plaintiff because he showed no signs of being a danger to himself or to others. The defendants in this case were aware of that information at the time they abducted and held the plaintiff. . . .

In considering the plaintiff's motion for a directed verdict, the Court is required to view the evidence in the light most favorable to the defendants and to resolve all conflicts in the evidence in the defendants' favor. *Dace v. ACF Industries, Inc.,* 722 F.2d 375 (8th Cir. 1983). A directed verdict motion should be granted only when reasonable jurors could not differ as to the conclusions to be drawn from the evidence. *Id.* . . .

. . . [G]iven that the defendants falsely imprisoned the plaintiff, were their actions legally justified so as to preclude liability for false imprisonment? As justification for their actions, the defendants rely on the defense of necessity. They claim that the confinement and attempted deprogramming of the plaintiff [were] necessary to prevent him from committing suicide or from otherwise harming himself or others. . . .

The defense of necessity has three elements. The first element is that the defendants must have acted under the reasonable belief that there was a danger of imminent physical injury to the plaintiff or to others. *State v. Johnson,* 289 Minn. 196, 199-200, 183 N.W.2d 541, 543 (1971); *People v. Patrick,* 126 Cal. App. 3d 952, 961, 179 Cal. Rptr. 276, 282 (1981); *People v. Patrick,* 541 P.2d 320, 322 (Colo. Ct. App. 1975); Restatement (Second) of Torts § 892(D) comment *a* (1979).

It is not clear that such a danger existed on August 16, 1982. The alleged threats of suicide made by the plaintiff were contained in a letter dated June 14, 1982, and that letter recounted impressions the plaintiff had had some time earlier. Moreover, Joyce Peterson, the psychiatric social worker who personally interviewed the plaintiff on July 26, 1982, concluded in her report, and reported to the plaintiff's relatives, that the plaintiff was not dangerous to himself or to others. Nevertheless, viewing the evidence in the light most favorable to the defendants, the Court will assume for purposes of this motion that the plaintiff was in imminent danger of causing physical injury to himself or to others.

The second and third elements of the necessity defense are intertwined. The second element is that the right to confine a person in order to prevent harm to that person lasts only as long as is necessary to get the person to the proper lawful authorities. *See State v. Hembd,* 305 Minn. 120, 130, 232 N.W.2d 872, 878 (1975) (dictum). . . . The third element is that the actor must use the least restrictive means of preventing the apprehended harm. *People v. Patrick,* 126 Cal. App. 3d 952, 960, 179 Cal. Rptr. 276, 282 (1981); W. LaFave and A. Scott, *Criminal Law* 387 (1972); *cf. Peterson v. Sorlien,* 299 N.W.2d 123, 129 (Minn. 1980) (where religious beliefs are implicated, first amendment requires resort to least restrictive alternative).

In this case, the defendants' conduct wholly fails to satisfy either of these elements of the necessity defense. Once having gained control of the plaintiff, the defendants had several legal options available to them. They could have:

(1) turned the plaintiff over to the police;

(2) sought to initiate civil commitment proceedings against the plaintiff pursuant to Minn. Stat. § 253B.07 (1982);

(3) sought professional psychiatric or psychological help for the plaintiff with the possibility of emergency hospitalization if necessary pursuant to Minn. Stat. § 253B.05 (1982).

At no time did the defendants attempt, or even consider attempting, any of these lawful alternatives during the five and one-half days they held the plaintiff, the first five of which were business days. Instead, they took the plaintiff to a secluded location with boarded-up windows, held him incommunicado, and proceeded to inflict their own crude methods of "therapy" upon him — methods which even the defendants' own expert witness has condemned. Well aware that the police were searching for the plaintiff, the defendants deliberately concealed the plaintiff's location from the police.

It must be emphasized that the Minnesota Legislature has prescribed specific procedures that must be followed before a person can be deprived of his or her liberty on the basis of mental illness. Minn. Stat. § 253B.07 et seq. (1982). . . . Those procedures include examination of the proposed patient by qualified professionals, Minn. Stat. § 253B.07, subd. 1 (1982), and a judicial determination that the proposed patient is dangerous and in need of treatment, id., subd. 6. Manifold procedural protections, including the right to counsel, Minn. Stat. § 253B.03, subd. 9 (1982), are afforded the proposed patient at all stages of this civil commitment proceeding. Obviously, none of these protections were afforded the plaintiff in this case.

Minnesota law also provides that, in situations where there is not time to obtain a court order, a person may be admitted or held for emergency care and treatment in a hospital, without a court order, upon a written statement by a licensed physician or psychologist that the person is mentally ill and is in imminent danger of causing injury to himself or to others. Minn. Stat. § 253B.05, subd. 1 (1982). The defendants in this case — unlicensed and untrained individuals — made no effort to obtain any such statements from a licensed physician or psychologist.

The defendants' failure to even attempt to use the lawful alternatives available to them is fatal to their assertion of the necessity defense. Where the Legislature has prescribed specific procedures that must be followed before a person can be deprived of his or her liberty on the ground of mental illness, not even parents or their agents acting under the best of motives are entitled to disregard those procedures entirely.

The Court has assumed for the purpose of this motion that the defendants were justified in initially restraining the plaintiff based upon their belief that he was in imminent danger of harming himself or others. But even under those circumstances, the defense of necessity eventually dissipates as a matter of law. No specific time limit can be set, because the

period during which an actor is acting out of necessity will vary depending on the circumstances of each case. In this particular case, however,
where the defendants held the plaintiff, a 24-year-old adult, for five and
one-half days with no attempt to resort to lawful alternatives available to
them, the Court could not sustain a jury verdict in the defendants' favor
on the issue of false imprisonment. Accordingly, the Court rules as a
matter of law that the plaintiff was falsely imprisoned without justification. The issue of what amount of damages, if any, the plaintiff suffered
from this false imprisonment is a question for the jury. . . .

Based on the foregoing, . . . the plaintiff's motion for a directed verdict is granted as to his claim for false imprisonment. . . .

After briefing a decision, ask yourself how it fits into the subject you are
learning. Why did the editor of the casebook include the decision you
briefed? What lesson does it teach you about the law? If the preceding
decision or decisions involve similar issues, how does the one you have just
briefed expand on what you learned from the others? What, for example, did
you learn about false imprisonment from *Meints,* and how does *Eilers* add to
that? In other words, step back far enough to see the larger picture.

II

INTRODUCTION TO LEGAL WRITING

3 The Art of Legal Writing

§3.1   The Language as a Professional Tool

Contrary to the aphorism, a lawyer's stock-in-trade is neither time nor advice. It is words: writing them, speaking them, and interpreting them. That is true not only because legal work involves so much reading and writing, but — more important — because words are the most fundamental tool lawyers use to gain advantage for their clients. The constant question for a lawyer is how to use words to cause a result, whether in court, in negotiation, in drafting a contract or a will, or in writing an appellate brief. And the written word is the most common medium through which lawyers exercise control over events.

A lawyer begins most situations as a prisoner of words that other people have written into statutes, opinions, contracts, and other things that govern. An effective lawyer tries to interpret those words to the advantage of the client and then, with the lawyer's own words, tries to persuade judges, jurors, and negotiating adversaries that the favorable interpretation is correct. An unsuccessful lawyer is not only ineffectual at using words to break out of the word-prison that others have built, but builds still more confining walls with poorly chosen words in briefs, memoranda, contracts, and other documents, at times making matters worse than they were in the first place.

Lawyers are fond of comparing words to surgeons' tools: "Words are the principal tools of lawyers and judges, whether we like it or not. They are to us what the scalpel and insulin are to the doctor."[1] Law is "one of the principal literary professions. One might hazard the supposition that the

---

§3.1   1. Chafee, *The Disorderly Conduct of Words*, 41 Colum. L. Rev. 381, 382 (1941).

average lawyer in the course of a lifetime does more writing than a novelist. . . . He must use that double-edged tool, the English language, with all the precision of any surgeon handling a scalpel." [2] "Language is the lawyer's scalpel. If he cannot use it skillfully, he is apt to butcher his suffering client's case." [3]

Because litigation is not done in secret, a surprising number of a lawyer's writings become public records, available in courthouses for anyone who is interested. Every law library holds thousands of volumes of opinions in which courts quote and interpret the written words of lawyers, both great and ordinary. And, for reasons that you will soon understand, much of this writing is done according to standards and conventions that are not consistent with the way you were taught to write before coming to law school.

Because lawyers do so much writing, an ability to write well is often essential to a young lawyer looking for a job. Employers routinely require applicants to submit writing samples. When you scan employment announcements looking for your first job, you will see phrases like the following over and over: "seeks attorney with proven writing ability," "excellent research and writing skills required," "recruiting for associate with superb writing skills."

As a professional tool, what kind of language is English? Once you learn how to use it—and do not assume that you already know that in a professional sense—you will find it remarkably adaptable. Far less rigid than many other languages, English often provides dozens of different methods of expressing roughly the same idea, each one conveying nuances slightly different from the others. That is possible because English allows sentences and clauses to be constructed in a multitude of ways and because English has a huge vocabulary, having inherited from Norman French and Old English and having borrowed heavily from Latin and Greek. But that very flexibility creates risks each time you try to write precisely. Because English provides so many options in structure, vocabulary, and nuance, a careful writer can find the means to express a difficult idea that might be inexpressible in a more rigid language, but for the same reasons a careless writer of English is easily tempted into writing mush. In few fields is that as true as it is in law.

A difficult idea takes much effort to express at all and even more to express in a way that is quickly and fully grasped by the busy people who are a lawyer's readers. Legal writing works well only if it transmits the ideas at hand with the clarity of Orwell's pane of glass.[4] If your reader's attention is drawn to the obscurities and other faults in your writing, you and your client will suffer for several reasons. First, the typical reader begins to resist and may not finish reading because lawyers and judges are busy people who do not have time to wade through difficult writing. Second, the reader is tempted to consider you unreliable because mediocre use of the language

2. Prosser, *English As She Is Wrote*, 7 J. Leg. Ed. 155, 156 (1954).
3. Kaufman, *Appellate Advocacy in the Federal Courts*, 79 F.R.D. 165, 170 (1978).
4. "Good prose is like a windowpane." G. Orwell, *Why I Write* (1947), in *The Orwell Reader* 390, 395 (1956).

implies general mediocrity as a lawyer. Third, the busy reader may misunderstand what you are trying to say. That is a danger that students often underestimate because most students have very little, if any, experience making important decisions based on the rapid reading of complex documents. Legal writing should give the viewer a quick and clear view, without distractions, of the idea behind it.

The demands of lawyerly writing come as a shock to many law students. That is because undergraduate education does not normally require writing that *functions* well. College writing need only *sound* nice. Its sole role is to provoke a satisfying grade by massaging a teacher with important-sounding resonances that suggest that the student's brain was alive and operating. College writing is not put to practical tests in a real world. It need not provide everything needed to advise a client or plan litigation (as office memoranda must); it is not asked to persuade people to make important decisions (as persuasive memoranda and appellate briefs are); and it never approaches the task of creating or defining legal rights and obligations (as statutes, opinions, regulations, contracts, wills, and deeds do). If these documents are to do their jobs, the lawyer's language must be used with a level of skill not often imagined in undergraduate school. Unlike a college student, a lawyer must write material that can withstand attack from what has been called the "reader in bad faith"—the opposing attorney who would like to distort an ambiguous phrase into something the writer never meant, the unsympathetic judge looking for a misstatement on which to base an adverse ruling, "and all the others who will want to twist the meaning of words for their own ends." [5] In law, good writing is power. If other lawyers are better at it than you are, you will be at their mercy.

There is another reason why legal writing is much more demanding than college writing. Higher levels of expression are needed for higher levels of thinking, and most law students quickly conclude that lawyerly reasoning outstrips anything that they had ever imagined in college. In other words, you will need to write better because you will need to think better. And because "trouble in writing . . . invariably reflects troubled thinking," [6] instruction in legal writing cannot be separated from instruction in legal reasoning.

On the road to becoming a professional, you will discover that some of the customs of youth come to an end. A custom encouraged by undergraduate education is the game of trying to "psych out" what the writing teacher "wants," composing in that style to get a nice grade, and then reverting to old habits as soon as the course is over. If you have done this in college, perhaps the blame is not yours. The structure of undergraduate education, after all, promotes it. One teacher may have told you that your paragraphs were too long, while another may have told you that your paragraphs were too short, but typically nobody told you how to tell the difference between a paragraph that is too short and one that is overly long. Put another way, nobody told you how to make a paragraph decision. Not only are college

---

5. H. Weihofen, *Legal Writing Style* 8 (2d ed. 1980).
6. B. Tuchman, *Practicing History* 284 (1981).

teachers unable to agree on objective standards, but the goals of a college education do not include teaching you how to handle a practical responsibility. As a lawyer, however, you will be required to produce practical writing on which clients, supervising attorneys, judges, and others can rely. Your law writing must be able to carry burdens that college simply does not address.

In college, what counted was what made the teacher happy. In law and in law school, what counts is what *works*. No one will try to straightjacket you into a single style of writing: there are many different ways of doing any legal writing chore effectively and many more of doing it badly. But lawyers and law school teachers do have objective standards that can be used to separate writing that works from writing that does not. Although reasonable lawyers, teachers, and judges might disagree about a few small points, you will find among them a surprising amount of agreement on professional standards of writing. That should hardly be surprising, since all these people must use writing for practical purposes, and since all of them are familiar with the consequences of mediocre writing.

Although there is a general agreement about standards of effectiveness, there is no easy, simple, cookbook-like formula for doing legal writing well. Instead, you will always be confronted with a range of things that you might do on paper. Not only are some of those choices more appropriate to a given situation than others are, but as the situation changes—even slightly and subtly—a good choice might become ineffectual, and a previously marginal choice might become one of the best things you can do. Professional work differs from other methods of earning a living partly through the professional's pervasive need to decide—in the face of all this subtlety—how to proceed. And as you learn lawyerly writing, you will begin to learn how a professional makes decisions.

In short, your goal now is to learn a skill college rarely teaches: *how to write to cause something to happen* in the real world. Consequently, *none* of the following is an affirmative defense to a teacher's critique of your writing:

"All through college, no one ever told me there was anything wrong with my writing."

"Several of my college teachers told me I was a good writer."

"I was an English major."

"I've never been able to write well, but I have other strengths that make up for it."

"After all these years, it's really too late to learn punctuation [or sentence structure, or noun-verb agreement, or any other issue of grammar]."

"The error you're pointing to must be a typo. I guess I missed it in proofreading."

"I really hadn't understood what you wanted."

If your writing lacks sound organization, clarity, conciseness, or forceful-ness, or if you have not fully mastered the rules of English grammar, or if you do not habitually plan and rewrite your material well, now is the time to learn to do it right. In fact, this is probably your *last* opportunity before your writing begins to affect your career.

§3.2 Predictive Writing and Persuasive Writing[1]

Lawyers make predictive judgments for two purposes: to advise clients and to plan litigation. A newspaper that is considering publishing a contro-versial article might ask its attorneys whether the newspaper would have to pay damages for defamation or invasion of privacy. If the answer is yes, the newspaper will probably want to know what changes in the article could solve the problem. Even if the answer is no, the newspaper may inquire whether it is likely to be sued (regardless of who would win), and, if the answer to that question is yes, whether any unessential changes in the article could minimize even that risk. Clients also ask attorneys to investi-gate the value of bringing a lawsuit. For instance, after the article is pub-lished, a person mentioned in it might ask an attorney whether a lawsuit is worth bringing. In each of these situations, a client will make a decision relying on an attorney's prediction of how the law will react. And if the newspaper is sued, lawyers on both sides will make further predictions in order to develop their litigation strategies.

Predictions are reduced to writing for two additional reasons. The first is to memorialize them and the reasoning behind them for the future. Predic-tions tend to be used more than once. The same prediction (and the reason-ing supporting it) might be used in deciding whether to sue, in drafting the complaint, in responding to motions to dismiss or for summary judgment, in conducting discovery, in negotiating with opposing counsel, in planning the presentation of evidence and arguments at trial, and in pursuing an appeal, all of which may stretch over a period of years. In addition, two or more lawyers often work together or sequentially in representing a client, and the lawyer who makes the initial prediction will need to record it in detail for supervisors and colleagues.

The second reason for reducing predictions to writing is that the act of writing improves the quality of the prediction. Not only are *the writing process and the thinking process inseparable,* but the number of variables to be taken into account can make predictive judgments so complex that an attorney is lost unless thoughts can be worked out on paper. It is not unusual for an attorney to start writing on the basis of a tentative prediction already

---

§3.2 1. Predictive writing is sometimes called objective writing, but objectivity only partly defines the genre. Any writing that makes a disinterested report of what the law is can be classified as objective. Predictive writing does that and more: it foretells how the law will resolve a particular controversy.

made, only to find, after much writing—and rewriting—that the prediction "won't write" and must be changed.

A different kind of writing is aimed at persuading a court to rule favorably. When a lawyer seeks a ruling from a court, the lawyer submits a memorandum or brief arguing the client's position. The document's intended audience is the judge (in the trial court) or the judges (on appeal) who will rule on the client's case, together with the law clerks or research attorneys who assist in judicial decision-making.

Persuasive writing and predictive writing have some things in common. For both, the audience is the same skeptical, busy, and cautious reader described throughout this chapter, and, in both situations, that person reads for the purpose of making a decision and expects the document to be helpful. The supervisor who reads an office memorandum from a junior lawyer must decide how to advise a client or how to conduct litigation. The judge who reads a brief or persuasive memorandum must decide how to rule on a motion or an appeal.

But persuasive writing and predictive writing also differ in fundamental ways. The aim of predictive writing is to foretell what will really happen, pleasant or unpleasant. If the newspaper will become liable for damages, it can limit its exposure if the editors are so advised beforehand. If, on the other hand, a lawsuit is destined to fail, the person mentioned in the article will want to know that in time to decide not to sue. In persuasive writing, however, the aim is to influence the reader to make a decision in the client's favor. Persuasive writing requires all the skills needed for predictive writing, but it also requires others: strategic thinking, for example, and the ability to lay out compelling theories and arguments.

§3.3   The Art Forms of Legal Writing

The most common document in which a lawyer writes predictively is called an office memorandum. Persuasive writing most commonly appears in two kinds of documents. One is a persuasive memorandum submitted to a trial court; its customary form is, depending on the author's position, a memorandum in support of a motion or a memorandum in opposition to a motion. The other kind of document is an appellate brief.[1]

Memoranda and briefs are manuals to guide decision-making. An office memorandum provides a basis for litigation planning, for client counseling, and for other decisions reached in a law office. A brief or persuasive memorandum is intended to lead a court to the decision urged by the attorney. Generally, memoranda and briefs, like manuals, are read intermittently and piecemeal. Unlike essays, they are not read from beginning to end. The reader may open up a particular memorandum or brief on several different

---

§3.3   1. Although a memorandum or brief submitted to a court becomes a public record, an office memorandum is a confidential document not normally distributed outside the lawyer's place of work.

occasions, and the reader's purpose at any given time determines the portions of the document that will be read and the order in which they will be read. In that way, these documents are very much like an owner's manual for an appliance or for an automobile. The reader's need at the moment may be limited, and it must be satisfied without having to read the entire document.

Although there are substantial differences among briefs and predictive and persuasive memoranda, all these documents are variations on a single and very logical structure of presentation. Each of them includes the following:

1. *opening material* to help the reader get into and use the document
2. a definition of the *issue* (or issues) addressed by the document
3. a recitation of the *facts* out of which the issue or issues arise
4. an analytical *summary*
5. an *analysis* of how the law treats those facts
6. *closure*

Even though these documents all tend to be organized around the structure outlined above, the details of format are not absolutely rigid. Memorandum format may differ somewhat from law office to law office and — within a law office — from memorandum to memorandum, according to the needs of the case. Similarly, the format of persuasive memoranda and briefs may vary slightly from jurisdiction to jurisdiction, and a given jurisdiction's customs and court rules may permit some variation from case to case.

The chart on page 46 lists the components of a thorough version of each type of document. (You can see a sample office memorandum in Appendix C, a sample persuasive memorandum in Appendix D, and sample appellate briefs in Appendices E and F.)

The largest and most complex part of each document is the Discussion or Argument, and together they represent the heart of what you will learn in this course. Chapters 6 through 13 explain everything you will need to know to write a Discussion: how to use the structure of rules; how to organize your analysis; how to select authority; how to integrate research into the writing process; how to work with precedent, statutes, and facts; and how to use citations and quotations. Chapters 14 and 15 describe additional skills needed to write an Argument: thinking strategically, developing a theory, understanding the judicial audience, using argumentation techniques, and staying within the rules of argumentation ethics. Chapters 16 through 21 explain how to build the rest of the document around the Discussion or Argument. And Chapters 4 and 5 and the remainder of this chapter prepare you for all of this by explaining legal writing style, paragraphing, and the process of planning, writing, and rewriting.

Lawyers write a wide range of other things too: contracts, wills, trusts, pleadings, motions, interrogatories, affidavits, stipulations, judicial opinions, orders, judgments, opinion letters for clients, statutes, administrative regulations, and more. But with the possible exception of opinion letters and judicial opinions — which have some things in common with the Discussion portion of an office memorandum — instruction in these other

	Office Memoranda	*Persuasive Memoranda*	*Appellate Briefs*
opening material to help the reader get into and use the document	memorandum heading	cover page	cover page
		Table of Contents	Table of Contents
		Table of Authorities	Table of Authorities
		Preliminary Statement	Statutes Involved
			Preliminary Statement
definition of the *issue* (or issues) addressed by the document	Question Presented	Question Presented	Question Presented
recitation of the *facts* out of which the issue or issues arise	Statement of Facts	Statement of the Case	Statement of the Case
analytical *summary*	Brief Answer	—	Summary of Argument
analysis of how the law treats those facts	Discussion	Argument	Argument
closure	Conclusion	Conclusion	Conclusion
	signature	indorsement	indorsement

forms of legal writing must wait until after you have learned much more about law and procedure and are able to enroll in upper-class drafting courses, clinics, and simulation courses.

§3.4 *Planning, Rewriting, and Work Habits*

Writing is easy. You just sit at a typewriter until blood appears on your forehead.

—*Red Smith*

There is no such thing as good writing. There is only good rewriting.

—*Justice Louis Brandeis*

Writing is hard work. A clear sentence is no accident. Very few sentences come out right the first time, or the third.

—*William Zinsser*

Some students make the disastrous mistake of sitting down to write in the hope that, as they go along, thoughts will come to them and the writing will compose itself. That does not happen, even to people who are well known for their ability to write. It does not happen to sports journalists (Red Smith), to Supreme Court justices (Louis Brandeis), or to authors of popular books (William Zinsser). There are many reasons why, among them the following:

First, creativity simply does not work that way. In real life, a writer begins by putting down on paper ideas so fragmentary that one might be ashamed of them. They might not even be quarter-baked—much less half-baked—but on paper they will at least be out in the open. The writer then reads over that fragmentary attempt, preferably after doing something else for a few hours or even a day or more. At that point, a writer who is satisfied is engaged in self-delusion. An undeluded writer rewrites, and rewrites, and rewrites—and rewrites again. After a while, the product becomes moderately lucid and perhaps only then does the writer even begin to understand the ideas being written about. Because new nuances and ramifications appear for the first time in each new draft, the whole thing has to be done over again—and again and again. Finally, after much reworking, the product becomes useful, and at that point it often cannot be recognized as a descendent of the first effort. The amount of understanding reflected in the final draft is many, many times the amount that surfaced in the first draft because the writing process and the thinking process are inseparable, each stimulating and advancing the other. When you try to write clearly and precisely about an idea, you discover how much of it you do not understand, and then you begin wrestling with the writing and the thinking simultaneously. And you will tap only a fraction of your ability to think unless you start with an outline and then write and rewrite over and over and over again.

The second reason for assiduous planning and rewriting is that legal writing is a highly *structured* form of expression. A lawyer develops a statement of the controlling rule or rules, proves that the statement is accurate, and applies the rules to a set of facts. Rules of law themselves are by nature rigorously structured ideas, and certainly their proof and application—and any discussion of their proof and application—are also unavoidably structured. A writer can hardly deploy all these structures without advance planning, just as a house cannot be built without blueprints supplied by the architect. Your planning will be more effective if you analogize it to putting up a building; if you discipline yourself not to begin construction until you have completed the architectural phase with a detailed outline; and if, throughout the work, you understand that you have a multitude of decisions of your own to make.

When you meet with a teacher to discuss your writing on a particular assignment, be prepared to discuss your plan, whether it was effective, and whether you executed the plan effectively. Your teacher might ask you to bring your notes and outline to the conference, which may focus on the decisions you made in handling the law's intellectual structures. In fact, because undergraduate education underemphasizes — if it even mentions — the concept of working within the structure of an idea, you will find that a fair amount of the first year of law school is devoted to teaching that skill.

The third reason for planning and rewriting is that legal writing is judged entirely by how well it educates and convinces the reader that the writer's reasoning is correct. The final product must be designed so that it can be most easily absorbed by the reader. In planning, you can most effectively do that through good organization. In college, teachers rarely critique organization in writing. But practical writing in any field is very different from the kind of abstract and academic essays submitted in college because the practical reader is by nature different from the reader for whom college essays are written. To a practical reader, unplanned writing resembles an irritating and inaccessible stream-of-consciousness, rather than something useful in making decisions.

You are, of course, at somewhat of a disadvantage in the beginning because you have no firsthand experience with the type of reader you are planning for. Whether judge or supervisor, however, the typical reader of your future work is marked by five characteristics. First, the reader must make a decision and wants from you exactly the material needed for the decision — not less and not more. Second, the reader is a very busy person, must read quickly, and cannot afford to read twice. Third, the reader is aggressively skeptical and — with the predatory instincts of a shark — will search for any gap or weakness in your analysis. (That is not because lawyers are particularly nasty people: skepticism simply causes better decisions.) Fourth, the reader will be disgusted by sloppiness, imprecision, inaccuracy, or anything that impedes the reader's decision-making process or hints that you might be unreliable. And fifth, the reader will be conservative about matters of grammar, style, citation form, and document format.

How do you start planning? The standard method is to make a list of what you think you will need to discuss; reorganize that list into a more logical order; find and plug the holes that appear where logic tells you that a previously unlisted thing must be explained; delete items you now find not useful; and, finally, compartmentalize the various items on the list into discrete sub-discussions. All this should produce an outline. If your mind does not easily get started this way, you might try explaining the material to someone else and taking note of what you say and the order in which you say it. That alone will not create an outline, but it will produce at least a beginning list and get you started on organizing it logically. You will need to do much adding and reorganizing, and probably some subtracting as well, but at least you will have started. In later chapters we will explore the ways in which the outline can be crafted to the type of decision the reader must make.

In rewriting, you can help the reader through attention to detail: wording, sentence structure, and paragraphing that is clear, concise, and forceful and that expresses exactly what the reader needs to know. One of the keys to efficient rewriting is allowing time between drafts, so that when you start a new draft, you can start "cold"—imitating the frame of mind of the person on whom the writing is meant to have an effect. This requires disciplining yourself to start early within the time allotted, to work at regular intervals during that time, and to avoid frantically putting the document together at the last minute. Allow plenty of time to stop writing for a day or two after each draft, clear your mind by working on something else, and come back to do the next draft both "cold" and "fresh." In rewriting, ask yourself at least the following questions:

1. Is what you have written well organized? Have you put things in a logical order, considering the needs of the reader? (Chapter 7 explains a variable paradigm for organizing proof of a conclusion of law, and §7.3 will help you scrutinize your writing for organizational effectiveness.)
2. Is it complete? Will the skeptical reader see gaps that you have not addressed?
3. Is it clear? Is it understandable to the reader who does not already know what you are trying to say? (See §4.1.)
4. Is it concise? Where are you using too many words to say something? Where can you use a few words in place of many, or cut out words completely, without reducing needed meaning? (See §4.2.)
5. Is it forceful enough to lead the reader through the analysis? (See §4.3.)
6. Is it accurate and precise? Have you explained the cases, the statutes, and the facts as they really are or can reasonably be interpreted? If others could reasonably disagree, have you shown how they would be wrong?   .
7. Have you scrutinized your writing in terms of the questions listed inside the front cover of this book?
8. Have you eliminated *all* of the following:
   a. poor usage of legal terminology (which can be eliminated by studying Appendix A and by using a legal dictionary while writing),
   b. punctuation errors (see Appendix B),
   c. poorly structured sentences (see §4.5),
   d. poorly structured paragraphs (see Chapter 5),
   e. awkward phrasing,
   f. misspellings,
   g. typographical errors, and
   h. citation form errors (see Chapter 13 and the Bluebook[1])?

As you write and rewrite, avoid the temptation to imitate unquestioningly whatever you happen to find in the judicial opinions that appear in

---

§3.4   1. The Bluebook, more formally known as *A Uniform System of Citation,* is a legal citation manual with which you will soon become familiar.

your casebooks. Those opinions have been placed in casebooks for what they tell you about the law — not for what they tell you about how to write. In the last decade or so, there has been a revolution in the way lawyers and judges look at writing. Verbosity, obscurity, arcaneness, and disorganization that were tolerated a generation ago are now viewed as flatly unacceptable because they make the reader's job harder and sometimes impossible. That means that before you adopt a practice or device that you have seen in an opinion, you should ask yourself *whether you are tempted to do so because it actually accomplishes your purpose or because you feel safer doing what a judge has done.* The latter is not a sound basis for a professional decision. To understand how things have changed since many of the opinions in your casebooks were written, read the opening paragraphs below of two decisions on the same issue.[2] One opinion is written in a style that was once common, while the other has the clarity and forthrightness that supervisors and judges will expect of you:

UNITED STATES v. ASKEY	UNITED STATES v. PALMER
108 F. Supp. 408	*864 F.2d 524*
(S.D. Tex. 1952)	*(7th Cir. 1988)*

ALLRED, District Judge. Counts 1 and 2 of the indictment charged defendant with violating 18 U.S.C. § 1708. Counts 3 and 4 charged violation of 18 U.S.C. § 495. The court sustained a motion to dismiss Count 2 and submitted the remaining counts to a jury which found defendant guilty as charged. The court had carried defendant's motion for judgment of acquittal on Count 1 along with the case. After receiving the verdict, the court announced that the verdict would be set aside as to Count 1. Defendant was sentenced on Counts 3 and 4. The purpose of this memorandum is to reflect the basis of the court's ruling on Counts 1 and 2. . . .

Omitting formal parts, Count 2 charges that defendant unlawfully abstracted and removed "from a letter addressed to Annice Beatrice Brown . . . the contents of such letter"—a described Trea-

EASTERBROOK, Circuit Judge. About a month after settling into a house, Mildred Palmer found in her mailbox three envelopes addressed to Clifton Powell, Jr., the former occupant. Instead of returning the envelopes to the Postal Service, Palmer opened them. She found three checks (technically, warrants on Illinois's treasury)— no surprise, for the envelopes in which Illinois mails checks are distinctive. The district court described what happened next:

Richard Morrison was present when Palmer brought the mail into the house and knew she had received the state warrants. Palmer and Morrison discussed negotiating the warrants and getting the proceeds. Someone endorsed Clifton Powell, Jr.'s name without his authority on the reverse side of each warrant. The warrants were then delivered by Morrison to a man named

---

2. The issue is whether a person who steals mail after it has been delivered by the post office has violated 18 U.S.C. § 1708, which penalizes stealing "from or out of any mail, post office, or station thereof, letter box, mail receptacle, or any mail route or other authorized depository for mail matter, or from a letter or mail carrier."

sury check. There is no allegation that the letter, from which defendant abstracted the Treasury check, was a *mailed* letter or one which had been removed from some office, station, letter box, receptacle or authorized depository. The language . . . from the statute prohibits the abstracting or removing from "such letter," clearly referring back to the first part of the statute, dealing with letters *in the mails,* or taken from some post office, receptacle or depository. In other words, it would be no offense to remove the contents of a letter never deposited for mailing or transmitted through the mails; yet, that is all that is charged in Count 2. It charges no offense.

Count 1 sufficiently charges the taking of a described letter from an authorized depository for mail. The motion for verdict of acquittal goes to the sufficiency of the evidence as to whether the place from which defendant removed the letter was an authorized depository for mail matter.

The letter in question, containing a Treasury check, was addressed to Annice Beatrice Brown, 1608 Chipito Street, Corpus Christi, Texas. It was delivered by a city carrier, at the address given, by dropping it through a small letter slot in the wall at the left of the door. It simply dropped on the floor, as did all other mail at this address. No receptacle or box or container was provided.

Annice Beatrice Brown formerly received her mail at this address but had removed from Corpus Christi. Defendant lived with two other men at the Chipito Street address but received his mail at 2310 Nueces Street. He picked up the letter in question. . . .

Lawrence Armour, Sr. Armour had something which neither Palmer nor Morrison had: a bank account. For a fee Armour negotiated the three state warrants through his bank account and returned the balance of the proceeds to Morrison who shared them with Palmer.

The United States charged Palmer and Morrison with possession of checks stolen from the mails, in violation of 18 U.S.C. § 1708. The jury found them guilty. . . . We must decide whether converting the contents of an envelope violates § 1708 when the envelope was delivered to an outdated address. . . . The prosecutor believes that the three envelopes were stolen from the "mail" because they had not been delivered to Powell. The defendants emphasize that the envelopes had been delivered to the address they bore and that when Palmer took the envelopes out of the mail box, she did not intend to steal them — for she reasonably believed that everything in the mailbox was hers. When Palmer discovered that the envelopes were not, she purloined their contents, but by then the envelopes were no longer part of the mail. If the checks had been addressed to Palmer and had been stolen from her on the way to the bank, the theft would not have violated § 1708; no more does her larceny, she insists.

Palmer and Morrison were not charged with stealing out of a "letter box [or] mail receptacle," which would make Palmer's intent at the time of the withdrawal pertinent. They were charged with stealing out of the "mail." . . .

Which opinion would you rather finish reading? Has one of these judges simply written out the material without seeming to think much about your needs as a reader? If so, what in the opinion prevents you from easily understanding what the judge is trying to say? If the judge were asked to rewrite the opinion, what changes should be made and why? If you understand the issue better from the other opinion, what did that judge do to make it easier for you? By the way, are you more curious about the outcome of one of these cases than you are about the other?

4 Effective Legal Writing Style

JAMES P. DEGNAN, THE PH.D. ILLITERATE
The Washington Post, Sept. 12, 1976

The scene is my office, and I am at work, doing what must be done if one is to assist in the cure of a disease I have come to call straight-A illiteracy. I am interrogating, I am cross-examining, I am prying and probing for the meaning of a student's paper. The student is a college senior with a straight-A average, an extremely bright, highly articulate student who has just been awarded a coveted fellowship to one of the nation's outstanding graduate schools. He and I have been going over his paper sentence by sentence, word by word, for an hour.

"The choice of exogenous variables in relation to multi-colinearity," I hear myself reading from his paper, "is contingent upon the derivations of certain multiple correlation coefficients." I pause to catch my breath. "Now that statement," I address the student—whom I shall call, allegorically, Mr. Bright—"that statement, Mr. Bright—what on earth does it mean? " Mr. Bright, his brow furrowed, tries mightily. Finally, with both of us combining our linguistic and imaginative resources, we decode it. We decide exactly what it is that Mr. Bright is trying to say, which is: "Supply determines demand."

Bright's disease attacks the best minds and gradually destroys the critical facilities, making it impossible for the sufferer to detect gibberish in his own writing or in that of others. During the years of higher education it grows worse, reaching its terminal stage, typically, when its victim receives his Ph.D.

The ordinary illiterate—perhaps providentially protected from college and graduate school—might say: "Them people down at the shop better stock up on what our customers need, or we ain't gonna be in business long." Not our man. Taking his cue from years of higher education, years of reading the textbooks and professional journals that are the major sources of his affliction, he writes: "The focus of concentration must rest upon objectives centered around the knowledge of customer areas so that a sophisticated awareness of those areas can serve as an entrepreneurial filter to screen what is relevant from what is irrelevant to future commitments."

§4.1   *Clarity and Vividness*

Degnan does not misuse the term *illiterate.* It means a person who lacks the ability to communicate through the written word, and that is true of the student described. What causes such a condition in a supposedly educated person? Three things combine.

The first is the English language's two storehouses of vocabulary: one from the Anglo-Saxon and Scandinavian languages and the other from Latin and French. These alternative storehouses give English an almost unique capacity to express precisely a wide range of nuance if the writer is skilled enough to find the "right" word. On the other hand, the alternative storehouses create untold traps of obscurity where the writer unwarily selects the "wrong" word.

The second cause is a compulsion many people feel to go straight for the "wrong" word—the word that blurs meaning, rather than sharpening it— because the storehouses are presumed to have different statuses. The Latin/French vocabulary has traditionally been considered to have a higher status because it is a remnant of the ruling structure of medieval England: monarchy, aristocracy, courts, and church. The Anglo-Saxon/Scandinavian vocabulary, on the other hand, is sometimes felt to be vulgar and undignified, the words of people who are neither subtle nor influential: construction workers *sweat,* but people who ride to the hounds *perspire.* But in many languages the verbiage of the governors tends to become euphemistic and fuzzy, while the vocabulary of the governed remains crisp and vivid.[1] A student might try to *sound* like a lawyer but fail to *communicate* like one—for example, by writing "ingested" instead of a word that would tell exactly what happened, such as "ate," "drank," or "swallowed."

And because law depends on clarity, precision, and readability, judges and senior lawyers want straightforward English and treat pretentiously vague diction as evidence of the writer's mediocrity. In one experiment, appellate judges and their law clerks were asked to appraise material written in a contorted style that might be called "legalese," while other judges and their law clerks were asked to evaluate the same material rewritten into

§4.1   1. Both tendencies are described in George Orwell's most famous essay, *Politics and the English Language.*

straightforward "plain English."[2] The original legalese was considered "substantively weaker and less persuasive than the plain English versions."[3] And the judges and law clerks assumed that the traditional legalese had been written by lawyers working in low-prestige jobs.[4]

The third cause of educated illiteracy is fear. The insecure writer who is not sure what to say may try to hide that insecurity in a fog of convoluted constructions, writing

> the above captioned appeal is maintained by the defendant as a direct result of

rather than

> the defendant appeals because

This kind of camouflage does not, however, actually reduce a writer's fear. The only real way to reduce fear is to figure out exactly what should be said and then to say precisely that.

To understand the importance of clarity in law, consider two things. First, you must prove everything you say, because the law-trained mind considers every unsupported assertion to be untrue. Second, no matter how important the issue, your reader will be able to spare only a limited amount of time to ponder what you write. The more time that must be spent trying to figure out what you are saying, the less time the reader will have to think about your message and to consider agreeing with it. Where poor writing obscures the message or makes the reading troublesome, you may get rejection even if entitled to agreement. When it comes to clarity, *you will never get the benefit of doubt.*

§4.2   Conciseness

> The present letter is a very long one simply because I had no time to make it shorter.
>
> *—Pascal*

First drafts are not lean. Rewriting is the program of exercise and diet that trims a passage down to something easily read and understood. And conciseness is an important issue in legal writing for three reasons. First, concise writing is by nature more clear and often more precise. Second, the typical reader of legal writing has no time to spare and either will resent

2. Benson & Kessler, *Legalese v. Plain English: An Empirical Study of Persuasion and Credibility in Appellate Brief Writing*, 20 Loyola L.A.L. Rev. 301, 301 (1987).
3. *Id.*
4. *Id.* at 301-02.

inflated verbiage or will simply refuse to read it. Third, something about legal work paradoxically creates a temptation to swell a simple expression into something ponderous and pretentious.

For example, compare two versions of the same analysis:

It is important to note that, at the time when the parties entered into the agreement of purchase and sale, neither of them had knowledge of the cow's pregnant condition.	When the parties agreed to the sale, neither knew the cow was pregnant.
Because of the fact that the cow, previous to the contract, had not become pregnant, despite planned and observed exposure to bulls whose reproductive capacities had been demonstrated through past experience, the seller had made the assumption that the cow would not be able to produce offspring.	The seller had assumed that the cow was infertile because she had not become pregnant when he tried to breed her with known stud bulls.
Due to the fact that the seller had made a statement to the buyer describing the cow's opportunities to reproduce and the failures thereof, there would have been, in the buyer's thinking, no purpose to any further investigation or inspection he might have considered making.	Because the seller had told the buyer about the cow's history, the buyer did not investigate further.
For these reasons, the contract did not include a provision for an upward modification in the payments to be made by the buyer to the seller in the event that the cow should later prove to be capable of reproduction.	Thus, the contract did not provide for an increase in the purchase price if the cow should turn out to be fertile.

How did the verbose rough draft on the left become the concise, finished product on the right?

First, some sentences were rewritten so that a person or a thing did something. Although the verbose draft is weighted down with modifiers, the concise version focuses on carefully chosen nouns and verbs, and many modifiers became unnecessary because their meaning has been incorporated into nouns and verbs (and sometimes into more succinct modifiers):

56

the cow's pregnant condition	*became*	the cow was pregnant
despite planned and observed exposure to bulls whose reproductive capacities had been demonstrated through past experience	*became*	when he tried to breed her with known stud bulls
there would have been, in the buyer's thinking, no purpose to any further investigation or inspection he might have considered making	*became*	the buyer did not investigate further

Second, words and phrases were eliminated if they could not justify themselves:

It is important to note that	*was deleted because the "importance" is communicated by the sentence's placement and, ironically, by the rewritten version's brevity*
previous to the contract	*was deleted because it is communicated by the context*

Third, each word and phrase was weighed to see if the same thing could be said in fewer words:

at the time when	*became*	when
entered into the agreement of purchase and sale	*became*	agreed to the sale
neither of them	*became*	neither
had knowledge of	*became*	knew
Because of the fact that	*became*	because
had made the assumption	*became*	assumed
would not be able to produce offspring	*became*	was infertile

57

Due to the fact that	*became*	Because
had made a statement to	*became*	told
describing the cow's opportunities to reproduce and the failures thereof	*became*	about the cow's history
For these reasons	*became*	Thus
include a provision for	*became*	provide for
an upward modification in the payments to be made by the buyer to the seller	*became*	an increase in the purchase price
in the event that	*became*	if
the cow should later prove to be capable of reproducing	*became*	the cow should turn out to be fertile

Be careful, however, not to edit out needed meaning. In the material above, it would be folly to eliminate so much verbiage that a reader would not know that the cow was pregnant when sold; that the parties did not know of the pregnancy at the time; how each party acquired his ignorance; that the contract did not provide for an adjusted price; and why it did not do so. But not all meaning is needed: "an upward modification in the *payments* to be made by the buyer to the seller" tells us that the money was to be tendered in installments, but that meaning does not survive into the rewritten version because it has nothing to do with the issue under discussion.

§4.3   Forcefulness

Forcefulness is not a writer's version of table-pounding. Rather, forceful writing leads the reader through ideas by specifying their relationships with one another and by identifying the ideas that are most important or compelling.

Relationships between ideas can be made clear through transitional words and phrases and through demonstrative sentence structure. Careful legal writing abounds with transitional words and phrases such as the following:

accordingly	in fact
additionally	(in order) to
although	in spite of
analogously	in that event
as a result	instead
because	moreover
but	nevertheless
consequently	not only . . . , but also
conversely	on the contrary
despite	on the other hand
even if	on these facts
even though	rather
finally	similarly
for example	since
for instance	specifically
for that reason	such as
furthermore	there
hence	therefore
here	thus
however	under these circumstances
in addition (to)	while
in contrast	

Some transitional words and phrases are stronger than others. Be careful to select those that accurately represent the relationship at hand and that claim neither too little nor too much.

Where several ideas are discussed collectively, the reader is forcefully led if that is made clear, perhaps through some sort of textual list. The list need not be diagrammed. In fact, it is usually more economical to incorporate a list into the text with a transition sentence ("There are four reasons why . . . "), followed by sentences or paragraphs coordinated to the transition sentence ("First . . . " or "The first reason . . . ").

An absence of these transitional words and phrases produces a tone of choppiness. Compare the following with the second paragraph of Chapter 1:

> In December, he had himself crowned king of England. William controlled only a small part of the country. In the following years, he had to embark on what modern governments would call campaigns to pacify the countryside. In 1069, his army marched to York. . . .

Demonstrative sentence structure—the other tool for showing logical relationships—includes, among other things, the following:

subordinate sentence elements showing affirmative relationships	The amended court rule provides for such sanctions, *which eliminates the need to rely on any inherent powers the court might or might not have to punish attorneys whose vexatious conduct multiplies the court's work.*

subordinate
sentence
elements
showing nega-
tive relation-
ships

Although the attorney here argues that he made these motions only after a thorough review of this court's precedents, he has not been able to cite a single decision in support of his position.

joinder of
independent
sentence
elements to
emphasize log-
ical relation-
ships

The conduct of this attorney is at least as egregious as that of other attorneys who have been so punished: *not only* has he served and filed a frivolous pleading, *but* he has made several equally frivolous motions.

In each of these examples, the reader is led economically through the interrelationships the writer is trying to convey. In the first, the italicized[1] dependent clause, when joined to the main clause of the sentence, aggressively ties together the ideas that sanctions are now provided for by court rule and that the court therefore need not face the difficult issue of whether it has an inherent power to punish. In the second example, the dependent clause raises a target that the rest of the sentence knocks down. In the third, the colon helps to show that the conduct arises to a level of egregiousness, while "not only" and "but" tie the conduct together into a pattern.

The second goal of forcefulness in legal writing is to identify the ideas that are most important or compelling, and there are several ways of getting that across. One is simply to say it:

> The attorney's most reprehensible act was to make a motion for a preliminary injunction where his clients were not in any way threatened with harm.

Other methods are more subtle. An emphasized idea can be placed at the beginning of a sentence, paragraph, or passage, where it will be most quickly noticed. Or a series of sentences can be arranged so that the shortest and simplest of them conveys the emphasized idea:

> This attorney served and filed a pleading alleging extremely unlikely facts without making any factual investigation and under circumstances indicating that his clients' only motive for litigation was harassment. He made numerous frivolous motions, including one for a preliminary injunction where his clients were in no way threatened with harm. He has now brought an appeal without any basis in statute

§4.3 1. Italics appear in these examples only to identify parts of the sentences for discussion, not to suggest that you italicize (or underline) for emphasis. Although italics or underlining for emphasis might be effective if done sparingly and carefully, it is too easily overdone and seldom has the desired effect on a reader.

or precedent, and he has submitted a record and brief not in compliance with the court's rules. *He has thoroughly disregarded the professional obligations of an attorney.*

Notice the differences in tone among the examples on the preceding pages. The paragraph quoted immediately above might be appropriate for a brief in which an adversary urges that the attorney be punished or that a punishment meted out below be sustained; it might also be appropriate to an opinion in which a court justifies a punishment. The tone is one intended to convince. The four preceding examples, however, are stated in a more objective tone, in which analysis is merely reported, although the same passages might appear in a persuasive or justifying document to provide a foundation for other, more rhetorical statements. While forcefulness is desirable in all legal writing—simply to help the reader understand what is important and how ideas are related—a rhetorical tone is reserved for documents intended to persuade or justify and is inappropriate where the writer is asked merely to report how the law will resolve a given set of facts.

§4.4   Punctuation and Other Rules of Grammar

SAWYER v. STATE
382 A.2d 1039 (Me. 1978)

McKUSICK, Chief Justice. Petitioner Robert Earl Sawyer stands indicted by a grand jury in Chautauqua County, New York, for second degree murder and first degree robbery arising from events which the indictment alleges occurred in Stow, Chautauqua County, New York, on or about February 11, 1977. He was arrested in Maine pursuant to a rendition warrant issued by the Governor of Maine, and he then petitioned in the Cumberland County Superior Court for a writ of habeas corpus to test the legality of his arrest as a fugitive under the Maine Uniform Criminal Extradition Act, 15 M.R.S.A. § 210 (1964). After an evidentiary hearing, a justice of the Superior Court denied the writ, entered judgment for the respondents, and ordered the rendition warrant to be executed. Petitioner appeals [on two grounds, one of which is] that the documentation accompanying the requisition of the Governor of New York State was legally insufficient to support his arrest and extradition.

We deny the appeal. . . .

The requisition from the Governor of New York was accompanied by a copy of the Chautauqua County grand jury indictment and an affidavit by the Acting District Attorney for Chautauqua County attesting to certain facts, but not such as would constitute probable cause for the petitioner's arrest. 15 M.S.R.A. § 203 (1964) provides, in the part here critical, that:

> [The] demand for the extradition of a person charged with crime in
> another state . . . shall be accompanied by a copy of an indictment
> found, or information, supported by affidavit in the state having jurisdic-
> tion of the crime, or by a copy of an affidavit made before a magistrate in
> such state, together with a copy of any warrant which was issued there-
> upon. . . ."

[Section 3 of the Uniform Criminal Extradition Act, as adopted by the
National Conference of Commissioners on Uniform State Laws provides, in part, that the demand shall be "accompanied by a copy of an
indictment found or by information supported by affidavit in the state
having jurisdiction of the crime, or by a copy of an affidavit made
before a magistrate there, together with a copy of any warrant which
was issued thereupon. . . ."]

Pointing to the commas placed in the Maine Act around the words
"or information" and to the absence of comparable commas in the
parallel section 3 of the Uniform Criminal Extradition Act . . . , petitioner argues that an "indictment found" (as well as an information)
must be supported by an affidavit sufficient to establish probable
cause to believe that the fugitive committed the charged offense.

We disagree.

The legislature mandates, in no uncertain terms, that Maine's Act,
expressly denominated the "Uniform Criminal Extradition Act," 15
M.R.S.A. § 229 (1964), "shall be so interpreted and construed as to
effectuate its general purpose to make uniform the laws of those states
which enact it." *Ibid.* This particular uniform law has been adopted, in
its original or revised form, in all but three states. . . . [T]he need for
uniformity among the states is particularly acute in this area of law,
involving as it does principles of interstate comity under an umbrella
of controlling federal law. . . .

The federal act, 18 U.S.C. § 3182 (1948), implementing article IV,
§ 2, of the United States Constitution, by its language, which the Uniform Act parallels, appears to make *either* an indictment *or* a probable
cause affidavit adequate documentation. We need not, however,
reckon with any conflict between what is adequate documentation to
require the asylum state to respond under the federal statute and what
is required by the Maine Uniform Criminal Extradition Act. We find no
conflict. As a matter of construction of our section 203, a copy of the
indictment, when based on a grand jury's determination of probable
cause, is all that is required. As held by the Colorado Supreme Court in
rejecting a contention that an affidavit alleging probable cause must
accompany an indictment:

> It is clear that an affidavit is not required where the charge is made by
> action of the grand jury, as it was here. The indictment imports *probable
> cause;* it embodies a grand jury's judgment that constitutional probable
> cause exists. . . .

Our examination of the relevant history of Maine's extradition statute shows that, despite the difference in punctuation, the legislature

did not mean any substantive departure from the Uniform Act. The promptness with which Maine enacted both the original 1926 Uniform Act and the 1936 revision evinces our legislators' eagerness to achieve and maintain uniformity in this important area of interstate cooperation. When the Maine legislature in 1929 first enacted the Uniform Act, it followed in section 3 the exact language and punctuation of the Commissioners' Act, namely:

> No demand for extradition of a person charged with crime in another state shall be recognized by the Governor unless in writing and *accompanied by a copy of an indictment found or by an information supported by affidavit in the state having jurisdiction of the crime, or by a copy of an affidavit made before a magistrate there,* together with a copy of any warrant which was issued thereon. . . .

The 1926 report of the Commissioners' committee that drafted the original Uniform Act leaves no doubt that they meant the phrase "supported by affidavit" to qualify "information" only. That report states:

> Following the instruction of the last conference, your committee have incorporated the provision [for extradition on information] in this draft, and suggest that it may be generally accepted on the theory of comity. But we provide that the information must be supported by somebody's affidavit to the facts, as otherwise it is sure to meet more or less objection in many legislatures. . . .

The commas setting apart the phrase "or information" first appeared in the Maine statute when the legislature adopted the 1936 revision of the Uniform Act. . . . That enactment was manifestly designed to track the revisions made in the uniform law, and not intended to produce any substantive differences. The Legislative Record of that 89th legislature is searched in vain for the slightest indication that the Maine lawmakers meant to deviate from revising the Maine Uniform Criminal Extradition Act in the same respect as the Commissioners had done in 1936. . . . Although in general punctuation can help in construing an unclear statute . . . , the two commas inserted in section 3 of Maine's version of the Uniform Act are themselves the sole cause of any ambiguity at all in that section.[1] That ambiguity is completely swept away by the express command that section 3 be construed to promote uniformity of law among the states and by considerations of the practical dealings among the states on extradition matters.

Under New York law, the grand jury, by returning an indictment, has

---

§4.4 1. [*Court's footnote:*] The State argues that the first comma serves merely to separate the series of alternatives ("indictment found, or information, supported by affidavit in the state having jurisdiction of the crime, or . . . an affidavit . . . before a magistrate") and that the second and third commas set off the modifying clause "supported by affidavit in the State having jurisdiction of the crime" which applies only to the "information" alternative and not to the "indictment found" alternative. Although we find it unnecessary to engage in such exegesis, the State's reading of the punctuation is as plausible as that of the petitioner and is consistent with the common-sense meaning of the statute, as the petitioner's reading of the punctuation is not.

found probable cause. . . . . A copy of that indictment was before the Governor of Maine when he issued his rendition warrant. To require that New York in addition furnish an affidavit establishing probable cause would force the demanding state to paper the same wall twice. This we need not, and will not, do. . . .

Although not willing to require New York to paper the same wall twice, the *Sawyer* court itself had to write and quote approximately two thousand words while examining legislative history going back half a century—all to resolve the ambiguity caused by two commas that somehow ended up in the wrong place. And the opinion printed here is only a small part of the fuss the commas caused. The defendant's attorney apparently spotted the commas and argued in the Superior Court for Cumberland County that his client could not be extradited. The attorneys for both sides probably submitted written argument in that court, and the judge there probably wrote an opinion. In the Maine Supreme Court, the attorneys undoubtedly submitted extensive written argument and appeared before the judges to make oral arguments. And all along the way, lawyers and judges' law clerks had to research the records of the Maine legislature and the National Conference of Commissioners on Uniform State Laws, as well as the corresponding statutes in other jurisdictions. This entire process would have taken many months; throughout that time the defendant was able to stay in Maine, and the New York authorities were not able to put him on trial for murder.

In another case, a trucking company and the Interstate Commerce Commission battled for 19 years over the absence of a single comma.[2] The Commission had issued a certificate authorizing the trucking company to ship

[b]etween points in Connecticut, Pennsylvania, New Jersey, and New York within 100 miles of Columbus Circle, New York, N.Y., on the one hand, and, on the other, points and places in Connecticut, Delaware, Maryland, Massachusetts, Pennsylvania, New Jersey, New York, and Rhode Island.[3]

The trucker claimed that the limitation "within 100 miles of Columbus Circle" applied only within New York state because that phrase was not preceded by a comma. The Commission argued that the limitation applied not only within New York, but also within Connecticut, Pennsylvania, and New Jersey. The difference meant enough money to the trucker to cause an endless series of administrative disputes and two lawsuits. Finally, a divided three-judge United States District Court held for the trucker, partly "as a matter of grammatical construction,"[4] even though the dissent pointed to evidence that both parties seemed to have known at the beginning of litigation that the Commission's interpretation was what had been intended all

2. *T. I. McCormack Trucking Co. v. United States*, 298 F. Supp. 39 (D.N.J. 1969).
3. *Id.* at 41.
4. *Id.*

along.[5] Here the absence of a single comma did more than make a sentence hard to understand: it caused an interpretation that appears to have been the direct opposite of what the writer intended.

A few years ago, a fad that could have been called "optionalism" occurred in lower education: it became "optional" to observe the conventional rules of punctuation. That fad is now dying out in lower education for the same reason that it never reached law schools: correct punctuation makes writing clear and easier to understand and is not mere decoration. It is not an excuse for a lawyer to say that a reader could figure out the meaning of a poorly punctuated sentence if only the reader would think about it. As *Sawyer* and *McCormack Trucking* illustrate, the antagonistic reader can make much trouble out of ambiguity caused by bad punctuation. And even where a reader is neutral or friendly, the lawyer's job is to make meaning so plain that the reader need not read the sentence twice to edit in punctuation carelessly left out.

Not only are punctuation and other grammar skills essential to conveying meaning clearly and precisely, but they have an important effect on your credibility and reputation. Readers—including readers of law school examinations—will question your analytical abilities and general competence if you do not observe the accepted rules of English grammar. "Where lumps and infelicities occur," the novelist John Gardner wrote, "the sensitive reader shrinks away a little, as we do when an interesting conversationalist picks his nose."[6]

Thus, if you have not already mastered the rules of punctuation and of grammar generally, you will have to do so in this course. Now and while writing and rewriting, consult Appendix B, which summarizes the more important rules of punctuation. Make sure that you understand *every* rule in Appendix B: your law school writing will be scrutinized for solid grammar in a way that you probably never experienced in college.

§4.5 How to Scrutinize Your Writing for Effective Style

During rewriting, ask yourself the following questions:[1]

Have you built sentences around concrete nouns and verbs? Compare the following:

> In *Smith,* there was no withdrawal of the guilty plea, based on the court's determination of a lack of evidence of coercion.

---

5. *Id.* at 42-46.
6. *The Art of Fiction: Notes on Craft for Young Writers* 99 (1984).
§4.5 1. Your teacher may mark your work in part by referring to some of these questions by the number-letter codes used here.

> In *Smith,* the court denied the defendant's motion to withdraw her guilty plea because she submitted no evidence that the plea had been coerced.

The first example clouds meaning in two ways. First, although the sentence includes nouns and a verb, it is not built on them: they do not seem important to the sentence's structure or to the way the sentence works. Second, the nouns and verb that do appear are vague, rather than concrete. The result is that the reader can hardly tell who has done what to whom. The second example is more vivid. Because the obscure "court's determination" has become the concrete "the court denied the defendant's motion," the reader immediately knows exactly what is going on. Similarly, the vague "lack of evidence of coercion" has become the precise "she submitted no evidence that the guilty plea had been coerced."

In law, people do things to other people and to ideas and things. The only way to describe that is with nouns and verbs that are straightforward and often fairly plain and simple. As with so many other legal writing faults, rewriting is the key to solving this one. Your early drafts might have sentences in it like the first example above, but your final draft should more closely resemble the second example. As you rewrite, have people, ideas, and institutions *do* things.

| 4-B | Have you rewritten sentences so that none are front-loaded? For example: |

> The defendant's solicitation of contributions through an organization with a misleading name, immediate deposit of the funds in a bank account in the Bahamas, and eventual use of the money to buy a vacation home in his own name constitutes fraud.

Latin and German routinely place the verb at or near the end of the sentence. Readers in those languages can afford to wait for the verb because earlier in the sentence the nouns show their relationships to one another by declining (changing form, depending on whether they are subjects, direct objects, indirect objects, and so on). Although word order means little in those languages, it means a lot in English because our nouns do not change form very much to show how they are being used.

The verb is what ties an English sentence together. In English, a sentence is incomprehensible until the reader has identified both a subject *and* a verb. And the most easily understood sentences in English bring the reader to the verb as quickly as possible. The example above cannot be understood in a single reading because the verb and object (together, a mere two words) are not reached until after the reader has plowed through a subject that is 39 words long.

Sentences like the example are caused by the habit of automatically making whatever you want to talk about the subject of the sentence. You sit at a table, writing. "What shall I talk about next?" you ask yourself and then write down the answer. That becomes the subject of a sentence, no matter how unreadable the result. Perhaps this process is inevitable in first drafts, but before the product is finished you should be able to recognize the problem and correct it.

There are two easy ways to fix such a sentence. The first is to find a way to make the subject simple and bring the reader to the verb quickly:

> The defendant committed fraud by soliciting contributions through an organization with a misleading name, immediately depositing them in a Bahamaian bank account, and eventually using the money to buy a vacation home in his own name.

The other cure, sometimes a bit less effective, is to break the original sentence in two:

> The defendant solicited contributions through an organization with a misleading name, immediately deposited them in a Bahamaian bank account, and eventually used the money to buy a vacation home in his own name. Taken together, this conduct was fraud.

You will lose control of your sentences if you just let them happen. Each sentence must be *built* if it is to communicate well.

Have you used transitional words and phrases to show how ideas are related?   Beginners often underestimate the reader's | **4-C** |
need to be told explicitly how ideas fit together or contrast with one another. You can do this economically with transitional words and phrases. See those listed in §4.3.

Have you streamlined unnecessarily wordy constructions? | **4-D** |
Effective rewriting depends in part on the ability to pare a convoluted construction down to something straightforward:

cross out	*and replace it with*
at the time when	when
because of the fact that	because
during such time as	during
for the purpose of	to
for the reason that	because
in the situation where	where
in the event that	if
previous to	before
with specificity	specifically
subsequent to	after
the reason being that	because
until such time as	until
with regard to	regarding

4-E Have you replaced nominalizations? A nominalization is a verb that has been turned into a noun but is still asked to do a verb's work. "The search *was a violation of* the defendant's rights" should be rewritten as "the search *violated* the defendant's rights." The nominalized phrase *was a violation of* is weaker and more verbose than the blunt verb *violated*. The same problem occurs when you turn a verb into an adjective and then try to use it as you would a verb ("was violative of"). Some other examples:

cross out	*and replace it with*
is able to	can
enter into an agreement	agree
make the argument that	argue that
make the assumption that	assume that
is aware of	knows
is binding on	binds
give consideration to	consider
make an objection	object
make payment to	pay
make provision	provide

4-F Have you deleted throat-clearing phrases (also known as "long windups")? Phrases like the following waste words, divert the reader from your real message, and introduce a shade of doubt and an impression of insecurity:

It is significant that . . .

The defendant submits that . . .

It is important to note that . . .

The next issue is . . .

Of the following two examples, why would the plaintiff's attorney feel more comfortable writing the first than the second?

The plaintiff contends that the judgment should be reversed because . . .

The judgment should be reversed because . . .

The superfluous words in the first example shift emphasis from the idea propounded to the obvious but irrelevant fact that the writer is the one doing the propounding. (But it is not ineffectual to begin an attack on an adversary's argument by beginning with phrasing like "Although the defendant has argued . . . .")

Have you broken up or streamlined unnecessarily long sen- | **4-G**
tences? They obscure meaning. If a sentence is too long to be
understood easily on the first reading, express the sentence's ideas in fewer
words, or split the sentence into two (or more) shorter sentences, or do
both. If you decide to reduce the sentence's verbiage, see questions 4-D,
4-E, and 4-F and review §4.2. If you decide to break up the sentence, be sure
to avoid the "sing-songy" style described in question 4-H.

Have you rewritten sentences so that none are "sing-songy"? | **4-H**
For example:

> The defendant solicited contributions through an organization with a
> misleading name. He immediately deposited the funds in a bank ac-
> count in the Bahamas. Eventually, he used them to buy a vacation
> home in his own name. This conduct was fraud.

These are four simple sentences, three of them beginning with a subject. Not
only does the passage sound naive, but the effect on the reader is boredom
and sometimes sleep. The cause is a tendency to write down one thing at a
time, without describing the relationships between or among the things
mentioned. At its most extreme, the result is a series of simple sentences, all
beginning with the subject.

There are two kinds of cure. One is to focus on the relationships, especially causal ones, using some of the transitional words and phrases listed in
§4.3:

> Not only did the defendant solicit contributions through an organiza-
> tion with a misleading name, but he immediately deposited the funds
> in a bank account in the Bahamas. Moreover, he used them to buy a
> vacation home in his own name. Therefore, he has committed fraud.

The other cure is to vary three things periodically: the types of sentences
(some simple, some compound, some complex); the lengths of sentences
(some long, some short, some medium); and the way sentences begin (some
with the subject, some with a prefatory word or phrase, some with a dependent clause). Closely related material can be combined into fewer sentences, where the sentence structure itself can demonstrate relationships
between ideas:

> Having solicited contributions through an organization with a mislead-
> ing name and deposited them in a Bahamian bank account, the defen-
> dant used the funds to buy a vacation home in his own name. Taken
> together, this conduct was fraud.

This example uses a subordinate sentence element ("Having solic-
ited . . . bank account") to achieve the desired effect. (See question 4-B
for other examples based on the same material as the examples above.)

To avoid the sing-songy effect, you must understand and be able to use the full range of sentence structures available in English.

4-I | **Have you avoided the passive voice unless you have a good reason for using it?**   In the active voice, the subject of the sentence acts ("Maguire sued Schultz"), but in the passive voice the subject of the sentence is acted upon ("Schultz was sued by Maguire"). More often than not, the passive is best avoided because of its three disadvantages: it is often more verbose; it tends to vagueness; and it is usually weaker and more boring to read.

But the passive may be the more effective voice where the identity of the actor is unknown, unimportant, or better left unemphasized. For example, compare the following:

> Ms. Blitzstein's aid-to-dependent-family benefits have been wrongfully terminated fourteen times in the last six years.

> The Department of Public Welfare has wrongfully terminated Ms. Blitzstein's aid-to-dependent-family benefits fourteen times in the last six years.

Here the passive is actually more concise. Depending on the context, the passive might not be vague because the reader might be likely to know that the Department is the only agency capable of terminating aid-to-dependent-family benefits, or at least that the Department is being accused of doing so in this instance. And, again depending on the context, the passive sentence may be the stronger and more interesting of the two. If the reader is a judge who is being asked to order the Department to stop this nonsense, the passive will be the stronger sentence because it emphasizes the more appealing idea. (Generally, a judge is more likely to sympathize with a victim of bureaucratic snafus than to condemn a government agency for viciousness or incompetence.)

In some circumstances, the passive voice is also a good way of avoiding sexist pronouns. See question 4-S.

4-J | **Have you avoided placing subjects far from verbs or verbs far from objects?**   A sentence is hard to understand if you insert a clause or phrase between a subject and a verb or between a verb and an object:

> Federenko, since her attorney neither requested an instruction on self-defense nor objected to the instruction that was actually given, cannot complain on appeal that the jury was improperly instructed.

> Myers was awarded, after four years of litigation involving two trials and an appeal, damages that equalled only half his losses.

The solution is to move the clause or phrase to the end or to the beginning of the sentence, leaving the subject and verb (or the verb and object) relatively close together:

dependent clause AFTER subject and verb	Federenko cannot complain on appeal that the jury was improperly instructed, since her attorney neither requested an instruction on self-defense nor objected to the instruction that was actually given.
dependent clause BEFORE subject and verb	Because her attorney neither requested an instruction on self-defense nor objected to the instruction that was actually given, Federenko cannot complain on appeal that the jury was improperly instructed.
phrase BEFORE subject and verb	After four years of litigation involving two trials and an appeal, Myers was awarded damages that equalled only half his losses.
phrase AFTER subject and verb	Myers was awarded damages that equalled only half his losses, after four years of litigation involving two trials and an appeal.

The clause or phrase should begin the sentence only if you want to emphasize it. Federenko's dependent clause belongs at the end of the sentence because it deserves less emphasis than the subject and verb. Where should the phrase in Myers' sentence go?

Have you avoided placing modifiers so that the reader will wonder what they modify? In speech, modifiers tend to wander all over sentences, regardless of what they are intended to modify. But in formal writing, more precision is required. These sentences all mean different things:

| **4-K** |

> The police are authorized to arrest *only* the person named in the warrant.
> [They are not authorized to arrest anyone else.]

> The police are authorized *only* to arrest the person named in the warrant.
> [They are not authorized to torture him or deport him.]

> The police are *only* authorized to arrest the person named in the warrant.
> [The warrant gives them some discretion in the matter: although they have the right to arrest, they may instead choose not to.]

Only the police are authorized to arrest the person named in the warrant.
[Civilians are not so authorized.]

Make sure that the modifier's placement communicates what you really want to say, and do not assume that a busy reader will be willing or even able to figure out the meaning from the context.

4-L Have you used parallel construction when expressing a list? Parallelism requires that even implied lists be expressed in some sort of consistent structure. Each item or idea must be phrased in the same grammatical format. Compare the following:

> This attorney should be disbarred because of his neglect of a matter entrusted to him, for pleading guilty to the felony of suborning perjury, and because he disclosed a client's confidences without the client's consent.

> This attorney should be disbarred because he neglected a matter entrusted to him, because he pleaded guilty to the felony of suborning perjury, and because he disclosed a client's confidences without the client's consent.

In the first example, the first listed item is expressed as a noun possessed by a pronoun ("his neglect"); the second as an unpossessed gerund ("for pleading"); and the third as a dependent clause, complete with subject, verb, and object ("because he disclosed . . . confidences"). Although the first and third items are preceded by the word "because," the second is not. Each form alone is grammatical, but the inconsistencies among them make the whole sentence sound illiterate. That would not have been true if each item in the list had been expressed in the same format. By contrast, the second example uses clauses for all three items. (Clauses are not necessarily preferred: here the writer of the second example could have used another format for each item, so long as all three items were expressed consistently.) Be careful also about the introduction to the list: it must be phrased so that it is appropriate to each item listed. If a verb appears in the introductory part of the sentence, a replacement verb should not appear in one of the listed items.

4-M Have you used terms of art where appropriate? Where an idea peculiar to the law is customarily expressed through a term of art, that term should be used because it conveys the idea as precisely as the law can manage and often makes long and convoluted explanations unnecessary. Do not write "the plaintiff asked the court to tell the defendants to stop building the highway." It is much more precise to write "the plaintiff moved for an order preliminarily enjoining . . . ."

But do not confuse terms of art with legal argot. A term of art is the law's symbol for an idea that frequently cannot be expressed with precision in any other way. Legal argot, on the other hand, has no special meaning peculiar to the law. Rather, it is pretentious verbiage used for everyday concepts by a writer who wants to sound lawyer-like, but instead creates an impression of mediocrity. (See question 4-O.)

Have you edited out inappropriately used terms of art? Terms of art ought to be used only to convey the precise meaning the law holds for them. Where you use a term of art (perhaps because it sounds lawyer-like) but do not really intend to communicate the idea the term of art stands for, the reader will assume that you do not know what you are talking about.

Have you edited out imitations of lawyer noises? Said noises found in and about a lawyer's writing have heretofore caused, resulted in, and led to grievous injury with reference to said lawyer's readers, clients, and/or repute, to wit: by compelling the aforesaid readers to suffer confusion and/or consternation at the expense of the aforementioned clients and consequently rendering said repute to become null, void, and nugatory.

Good legal writing and good writing in other fields have the same characteristics of clarity and smoothness in reading. Thinking like a lawyer is not the same as imitating lawyer noises. Expressions like "to wit," "hereinbefore," and "aforesaid" are argot—not terms of art (see question 4-M) —and they do not convey anything that ordinary English cannot communicate more clearly and less awkwardly. The most influential memos and the most persuasive briefs are written in the real English language.

Have you edited out contractions and other conversational language? They may be appropriate to a letter to a friend, but they have no place in lawyerly documents.

Have you edited out inappropriate abbreviations? In formal documents, a lawyer does not write "the N.C. Supreme Court has held . . . ." Spell words out unless the abbreviation is generally used at least as often as the full name (for example, "NAACP" and "FCC"). Otherwise, abbreviate only in citations.

Have you avoided rhetorical questions? They are ineffective. Your job is to lead—not jab—the reader.

Have you avoided sexist wording? In the way all languages evolve, English is now shedding many centuries of sexist phrasing, a process that is particularly important in legal writing because law is one of the dialects of government. Perhaps a decade or two from now, the language might settle into phrasings that are both gender-neutral and fluid. In the meantime, writers must struggle a bit.

The thorniest problem is English's use of the pronouns *he, his,* and *him* to refer generally to people of either gender. The problem would not exist if

English had a third-person pronoun that meant "any person," regardless of gender. But English lacks such a pronoun and is not likely to develop one. The ersatz pronoun *s/he* has not gained acceptance, and it offends most readers. The ritual incantations *he or she, his or her,* and *him or her* are wordy and, if repeated often, tedious.

The best solution is to eliminate the need for a pronoun. If that cannot be done, recast both the pronoun *and* its noun in the plural. The result can sometimes be a more concise wording:

	To calendar a motion, an attorney must file *his* moving papers with the clerk.
pronoun replaced with "the"	To calendar a motion, an attorney must file *the* moving papers with the clerk.
actor made plural	To calendar motions, attorneys must file *their* moving papers with the clerk.
actor eliminated from sentence	A motion is calendared by filing the motion papers with the clerk.

Here the most concise solution is to eliminate the actor entirely and cast the sentence in the passive voice. But that may not be true with other sentences. And even here, the most concise solution might not be the best one. If the sentence is meant to warn attorneys who forget to file their moving papers, that point is lost if the attorneys themselves are not even mentioned.

Make sure that the remedy you choose makes sense in the context. For example, substituting "the" for "his" works here only because the moving attorney would be the only one to calendar the motion. And if you recast in the plural, recast the whole construction that way. The following is wrong because the pronoun is plural but the noun to which it refers is singular:

To calendar a motion, an attorney must file their moving papers with the clerk.

Fall back on "he or she" only as a last resort.

Gender-biased nouns are usually easier to avoid. The "reasonable man" in negligence law can as easily be the "reasonable person"; a "juryman" might just as well be a "juror"; and, depending on the context, "manpower" might be replaced with "effort," "personnel," "workers," or something else. Some nouns, such as "businessman," are harder, however. Unless gender truly matters ("the corporation specializes in the manufacture of businesswomen's clothing"), it is sexist to refer to a woman in business as a "businesswoman." Unless the awkward term "businessperson" gains acceptance, the only solution is to rephrase the sentence so that you need not rely on a word like "businessman" or "businesswoman."

Exercise I.   Kalmar's Driveway (Clarity and Conciseness)

Rebuild the following sentences around concrete nouns and verbs. Make sure that each sentence is of comprehensible length. Eliminate throat-clearing phrases, and replace nominalizations, unnecessary passives, and unnecessarily wordy constructions. (See §§4.1 and 4.2 and questions 4-A, 4-D, 4-E, 4-F, 4-G, and 4-I in §4.5.)

1. It is evident that Kalmar is likely to be convicted of accepting a bribe because all the elements of bribery are susceptible of proof beyond a reasonable doubt.

2. A person is guilty of accepting a bribe if that person is an employee of the government and "requests or receives from any other person anything of value, knowing it to be a reward or inducement for an official act," Crim. Code § 702, and a conviction may occur only if evidence is presented by the prosecution that persuades the finder of fact beyond a reasonable doubt that the defendant is guilty.

3. The initial element that can be established is that Kalmar is an employee of the government.

4. The facts indicate that in his capacity as Roads Commissioner, Kalmar had occasion from time to time to purchase, on behalf of the government, quantities of cement, asphalt, and other road construction materials from Phelps, who caused these materials to be delivered to road-repair sites on trucks owned by Phelps.

5. Kalmar had need for a new driveway at his own home, and he made a request to Phelps for a recommendation of a contractor who would do a good job at a reasonable price.

6. Phelps told Kalmar that she would look into the matter, but, without Kalmar's knowledge, a new driveway was built at his home by her employees the next day.

7. The circumstances fit into a pattern showing that Kalmar had knowledge that he was being offered a reward or inducement by Phelps for official acts directly relating to his job, and although the statute does not specify that a defendant must know at the time the thing of value is actually delivered or physically taken that it is a reward for official acts, Kalmar both accepted and continued to receive the bribe when, according to the facts, he did not undertake any effort to compensate Phelps for the cost of the driveway.

8. Because the cost involved is such that it could not have been accidentally overlooked by Kalmar, there can be no innocent explanation for the fact that he had an opportunity every day to see that he had a new driveway for which nothing had been paid, and there is therefore no reasonable doubt about his guilt.

Exercise II.   Smolensky at the Plate (Clarity and Forcefulness)

Edit the following to produce sentences that are not front-loaded or "sing-songy." Use transitional words and phrases to show how ideas are related. Make sure that subjects, verbs, objects, and modifiers are appropriately placed. (See §§4.1 and 4.3 and questions 4-B, 4-C, 4-H, 4-J, and 4-K in §4.5.)

1. Vargas, when Smolensky, who was batting, turned around and attacked him with a baseball bat, was playing catcher.

2. In *Crawford v. Bender,* the Court of Appeals held that a person who engages in a sport, has an opportunity to know beforehand of the types of bodily contact customary in that sport, and suffers an injury as a result of such a contact, cannot recover damages.

3. Some physical contact is inevitable in athletics. Assault is not inevitable and is prohibited by the rules of virtually every team sport.

4. Vargas participated in the game of baseball. He consented to those bodily contacts that are customary in baseball or permitted by the rules of the game. Baseball players are rarely beaten with baseball bats. In the past, Vargas has only been hit with a bat by accident. League Rule 19 specifically prohibits "striking another player."

5. To hold that Vargas will not be able to recover when Smolensky will not be able to offer any evidence that would show that Vargas intended to consent to be attacked with a bat would be inconsistent with the rule of *Crawford.*

5 Paragraphing

§5.1 Organization and Paragraphing

Before law school, your paragraphing practices may have amounted to writing until you seemed to have written a lot, stopping, and then starting a new paragraph. Paragraphs put together that way will confound and annoy readers who must find your meaning quickly. Those readers will count on you to use paragraphing to make your thinking more clear. They will assume that each paragraph substantiates a separate and distinct idea or discusses a single subject. And they will assume that the first or second sentence in each paragraph will state or imply that idea or subject and, if necessary, will also show how it is related to ideas you have already considered. To the extent you frustrate these assumptions, your writing will be less helpful and less influential.

Paragraphing has three goals. The most obvious is to break your material up into digestible chunks. The second is to help you discipline yourself to confront and develop each theme inherent in the material. The third is to tell the reader where he or she is in your logic, how that place was arrived at, and where you are headed — in other words, to make your organization apparent. If the reader feels lost or does not immediately know what the paragraph's thesis or topic is or how it differs from that of the preceding paragraph, there is something wrong with the paragraph's length or structure or with the wording of individual sentences. As you will see in §5.2, the paragraph's first sentence is the one most often botched.

How can you tell the difference between a paragraph that accomplishes these goals and one that does not? An effective paragraph has five characteristics. First, it has *unity:* it proves one proposition or covers one subject.

Material that is more relevant to other propositions or subjects has been removed and placed elsewhere. Second, an effective paragraph has *completeness:* it includes whatever is necessary to prove the proposition or cover the subject. Third, an effective paragraph has *internal coherence:* ideas are expressed in a logical sequence that the reader is able to follow without having to edit the paragraph mentally while reading. Fourth, an effective paragraph is of *readable length:* it is neither so long as to be indigestible nor so short as to seem trivial. Fifth, an effective paragraph *announces or implies its purpose* at the outset: its first or second sentence (or both) states its thesis or topic and, if necessary, makes a transition from the preceding material.

§5.2   Thesis Sentences, Topic Sentences, and Transition Sentences

In college, you may have been told that each paragraph begins with a topic sentence. Although a topic sentence is appropriate to the bulk of what is written in college, most — though not all — paragraphs in good legal writing begin with something more definitive than a topic sentence. College writing is largely *descriptive:* for the most part, it describes conditions or events or conveys largely unanalyzed information. Although some portions of a memorandum of law or an appellate brief are descriptive, the most critical passages are *probative:* they prove propositions that resolve issues. In descriptive writing, the paragraph recites facts or events, and the first or second sentence tells the reader the paragraph's topic or theme, to the extent that is not already evident from the context. But in probative writing, the paragraph exists to *prove* the validity of its first or second sentence, which states the paragraph's *thesis.* A topic is merely a category of information ("weather in Death Valley"), but a thesis is a proposition capable of proof or disproof ("the climate of Death Valley is brutal"):

Descriptive	*Probative*
In January in Death Valley, the average high temperature is about 65°, and the average low is about 37°. Spring and fall temperatures approximate summer temperatures elsewhere. In April and in October, for example, the average high is about 90°, and the average low about 60°. July is the hottest month, with an average high of about 116° and an average low of about 87°. The highest tempera-	The climate in Death Valley is brutal. At Furnace Creek Ranch, the highest summer temperature each year reaches at least 120° and in many years at least 125°. The highest temperature recorded in Death Valley — 134° — is also the highest recorded in the Western Hemisphere and the second highest recorded anywhere on earth. (The highest is 136° — in the Sahara.) In the summer sun, a person

ture ever recorded in Death Valley was 134°F on July 10, 1913. Average annual rainfall is about 1½ inches. — can lose four gallons of perspiration a day and — in 3% humidity — die of dehydration.

A confused reader of descriptive writing might ask, "What is this paragraph about?" But a confused reader of probative writing asks instead, "What is this writer trying to prove?"[1]

Probative and descriptive writing can occur in the same document. In college writing, you might typically have written many descriptive paragraphs setting out an abundance of raw data and then concluded with a short passage expressing one or more inferences that the data supported.[2] Although the document as a whole might tend to support the inferences, probative writing in college tends to be limited to the final passage — if it occurs even there.[3] But in an effective Discussion or Argument in a memorandum or a brief, the writing is largely probative, with only occasional digressions into description. Some other parts of a memorandum or brief, however, are predominantly description. The best examples are the Statement of Facts in an office memorandum and the Preliminary Statement in a persuasive memorandum or appellate brief.[4]

Unless the topic is implied by the context, a descriptive paragraph states its topic in the first or second sentence, and that sentence is the *topic sentence*. A probative paragraph states its thesis in its first or second sentence, and that sentence is the *thesis sentence*.[5] (Although a topic can often be implied, a reader is greatly helped if a thesis is always stated and never implied.) With either kind of paragraph, a *transition sentence* helps show the reader how the paragraph is connected to the material before it or the material after it.[6]

§5.2 1. The text paragraph attached to this footnote is probative. It is not merely *about* first sentences in paragraphs. It proves the proposition that most paragraphs in legal writing must begin with something more definitive than a topic sentence. The paragraph's thesis is expressed in its second sentence. The first sentence makes a transition.

2. You will learn in Chapters 6 and 7 that in law that kind of organization will frustrate your readers to the point of impatience. The law-trained reader needs to learn *at the beginning* what you intend to prove and needs to be told, at *each* step along the way, *how* the data support the proposition you are trying to prove.

3. Unless the reader is told *how* the data support the inference, the writing is not probative: the essence of proof is a *demonstration* of how the data support the inference. A mere recitation of data is not a proof. Although in college you might not have been criticized for omitting that kind of demonstration, you will be strongly criticized for it in law school because in law the reader will agree with you only if the proof is convincing. The largest part of this text is devoted to showing you what a proof is and how to make one.

4. This paragraph is probative. The first sentence states a thesis (like "the climate of Death Valley is brutal"), which the rest of the paragraph proves.

5. In college, "thesis sentence" is sometimes used to refer to a sentence that sums up the meaning of an entire essay. Here, it has a different meaning.

6. This is a descriptive paragraph. Its topic is the three kinds of sentences that tell a reader a paragraph's purpose and relationship to its surroundings. Although the paragraph could have begun with a sentence expressing that, the topic sentence was omitted on the grounds that it would have blocked the flow into the paragraph; that too many announcements of paragraphs' purposes can become tedious; and that this paragraph's purpose is implied by the context. From your point of view as the reader, was that the best writing decision? Does the context make the topic clear enough without a topic sentence? Or would you rather have been told at the beginning what the paragraph is about?

These sentences can be worked into a paragraph in several different ways. A transition sentence most often appears at the beginning of a paragraph, less often at the end (as a bridge into the next paragraph), rarely in the middle, but not at all if a transition is unnecessary. The first sentence in a paragraph can often do double duty. It might state a thesis or topic and — perhaps in a dependent clause — make a transition. Or a transition sentence at the beginning of a paragraph can imply a topic while making a transition from the previous paragraph. If the paragraph begins with a transition sentence that does not also state a thesis or state or imply a topic, the paragraph's second sentence can express the thesis or topic. Where a paragraph's thesis or topic is complex, the paragraph might end with a closure sentence that ties up loose ends.

The two most common problems beginners have in this respect are (1) omitting topic and thesis sentences entirely and (2) using topic sentences for probative paragraphs. If a topic or thesis sentence is omitted, the reader will have to read the paragraph two or three times to try to figure out its purpose, unless the purpose is implied by the context. Generally, that kind of omission happens when the writer does not know the purpose of the paragraph. The result is often something like this:

(a) Instructor identifies a murky paragraph in student writing.

(b) Instructor asks student, "Tell me in a sentence what you are trying to say in this paragraph."

(c) Student reads paragraph — ponders — and, generally, comes up with a one-sentence statement.

(d) Instructor says, "Well, would it help the reader if you *said that* at the front end of the paragraph?"

(e) Light bulb flashes over student's head.

(f) Instructor then asks, "Now if that's your main idea, how does *this* sentence [indicating one whose function is unclear] tie in to that idea?"

(g) If the student suggests a function, the instructor asks, "Is there any way you could make that function clearer to the reader?"

(h) If the student does not see a function, the instructor asks, "Does that sentence belong in the paragraph?"

As the author of this familiar scene concludes, *"There is no reason why you, the writer, cannot carry on that conversation inside your own head as you [rewrite]."* [7]

Thesis and topic sentences can help you give each paragraph unity, coherence, and completeness. The habit of announcing or alluding to a paragraph's purpose at the beginning is a kind of self-discipline. Because it forces you to articulate the paragraph's reason for being, it will encourage you — especially during rewriting — to limit the paragraph to one thesis or topic (unity), to do whatever is necessary inside the paragraph to prove that thesis or cover that topic (completeness), and to express the ideas in the paragraph in a sequence appropriate to the thesis or topic (coherence).

7. Gross, *California Western Law School's First-Year Course in Legal Skills*, 44 Alb. L. Rev. 369, 389-90 (1980).

The other basic mistake made by beginners is using a topic sentence for a probative paragraph (which should have a thesis sentence instead). Consider the following:

> The federal bank robbery statute penalizes obtaining anything of value from a bank "by force and violence, or by intimidation." 18 U.S.C. § 2113 (1982). Several cases have defined "intimidation." For example, a defendant takes by intimidation when he hands a bank teller a note reading, "Put all your money in this bag and nobody will get hurt." *United States v. Epps,* 438 F.2d 1192 (4th Cir. 1971). The same is true where a defendant, while holding his hand in his pocket to suggest that he has a weapon, hands a teller a note reading, "This is a holdup." *United States v. Harris,* 530 F.2d 576 (4th Cir. 1976). And even where a teller never sees a weapon, intimidation is proved where a defendant produces a note stating, "I have a gun. Give me all the bills or I will shoot you." *United States v. Jacquillon,* 469 F.2d 380 (5th Cir. 1972), *cert. denied,* 410 U.S. 938 (1973).

This paragraph is probative and not descriptive. Its purpose is to prove a definition of "intimidation." But the first sentence does not tell you what that definition is and therefore is not a thesis sentence. It announces only a topic — the federal bank robbery statute — and does not accurately communicate what the paragraph is meant to accomplish. In fact, the definition the quoted paragraph is meant to prove is not articulated in *any* sentence. To the reader who needs to know what "intimidation" is, a paragraph like this is very frustrating. Not only does the law-trained reader need to know what the writer intends to prove, but the reader needs to know it *before proof begins.* Most of the problem could be solved with an accurate thesis sentence like this:

> Under the federal bank robbery statute, 18 U.S.C. § 2113 — which penalizes obtaining anything of value from a bank "by force and violence, or by intimidation" — the courts have defined "intimidation" as conduct reasonably calculated to produce fear, even in the complete absence of physical violence.

To the law-trained reader, the last fourteen words of this sentence give the whole paragraph meaning because they *synthesize the holdings of the cases* into a definition that the paragraph proves to be accurate.

If you have begun a probative paragraph with a topic sentence, in all likelihood you did not know — at the moment you started to write the paragraph — what you intended to prove within that paragraph. In a first draft, there is nothing wrong with that: in a first draft, you are still working out the analysis because the writing and thinking processes are inseparable. But during rewriting, when you find a topic sentence atop a probative paragraph, that is a clue to you that you have not, in your own mind, completed the analysis. And drafting a replacement thesis sentence will force you to begin finishing the job.

Once you have replaced a topic sentence with a thesis sentence, some rewording and reordering of other sentences might be needed to give the paragraph coherence — to show, in other words, *how* the rest of the paragraph proves the thesis. Mark each way in which the earlier version has been changed here:

> Under the federal bank robbery statute, 18 U.S.C. § 2113 — which penalizes obtaining anything of value from a bank "by force and violence, or by intimidation" — the courts have defined "intimidation" as conduct reasonably calculated to produce fear, even in the complete absence of physical violence. For example, although a teller never actually sees a weapon, intimidation is proved where a defendant produces a note stating, "I have a gun. Give me all the bills or I will shoot you." *United States v. Jacquillon,* 469 F.2d 380 (5th Cir. 1972), *cert. denied,* 410 U.S. 938 (1973). More vaguely expressed threats are treated the same way. A defendant takes by intimidation when he hands a bank teller a note reading, "Put all your money in this bag and nobody will get hurt." *United States v. Epps,* 438 F.2d 1192 (4th Cir. 1971). And the result is the same even where the threat is entirely implied — for example, where a defendant, while holding his hand in his pocket to suggest that he has a weapon, hands a teller a note reading, "This is a holdup." *United States v. Harris,* 530 F.2d 576 (4th Cir. 1976).

If your prior writing experience has primarily been descriptive — and that is true of most law students — you will have to discipline yourself to see the difference between a descriptive paragraph and a probative one. And you will have to be careful to begin a probative paragraph with a thesis sentence. You will probably find that this kind of self-discipline forces you to make your meaning more clear to the reader throughout the paragraph — and that consequently you will analyze more deeply.

§5.3   *How to Scrutinize Your Writing for Effective Paragraphing*

During rewriting, ask yourself the following questions:[1]

5-A **Have you given each paragraph a unified purpose?** Prove one proposition or cover one subject. Remove and place elsewhere material that is more relevant to other propositions or subjects.

5-B **Have you made each paragraph complete?** The paragraph should include whatever is necessary to prove the proposition or cover the subject. Show the reader each step in your analysis.

§5.3 1. Your teacher may mark your work in part by referring to some of these questions by the number-letter codes used here.

Have you — within each paragraph — expressed your ideas in an effective sequence? 5-C Where a paragraph is confusing but nothing is wrong with its size or with the wording of individual sentences, the problem is usually that the paragraph lacks internal coherence. That happens when ideas within the paragraph are presented in a sequence that makes it hard for the reader to understand them or how they fit together to prove the thesis or illuminate the topic.

Have you broken up paragraphs that are so large that the reader cannot discern your organization? 5-D Although there are no set rules on paragraph length, paragraphs that wander aimlessly or endlessly do not accomplish the goals of paragraphing. If paragraphs are so large that the material is not broken up into digestible chunks, the reader will not be able to discern your organization. Where this happens, you have probably tried to develop two or more complex and separable themes in a single paragraph, perhaps without being aware of it. The cure is to identify the individual themes and to divide the material into separate paragraphs.

Have you rewritten paragraphs that are so short that no thesis or topic is developed? 5-E Generally, one- and two-sentence paragraphs are ineffective unless you have a special reason for separating out uncomplicated material for emphasis. If a paragraph is so short that no thesis or topic is developed, the problem could be either of two things. The first is that you might have missed the complexities of the thesis or topic. The second is that the thesis or topic might be so simple that it does not merit treatment in a separate paragraph; it might, in fact, be part of some other thesis or topic.

Have you introduced each paragraph with a thesis or topic sentence, except for descriptive paragraphs where the topic is clearly implied by the context? 5-F If the reader does not learn the paragraph thesis or topic at the beginning, the reader will have to read the paragraph two or three times to figure out its purpose. (See pages 78-80.)

Have you been careful not to begin a probative paragraph with a topic sentence? 5-G A probative paragraph has a thesis, not a topic. If you are unsure whether a particular paragraph is probative or descriptive, ask yourself two questions. First, does the material in the paragraph — standing alone — prove something that is relevant to your analysis? Second, if so, what proposition does it prove? If you have an answer to the second question, your answer is a rough draft of a thesis sentence. If you are trying to prove the accuracy of a rule of law, the thesis sentence should generally state the rule. (See pages 81-82.)

Have you shown how the paragraph is related to the surrounding material, unless the relationship is implied by the context? 5-H There are several ways of doing this. The paragraph can begin with a transition sentence. Or it can begin with a sentence that both makes a transition and states a thesis or topic. Or the last sentence of the preceding paragraph can build a bridge between the two paragraphs: that sentence can raise an expectation, for example, that the second paragraph satisfies.

5-1 Have you deleted throat-clearing introductory sentences? These obscure, rather than explain. They bump into the paragraph's thesis or topic backward. For example:

> The Court of Appeals considered this question in *Bellamy*. There, the court held that, under some circumstances, a promissory note can be a security subject to regulation under this state's Blue Sky Law.

Why not combine these two sentences into a single thesis or topic sentence that goes straight to the point:

> The Court of Appeals held in *Bellamy* that, under some circumstances, a promissory note can be a security subject to regulation under this state's Blue Sky Law.

Exercise I.   The First Weeks of Law School (Probative and Descriptive Paragraphs)

Write two paragraphs—one descriptive and the other probative—about the first weeks of law school.

Descriptive paragraph: Summarize what happened during your first weeks in law school. Describe only what you saw, heard, read, and wrote. Do not try to prove any belief you might have about the first weeks of law school.

Probative paragraph: The opening sentence of this paragraph should be "The first weeks of law school are hard" (or "puzzling" or "exciting" or "brutal" or "challenging" or any other characterization you choose) "because"—and here you complete the sentence by stating whatever you believe to be the cause of your characterization. The rest of the paragraph should prove the thesis expressed in this sentence.

Exercise II.   Maldonado's Citrus Croissants (Thesis and Topic Sentences, Paragraph Coherence)

Is the paragraph below probative or descriptive? What is the thesis or topic? Is it adequately expressed in the first or second sentence? If not, write an appropriate thesis or topic sentence. Within the paragraph, are ideas expressed in a logical sequence so that you do not have to edit the paragraph mentally while reading? If you believe the sentences in the paragraph should appear in a different order, rearrange them and write out separately your reasons for doing so. Decide whether any sentence's wording should be altered to improve the flow from sentence to sentence and from idea to idea.

> A matter of general knowledge within an industry is not protectable as a trade secret because it lacks a trade secret's novelty or uniqueness.

Wright v. Palmer, 11 Ariz. App. 292, 464 P.2d 363 (1970); Restatement of Torts § 757 comment *b* (1939). "Matters which are completely disclosed by goods which one markets cannot be his secret." Restatement § 757 comment *b.* Maldonado's Citrus Croissants recipe is not a trade secret. Although the recipe for Citrus Croissants was unique and novel and had not been developed by any other baker, anyone in the baking industry could have purchased Citrus Croissants from a store and discovered their ingredients and baking process through reverse engineering, a relatively time-consuming and expensive process. Thus, the recipe could have been discovered, although not easily. Since the recipe could have been disclosed through marketed croissants, it does not constitute a trade secret.

Exercise III.   Escape from Prison (Paragraph Unity, Coherence, and Length)

Is the paragraph below limited to proving a single proposition or covering a single subject? If not, what material is extraneous? Is the paragraph of appropriate size? If you believe it is too long, how should the problem be solved? Are the ideas expressed in a sequence that enables you to understand the meaning of the paragraph without reading it twice? If not, what sequence would be better? Rewrite the paragraph in light of your answers to these questions. Be sure to include any thesis, topic, or transition sentences that would be needed.

A prisoner who leaves a prison without permission is guilty of a crime of escape. Until relatively recently, the defense of necessity was not available in California to a prisoner who claimed that prison conditions were so intolerable as to require escape. An early case, for example, affirmed a conviction for escape, conceding that "if the facts were as stated by the defendant, he was subjected to brutal treatment of extreme atrocity" in a "remote" mountain prison camp far from any authorities to whom he might complain. *People v. Whipple,* 100 Cal. App. 261, 266, 279 P.2d 1008, 1010 (2d Dist. 1929). And a more recent case affirmed a conviction where the defendant offered evidence that other prisoners had threatened to kill him, and that prison guards had refused to protect him. *People v. Richardson,* 269 Cal. App. 2d 768, 75 Cal. Rptr. 597 (1st Dist. 1969). Both *Whipple* and *Richardson* cited 1 Hale P.C. 611 for the proposition that escape from prison can be excused only to avoid death as immediate as that threatened when the prison itself is engulfed in fire. But drawing on decisions from other jurisdictions, the Court of Appeal for the Fourth District has held that, through a "limited defense of necessity," a prisoner can defeat a prosecution for escape if the prisoner can demonstrate (1) that he or she was "faced with a specific threat of death, forcible sexual attack or substantial bodily injury in the immediate future," (2) that a complaint to the authorities would have been futile or not possible, (3) that the same was true regarding resort to the courts, (4) that the prisoner used no "force or violence" in escaping, and (5) that the prisoner surrendered to the authorities "when he [had] attained a position of safety from the immediate threat.'' *People v. Lovercamp,* 43 Cal. App. 3d 823, 831-32, 118 Cal. Rptr. 110, 115 (4th Dist. 1974). Even under this test, Victor Minskov does not have a defense to the charge of escape. He had been beaten twice by a group of prisoners who threatened to attack him as long as he remained in the same prison. He scaled the prison wall at 4 A.M. immediately after the second beating and while being chased by the same group. After the first beating, he had complained to prison guards, who laughed at him, and during the second beating his cries for help brought no response. The courts would not have been able to protect him from such an assault, and he used no force or violence in escaping. But after leaving the prison he hid under an assumed name for 16 months and was finally captured at the Los Angeles airport trying to leave the country. Thus, he will not be able to show that he complied with the last element of the *Lovercamp* test by surrendering to the authorities upon attaining ''a position of safety from the immediate threat.''

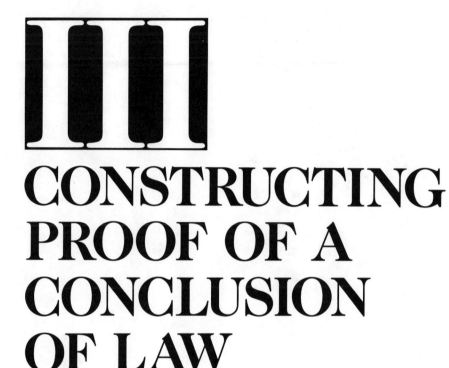

III
CONSTRUCTING PROOF OF A CONCLUSION OF LAW

6 Working with Rules

§6.1 Rules of Law: Introduction

A rule is a general principle on which decisions are to be based. Some rules might be thought of as *mandatory* ("any person who pays a fee of ten thousand lire shall be entitled to a beach permit"), while others are *prohibitory* ("no person shall transfer more than two million pesos to another country without a license from the Ministry of Finance") or *discretionary* ("the curator of the Louvre may permit flash photographs to be taken when, in his or her judgment, no damage to art will result"). Some appear to be one kind of rule, but on examination turn out to be something else. For example, the following seems mandatory but would actually be discretionary if a correlated rule empowers the judge to suspend sentence: "a person in charge of a dog that fouls the footway shall be fined ten pounds."

You might think that making decisions through rules is an easy endeavor, but for several reasons that is hardly so. First, rules must be expressed in terms of categories of actions, things, conditions, and people, and you have already had a taste—in Chapter 2 and in your other courses—of how slippery those kinds of definitions can be. Some of the slipperiness is there because precision takes constant effort, like clearing ice and snow in winter. But some of it is there to give law the flexibility needed for sound decision-making. The language "in which law is necessarily expressed . . . is not an instrument of mathematical precision but possesses what has been happily described as an 'open texture.'" [1] That is because a rule's quality is mea-

---

§6.1 1. D. Lloyd & M. Freeman, *Lloyd's Introduction to Jurisprudence* 1139 (5th ed. 1985).

sured not by its logical elegance — few rules of law have that — but by how well the rule guides a court into making sound decisions. "Rules of law are not linguistic or logical rules but to a great extent *rules for deciding.*"[2]

Second, the rule and its expression are not easily equated because a given rule might be expressed in any of a number of ways. Where law is made through precedent — as much of our law is — different judges, writing in varying circumstances, may enunciate what seems like the same rule in a variety of distinct phrasings. At times, it can be hard to tell whether the judges have spoken of the same rule in different voices or instead have spoken of slightly different rules. In either situation, it can be harder still to discover — because of the variety — exactly what the rule is or what the rules are. All this may at first seem bewildering, but in fact it opens up one of the most fertile opportunities for a lawyer's creativity because in litigation each side is free to argue a favorable interpretation of the mosaic of rule statements found in the precedents and courts are free to mutate the law through their own interpretation of the same mosaic.

Third, even where the rule is expressed in one voice, ambiguity and vagueness can obscure intended meaning unless the person stating the rule is extraordinarily careful in using and defining language. The classic example asks whether a person riding a bicycle through a park violates a rule prohibiting the use there of "vehicles." (What had the rule-maker intended? How could the intention have been made more clear?) Even where the rule-maker is careful with language, the structure of a rule does not always easily accommodate an expression of the rule's purpose — or, as lawyers say, the policy underlying the rule — even though the rule's policy or purpose is the key to unravelling ambiguities within the rule. (Is a self-propelled lawn mower a prohibited "vehicle"? How could the rule make that clear? Does your solution also determine whether the rule prohibits an excavator owned by the Parks Department?) Not only is it difficult to frame a rule so that it controls all the rule-maker wishes to control, but after a rule is framed situations inevitably crop up that the rule-maker did not contemplate or could not have been expected to contemplate. (Is a baby carriage powered by solar batteries a "vehicle"?)

Fourth, the parts of a rule may be so many and their interrelationships so complex that it may be hard to pin down exactly what the rule is and how it works. And this is compounded by interaction between and among rules. A word or phrase in a rule may be defined, for example, by another rule. Or the application of one rule may be governed by yet another rule — or even a whole body of rules. There are ways, however, of organizing and diagramming a rule (and its related rules) to discover meaning, and these are explained in the pages that follow.

Fifth, even where the rules are clear, a set of facts may at first seem so complicated as to be impenetrable, unyielding of a place to start applying the rule. But just as there are ways of organizing the rule, so are there ways of organizing the facts, and these, too, are explained later in this chapter.

2. *Id.* at 1140 (emphasis in original).

More than any others, two skills will help you become agile in the lawyerly use of rules. The first skill is language mastery, including an "ability to spot ambiguities, to recognize vagueness, to identify the emotive pull of a word . . . and to analyze and elucidate class words and abstractions."[3] The second is the capacity to think structurally. A rule is, after all, an idea with structure to it, and—even though the *words* inside a rule might not have mathematical precision—the rule's *structure* is more like an algebraic formula than a value judgment. The skill needed is that of perceiving the structure of an idea, breaking it down into sub-ideas, organizing the sub-ideas usefully and accurately, and applying the organized idea to facts.

§6.2   The Inner Structure of Rules

At this moment the King, who had for some time been busily
writing in his notebook, called out "Silence!" and read from his book,
"Rule Forty-two. *All persons more than a mile high to leave the court.*"
Everyone looked at Alice.
"*I'm* not a mile high, said Alice.
"You are," said the King.
"Nearly *two* miles high," added the Queen.

—*Lewis Carroll*,
Alice in Wonderland

Every rule has three distinct components: (1) a set of elements, collectively called a *test;* (2) a result that occurs when the test is satisfied by the presence of all the elements; and (3) what, for lack of a better expression, could be called a causal term that determines whether the result is mandatory, prohibitory, or discretionary. (As the examples on the next page illustrate, the result and the causal term are usually integrated into the same phrase or clause.) Additionally, many rules have (4) one or more exceptions that, if present, would defeat the result, even if all the elements are present.

Consider Alice's situation. She was confronted with a test of two elements. The first was the status of being a person, which mattered because at the time she was in the company of assorted small animals, some playing cards with arms and legs, and a beast with the head and wings of an eagle and the body of a lion—all of whom seem to have been exempt from any requirement to leave. The second element went to height—specifically a height of more than a mile. The result would have been departure from the court, and the causal term was mandatory ("*All* persons . . . *to* leave . . ."). No exceptions were provided for. Alice has denied the second element (her height), impliedly conceding the first (her personhood). The Queen has offered to prove a height of two miles. What would happen if the

3. W. Twining & D. Miers, *How to Do Things with Rules* 120 (1976).

Queen were unable to make good on her promise and instead produced evidence showing only a height of 1.241 miles? (Read the rule.) What if the Queen were to produce no evidence and if Alice were to prove that her height was only 0.984 miles?

A causal component is always mandatory (such as "shall"), prohibitory ("shall not"), or discretionary or permissive ("may"). The following extracts from the Freedom of Information Act[1] illustrate each type of causal term:

> Except with respect to the records made available under paragraphs (1) and (2) of this subsection, each agency, upon any request for records which (A) reasonably describes such records and (B) is made in accordance with published rules stating the time, place, fees (if any), and procedures to be followed, *shall* make the records promptly available to any person.[2]

> The Court *may* assess against the United States reasonable attorneys' fees and other litigation costs reasonably incurred in any case under this section in which the complainant has substantially prevailed.[3]

> Except to the extent that a person has actual and timely notice of the terms thereof, a person *may not* in any manner be required to resort to, or be adversely affected by, a matter required to be published in the Federal Register and not so published.[4]

To make sense out of rules as complex as these, a lawyer might diagram them out on scratch paper. If trying to help someone else understand them, the lawyer might also reorganize the phrasing of one or more of the rules. (Be careful, though: reorganizing phrasing is not the same as *re*phrasing. The words of a rule are subject to interpretation, and rephrasing can change meaning, rather than assist comprehension.)

The third example above could be diagrammed as shown on page 93. The diagrammed rule has not only two elements, but also two results, each of which is prohibited ("may not").

The conjunctions *and* and *or* reveal some of the rule's structure. In the diagrammed rule, "and" means that the elements are cumulative: if either of them is not substantiated in the facts, the rule will not operate. If "and" were to be replaced with "or," the elements would become *alternative:* either of them — even in the absence of the other — would cause the result. But "or" appears here not in the test, but instead in the result component. If the causal component had been mandatory ("shall") or permissive ("may"), the word "or" would have meant that the items listed in the result were alternative ("shall be required . . . or adversely affected," "may be required . . . or adversely affected"). That could not, however, be so where, as here, the causal term is prohibitory ("may not"): if "a person may not" be subject to either of the results set out, that person is free from both of them.

§6.2   1. 5 U.S.C. § 552 (1982 & Supp. IV 1986).
2. 5 U.S.C. § 552(a)(3) (1982) (emphasis supplied).
3. 5 U.S.C. § 552(a)(4)(E) (1982) (emphasis supplied).
4. 5 U.S.C. § 552(a)(1) (1982) (emphasis supplied).

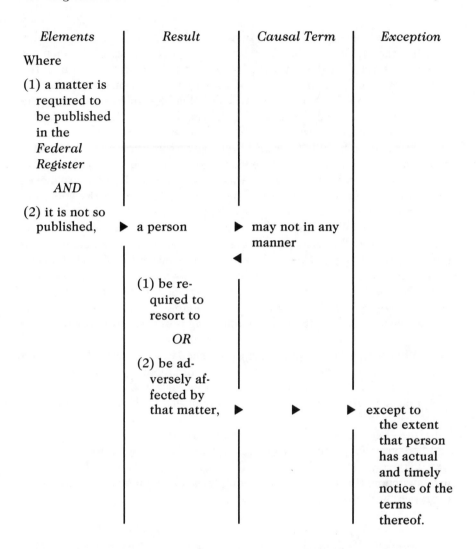

Elements	Result	Causal Term	Exception
Where			
(1) a matter is required to be published in the *Federal Register*			
AND			
(2) it is not so published, ▶	a person	▶ may not in any manner ◀	
	(1) be required to resort to		
	OR		
	(2) be adversely affected by that matter, ▶	▶	▶ except to the extent that person has actual and timely notice of the terms thereof.

You might think that exceptions need not be listed separately from elements, since an exception could just as easily be stated negatively among the elements. For example:

Elements

Where (1) a matter is required to be published in the *Federal Register*

AND

(2) it is not so published

AND

(3) a person does not otherwise have actual and timely notice of the terms thereof . . .

Certainly, if Congress had wanted to, it could have formulated the rule this way, but the effect probably would not have been the same. An element usually must be alleged and proved by the party claiming the benefit of the test and its results. Generally (but not always), the creation of an exception places on the opposing party the burden of pleading and persuasion, in the form of an affirmative defense. The distinction between elements and affirmative defenses is important in the way a rule *operates*. Here a person logically ought to be able to escape being adversely affected by a matter if that person can prove (1) that the matter was required to be published in the *Federal Register* and (2) that it was not so published. But it also makes especially good sense that a person should not gain that benefit where the government can prove that the person had actual and timely notice of the matter in some other way. You would not know for certain, however, whether an exception is a negative element or an affirmative defense without reading the precedents that have interpreted and enforced the rule.

Diagramming the rule not only breaks it down so that it can be understood, but, where properly done, it also permits putting the rule back together in a reorganized form more understandable to a reader and easier for the reader to apply. Notice how the following is derived from the diagram:

> Where a matter is required to be published in the *Federal Register* and is not so published, a person may not in any manner be required to resort to or be adversely affected by that matter, except to the extent that the person has actual and timely notice of the terms thereof.

Here the elements are best listed first because there are only two of them and because this particular rule can be more concisely expressed in that way. (Try stating this rule coherently with the elements listed last.) A rule with an uncomplicated result but a complex set of elements might be better expressed with the elements at the end:

> A person is guilty of common law burglary when he or she breaks and enters the dwelling of another in the nighttime with intent to commit a felony therein.

The sentence above illustrates the general principle — applicable to all writing but especially important in legal writing — that a sentence made up of one complex construction and one simple construction is usually best put together with the simple construction first. Where a complex construction appears at the beginning of the sentence, the reader is deprived, until after the complex construction has been read, of the context necessary to make sense out of it:

> When a person breaks and enters the dwelling of another in the nighttime with intent to commit a felony therein, he or she is guilty of burglary.

Because the reader does not learn until the end of the sentence what this list of elements is all about, a sentence like this can be understood only by reading it at least twice. An even greater problem is created by placing the complex construction in the middle of the simple construction:

> A person who breaks and enters the dwelling of another in the night-time with intent to commit a felony therein is guilty of burglary.

How does one determine how many elements are in a rule? Think of an element as an integral fact, the absence of which in any set of facts would prevent the rule's operation, and then explore the logic behind the rule's words. For example, is "the dwelling of another" one element or two? A person might be guilty of another crime, but she is not guilty of common law burglary where she breaks and enters the restaurant of another, even in the nighttime and with intent to commit a felony therein. "The dwelling of another" thus includes two factual integers — the nature of the building and the identity of its resident — and therefore two elements. If you can think of a reasonably predictable scenario in which only part of what you believe to be one element could be true, then you have inadvertently combined two or more elements.

Often you cannot know the number of elements in a rule until you have consulted the cases interpreting it. Is "breaking and entering" one element or two? The cases define "breaking" in this sense as the creation of a gap in a building's protective enclosure, such as by opening a door, even where the door was left unlocked and the building is thus not damaged. The cases further define "entering" for this purpose as placing inside the dwelling any part of oneself or any object under one's control, such as a crowbar.[5] Can a person "break" without "entering"? A would-be burglar would seem to have done so where she has opened a double-hung window by pushing it up from the outside, and where, before proceeding further, she has been apprehended by an alert police officer — literally a moment too soon. "Breaking" and "entering" are therefore two elements, but one could not know that without discovering precisely how the courts have defined the terms used.

Where the elements are complex or ambiguous, an enumeration may add clarity to the list:

> A person is guilty of common law burglary when he or she (1) breaks and (2) enters (3) the dwelling (4) of another (5) in the nighttime (6) with intent to commit a felony therein.

---

5. This sentence contains an example of what might be thought of as a definitional rule — a rule that defines an element of another rule (in this instance the element of an "entering"). (The preceding sentence does the same thing for the "breaking" element.) You might think of these definitions as sub-rules, since their purpose is to assist analysis based on the rule for common law burglary. Both sentences also contain ideas that at first do not seem very rule-like. The "entering" sentence contains an example ("such as a crowbar"), and the "breaking" sentence contains both an example and two qualifications ("such as by opening a door, even where the door was left unlocked and the building is thus not damaged"). But courts are asked to decide questions like whether opening a door creates a gap in a building's protective enclosure, and a court's decision on such an issue creates a new rule (which you might think of as yet another sub-rule). Try reformulating the "breaking" and "entering" sentences into the elements/causal term/result format. Because of the examples and qualifications, you might find that each sentence evolves into two or three or even four sentences.

Instead of elements, some rules have criteria or guidelines. These tend to be rules that empower a court or other authority to make discretionary decisions, and the criteria define the scope of the decision-maker's discretion. For example, under a typical modern divorce statute,[6] marital property is distributed as follows:

> Marital property shall be distributed equitably between the parties, considering the circumstances of the case and of the respective parties.
>
> In determining an equitable disposition of property . . . , the court shall consider:
>
> (1) the income and property of each party at the time of marriage, and at the time of the commencement of the action;
>
> (2) the duration of the marriage and the age and health of both parties;
>
> (3) the need of a custodial parent to occupy or own the marital residence and to use or own its household effects;
>
> (4) the loss of inheritance and pension rights upon dissolution of the marriage as of the date of dissolution;
>
> (5) any award of maintenance;
>
> (6) any equitable claim to, interest in, or direct or indirect contribution made to the acquisition of such marital property by the party not having title, including joint efforts of expenditures and contributions and services as a spouse, parent, wage earner and homemaker, and to the career or career potential of the other party;
>
> (7) the liquid or non-liquid character of all marital property;
>
> (8) the probable future financial circumstances of each party;
>
> (9) the impossibility or difficulty of evaluating any component asset or any interest in a business, corporation, or profession, and the economic desirability of retaining such asset or interest intact and free from any claim or interference by the other party;
>
> (10) the tax consequences to each party;
>
> (11) the wasteful disposition of assets by either spouse;
>
> (12) any transfer or encumbrance made in contemplation of a [divorce] action without fair consideration;
>
> (13) any other factor which the court shall expressly find to be just and proper.

Only seldom would all of these criteria tip in the same direction. With a rule like this, a judge does something of a balancing test, deciding according to the tilt of the criteria as a whole, together with the angle of the tilt. If the criteria favor a party only slightly, he or she may get most of the marital property, but less than if the party had been favored overwhelmingly.

You will meet few of these criteria rules in the first year of law school, except perhaps in courses on civil procedure and constitutional law. They are a relatively new development in the law and grow out of a recent tendency to define more precisely the discretion of judges and other officials. You will see criteria rules more often in the second and third years of law school, where the focus is on parts of the law dominated by the innovations of modern statutes and recent constitutional law. The first year, however, is largely devoted to subjects closer to the common law: property, contracts,

6. N.Y. Dom. Rel. Law § 236, Part B(5)(c) & (d) (McKinney 1986).

torts, and criminal law. In those fields, and in the law as a whole, the prevalent rule structure is that of a set of elements, the presence of which leads to a particular result in the absence of an exception.

§6.3   Organizing the Application of a Rule

Welty and Lutz are students who have rented apartments on the same floor of the same building. At midnight, Welty is studying, while Lutz is listening to heavy metal with his new four-foot speakers. Welty has put up with this for two or three hours, and finally she pounds on Lutz's door. Lutz opens the door about six inches, and, when he realizes that he cannot hear what Welty is saying, he walks back into the room a few feet to turn the volume down, leaving the door open about six inches. Continuing to express outrage, Welty pushes the door completely open and strides into the room. Lutz turns on Welty and orders her to leave. Welty finds this to be too much and punches Lutz so hard that he suffers substantial injury. In this jurisdiction, the punch is a felonious assault. Is Welty also guilty of common law burglary?

You probably say "no," and your reasoning probably goes something like this: "That's not burglary. Burglary happens when somebody gets into the house when you're not around and steals all the valuables. Maybe this will turn out to be some kind of trespass." But in law school a satisfactory answer is never merely "yes" or "no": an answer necessarily includes a sound *reason,* and, regardless of whether Welty is guilty of burglary, this answer is wrong because the reasoning is wrong. The answer can be determined only by applying the rule on burglary found in §6.2. Anything else is a guess.

Where do you start? Remember that a rule is a structured idea: the presence of all the elements causes the result, and the absence of any of them causes the rule not to operate. The elements of burglary are

1. a breaking
2. and an entry
3. of the dwelling
4. of another
5. in the nighttime
6. with intent to commit a felony therein

To discover whether each element is in the facts, simply annotate the list:

1. *a breaking:* If a breaking can be the enlarging of an opening between the door and the jam without permission, and if Lutz's actions do not imply permission, there was a breaking.
2. *and an entry:* Welty "entered," for the purposes of the rule on burglary, by walking into the room, unless Lutz's actions implied permission to enter.

3. *of the dwelling:* Lutz's apartment was a dwelling.
4. *of another:* And it was not Welty's dwelling: she lived down the hall.
5. *in the nighttime:* Midnight is in the nighttime.
6. *with intent to commit a felony therein:* Did Welty intend to assault Lutz when she strode through the door? If not, this element is missing.

You can see how much the first answer ("it doesn't sound like burglary") was a guess. By examining each element separately, you find that elements 3, 4, and 5 are present, but that you really do not know about the others without some hard thinking about the facts and without consulting the precedents in this jurisdiction that have interpreted elements 1, 2, and 6.

The precedents might turn up a variety of results. Suppose that, although local precedent defines Welty's actions as a breaking and an entry, the cases on the sixth element strictly require corroborative evidence that a defendant had a fully formed felonious intent when entering the dwelling. That kind of evidence might be present, for example, where the accused was in possession of safecracking tools when she broke and entered, or where, before breaking and entering, the accused had confided to another that she intended to murder the occupant. Against that background, the answer here might be something like the following: "Welty is not guilty of burglary because, although she broke and entered the dwelling of another in the nighttime, there is no evidence that she had a felonious intent when entering the dwelling."

Suppose, on the other hand, that under local case law Welty's actions again are a breaking and an entry; that the local cases do not require corroborative evidence of a felonious intent; and that local precedent defines a felonious intent for the purposes of burglary to be one that the defendant could have been forming, even if not yet consciously, when entering the dwelling. Under those sub-rules, if you believe that Welty had the requisite felonious intent, your answer would be something like this: "Welty is guilty of burglary because she broke and entered the dwelling of another in the nighttime with intent to commit a felony therein, thus meeting all the elements of common law burglary." These are real answers to the question of whether Welty is guilty of burglary: they state not only the result, but the reason why.

§6.4 Applying a Rule in Writing

When reading the kind of probative writing that occurs in the Discussion portion of an office memorandum or the Argument portion of a persuasive memorandum or appellate brief, a lawyer or judge needs first to be told of the conclusion the document is intended to prove. If the conclusion is mentioned for the first time after the analysis that supports it, or in the middle of that analysis, some or all of the analysis seems pointless to the reader who does not yet know what it was intended to substantiate. Effective writers usually state their conclusions baldly at the beginning of a Discussion or Argument ("The plaintiff does not have a cause of action because . . ."). This may take some getting used to. Not only is it contrary to the way writing is generally done in college, but most of us have been socialized since childhood to state a conclusion only after a proof—even in the most informal settings—to avoid appearing opinionated, arrogant, or confrontational. Far from being offended, however, the reader who has to make a decision is grateful not to be kept in suspense. Such a reader becomes frustrated and annoyed while struggling through passages the relevance of which cannot be understood because the writer has delayed announcing the conclusion the passages are intended to prove.

Having read a conclusion, the law-trained reader is next most curious about the rule or rules[1] that compel it. After all, the idea of law is that things are to be done only if they can be justified through one or more rules.[2] At this point, the reader usually is not yet interested in a prefatory recitation of the facts, because the determinative facts can be identified only through analysis of the elements of the rule.[3] After the conclusion and supporting rule or rules have been stated, your task is to substantiate the conclusion by showing how it results from an application of the rules to the facts at hand. If reasonable arguments could be made against your conclusion—and there usually are such arguments—they should be evaluated.[4]

If there are several issues, each will have a conclusion, which must be proved separately in approximately the sequence described above. Even a single issue might devolve into several sub-issues, each requiring a sub-conclusion that, unless incontestable, must be separately demonstrated. For example, the facts at the beginning of §6.3 present only one issue ("Is Welty guilty of burglary?"), but at least six sub-issues—one for each of the elements of common law burglary. Three of those elements are contestable, and a writer's conclusion as to each would have to be demonstrated separately.

Assume that, in the jurisdiction in question, the crime of common law burglary has been reduced to statute in the following form:

---

§6.4 1. Although a conclusion is sometimes based on a single, simple rule, more often it grows out of two or more rules. A rule might, for example, have an entourage of subordinate rules: you have already seen examples of that in the rules defining various elements of burglary. Or a conclusion might be based on rules that are entirely independent of each other. You have seen an example of that as well: although the rules on burglary and assault define two separate crimes, both are needed to determine whether Welty is guilty of burglary. A comprehensive organization (explained in Chapter 7) may be needed where a conclusion is proved through several rules. In this chapter, however, the examples are a little more simple. For conciseness here, "rule" should be understood to mean the rule or rules essential to proving the conclusion.

2. In practice, it is not enough merely to state the rules: they must be proved through citation to and discussion of cases and statutes. That is a complex task requiring a multitude of skills explained in Chapters 7-11 and 13. For the moment, however, let us concentrate on rule application, rather than on rule proof.

3. Facts are examined extensively in a Discussion or Argument. But because a memorandum or brief includes a separate fact statement, a *recitation* of unanalyzed facts at or near the beginning of a Discussion or Argument often wastes space and effort.

4. Law school teachers—but not practicing lawyers—call this kind of evaluation a counter-analysis.

> *Criminal Code § 102:* "A person commits burglary by breaking and entering the dwelling of another in the nighttime with intent to commit a felony therein."

And assume that the elements of burglary have been statutorily defined as follows:

> *Criminal Code § 101(c):* A "breaking" is the making of an opening, or the enlarging of an opening, so as to permit entry into a building, or a closed off portion thereof, provided that neither owner nor occupant has consented thereto.

> *Criminal Code § 101(g):* An "entering" or an "entry" is the placing, by the defendant, of any part of his body or anything under his control within a building, or a closed off portion thereof, provided that neither owner nor occupant has consented thereto.

> *Criminal Code § 101(e):* A "closed off portion" of a building is one divided from the remainder of the building by walls, partitions, or the like so that it can be secured against entry.

> *Criminal Code § 101(f):* A "dwelling" is any building, or any closed off portion thereof, in which one or more persons habitually sleep.

> *Criminal Code § 101(n):* A dwelling is "of another" if the defendant does not by right habitually sleep there.

> *Criminal Code § 101(m):* "Nighttime" is the period between sunset and sunrise.

> *Criminal Code § 101(k):* "Intent to commit a felony therein" is the design or purpose of committing, within a building or closed off portion thereof, a crime classified in this Code as a felony, provided that the defendant had such design or purpose at the time both of a breaking and of an entering.

Assume further that the statutes also include the following:

> *Criminal Code § 11:* No person shall be convicted of a crime except on evidence proving guilt beyond a reasonable doubt.

> *Criminal Code § 403:* An assault causing substantial injury is a felony.

Finally, assume, for the sake of simplicity, that none of these sections has yet been interpreted by the courts — probably a unique situation — and that you are therefore limited to reliance on the statute.

An analysis of whether Welty is guilty of burglary could be organized into something like the following (notice the organization):

Welty will not be convicted of burglary because the evidence does not show beyond a reasonable doubt that she had formed the intent to commit a felony when she broke and entered Lutz's apartment. Under § 102 of the Criminal Code, a person is guilty of burglary if he or she (1) breaks and (2) enters (3) the dwelling (4) of another (5) in the nighttime (6) "with intent to commit a felony therein." Under § 11, a defendant can be convicted only "on evidence proving guilt beyond a reasonable doubt."

Although (as shown below) Welty broke and entered Lutz's dwelling in the nighttime, and although the assault she committed there is classified as a felony by § 403, the evidence does not prove beyond a reasonable doubt that she had formed the intent to assault Lutz when she broke and entered. Section 101(k) defines "intent to commit a felony therein" as "the design or purpose of committing, within a building or closed off portion thereof, a . . . felony, provided that the defendant had such design or purpose at the time both of a breaking and of an entering." When Lutz turned around and ordered her to leave while she was protesting his noise, she found this to be "too much" and punched him. A reasonable explanation for her intent is that it was formed after she was already in the room, and no words or action on her part show that she had the intent to punch Lutz before she actually did so. Although, in her rage, she might have contemplated an assault before or when she broke and entered, there is a difference between considering an act and having the "design or purpose of committing" it, and her actions before she struck Lutz show no more than an intent to complain.

Welty's pushing open Lutz's apartment door was, however, a breaking, which § 101(c) defines as "the making of an opening, or the enlarging of an opening, so as to permit entry into a building, or a

---

The first sentence expresses the ultimate conclusion that the entire Discussion is intended to support.

The basic rule governing the controversy.

In a longer Discussion, tell the reader the order in which you will address the issues; here some of that is implied.

A rule of application that permeates the Discussion.

The determinative issue is considered first. Why consider first an element that the statute lists last? If one element is unprovable, it becomes the most important element because Welty can be convicted only if all the elements are proven. Why, then, bother to consider the other elements at all? You might be wrong about the element you think is dispositive, and, for reasons explained in Chapter 7, the reader is entitled to a full accounting.

A counter-analysis.

Notice how this paragraph begins with the writer's conclusion on the breaking issue, followed by the rule defining a breaking, an application of the rule to the facts, and more than one counter-analysis.

closed off portion thereof, provided that neither owner nor occupant has consented thereto." Lutz's apartment is a "closed off portion" of a building, which is defined by § 101(e) as "one divided from the remainder of the building by walls, partitions, or the like so that it can be secured against entry." Although Lutz's apartment is not described, it would be difficult to imagine an apartment that is not thus divided from the building in which it is located. During the incident in question, Lutz opened his front door about six inches after Welty knocked on it to complain of noise, and, when she walked into his apartment moments later, he immediately ordered her out. The initial opening of six inches would not have been enough to admit Welty, and Lutz's prompt order to leave shows beyond a reasonable doubt that he had not consented to her opening the door farther. And nothing suggests that Welty had consent from an owner of the apartment, who conceivably might have been someone other than Lutz.

Welty's walking into Lutz's apartment was an entry, which § 101(g) defines as "the placing, by the defendant, of any part of his body or anything under his control within a building, or a closed off portion thereof, provided that neither owner nor occupant has consented thereto." Welty walked into Lutz's apartment, and the circumstances do not show consent to an entry for the same reasons that they do not show consent to a breaking.

This paragraph is structured like the preceding one, except that for economy it incorporates by reference the parallel analysis set out earlier.

The other elements are all substantiated beyond a reasonable doubt. First, Lutz's apartment is a dwelling. Section § 101(f) defines a dwelling as "any building, or closed off portion thereof, in which one or more persons habitually sleep," and nothing suggests that Lutz does not habitually sleep in his own apartment. Additionally, that apartment is, to Welty, the dwelling of another, as defined by § 101(n), because

On these facts, it is not easy to determine whether Welty broke or entered Lutz's apartment, or whether she intended, while doing so, to commit a felony inside. Above, a paragraph has justifiably been devoted to each of those issues. But the other elements are easier: a reader can quickly agree that Lutz's apartment is the dwelling of another and that the incident happened in the nighttime. Al-

nothing suggests that she herself habitually sleeps there. Finally, all these events transpired between sunset and sunrise, and therefore within § 101(m)'s definition of nighttime.

though the reader must be told enough about these elements to create confidence in the ultimate conclusion, the analysis can be compressed.

This discussion could have been organized effectively in many different ways, and the example given here is only one of them.[5] Any effective organization of this material will emerge from a preliminary outline in which each element is itemized separately, together with a list of facts and subissues relevant to that element. Be careful, however: the issues here are not terribly subtle, and the facts given were few. *Even the earliest writing you will do in law school will require both more extensive discussion and deeper analysis.* In Chapter 7, you will learn how to expand this type of organization into a paradigm that can be varied in several ways to structure almost any kind of practical discussion involving the application of law to facts.

§6.5   *Using Rules Predictively*

> The prophecies of what the courts will do . . . are what I mean by the law.
>
> *—Oliver Wendell Holmes*

The Discussion in an office memorandum is predictive writing,[1] which foretells a court's ruling by evaluating the quality of arguments on each side of an issue. Some lawyers express the prediction openly ("Welty will not be convicted of burglary"), while others imply the prediction by stating the conclusion on which it is based ("The evidence does not establish beyond a reasonable doubt that Welty is guilty of burglary").

For precision, a prediction should at least imply the degree of accuracy ascribed to it by the writer. Is the underlying rule a matter of "settled law" and are the facts clear-cut? If the law is not settled, is that because different courts have interpreted it differently or because the authority is scanty? Is the prediction "iffy" or confident? Overt qualifications of accuracy are usually not necessary, since the prediction can be stated in a way that implies the writer's confidence in it. The implication comes not from "weasel words" like "seems to" or "perhaps," but instead from a precise statement of the variables on which the prediction is based ("The defendant should prevail unless . . .").

Occasionally, the law has gaps — holes that have not yet been filled in by

---

5. When you write, resist the temptation to copy uncritically the format in this example. It might not be appropriate to your assignment or to a reasonable analytical approach that you might choose to adopt with that assignment. On the other hand, the example does illustrate important lessons about rules and subordinate rules, elements and facts, burdens of proof, organization, outlining, and paragraphing.

§6.5   1. See § 3.2.

legislation or by precedent. Max Weber wrote that, unlike some of the legal structures of continental Europe, the English system of common law has never made a pretense of being a "gapless system of rules."[2] He might have added that one of the glories of the common law is the way it routinely fills in gaps by analogizing from precedent and by synthesizing different holdings.[3] To an effective lawyer, gaps present creative opportunities to make new law while obtaining what a client wants. If the lawyer can persuade a court to rule for the client in a case of first impression in the lawyer's jurisdiction, the new precedent thus set fills part — and sometimes all — of a gap, and new law is thus made. Few things are more professionally satisfying to a litigator. On the other hand, students tend to want more certainty in the law and to view these gaps with terror because they make prediction difficult. One of the signs of growing confidence and maturity in a young lawyer is an increasing ability to feel comfortable with gaps in the law and to make reliable predictions in spite of them. For that to happen, each gap must be defined and explained, rather than glossed over.

You will also encounter gaps in facts. What can you do when a critical or apparently critical fact cannot be learned before analysis must be committed to paper? Often you can determine that the unknown fact is limited to certain possibilities, and you can analyze each of these possibilities in writing. For example, if the client is a defendant charged with burglary, he might not know whether the structure involved was used as a dwelling at the time of the alleged breaking and entry: the structure may be in a secluded location, and the owner may refuse to discuss the matter with anyone representing the client. Under local law, although breaking and entering a non-dwelling is undoubtedly criminal, it may be a lower degree of crime — with a less severe punishment — than burglarizing a dwelling. If a memorandum must be written now, you can explore both possibilities, and, when the fact is ultimately learned, the answer will already have been analyzed in writing. When this happens, the conclusion can be expressed either alternatively ("If the building turns out to be a dwelling, . . . ; if not, . . .") or conditionally ("Unless the building turns out not to be a dwelling, . . ."). The factual gap and all the possibilities that might fill it must be clearly identified. Sometimes, the process of analyzing each possibility will lead you to discover that the unknown fact cannot affect the result because all the possibilities lead to the same answer.

Good predictive writing squarely faces two sources of unhappiness. One is weaknesses in the client's case, and the other is arguments that might challenge the writer's conclusion. No one is helped where a prediction turns out to be inaccurate because unpleasant possibilities have been avoided, and these kinds of avoidances are easily spotted by the typical reader, who has learned through experience that few legal conclusions are immune from attack, that every client's case has weaknesses, and that the client is always best protected when the *complete* situation is known from the beginning. That kind of reader is worried by writing that too easily reaches the conclu-

2. *On Law in Economy and Society* 62 (E. Shils & M. Rheinstein trans. 1954).
3. These techniques are explored in Chapter 10.

sion that the client is in the right, as well as by writing that does not fully consider arguments that could challenge the writer's conclusion. A writer shows maturity and dependability by exploring in depth both ideas that might put the client in the wrong and ideas that could show the writer to be incorrect. Predictive writing is frank and disinterested *diagnosis*. Advocacy has another time and place.

§6.6 How to Scrutinize Your Writing for Effective Rule Usage

During rewriting, ask yourself the following questions:[1]

Have you stated explicitly every rule on which your analysis is based? If the cases have not formulated an explicit statement of the rule, you must do it—and prove your formulation through the cases. | **6-A**

Have you come to a precisely stated conclusion? To convince the reader that your conclusion is correct, start by stating the conclusion precisely, succinctly, and in such a way that the reader knows from the very beginning what you intend to demonstrate. | **6-B**

Have you shown why the conclusion is true? Every conclusion of law must be proved by reasoning from statutes, cases, or other authority. A proof is a complete explanation of how the conclusion is derived from rules and facts and how the rules are derived from authority. Conclusory writing is writing in which the proof is either incompletely stated or missing altogether. It is conclusory writing to state the facts, the applicable rules, and your conclusion without explaining how the rules are supported by authority or how the facts and rules add up to the conclusion. Sometimes you need not—and even should not—give a full explanation of your reasoning, but those instances are more or less limited to preliminary and ancillary matters with which the reader can easily agree. Since most students underestimate the skepticism of readers, you would do better—where you do not know how much to explain—to err on the side of making a more complete explanation until you have gained a better sense of what must be fully proven and where proof can to some extent be implied. | **6-C**

Have you edited out waffling? Unless you take a position and prove it, your thinking will not be valuable. Because the law's purpose is to resolve disputes, it does not permit the leisure that other disciplines do to play with gray areas of analysis. The adversary process requires that conclusions and explanations be stripped of qualifications that | **6-D**

---

§6.6 1. Your teacher may mark your work in part by referring to some of these questions by the number-letter codes used here.

are not strictly required by logic. A qualification required by logic is not the same as the kind of vague and mushy waffling injected by words like "seems to," "appears," and their synonyms. In college, students discover that conclusion-hedging can be a defense against criticism, but that is not so in law school. Waffling makes a lawyer's advice less meaningful to clients and supervising attorneys and a lawyer's advocacy less persuasive in court. When a lawyer is disagreed with, the heavens do not darken so that lightning can strike the lawyer down on the spot. To the contrary, supervisors and judges are grateful for forthrightness and impatient with hedging.

| 6-E | **Have you concentrated on solving a problem, rather than writing a college essay?** The most charitable thing that can be said |

about a college essay is that it is a forum for what a scientist would recognize as "pure" analysis — that is, analysis to satisfy curiosity — rather than "applied" analysis, which is practical inventing and problem-solving. In a college essay, a writer is rewarded for reasoning in almost any logical manner toward any sensible goal the writer selects, even at whim. Legal writing is practical work, however, and, although curiosity is a valuable means to the end of problem-solving, it is not an end in itself. Rather, *your discussion must be directed toward resolving specific questions.* Words not helpful in resolving these questions should be cut.

| 6-F | **Have you ignored red herrings?** Students sometimes think they must discuss every fact, rule, case, and statue available because |

they do not want the teacher to think they have not done a complete job. "Why is it there if you didn't want us to talk about it?" a student might ask a teacher. Sometimes, "it" is there to test your ability to distinguish between that which is critical and that which does not matter. At other times, "it" is there merely to duplicate the mosaic of real life, in which the relevant and the irrelevant mingle freely. Because a lawyer is responsible for separating one from the other, you should be able, if asked, to explain how you differentiated between the relevant and the irrelevant. In your writing, address every true issue, but do not waste valuable time and space discussing things that will not affect how the controversy is resolved.

Exercise I.   Ada Warren and the Pride of Gloucester

1. With the aid of §§ 101(d)-(f) of the Obligations Code and § 10(b) of the Criminal Procedure Code, break down the rule in Obligations Code § 102 into an outline of the test and its exceptions. Be careful: the definition of an element might itself have elements, and an exception might be divided into elements. (Under each element you list, leave lots of white space. When you do the second part of this exercise, you will need room to write more.)

> *Obligations Code § 101(d):* As used in this chapter, "harm" means physical injury or economic loss.

> *Obligations Code § 101(e):* An intent to confine is the state of mind in which one knowingly or deliberately confines another.

Obligations Code § 101(f): A person is confined if he is restrained within fixed boundaries and either is harmed by the restraint or is contemporaneously conscious of it.

Obligations Code § 102: A person who intends to and does confine another is liable for false imprisonment unless the confinement results from an arrest, as that term is defined in section 10(b) of the Criminal Procedure Code.

Criminal Procedure Code § 10(b): An "arrest" is the taking into custody, by a law enforcement officer, of a person whom the officer intends to charge with a crime.

2. Your client is Ada Warren of Lincoln Notch, Vermont. She was born on April 21, 1920. When the Lincoln Creamery fell on hard times in 1984, she lost her job as office manager and lived thereafter on social security. When her cousin Virgil died last year, she inherited his farm in Grafton, which she sold to a Boston developer for a half million dollars. She then booked a cruise on the *Pride of Gloucester,* a six-cabin sailing yacht.

Ms. Warren boarded the *Pride of Gloucester* at 8:30 on a Friday night. The boat cast off at 9:00, and, after watching it clear the harbor, she went below at 9:30, drew her cabin curtains, and was asleep by 10:15. At 10:45, the boat was boarded by Officers Magrane and Kroyer of the State Marine Police, who had been told by an informer that Wilbur Blaisdell, a crew member, had marijuana hidden behind his bunk. Behind Blaisdell's bunk, Officers Magrane and Kroyer found a substance that smelled, looked, and felt like marijuana. Magrane placed Blaisdell's wrists in handcuffs and told him that he was under arrest. Kroyer ordered the captain to sail to the Marine Police dock where the boat would be impounded. There, at about midnight, Blaisdell was taken off the boat. He made such a ruckus that all of the crew and passengers, except Ms. Warren, awoke and came on deck, where they were told by Officer Kroyer that they would have to leave the boat. The crew all lived nearby and, except for Blaisdell, they found ways to get home. Officer Magrane drove the passengers (except Ms. Warren) in a Marine Police van to a hotel, where they put up for the night at their own expense. In the commotion, everyone had forgotten about Ms. Warren. The captain did not give the Marine Police a passenger list, and they did not know that she was still on board.

At 12:15, Officer Kroyer sealed the boat. He locked every outer door and hatch (including the door separating the deck from the passageway on which the passengers' cabins were situated), removed the gangway, locked it in a shed, and went home. The result was that, even though Ms. Warren's cabin was unlocked, she would not have been able to get to the deck because all the doors and hatches were locked from the outside, and even if she had been able to get to the deck, she would not have been able to walk off the boat. No one else was at the dock until Officer Tedescu arrived at 6:30 on Saturday morning. Tedescu found a note from Kroyer that the boat had been impounded but that (except for Blaisdell's bunk) it had not yet been searched. He rolled out the gangway, walked on board, and at 6:45 unlocked the door to the passageway outside Ms. Warren's cabin.

Ms. Warren had slept soundly through the night. She woke up at 7:00, thought the boat must be sailing in especially calm water, dressed, opened her cabin door, found Officer Tedescu standing in the passageway, and ordered breakfast. Officer Tedescu apprised her of her situation, and she fainted. Officer Tedescu caught her as she fell. She revived in a moment or two, and he drove her to a nearby hospital, where an emergency room physician decided that she needed no treatment. Officer Tedescu then drove her to the Gloucester Cruise Company office. The company refused (and continues to refuse) to refund the $3,500 that she had paid for a two-week cruise.

When you asked whether Ms. Warren had suffered any physical harm while locked in the boat, she replied, "You may be a sweet young whippersnapper, but surely I can get through a good night's sleep without suffering medical deterioration." When you asked her why she fainted, she said, "I was literally floored by what this man Tedescu told me. Dignified ladies do not spend the night under police lock and key. This is shocking, shameful, and outrageous, and I understand that lawyers get their money by making people like this fellow Kroyer pay damages for things like locking me up in a police boatyard."

With the aid of Criminal Code §§ 4002 and 4029, annotate your outline of elements factually. Under each element, list the facts that are relevant to that element.

> *Criminal Code § 4002:* A person is guilty of criminal possession of a controlled substance if that person possesses any quantity of the following: (a) marijuana [other subsections of § 4002 are omitted].

> *Criminal Code § 4029:* A motor vehicle, aircraft, boat, or ship on which a controlled substance is discovered shall be seized and impounded, and, after the District Attorney certifies that it is no longer needed as evidence, it shall become the property of the State, to be disposed of as the Director of General Services directs.

3. You have been asked to determine whether Ms. Warren has a cause of action for false imprisonment against Officer Kroyer. (Do not consider whether she has a cause of action against the cruise company or any of its employees.) Make an outline of a Discussion in which you explain your prediction in writing. Use as a resource your factually annotated outline of elements and exceptions. Discuss the elements in the order most appropriate to this case, not the order in which they appear in the statute.

4. If your teacher has instructed you to do so, write the Discussion you have just outlined.

Exercise II. Nansen and Byrd

1. With the aid of §§ 16 and 221(a) of the Criminal Code, break down the rule in § 220 into an outline of the test and its exceptions. Be careful: the definition of an element might itself have elements, and an exception might be divided into elements. (Under each element you list, leave lots of white space. When you do the second part of this exercise, you will need room to write more.)

Criminal Code § 16: When a term describing a kind of intent or knowledge appears in a statute defining a crime, that term applies to every element of the crime unless the definition of the crime clearly indicates that the term is meant to apply only to certain elements and not to others.

Criminal Code § 220: A person is guilty of criminal sale of a controlled substance when he knowingly sells any quantity of a controlled substance.

Criminal Code § 221(a): As used in section 220 of this code, "sell" means to exchange for goods or money, to give, or to offer or agree to do the same, except where the seller is a licensed physician dispensing the controlled substance pursuant to a permit issued by the Drug Enforcement Commission or where the seller is a licensed pharmacist dispensing the controlled substance as directed by a prescription issued by a licensed physician pursuant to a permit issued by the Drug Enforcement Commission.

2. You have interviewed Nansen, who lives with Byrd. Neither is a licensed physician or a licensed pharmacist. At about noon on July 15, both were arrested and charged with criminal sale of a controlled substance. Nansen has told you the following:

"Byrd keeps a supply of cocaine in our apartment. He had been out of town for a month, and I had used up his stash while he was gone. I knew that was going to bend Byrd completely out of shape, but I thought I was going to get away with it. I had replaced it all with plaster. When you grind plaster down real fine, it looks like coke. For other reasons, I had decided to go to Alaska on an afternoon flight on July 15 and not come back. Byrd was supposed to get back into town on July 16, and by the time he figured out what had happened, I would be in the Tongass Forest.

"But on the morning of the 15th, Byrd opened the door of the apartment and walked in, saying he had decided to come back a day early. I hadn't started packing, yet—I wouldn't have much to pack anyway—but I didn't know how I was going to pack with Byrd standing around because of all the explaining I'd have to do. I also didn't want Byrd hanging around the apartment and working up an urge for some cocaine that wasn't there. So I said, 'Let's go hang out on the street.'

"We had been on the sidewalk about ten or fifteen minutes when a guy came up to us and started talking. He was dressed a little too well to be a regular street person, but he looked kind of desperate. I figured he was looking to buy some drugs. Then I realized that that was the solution to at least some of my problem. I took Byrd aside and said, 'This guy looks like he's ready to buy big. What do you think he'd pay for your stash?' Byrd looked reluctant, so I turned to the guy and said, 'We can sell you about three ounces of coke, but we have to have a thousand for it.' When the guy said, 'Yeah,' Byrd said, 'Wait here' and ran inside the apartment building. A thousand was far more than the stuff was worth.

"Byrd walked out onto the stoop with the whole stash in his hand in

109

the zip-lock bag he kept it in, and while he was walking down the steps, about ten feet away from me and the guy who wanted to buy, two uniforms appeared out of nowhere and arrested Byrd and me."

The "guy" turned out to be Officer D'Asconni, an undercover policeman who will testify to the conversation Nansen has described. The police laboratory reports that the bag contained 2.8 ounces of plaster and 0.007 ounce of cocaine. When you told Nansen about the laboratory report, he said the following:

"I didn't think there was any coke in that bag. What they found must have been residue. I had used up every last bit of Byrd's stuff. I clearly remember looking at that empty bag after I had used it all and wondering how much plaster to put in it so that it would at least look like the coke Byrd had left behind. I certainly didn't see any point in scrubbing the bag with cleanser before I put the plaster in it."

With the aid of § 221(b), annotate your outline of elements factually. Under each element, list the facts that are relevant to that element.

Criminal Code § 221(b): As used in section 220, "controlled substance" includes any of the following: . . . cocaine . . . .

3. You have been asked to determine whether Nansen or Byrd is likely to be convicted of criminal sale of a controlled substance. The question is not whether Nansen or Byrd criminally sold a controlled substance, but whether either of them is likely to be convicted of doing that. To make that prediction, you will need to take into account the provisions of § 10(a) of the Criminal Code.

Criminal Code § 10(a): A person may be convicted of a crime only if the finder of fact is convinced beyond a reasonable doubt, from the evidence admitted at trial, that the prosecution has proved every element of the offense.

Now make an outline of a Discussion in which you explain your prediction in writing. Use as a resource your factually annotated outline of elements. Discuss the elements in the order most appropriate to this case, not the order in which they appear in the statute.

4. If your teacher has instructed you to do so, write the Discussion you have just outlined.

7 Organizing Proof of a Conclusion of Law

§7.1 A Paradigm for Structuring Proof

Because each needs to make a decision, a lawyer reading predictive writing and a judge reading persuasive writing look for the kind of tightly constructed proof that makes your conclusion seem inevitable. As you have already learned, the typical reader needs to know first what that conclusion is; then the rule or rules on which the conclusion is based; next, proof that the rules have been stated accurately; and, finally, the application of rules to the facts. The law-trained mind does not accept a statement of a rule as genuine until the rule itself is proved with authority, such as precedent, statutes, court rules, administrative regulations, treatises, and the like.

Thus, to the reader who must make a decision, analysis is most easily understood if it is organized into the paradigm on the top of page 112 or into some variation of that paradigm, the steps of which are the components of a proof of a conclusion of law.

Authority, policy discussions, and counter-analyses[1] appear both in *rule proof* (the third component) and in *rule application* (the fourth component) but for different purposes. In rule proof, authority and policy show that your statement of the rule is accurate, while in rule application authority and policy—sometimes the same authority and policy—are used to

---

§7.1 1. Law-school teachers—but not practicing lawyers—apply the expression *counter-analysis* to an evaluation of the arguments that might reasonably be raised to challenge the writer's conclusion. A counter-analysis in persuasive writing is sometimes called a counter-argument.

---

1. a statement of your **conclusion;**

2. a statement of the **rule** that supports the conclusion;

3. **proof of the rule** through citation to authority, through explanations of how the authority stands for the rule, through analyses of policy, and through counter-analyses; and

4. **application of the rule's elements to the facts** with the aid of supporting authority, policy considerations, and counter-analyses, thus completing proof of the conclusion.

---

confirm that your application is what the law has in mind. In rule proof, the counter-analysis is directed at arguments that might challenge the rule's validity or the accuracy of your formulation of the rule. But in rule application, the counter-analysis considers arguments that could be made against your application of the rule. In predictive writing, the counter-analysis is an objective evaluation of each contrary argument with an honest report of its strengths and weaknesses. In persuasive writing, a counter-argument is equally thorough, but not open-minded: you must stress the weaknesses of each contrary argument, and you must show the strengths to be unconvincing.

Like any structure for expression, this paradigm can be mutated according to need. That can happen in three ways: you can vary the sequence of the components; you can vary the depth at which the material is explored; and you can combine separately structured discussions into a unified explanation of several issues and sub-issues.

§7.1.1 Variations of Sequence

In some situations, you might vary the sequence of the paradigm components—for example, by stating the rule first and the conclusion second—although the order should not be illogical or confusing. You might vary the order, for instance, where the most effective transition from a preceding passage requires mentioning the rule before the rest of the new discussion. But *rule proof should generally be completed before rule application begins.* A beginner should think long and hard before deciding to vary the sequence given above, and, if you vary the sequence, you should be able, if asked, to give a good reason for doing so.

§7.1.2 Variations in Depth

A somewhat more complicated kind of variation involves depth. Most variations in depth go to rule proof, to rule application, or to both. Each can be given an explanation that is *conclusory, substantiating,* or *comprehensive.*

A *conclusory explanation* does no more than allude to some basis for the deduction made by the writer:

> Gaedel has no cause of action for false imprisonment because he did not learn of the restraint until it had ended. A person has not been confined, and therefore has not been falsely imprisoned, unless he knew of the restraint at the time it happened. *Herring v. Boyle,* 1 Cr. M. & R. 377, 149 Eng. Rep. 1126 (Ex. 1834).[2]

Here the rule (the second paradigm component) is clearly set out, but the only proof of it (the third component) is a citation to a decision, without any explanation of the court's reasoning or of the facts there adjudicated. The conclusion (the first component) is also plainly stated, but the only explanation for the way the conclusion is derived from the rule (the fourth component) is an allusion to a single fact: Gaedel did not contemporaneously know that he had been restrained. In addition, there are no counter-analyses and no discussion of policy.

A conclusory explanation is appropriate only where the reader will be quick to agree with your conclusion, or where the point is peripheral to your analysis. There, a more detailed analysis would seem tedious to the reader who is interested in more significant material. In other situations, however, a merely conclusory explanation will keep from the reader information essential to the decision the reader must make. For example, a judge who has been asked to grant summary judgment against Gaedel could hardly, from the passage above, have the kind of confidence needed for such a decision: at the very least, the judge would need to know how the facts of *Herring* are analogous to Gaedel's, together with the reasoning relied on by the *Herring* court, the relevant policy, and any useful counter-analyses. In predictive writing, the same information would be needed by a lawyer who must decide whether to recommend suit or how to conduct it (if representing Gaedel) or how to resist a suit already brought (if representing the person about whom Gaedel complains).

A *substantiating explanation* goes more deeply into the writer's reasoning, but still does not state the analysis completely:

> Gaedel does not have a cause of action for false imprisonment. A person has not been confined — and therefore has not been falsely imprisoned — unless he knew at the time of the restraint that he would

---

2. Assume that *Herring* is the only relevant appellate case in the jurisdiction where these events take place.

not be able to move about freely. In *Herring v. Boyle,* 1 Cr. M. & R. 377, 149 Eng. Rep. 1126 (Ex. 1834), a plaintiff was held not to have proved confinement where there was no evidence that he knew of the restraint at the time it allegedly occurred. He "may have been willing to stay," *id.* at 381 (Bolland, B.), and "[t]here was no evidence [of] compulsion upon" him, *id.* at 382 (Gurney, B.). Similarly, in the present case, Gaedel, out of his own free will, entered Lopez's office and remained there, unaware until after he had left that the door had been locked from the outside.

This passage provides more rule proof and more rule application. Although we are still not told the facts of *Herring,* we learn a little about the court's reasoning. And although the passage lacks a policy discussion and a counter-analysis, it includes at least some statement about how *Herring* should govern the writer's facts.

A substantiating explanation is appropriate where the reader needs more than a conclusory explanation, but where the point being made is not central to the analysis. Although a substantiating analysis is often enough, a deeper explanation is necessary where the issue is particularly important or where the reader's skepticism is likely to be aggressive. The substantiating passage above would not, for example, satisfy the lawyer who must decide whether to recommend a lawsuit to Gaedel; the lawyer on either side who must decide how to conduct litigation; or the judge who has been asked to grant summary judgment against Gaedel. These are difficult decisions, and each of these people would need more information.

A *comprehensive explanation* includes whatever analyses are necessary to satisfy an aggressive skepticism. Rule proof and rule application can be augmented with further detail about the law and the facts, with added or expanded counter-analyses, and with policy discussions sufficient to give the skeptical reader confidence that the law's goals would be achieved through your conclusion:

Gaedel does not have a cause of action for false imprisonment.	The writer's conclusion.
A person has not been confined—and therefore has not been falsely imprisoned—unless he knew at the time of the restraint that he would not be able to move about freely.	The rule on which the conclusion is based.
In *Herring v. Boyle,* 1 Cr. M. & R. 377, 149 Eng. Rep. 1126 (Ex. 1834), a ten-year-old boy attended the defendant's boarding school. When his mother sought to take him home for the Christmas holidays, the defendant refused even to let her see her son unless the tuition bill was paid. This continued for seventeen	Rule proof begins with an explanation of the controlling case.

days and ended only after the mother sued for a writ of habeas corpus. There was, however, no evidence that the child knew of his mother's attempts to take him home, or that he wished to leave or felt himself restrained. "[T]he boy may have been willing to stay. . . . " *Id.* at 381 (Bolland, B.). "There was no evidence . . . which showed that there was any compulsion upon the boy." *Id.* at 382 (Gurney, B.).

Although the Restatement (Second) of Torts, § 42, would provide liability wherever the plaintiff is harmed by a restraint, even if not contemporaneously aware of it, the Restatement's position has not been adopted in this jurisdiction, *Herring* being the only case on point. And *Herring* represents the sounder view. False imprisonment law protects both physical freedom of movement and the emotion of freedom. A person unaware of any restraint has been deprived of neither. If a plaintiff is truly prevented from moving about as much as he wants, he will learn of that when he reaches the boundaries of the restraint. And if a person is restrained but does not know of it at the time, he has not suffered the emotion of imprisonment. While it might seem attractive to compensate a plaintiff who was tricked, for example, into contemporaneous ignorance of the restraint, the unpleasantness that person might suffer on later learning the truth is both too slender and too intangible to quantify into damages.

Here Gaedel did not learn of the restraint until a week after it happened. He was summoned by Lopez, his employer, into her office for questioning about thefts from the workplace. Lopez, unknown to Gaedel, had ordered her security guard to keep the office door locked from the outside throughout the interrogation. Although Gaedel might have been shocked and suffered unhappiness when he eventually learned of this restraint, his ignorance

If you had to make a decision based on this writer's analysis, would the explanation of Herring *convince you — or would you want to know more about the court's reasoning?*

A counter-analysis of an argument that could challenge the writer's rule proof. Herring, *the controlling case, is old enough that it might be infirm, and the Restatement's position suggests that the common law elsewhere has evolved away from* Herring. *The writer says that* Herring *represents the sounder policy. Does this explanation satisfy you? Would you want to know whether these theories about policy have been adopted by courts in this jurisdiction or in others?*

Rule application begins with a sentence that points to the most determinative fact.

of it while it was happening deprives him of a cause of action.

Even if *Herring* were to be repudiated and the Restatement view adopted, Gaedel's loss was not the type of harm contemplated by the Restatement. The Restatement illustrates the required harm with three hypotheticals: a six-day-old baby who suffers medically while locked for two days in a bank vault; a "wealthy idiot" kidnapped for ransom and deprived of his family's care; and a diabetic in insulin shock who is jailed mistakenly as a drunkard and suffers both medically and emotionally. Restatement (Second) of Torts § 42 (1965) comment *a*. Gaedel's only injury is the humiliation he felt when he later learned that he had been locked inside Lopez's office. Gaedel suffered no physical injury, and, because he would have been in Lopez's office anyway, he was not cut off from his family or friends or anything he would have wanted or needed to do. Although he is unhappy about knowing that he was locked in an office by a security guard, that event is not comparable to the jailing of a diabetic in insulin shock. The stigma of the jailing is much greater, and the diabetic suffered medically, as well as emotionally.

> A counter-analysis of an argument that could challenge the writer's rule application. What will happen if the prediction in the writer's rule proof turns out to be wrong? In other words, what will happen if the local courts adopt the Restatement's rule? The writer shows that the result would be the same under either rule.

Beginning students sometimes write explanations so *cryptic* as to be less than conclusory. The writer of a passage as cryptic as this one has tried to put too much into a small bottle:

> Gaedel, who did not know he was restrained, does not have a cause of action for false imprisonment. *Herring v. Boyle,* 1 Cr. M. & R. 377, 149 Eng. Rep. 1126 (Ex. 1834).

A cryptic explanation is never enough — even in a situation where a conclusory explanation would suffice — because a cryptic explanation omits any statement of the rule on which the conclusion is to be based. Compare this cryptic passage to the conclusory one on page 113. The reader of the conclusory passage might agree with it if he or she is willing (1) to believe, without further explanation, that *Herring* stands for the rule stated and (2) to assume that the only determinative fact in the present case is Gaedel's contemporaneous ignorance of the restraint. But even if willing to make those assumptions, a reader cannot agree with a conclusion without even knowing what the controlling rule is, which is exactly what the cryptic passage asks the reader to do.[3]

How can you tell how much depth is needed? Ask yourself two other questions. First, how much explanation will convince the reader that the conclusion is correct? That depends on the reader's level of skepticism, which in turn depends on how important the issue is to the decision the reader must make, and on how many possibilities for error the reader would predictably see in the conclusion. Second, how much explanation will prevent gaps the reader would have to fill by independently studying the authorities relied on? The second question poses what might be called the need-to-read test: you have not explained enough if your reader would find it hard to agree with you without actually studying the authorities you have cited. A reader's need to go to the books is predicated on the context. A reader is more likely to feel that need with a critical, difficult, or obscure point than with a simple, peripheral, or routine one. A reader's need to know more is particularly great for authority that is the only support or the central basis for your conclusion.

But do not explore an issue in more depth than a reader would need. Remember that the reader is apt to be a busy person, almost as intolerant of too much explanation as of too little. Where you devote much detail to peripheral, routine, or easily accepted propositions, the writer gets bogged down in tedium.

§7.1.3 Combinations of Separately Structured Explanations

The third type of paradigm variation combines separate explanations into a unified whole. This is necessary wherever any of the following is true: (1) more than one element of a rule is at issue; (2) your conclusion depends on two or more separate rules; or (3) your conclusion can be justified separately through two or more independent theories, which you propound in the alternative. In each instance, the material can be organized only by breaking the conclusion down into sub-conclusions, each of which will have to be proved separately through a paradigm-structured discussion.

The most common situation occurs where more than one element is in question. In all the passages quoted earlier, only one of the several elements of false imprisonment was at issue. But if you must resolve every element,

---

3. In addition, the citation in the cryptic passage cannot possibly prove the literal truthfulness of the sentence that precedes it. Rule 2.2 in *A Uniform System of Citation* (the "Bluebook") permits citation without a signal (such as "E.g.," "Cf.," etc.) only where the authority "states the proposition" that precedes the citation, or is the source of a quotation, or is named in text and cited to in a footnote. The second and third possibilities are not relevant here. And although signals are strongly discouraged in practical writing (because they tell less than the reader needs to know), *Herring* does not "state the proposition" that Gaedel—whom the *Herring* court had never heard of—has no cause of action. When a citation "states the proposition," it proves the literal truthfulness of the words that precede it.

you will have an ultimate conclusion for the rule as a whole, together with a sub-conclusion for each element:

Ultimate Conclusion:

"Lopez is not liable for false imprisonment."

Sub-Conclusions:

Element #1: "Gaedel *was restrained within fixed boundaries.*"

Element #2: "Gaedel was restrained within fixed boundaries *by Lopez or at her direction.*"

Element #3: "Lopez *acted with the intent to confine.*"

Element #4: "But Gaedel *was not contemporaneously aware of the restraint.*"

Element #5: "Lopez *did not act within the scope of a lawful authority to arrest.*"

If this analysis were to be written out, the opening paragraph would state the conclusion ("Lopez is not liable for false imprisonment") and recite the rule on which it is based (the elements of false imprisonment). If the rule is settled law, it might be proven in the opening paragraph; otherwise, rule proof would require one or more additional paragraphs. Then each element, as a sub-conclusion, would have to be proved separately through an independent but paradigm-structured discussion. Each element would have to be defined (through a definitional rule); the definition would have to be substantiated through authority (rule proof); and the facts would have to be analyzed in light of the definition (rule application).

In such an analysis, the opening paragraph—or paragraphs, if the underlying rule is hard to prove—would at first seem to be an incomplete paradigm structure because it lacks rule application and definitions of the elements. But the opening paragraph or paragraphs would actually function as an "umbrella" paradigm structure that covers, organizes, and incorporates the subordinate, structured proofs of the elements.

The most dispositive issues usually—but not always—should be addressed first, and the same for sub-issues within issues. Here, because the fourth element of false imprisonment is the dispositive one, in most situations its proof would probably precede that of the others. In predictive writing either lawyer might first address the fourth element because each lawyer can recognize that it will be the heart of the dispute in court. But if Gaedel's lawyer believes that all the elements of the offense can be proven, he or she could instead analyze them in the order in which they appear in the rule. That might be easier for the reader to follow if no element takes vastly more space than another to explain. But the situation would be different if the fourth element consumes, for example, three-quarters of the Discussion. There the reader would be able to follow the contours of the analysis more easily if Gaedel's lawyer were to begin with the fourth element because it will be the one most in controversy. And if the fourth element takes up, say, 90 percent of the Discussion, Gaedel's lawyer might even consider disposing of the other elements first to set up the context. In persuasive writing, Lopez's lawyer would draw the court's attention first to the fourth element because Lopez will win if the court decides that that element has not been satisfied. But, for strategic reasons, Gaedel's lawyer might want to explain to the court the strength of Gaedel's case on some of the other elements before tackling the fourth one.

You might be tempted to focus on one issue or sub-issue, resolve it, and then dismiss the other issues or sub-issues as moot on the theory that the one you have focused on disposes of the whole controversy. That will not work because you may be wrong about the issue or sub-issue you believe to be central. Here, for example, you cannot ignore the other elements of false imprisonment merely because you believe that the fourth element (contemporaneous awareness) is unsatisfied. The reader of predictive writing is entitled to know what will happen if you turn out to be wrong. If, for instance, you believe that all of the other elements are unquestionably satisfied, the fourth element becomes all the more important, and litigation planning may have to center on acquiring evidence relevant to that element. That is the kind of resource-allocation decision that should be reached only on a clear demonstration that the other four elements will inevitably be proved at trial. And in persuasive writing you will want to make arguments on each truly debatable element on the possibility that the court might disagree with you about the one you believe to be dispositive.

Somewhat more difficult are the other two situations requiring combined paradigm-structured analyses. One of these situations occurs where the conclusion results from a combination of two or more independent rules — often one procedural and the other substantive.[4] The other occurs where the conclusion can be proved through alternative theories. Students see this most often in moot court assignments where the jurisdiction has no rule on point, where it could choose between or among competing rules, and where one can argue that either of two or more competing rules will, independently of one another, justify the conclusion. Although these are more complex situations than the one where more than one element of a single rule is at issue, they are resolved in the same way: an umbrella paradigm-structure is constructed, and underneath it the sub-conclusions are proved through separate, subordinate paradigm-structured analyses.

A well-organized presentation of analysis is immediately recognizable. Issues and sub-issues are handled separately, and each issue is clearly resolved before the next is taken up. Inside each issue and each sub-issue, the material is organized around the elements of the controlling rule or rules,

4. In §12.5 and §15.5, you will learn how procedural and substantive rules interact.

and not around individual court decisions.[5] Each issue and each sub-issue is explored through a well-chosen variation of the paradigm explained in this chapter. The reader is given neither too little nor too much explanation, but instead is able to read quickly and finish confident that the writer's conclusion is correct. Authority is discussed in the order of its logical importance, not necessarily in the chronological order in which it developed. Paragraphing is used to reflect the structure of the writer's analysis. Finally, the writer's organization is apparent throughout: the reader always knows where he or she is and how everything fits together. These things all come from sound *architecture:* from a wisely chosen building plan that the writer can explain and justify if asked to do so.

§7.2   *How to Scrutinize Your Writing for Organizational Effectiveness*

After you have written a first draft—and before you start on later drafts—ask yourself the following questions:[1]

7-A   **Have you included every component of the paradigm for structuring proof?** Where are your conclusion, the rules on which you rely, their proof, and their application? If you cannot easily find all of them, you have either hidden something or—more probably—left something out.

7-B   **Have you completed rule proof before starting rule application?** If you let the material get out of control, the result will be a little rule proof, followed by a little rule application, followed by a little more rule proof, followed by a little more rule application—and so on, back and forth. Finish proving the rule before you apply it. A reader's heels dig in when you try to apply a rule before rule proof is complete.

7-C   **Have you varied the sequence of the paradigm only where truly necessary?** If you have varied the sequence of the components of the paradigm, what was your goal? Could it have been achieved in another way? If not, was the goal more valuable than any clarity you might have sacrificed by varying the sequence?

7-D   **Have you chosen an appropriate depth for your explanation of rule *proof*?** Is your rule proof conclusory, substantiating, or comprehensive? Whatever the depth, how did you choose it? If you were in

---

5. The law is, after all, the rules themselves, and a decision merely proves a rule's existence and accuracy. The integers of the law are the rules and their elements, not items of authority.

§7.2 1. Your teacher may mark your work in part by referring to some of these questions by the number-letter codes used here.

the decision-maker's position, would you need more rule proof? Less? Is policy accounted for? (If the rule seems arbitrary, the reader will resist agreeing that it is the correct one to use. The reader will more easily agree if you at least allude to the policy behind the rule and the social benefits the rule causes.) Have you counter-analyzed attractive arguments that might challenge your choice or formulation of the rule?

Have you chosen an appropriate depth for your explanation of rule *application*? Is your rule application conclusory, substantiating, or comprehensive? Whatever the depth, how did you choose it? If you were in the decision-maker's position, would you need more rule application? Less? Is policy accounted for? Have you counter-analyzed attractive arguments that might challenge your application of the rule? | **7-E**

Have you organized a multi-issue presentation so that the reader understands how everything fits together? If you have combined separately structured explanations, did you identify separate sub-conclusions? Are the combined paradigms covered by an umbrella paradigm? Is the result crystal-clear to the reader? If not, how could it be made so? | **7-F**

Have you organized around tests and elements, rather than cases? Your goal is not to dump before the reader the cases you found in the library. The cases are only raw materials, and your job is not complete until you have synthesized them together into a coherent discussion organized around the applicable tests and their elements. A mere list of relevant cases, with discussion of each, is not helpful. This fault is easy to spot in a student's paper: the reader sees an unconnected series of paragraphs, each of which is devoted to discussion of a single case. The impression made is sometimes called "show-and-tell." A student not making this mistake might use five cases to analyze the first element of a test, one case — if it is dispositive — to analyze the second, three for the third, and so on, deploying cases where they will do what is needed. | **7-G**

Have you avoided presenting authority in chronological order unless you have a special need to do so? The reader wants to know what the current law is and how it governs the facts at hand. Although a little history might be useful somewhere in the discussion, you will waste the reader's time if you begin with the kind of historical background typical of a college essay. Unless there is some special need to do otherwise, present authority in the order of its logical importance, not the order in which it came to be. | **7-H**

Have you collected closely related ideas? If there are three reasons why the defendant will not be convicted, list them and then explain each in turn. The reader looking for the big picture cannot follow you if you introduce the first reason on page 1; mention the second for the first time on page 4; and surprise the reader with the third on page 6. If you | **7-I**

have more than one item or idea, listing them at the beginning helps the reader keep things in perspective. It also forces you to organize and evaluate your thoughts: sometimes, in the act of listing, you may find that there are really fewer or more reasons — or whatever else you are listing — than you had originally thought.

Exercise.　*Griggs and the Anti-Bandit*

Griggs has been charged in Maryland with receipt of stolen goods,[1] specifically a BMW floor mat and a Banzai Anti-Bandit automobile tape deck. He told Officer Ochs that he had driven onto the shoulder of a rural road after realizing that he was lost, and that he had attempted to turn around by backing his van up a few feet into the woods, where it became stuck in the mud. According to Griggs, he got out, tried to rock the van out of the mud, and noticed the mat and the Anti-Bandit lying on the ground. The Anti-Bandit comes with a handle and is designed to be removed and carried away at the owner's convenience. Griggs maintains that he did not notice, twenty feet further into the woods, a BMW stripped of everything that could be removed. (The police have found nothing else taken from the BMW.) Griggs says that he worked the mat under one of his rear wheels to gain traction, and that, when his baby woke up in the front seat and started screaming, he slid the Anti-Bandit into his dashboard (from which his own had been stolen some weeks before) and started playing the Everly Brothers' "Bye Bye Love," which his daughter finds soothing. Appearing just as Griggs was about to drive his van away with the mat and the Anti-Bandit inside, Officer Ochs believed none of this and placed Griggs under arrest.

Using the questions outlined in §7.2, scrutinize the Discussion below for organizational effectiveness. You might find this easier if you mark it up, dividing it into the components of the paradigm. Do you agree with the writer's analysis? (Put another way, is your skepticism allayed?) If yes, what convinces you? If not, what causes doubt? If you need to know more in order to be convinced, what should the writer have told you? What effect does the writer's organization have on you as a skeptical reader? How would you rewrite this passage? Be prepared to discuss your thinking in class.

> In Maryland, a person is guilty of receiving stolen property when he (1) receives from another person (2) property that at the time of receipt had been stolen (3) knowing that it has been stolen and (4) with a fraudulent intent in receiving it. *Carroll v. State,* 6 Md. App. 647, 252 A.2d 496 (1969).
>
> At about 1 A.M. Officer Ochs found Griggs in possession of the floor mat and the Anti-Bandit. Both were later shown to have come from a BMW that was stolen between 9 and 10 o'clock the previous evening. Griggs admitted that the radio and floor mat were not his. Hence, Griggs was in exclusive possession of a stolen radio and a stolen floor mat, and,

---

1. Normally, a modern criminal law issue centers on a statute, such as one defining a crime. But that will not be true here because the state involved follows the unusual practice of defining this crime (and a few others) through the common law and not by statute.

since they were recently stolen, the receipt element is satisfied. Where a defendant is found in unexplained and exclusive possession of recently stolen property, a receipt from another person will be inferred. *Mills v. State*, 3 Md. App. 693, 241 A.2d 166 (1968).

In *Carroll*, the defendant met an acquaintance on a deserted back road and purchased a car engine from him at substantially below market value. While driving off with the engine in his truck, the defendant was arrested and subsequently convicted of receiving stolen goods. On appeal, he argued that because he had no direct knowledge that the property was stolen, he could not be convicted of receiving stolen goods. The Court of Special Appeals rejected this argument and held that a defendant's knowledge of property's stolen character can be proved by evidence showing that under the circumstances the defendant "knew or could reasonably have suspected that the property in his possession was stolen." *Carroll*, 6 Md. App. at 650, 252 A.2d at 498. The court further held that mere possession itself can be significant circumstantial evidence of guilty knowledge, although it is not alone dispositive. *Id.* Because of the prosecution's obligation to prove guilt beyond a reasonable doubt, a conviction can be based solely on circumstantial evidence only where "the circumstances, taken together . . . exclude every reasonable hypothesis or theory of innocence." *Mills*, 3 Md. App. at 697, 241 A.2d at 168. Therefore, Griggs knew or could reasonably have suspected that the BMW floor mat and the Banzai Anti-Bandit radio were stolen property.

For intent to be fraudulent it "need not be *lucri causa* [for the sake of gain], but . . . merely hostile to the title of the true owner." *Carroll*, 6 Md. App. at 650-51, 252 A.2d at 498. In *Carroll*, the defendant's possession of the engine was fraudulent because he planned on installing it in his own car, which was certainly hostile to the title of the true owner. Here Griggs's actions show a similar intent. First, he had the radio and floor mat in his van. Second, he had used the Anti-Bandit to quiet his baby and the floor mat to free his van from the mud. Third, although Griggs told Officer Ochs that he "hadn't had a chance" to decide what he intended to do with these items eventually, he had started the van's engine and was beginning to drive off. Therefore, Griggs had a fraudulent intent when he received the Anti-Bandit floor mat. Although a defendant is presumed innocent and the prosecution must prove guilt beyond a reasonable doubt, "the trier of facts in a criminal case . . . is not commanded to be naive and to believe without scrutiny every glib suggestion or farfetched fairy tale." *Berry v. State*, 202 Md. 62, 67, 95 A.2d 319, 321 (1952).

Therefore, Griggs will be convicted of receiving stolen goods.

§7.3 Organizing an Examination Answer

In law school examinations, the teacher will provide a set of facts and ask you to write according to an assigned role. Most commonly, you will be asked either to analyze objectively the rights and liabilities of various characters in the fact-story or to make the best arguments available to one or more of the characters. You will be graded on how well you identify genuine issues, determine the governing rules, state those rules accurately, and apply the rules to the facts. The teacher is less interested in your conclusions than in the skills and understanding you show in arriving at and explaining those conclusions. The teacher will give you credit only for what is plainly written in the examination booklet and will give you no credit for things that you know but do not clearly express.

Think of a law school examination as a computerized cash register in a grocery store. The cashier places each item above an electronic "eye" that "sees" the item's universal product code and rings up the price. If the cashier does not hold an item at exactly the proper angle, the eye sees nothing and registers nothing. The cashier is able to try again and again and, if necessary, can even ring up a purchase manually. Like the electronic eye, the teacher will give you credit for what you show in the proper format, but, unlike the cashier, you get only one chance.

In an examination answer, the proper format is one that clearly shows the teacher the things he or she is grading: issue spotting, rule fluency, and analysis. Although a permutation of the paradigm for proving conclusions of law might be helpful, remember that the teacher, unlike a judge or supervising attorney, will not read your work for the purpose of making a decision.

Each exam question will include several issues. For each issue, you might write a permutation of the paradigm that goes something like this:

1. Since the teacher is more interested in your issue-spotting ability than in your conclusion, start by stating the *issue.*
2. The governing *rule or rules* should follow.
3. Proof of a rule is usually not necessary (because the teacher is in part testing your ability to remember rules that have been more or less proven in class) and often not possible (because the facts tend to be set in mythical jurisdictions). However, in some subjects dominated by uniform or federal statutes, the teacher may be willing to give you a little credit if you are able to refer to specific sections of a code, although such a teacher will not give you credit for good citation form.
4. Having stated the rule, *apply* it to the facts. You can show analytical depth by including a counter-analysis, and you usually cannot get full credit without one.
5. If you have not already done so, state your *conclusion* before moving on to the next issue.

Students have traditionally tried to remember this formula by calling it "IRAC": *I*ssue, *R*ule, *A*nalysis/counter-analysis, *C*onclusion. The answer to each question in the examination should include several IRAC-structured discussions, one for each issue you identify. But limit the IRAC formula to exam-taking: it does not work well in documents written to guide practical decision-making.

There are some other things to keep in mind about law school examinations. First, the goal is not to find the largest number of issues in each question. Instead, the goal is to identify the issues actually presented by the question, no more and no less. You will lose credit for missing issues, but many teachers will also reduce your grade if you "spot" issues that are not fairly suggested by the facts.

Second, analyze each genuine issue, even where you believe that the result on one issue would make the others moot. Not only must you do that in law practice anyway, but you cannot get full credit on examinations without handling every issue.

Third, budget your time carefully during the examination. The teacher will usually tell you either how much time to spend on each question or the weight each question will have on the final grade. Not only should you stay within the stated or implied time allocation, but for each question spend about *half* the time reading the question, thinking, and outlining your answer. Throughout law, planning is essential to success. One of the tragedies of the examination room is the student who realizes halfway through writing an answer that he or she has misunderstood the question by not thinking and outlining before writing.

Fourth, start preparing for exams long before the end of classes. The best preparation is to make your *own* outline of the subject matter of the course. Make the outline during the semester from class notes, from case briefs made for class, and from those portions of the text covered by the teacher. The casebook's table of contents is more helpful than most students realize. You will do better on examinations if you make your own outline, because the act of outlining is an irreplaceable self-teaching experience.

Fifth, teachers hate gimmicks in exam answers. Instead, in a business-like manner, simply write down what the teacher must see if you are to get credit.

Finally, although teachers differ from one another on examination philosophy, most teachers tell their classes something of their own views on examinations and grading. Take seriously what each teacher tells you.

8 Selecting Authority

§8.1 Introduction

You will need authority both in rule proof—to show that your formulation of the rule accurately states the law—and in rule application—to show that your resolution of the facts conforms to what the law intends. Authority, as you know by now, is evidence for a rule's existence, for its content, and for the goals it is meant to further. This chapter explains how to select the best available authority. Chapter 9 explains how to integrate library work with your analysis and writing. And Chapters 10 and 11 explore use of two types of primary authority: case law on the one hand and statutes and statute-like material on the other.

To select the best available authority, you need to understand a complicated set of preferences that courts use in determining which authority they will follow. A hierarchy (explained in §8.3) ranks authorities so that, in the event of conflict, one can be chosen over another. There are special problems with dicta (§8.4), with precedent from other jurisdictions (§§8.5-8.6), and with the selection of nonmandatory precedent (§8.7). But to understand all this, you need some detailed information about how courts are organized.

§8.2 How Courts Are Organized

Because the United States has a federal system of government, it has two different kinds of court systems. Each state has its own courts, enforcing that state's law, and in addition the federal government has courts throughout the country, enforcing federal law.[1] The Constitution allocates certain responsibilities to the federal government and reserves the rest to the states. As a result, state court systems tend to be organized as variations, from state to state, on similar themes, while the federal courts operate rather differently.

§8.2.1   State Courts

You already know that a trial court determines the facts of a case and issues a judgment setting out the rights of the parties, while an appellate court decides whether the trial court made any errors of law prejudicial to a party that lost below. A very simple state court system might include trial courts of equal rank in county seats throughout the state, together with an appellate court in the state capital to hear appeals arising out of the work of the trial courts. Although that was once the system in most states, so simple an organization would be unrealistic under modern conditions. Virtually every state now has several different kinds of trial court, and most now have more than one appellate court.

The usual pattern goes something like this: A trial court of *general jurisdiction*—called the Circuit Court, the Superior Court, the Court of Common Pleas, or something similar—will try cases that do not come within the *limited jurisdiction* of some specialized trial court. A state might provide, among its specialized trial courts, for a Court of Claims to hear suits against the state government; a Probate Court or Surrogate's Court to adjudicate questions involving wills and inheritances; a Family Court to settle matters of support and child custody; a Juvenile Court to determine whether minors have committed crimes or are otherwise in need of special supervision; a Small Claims Court to decide (perhaps without lawyers) disputes where the value at stake is not large; a Magistrate's Court or the like to try some misdemeanors and other offenses; or a Housing Court to resolve litigation between landlords and tenants. Often these functions are merged. A Family Court, for instance, might have jurisdiction not only over support and custody, but also over matters that, in another state, would be adjudicated by a Juvenile Court. A Small Claims Court might not be a separate court, but instead a Small Claims Division of the court of general jurisdiction. Generally, except for a Court of Claims, state trial courts tend to be organized by county.

About two-thirds of the states have created intermediate courts of appeal, which stand organizationally between the trial courts and the appellate court that is the court of last resort. In some states, such as Pennsylvania and Maryland, the intermediate court of appeals hears appeals from every part of the state, while in others, such as California and Florida, the intermediate appellate court is divided geographically into districts, departments, or the equivalent, which function as *coordinate courts* of equal rank. In any event, a party dissatisfied with the result in an intermediate

§8.2 1. As you will learn in the course on civil procedure, federal courts on occasion will enforce a state's law, and vice versa.

court of appeals can attempt to appeal to the highest court in the state, although there are usually limitations on the right to appeal above the intermediate appellate court. The principal reason for creating an intermediate court of appeals is the need to free the highest court in the jurisdiction from an oppressive caseload.

The names of these courts are not consistent from state to state. In California and many other states, the Superior Court is the trial court of general jurisdiction, but in Pennsylvania the Superior Court is the intermediate court of appeal. In Maryland and New York, the Court of Appeals is the highest court in the state, but in many states the intermediate appellate court has that name or a similar one. In New York, the trial court of general jurisdiction is called the Supreme Court, but in most states that is the name of the highest court in the state.

§8.2.2   Federal Courts

The federal court system is organized around a general trial court (the United States District Court); a few specialized courts (such as the United States Tax Court); an intermediate appellate court (the United States Court of Appeals); and the highest appellate court (the United States Supreme Court).

The United States District Court is organized into approximately one hundred districts. Where a state has only one district, the court is referred to, for example, as the United States District Court for the District of Montana. Some states have more than one district court. California, for instance, has four: the United States District Court for the Northern District of California (at San Francisco), the United States District Court for the Eastern District of California (at Sacramento), the United States District Court for the Central District of California (at Los Angeles), and the United States District Court for the Southern District of California (at San Diego).

The United States Courts of Appeals are organized into thirteen circuits. Eleven of the Circuits include various combinations of states: the Fifth Circuit, for example, hears appeals from the district courts in Louisiana, Mississippi, and Texas. There is also a United States Court of Appeals for the District of Columbia and another for the Federal Circuit, which hears appeals from certain specialized lower courts.

The United States Supreme Court hears selected appeals from the United States Courts of Appeals and from the highest state courts in cases where the state court's decision has been based on federal law. The United States Supreme Court does not decide questions of state law.

§8.3   The Hierarchy of Authority

There are two kinds of authority. *Primary authority* includes decisions, statutes, and statute-like materials such as constitutions, court rules, and administrative regulations. (For brevity, we can refer to statutes and statute-like materials collectively as "enactments.") Treatises, law review articles, and other commentaries on the law are *secondary authority*. Primary authority is produced by a legislature, a court, or some other unit of a sovereignty (a state or federal government) acting within its official capacity to make or determine law. Secondary authority, on the other hand, is only description of what a private person believes the law to be; the author of secondary authority may be knowledgeable, but he or she lacks the power to create law.

Primary authority is divided in turn into two sub-varieties. *Mandatory authority*—which must be obeyed—includes enactments of the sovereignty whose law governs the question to be resolved, as well as the decisions of the appellate courts to which an appeal could be taken from the trial court where the issue is being or could be litigated. *Persuasive primary authority*—which need not be obeyed—has been produced by an entity empowered to make law, but not by the entity whose law controls the matter at issue.

Within a single sovereignty, some mandatory authority outranks other mandatory authority. First, a constitution prevails over an inconsistent statute, and either a constitution or a statute trumps an inconsistent regulation promulgated by an administrative agency. That is basic civics: a constitution is the fundamental law creating a government in the first place; a legislature can enact only those kinds of statutes allowed by a constitution; and an administrative agency is still more subservient and is allowed to regulate only to the extent permitted by statute. Second, later enactments prevail over earlier ones of the same rank. A later statute, for example, prevails over an earlier one, but not over an earlier constitutional provision. Third, a constitution or a statute will prevail over an inconsistent common law precedent. Fourth, case law made by higher courts prevails over inconsistent case law made by lower courts. Finally, later decisions prevail over inconsistent earlier ones from the same court.

Persuasive primary authority occurs in four forms: (1) decisions by the courts of sovereignties whose law does not govern the particular dispute in question (for example, a decision from another state); (2) decisions by coordinate appellate courts, to which an appeal could not be taken from the trial court where the issue would be or is being litigated (an example is given in the next paragraph); (3) decisions made by trial courts, regardless of the sovereignty; and (4) dicta in any decision.

A precedent is not mandatory merely because it was made by an appellate court in the jurisdiction where a present controversy is being or would be litigated. To be mandatory, a decision must have been made by an appellate court to which the matter at hand could be or already has been appealed. For example, the United States Court of Appeals for the Sixth Circuit hears appeals from federal trial courts in Kentucky, Michigan, Ohio, and Tennessee, while the coordinate court for the Third Circuit decides appeals from federal trial courts in Delaware, New Jersey, and Pennsylvania. An opinion by the Sixth Circuit is mandatory authority to a United States District Court in Cleveland, because the Sixth Circuit can reverse, on appeal, a decision of that trial court. The same opinion is mandatory to the Sixth Circuit itself, which is bound by its own prior decisions. But that opinion is only persuasive authority to a United States District Court in Pittsburgh, because the Third Circuit — not the Sixth — hears appeals from federal trial courts in Pennsylvania.[1] And that opinion is only persuasive authority in the Court of Appeals for the Third Circuit (a coordinate court to the Sixth Circuit) and in the Supreme Court of the United States (which is superior to all the circuits).

Decisions by the United States Supreme Court, on the other hand, are mandatory in every federal court because the Supreme Court has the power ultimately to reverse a decision by any federal court.[2] But decisions of the United States Supreme Court are mandatory authority in a state court only on issues of federal law because the United States Supreme Court has no jurisdiction to decide matters of state law.

In contrast to primary authority, which may be either mandatory or persuasive, secondary authority is always persuasive and never mandatory. The most significant forms of secondary authority are (1) restatements, which are formulations of the common law drafted by scholars commissioned by the American Law Institute; (2) treatises written by scholars; and (3) articles and similar material published in law reviews. If secondary authority is both on point and needed to fill a gap in the law, a court is most likely to be influenced by a restatement. On an issue not considered by the restatements, the most influential secondary authority will usually be a treatise or article written by a renowned scholar.

Since 1923, the American Law Institute has commissioned restatements in contracts, property, torts, and several other fields in an attempt to express some consensus about the common law as it has developed in the fifty states. When a restatement is no longer up-to-date, it is superseded by a second version. Thus, the Restatement (Second) of Torts has replaced the Restatement of Torts. A restatement consists of a series of black-letter law rules organized into sections, to which commentary is appended. Although

§8.3 1. This is not the situation in every jurisdiction with coordinate intermediate appellate courts. For example, the New York state intermediate appellate court, misleadingly called the Appellate Division of the state Supreme Court, is divided geographically into four Departments, which operate independently of one another. This may seem analogous to the federal circuits, but it is not, because — even though administratively divided into Departments — the Appellate Division is, under New York law, technically one court. Thus, a trial court within geographical limits of the First Department must follow a decision of the Appellate Division, Fourth Department, if there is no dispositive precedent from the Appellate Division, First Department, or from the state's highest court, the Court of Appeals. On the other hand, the First Department itself is free to reject a precedent set by the Fourth Department.

2. Beginners sometimes form the misimpression that the Supreme Court's refusal to grant a writ of certiorari in a particular case is authority. A petition for certiorari is a request for permission to appeal to the Supreme Court. The overwhelming majority of these petitions are denied simply because the Supreme Court cannot possibly decide the thousands of cases annually that various parties want to appeal to the nation's highest court. Because, in deciding these petitions, the Supreme Court performs a kind of triage, the Court itself has held that "the denial of a writ of certiorari imports no expression of opinion upon the merits of the case." *United States v. Carver*, 260 U.S. 482, 490 (1922). On the other hand, if you cite to a decision below from which the Supreme Court has "denied cert," you are required by rule 10.7 in *A Uniform System of Citation* (the Bluebook) to incorporate the denial into the citation as subsequent history.

some states' courts are relatively unimpressed by restatements, other states give special respect to one or another of the restatements. You can find out whether a state's courts defer to a particular restatement by checking the manner and frequency with which the restatement is cited in the state's decisions.

The authoritativeness of a treatise depends on the reputation of its author and on whether the treatise has been kept up-to-date. Some of the outstanding treatises have been written by Wigmore (evidence), Corbin (contracts), Williston (contracts), Prosser and Keeton (torts), and Davis (administrative law). Some of the renowned but older treatises have not been—and could not possibly be—revised to reflect current law. These include the commentaries written in the nineteenth century by Story and by Kent, those written in the eighteenth century by Blackstone, Coke's seventeenth-century *Institutes,* and Littleton's *Tenures,* written in the fifteenth century. Some treatises are multivolume works; some are in a single volume; some double as hornbooks; some are hardbound with pocket parts or other annual supplements; and some are in looseleaf binders for easier updating.

Law reviews print two kinds of material: articles (written by scholars, judges, and practitioners) and comments and notes (written by students). If an article is thorough, insightful, or authored by a respected scholar, it may influence a court and may therefore be worth citing. Most articles, however, do not fit that description, and an article's publication should not be taken to mean that it will be influential.[3] Only in the most unusual of circumstances does a student comment or note influence a court. But even where law review material will not be influential (and therefore would not be worth citing), it might nevertheless stimulate your thinking, and its footnotes can help you find cases, statutes, and other authority.

Legal encyclopedias, legal dictionaries, digests, and *American Law Reports* are not authority. These publications are not written by scholars, and their only function is to collect cases and to summarize parts of them. The definitions in legal dictionaries are taken from opinions, often verbatim. Not only is the true authority the decision itself, but the dictionary rarely uses a case from the jurisdiction where the writer's issue arises. Legal encyclopedias discuss more complex material but suffer from the same fault. Although digests and *American Law Reports* are more exhaustive, the true authority is still the cases they cite.[4]

---

3. The following is a typical appellate judge's approach to law review articles as authority: "My experience teaches . . . that too few law review articles prove helpful in appellate decision making. They tend to be too talky, too unselective in separating the relevant from the irrelevant, too exhaustive, too exhausting, too hedged, too cautious about reaching a definite conclusion. When they do, they strive too hard for innovation or shock effect at the expense of feasibility or practicality." Wald, *Teaching the Trade: An Appellate Judge's View of Practice-Oriented Legal Education,* 36 J. Leg. Ed. 35, 42 (1986).

4. In a prior era, lawyers and judges were in the habit of citing to legal encyclopedias and dictionaries, even though they were not authority, and you will see that done occasionally in opinions printed in your casebooks. That practice is no longer considered acceptable. Today lawyers and judges seek greater precision from real authority, and if you cite to a legal dictionary or encyclopedia, you risk creating an impression of sloppiness and perhaps mediocrity.

§8.4   How Courts Use Dicta

As you already know, a dictum is not a holding and thus cannot be controlling authority, no matter what court it comes from. Once, after hearing an argument based on dicta from *Marbury v. Madison* — the single most important decision in American constitutional law — the Supreme Court held that

> general expressions [that] go beyond the case . . . may be respected, but ought not to control the judgment in a subsequent suit, when the very point is presented for decision. The reason . . . is obvious. The question actually before the Court is investigated with care, and considered in its full extent. Other principles which may serve to illustrate it, are considered in their relation to the case decided, but their possible bearing on all other cases is seldom completely investigated.[1]

If that is so, why do courts write dicta in the first place?

Sometimes it adds clarity to an opinion. A court may want, for example, to make clear what the case is *not* ("if the plaintiff had presented evidence of injury to his reputation, he might be entitled to damages"). Or the court may wish to illustrate the possible ramifications of its decision ("when a minor is at the controls of a power boat, or for that matter an automobile or an airplane, she is held to the standard of care expected of a reasonable adult if sued by a plaintiff who, like this one, is struck in the water and injured"). Occasionally, a court will add dicta to justify an apparently harsh decision ("although these facts perhaps constitute a cause of action for defamation, which the plaintiff did not bring, they do not substantiate the invasion of privacy cause of action asserted in the complaint") or to make a suggestion to a lower court on remand ("although the parties have not appealed on the question of appropriate damages, that issue will inevitably arise in the new trial we order, and we believe it necessary to point out . . .").

Sometimes a dictum is inadvertent. A judge might get a bit carried away or might formulate the issue or the rule or the determinative facts so that it is not clear whether a particular comment is really within the scope of the decision. Even when a judge is careful in defining the issue, rule, and determinative facts, readers might reasonably disagree about whether a particular comment is necessary to the resolution of the issue at hand.[2]

In any event, a dictum can never be mandatory authority. If it comes from a court not able to reverse the court to which it is cited, a dictum is persuasive authority on two counts (once because it is dicta and again because it is not from a mandatory court). On the other hand, if the court that wrote the dictum can reverse the court in which the current matter is now being litigated, the dictum, though still not mandatory, becomes more influen-

§8.4   1. *Cohens v. Virginia,* 19 U.S. (6 Wheat.) 264, 399-400 (1821).
2. If a court decides an issue on two independent grounds, either of which would alone have been sufficient, neither is dictum. Both were the basis of the decision, even if only one would have been needed.

tial.[3] That is particularly so where the court that produced the dictum went out of its way to express it in a deliberative fashion:

> While we can agree that what Mr. Justice Marshall volunteered in Part III of his opinion is dictum, it does not at all follow that we can cavalierly disregard it. There is authority for the proposition that a distinction should be drawn between "obiter dictum," which constitutes an aside or an unnecessary extension of comments, and considered or "judicial dictum" where the Court, as in this case, is providing a construction of a statute to guide the future conduct of inferior courts. While such dictum is not binding upon us, it must be given considerable weight and cannot be ignored in the resolution of the close question we have to decide.[4]

Thus, it is not wrong to use a dictum, but it is wrong to use it inappropriately. Although a dictum can be used to supplement reliance on unclear or incomplete holdings, it can never take the place of a holding, and it is inappropriate to treat it as though it could. And where a dictum is used, it must be identified as such or the result can be viewed as an attempted deception.

§8.5   How Courts React to Foreign Precedent

Lawyers and judges use the term "foreign law" usually to mean law from another state (not law from overseas). In addition, it may help here to use four phrases not common among lawyers and judges. For brevity, we can call the court that authored a precedent the "precedential court," and we can use the expression "decisional court" for the court that has been or could be asked to adjudicate a current controversy in which the precedent might be used.[1] Where the courts are in different states, we can refer to one as the "precedential state" and the other as the "decisional state."

Cases from other jurisdictions are consulted only for guidance and only where a gap appears in local law.[2] Although some courts prefer to fill a gap by analogizing to existing local law,[3] most courts are curious about foreign

---

3. "[A] federal district court is required to give great weight to the pronouncements of its Court of Appeals, even though those pronouncements appear by way of dictum. 'While not excused from making an independent examination of the precise issue presented, we cannot assume that our Court of Appeals writes merely for intellectual exercise.'" *Max M. v. Thompson*, 585 F. Supp. 317, 324 (N.D. Ill. 1984) (citation omitted).

4. *United States v. Bell*, 524 F.2d 202, 206 (2d Cir. 1975).

§8.5   1. These terms come from Hardisty, *Reflections on Stare Decisis*, 55 Ind. L.J. 41, 45 (1979).

2. "Absent any Florida case directly in point, we may look elsewhere for persuasive authority." *Tonkovich v. South Florida Citrus Indus., Inc.*, 185 So. 2d 710, 715 (Fla. Ct. App. 1966).

3. "In cases of first impression in Alabama we believe it our duty to draw upon well established principles that have been long adhered to by our Supreme Court, if they provide a solution to the problem, before going to the law of other states for guidance." *Lammers v. State Farm Mutual Automobile Ins. Co.*, 48 Ala. App. 36, 40, 261 So. 2d 757, 761 (Civ. App.), *cert. denied*, 288 Ala. 745, 261 So. 2d 766 (1972).

precedent when local law is not dispositive.[4] Even then, a decisional court will not be influenced by foreign holdings that are inconsistent with policies embedded in the decisional court's own local law.[5]

A decisional court will not be persuaded merely because a court in another state has taken a particular position.[6] Although a court might be impressed because a doctrine is the rule of a majority of states that have ruled on the matter, or because there is a trend among recent decisions toward or away from a rule, a court will nevertheless reject a rule it believes unwise. In determining the majority and minority rules and any recent trend, a court considers the number of states that have taken a particular position, not the number of courts or the number of decisions.[7] A precedential state's law becomes settled only when so held by that state's highest court.[8] Until a precedential state's highest court has ruled, the opinion of a lower court, while significant, is only a tentative expression of that state's law on the point.

Precedent interpreting statutes in other jurisdictions is treated somewhat differently from precedent interpreting the common law. That is because decisions interpreting statutes are not free-floating authority for what the law is in some generalized sense: they are authority for the meaning of specific words found in specific statutes, and they have no life independent of the words interpreted. If, for example, a statute were to be repealed, the cases interpreting it would no longer represent current law.

Opinions interpreting statutes in another state can be persuasive authority, but only if the statutory provisions are facially similar or identical.[9] Foreign precedent has an especially strong impact where the local statute is derived from the foreign one interpreted by the precedential court and where the foreign decision predates enactment of the derivative statute in the decisional state.[10] Less weight is given to foreign precedent that interprets the original statute after the derivative version was enacted in the

4. "Comparable court decisions of other jurisdictions, while not determinative of issues before an Illinois court, are persuasive authority and entitled to respect." *In re Marriage of Raski,* 64 Ill. App. 3d 629, 633, 381 N.E.2d 744, 748 (App. Ct. 1978).

5. "[D]ecisions setting forth the public policies of other jurisdictions will not be followed if not harmonious with the judicially declared public policy of Illinois." *Galler v. Galler,* 32 Ill. 2d 16, 26, 203 N.E.2d 577, 583 (1964).

6. "Decisions of courts of other jurisdictions, even if based upon identical facts, are no more than persuasive, and they are persuasive only to the extent that their reasoning is regarded as logical." *Mauzy v. Legislative Redistricting Bd.,* 471 S.W.2d 570, 573 (Tex. 1971).

7. "Like witnesses, foreign authorities should be weighed and not counted." *Michigan Mutual Liability Co. v. Stallings,* 523 S.W.2d 539, 545 (Mo. Ct. App. 1975).

8. "The decision of a court not of last resort in other jurisdictions, while entitled to respect, is not determinative of the law of the state in which the decision is rendered." *Van Wagenberg v. Van Wagenberg,* 241 Md. 154, 215 A.2d 812, 821 (1966).

9. "[W]e remain unpersuaded. . . . [A]ppellants cite no direct Arizona authority for their concept. They cite instead a number of cases from other jurisdictions which may or may not have use tax exemptions similar to our A.R.S. § 42-1409(B)(2). No direct comparison is made [in appellants' brief] between the statutes. . . ." *State Tax Comm'n v. Anderson Dev. Corp.,* 117 Ariz. 555, 557, 574 P.2d 43, 45 (Ct. App. 1977).

10. "[W]hen Arizona adopts a statute from another state, it will be presumed to have been adopted with the construction previously placed on it by the courts of that state." *England v. Ally Ong Hing,* 105 Ariz. 65, 68, 459 P.2d 498, 501 (1969).

decisional state.[11] Where the source of the local statute is a model or uniform draft, such as the Uniform Commercial Code, a local court can be persuaded not only by the interpretations of the same statute in other states, but also by the commentaries written by the drafters and published with the model statute.[12]

Be careful: different states have formulated different principles on the reception of foreign precedent, and only the case law of the decisional state will explain the terms on which it is willing to receive foreign precedent. The comments and quotations here merely illustrate the intellectual process; they do not define the approach a particular state will take.

§8.6   How to Write About Foreign Precedent

Because foreign precedent is used only to help fill a gap in local law, you must *lay a foundation for it* by clearly defining a gap and by specifying how local law is not definitive. A particularly deep gap occurs where the issue is one of "first impression" in the decisional state, which means that the appellate courts there have never before had occasion to resolve it. Even if some local courts have ruled, a gap would still exist if the rulings are all from nonmandatory courts. If those courts have ruled infrequently or are in disagreement, the gap is deep, and foreign precedent may have a significant role in resolving it. If, however, the lower courts have ruled often and agree with each other, the gap is shallower, and the role of foreign precedent is limited to providing context for a discussion of whether the jurisdiction's highest court will or should overrule the lower courts, despite the consensus below. Another possibility is that local cases, even from the highest court in the jurisdiction, may be so infirm from age or poor reasoning that foreign precedent can again provide context for a discussion of whether the decisional jurisdiction will or should change course. Finally, local cases might have come very close to the issue but might not have resolved it directly. Because analogies to and syntheses of local authority[1] might dispose of the issue, this kind of gap is shallow, and the role of foreign precedent is limited to noting whether the resulting analogy or synthesis is consistent with what has happened elsewhere. Wherever the gap is shallow, an evaluation of foreign authority is only an adjunct to a main discussion of local cases.

---

11. "Appellants correctly point out that our statutes of limitations were adopted from Texas, and that a Texas court has held that the statute of limitations for libel did not apply to an action for damages to business caused by false statements. . . . Since that case was decided after the statute was adopted by Arizona, however, its holding, although persuasive, is not controlling." *Gee v. Pima County*, 126 Ariz. 116, 117, 612 P.2d 1079, 1080 (Ct. App. 1980).

12. "While we are not bound by the interpretation of the Commissioners on Uniform State Laws in their prefatory note to the draft of 1939 of the Uniform Acknowledgment Act, it is highly persuasive and should be adopted unless it is erroneous or contrary to the settled policy of this State." *Valley Nat'l Bank v. Avco Dev. Co.*, 14 Ariz. App. 56, 60, 480 P.2d 671, 675 (1971).

§8.6   1. Analogy and synthesis are explained in Chapter 10.

To lay a foundation for the reception of foreign precedent, describe the topography of local law and define the local gap precisely:

> In Vermont, the issue of whether or not violation of § 1111 is negligence per se has not been the subject of any reported decisions. But Massachusetts and New York have enacted similar statutes, and courts in those states have held . . . .

> No court in Alaska has decided the question of whether the purchase of a newly built home implies a warranty of habitability, and the legislature has enacted no statute that would resolve the issue. However, a majority of the jurisdictions that have ruled on this point have held that . . . .

Do not lecture the reader on basic principles of the hierarchy of authority ("since there are no reported decisions in this state on this issue, it is necessary to look to the law of other jurisdictions"). The reader long ago learned that foreign law can be helpful in filling local gaps.

Once this kind of foundation has been laid, describe precisely the topography of foreign authority, identifying majority and minority rules and any recent trend; analogizing where necessary; and synthesizing the foreign precedent into a pattern where possible. You will need to substantiate your description of foreign precedent with some pretty detailed citation. It may be powerful to say that 39 states have adopted the position you believe to be correct, but you cannot substantiate that kind of claim merely by citing to a law review article or even to an opinion. For three reasons, you must cite to a case from *each* of those 39 states. First, the law review article or opinion may be a few years old, and in the interim the number of states may have shrunk or grown. Second, courts and supervisors depend on you to report what *you* have found, rather than secondhand information that you have not yourself verified. Third, the reader who wants to check your authority is entitled to know directly from your writing where to find it, and that reader should not have to trace your research through second and third sources. But do not avoid foreign precedent just because it may involve substantial research: if mandatory authority is not dispositive, the reader will expect you to explain what the box score is elsewhere. That is part of a lawyer's job.

§8.7 How to Select Nonmandatory Precedent

So many opinions have been published that they occupy millions of pages in thousands of volumes of reporters, filling shelf after shelf in law libraries. The mass is so large that computers are increasingly used to keep track of it. After you have isolated those opinions that touch on the subject to be written about, how do you choose, first, the opinions to rely on and, second, those to emphasize?

If you have mandatory authority, it will have to dominate your analysis. If local but not mandatory precedent is to be considered, or if you need to refer to foreign precedent, you must make some difficult choices unless the available precedent is so sparse that you have no choice but to discuss it all. Since your goal is either to predict a court's action or to persuade a court to act, your criteria for selecting nonmandatory precedent will have to be the same criteria the courts use.

The task would be easier if courts were to adopt uniform and well-defined rules on the selection of nonmandatory precedent on which to rely, but any such rules would deprive judges of some of the flexibility and creativity so valuable to judicial decision-making. Instead, without having made any overt rules on the subject, most courts, in most cases, apply a relatively uniform set of criteria. Generally, courts are impressed as follows, in approximately this order of priority:

First: whether a precedent is on point with the issue before the decisional court, or, if not on point, whether a sound analogy or synthesis makes it relevant. If the opinion is easily distinguished, or if a synthesis would be logically faulty, the decisional court will not be influenced.

Second: the quality of the precedent's reasoning. Is the logic of the holding sound? Is it based on a reasonable interpretation of other authority? Is it based on public policy agreeable to the decisional court? Even long-standing precedent will not persuade if it does not make good sense. "It is revolting," Justice Holmes once wrote, "to have no better reason for a rule of law than that so it was laid down in the time of Henry IV. It is still more revolting if the grounds upon which it was laid down have vanished long since, and the rule simply persists from blind imitation of the past." [1]

Third: the identity of the precedential court. Is it the highest court in its jurisdiction? Is it a court with recognized expertise or leadership in the field (such as the New Jersey and California supreme courts in negligence law)? Is it a court that has in the past influenced the courts of the decisional state? Is it in a state where the relevant conditions are similar to those prevailing in the decisional state? Is it a court philosophically compatible with the decisional court? (California negligence decisions, for example, are not influential in New York.)

Fourth: the treatment of the precedent in other reported opinions. Is it discussed with approval or with skepticism? Of course, if in its own state the precedential opinion has been overruled, even if only impliedly,[2] this criterion becomes the most important.[3]

---

§8.7 1. *The Path of the Law,* 10 Harv. L. Rev. 457, 469 (1897).

2. A court does not usually list each prior decision it overrules when the law alters course. There is just too much reported precedent in law books for that kind of orderly housekeeping: a line of overruled cases is often much too long to recite, in its entirety, in the overruling opinion. And sometimes the law is changed more than an opinion reveals, either because the court chooses not to emphasize its modification or rejection of prior law or because the logical or practical ramifications of the decision are not immediately apparent even to the court itself.

3. Scholarly commentary on an opinion may be persuasive in court, but not as frequently as students sometimes believe, except where the scholarly opinion is sharp and insightful, widely shared, or the product of a well-known scholar in the field.

Fifth: the clarity with which the holding is expressed. If the rationale for the holding is unstated or vaguely stated, the opinion is, to that extent, less probative of what the law is.

Sixth: when the precedent was decided. Judges are predisposed to treat newer opinions as more authoritative than substantially older ones, simply because changing social conditions can make a rule inapt. On the other hand, a holding so new as not to have been tested through experience may be treated a little warily at first. A minority rule may be especially persuasive if the recent case law shows a trend toward it, making it the "emerging" rule.

Seventh: positions taken by judges in the precedential court. Was the decision unanimous? If not, was the dissent well reasoned and eloquent or written by a respected judge? For that matter, was the majority opinion written by an influential judge?[4]

4. Like scholarly comment on precedent, the answers to these questions are often overrated by students. The other criteria are harder to apply than this one, but they also have much more effect.

9 Working in the Library

§9.1 Introduction

In the library, your goal is to discover all *useful* mandatory authority, and, where mandatory authority has a gap, to fill it with persuasive authority. Students often ask how much authority will be "enough." You have enough when you are able to lay out for the reader a precise topography of the law on the issue at hand, supplying whatever detail the reader will need—not more and not less.

In the unusual situation where you have clear mandatory authority on point, the topography might be nothing more than an analysis of one or two cases that are on point and decided by the highest court of your jurisdiction. In the more common situation where mandatory authority is ambiguous or nonexistent or disposes of only part of the issue, the topography will be much more complex. If the gap is a matter of common law and if it is important to the case, you may need to be able to show the reader the number of states that have adopted one rule, the number that have adopted a rival rule, and the number that have not ruled. If the gap is a matter of state statutory interpretation, you might in some instances even need to be able to show the reader the number of states that have enacted similar statutes and how those states have interpreted their statutes. If the gap is a matter of unsettled federal law, you may need to show the reader how each of the circuits has ruled.

When you are assigned to write a memorandum or brief, where do you begin in the library? What do you do next? And what after that? First, determine whether the issue or issues to be researched are matters of state law or of federal law. If you are researching state law, follow some variation of the sequence laid out in §9.2. If the issue is federal, do the same with §9.3.

§9.2 How to Organize a Comprehensive Search on an Issue of State Law

You will usually find appropriate authority most quickly if research is done in approximately the following sequence, which should be varied where appropriate.[1] Rely on your research text for detailed information about each of the research tools mentioned here.

Step 1: Educational material. If you know little about the field you are researching, a brief look at some of the following can help you get oriented:

a. For some of the larger states, encyclopedias have been published, limited to the state's law.
b. Otherwise, the national encyclopedias — *American Jurisprudence 2d* (Am. Jur. 2d) and *Corpus Juris Secundum* (C.J.S.) — are available.
c. One of the classic treatises, such as Williston on *Contracts,* may provide an overview.

If you already have a basic understanding of the field, skip this step, which will do no more than give you a quick understanding of the intellectual terrain around you. Encyclopedias have almost no other function and should otherwise be ignored. Unlike treatises, they are not written by scholars and are not recognized as authority. Moreover, encyclopedias tend to underemphasize statutes, and they are not valuable as case finders because their footnotes skim the surface of the case law, sometimes misleadingly.

Step 2: Statutes and statute-like material from the jurisdiction in question. These include the state's

a. code of statutes;
b. constitution;[2]
c. court rules (if the issue is procedural or has procedural overtones);
d. administrative regulations (if the issue is regulatory); and
e. rules of legal ethics (if relevant).

In searching for mandatory authority, you begin here because a statute, to the extent of its coverage, supersedes the common law. To learn the *current* law, you have to read (1) the bound volumes of the state codification, (2) the pocket parts, (3) any paperback supplements that were printed after the pocket parts, and (4) the session laws, if available, for the months after

§9.2 1. If you are researching a matter already in litigation—where the procedural posture will be important—see §15.6.
    2. State constitutions sometimes dispose of more than one might think. The federal constitution is a relatively short document drafted, for the most part, in broad terms. But most state constitutions are more detailed and at times contain provisions that do not seem so fundamental that we would normally think of them as "constitutional."

the paperback supplements. You can usually find a state's constitution, court rules, and ethics code published together with the state's statutory codification.

Step 3: Precedent from the jurisdiction in question. Case law can be found by searching the following:

    a.   annotations ("notes of decisions") in the state's statutory codes — but only if you found a relevant enactment through Step 2;

    b.   the state's digest (even if you have already discovered some cases through statutory annotations); and

    c.   *Shepard's* — in which you look for cases that have cited significant decisions found through items (a) and (b).

Again, it is not enough just to read a bound volume. If you are looking for cases interpreting a statute, there may be more in the codification's pocket part and, in some states, in a paperback supplement (although not in the session laws). If you are looking for common law cases, you must check the digest's pocket part, its paperback supplement (if there is one), and the relevant reporter's advance sheets (which are digested in the front of each volume). Even *Shepard's* has paperback supplements, and you must usually check more than one.

Step 4: Legislative history. Consult the legislative history if a statute controls, if the legislative intent is in question, and if the state publishes legislative histories (many do not).

Step 5: Case law from other jurisdictions. If Steps 2, 3, and 4 have not disposed of the issue, seek guidance from precedent elsewhere. If the issue is statutory, look for cases interpreting *similar* statutes in other jurisdictions. If the issue is part of the common law, look for common law precedent. The case law of other jurisdictions can be found through the following:

    a.   *American Law Reports* (A.L.R.), which can be very comprehensive if it annotates the *precise* issue;

    b.   treatises and their abundant footnotes;

    c.   law review articles and their abundant footnotes.

If you have a large number of cases after you complete item (c), omit the rest of this step: your goal is not to find all the cases, but instead to find and analyze the *most important* ones. But if your authority is sparse or has gaps, continue with the following:

    d.   if the issue is statutory, the statutory codifications of other states (look for similar statutes and for cases that interpret them — and do not forget to use pocket parts and paperback cumulative supplements);

    e.   if the issue is one of common law, the relevant restatement, its footnotes and interim case service, and *Shepard's Restatement of the Law Citations;*

    f.   national digests; and
    g.   *Shepard's* (look for cases that have cited significant decisions found through items (a) through (f)).

A.L.R. is updated with pocket parts; digests with pocket parts and paperback supplements; and *Shepard's* with paperback supplements, of which you must usually check more than one.

Step 6: Commentaries. Even if Steps 2, 3, and 4 seem to have entirely disposed of the issue, seek guidance from scholarly commentaries. The following can help you understand the larger picture, including trends in the law that are not immediately obvious from your review of the primary authorities:

    a.   treatises
    b.   the relevant restatement
    c.   law review articles

In this step, treatises, restatements, and law review articles are not consulted for the same reason they were in Step 5. In Step 5, their footnotes were used as devices to find primary authority. Here they are treated as authority in their own right, not merely as case-finding devices. (You will be a more efficient researcher if you can separate in your own mind the functions each book can accomplish.)

Step 7: Other research tools. If the steps above have not entirely disposed of the issue, look through your research text for other, less commonly used tools that might assist in losing the gap.

Step 8: Shepardize. Check all cases, statutes, administrative regulations, and court rules on which you rely. Look for reversals, affirmances, repeals, amendments, and other events that alter or might alter the quality of the authority. Here, you are not using *Shepard's* to find cases, as you did in Steps 3 and 5. Instead, you are verifying the pedigree of authority that you have already found.

§9.3   *How to Organize a Comprehensive Search on an Issue of Federal Law*

You will usually find appropriate authority most quickly if research is done in approximately the following sequence, varying it where appropriate.[1] Rely on your research text for detailed information about each of the research tools mentioned here.

Step 1: Looseleaf services. If the issue is one of federal regulation in a specialized field, such as antitrust, aviation, communications, labor, securi-

---

§9.3. 1. If you are researching a matter already in litigation—where the procedural posture will be important—see §15.6.

ties, tax, or environmental law, a looseleaf service is the most efficient way to get started. If there is a thorough and well-organized looseleaf, you can skip Step 2, even if you know little about the field, and you will find that many parts of Steps 3, 4, and 5 will be easier—some even unnecessary.

Step 2: Educational material. See §9.2, Step 1.

Step 3: Federal statutes and statute-like material. These include the following:

a. the United States Code in either annotated edition: *United States Code Annotated* (West) or *United States Code Service* (Lawyers Co-operative)—unless you are certain that the issue is purely constitutional and involves no federal statute;

b. if the issue is constitutional, the United States Constitution—but you are more likely to find the dispositive law in precedent interpreting the Constitution (see Step 4);

c. if the issue is one of administrative regulation, the *Code of Federal Regulations,* updated by the *Federal Register;*

d. if the issue is procedural or has procedural overtones, the Federal Rules of Civil Procedure, Federal Rules of Criminal Procedure, Federal Rules of Evidence, or Federal Rules of Appellate Procedure.

To learn the *current* law, you have to read (1) the bound volumes of the state codification, (2) the pocket parts, (3) any paperback cumulative supplements that are printed after the pocket parts, and (4) the session laws, if available, for the months after the paperback cumulative supplements. The Constitution is printed in each of the two annotated editions of the United States Code, as are the federal procedural rules. In a specialized field, such as environmental regulation, the statutory material might also be found in a looseleaf.

Step 4: Federal case law. This can be found through the following:

a. *American Law Reports Federal* (A.L.R. Fed.), which can be very comprehensive if it annotates the *precise* issue;

b. looseleaf services, if the issue involves federal regulation in a specialized field;

c. annotations ("notes of decision") in *United States Code Annotated* or in *United States Code Service;*

d. the various federal digests (even if you have already discovered some cases through A.L.R. Fed., looseleafs, and statutory annotations);

e. treatises and their abundant footnotes;

f. law review articles and their abundant footnotes; and

g. *Shepard's,* in which you look for cases that have cited significant decisions found through items (a) through (f).

With A.L.R. Fed., statutory annotations, and digests, it is not enough just to read the hardback volume. A.L.R. Fed. is updated with pocket parts. Digests and the annotated codes are updated with pocket parts and by periodic supplements during the year. Even *Shepard's* has paperback supplements, and you must usually check more than one.

Step 5: Legislative history. If a statute controls and if the legislative intent is in question, check the legislative history.

Step 6: Commentaries. Even if Steps 3, 4, and 5 seem to have entirely disposed of the issue, seek guidance from scholarly commentaries. The following can help you understand the larger picture, including trends in the law that are not immediately obvious from your review of the primary authorities:

a. treatises
b. law review articles

Treatises and law review articles are not used here for the same purpose they were in Step 4, where their footnotes were used as devices to find primary authority. Here they are treated as authority in their own right, not merely as case-finding devices.

Step 7: Other research tools. If the steps above have not entirely disposed of the issue, look through your research text for other, less commonly used tools that might assist in closing the gap.

Step 8: Shepardize. Check all cases, statutes, administrative regulations, and court rules on which you rely. Look for reversals, affirmances, repeals, amendments, and other events that alter or might alter the quality of the authority. Here you are not using *Shepard's* to find cases, as you did in Step 4. Instead, you are verifying the pedigree of authority that you have already found.

§9.4   How to Work Effectively in the Library

Prepare yourself for the library. You will not work efficiently if you research like a vacuum cleaner. Instead, look carefully at the facts you have been given and define, as precisely as you can, the issue or issues you have been asked to resolve. While in the library, be conscious of what you are looking for. Focus on that and not on extraneous material, no matter how interesting it may be. Aimless exploring wastes time and will only increase your anxiety. Remember also that your goal is to discover authority *against*—as well as for—your conclusion because you cannot predict without counter-analyzing that authority, and you cannot persuade a court without arguing against it.

How should you store all the things you find in the library? To take notes and brief cases, many lawyers use large index cards or pages in a binder, usually putting only one case on a card or page. The advantage of cards is that they can be shuffled easily while researching and writing. The advantage of pages is that more can be written on them.

Another medium for storage is the photocopying of critical or quotable authority. Brief all cases, whether you photocopy them or not, because while briefing you analyze as well as record. For the same reason, you should outline statutes, photocopied or not. The advantage of photocopying the most critical authority is that you can return to it again and again, as you write outside the library, at times when you realize that you have not fully understood the authority's possibilities. The advantage of photocopying pages from which you might quote is that your quotations are more likely to be accurate. Photocopying, however, is much overrated by students, many of whom try to reduce their anxiety at the library's photocopy machines. Although photocopied cases look impressive, the student who copies dozens of barely read cases only defers thinking about them until a later time, when they will be briefed and the photocopies thrown out. The wiser student is the one who copies only what is truly needed and who does much of the analysis while reading authority in the original books at a library table.

While making notes in the library, *accurately* write down what you need, both the substance of the authority and its full citation. (For the latter, keep a copy of *A Uniform System of Citation* close at hand so that you can write out the citation in complete form while you are using the books in the library.) Be sure that your notes are complete enough to include all the citation information you will need when you start to write.

Read several authorities before you start taking detailed notes. You will not know what is really important until you have strolled around a bit in the landscape of authority that you must eventually explain to the reader. But even if you defer briefing until you know some of the lay of the land, you will still find that your earliest briefs are the least well done. Near the end of the research, go back to some of the important authorities you read first: you may be surprised at what you missed. If, when you return to them, you find your first notes seem a little naive, do not be discouraged: that happens even to experienced lawyers when they research a field that is new to them.

Start writing before you have finished the research. You will find that you are most productive if, as you go along, you spend an increasing proportion of your time writing and a progressively smaller proportion researching. Early in your research, snatches of what you will say — a paragraph or two, perhaps — will come to you in the library. They are worth writing down, although you will certainly change them substantially later. Eventually, you will be writing so much that you will visit the library only to verify something in your notes or to fill a small gap in your research that you had not noticed before.

If you try to do "all" the research before beginning to write, you will waste large amounts of time in the library, the writing will only be harder, and the document you produce will probably be inferior. You will do unnecessary library work because you will not be able to know when you have already found everything you need. The writing will be harder because you will barely know where to begin writing, and your pile of notes and photocopies will seem monolithic, impenetrable, and intimidating. And your document will be inferior because of so much wasted time and effort. Research, thinking, and writing are not really separable activities. They are all part of a single process of creation.

Perhaps the most important way of integrating writing and research is to start outlining the entire Discussion or Argument as soon as your research has begun to show you the contours of what you will say. The outline will give you strong clues about what still must be found in the library. And eventually it will help you identify the point at which you have found what you need and at which research should therefore stop.

10 Working with Precedent

§10.1 Eight Skills for Working with Precedent

Perhaps once in a blue moon, a lawyer might find that an issue is entirely resolved by mandatory precedent on point—precedent from a mandatory appellate court that has decided the same issue on mirrored facts. More often, the law is less certain, and the lawyer must construct an answer from more tangential precedent, using at least some of eight different skills. They are (1) ranking precedent according to the hierarchy of authority and the principles that are derived from it; (2) formulating rules along a continuum from the broadest to the narrowest interpretations arguable from the facts and wording of precedent; (3) analogizing; (4) distinguishing; (5) eliciting policy; (6) synthesizing fragmented authority into a unified whole; (7) reconciling conflicting or adverse authority; and (8) testing the result of the first seven skills for realism and marketability to the judicial mind.[1]

In Chapter 8, you learned about the *hierarchy of authority* and the principles that are derived from it. The other skills are explained in this chapter.

---

§10.1 1. In this chapter—as in Chapter 8—the "precedential court" is the court that authored the precedent under discussion, and the "later court" or "decisional court" is the court that has been or could be asked to adjudicate a current controversy to which that precedent might be applied. Similarly, the "precedential facts" are the facts of the precedent itself—as opposed to the facts of the current case.

§10.2   Formulating a Variety of Rules from the Same Precedent

In this course[1] and in others, you have already learned something about *formulating rules along a continuum from the broadest to the narrowest interpretations.* For example:[2]

> A's father induces her not to marry B as she promised to do. On a holding that the father is not liable to B for so doing, a gradation of widening propositions can be built, [the first of which is the following:]

   1.   Fathers are privileged to induce daughters to break promises to marry.

This would be a rule limited strictly to the precedential facts. How likely is it that the law would give fathers a privilege denied to others? What purpose might the law have had for doing such a thing? How likely is it that only daughters would be inducible within the scope of such a privilege? Why would the law have singled them out? And how likely is it that only promises to marry would be the object of such treatment? What reason might the law have to treat those kinds of promises specially? If you cannot answer these questions, one or more elements of this narrow formulation are inaccurate.

   2.   Parents are so privileged.

Here the father in the precedent is only an example of the class of privileged people. Even if the precedential court had written much about a special and valuable role for fathers in the family, that would not prevent a later court from deciding—in an era in which gender roles have come to be treated differently—that the rule privileges all parents, regardless of gender. A later court might do that overtly, by recognizing that the precedential court intended to limit the privilege to fathers and by deciding that such a limitation offends modern policy. Or a later court might do it more subtly, by concluding that the precedential court meant the privilege to extend to both parents and that the father was spoken of merely because he was the parent at issue in the precedent.

   3.   Parents are so privileged as to both daughters and sons.

Here the daughter in the precedent is only an example of the class of people who can be induced within the scope of the privilege. All that has been said about the father's gender applies equally to the daughter's.

---

§10.2   1. See §2.2.
2. The example and the sample rules derived from it are from Oliphant, *A Return to Stare Decisis*, 14 A.B.A.J. 71, 72 (1928).

4.   All persons are so privileged as to promises to marry.

The father and daughter are no longer examples because the rule is not limited to classifications of people. Rather, the relationship between father and daughter would have been mere coincidence. This formulation is a pretty drastic expansion of formulation 3. There could have been some intermediate steps: blood relatives are privileged to induce other blood relatives; relatives (blood or not) are privileged to induce other relatives; people who have reason to care about each other (friends, for example) are privileged to induce one another; and so on.

5.   Parents are so privileged as to all promises made by their children.

We are back to parents and children, but now the contemplation of marriage has become coincidental: the promise might as well be one to buy a motorcycle or to climb the Himalayas. A later court might be wary of such a broad rule. Are there reasons why a parent should be privileged to induce a child to break *any* promise? How is society or—some valuable part of it—protected by such a privilege? Conversely, is there anything about a promise to marry that makes it fit for special treatment? (As you can see, policy considerations are important in selecting the most plausible rule formulation.)

6.   All persons are so privileged as to all promises made by anyone.

Under this formulation, no one can be liable for inducing another person to break a promise. If that were the rule, the law would have no need in this kind of controversy for a concept like a privilege. But the law has plainly used that concept, implying rather strongly that there is liability in some situations but not in others. Certainly, formulations 5 and 6 are so broad as to be unreasonable and unrealistic, just as formulations 1 and 2 are so narrow as to be unreasonable and unrealistic. The hard task is figuring out which of the other formulations is most likely to be adopted by a decisional court. Be careful when you consider such a question: you cannot do whatever you please. In predictive writing, you must formulate the rule as you believe the courts are most likely to in the case you are trying to predict. And in persuasive writing, you must select a formulation that both favors your client and is likely to be accepted as valid by the court you are trying to persuade. In addition, if the rule has been stated over and over again in many mandatory decisions and in pretty much the same wording, you do not have much room for interpretive maneuver. In fact, you might not have any at all. Your room for maneuver grows where the law has a gap: where the courts have implied but not fully stated the rule, where the decisions are inconsistent or sparse, and so forth.

§10.3   *Analogizing and Distinguishing*

An *analogy* is a demonstration that two situations are so parallel that the reasoning that justified the decision in one should do the same in the other. When a decisional court is persuaded by an analogy to precedent, the decisional court is said to "follow" the precedent. *Distinguishing* is the opposite of analogy: a demonstration that two situations are so fundamentally dissimilar that the same result should not occur in both. Analogizing and distinguishing have been two of the most important intellectual tools in the slow and gradual construction and evolution of the common law. Both help find and state the rule for which a precedent stands, together with something about how that rule is to be applied. (Distinguishing does so by showing what the rule is not and how it is not to be applied.) There are three steps in analogizing or distinguishing. First, make sure that the issue in the precedent is the same one you are trying to resolve. Second, identify the precedent's determinative facts. Do not look for mere coincidences between the precedent and the current case; look instead for facts on which the precedential court really relied. Finally, compare the precedent's determinative facts to the facts you are trying to resolve. Although you should strongly consider what the precedential court has said about its reasoning, your conclusion need not necessarily be one that was within the stated or even conscious contemplation of the precedential court, since a court cannot always predict every one of the reasonable consequences of each precedent it sets. Your conclusion should, however, be the most logical and plausible one that is consistent with the heart of the precedential court's reasoning and with public policy. For example:

> Suppose a College Dean has a power to make and enforce rules of conduct in his College, and that he does not publish a set of carefully drafted rules, but applies a rough and ready doctrine of precedent. He fines Jones £5, and explains to him that he has done so because Jones kept Miss Doe, his girlfriend, in the College until 9:30, and that he has always fined undergraduates £5 if they allow ladies to stay in College after 9 P.M. Two days later he discovers that Smith allowed Miss Styles to remain in until 9:10 P.M. because she had been stung by a bee and was in considerable pain. It would surely be justifiable for the Dean to excuse Smith, and distinguish his earlier decision, without having to show that in Jones' case he emphasized the [good] health of Miss Doe, or treated it in any way material to the issue of Jones' guilt. For what he does in Smith's case is not to pretend that he previously regarded Miss Doe's health as material—which would be untrue—but only that in Smith's case he finds a circumstance which makes it very different from Jones' case, which is not in the least untrue, and indeed quite sensible of him.[1]

---

§10.3   1. Simpson, *The Ratio Decidendi of a Case and the Doctrine of Binding Precedent,* in *Oxford Essays on Jurisprudence* 174 (Guest ed. 1961).

§10.4   Eliciting Policy from Precedent

Policy is elicited from authority that explains the underlying goals that the rules in question are intended to advance. Remember how revolting it was to Holmes, "to have no better reason for a rule of law than that so it was laid down in the time of Henry IV." [1] Not only is policy important in clearing up ambiguities in the law, but judges are guided by policy concerns even in applying law that seems on the surface to be unambiguous. A court needs confidence that a contemplated decision really is consistent with the law's goals. Thus, legal analysis persistently asks what the rules are meant to accomplish, whether the proposed result would accomplish that, and whether the rules and the result would create more problems than they would solve. And where a jurisdiction has no settled rule and therefore must choose between or among competing rules, the rule selected must be one that is consistent with the jurisdiction's policies. Although you may find policy openly stated in precedent, it is perhaps more often implied through the court's reasoning.

§10.5   Synthesis and Reconciliation

Synthesis is the binding together of several opinions into a whole that stands for a rule or an expression of policy. By focusing on the reasoning and generic facts that the cases have in common, synthesis finds and explains collective meaning that is not apparent from the individual cases themselves. As with analogizing and distinguishing, a synthesis must be realistic enough to work. Its plausibility will be measured by the extent to which it is logical, reasonable, and consistent with public policy. In predictive writing, a synthesis must be one the courts are likely to adopt. And in persuasive writing, it must be that *and* one that favors your client. In persuasive writing, the essence of this skill is the turning of weakness into strength by looking beneath the surface of precedent to find underlying consistencies in reasoning and policy.

Beginners sometimes think they have synthesized authority when in fact they have not. A passage does not explain a synthesis merely because several cases are mentioned, one after another. It is not a synthesis to describe Case A, describe Case B, describe Case C, describe Case D, and then stop. That is nothing more than an amplified list: the raw materials have been held up to view, but they have not been sewn together. To turn it into a unified whole, you would have to identify the threads that appear in all the cases, stitch the cases together by joining the threads, and organize the

---

§10.4   1. *The Path of the Law*, 10 Harv. L. Rev. 457, 469 (1897). (See §8.6.)

analysis around the threads themselves (rather than around the individual cases). The reader cares more about the threads than about the individual cases, and an individual case is important only to the extent that it teaches something about a thread. It may turn out that Case B sets out the most convincing proof of whatever is at issue; Cases A and D agree and are the only out-of-state cases to have decided the issue; and Case C is a much older decision standing for the same rule but on the basis of reasoning that is less complete than that expressed in Case B. An effective synthesis might explain Case B in full; use Cases A and D to show that foreign authority agrees; and then use Case C only if needed to fill in a remaining gap. Your choice of a formula of synthesis like this one will depend on the issue and on the topography of authority available to you. That choice is an important decision, and you should be prepared to explain how you made it.

Some students go to all the trouble of working out a synthesis, but then fail to make the synthesis clear to the reader. First, state the synthesis in a thesis sentence that sets out the synthesized rule or statement of policy:

> Although the Supreme Court has not ruled on the question, the trend in the Courts of Appeal is to hold that such a prosecution is dismissable where any of four kinds of government misconduct has occurred: . . .

(A synthesis like this could take several pages to prove because, typically, no case will consider more than one form of misconduct.) Remember that the reader will most easily understand the synthesis in the reverse of the order in which you developed it. Although in developing the synthesis you might start from the case details and work up to a synthesized rule or statement of policy, things will be most clear to the reader if you start with the synthesized rule or policy and work down to the supporting details.

Second, organize your explanation around some variation of the paradigm for structuring proof of a conclusion of law,[1] and use the techniques of forceful writing[2] to show the reader how the synthesis fits together. Finally, read your explanation pretending to be a person who is ignorant of the cases and of your synthesis. If the structure of your synthesis is not instantly clear to that kind of reader, find the problem and fix it.

A hybrid skill is that of *reconciliation*. If two decisions seem on the surface to be in conflict, you might be able to demonstrate that the conflict does not exist because on closer examination the two decisions actually stand for the same rule, espouse the same policy, or can be harmonized in some other way. Used in that way, reconciliation has much in common with synthesis. In another situation, a precedent might seem on the surface to conflict with a decision favorable to your client in a current case. There you might be able to demonstrate that the seemingly adverse precedent does not actually conflict with the decision your client would prefer — and in some instances even supports a decision in your client's favor. (But if the precedent seems on the surface to be helpful to your client, your adversary might

§10.5 1. See §7.1.
2. See §4.3.

be able to demonstrate that it really stands for something entirely different and actually hurts your client and helps your adversary.) Used in these ways, reconciliation is sometimes — but not always — related to the skills of analogy and distinguishing. The seemingly adverse precedent might lose its adversity if it turns out to be distinguishable, for instance, but the same result might also happen in other ways. The seemingly adverse precedent might actually reflect favorable policy, for example.

§10.6   Testing for Realism and Marketability

The last skill is that of *testing the result of your reasoning for its realism and marketability to the judicial mind*. Some issues can be resolved without an analogy, others without a reconciliation or a synthesis. But whatever skills you might use in assembling your analysis, you *must* step back from what you are doing and ask yourself whether the result will seem reasonable and just to the typical judge. The experience of adjudicating creates what Roscoe Pound called "the trained intuition of the judge," [1] an instinct for how the law ought to treat each set of facts that ends in dispute. If the result of your reasoning would strike the judicial mind as unrealistic and unreasonable, that mind will reject what you have done, even if you have used all the other skills with gymnastic agility. Because the law is hardly ever certain, a judge can always fold back your reasoning and make other analogies, build other syntheses, and so forth — or, more likely, adopt the analogies, syntheses, and other constructs proposed by your adversary. The skill of testing requires, of course, that you have some understanding of how the judicial mind operates. That may take a long time to come to know fully, but you are learning it now through the decisions you read in casebooks and through the writing you do in this course. (Although lawyers often write arguments based on equity, justice, and reasonability, they *never write down* the kind of *testing* described here. It should be easy to see why: how could you reduce to writing a testing for realism? If a lawyer concludes that the result of his or her reasoning would offend the judge's trained intuition, the lawyer simply starts over again and builds another analysis.)

Instructions for Exercises I and II

In this course and others, you are beginning to learn how to analogize, distinguish, formulate rules, elicit policy, synthesize, reconcile, use the hierarchy of authority, and test analysis for its realism and marketability to the judicial mind. Although these are certainly difficult skills to master, many students say that what is even harder is the *process* of putting these skills together into an integrated whole that resolves an issue. The exercises in this chapter will show

§10.6   1. *The Theory of Judicial Decision*, 36 Harv. L. Rev. 940, 951 (1923).

you how that process works in situations where the issue is resolved entirely on the basis of precedent.

Using the skills discussed in this chapter, make the prediction asked for in each exercise. Assume that your library research has told you that the prediction will rest on the decisions reproduced in the exercise.[1]

Outline issue by issue: Write out an outline of your reasoning, broken down into the various issues that would be put before the court. Under each issue, list the facts that are most critical to your analysis and the cases the court would rely on in making the ruling. (You might list some cases and some facts under more than one issue.)

Consider the various rules for which each case might stand: For each case listed under a given issue, formulate a broad rule that is reasonable and realistic, a narrow rule that is reasonable and realistic, and an intermediate rule that fits the same description; write those rules on your outline; mark the one a court would be most likely to accept; and write the reason.

Consider the ways in which each case might be analogized or distinguished: Where you believe a court would be persuaded by an analogy to a case, write a statement of the analogy next to the case and under the issue where it is relevant, and write why you believe the analogy is persuasive. Where you predict that a court is likely to distinguish a case, write that next to the case under the issue where it is relevant and record the reason for your prediction.

Consider policy: Where you think a case announces policy that would persuade a court, write that policy next to the name of the case and under the issue to which it is relevant, and record the reason for its persuasiveness.

Consider the possible syntheses: Where you predict that a court is likely to synthesize two or more holdings into a single statement of a rule or of policy, note that under the issue where it is relevant and state the synthesis, the cases that would support it, and the reason the synthesis is persuasive.

Consider the possible reconciliations: Where you believe a court is likely to reconcile inconsistent cases or a case that is adverse to your client, write that under the issue where it is relevant, together with the basis for the reconciliation and the reason for its persuasiveness.

Consider the hierarchy of authority: Where a court would have to use the hierarchy of authority to resolve an inconsistency in the case law, write the names of the cases on your outline under the issue where they are relevant; note the inconsistency; mark the case that you believe the court would follow; and write the reason for your prediction.

Throughout your outline, test your thinking in several ways.

Consider counter-arguments: Ask yourself whether a reasonable argument could challenge any part of your analysis. If so, note the argument at the relevant point in the outline and write your prediction of whether the argument is likely to persuade a judge. If you believe that an argument, even though reasonable, is not likely to persuade, write the reason for your prediction. If, on reflection, you conclude that the argument is likely to persuade, modify your analysis accordingly.

1. The decisions are reproduced in alphabetical order. Where citations are omitted, assume that you have read the authorities cited to and found that they do not add anything to the decisions reproduced here. Dissents and concurrences, if any, are omitted.

Consider troublesome facts: Ask yourself whether a fact has a reasonable chance of causing a judge to doubt your analysis. If so, note that fact and why it would create doubt. If you conclude that, in spite of the doubt, the judge would rule as you have predicted, state the reason. If, on reflection, you believe that the doubt overcomes your analysis, modify your analysis accordingly.

If you cannot find arguments or facts that work against your analysis, you may be avoiding problems.

In addition, ask yourself whether your analysis will seem *reasonable, just, and realistic to the judicial mind.*

Finally, *predict* how the court will rule.

The diagram below might help you see this process as a whole.

identify the issues
analyze each issue
- ▶ identify the determinative facts
- ▶ identify the cases on which the court will rely
- ▶ for each case, consider
  - ▷ along a spectrum from broad to narrow, the most likely rule for which the case stands
  - ▷ ways of analogizing or distinguishing
  - ▷ policy for which the case stands
  - ▷ possible syntheses with other cases
  - ▷ possible reconciliations
  - ▷ how the court will use the hierarchy of authority to resolve inconsistencies in the case law
- ▶ test by considering
  - ▷ counter-arguments
  - ▷ troublesome facts
  - ▷ whether your analysis will seem reasonable, just, and realistic to the judicial mind
- ▶ predict how the court will resolve the issue
predict how the court will resolve the entire controversy

If your teacher has assigned the exercise as preparation for a class, be prepared to speak in class from your outline. During class, your teacher may ask you to transform your outline into some variation of the paradigm described in Chapter 7 (see page 112). Be prepared to explain how you would vary the paradigm in sequence and depth and how you would combine separately paradigmed explanations into a unified whole.

If, on the other hand, your teacher has assigned the exercise as work to be done entirely at home, complete the exercise at home by reorganizing your outline into some variation of the paradigm described in Chapter 7, varying the paradigm as appropriate in sequence and depth and, if necessary, combining separately paradigmed explanations into a unified whole.

Regardless of whether you complete the exercise in class or at home, you can treat it as a dry run of the kind of planning you will need to do in order to write a Discussion in an objective memorandum (or an Argument in a persuasive document).

Consider three suggestions: First, start with a lot of paper and leave much blank space because you will probably find yourself going back and adding to what you have already done. The process of organizing will inevitably generate more insights than you had when you started out. Second, do not be afraid to change your mind as you go along. Some of the insights you gain may persuade you to change your analysis. Third, make an objective prediction and do not take sides. Your prediction is for the benefit of a supervisor, such as a senior partner, who really wants to know what will happen in court. You are not being asked for courtroom advocacy. (That will be covered in later chapters.)

Exercise I.   Emil Risberg's Diary[1]

Returning from an expedition across the Arctic ice cap in the last century, Emil Risberg and his companions became stranded at the northern tip of Greenland, and after several weeks they all died of scurvy and exposure. A few years later, their hut was found, their bodies were buried at sea, and their possessions were returned to their families. Emil Risberg's widow received, among other things, his diary.

Risberg had measured the group's geographic position every day during the expedition, and he recorded those measurements, as well as a mass of other detail, in his diary. His measurements showed that he and the group he led had travelled farther north than anyone else had gone at the time. The diary brought Risberg much posthumous fame, and it was not until early in this century that any explorer got closer to the north pole. The diary was passed on in Risberg's family through inheritence. Four years ago, when the diary became controversial, it was owned by Risberg's great-granddaughter, Olga Risberg.

The controversy began when a researcher named Sloan announced that Risberg had faked his measurements and that he could not possibly have gotten as far north as the diary showed. Sloan supported his argument with a large amount of scientific evidence involving things like the ocean currents that shift the ice pack and the distances that can be travelled in a day over ice. Olga Risberg took this very badly.

Within a month or two, she went to the officers of the New York Geographical Society, whom she had never met before, and gave them the diary, together with a letter that contained the following sentence:

> I donate my great-grandfather's diary to the Society because I believe the Society is best situated to evaluate the measurements recorded in it and to establish once and for all that Emil Risberg went where he claimed to have gone.

The Society had not asked Olga to make a gift of the diary, and no one at the Society said anything to her about conducting a study or about her motivation for the gift. At the time, the diary had been appraised at a value of $15,000.

1. See the instructions on page 155.

The Society did nothing to evaluate the diary. Two years ago, Olga demanded that the Society either resolve the controversy or return the diary to her. The Society replied in a letter that, among other things, stated the following:

> When you donated the diary to the Society, you expressed some hope that it would be studied. But the Society made no promise — orally or in writing — to study the controversy surrounding the diary. If and when our board of directors chooses to go ahead with a study, we will do so, but you made a gift which we accepted without conditions.

Sloan has just died. In his papers are notes showing that he had faked his own measurements, that he had started the controversy to build his reputation, and that all along he had believed that Risberg's diary was accurate. Olga has been beseiged with offers to buy the diary from people who were unaware that she had donated it to the Society. All of the offers are in six figures.

You have concluded that the gift cannot be set aside on the grounds of fraud. Will Olga Risberg be able to persuade a court to impose a constructive trust on the Society's title to the diary?

SHARP v. KOSMALSKI
40 N.Y.2d 119, 351 N.E.2d 721, 386 N.Y.S.2d 72 (1976)

GABRIELLI, J. Plaintiff commenced this action to impose a constructive trust upon property transferred to defendant on the ground that the retention of the property and the subsequent ejection of the plaintiff therefrom was in violation of a relationship of trust and confidence and constituted unjust enrichment. The Trial Judge dismissed plaintiff's complaint. . . . [This was error.]

Upon the death of his wife of 32 years, plaintiff, a 56-year-old dairy farmer whose education did not go beyond the eighth grade, developed a very close relationship with defendant, a school teacher and a woman 16 years his junior. . . . Plaintiff came to depend upon defendant's companionship and, eventually, declared his love for her, proposing marriage to her. Notwithstanding her refusal of his proposal of marriage, defendant continued her association with plaintiff and permitted him to shower her with many gifts, fanning his hope that he could induce defendant to alter her decision concerning his marriage proposal. Defendant was given access to plaintiff's bank account, from which it is not denied that she withdrew substantial amounts of money. Eventually, plaintiff . . . executed a deed naming her a joint owner of his farm. The record reveals that numerous alterations in the way of modernization were made to plaintiff's farmhouse in alleged furtherance of "domestic plans" made by plaintiff and defendant.

In September, 1971, while the renovations were still in progress, plaintiff transferred his remaining joint interest to defendant. At the time of the conveyance, a farm liability policy was issued to plaintiff naming defendant and her daughter as additional insureds. Furthermore, the insurance

159

agent was requested by plaintiff, in the presence of defendant, to change the policy to read "J. Rodney Sharp, life tenant. Jean C. Kosmalski, owner." In February, 1973, the liaison between the parties was abruptly severed as defendant ordered plaintiff to move out of his home and vacate the farm. Defendant took possession of the home, the farm and all the equipment thereon, leaving plaintiff with assets of $300.

Generally, a constructive trust may be imposed "[w]hen property has been acquired in such circumstances that the holder of the legal title may not in good conscience retain the beneficial interest" [citations omitted]. In the development of the doctrine of constructive trust as a remedy available to courts of equity, the following four requirements were posited: (1) a confidential or fiduciary relation, (2) a promise, (3) a transfer in reliance thereon and (4) unjust enrichment [citations omitted].

. . . The record in this case clearly indicates that a relationship of trust and confidence did exist between the parties and, hence, the defendant must be charged with an obligation not to abuse the trust and confidence placed in her by the plaintiff. . . .

Unquestionably, there is a transfer of property here. . . . Even without an express promise . . . courts of equity have imposed a constructive trust upon property transferred in reliance upon a confidential relationship. In such a situation, a promise may be implied or even inferred from the very transaction itself. As Judge Cardozo so eloquently observed: "Though a promise in words was lacking, the whole transaction, it might be found, was 'instinct with an obligation' imperfectly expressed (*Wood v. Duff-Gordon*, 222 N.Y. 88, 91)" (*Sinclair v. Purdy*, 235 N.Y. 245, 254 . . .). . . .

. . . Indeed, in the case before us, it is inconceivable that plaintiff would convey all of his interest in property which was not only his abode but the very means of his livelihood without at least tacit consent upon the part of the defendant that she would permit him to continue to live on and operate the farm. . . .

The salutary purpose of the constructive trust remedy is to prevent unjust enrichment. . . . A person may be deemed to be unjustly enriched if he (or she) has received a benefit, the retention of which would be unjust [citation omitted]. . . . [W]hether defendant's conduct following the transfer . . . resulted in the unjust enrichment of the defendant . . . must be determined from the circumstances of the transfer since there is no express promise concerning plaintiff's continued use of the land. . . . This case seems to present the classic example of a situation where equity should intervene to scrutinize a transaction pregnant with opportunity for abuse and unfairness. . . .

SINCLAIR v. PURDY
235 N.Y. 245, 139 N.E. 255 (1923)

CARDOZO, J. . . . Elijah F. Purdy [owned a half] interest in real estate in the city of New York. . . . Elijah was a clerk of what was then known as the Fifth District Court. His ownership of real estate subjected him to constant importunities to go bail for those in trouble. The desire to escape these importunities led him to execute a deed conveying his undivided half interest to his sister Elvira [who already owned the other half]. . . . The record does not make it plain whether at this time brother and sister made their home together. The relation between them in any event was one of harmony and affection, and so continued till the end. . . . There is evidence of repeated declarations by Elvira that, though the [whole] title was in her name, a half interest was his. . . . Elijah died at the age of 80 in 1914. [A niece, who would have inherited from Elijah, has brought this suit to establish a trust in favor of Elijah (and therefore in favor of the niece) over the property deeded to Elvira.]

. . . The sister's deposition shows that her brother disclosed his plan to her before the making of a deed. Someone, he said, had advised him to place his share of the property in her name. He told her that he intended to follow the advice. It was an expedient adopted to save him the bother of going upon bonds. She does not remember that she made any promise in return. He trusted, as she puts it, to her sense of honor. A little later she learned that the title was in her name.

We think a confidential relation was the procuring cause of the conveyance. The grantor could not disclose the trust upon the face of the deed. If he had done so, he would have defeated the purpose of the transfer, which required that title, to outward appearance, be vested in another. He found, as he thought, in the bond of kinship a protection as potent as any that could be assured to him by covenants of title. . . . "The absence of a formal writing grew out of that very confidence and trust, and was occasioned by it." [Citation omitted.]

In such conditions, the rule in this state is settled that equity will grant relief. [Citations omitted.] . . .

. . . Here was a man transferring to his sister the only property he had in the world. He was transferring it in obedience to advice that embarrassment would be avoided if he put it in her name. He was doing this, as she admits, in reliance upon her honor. Even if we were to accept her statement that there was no distinct promise to hold it for his benefit, the exaction of such a promise, in view of the relation, might well have seemed to be superfluous. . . . Though a promise in words was lacking, the whole transaction, it might be found, was "instinct with an obligation" imperfectly expressed *Wood v. Duff-Gordon,* 222 N.Y. 88, 91. It was to be interpreted, not literally or irrespective of its setting, but sensibly and broadly with all its human implications. . . .

TEBIN v. MOLDOCK
19 A.D.2d 275, 241 N.Y.S.2d 629 (1963)

BREITEL, J.P. Plaintiffs appeal from a judgment dismissing their complaint after a trial without a jury. Plaintiffs are the son, sister and two brothers of a New York decedent, all of whom are residents of Poland.

Defendant is decedent's niece, and a native-born American. Decedent emigrated to the United States from Poland in 1913. She died in 1956, a widow, leaving only plaintiff son as a surviving descendant. The action was to impose a constructive trust, in favor of plaintiffs, of certain funds deposited in savings institutions, and a multiple dwelling. The assets had once belonged to decedent but she, in the last five years of her life, had transferred them to defendant niece.

Plaintiffs charged defendant with having obtained the assets . . . by promises made to hold the property for the benefit of plaintiff son. . . .

[We hold that] a constructive trust [must] be imposed on the . . . assets of decedent in the hands of defendant niece. While the evidence does not establish fraud or undue influence, it does inescapably establish that the assets were transferred on certain promises to hold for the benefit of the son, which promises were made in a confidential relationship. These promises were relied upon, and for their breach equity is bound to provide appropriate relief.

Hermina Tebin, the decedent, was born in Poland in 1882. She married there, but later separated from her husband, left her two sons with her parents, and emigrated to the United States in 1913. One son died in 1920 without issue. The other, who was born in 1904, is the first-named plaintiff in this action.

Since coming to this country decedent lived in New York, earned her livelihood as a midwife, acquired the lower east side multiple dwelling in which she lived, and accumulated cash funds in the amount of about $19,000. During this period of over 40 years, she saw her son in Poland once when she travelled there in 1928, and stayed for some two months. She maintained an intermittent correspondence with him throughout and until the end of her life. . . .

In 1920, decedent brought her sister Aniela to the United States. . . . Defendant niece is Aniela's daughter, whom decedent knew as a growing child, befriended and assisted as a young woman training for an educational career, and who, in decedent's later years, handled her moneys and affairs when illness and age closed in.

[Decedent's health began to deteriorate in 1947.]

Starting in 1951 [decedent began transferring her bank accounts to defendant niece]. In December, 1951 the real property was transferred . . . to the niece, [who, at the same time, signed an] agreement [providing] that decedent should retain the use, free, of her apartment, and receive for her life the net income from the property less a management fee to the niece. The [agreement] recited that the niece was the sole and entire owner of the property.

In August, 1951 decedent made a will in which the niece was named as the sole beneficiary of her estate. It contained the following clause: "Third: I have given certain oral instructions to my said niece, with respect to my son Kazimierz Tebin, and having full faith and confidence in her honesty and integrity, I feel certain that she will carry out my instructions. Nonetheless, in the event that she fails to carry out my instructions, it shall be a matter for her own conscience and not otherwise."

As decedent's end approached, the niece handled more and more of the aunt's affairs, faithfully, and paid all her expenses of living, hospitalization and medical services, out of the funds theretofore transferred to the niece. After the aunt's death, the niece from the same sources paid the funeral expenses. . . .

Presently, the niece holds the real property and about $14,000 of roundly $19,000 transferred to her.

Plaintiffs assert that the niece and her mother frightened decedent with the representation that if any assets were ever received by the son, he being in a Communist country, the assets would be taken from him and that Stalin would kill him. . . .

Plaintiffs also claim that the assets were transferred to the niece on her promise that she would hold them for decedent's son and advance funds as he needed and could profitably use them.

The niece and her mother assert that the relation between the decedent and her son was not a close one, the decedent often complained of the greediness of the son and his persistent and exclusive interest in receiving remittances and gifts. Moreover, it is asserted that the niece was to send moneys to the son only in her exclusive discretion and judgment, and never in excess of $25 in any one month. It is pointed out that the niece was the godchild of decedent, the relationship intimate, and that the American-born niece was the special pride and object of affection of decedent. In short, the gifts were absolute; there were no promises except acquiescence in precatory requests of minimal effect in relation to the assets involved. . . .

[I]t is clear by documents, reliable witness testimony, and circumstances that the niece made or acquiesced in promises which induced the transfer of assets. Indeed, her testimony confirms pivotal facts. . . .

In July, 1952 decedent came to Mr. Solon, a lawyer, and retained him to recover her property. . . . Decedent had told Mr. Solon the Stalin story and that she had transferred the assets to the niece to provide her lifetime needs and take care of her son. While there were some ensuing conversations about bringing a lawsuit nothing further was done to prosecute the matter. . . .

The niece testified that decedent told her: "that she was an older woman, that she wanted someone who would take care of her, who would look after her needs while she was alive. . . . She spoke to me also about her son, and she said that all during her lifetime he had always written to her and asked her to help, and that since she was giving me everything she had, she thought that he probably would, after her death, seek me out and ask me for help, and she asked me to see that he never got his hands on any lump sum of money. That is why she was giving it to me. But she knew that if he would write to me and ask me for help, and if I felt that he needed it, that I would help him." . . .

In August, 1952 decedent wrote to her son in Poland:

> I was very sick with my heart [because] Aniela and her daughter Janina scared me by telling me that if I leave my estate to you Stalin will take it

away from you after I die and that . . . you may be shot to death. So I gave all to Janka — $14,000 and a house and now they are trying to commit me to an insane asylum so they could keep everything for themselves. I will try to have you come here and take it all back because they stole it from me by fraud and they bribed the lawyer.

Keep this letter so that you could appear as a witness if necessary. . . .

It is evident, beyond persuasive contradiction, that a secret agreement had been effected between aunt and niece for the benefit of the aunt during her lifetime, and the son. . . .

[A constructive trust will be imposed where] the one who entrusted property did so because of certain understandings, and the one to whom the assets are given acquiesced even in silence (e.g., *Sinclair v. Purdy*, 235 N.Y. 245, 253-254 . . .). . . .

In dealing with the problem of a secret trust or the breach of a confidential relationship the ordinary rules imposed by the Statute of Frauds . . . are not applicable. Equity in this area has always reached beyond the facade of formal documents, absolute transfers, and even limiting statutes on the law side. . . .

. . . Under recent decisions it has been held that the Polish regime does not prevent [Polish citizens from receiving money inherited in capitalist countries] [citations omitted].

Accordingly, the judgment . . . should [provide] for a constructive trust in [the son's] favor. . . .

TEBIN v. MOLDOCK
14 N.Y.2d 807, 200 N.E.2d 216, 251 N.Y.S.2d 36 (1964)

PER CURIAM . . . The judgment should be modified to limit the scope of the constructive trust imposed on defendant Janina Moldock to an obligation to pay $25 a month for the benefit of Kazimierz Tebin. . . . [W]e conclude the record supports a finding that defendant, occupying a relationship of confidence and trust with decedent, undertook to devote a small part of the property given to her for the benefit of plaintiff. On the basis of defendant's own testimony this would approximate $25 a month. No such breach of confidence or of fiduciary obligation, either before or after decedent's death, has been established as would warrant forfeiture by defendant of the major interest in decedent's property which it was clearly decedent's intent that defendant should have.

Exercise II. Teddy Washburn's Gun[1]

In his prime, Gorilla Morrell was often on the bill at Friday Night Wrestling. Now he is reduced to hanging around Washburn's Weights Room & Gym, which is adjacent to Washburn's Bar, Grill & Billiards on Rappahannock Street in Richmond, Virginia. Gorilla is good for Teddy Washburn's business because

1. See the instructions on page 155.

customers in the Weights Room try to take Gorilla on. When this happens, customers in Washburn's other establishment wander into the Weights Room to watch. There they order more drinks, which Washburn passes through a hole he has cut through the wall. Afterward, Gorilla, his adversary, and the spectators tend to adjourn back to the Bar, where the spirit of conviviality usually leads to games of billiards accompanied by further orders of food and drink.

Washburn has let Gorilla build up a bill of $183.62, dating back over several weeks. Last night, they had words over the matter. Gorilla took a swing at Washburn, who came out from behind the bar and chased Gorilla out into the street. There Gorilla took another swing at Washburn, and Washburn, demanding his money, pulled out a gun (for which he has title and a license).

Gorilla grabbed for the gun, but it fell out of Washburn's hand, sliding five or six feet along the sidewalk and coming to rest at the feet of Snare Drum Bennett, a mechanic who was returning from work. Bennett happened onto this scene only in time to hear Washburn demand money and to see him pull out the gun and have it knocked from his hand.

Bennett, Washburn, and Gorilla looked at the gun, then at each other, and then at the gun again. Finally, Bennett crouched down, picked up the gun, checked to make sure the safety was on, and put it in her coat pocket. "Washburn," she said, "you haven't paid *me* yet for the front end work I did on your car."

"I will," said Washburn.

"It's $275," said Bennett, "and it's been three weeks. I think you should go back inside. You ought to pay your own debts before you accuse other people of welshing out on you."

"How can I pay you," exclaimed Washburn, "if he won't pay me?"

"That's your problem," said Bennett, "I'm holding on to the gun. You can't seem to handle it right now, and I want my money."

At that point, Gorilla clobbered Washburn in the face and sent him staggering. Bennett turned around, walked a half-dozen steps, and began to turn into a dark alley. Washburn started to get up, called out "Hey, you!" and took a step in Bennett's direction. Bennett took the gun from her coat, pointed it at Washburn, smiled, and said, "Back off, bucko."

Washburn froze, and Bennett walked into the alley. As soon as she was out of sight, she dropped the gun into an open but full trash dumpster. The dumpster belongs to a grocery store and is about five feet inside the alley, which in turn is about twenty feet from the front door of Washburn's bar.

An hour or so later, the police came to Bennett's home and arrested her for robbing Washburn of his gun. Bennett told them where she had dropped it. The police went straight to the dumpster but found nothing inside, not even the trash that had muffled the gun's fall.

Is Bennett likely to be convicted of robbing Washburn of his gun?[2]

---

2. The question is not whether Bennett robbed Washburn of his gun, but whether she is likely to be convicted of robbery. To make that prediction, you will need to take into account the prosecution's burden of proof beyond a reasonable doubt.

BUTTS v. COMMONWEALTH
145 Va. 800, 133 S.E. 764 (1926)

BURKS, J. Louis Butts [appeals his conviction for attempted] robbery. . . .

. . . [T]he accused had worked for the Royal Guano company for two days and a half at $2 a day, when he was discharged. . . . He thereupon demanded immediate payment of the amount due him, but was told that Saturday was pay day, and that he would have to return on Saturday to get his money, and he was ordered off the premises. He objected [to waiting for his pay]. He left the premises, however, peaceably, but, after changing his clothes, he put his pistol in his pocket, and returned to the plant in quest of the superintendent. When he found the superintendent, he stated to him the facts about his discharge, and demanded payment of what was due him. He was again told that Saturday was pay day, and that he would have to return on that day to get his money. There was no controversy over the amount due, and it is conceded on behalf of the Commonwealth that the amount was $5. Upon refusal of payment until Saturday, the accused became profane, and pointed a pistol at the superintendent and demanded that "he be paid his wages then and there." The accused and the superintendent then went to the latter's office, the accused still holding the pistol in his hand, to ascertain from the accused's time card how much he had earned. The card was produced, and the superintendent "thereupon took $5 of his own money out of his pocket and handed it to the accused, who thereupon at once left the premises." Was this an attempt at robbery?

Our statute does not define robbery, so that we have to look to the common law for the definition. [Citation omitted.]

> Robbery is an aggravated form of larceny, but is treated as a distinctive crime. It is the taking, with intent to steal, of the personal property of another, from his person or in his presence, against his will, by violence or intimidation. . . .

[Citations omitted.]

. . . But there can be no [robbery] of the property taken if it, in fact, is the property of the taker, or if he, in good faith, believes it is his for there is lacking the criminal intent which is an essential element of larceny. . . .

The taking must . . . be animo furandi . . . generally translated as "an intent to steal." But what is an intent to steal? It is an intent to feloniously deprive the owner permanently of his property. But "feloniously" in this connection simply means "with criminal intent." [Citation omitted.] . . .

. . . [The accused] had the right to suppose that [when] he was discharged . . . and ordered off the premises, he . . . was entitled to his pay when his connection with the company was severed. This belief of the accused was entirely reasonable, and, even if unsound, [his mistake] should not of itself have furnished ground for refusal to set aside the verdict. He apparently acted in good faith, and there is nothing in the record to contradict him. His good faith negatived the idea of a felonious intent. . . .

Reversed.

GREEN v. COMMONWEALTH
133 Va. 696, 112 S.E. 562 (1922)

BURKS, J. The plaintiff in error was convicted of robbing Mrs. Lillie Priddy [and appeals on the ground] that the verdict is contrary to the evidence. . . .

[Although there was evidence that the accused assaulted Mrs. Priddy, that] did not relieve the Commonwealth of the burden of proving the robbery beyond a reasonable doubt. The only witness who testified as to the alleged robbery was Mrs. Priddy. Her account of what took place is substantially as follows: About 3:30 o'clock on the afternoon of May 14, 1921, she was walking along a private road . . . ; that she saw the accused approaching . . . at a distance of about a city block; that at the time she had her pocketbook in her hand in which there was a ring of the value of $30, a fountain pen of the value of $2, and $3.75 in money; that when she saw him approaching, she from force of habit wrapped the chain of the pocketbook around her wrist; that as he passed her, distant about five feet, he tipped his hat and said, "Good evening". . . ; that just after he passed her he struck her "right down across the neck and shoulder with a stick"; that she must have been unconscious for a minute or two, and when she came to herself he was standing over her, and she thought he was going to choke her, and she kicked him with both feet between the knee and hip; that she began screaming, and he ran off up the road in the direction from which she had come. She further testified that the chain of the pocketbook was not broken before she fell, and that "I had it in this hand, and it fell across the road, and I was lying across the road, my shoulders were in the mud in a rut," and that she did not know how the pocketbook was taken from her hand. On cross-examination, she testified as follows:

Q. When the pocketbook was found there, it had the ring in it, didn't it?
A. Had everything in it.
Q. There wasn't anything taken from the pocketbook?
A. There was nothing taken from it.
Q. Did you see him put the pocketbook down?
A. No; I did not.
Q. Didn't see him with it at all, did you?
A. No; I did not.
Q. Did you know whether the pocketbook fell from your hand?
A. No; it didn't fall.
Q. How far was it from you when it was picked up?
A. Just right across the road.
Q. I asked you how far it was.

A.   I don't know how far it was. I think it was about five or six feet. . . .

Q.   Mrs. Priddy, do you know whether or not this pocketbook was taken from your hand, or whether it fell when you fell?

A.   It must have been snatched from my hand, because it could not have fallen because I had the chain wrapped around my wrist just like this (demonstrating), and somebody pulled the pocketbook and broke the chain.

Of course, if she was unconscious at the time she could not know. . . . The only fact stated is that she had the chain wrapped around her wrist, and that the chain was broken. There is nothing in the record to indicate what the strength of the chain was. The testimony does not show that the accused ever, for a moment of time, had the pocketbook and its contents in his absolute control. The testimony of Mrs. Priddy, if credited by the jury, showed a very violent assault and battery upon her by the [accused], but does not establish a robbery.

Robbery is the taking, with the intent to deprive the owner permanently, of personal property, from his person or in his presence, against his will, by violence or intimidation. [Citations omitted.] The taking must be the securing dominion or absolute control of the property. The absolute dominion must exist at some time, though it be only momentary. [Citation omitted.] . . .

The testimony in this case does not measure up to these requirements. . . .

Reversed.

JORDAN v. COMMONWEALTH
25 Gratt (66 Va.) 943 (1874)

STAPLES, J. . . . The taking must in all cases be accompanied with the felonious intent, and no subsequent felonious purpose will render the previous taking felonious. As expressed by Lord Coke, "the intent to steal must be when it cometh to his hands or possession; for if he hath the possession of it unlawfully, though he hath animum furandi afterward and carrieth it away, it is no larceny." . . .

. . . [I]n the case at bar, the prisoner and his associates in snatching the pistol from the prosecutor may not have intended at the time to steal it. If they did not so intend, if the only object was to prevent its being used against them, then the subsequent carrying away and conversion would not constitute robbery. On the other hand, if the intention at the time was to deprive the prosecutor wholly of the pistol, the offence is robbery, although the assailants on snatching the pistol, may also have intended to prevent its being used against them. Both intents may have existed at the time. The jury may infer the felonious intent from the immediate asportation and conversion of the property, in the absence of satisfactory countervailing evidence. . . .

LINDSAY v. COMMONWEALTH
135 Va. 580, 115 S.E. 516 (1923)

PRENTIS, J. The accused has been found guilty of murder in the first degree. . . . The only question which requires our consideration is whether the evidence is sufficient to support the verdict.

. . . On the morning of July 4, 1921, at about 10 o'clock A.M., Betty Mills, with whom the petitioner lived . . . was shot in the abdomen, and died on the afternoon of the same day. The accused was seen and accosted on the highway in the immediate vicinity of and going towards the house in which he and the deceased lived, and was seen in the house just after the shot was heard. There is evidence that he had cursed the deceased on that morning at about 7 o'clock; that just before the occurrence a witness near by heard "a sound like somebody was fussing, and heard a man say to a woman, 'Shut up, God damn you' "; and this witness said he had gone about 20 steps further when he heard the report of the gun. Another witness, fixing the time about 8 or 9 o'clock in the morning, saw the accused go towards their joint dwelling, and shortly thereafter heard the deceased say, "Oh John, Oh John!" and then heard a gun shot. Another witness heard the accused tell the deceased between 6 and 7 o'clock in the morning that "if she didn't shut up he would take something and kill her." These witnesses were not in the actual presence of the parties, but outside of their dwelling, and near enough thereto to recognize their voices. . . . The physician testified that the wound was about 10 inches long, beginning above the pelvic bone, extending to such bone, and about one inch to the right of the median line. . . .

He also expressed the opinion that this wound could have been made either in an attempt to commit suicide or in a struggle for the possession of the gun, as well as deliberately by the accused, but if thus killed by the accused she must have been either sitting down, or down upon her hands and knees; that from the character of the wound it was just as probable that the deceased was accidentally shot, or shot herself, as that she was shot by the accused; that she stated to him (the physician) that she was down on the floor when shot, and repeatedly stated to him in the presence of several others during the day that the wound was the result of an accident, and that the accused was not present when she was shot. . . .

The only witness for the defense was the sheriff [who testified that the deceased, before dying, had told him that] "she started to housecleaning, and . . . she was carrying that gun from the washstand over to the bureau, and struck the gun against the rocker, or her foot, she didn't know which, and caused it to go off " [and that her] "words were these: 'I shot myself; John was not here'; or 'John was not here, I shot myself.' " . . .

. . . The woman's statement that the accused was not there may be easily reconciled with the statements of the other witnesses that they saw him enter the house at or about the time the shot was heard, because there was more than one room on the bottom floor of their dwelling, and another one upstairs. We are always most reluctant to disturb a verdict which has been approved by the trial court, but, giving all of the evidence in this record our most careful consideration, we are driven to the conclusion that, unless the rule which requires the commonwealth to prove crime to the exclusion of every reasonable doubt is to be abrogated, this judgment must be reversed. . . . [T]he chief question is not as to which of the witnesses who testified are to be believed, for there is no reason for disbelieving any of them. That there may be good reason for fair-minded men to differ as to whether or not the accused is the guilty agent is not sufficient to support the conviction for a criminal case, which is not to be determined by the preponderance of the evidence. That there is a reasonable doubt of the guilt of the accused is believed to be evident. . . .

Reversed.

STATE v. SMITH
268 N.C. 167, 150 S.E.2d 194 (1966)

[The defendant appeals from a conviction for robbery.] The evidence for the State tended to show these facts:

. . . Adams was awakened by the noise of breaking glass in his service station, which was located about 40 yards from his home. The noise came over an intercom system connecting his bedroom with the service station. He dressed quickly, took his rifle, and set out for the station. Halfway there, he observed one Thomas Henry coming from the station toward him. Henry told Adams that someone had his car and wouldn't give it back to him. Adams held the rifle on Henry and marched him to the street to see "where his partner was." On the street he saw a police car parked below a 1960 Chevrolet. Policeman Spikes and defendant were standing side-by-side near the parked cars. Adams, "thinking everything was under control," went up to the two with his rifle. When he was within three or four steps of them, defendant pushed the policeman in front of him, pointed a 38 caliber pistol in Adams' face and ordered him to drop the rifle. Adams failed to obey the order and defendant said, "If you don't drop it, I'll kill you." After saying this twice, defendant fired a shot, which struck not far from Adams' feet. Adams then dropped his rifle. Defendant picked it up, [and he and Henry,] carrying the rifle and the pistol with them, then drove off towards Vanceboro. . . .

About 40 minutes after defendant and Henry had driven off with the . . . rifle, police found Henry standing by the wrecked car . . . and Adams' rifle was beside a telephone pole just below the place where the car had [been] wrecked. . . .

SHARP, J. . . . Assuming the truth of the State's evidence, does it show that the offense committed upon Adams was . . . robbery . . . ? . . .

Robbery, a common-law offense not defined by statute in North Carolina, is merely an aggravated form of larceny. [Citation omitted.] . . . Robbery is " 'the taking, with intent to steal, of the personal property of another, from his person or in his presence, without his consent or against his will, by violence or intimidation.' " [Citation omitted.] The taking must be done *animo furandi,* with a felonious intent to appropriate the goods taken to some use or purpose of the taker. . . .

In robbery, as in larceny, the taking of the property must be with the felonious intent *permanently* to deprive the owner of his property. [Citations omitted.] Thus, if one disarms another in self-defense with no intent to steal his weapon, he is not guilty of robbery. [Citation omitted.] If he takes another's property for the taker's immediate and temporary use with no intent permanently to deprive the owner of his property, he is not guilty of larceny. [Citations omitted.]

. . . The narrow question here is whether the circumstances under which defendant took the rifle are susceptible to the inference that he had any intent other than that of permanently depriving Adams of the weapon. . . .

It would be unreasonable to assume that defendant, fleeing from arrest for the crime of felonious breaking and entering, had any expectation of returning the rifle he had taken in order to effect his escape. To do so by any certain means would be to invite detection and capture. For the purpose of decision here, we assume that defendant took the rifle "for temporary use" and that after it had served his purpose of escape, he intended to abandon it at the first opportunity lest it lead to his detection. Such procedure, however, would leave Adams' recovery of his rifle to mere chance and thus constitute "such reckless exposure to loss" that it is consistent only with an intent permanently to deprive the owner of his property. [Citation omitted.] In abandoning it, defendant put it beyond his power to return the rifle and showed total indifference as to whether Adams ever recovered his rifle. When, in order to serve a temporary purpose of his own, one takes property (1) with the specific intent wholly and permanently to deprive the owner of it, or (2) under circumstances which render it unlikely that the owner will ever recover his property and which disclose the taker's total indifference to his rights, one takes it with the intent to steal *(animus furandi).* A man's intentions can only be judged by his words and deeds; he must be taken to intend those consequences which are the natural and immediate results of his acts. If one . . . has taken property from its owner without any color of right, his intent to deprive the owner wholly of the property "may, generally speaking, be deemed proved" if it appears he "kept the goods as his own 'til his apprehension, or that he gave them away, or sold or exchanged or destroyed them. . . ." [Citation omitted.] . . .

No Error.

11 Working with Statutes

§11.1 Ten Tools of Statutory Interpretation

Interpretation is the art of finding out . . . what [the drafter] intended to convey.

—*Francis Lieber*

I don't care what their intention was. I only want to know what the words mean.

—*Oliver Wendell Holmes*

As you have realized by now, "learning law" is less learning what the rules of law are (a body of information) than it is learning how to discover and use the rules (a repertory of intellectual skills). And you have learned that a common law country has two types of sources of law: judicial precedent, on one hand, and, on the other, statutes and statute-like material, such as constitutions, administrative regulations, and court rules. Chapter 10 inventoried the skills used in writing about precedent. This chapter does the same thing for the tools used to interpret and explain statutes and statute-like material.

The two quotations at the beginning of this section might seem to express contradictory approaches to interpreting any source of law, the first focusing on what the lawmaker intended to do and the second on what the lawmaker did. The first approach might use any reliable evidence of intent, but the second concentrates on the words actually used. This is a classic tension in statutory interpretation, and it grows partly out of a history of struggle—now mostly halted—between legislatures and courts. As you know, in English common law, courts were the original lawmakers, and legislatures arose afterward, acquiring the power to make new law and to change law already made by courts. Courts, of course, retained the ultimate power to enforce all law. And, because interpretation is essential to enforcement, courts used their power to limit the effect of intrusive statutes, which judges treated with suspicion and even condescension until well into this century.[1]

Some practices of statutory construction grew out of this struggle and survive today because they still accomplish some logical purpose — although not necessarily the same purpose for which they were invented. For example, statutes in derogation of the common law are still strictly construed. Long ago, courts used this and other rules to limit the invasion of legislatures onto the courts' lawmaking turf. Today the reason is different: since the pre-statutory common law was a complete and fairly stable system of rules, one can fairly conclude that, unless a legislature announces otherwise, it intends to tinker with that system only in small ways.

The search for meaning or intent begins with the words of the statute. At one time, nearly every jurisdiction in the United States followed the "plain meaning" rule, which permits inquiry into other evidence of legislative intent only where the words of the statute do not plainly convey meaning. In recent decades, however, a number of courts have modified or abandoned the plain meaning rule and now search outside the statute for evidence of intent even where the statutory wording seems clear and unambiguous. Those courts that still adhere to the plain meaning rule do so not because they would rather not know how statutes or sausages are made,[2] but because they believe legislative intent can most efficiently be established by finding meaning in the words of the statute itself and by inquiring further only when those words are ambiguous. Those courts that examine other evidence of intent even when the statutory words are clear do so because they believe that the words' meaning is not good enough if other evidence shows that the legislature intended something else. (Are you beginning to understand the tension between what words mean and what their author intended them to mean? If the legislature wanted to communicate one thing but instead communicated another, which message should a court choose to receive — the one sent or the one intended to be sent?)

Aside from reading the statute, what kind of inquiry could a court make? You might think that the sensible thing would be to ask the legislature what it had in mind. But most state legislatures are made up of between one and two hundred voting members, and Congress includes 100 Senators and 435 Representatives. Even if a group could have a collective state of mind, these groups are just too large to be able to tell you what, as groups, they were thinking some time before. In addition, legislatures consider such a stagger-

---

§11.1 1. There are many reasons why this kind of struggle is mostly behind us, but perhaps the most important is this: modern life is so complex and so difficult as to humble anyone who undertakes to make law, and judges today are grateful for a partnership with legislatures, which are better equipped to gather masses of detailed information and to work out compromises between competing interest groups.

2. "If you like laws or sausages, you should never watch either one being made" (attributed to Bismarck).

ing number of bills that most members are not likely to have clear memories of what they thought a bill meant when they voted for or against it. And even on the day of a vote, most legislators have no more understanding of a bill than they can get from a quick reading of it or—more likely—from reading a short synopsis of it. Finally, many questions of statutory interpretation arise long after enactment, when many of the enacting legislators are no longer in office or even alive.

How, then, can the meaning be found? Where the meaning of a statute has not been settled, courts use ten tools:

1. the *wording* of the statutory section at issue;
2. any *statutory context* that might indicate the legislature's intent: other sections of the same statute,[3] other statutes addressed to the same subject matter, the heading of the section at issue, and the statute's title and preamble (if any);
3. the historical context: the *events and conditions that* might have *motivated* the legislature to act;
4. the context created by announcements of *public policy in other statutes and in case law*;
5. *interpretations of the statute by lower or collateral courts;*[4]
6. the statute's *legislative history,* which consists of the documents and records created by various parts of the legislature during the course of enactment;
7. a collection of maxims known as the *canons of statutory construction;*
8. *comparison with parallel statutes in other jurisdictions,* focusing on judicial interpretation of those statutes,[5] as well as the circumstances in which they were enacted;
9. *interpretations of the statute by administrative agencies* charged with enforcing the statute; and
10. *interpretations of the statute by scholars* who are recognized experts in the field.[6]

Beginners sometimes overlook the possibility that terminology in a particular section of a statute may be defined in another section of the same statute, or even in a definitions section that applies to an entire code. In addition, a relatively mundane word is sometimes defined, for the purposes of the statute, in a surprising way. And a term may have different meanings in different statutes. As versatile as the English language is, the number of ideas needing to be expressed seems to exceed the number of concise words

---

3. For example, if you ignore context, you might waste much effort trying to figure out the meaning of a statutory word or phrase, only to learn later that it is crisply defined in a definitions section at the beginning of the statute.

4. If, as to the issue at hand, the statute has been definitively interpreted by *higher* courts, its meaning would be settled through mandatory authority, and none of these tools would be needed.

5. See pages 135-36.

6. Mere publication of a law review article—without more—does not create recognized expertise. See page 132.

and phrases available to be symbols for them, and some expressions have to do double or triple duty.

For example, § 6-201 ("Franchises") of the Administrative Code of the City of New York defines "the streets of the city" as

> streets, avenues, highways, boulevards, concourses, driveways, bridges, tunnels, parks, parkways, waterways, docks, bulkheads, wharves, piers, and public grounds or waters within or belonging to the city

while § 16-101(3) ("Department of Sanitation") defines "street" to include any

> street, avenue, road, alley, lane, highway, parkway, boulevard, concourse, driveway, culvert and crosswalk and every class of public road, square and place, except a wharf, pier, bulkhead or slip by law committed to the custody and control of any other agency.

Why might a wharf be a "street" for one purpose, but not for another? In § 6-201, the word "street" is a symbol for a place where activity might require getting a franchise from the city. In § 16-101(3), the same word is a symbol for a place for which the Department of Sanitation has the responsibility of cleaning, sweeping, sanding, and removing ice, snow, and garbage.[7] In each case, the statute would be unreadable if the idea were fully described every time it is mentioned.

Beginners often make the mistake of focusing solely on a rule's phrasing (whether found in a statute or elsewhere) and ignoring the policies underlying the rule. The result is an overly mechanical application, often far from the contemplation of the legislature or the policies the rule is meant to advance. Remember that words are merely symbols for concepts, and that interpretation is the art of seeing through the words to locate the ideas represented. Courts will not mechanically apply a statute in a literal way if that would undermine the approach the legislature has taken to solving the problem in dispute. Learned Hand wrote that "statutes always have some purpose or object to accomplish, whose sympathetic and imaginative discovery is the surest guide to their meaning."[8]

Although legislative history is often resorted to and would seem to be the most direct evidence of the legislature's purpose, it is sometimes viewed with suspicion. It is often incomplete, especially with state statutes, and, because of the chaotic nature of legislative work, it can be internally contradictory. It is also vulnerable to manipulation by legislators who may not share the views of a majority of their colleagues. And the collective intent of a legislature (or any other large group of people) may simply be more a metaphysical idea than something ever provable through evidence. On the other hand, some portions of the typical legislative history tend to be viewed

---

7. "A word is not a crystal, transparent and unchanged, it is the skin of a living thought and may vary greatly in color and content according to the circumstances and the time in which it is used." *Towne v. Eisner,* 245 U.S. 418, 425 (1918) (Holmes, J.).

8. *Cabell v. Markham,* 148 F.2d 737, 739 (2d Cir.), *aff'd,* 326 U.S. 404 (1945).

by the courts as particularly reliable. Those are the reports of the committees that considered and reported the bill and the floor comments of the sponsors of the bill, except as to amendments not considered by the committees and not endorsed by the sponsors.

Although scholars have frequently criticized many of the canons of construction, courts continue to use them regularly. It is certainly true, as Judge Posner has pointed out, that the courts have no way of knowing whether legislators have enacted a particular statute with the canons in mind, or even whether legislators have ever heard of the canons of construction.[9] It is also true, as Karl Llewellyn showed, that canons tend to be inconsistent with one another and that courts may invoke them to justify decisions rather than to help in making decisions.[10] On the other hand, few scholars would reject all the canons, and some canons are rarely criticized. Among this favored category are the following:

- A statute is to be construed in light of the harm the legislature meant to remedy.

- Statutory words and phrases are to be construed in the context of the entire statute of which they are a part.

- Statutes on the same subject (in Latin, *in pari materia*) are to be construed together.

- Where possible, statutes are to be construed so that their constitutionality is preserved.

- Penal statutes are to be narrowly construed.

- Statutes in derogation of the common law are to be narrowly construed.

In a less certain category are maxims—many of which contradict each other—on whether repeals by implication are favored; on whether the expression of one thing in a statute necessarily excludes another not mentioned; on the construction to be given to words of permission and to words of command; on whether words and phrases judicially construed in other contexts before enactment are to be given the same meaning in a statute; on the effect of grammar on interpretation; on the effect of statute titles, section headings, and preambles on interpretation; on the treatment to be given to legislative history; on the effect of interpretations by administrative agencies; on the effect of judicial interpretations in which the legislature, by not amending, might have acquiesced; and on a host of other issues.

Canons are rules of a sort and must be proved with authority, usually case law to be found in the digests under the topic heading of "Statutes." But be careful: the lawyer hurling a canon as an epithet is apt to find a contradictory one thrown right back. Instead, the convincing argument is a thoughtful and

9. *Statutory Interpretation—in the Classroom and in the Courtroom,* 50 U. Chi. L. Rev. 800, 806 (1983).
10. *The Common Law Tradition* 521-35 (1960).

thorough analysis of the statute. Canons play a part in that, but not the largest part.

Let us examine two decisions from the same litigation to see seven of the ten tools in operation.

McBOYLE v. UNITED STATES
43 F.2d 273 (10th Cir. 1930)

PHILLIPS, Circuit Judge. William W. McBoyle was convicted and sentenced for an alleged violation of the National Motor Vehicle Theft Act, section 408, title 18, U.S. Code. The indictment charged that on October 10, 1926, McBoyle caused to be transported in interstate commerce from Ottawa, Ill., to Guymon, Okl., one Waco airplane, . . . which was the property of the United States Aircraft Corporation and which had theretofore been stolen; and that McBoyle then and there knew it had been stolen. . . .

> In the movies, when you hear someone say, "They've crossed the state line — call the FBI," this is the kind of statute that creates federal jurisdiction.

The primary question is whether an airplane comes within the purview of the National Motor Vehicle Theft Act. This act defines the term "motor vehicle," as follows:

> The term "motor vehicle" when used in this section shall include an automobile, automobile truck, automobile wagon, motor cycle, or any other self-propelled vehicle not designed for running on rails.

Counsel for McBoyle contend that the word "vehicle" includes only conveyances that travel on the ground; that an airplane is not a vehicle . . . ; and that, under the doctrine of ejusdem generis, the phrase "any other self-propelled vehicle" cannot be construed to include an airplane.

> A *canon of construction:* Where general language follows a list of specific examples, the general language's meaning is limited to the same nature [*ejusdem generis*] as the specific, unless there are clear indications to the contrary.

[In a passage deleted here, the court traces various meanings ascribed to the word "vehicle" in both legal and popular

> The court focuses on the *words of the statute* and considers the canon of

usage, quoting authorities that define a vehicle as an object that travels and carries things or people. One of the definitions specifies that a ship is a vehicle; according to another, a vehicle carries things or people, "especially on land."]

Both the derivation and the definition of the word "vehicle" indicate that it is sufficiently broad to include any means or device by which persons or things are carried or transported, and it is not limited to instrumentalities used for traveling on land, although the latter may be the limited or special meaning of the word. We do not think it would be inaccurate to say that a ship or vessel is a vehicle of commerce.

An airplane is self-propelled [and] is designed to carry passengers and freight from place to place. It runs partly on the ground but principally in the air. It furnishes a rapid means for transportation of persons and comparatively light articles of freight and express. It therefore serves the same general purpose as an automobile, automobile truck, or motorcycle. It is of the same general kind or class as the motor vehicles specifically enumerated in the statutory definition and, therefore, construing an airplane to come within the general term, "any other self-propelled vehicle," does not offend against the maxim of ejusdem generis.

Furthermore, some meaning must be ascribed to [Congress's use of the] phrase "any other self-propelled vehicle" [immediately after Congress had specifically listed] all of the known self-propelled vehicles designed for running on land. . . .

We conclude that the phrase, "any other self-propelled vehicle," includes an airplane. . . .

ejusdem generis only long enough to decide that the court's interpretation of the statute would not offend the canon.

Are you convinced by the court's interpretation of the statutory wording?

COTTERAL, Circuit Judge (dissenting). I feel bound to dissent on the ground that the National Motor Vehicle Theft Act should not be construed as relating to the transportation of airplanes.

A prevailing rule is that a penal statute is to be construed strictly against an offender and it must state clearly the persons and acts denounced. [Citations omitted.]

Another canon of construction. The dissenter will soon try to link this one up with *ejusdem generis.*

It would have been a simple matter in enacting the statute to insert, as descriptive words, airplanes, aircraft, or flying machines. If they had been in the legislative mind, the language would not have been expressed in such uncertainty as "any other self-propelled vehicle not designed for running on rails." The omission to definitely mention airplanes requires a construction that they were not included. Furthermore, by excepting vehicles running on rails, the meaning of the act is clarified. These words indicate it was meant to be confined to vehicles that *run,* but not on rails, and it did not extend to those that *fly.* . . .

Now the dissenter takes on the *words of the statute,* but in a way the court did not. The dissenter asks what Congress could have written into the statute but chose not to.

The rule of ejusdem generis has special application to this statute. General words following a particular designation are usually presumed to be restricted so as to include only things or persons of the same kind, class, or nature, unless there is a clear manifestation of a contrary purpose. [Citation omitted.] The general description in this statute refers to vehicles of the same general class as those enumerated. We may assume an airplane is a vehicle, in being a means of transportation. And it has its own motive power. But is an airplane classified generally with "an automobile, automobile truck, automobile wagon, or motor cycle"? Are airplanes regarded as *other types of automobiles* and the like? A moment's reflection demonstrates the contrary.

The dissenter turns to the *canon* considered in the court's opinion.

Counsel for appellant have referred us to debates in Congress when the act was pending as persuasive of an interpretation in his favor. [Citations to the Congressional Record omitted.] . . . The discussions of the proposed measure are enlightening . . . in showing that the theft of automobiles was so prevalent over the land as to call for punitive restraint, but airplanes were never even mentioned.

Because this question was not addressed in the reports of the committees that drafted the statute, the only relevant *legislative history* is the floor debates. Floor debates are a notoriously unreliable form of legislative history because they can include remarks by legislators who took no part in drafting the statute in committee, who might not have thought much about it, and who may not even have read it. But here the floor debates reveal surprising evidence of legislative intent: no legislator complained about a need to do something about airplane theft.

It is familiar knowledge that the theft of automobiles had then become a public menace, but that airplanes had been rarely stolen if at all, and it is a most uncommon thing even at this date. The prevailing mischief sought to be corrected is an aid in the construction of a statute. [Citation omitted.] . . .

Finally, the dissenter takes up the *historical context*.

McBOYLE v. UNITED STATES
283 U.S. 25 (1931)

Mr. Justice HOLMES delivered the opinion of the Court. . . . The question is the meaning of the word "vehicle" in the phrase "any other self-propelled vehicle not designed for running on rails." No doubt etymologically it is possible to use the word to signify a conveyance working on land, water or air, and sometimes legislation extends the use in that direction, e.g., land and air, water being separately provided for, in the Tariff Act [of] 1922 [citation omitted]. But in everyday speech "vehicle" calls up the picture of a thing moving on land. Thus in Rev. Stats. § 4, intended, the Government suggests, rather to enlarge than to restrict the definition, vehicle includes every contrivance capable of being used

While dissecting the *words of the statute*, Holmes considers the *statutory context*.

"as a means of transportation on land."
And this is repeated, expressly exclud-
ing aircraft, in the Tariff Act [of] 1930
[citation omitted]. So here, the phrase
under discussion calls up the popular
picture. For after including automobile
truck, automobile wagon and motor
cycle, the words "any other self-
propelled vehicle not designed for running on rails" still indicate that a vehicle
in the popular sense, that is a vehicle
running on land, is the theme. It is a vehicle that runs, not something, not commonly called a vehicle, that flies.
Airplanes were well known in 1919,
when this statute was passed; but it is
admitted that they were not mentioned
in the reports or in the debates in Congress. It is impossible to read words that
so carefully enumerate the different
forms of motor vehicles and have no reference of any kind to aircraft, as including airplanes under a term that usage
more and more confines to a different
class. The counsel for the petitioner
have shown that the phraseology of the
statute as to motor vehicles follows that
of earlier statutes of Connecticut, Delaware, Ohio, Michigan and Missouri, not
to mention the late Regulations of Traffic for the District of Columbia [citation
omitted], none of which can be supposed
to leave the earth.

   . . . When a rule of conduct is laid
down in words that evoke in the common
mind only the picture of vehicles moving
on land, the statute should not be extended to aircraft, simply because it may
seem to us that a similar policy applies,
or even upon the speculation that, if the
legislature had thought of it, very likely
broader words would have been used.
[Citation omitted.]

   Judgment reversed.

Historical context and
legislative history are
considered together.

Again, Holmes
simultaneously uses two
tools — this time *legislative
history* and *comparison
with parallel statutes*. The
point is that Congress seems
to have modelled the Act on
statutes that clearly are not
addressed to aircraft theft.
The most telling comparison
— and perhaps the most
enjoyable for its irony — is
with a *city's* traffic
regulations, which certainly
could not have been meant
to penalize the stealing of
airplanes.

As important as *policy* is, it
also has its limitations. Here
Holmes notes that his court
is permitted to construe the
statute only to accomplish
the goal Congress had
selected for it — and not
some other goal the court
might think equally valid.

What do you think caused the Supreme Court to reverse? That question can be divided into two sub-questions: First, what idea or ideas most persuaded the Supreme Court to see the statute differently? And second, which tool or tools of statutory analysis led the Court to whatever answer you gave to the first sub-question?

Missing from these opinions are the three tools that use interpretations of the statute by others: by lower or collateral courts, by administrative agencies, and by scholars expert in the field. Each tool's absence has an explanation. First, the judges themselves tell us why they have no precedent on point to guide them: airplane theft seems to have been exceedingly rare at the time. Second, no administrative agency would have had a reason to interpret the statute because no administrative agency was charged with enforcing it.[11] And finally, the modern explosion in published scholarship on statutes had not yet begun when these opinions were written. Only a very few law reviews were then being published, and scholarship had not yet begun to concentrate on statutes, as it does today.

Parenthetically, Congress later amended the statute so that it now penalizes anyone who "transports in interstate or foreign commerce a motor vehicle *or aircraft,* knowing the same to be stolen."[12] Having learned something about how overly specific wording can make a statute like this at least partly obsolete, Congress defined "aircraft" so that the statute could adapt to changing technology: " 'Aircraft' means any contrivance now known *or hereafter invented* . . . for flight in the air."[13] Although the amendment was enacted when airplanes were still driven by piston engines and propellers, it probably penalizes the act of knowingly moving a stolen space shuttle across a state line.

§11.2   How to Present Statutory Analysis

Writing about a statutory question focuses on the words of the statute because the words are what is to be interpreted. The crucial term or phrase should appear, inside quotation marks, when you state the issue, your con-

---

11. An administrative agency is, by statute, given the responsibility of developing and enforcing detailed regulation of a particular aspect of the business world. Examples are the National Labor Relations Board, the Environmental Protection Agency, and the Equal Opportunity Employment Commission.

12. 18 U.S.C. § 2312 (1982) (emphasis supplied). An adjacent section penalizes anyone who knowingly "receives, possesses, conceals, stores, barters, sells, or disposes of any motor vehicle *or aircraft,* which has crossed a State or United States boundary after being stolen." 18 U.S.C. § 2313 (Supp. II 1984) (emphasis supplied). (Stealing a vehicle or an airplane would, of course, be punished under the law of the state where the theft took place. But once a stolen vehicle or airplane is moved out of state, it will be much harder for the local authorities to prosecute the thieves or those who received the stolen property from them. To make available the resources of the federal government, Congress made it a separate federal offense to move such stolen property across state lines.)

13. 18 U.S.C. § 2311 (1982) (emphasis added).

clusion, the rule on which you rely, and the most important steps of logic in the analysis:

> The question of whether the Interborough Repertory Theatre must get a franchise to present entertainment on the Staten Island ferry depends in part on whether the ferry is one of the "streets of the city"

But your obligation to tell the reader the *rule* on which you rely usually cannot be satisfied merely by quoting the statute in unedited form. Because statutes must be drafted to govern wide ranges of factual possibilities, a rule expressed entirely in statutory language may need to be reformulated for practical application. If, for example, you are asked to determine whether moving a stolen "boat" across a state line violates the National Motor Vehicle Theft Act, you will not be able to express the controlling rule by quoting the statutory sentence on which your reasoning will be based: "The term 'motor vehicle' when used in this section shall include an automobile, automobile truck, automobile wagon, motor cycle, or any other self-propelled vehicle not designed for running on rails." For the purpose of resolving an issue like that, this sentence does not fully communicate the governing rule. It does not even contain a list of elements. A far more useful formulation, supportable by *McBoyle,* would be something like this: "For the purposes of the Act, a 'motor vehicle' is a conveyance that is 'self-propelled,' that operates primarily on land, and that does not run on rails." Do you see how much more practical and easy to apply this formulation is? A boat does not run on rails, it might be self-propelled, but, alas, it hardly ever transports things or people across land. What the reader needs is a statement of the rule *embodied* in the statute. Do not be careless, however, in reformulating the statutory language into a useful expression of a rule: you want something that you can apply to facts, but you also want something that accurately pronounces the statute's meaning. If you oversimply or distort, trouble awaits. It helps to use the key phrases of the statute. "Self-propelled" is a key phrase here because not all boats are that. A barge, pushed by a tug, is not self-propelled. But what if the "boat" at issue is a rowboat, a canoe, or a kayak? If an ocean liner is permanently moored, with its engines removed, and used as a hotel, we would say it is no longer self-propelled — and probably not even a conveyance. But what about an ocean liner that sits at dockside as a derelict, its engines broken but repairable?

The two most important differences between the presentation of common law precedent and the presentation of statutory analysis are in the way the presentation is organized and in the role played by case law.

You already know that some precedent interprets the common law, while other precedent interprets statutes and statute-like authority. In using either kind of precedent, later courts will analogize, distinguish, elicit policy, reconcile seemingly adverse authority, and synthesize fragmented authority. Interpretation of common law precedent focuses less on the intent of prior courts and more on reasonably applying rules that have been created through precedent. A court can thus make a significant change in the direction of the common law without invading the power of another branch of government. But a court's freedom of interpretive maneuver is more limited where a statute is involved because with statutes the aim is to discover the intent of the legislature. Not only is the legislature a coordinate branch of government with a right to have its enactments respected by the courts, but the legislature has the power to redraft a statute and thus obliterate judicial interpretations that the legislature finds annoying.

Although some statutes are carefully drafted with the kind of explicitness that makes intent obvious and application relatively mechanical, at times a legislature will deliberately leave gaps in a statute that the courts, through precedent, will be expected to fill. An example of the latter is 15 U.S.C. § 1, which prohibits any "combination . . . in restraint of trade." What do you think that means? Congress might have had a rough idea when it enacted the Sherman Anti-Trust Act in 1890, but it left to the courts the task of discovering the full sense of the phrase. In the West Publishing Company's annotated edition of the United States Code, over 500 pages in small print are devoted to notes of decisions in which courts have attempted to discover the precise meaning of these four words. On the other hand, 39 U.S.C. § 3009 provides that "unordered merchandise" received in the mail "may be treated as a gift by the recipient," and the statute defines "unordered merchandise" as "merchandise mailed without the prior expressed request or consent of the recipient." Here, perhaps because the subject matter is much more simple conceptually, politically, and economically, Congress left far fewer gaps in the enactment, although at least one appellate court has had to resolve the question of whether an offer to insure is "merchandise" within the meaning of the statute.[1]

Statutory and common law analysis differ in the way you will organize authority in rule proof and in rule application.[2] If the issue is resolved purely by common law precedent, you might, for example, find one or more decisions that set out the fundamental rules, surrounded by an entourage of other decisions that each explain some specific aspect of a rule or its application—together with various relevant secondary authority, such as restatements, treatises, leading law review articles, and so forth. The precedent at the center of this throng is the basic source for the overall rule or rules, and parts of the entourage can be used to answer questions left open after the overall rule is set out. The division of emphasis between the basic authority and parts of the entourage depends on the issue you must resolve, the facts, and the quality of the authority. At one extreme, the basic authority might be so comprehensive that you can focus on it almost entirely, using entourage material only to fill small gaps. At the opposite extreme—with another issue and different facts and authority—you might be able to use the basic authority only as a starting point and be forced to focus mostly on entourage material that fills large gaps left open by the more basic authority.

But if the issue is statutory, the central decisions are replaced by one or more statutes, and the entourage is made up of decisions interpreting those

---

§11.2   1. *See Kipperman v. Academy Life Ins. Co.*, 554 F.2d 377 (9th Cir. 1977).
2. See §7.1.

statutes, as well as any useful legislative history, interpretations by administrative agencies, commentaries by scholars, decisions interpreting sufficiently similar statutes in other jurisdictions, and so forth. Some authority appropriate to statutory analysis is inappropriate to common law analysis, and vice versa. For example, if a state has codified a common law rule addressed in a restatement — and has done so in a way that is inconsistent with the restatement's view — the restatement, to the extent of the inconsistency, is irrelevant to an interpretation of the statute.

Instructions for Exercises I and II

You have probably discovered that one of the hardest things about legal writing is the organizing of scattered insights into an integrated whole that resolves an issue. The exercises in this chapter show you how to do that in situations where the issue is resolved at least partly on the basis of a statute.

Using the tools discussed in this chapter and the precedent skills explained in Chapter 10, make the prediction asked for in each exercise. Assume that your library research has told you that the prediction will rest on the statutes and decisions reproduced in the exercise.[1]

Outline issue by issue: Write out an outline of your reasoning, broken down into the various issues that would be put before the court. Under each issue, list the facts that are most critical to your analysis and list the authorities the court would rely on in making the ruling. (You might list some authorities and some facts more than once.)

Consider the various rules for which each authority might stand: For each authority listed under a given issue, formulate a reasonable and realistic broad rule, a reasonable and realistic narrow rule, and a reasonable and realistic intermediate rule; write those rules on your outline; mark the one a court would be most likely to accept; and write the reason. (If the authority is a statute, pay close attention to its wording.)

Consider policy: Where you think an authority announces policy that would persuade a court, write that policy next to the name of the authority and under the issue to which it is relevant, together with the reason for its persuasiveness.

Consider other statutory interpretation tools: Interpretations by lower or collateral courts; the events and conditions that are likely to have motivated the legislature to act; the canons of statutory construction; the legislative history (if any); the statutory context (other sections of the same statute, other statutes addressed to the same subject matter, the heading of the section at issue, the statute's title, and so forth); and comparison with parallel statutes in other jurisdictions. (The exercises in this chapter do not involve interpretations by administrative agencies or by scholars who are experts in the relevant field.)

Consider the ways in which each case might be analogized or distinguished: Where you believe a court would be persuaded by an analogy to a case, write a

---

1. The decisions are reproduced in alphabetical order (ignoring the terms *State* and *People*, which indicate that one of the parties is a government). Where citations are omitted, assume that you have read the authorities cited to and found that they do not add anything to the decisions reproduced here. Dissents and concurrences, if any, are omitted.

statement of the analogy next to the case and under the issue where it is relevant, together with the reason for its persuasiveness. Where you predict that a court would be likely to distinguish a case, write that next to the case under the issue where it is relevant and record the reason.

Consider the possible syntheses: Where you predict that a court is likely to synthesize the meaning of two or more authorities into a single statement of a rule or of policy, note that under the issue where it is relevant and state the synthesis, the authorities that would support it, and the reason for its persuasiveness.

Consider the possible reconciliations: Where you believe a court is likely to reconcile inconsistent authority or authority adverse to your client, write that under the issue where it is relevant, together with the basis for the reconciliation and the reason for its persuasiveness.

Consider the hierarchy of authority: Where a court would have to use the hierarchy of authority to resolve an inconsistency in two or more statutes or cases, note the authorities on your outline under the issue where they are relevant; note the inconsistency; mark the authority that you believe the court would follow; and write the reason for your prediction.

Throughout your outline, test your thinking in several ways.

Consider counter-arguments: Ask yourself whether a reasonable argument could challenge any part of your analysis. If so, note the argument at the relevant point in the outline and write your prediction of whether the argument is likely to persuade a judge. If you believe that an argument, even though reasonable, is not likely to persuade, write the reason for your prediction. If, on reflection, you conclude that the argument is likely to persuade, modify your analysis accordingly.

Consider troublesome facts: Ask yourself whether a fact has a reasonable chance of causing a judge to doubt your analysis. If so, note the fact and why it would create doubt. If you conclude that, in spite of the doubt, the judge would rule as you have predicted, state why. If, on reflection, you believe that the doubt overcomes your analysis, modify your analysis accordingly.

If you cannot find arguments or facts that work against your analysis, you may be avoiding problems.

In addition, ask yourself whether your analysis will seem *reasonable, just, and realistic to the judicial mind.*

Finally, *predict* how the court will rule.

The diagram on page 188 might help you see this process as a whole.

If your teacher has assigned the exercise as preparation for a class, be prepared to speak in class from your outline. During class, your teacher may ask you to transform your outline into some variation of the paradigm described in Chapter 7 (see page 112). Be prepared to explain how you would vary the paradigm in sequence and depth and how you would combine separately paradigmed explanations into a unified whole.

If, on the other hand, your teacher has assigned the exercise as work to be done entirely at home, complete the exercise at home by reorganizing your outline into some variation of the paradigm described in Chapter 7, varying the paradigm as appropriate in sequence and depth and, if necessary, combining separately paradigmed explanations into a unified whole.

identify the issues
analyze each issue
- ▶ identify the determinative facts
- ▶ identify the authorities on which the court will rely
- ▶ for each authority, consider
  - ▷ along a spectrum from broad to narrow, the most likely rule for which the authority stands
  - ▷ policy for which the authority stands
  - ▷ (for statutes only:) events and conditions that motivated the legislature to act; legislative history; canons of construction; other tools of statutory construction
  - ▷ (for cases only:) ways of analogizing or distinguishing
  - ▷ possible syntheses with other authorities
  - ▷ possible reconciliations
  - ▷ how the court will use the hierarchy of authority to resolve inconsistencies in the law
- ▶ test your analysis by considering
  - ▷ counter-arguments
  - ▷ troublesome facts
  - ▷ whether your analysis will seem reasonable, just, and realistic to the judicial mind
- ▶ predict how the court will resolve the issue

predict how the court will resolve the entire controversy

Regardless of whether you complete the exercise in class or at home, you can treat it as a dry run of the kind of planning you will need to do in order to write a Discussion in an objective memorandum (or an Argument in a persuasive document).

Consider three suggestions: First, start with a lot of paper and leave much blank space because you will probably find yourself going back and adding to what you have already done. The process of organizing will inevitably generate more insights than you had when you started out. Second, do not be afraid to change your mind as you go along. Some of the insights you gain may persuade you to change your analysis. Third, make an objective prediction and do not take sides. Your prediction is for the benefit of a supervisor, such as a senior partner, who really wants to know what will happen in court. You are not being asked for courtroom advocacy. (That will be covered in later chapters.)

[handwritten: who sold it to them?]

Exercise I.   Chesbro and the Ironwood Tract[1]

Fourteen years ago, Palo Verde Development Corporation purchased a deed to an Arizona parcel known as the Ironwood tract. The tract is unimproved terrain and has never been fenced or built upon. It is one mile from a paved road and 65 miles from downtown Phoenix. Today, the nearest residential development is Verde River Estates, nine miles from the tract, toward Phoenix along the same road. From the date of the purchase until this past September, no employee of Palo Verde had set foot on the tract.

Palo Verde built Verde River Estates during the last two years. When the last units were sold in September, the company sent a surveying team to the Ironwood tract, but they were chased off the land by Homer Chesbro, whose Black Canyon Ranch adjoins the Ironwood tract. Chesbro bought the Ranch eleven years ago from a person who told him that he was buying both the Ranch and the tract. Although the metes and bounds description in Chesbro's deed does not include the tract, that and most of the rest of the deed is in language that nonlawyers would find incomprehensible. For the past eleven years, Chesbro and his employees have grazed cattle on the Ironwood tract two or three times a month throughout the year. The tract cannot support more grazing, and the soil will not support farming or other intensive agriculture, although luxury housing could be built on it.

[handwritten right margin: 10-year statute of limitations has run out]

Chesbro had no idea that Palo Verde had a deed to the property. At the same time, Palo Verde had no idea that Chesbro was using the tract or that he thought his deed included it.

If Chesbro takes the position that he acquired title by adverse possession, *[handwritten: Issue]* will Palo Verde succeed in an action to eject him and quiet its own title? *[handwritten: no - statute has run out]*

ARIZONA REVISED STATUES

§ 12-521.   Definitions

A. In this article, unless the context otherwise requires:

1. "Adverse possession" means an actual and visible appropriation of the land, commenced and continued under a claim of right inconsistent with and hostile to the claim of another.

2. "Peaceable possession" means possession which is continuous, and not interrupted by an adverse action to recover the estate. . . .

§ 12-526.   Real Property in Adverse Possession and Use by Possessor; Ten-Year Limitation . . .

A. A person who has a cause of action for recovery of any lands, tenements or hereditaments from a person having peaceable and adverse possession thereof, cultivating, using and enjoying such property, shall

---

1. See the instructions on page 186.

commence an action therefor within ten years after the cause of action accrues, and not afterward. . . .

§ 12-527.   Effect of Limitation on Title

When an action for recovery of real property is barred by any provision of this article, the person who pleads and is entitled to the bar shall be held to have full title precluding all claims.

[These sections are descended from §§ 2938-2939, 2942-2945, and 2948 of the Arizona Civil Code of 1901, which in turn were modelled after Texas statutes.]

ADAMS v. LAMICO
118 Utah 209, 221 P.2d 1037 (1950)

WOLFE, J. This action was commenced by the appellant to quiet title to an eighty acre tract of land in Duchesne County, Utah. . . .

. . . [T]he respondents claimed title to the land . . . by virtue of seven years' adverse possession[, during which they used the land as a winter range for sheep].

The evidence establishes that the . . . tract in question consisted of unbroken and unimproved brush lands suitable only for grazing. . . . The property was uninclosed, although there was fencing along part of one end of the tract. It appears that . . . the respondents during the winter grazed all of the eighty acres. . . . They were actually upon . . . the tract . . . for about five to six months each year, entering thereon in November and remaining until April, at which time they moved their sheep onto higher grazing lands in Colorado for the summer and early autumn. The respondents did not leave anyone upon or in charge of the eighty acres during the summer months while they were away. . . .

Contrary to the appellant's contention the occupancy and possession of the unbroken brush land . . . was in law a continuous occupancy despite the fact that neither Brady nor the respondents grazed or made any use of those lands during approximately six months of the year. . . . Sec. 104-2-9, Utah Code Annotated 1943, provides: "For the purpose of constituting an adverse possession . . . , land is deemed to have been possessed and occupied in the following cases: . . . (3) Where, although not inclosed, it has been used for the supply of fuel, or of fencing timber for the purposes of husbandry, *or for pasturage,* or for the ordinary use of the occupant." (Italics added.)

In *Kellogg v. Huffman,* 137 Cal. App. 278, 30 P.2d 593, it was held under Sec. 323, subd. 3, Cal. Code Civ. Proc., which is identical to Section 104-2-9, subd. 3, quoted above, that pasturing during the entire grazing season of each year during which feed is available, if done to the exclusion of others, is a sufficient use and occupation of land, which is reason-

Who is Brady?

ably fit for grazing purposes only, to constitute the occupation and possession necessary to establish title by adverse possession. . . .

Thus we conclude that the respondents . . . had continuously claimed, occupied, and used [the property] for at least seven years prior to the commencement of this action. . . .

ARIZONA SUPERIOR MINING CO. v. ANDERSON
33 Ariz. 64, 262 P. 489 (1927), error dismissed, 278 U.S. 578 (1929)

ROSS, C.J. . . . John Carter Anderson sued the Arizona Superior Mining Company for the reasonable value of his services in examining and reporting on certain mining properties of the company. . . .

[The defendant unsuccessfully moved in the trial court to transfer the case from Pima County to Maricopa County on the ground that the latter had jurisdiction.]

Counsel for defendant have directed our attention to decisions holding jurisdiction to be as claimed by them, but in all such cases the language of the statute giving jurisdiction . . . is different from the wording of our statute. . . . Aside from the compelling force of the language of the statute itself, in adopting it from another state, we took it with the construction theretofore placed upon it. . . .

DE LAS FUENTES v. MACDONELL
85 Tex. 132, 20 S.W. 43 (1892)

GAINES, J. This was an action on trespass to try title. . . .

Appellants . . . complain that the court erred in sustaining the defendant's plea of the statute of limitations of five years. . . . The boundaries of the land were at one time marked out, but it was never inclosed. It is fit only for grazing purposes. There have never been any houses upon it. No part of it has ever had any inclosures upon it, except small pens, made of posts and brush, for the purpose of penning sheep. These were renewed every year. . . . The land was used for "grazing and lambing purposes." How many sheep were kept upon it does not appear. One witness states that in 1871 there were 13,000 sheep upon the land. How many were there during other years is not shown. Another witness says: "When we took the sheep off, we always left goats on it. The sheep and goats were in [the] charge of shepherds." Cattle belonging to others were permitted to graze upon the land. . . . There have been several cases decided in this court in which the effort has been made to show an adverse possession of land by merely grazing cattle and horses upon it, but it has uniformly been held that the possession was not sufficient to meet the requirements of the statute. [Citations omitted.] It must be conceded that in none of these cases were facts as strong in favor of the claim of adverse possession as in the case before us; yet we think them to

191

be sufficient to indicate the rule in this court to be that the mere occupancy of land by grazing live stock upon it, without substantial inclosures or other permanent improvements, is not sufficient to support a plea of limitation under our statutes. Uninclosed land, in this state, has ever been treated as commons for grazing purposes; and hence the mere holding of live stock upon it has not been deemed such exclusive occupancy as to constitute adverse possession. [We have held that t]here must be "an actual occupation of such nature and notoriety as the owner may be presumed to know that there is a possession of the land" [citation omitted]; "otherwise, a man may be disseised without his knowledge, and the statute of limitations run against him, while he has no ground to believe that his seizure has been interrupted" [citation omitted]. We think the testimony insufficient to show adverse possession. . . .

KELLOGG v. HUFFMAN
137 Cal. App. 278, 30 P.2d 593 (1934)

BARNARD, P.J. This is an action to quiet title to 160 acres of land in the Kettleman Hills in Fresno county. . . . This property was rough and arid and was situated in what was, until about 1929, a sparsely settled country used only for grazing purposes. . . .

The appropriate portion of section 323 of the Code of Civil Procedure reads as follows: ". . . For the purpose of constituting an adverse possession . . . land is deemed to have been possessed and occupied in the following cases: . . . (3) Where, although not inclosed, it has been used for the supply of fuel, or of fencing-timber for the purposes of husbandry, or for pasturage, or for the ordinary use of the occupant."

. . . To establish adverse possession it is only necessary that land be put to such use as can reasonably be made thereof, and such a use is sufficiently continuous if, during the required time, it be so used at all times when it can be used for the purpose to which it is adapted. [Citations omitted.] It is well settled in this state that pasturing during the entire grazing season of each year during which feed is available, if done to the exclusion of others, is a sufficient use and occupation of land, which is reasonably fit only for pasturage purposes, to constitute the occupation and possession necessary to establish a title by adverse possession. [Citations omitted.] . . . " . . . It is sufficient that the use is in accordance with the usual course of husbandry in the locality."

[There was ample evidence in the record of adverse possession through use of the land for grazing purposes.]

STATE v. McDONALD
88 Ariz. 1, 352 P.2d 343 (1960)

MURRY, J. This is an appeal by the State of Arizona . . . from a judgment in a condemnation suit wherein substantial damages were awarded

to . . . Rockwell and McDonald for properties condemned by the State
for highway purposes. . . .

. . . At the trial it was stipulated that the question of fees and expenses of expert witnesses was a matter, both of fact and law, to be
determined by the court. A cost bill totalling $1,375.50 was eventually
filed by defendants . . . and by a separate order the court allowed said
cost bill en toto. . . .

At first glance there appears to be a split of authority on the question
here involved. But after a careful reading of the cases, it becomes apparent
that those courts allowing costs for expert witnesses concern themselves
with the interpretation of their given statutes. [Citations omitted.] . . .

A.R.S. § 12-1128 [the governing Arizona statute] was adopted from
California [in 1901. Since then two California cases have] held that this
section (West's Ann. Cal. Code Civ. Proc. § 1255) meant the usual costs
attending trial allowed by statute. [Citations omitted.] . . .

Although we are not bound to follow the interpretation placed on a
statute by a state from which our statute was adopted, it is persuasive.
[Citation omitted.] . . .

WORK v. UNITED GLOBE MINES
*12 Ariz. 339, 100 P. 813 (1909), aff'd, 231 U.S. 595
(1914)*

So if someone uses your land for 10 years, it's theirs? I you do nothing

SLOAN, J. . . . It is contended by counsel for plaintiff in error that
adverse possession for the statutory period does not confer title so as to
permit one to maintain an action to quiet title based upon such adverse
possession. The argument is that under paragraph 2942, Civ. Code. 1901,
title by adverse possession is only available in suits which have for their
direct and immediate object the recovery of the possession of real property, and that, an action to quiet title under our statutes not being one
brought directly and immediately for the recovery of the possession of
real property, title by adverse possession may be neither pleaded as a
defense to such action, nor can it form a basis for affirmative relief by way
of cross-complaint. Said paragraph reads as follows: "Whenever in any
case the action of a person for the recovery of real property is barred by
any of the provisions of this title the person who pleads and is entitled to
the bar shall be held to have full title precluding all claims." The construction of this statute in its effect upon actions to quiet title is not now in this
territory an open question. The above paragraph, together with the body
of our statutes of limitations, was adopted from the statutes of the state of
Texas. The Supreme Court of that state, in *Moody v. Holcomb,* 26 Tex.
714, held that adverse possession of lands for the statutory period confers
title thereto which may be quieted in an action brought for that purpose
by the party asserting such title. This decision was rendered prior to the
adoption of the statute by this territory and after its enactment by the
Legislature of the state of Texas. . . .

We find no error in the record, and the judgment of the court below is
affirmed.

Exercise II.   Pappas and Ziegler at Sal's Auto Parts[1]

Joel Pappas has been arrested in Connecticut for robbery. The police have a written statement from Jonathan Chen:

> I am employed at Sal's Auto Parts. I run the cash register in the after-noon and evening. After 6 o'clock, I am the only employee there, and I do whatever needs to be done. I was at work at 6:30 p.m. last Tuesday. I was at the register when a man came in. This is the same man whom I have identified in a line-up and thereafter learned to be Joel Pappas. When he entered the store, he was wearing jeans and a t-shirt.
>
> This man came up to the register, where I was standing, looked me straight in the eye, and said, "Open up the register and there won't be any trouble." He's a huge guy and could easily have beaten me to a pulp. I am five feet, six inches, and I weigh 136 pounds. I opened up the register, and he scooped up all the bills and put them in a bag. He told me to lie down on the floor and count to a thousand. He said that if I stood up early, he'd pound my head into the countertop. I got down on the floor and counted to a thousand. Then I got up and called the police.
>
> There were no other customers or employees in the store, and during this whole thing I could see only one other person. That was a woman standing on the sidewalk just outside the front door. I have also picked her out of a line-up and learned her name to be Gail Ziegler. The front of the store is a large picture window, and I could see that she was just standing there, looking out at the parking lot, as though she was waiting for somebody to pick her up. She walked up to the front of the store three or four minutes before the defendant walked in. I did not see her leave. She was there when I hit the floor, and she was gone when I got up.
>
> While this man was at the register, I didn't know why the woman was standing there. She could have been just hanging around, or she could have been helping him out somehow. At no time did I see the two of them talk or gesture to one another. All I knew at the time was that she wasn't going to help me. Even if she wasn't helping him, she wouldn't have been able to realize that I was being held up.
>
> The distance between the register and the front door is 54 feet. When the police were in the store, I got a tape measure and measured it. The woman was at least a foot outside the door.

The police also have a statement from Ziegler:

> At 6:30 last Tuesday, I was at Sal's Auto Parts. Joel was going to rob the place, and I was going to stand lookout at the front door. I walked up to the front of the store a few minutes before Joel walked in. I looked out at the parking lot to make sure nobody would walk in. If somebody did start to walk in, I was going to ask them for a lot of directions and act lost to keep them busy until Joel walked out. I left as soon as I saw the guy at the cash register disappear. Joel left about a minute later.
>
> Joel is over six feet tall, and he works out with weights.

---

1. See the instructions on page 186.

In Connecticut, robbery is classified in three degrees. The highest is first-degree robbery, which requires aggravating factors not present in Pappas's case. Third-degree robbery carries the least severe penalty, and the prosecution therefore would prefer a conviction for second-degree robbery.

If the evidence at trial coincides with the statements Chen and Ziegler have given the police, is Pappas likely to be convicted of second-degree robbery?[2] *She admits she was an accomplice*

CONNECTICUT GENERAL STATUTES ANNOTATED

§ 53a-133.   Robbery Defined

A person commits robbery when, in the course of committing a larceny, he uses or threatens the immediate use of physical force upon another person for the purpose of: (1) Preventing or overcoming resistance to the taking of the property or to the retention thereof immediately after the taking; or (2) compelling the owner of such property or another person to deliver up the property or to engage in other conduct which aids in the commission of the larceny.

§ 53a-135.   Robbery in the Second Degree . . .

(a) A person is guilty of robbery in the second degree when he commits robbery and (1) he is aided by another person actually present; or (2) in the course of the commission of the crime or of immediate flight therefrom he or another participant in the crime displays or threatens the use of what he represents by his words or conduct to be a deadly weapon or a dangerous instrument. . . .

§ 53a-136.   Robbery in the Third Degree . . .

(a) A person is guilty of robbery in the third degree when he commits robbery. . . .

Commission to Revise the Criminal Statutes: Comment on § 53a-135 (1971)

Robbery in the second degree makes the presence of an accomplice an aggravating factor. The rationale is that the accomplice is equal to a person armed and therefore would generate a higher degree of fear in the victim. Robbery in the second degree is also aimed at circumstances where the actor or accomplice, although not armed with a deadly instrument, purports or represents to be so armed and threatens its use. For example, the actor threatens to use what appears to be a gun he holds in his hand; in reality the gun is only a toy pistol.

---

2. The question is not whether Pappas committed second-degree robbery, but whether he is likely to be convicted on that charge. To make that prediction, you will need to take into account the prosecution's burden of proof beyond a reasonable doubt.

195

STATE v. ARCHAMBAULT
146 Conn. 605, 153 A.2d 451 (1959)

MURPHY, J. . . . While it is of course true that a penal statute should be strictly construed, it is not the purpose of the rule of strict construction to enable a person to avoid the clear import of a law through a mere technicality. To enforce the rule beyond its purpose would be to exalt technicalities above substance. [Citation omitted.] The ordinary and reasonable construction of the statute is that accorded it by the trial court. [Citation omitted.] . . .

STATE v. EDWARDS
201 Conn. 125, 513 A.2d 669 (1986)

HEALEY, J. . . . The defendant . . . claims that . . . the state failed to prove beyond a reasonable doubt that [he] was guilty of being an accessory to robbery in the second degree. . . .

. . . [In a] supermarket parking lot, . . . Veda Johnson, seventy-eight years old, had just finished putting groceries from a shopping cart into her car when she heard footsteps behind her and was then pushed into the cart. At the same time, she felt someone tugging at the purse on her left arm and saw a man run toward the rear of the store. Johnson saw a car come from behind the supermarket building and slow down when it approached the man running toward it. The passenger door opened and the man entered a . . . station wagon. . . .

[While in custody, the defendant told the police that he had driven the station wagon and] that his partner had taken the pocketbook. . . .

General Statutes § 53a-135(a)(1) requires that the person who commits the robbery be "aided by another person *actually present*." (Emphasis added.) The defendant claims that the driver of the getaway car, "whose very existence is unknown until *after* the commission of the crime," cannot be actually present during the crime as a matter of law. We agree with the defendant.

Penal statutes must be strictly construed [citations omitted]; but such construction must accord with common sense and commonly approved usage of the language. [Citations omitted.] The Commission to Revise the Criminal Statutes comments that § 53a-135 "makes the presence of an accomplice an aggravating factor. The rationale is that the accomplice is equal to a person armed and therefore would generate a higher degree of fear in the victim. . . ." [Citation omitted.] The Comment implies that the presence of the accomplice must be both temporarily and physically proximate to the robbery such that the victim is aware of the accomplice during the robbery. The state claims that there is "no suggestion in the language of the statue that the concept of actual presence hinges on the victim's perception of such presence." . . . The offense of robbery in the second degree, as distinguished from robbery in the third degree, requires either of two additional elements—another person actually present or the display or threatened use of a deadly weapon or dangerous instrument. The [longer sentence of imprisonment] attached to robbery in the second degree indicates that the legislature considered it to be a more serious crime because it was likely to have a more severe effect upon the victim. The . . . sensory perception by a robbery victim of "another person actually present," be it by observation, feeling or belief, presents a factual determination in each case unless such a perception could not exist, as a matter of law, as it could not in this case. . . . If the victim is unaware of the accomplice at the time of the robbery or the defendant is armed with a deadly weapon but does not display or threaten its use, then the aggravating factor enhancing the offense to robbery in the second degree is absent because there has been no additional effect upon the victim. . . .

. . . [W]e conclude that the defendant, as the driver of the getaway car, was not "actually present" . . . until sometime after the commission of the robbery. *Cf. State v. Miller,* 14 Or. App. 608, 513 P.2d 1199, 1201 (1973) (defendant guilty of robbery in the second degree; aided by individual standing in the parking lot twenty-five feet from the victim whom she observed *during the course of the attack*).

Because the element of actual presence was not proven, this case must be remanded. . . .

HARRIS DATA COMMUNICATIONS, INC. v. HEFFERNAN
183 Conn. 194, 438 A.2d 1178 (1981)

SPEZIALE, J. [Harris Data seeks a refund of state sales and use taxes.]
[A statute] does not become ambiguous merely because the parties contend for differing meanings. [Citation omitted.] The intent of the legislature is to be found in the meaning of the words of the statute; that is, in what the legislature actually *did* say, not in what it *meant* to say. [Citations omitted.] Where the language of the statute is unambiguous, we are confined to the intention expressed in the actual words used and we will not search out any further intention of the legislature not expressed in the statute. [Citations omitted.] In the absence of ambiguity it is unnecessary to resort to principles of statutory construction such as the resolution of ambiguity in favor of the taxpayer. . . .

PEOPLE v. HEDGEMAN
70 N.Y.2d 533, 517 N.E.2d 858, 523 N.Y.S.2d 46 (1987)

HANCOCK, J. . . . [A] bank teller . . . testified that defendant came to her window [and] handed her a note which read: "Important. Follow to the letter. . . . Your life and others are in jeopardy. I have a bomb and demand the sum of $15,000. . . ." The teller informed defendant that she did not have that amount of money at her station and gave him the $200 in cash from her drawer. With the money in hand, defendant went out the front door. . . .

As defendant left, the teller pressed the silent alarm and went looking for the assistant manager whom she found near the rear of the tellers' area and informed of the robbery. . . . [H]e and the teller went to the window . . . and observed defendant. He was walking along the sidewalk on that side of the bank, around the corner from the front door, towards an automobile parked at curbside by a parking meter. The automobile was 15 feet from the bank window. Sitting in the driver's seat was a person whose gender, age and race the teller could not determine. When defendant entered the automobile on the passenger side, it drove off. . . .

As defined in the Penal Law, a simple taking of property by force, without any aggravating circumstances such as physical injury to a non-participant or use of a weapon, constitutes robbery in the third degree. . . . When the commission of the offense includes circumstances which cause, threaten to cause, or increase the risk of physical injury to another, the Legislature has deemed the crime to be more serious and deserving of greater punishment. Thus, when a participant in the robbery is armed with a deadly weapon, uses or threatens the immediate use of a dangerous instrument, displays what appears to be a firearm, or causes serious physical injury to a nonparticipant, the offense is upgraded to robbery in the first degree. . . . Where the robbery is accompanied by less serious circumstances, it is classified as robbery in the second degree — the crime involved here. [Section 160.10 of the] Penal Law defines robbery in the second degree as follows:

> A person is guilty of robbery in the second degree when he forcibly steals property and when:
>   1. He is *aided by another person actually present* [emphasis added]; or
>   2. In the course of the commission of the crime or of the immediate flight therefrom, he or another participant in the crime:
>   (a) Causes physical injury to any person who is not a participant in the crime; or
>   (b) Displays what appears to be a pistol, revolver, rifle, shotgun, machine gun or other firearm.

. . . The notion of "actual presence" pertains . . . to something other than presence which is merely "theoretical" or "constructive." To hold that the term "actual presence" means presence in the broader sense so as to include "constructive presence," as the People urge, would read the word "actual" out of the statute. It would denude the phrase of its plain meaning and, moreover, violate the accepted canon of construction, especially critical when interpreting penal provisions, that words which define or delimit the reach of statutory provisions may not be disregarded as superfluous, but must be given meaning and effect [citations omitted]. . . .

When the three aggravating factors in Penal Law § 160.10 are read together, they reflect a concern for the added element of physical harm, danger, and perceived threat of additional violence to the victims of the robbery. That concern is clearly present in situations involving physical injury or the apparent willingness to use a firearm. Likewise, it is present where the robber is joined by another in his use or threat of force or in his seizing or retaining another's property. No such concern exists, however, where the robber has but one accomplice, unknown and unseen to the victim at the time of the robbery, and limited in his participation to waiting for the robber and driving him from the area once the taking has been accomplished.

There is additional evidence in the statute that it was accessorial aid *at the crime scene* and not elsewhere which the Legislature considered sufficiently serious to be an aggravating factor. Two of the three aggravating factors, causing physical injury and displaying a firearm, operate to raise ordinary robbery to robbery in the second degree not only when the aggravating conduct occurs at the crime scene, but also when it occurs during the "immediate flight therefrom" (subd. [2]). By contrast, the aid rendered by an accomplice must, in order to operate as an aggravating factor, be rendered while that accomplice is *actually* present at the robbery (subd. [1]). Assistance rendered solely in the course of "flight therefrom" does not raise the offense to second degree robbery [citations omitted]. . . .

. . . [T]he Commission Staff Notes on the revised Penal Law . . . evince a legislative intent wholly consistent with the result we reach today. The use of a getaway car was included among the aggravating factors in the former robbery statute [citation omitted]. It was eliminated when the Penal Law was revised in 1965 because it was considered by the Legislature to be an insufficiently egregious factor to justify a more serious conviction and harsher sentence. The Commission Staff Notes explain that, where the robber acts alone, the use of an automobile simply does not seem "a highly significant item." And where the robber acts with "a group of bandits," regardless of whether an automobile is used, the robbery is *"in any event"* aggravated only "by virtue of the accomplice factor" [citation omitted]. The mere use of a driver, whose participation in a bank robbery is limited to waiting outside and operating the getaway vehicle, plainly does not constitute a "group of bandits." . . .

Here the evidence was that another person aided defendant in the course of his flight from the crime scene by driving him away. It showed nothing else. There was no suggestion that the driver was armed, prepared to assist defendant, or even observing defendant's actions, or that he was sufficiently close to defendant to be available to render him aid during the actual commission of the robbery. Under these facts, where there is no showing that the driver was ready, willing or able to aid defendant in the forcible stealing from the teller or the bank — let alone that he directly participated therein — it cannot be said that he was "actually present" within any fair construction of the statute.

. . . [The] defendant's conviction [should be] reduced to robbery in third degree, and the case remitted for resentencing.

STATE v. MILLER
14 Or. App. 608, 513 P.2d 1199 (1973)

THORNTON, J. Defendant was convicted after jury trial of robbery in the second degree. ORS 164.405.[3] On appeal he contends that . . . the state failed to offer sufficient evidence to establish that he was aided by a second person actually present during the course of the robbery, a necessary element of the crime.

The victim of the robbery, an elderly woman, had parked her automobile in a lighted parking lot of a Portland restaurant, intending to enter the restaurant. She stepped from her car, closed the door, and was in the act of locking the car door with her key when she was grabbed from behind. She testified that her assailant threw her against the car door, struck her on the jaw with his fist, pulled her purse from her grasp and ran from the scene. She also testified that during the course of the attack she observed another young man standing across the parking lot approximately 25 feet from her, and that the second young man and her assailant ran from the scene together following the purse snatching. The victim testified that the defendant was the person who struck her with his fist and took her purse. . . .

The term "aided by another person actually present" as used in ORS 164.405 includes a person who is at hand, or within reach, sight or call, and who presents an added threat to the victim's safety. *See* Proposed Oregon Criminal Code 154-57, Commentary, §§ 148 to 150 (1970).

We conclude that the jury could legitimately infer that 25 feet away across a parking lot would constitute easy access to aid the defendant, if necessary, and would be in sufficient proximity . . . to support the finding of the jury that defendant was aided by a second person actually present. [Citation omitted.] . . .

Affirmed.

---

3. ORS 164.405 provides:

(1) A person commits the crime of robbery in the second degree if he [commits robbery] and he:
(a) Represents by word or conduct that he is armed with what purports to be a dangerous or deadly weapon; or
(b) Is aided by another person actually present. . . .

12 Working with Facts

§12.1 What Is a Fact?

Consider the following statements:

1. *The plaintiff's complaint alleges* that, at a certain time and place, the defendant struck the plaintiff from behind with a stick.

2. At trial, *the plaintiff's principal witness testified* that, at the time and place specified in the complaint, the defendant struck the plaintiff from behind with a stick.

3. At the conclusion of the trial, *the jury found* that, at the time and place specified in the complaint, the defendant struck the plaintiff from behind with a stick.

4. At the time and place specified in the complaint, *the defendant struck* the plaintiff from behind with a stick.

5. At the time and place specified in the complaint, the defendant *brutally* struck the plaintiff from behind with a stick.

6. At the time and place specified in the complaint, the defendant *accidentally* struck the plaintiff from behind with a stick.

7. At the time and place specified in the complaint, the defendant *committed a battery* on the plaintiff.

Which of these statements expresses a fact?

Number 7 plainly does not: it states a *conclusion of law* because battery

201

is a concept defined by the law, and as a law student you have learned that you can discover whether a battery occurred only by consulting one or more rules of law. Numbers 5 and 6, however, are a little harder to sort out.

Statement 6 includes the word *accidentally*. The defendant might have wanted to cause violence, or he might have struck the plaintiff only inadvertently and without any desire to do harm. With both possibilities, an observer might see pretty much the same actions: the stick being raised, the stick being lowered, the collision with the back. There might be small perceptible differences between the two — the defendant's facial expression, for example, or the words spoken immediately before and after the incident. But even those differences might not occur. A cunning defendant intent on violence, for example, can pretend to act inadvertently. The difference between the two possibilities is in what the defendant might have been thinking or feeling when he struck the plaintiff. If we say that the defendant struck the plaintiff "accidentally," we have made a conclusion about what the defendant was thinking at the time. That conclusion is a purely factual one — lawyers would say a *conclusion of fact*. (It would be a conclusion of law if it were framed in terms the law defines, such as "intention to cause a contact with another person.") A conclusion of fact is not a fact: it is an inference derived from facts.

Statement 5 contains the word *brutally,* which is a value-laden and subjective *characterization*. If one is shocked by the idea of a stick colliding with a human being — regardless of the speed and force involved — even a gentle tap with a stick might be characterized as brutal. (Conversely, an observer who is indifferent to suffering and violence might call repeated lacerations with a stick "playful.") And a friend of the plaintiff or an enemy of the defendant might construe whatever happened as "brutal," while an enemy of the plaintiff or a friend of the defendant might do the reverse. Assuming that we have not seen the incident ourselves, we should wonder whether the word *brutally* accurately summarizes what happened, or whether it instead reflects the value judgments and preferences of the person who has characterized the incident as brutal. A characterization is not a fact; it is only an opinion about a fact.

We are left with statements 1 through 4. Do any of them recite a fact? There are two ways of answering that question. Although the two might at first seem to contradict each other, they are actually consistent, and both answers are accurate, although in different ways.

One answer is that statements 1, 2, and 3 are layers surrounding a fact recited in statement number 4: number 1 is an allegation of a fact; number 2 is evidence offered in proof of the allegation; number 3 is a conclusion that the evidence proves the allegation; and number 4 is the fact itself. This is an answer that might be reached by a perceptive lay person who has noticed what you now know to be a sequence inherent to litigation: the party seeking a remedy first alleges, in a pleading, a collection of facts that, if proven, would merit a remedy, and that party later at trial submits evidence to persuade the finder of fact that the allegations are proven. Notice that this first answer is built on the ideas that a "fact" is part of an objective, discoverable truth and that the purpose of litigation is to find that truth.

The other answer is that numbers 1 through 4 all recite facts, the first three being procedural events of the kind described in §1.3. This answer is derived from the requirement, inherent to litigation, that the decisions of the finder of fact be based not on an objective "truth" that occurred out of court, but instead on whether *in court* a party has carried his or her burdens to make certain allegations and to submit a certain quantum of evidence in support of those allegations. Because it lacks omniscience, a court cannot decide on the basis of what is "true." In a procedural sense, litigation is less a search for truth than it is a test of whether each party has carried burdens of pleading, production, and persuasion that the law assigns to one party or another.[1] Because of the adversary system, the court is not permitted to investigate the controversy: it can do no more than passively weigh what is submitted to it, using as benchmarks the burdens set out in the law. Thus, if a party does not allege and prove a fact essential to that party's case, the court must decide that the fact does not exist. And this is so even if the fact does exist. That is why experienced lawyers tend to be more confident of their abilities to prove and disprove allegations than they are of their abilities to know the "real" truth about what happened between the parties before litigation began.

Both answers are correct, but their value to you will change as time goes on. Right now, the first answer gives you a model of how facts are processed in litigation. But soon the second answer will become increasingly important. That is because, as you learn lawyering, you will have to learn the ways in which the law compels lawyers to focus on whether a party can carry or has carried a burden of pleading, production, or persuasion.

The nonexistence of a fact can itself be a fact. For example, consider the following:

8. The plaintiff's complaint does not allege that the defendant struck the plaintiff with a malicious intent to cause injury.

Here the absence of an allegation is itself a fact. If the complaint demands not only compensatory damages (intended to compensate the plaintiff for his loss), but also punitive damages (additionally intended both to punish the defendant for the outrageousness of his conduct and to warn others like him), the defendant might win a motion to dismiss the demand for punitive damages. But that depends on whether local law treats malice as significant: if the jurisdiction allows punitive damages even in the absence of malice, the missing allegation means nothing.

---

§12.1 1. These burdens are explained more fully later in this chapter. For the moment, it will be enough to understand the following: A *burden of pleading* is a party's obligation to allege in a pleading facts that, if proven, would entitle the party to the relief sought. A *burden of production* is a party's obligation to come forward with enough evidence about a particular issue to warrant a trial of it. And a *burden of persuasion* is a party's obligation at trial to introduce enough evidence to persuade the trier of fact that the allegations are accurate. The law assigns these obligations to one party or the other depending on factors such as the category of case (defamation, breach of contract, criminal, etc.), the stage within the case at which the issue is considered (motion challenging a pleading, motion for summary judgment, motion for directed verdict, etc.), and the nature of the issue.

9. At trial, no witness has testified that the plaintiff suffered any physical or psychological injury or even any indignity.

Now the absence of certain evidence is itself a fact. Consequently, the defendant might be entitled to a directed verdict on the question of damages: the judge might instruct the jury that it is permitted to award only nominal damages, such as one dollar. But that depends on whether the jurisdiction limits recovery to injuries that require medical treatment, produce pain and suffering, or cause humiliation or other dignitary loss.

You might by now have begun to realize that facts are not as simple as they at first seem. Facts have subtleties that can entangle you if you are not careful. Beginners tend to have difficulties with five fact skills: (1) separating facts from other things; (2) separating determinative facts from other kinds of facts; (3) building inferences from facts; (4) purging analysis of hidden and unsupportable factual assumptions; and (5) after litigation has begun, using facts in ways that are appropriate to the case's procedural posture. When you have mastered these skills, you will be able to make reasoned decisions about selecting, using, and describing facts. The last few pages have explained the first skill, and Exercise I will test it. The remainder of this chapter considers each of the other skills in turn.

Exercise I.   The Menu at the Courthouse Cafe

The following appear on the menu at the Courthouse Cafe. Decide what is a fact, what is a characterization, and what is a conclusion of fact. (If part of an item is factual and part is not, decide exactly where the fact ends and the non-fact begins.)

Hot, steaming coffee

Healthful oat bran muffins

Pure beef hot dogs

Garden-fresh vegetables

Hand-picked huckleberries

Home-made huckleberry pie

Delicious peanut butter ice cream

§12.2   Identifying Determinative Facts

Facts can be divided into three categories. The first are essential to a controversy because they will determine the court's decision: if a change in a fact would have caused the court to come to a different decision, that fact is determinative. The second is a category of explanatory facts that, while not determinative, are nevertheless useful because they help make sense out of a situation that would otherwise seem disjointed. The third category includes coincidental facts that have no relevance or usefulness at all: they merely happened. Part of life's charm is that all three categories of facts—the relevant and the irrelevant—occur mixed up together in a disorderly mess. And two of the most basic things lawyers do is to separate the determinative facts and to treat them as determinative.

You have already started learning how to do those things in this and other courses, mostly through the analysis of precedent. When, for example, you are asked to formulate the rule of a case, you have begun to develop the habit of isolating the facts the court considered determinative and then reformulating those facts into a list of generalities that—when they occur together again in the future—will produce the same result that happened in the reported opinion. But when you look at a given litigation through the lens of an opinion, you are looking at it *after* a court has already decided which facts are determinative: you are explicating the text of the opinion to learn what the court thought about the facts. We are concerned here with another skill: looking at the facts at the *beginning* of the case, before they are even put to a court, and predicting which facts the court will consider determinative.

Recall Welty's experience with Lutz, which you first considered in Chapter 6:

> Welty and Lutz are students who have rented apartments on the same floor of the same building. At midnight, Welty is studying, while Lutz is listening to heavy metal with his new four-foot speakers. Welty has put up with this for two or three hours, and finally she pounds on Lutz's door. Lutz opens the door about six inches, and, when he realizes that he cannot hear what Welty is saying, he walks back into the room a few feet to turn the volume down, leaving the door open about six inches. Continuing to express outrage, Welty pushes the door completely open and strides into the room. Lutz turns on Welty and orders her to leave. Welty finds this to be too much and punches Lutz so hard that he suffers substantial injury. In this jurisdiction, the punch is a felonious assault. Is Welty also guilty of common law burglary?

You already know that common law burglary is the breaking and entering of the dwelling of another in the nighttime with intent to commit a felony therein. Whichever way a court rules, the size of the opening between Lutz's door and the door frame is going to be one of the determinative facts because the size of the opening helps to determine whether, at the moment Welty walked in, Lutz's dwelling was surrounded by the kind of enclosure that can be broken. Depending on one's theory, Lutz's activities before Welty knocked on the door could be either explanatory or determinative: they help make sense out of the situation, but they also help explain Welty's actions and intent, which go to other elements of the test for burglary. But you have not been told that Lutz only recently got into heavy metal and that previously he had been a devotee of country and western music; those facts are omitted because they are purely coincidental and do not help you understand the issues. You have been told the time of day—because it determines one of the elements of burglary—but you have not been told the date because it is as coincidental as Lutz's history of musical taste.

Of the five fact skills considered in this chapter, isolating the determinative facts is probably the one about which you have already learned the most in this course and in others. The first few months of law school are designed to teach two things that are the heart of this skill: rule analysis and a heightened sense of relevance.

§12.3   Building Inferences from Facts

We will continue a bit further with Welty and Lutz.

One of the elements of burglary is the intent to commit a felony within the dwelling. The element can be satisfied only if a defendant had that intent at the time that any breaking and entering might have occurred. If the defendant formed the intent for the first time only after entering the dwelling, the element is not satisfied. Assuming for the moment that Welty broke and entered Lutz's apartment when she opened the door further and walked in,[1] did she—at the instant she stepped inside—intend to commit a felony there?

Your response may be "Well, let's ask Welty—she's the one who would really know." But things are not so easy. If you are the prosecutor, you may find that the police have already asked her that question and that she has refused to answer or has given an answer that the police consider self-serving. In fact, one rarely has direct evidence of a person's state of mind: people do not carry electronic signboards on their foreheads on which their thoughts can be read at moments the law considers important. Instead, as prosecutor you would have to prove Welty's state of mind through the surrounding circumstances—for example, through the things she did and the things she knew other people had done.[2] Although her state of mind would be easier to determine if she had appeared at Lutz's door with an arsenal of weaponry—or, in another situation, with safecracking tools—

---

§12.3 1. The breaking and entering issues may not be easy to resolve. See §§6.3-6.4. Let us focus here, however, only on the state-of-mind element: whether, at the time of any breaking and entering that *might* have occurred, she intended to commit a felony inside.

2. Once again, the nonexistence of a fact can be treated as a fact:

> "Is there any other point to which you wish to draw my attention?"
> "To the curious incident of the dog in the night-time."
> "The dog did nothing in the night-time."
> "That was the curious incident," remarked Sherlock Holmes. . . . "Obviously the midnight visitor was someone the dog knew well."

A. Conan Doyle, *Silver Blaze,* in *The Memoirs of Sherlock Holmes* 27 (1893).

inferences can be built from circumstances even without such dramatic displays of intent.

Even if you are Welty's defense lawyer and can freely ask her when she formed an intent to hit Lutz, you might not be much better off. She might tell you something like the following:

> I don't know when I decided to punch him. I had to listen to his loud music on his four-foot speakers for two or three hours while I was trying to study for civil procedure. At least once or twice during that time, I thought that it might be nice to punch his lights out, but I don't know that I had decided then to do it. When I knocked on his door, I thought, "This guy had better be reasonable, or else"—but at that instant I don't know whether I was committed to punching him. When I pushed the door open and stepped inside, I thought, "This joker might learn a little respect for the rest of us if something very emphatic happened to him—something that might help him remember in the future that other people have needs and that he shouldn't be so self-centered." Even then, I wasn't certain that I was going to do anything except try to reason with him. And when he ordered me out, I decked him. Nobody told me that I was supposed to make sure that my thoughts fit into this "state of mind" you're telling me about. I have no idea when I "formed an intent" to hit him. I can only tell you what my thoughts were at each step in the story. You're the lawyer: you tell me when I "formed an intent."

Now the problem is something else: a party's thoughts do not mesh nicely with the law's categories of states of mind. Welty's sequence of emotions somehow culminated in an action, but there seems to have been no magical moment at which anger crystallized into a decision that the law might recognize as "intent." A defense lawyer handles this problem in the same way that a prosecutor deals with the absence of direct evidence: each lawyer will build inferences from the circumstances surrounding Welty's actions. As Welty sees the arguments unfold, she might conclude that the law is doing strange and perhaps arbitrary things in categorizing her thoughts. But the law must have a way of judging states of mind, and it relies heavily on circumstances.

Albert Moore has used the term *inferential stream* to refer to the sequence of circumstantial conclusions that can grow out of a fact or piece of evidence.[3] Circumstantial evidence does not necessarily lead to only one stream of inferences. Consider the evidence in *Smith v. Jones*, where Smith claims that Jones caused an accident by running a red light:

> Jones testifies that his two children, ages five and six, were arguing in the back seat of his car just before the accident occurred. [This] is circumstantial propositional evidence that Jones entered the intersection against the red light because there is a series of valid generalizations that connects this evidence to

---

3. *Inferential Streams: The Articulation and Illustration of the Advocate's Evidentiary Intuitions*, 34 UCLA L. Rev. 611 (1987).

the factual proposition in question. These generalizations might be stated as follows:

> *Generalization 1:* People driving with children arguing in the back seat of the car sometimes pay attention to what is happening in the back seat.

> *Generalization 2:* People who are paying attention to what is happening in the back seat of the car are sometimes momentarily distracted from what is happening on the road in front of them.

> *Generalization 3:* People who are momentarily distracted from what is happening on the road in front of them sometimes enter an intersection against the red light.

> *Conclusion:* Jones entered the intersection against the red light.

Based on the foregoing, one might conclude that this circumstantial evidence tends to prove only that Jones entered the intersection against the red light. One could also, however, conclude that this evidence tends to disprove that Jones entered the intersection against the red light. This conclusion might be based on the following analysis:

> *Generalization 4:* People driving with children arguing in the back seat are sometimes conscious of the presence of children in the car.

> *Generalization 5:* People who are conscious of children in their car sometimes drive cautiously.

> *Generalization 6:* People who drive cautiously sometimes pay close attention to the road.

> *Generalization 7:* People who pay close attention to the road sometimes do not enter an intersection against the red light.

> *Conclusion:* Jones did not enter the intersection against the red light.

In *Smith v. Jones*, therefore, the evidence that Jones' children were arguing in the back of the car just before the accident, by itself, may tend to prove or disprove that Jones entered the intersection against the red light, depending on which set of generalizations is viewed as more reliable and accurate. . . . Thus, circumstantial propositional evidence may "cut both ways" in two situations: when the same evidence tends to prove or disprove the same factual proposition; or when it tends to prove one factual proposition while also tending to disprove another.[4]

§12.4   Identifying Hidden and Unsupportable Factual Assumptions

As David Binder and Paul Bergman have pointed out, "[i]f in medieval times there was 'trial by combat,' then today we have 'trial by inference.'"[1]

---

4. *Id.* at 625-27.
§**12.4** 1. Fact Investigation: From Hypothesis to Proof 82 (1984).

Your adversary and the court will mercilessly challenge your inferential streams, looking for weaknesses in the way they were put together. Consequently, you must purge your analysis of hidden assumptions that will not stand up to scrutiny when exposed. Consider the following:

> Detective Fenton Tracem rushes breathlessly into the office of the local prosecutor, Les Gettem, eager to persuade Les to issue an indictment. Fenton describes the evidence he has uncovered:
>
>> Les, we've got a good case for bank robbery against Clyde. The gun the robber used and dropped at the door was originally purchased by Clyde. The owner of A-1 Guns can definitely identify Clyde as the purchaser and the teller can identify the gun. Moreover, the day after the $10,000 was taken, Clyde deposits $7,000 cash in a bank account using the fictitious name of Dillinger. A teller at the bank can definitely identify Clyde. Then later that day, Clyde buys a $1,500 gold watch and pays for it in cash. The owner of A-2 Jewelry can also identify him. Finally, the next day — two days after the robbery — Clyde moves out without giving Ness, his landlord, his two neighbors, Capone and Siegel, or the post office his new address. Ness, Capone, Siegel and the post office clerk are all willing to testify. Les, we're rock-solid on this one.
>
> The detective has disgorged a mass of circumstantial evidence which appears in the aggregate to be quite convincing. The prosecutor cannot, however, be content to rely on this presentation. In order to analyze the probative value of the evidence, Gettem must first expressly articulate the generalization which links each item of evidence to an element. . . . [E]xpressly articulating generalizations is the key to determining just how strong a piece of evidence is.
>
> Consider, therefore, the generalization the prosecutor might articulate for the first piece of evidence, that the gun used and dropped by the robber was originally purchased by Clyde. The generalization might be something like, "People who have purchased a gun subsequently used in a robbery are more likely to have participated in the robbery than people who have not." [2]

How accurate is this generalization? See what happens when you combine it with *either* of two strings of other generalizations. This is the first one: "Robbers do not feel morally compelled to pay for what they acquire, and because guns can be stolen, a robber does not have even a practical need to pay for a gun." This is the second string: "Robbers tend to plan their crimes with at least some amount of forethought; some forethought would cause a robber to foresee that he or she might lose control of a gun during the robbery; other forethought would cause a robber to foresee that a gun legally purchased from a merchant might be traced back to the robber; Clyde is bright enough to have come to both of these foresights." Both strings seem more believable than "People who have purchased a gun subsequently used in a robbery are more likely to have participated in the robbery than people who have not" — and *either* string might overcome and negate the generalization on which the detective relies.

---

2. *Id.* at 92-93.

In the beginning years of practice, one must force oneself to articulate explicitly the generalizations on which one relies, for it is not a skill practiced in everyday life. In fact, there is a word for people who state the generalizations underlying all inferences they make: bores. But in the privacy of one's office, one should expressly identify the premises on which one relies [because] by articulating the underlying generalization one can consciously consider the question of how strongly it is supported by common experience.

This point may be seen more clearly if one is asked to evaluate another of Det. Tracem's pieces of evidence without the aid of an expressed generalization. "The day after the $10,000 was taken, Clyde deposits $7,000 cash in a bank account using the fictitious name of Dillinger." As D.A. Les Gettem, one is asked how strongly suggestive of Clyde's guilt this piece of evidence is. . . .

. . . If your answer is something like, "The evidence is strongly indicative of guilt" (or "isn't too probative of guilt"), you have had a knee-jerk reaction to the evidence. Undoubtedly some accumulation of common experience was implicit in whatever conclusion you reached. But unless the common experience is crystallized in an explicitly stated generalization, one has no focal point for considering how uniformly common experience supports the generalization.

If your conclusion did include a generalization, it may have been something like, "People who deposit $7,000 in a bank account under a fictitious name are likely to have gotten the money illegally." With this generalization explicitly stated, one has a basis for gauging with some degree of accuracy the probative value of the fictitious bank account evidence. One has an explicit premise which can be tested according to one's own and a factfinder's probable views as to how the world operates. . . .

There are other reasons for articulating generalizations. Their articulation may bring to mind potential exceptions. . . . [O]ne method of testing the degree to which common experience uniformly supports a generalization is to add "except when" to a generalization, and see how many reasonable exceptions one can identify. . . .

[For example, consider] a generalization that one might make in Clyde's case: "People who move without leaving a forwarding address are usually trying to avoid detection." By adding "except when," one sees that this generalization is subject to many exceptions and is therefore less likely to be persuasive. People may be trying to avoid detection, except when they simply forget to leave a forwarding address, or except when they do not yet know the permanent address to which they will be moving, or except when they will be moving around for a time and will not have a permanent address.[3]

As Binder and Bergman point out, only bores recite for the benefit of others all the generalizations underlying their inferences. Thus, when you build and test your own inferences, you will not commit to paper much of the analysis Binder and Bergman describe. As they suggest, it is thinking reserved for the privacy of your own office.

But things are different when you attack your adversary's inferences. If Clyde becomes your client, you might argue that a directed verdict should be—or, on appeal, should have been—granted because a rational jury would not be able to find guilt beyond a reasonable doubt. In a supporting

3. *Id.* at 93-96.

memorandum or in an appellate brief, you might write, "The evidence that he moved without leaving a forwarding address does not tend to prove guilty flight. It could just as easily prove that he forgot to leave a forwarding address, or that he did not yet know his new permanent address when he moved, or that he would be moving around for a time without a permanent address."

Exercise II.   Welty's State of Mind

This exercise has two parts. Complete the first one before doing any portion of the second one.

1. Develop whatever streams of inferences are necessary to determine Welty's state of mind from the facts given on pages 205 and 207. Write out each fact on which you rely and each inference in the stream flowing from that fact.

2. You are now no longer the person who completed the first part of this exercise. You are somebody else, and you have been hired to attack each of the inferential streams developed in the first part of the exercise. Write down every hidden assumption you can find in those inferential streams, and decide whether each assumption is probable enough to support the inferences that flow from it.

═══════════

§12.5   Using Facts in Ways Appropriate to the Case's Procedural Posture

Once litigation has begun, the facts are seen through filters that differ according to the case's procedural posture. The procedural posture is the procedural event or events that have placed an issue before the court. If you were asked to give the procedural posture in the trial court in *Meints v. Huntington*,[1] a reasonable answer might begin like this: "The defendants requested that the jury be instructed that . . . ." If you were asked to do the same for *Eilers v. Coy*,[2] you might start with the words "The plaintiff moved for a directed verdict . . . ." For *Sawyer v. State*,[3] the answer might begin "After he was arrested as a fugitive from another state, Sawyer petitioned for a writ of habeas corpus . . . ."

In one way or another, your teachers in other courses have probably suggested to you that the meaning of a judicial decision is qualified in part by the procedural posture in which the decision was rendered. In addition, you will see in the next few pages that a case's procedural posture limits the

---

§12.5   1. See Exercise I, Chapter 2 (page 18).
2. See Exercise III, Chapter 2 (page 32).
3. See page 61.

ways in which facts may be used and described. That is true not only of the already adjudicated facts in decisions you read in casebooks and in the library, but also of the not yet adjudicated facts in cases you are litigating or contemplating litigating.

In trial courts, an attorney requests a judicial order by making a motion for it, and most procedural postures are defined in terms of the motion that has been made.[4] Each type of motion is governed by procedural rules that control how the motion is to be decided. Motions in trial courts can be divided into three very generalized categories: motions that challenge the manner in which the litigation began, motions that challenge the quality of a party's evidence, and a catch-all category of miscellaneous case management motions. When a trial judge's decision is appealed, the case moves into yet another procedural posture, where the trial judge's decision is evaluated through a filter called the standard of review.

You will confront the procedural posture if you are asked to write any of the following: an office memorandum predicting the decision on a particular motion, a persuasive memorandum supporting or opposing a motion, an appellate brief, or (as a judge's law clerk) a draft opinion deciding a motion or an appeal. In each of these documents, you will have to use the facts in a way that is appropriate to the procedural posture.

§12.5.1   Motions Challenging the Manner in Which the Litigation Began

As a practical matter, the most important of these are motions testing the sufficiency of the pleadings. The *burden of pleading* is a party's obligation to allege, in its pleading, facts, that, if proven, would entitle the party to the judgment it seeks. In a civil case, the plaintiff's complaint must allege facts that, if proven, equal a cause of action. If a defendant pleads a counterclaim or an affirmative defense in the answer, the answer must allege facts that, if proven, equal a counterclaim or affirmative defense. And in a criminal case, the government's indictment or information must allege facts that, if proven, would constitute a crime.[5]

In a civil action, a defendant can, before answering a complaint, move to dismiss it for failure to state a cause of action. Because this motion tests the sufficiency of a pleading, the record is limited to the four corners of the complaint.[6] The question is not whether either party has proved anything.

---

4. You will find it easier to understand this material if you review §1.3. In some jurisdictions, some motions are known by names other than the ones used here.

5. A defendant does not file a written answer to an indictment. Because criminal defendants cannot constitutionally be required to make statements about the events at issue, they do not submit written pleadings. Instead, a criminal defendant pleads only "guilty" or "not guilty," orally in court and without elaboration.

6. This is an instance of a rule governing the disposition of a particular kind of motion. *See, e.g.,* Rule 10(c) of the Federal Rules of Civil Procedure. Like all rules, this one is capable of variation from jurisdiction to jurisdiction, the leading exception here being Rule 3211 of the New York Civil Practice Law and Rules. Because so many rules govern the disposition of motions, and because they so often vary from jurisdiction to jurisdiction, be careful to discover exactly what the local rules are. That knowledge comes only with time and thought in the library: guessing about local rules often leads to grief.

Instead, the court assumes—for the purpose of the motion only—that the factual allegations in the complaint can be proven, and the court then decides whether, if proven, those allegations would amount to a cause of action. If the court concludes that they could not, it strikes the cause of action from the pleading. If the court strikes all the causes of action pleaded in a complaint, the complaint itself is dismissed and the litigation is terminated unless the plaintiff can serve and file an amended complaint with additional or reformulated allegations that would survive a motion to dismiss. Similarly, a plaintiff can move to dismiss a counterclaim or an affirmative defense pleaded in the defendant's answer, and in a criminal case a defendant can move to dismiss one or more counts in the indictment or information, or the entire indictment or information.

In addition to the sufficiency of the pleadings, other aspects of the beginning of the litigation may be challenged by motion. A defendant, for example, might move to dismiss an action on the ground that the court lacks jurisdiction over the subject matter, or that the summons was improperly served, or that venue is improper, and so on. What unifies all these motions is that they are usually made during the pleading stage. Several of them are even waived unless made during that period, although rules vary somewhat from jurisdiction to jurisdiction.[7]

Because, at this stage in the litigation, no evidence has been submitted, lawyers do not describe the "facts" recited in the pleadings as things that actually happened. Until it receives evidence later in the litigation, a court has no idea whether the "facts" happened, and the "facts" therefore are described as allegations:

> Although the plaintiff has alleged that the defendant struck him from behind with a stick, he has not alleged that the defendant intended to cause him injury.

It is *absolutely wrong* in this procedural posture to write the following:

> Although the defendant struck the plaintiff from behind with a stick, the defendant did not intend to cause the plaintiff injury.

We will find out later—after evidence has been produced—whether the defendant struck the plaintiff or intended to cause injury.

§12.5.2 Motions Challenging the Quality of a Party's Evidence

These include motions for summary judgment, for a directed verdict, and for judgment notwithstanding the verdict. In contrast to the motions testing allegations in pleadings, these require the court to decide whether a party has sustained a burden to produce evidence.

---

7. *See, e.g.,* Rule 12 of the Federal Rules of Civil Procedure.

Do not confuse the *burden of production* with the *burden of persuasion*. The burden of persuasion is the obligation to persuade the trier of fact that a particular allegation is true. The burden of production (often called the burden of going forward) is the obligation to satisfy the judge—even in cases where the actual trier of fact is a jury—that the party who must shoulder the burden can provide enough evidence about a particular allegation to make it worth putting the question to the trier of fact.

The law has good reasons to avoid putting a question to a trier of fact unless the party with the burden of production has at least a threshold quantum of evidence. First, putting a question to a trier of fact is expensive and time-consuming. The only purpose of a trial is to ascertain the facts from conflicting evidence, and in modern litigation trials have become expensive and burdensome to the parties, the courts, and ultimately the public. Second, there are certain risks where the trier of fact is a jury. Although the right to trial by jury is one of the foundations of common law procedure—treasured as a vehicle for limiting the authority of government—jurors with no training in law are so capable of misunderstandings that many of the rules of evidence and procedure are designed to limit what juries can see, hear, and decide.

Although the difference between a burden of persuasion and a burden of production may seem technical, it is important in practice and in practical legal writing. A beginner may be confused not only because the two burdens at first seem similar, but also because the term *burden of proof* is occasionally but confusingly applied to both burdens collectively. You will be able to differentiate between them, however, if you remember some of the basic concepts of each burden.

You already know, for example, that when a civil case is tried, the plaintiff has the burden of persuading the fact finder of the existence of facts that substantiate each element of a cause of action pleaded in the complaint. You also know that the defendant can try to prevent the plaintiff from carrying that burden, or the defendant can raise one or more affirmative defenses, or the defendant can do both. You recall that a defendant who pleads an affirmative defense assumes the burden of persuading the fact finder of the existence of facts that substantiate each element of that defense. And you remember that in criminal cases the prosecution must carry a burden of persuasion as to every element of the crime, and the defendant assumes a similar burden for each element of any asserted affirmative defense.[8] It is the trier of fact who determines whether these burdens have been carried, and the trier does so only at the end of the trial. The trier of fact should find against a defendant if the plaintiff or prosecution has carried its burden of persuasion and if the defendant has not done so with an affirmative defense. But the trier of fact should find for a defendant if the defendant has substantiated an affirmative defense, even if the plaintiff or prosecution

---

8. In some jurisdictions, certain criminal defenses are called "affirmative" even if conceptually they are not. By nature, an affirmative defense is one for which the defendant assumes a burden of persuasion. Local law, however, might label a defense "affirmative" if the defendant assumes a burden of production, but not the burden of persuasion, which must be shouldered by the prosecution; these defenses might require a defendant to do something, but they are not true affirmative defenses because the "something" is less than carrying a burden of persuasion.

has carried all its burdens. If the trier of fact is a jury, the result is in the form of a verdict, and if the trier is a judge, the same kind of decision takes the form of the judge's findings of fact.

The concept that may now seem odd to you is that the parties might not even be allowed to try to carry these burdens of persuasion unless they have already shown that they can satisfy their burdens of production. The burden of production requires the party shouldering it to come forward with a minimum, threshold quantum of evidence, defined by the relevant rules of procedure and by the case law interpreting those rules. The question of whether a party has carried a burden of production is generally put to a judge through one of the three motions that challenge the quality of the other party's evidence.

These motions—for summary judgment,[9] for a directed verdict,[10] and for judgment notwithstanding the verdict[11]—exist so that parties, lawyers, and judges can avoid, where possible and appropriate, the effort and expense of trial, as well as the perils of juries. A motion for summary judgment can be made before trial. A motion for a directed verdict can be made during trial, after the opposing party has rested (finished presenting evidence) and before the jury has begun to deliberate. A motion for judgment notwithstanding the verdict is made—as its name suggests—after the jury has returned a verdict. Although these motions are governed by different procedural rules, all three are decided according to approximately the same logic: the motion should be granted if the opposing party has failed to satisfy a burden of production and if the law is such that the movant is entitled to a favorable judgment.[12]

Although motions for summary judgment are very common in civil practice,[13] they may at first perplex you. The judgment is "summary" because there is no trial. The evidence is put before the court not through testimony in a courtroom, but instead through the parties' written submissions, which include affidavits, deposition transcripts, exhibits, and answers to interrogatories. In virtually every American jurisdiction, a party is entitled to summary judgment if none of the material facts are genuinely in dispute and if that party is entitled to judgment as a matter of law.[14] Be careful: although

9. *See* Rule 56 of the Federal Rules of Civil Procedure.

10. *See* Rule 50(a) of the Federal Rules of Civil Procedure. Verdicts are, of course, the products of juries. In a bench trial, the corresponding device is a motion for involuntary dismissal. *See* Rule 41(b) of the Federal Rules of Civil Procedure.

11. *See* Rule 50(b) of the Federal Rules of Civil Procedure.

12. *See, e.g., Anderson v. Liberty Lobby, Inc.,* 477 U.S. 242, 250-52 (1986).

13. There are no summary judgments in criminal cases. Our constitutional concepts of procedural due process would not tolerate summary judgments in favor of the prosecution, and summary judgments in favor of the defendant are inconsistent with the limited scope of criminal discovery and with the understandable reluctance of criminal defense lawyers to reveal before trial their theories and evidence. In many jurisdictions, the government must carry a burden of production at a preliminary hearing, where the case is dismissed if the government does not bring forward a threshold quantum of evidence. In any event, a defendant can challenge the government's evidence at trial through a motion for a directed verdict or for a motion for judgment of acquittal despite a guilty verdict. In criminal trials, the prosecution's persuasive burden is *proof beyond a reasonable doubt,* which is the heaviest burden known to the law. The trial motions will be granted if, viewing the evidence in the light most favorable to the government, the judge concludes that a reasonable jury would necessarily find or have found reasonable doubt.

14. *See, e.g.,* Rule 56 of the Federal Rules of Civil Procedure.

this seems like a simple, two-element test, it has some deceptive subtleties. First, a fact is not material merely because it is logically related to the controversy: a fact is material in this sense only if it is determinative, and you already know that a determinative fact is one that, if different, would change the court's decision.

Second, a fact is not "in dispute" merely because the parties disagree about it. On a motion for summary judgment, a fact is genuinely disputed only if there is a real question about whether a burden of persuasion could be carried at trial. In federal cases, facts are not genuinely in issue unless they "properly can be resolved only by a finder of fact because they may reasonably be resolved in favor of either party." [15] In other words, a fact issue is genuine only if a reasonable jury could go either way.[16]

Finally, the second element of the test for summary judgment incorporates the relevant substantive rules at issue — primarily, the rules defining the cause of action and any affirmative defenses — because the only way a court can determine whether a party is entitled to judgment as a matter of law is to apply the substantive rules that define the parties' rights and obligations.

In any of these procedural postures, a description of the facts is framed in terms of the evidence submitted:

> The plaintiff testified that he was struck in the back and that the defendant was the only person who was behind him at the time. The defendant does not deny that he struck the plaintiff or that he used a stick to do it. Aside from the stick, the only evidence that might conceivably show that the defendant intended to cause injury is a letter, dated two days before the incident, in which the defendant complained that the plaintiff "had better keep his cattle off my land or I'll have to do something."

Notice how each fact is connected with evidence so that the reader can judge whether the evidence really proves it. That is because the provability of facts is still at issue. In these procedural postures, the only facts that can accurately be stated without any reference to evidence are those that are "true" because the parties do not disagree about them.

§12.5.3 Miscellaneous Case Management Motions

These are housekeeping motions, used to manage the progress of litigation, such as motions in discovery; motions for preliminary injunctions; and

---

15. *Anderson v. Liberty Lobby, Inc.,* 477 U.S. 242, 250 (1986).

16. At trial in the overwhelming majority of civil actions, the party charged with a burden of persuasion must satisfy it by a *preponderance of the evidence:* by evidence showing more likely than not that the alleged facts are true. A few burdens of persuasion in civil trials must be carried by *clear and convincing evidence;* these burdens are heavier because of a special need to protect some vulnerable interest. In federal courts and in several — but not all — states, the genuineness of a summary judgment fact issue is judged in part by the weight of the burden of

suppression motions in criminal cases.[17] What makes these motions different from the ones you have just read about is that the granting of a management motion does not terminate the litigation; instead, management motions regulate the litigation's progress. Burdens of production and burdens of persuasion are so effective at helping a court structure its decision-making that they are used not just to award judgments, but also to decide many of these motions as well.

For example, before trial, a criminal defendant who gave the police a statement might move to suppress it, arguing that the police wrongfully obtained the statement by failing to inform him first of his constitutional right to remain silent. If the court grants the motion, the statement cannot be used as evidence at trial. At or before the hearing on the motion, the defendant must carry a burden of production by submitting at least some evidence that he made a statement. That is a relatively easy burden for the defendant to satisfy,[18] especially because the prosecution is not likely to deny it. Once the burden of production has been met, however, the prosecution must shoulder a much heavier one: the prosecution must show beyond a reasonable doubt that the defendant was warned, in language he could understand, that he need not say anything to the police, that anything he says may be held against him, that he has a right to an attorney present during interrogation, and that if he cannot pay for an attorney, one would be appointed for him at government expense.[19]

Because these miscellaneous motions are generally decided on the basis of evidence, the facts are described in the same way as with motions for summary judgment, for a directed verdict, and for judgment notwithstanding the verdict.

§12.5.4 Appeal

In an appellate court, a standard of review is applied to the decision below. The standard varies from jurisdiction to jurisdiction, from court to court, and from case to case, depending on the nature of the decision appealed from. Some types of decisions, for example, will be reversed if "erroneous"; others only if "clearly erroneous"; and yet others only if "an abuse of discretion."[20]

On appeal, the facts are usually described just as they were in procedural posture in the trial court. If the appeal is from the dismissal of a complaint,

---

persuasion that would have to be carried at trial. In those jurisdictions, if a party at trial would have to prove a fact by clear and convincing evidence, that party will lose a pretrial summary judgment motion unless he or she can produce evidence when the motion is made that would later permit a reasonable jury to decide that the fact has been proven by clear and convincing evidence. *See Anderson v. Liberty Lobby, Inc.,* 477 U.S. 242, 252-56 (1986).

17. Although a request for jury instructions is not called a motion, in a technical sense it is one, and it is of the case management variety.

18. The defendant can carry the burden of production simply by stating in an affidavit or in testimony that he made a statement to the police.

19. *See Miranda v. Arizona,* 384 U.S. 436 (1966).

20. Chapter 20 explains appellate practice and standards of review.

for example, the facts are described as allegations. The facts are described as evidence if the appeal is from a judgment resulting from a motion challenging the quality of evidence or from an order resulting from a case management motion, unless the facts are undisputed or the trial judge made findings of fact that are not being challenged on appeal. If the facts are undisputed or the trial judge made unchallenged findings of fact, the facts are described as truth.

Exercise III.   Welty's Facts at Various Procedural Postures

1. Welty has been indicted for burglary. She has moved to dismiss the indictment, which alleges the events on page 205. Write a description of the facts in this procedural posture. (Before attempting this, you might reread §12.1.)

2. At trial, Lutz has testified to everything he saw and heard, and the prosecution has rested. Welty has not yet presented any evidence, and she has moved for a directed verdict. Write a description of the facts in this procedural posture.

3. At trial, Lutz has testified to everything he saw and heard; the prosecution has rested; Welty has testified to everything she saw, heard, and thought (see page 207); and she has moved for a directed verdict. Write a description of the facts in this procedural posture.

13 Citations and Quotations

§13.1 A Tour of the Bluebook

Legal writing has unique citation rules because the typical reader of legal writing needs very specific information about each authority and needs it expressed precisely and succinctly in "citation language" that can be quickly skimmed and understood. You will find that a properly constructed legal citation conveys a large amount of information in a very small space. Bad citation form, on the other hand, is instantly noticed and causes a reader to suspect that the writer is sloppy or ignorant—and therefore unreliable. Letter-perfect citation form not only provides necessary information unambiguously, but it also helps to create an impression of meticulousness and dependability.

From a citation, a reader expects to learn (1) *where* the authority can be found, (2) the authority's *weight* (whether it is mandatory and, if not, some of the factors on which its persuasiveness can be judged, such as its date and the name of the court that decided it); and (3) *your purpose* in using the authority. To show the reader where authority can be found, citations include, in formulated abbreviations, the names of publications, as well as volume numbers and page, section, or paragraph numbers. To show the weight of authority, citations identify courts and jurisdictions and include dates, subsequent histories, and explanatory parentheticals. And if the surrounding text does not make your purpose clear, the citation can include a signal defining the relationship between the text and the cited authority (although, as you will see, signals are disfavored in memoranda and briefs). All of these things are accomplished through *citation grammar:* words, abbreviations, and numbers that, when expressed in proper order, have precise meaning for the reader.

A *Uniform System of Citation,* also known as the Harvard Citator and the Bluebook, is a codification of the most commonly followed rules of legal citation.[1] The Bluebook is divided into three parts.[2] The first—titled "General Rules of Citation and Style" (rules 1 through 9)—governs matters common to all citations, regardless of the type of authority involved. Examples include citation structure, signals, short-form citations, quotations, typefaces, and the like. The second part—titled "Citation Forms for Specific Types of Authority" (rules 10 through 20)—sets out separate rules for citations to precedent, constitutions, statutes, legislative histories, administrative regulations, books, articles, and other material. The third—titled "Tables"—includes special citation rules for each jurisdiction. From the tables, you can learn the citation form for each state's statutory code, the names and abbreviations of the reporters to which a particular court's decisions must be cited, and even some of the details of changes where a state has restructured its court system (check Kentucky, for example).

Two kinds of tasks confront you in using the Bluebook: finding the applicable citation rule (a type of research chore) and discovering its meaning (a task of quasi-statutory interpretation). The research is not as hard as it looks. With the Bluebook index or table of contents, you can find the applicable rule once you are aware of what a citation is intended to communicate and how the Bluebook is organized. If you use the descriptive word method (in the Bluebook index) and the topic method (in the table of contents)—just as in researching any other kind of code—you can find the rules that govern the citation you are trying to put together. As with statutes, try the index before the table of contents, at least until you know the Bluebook thoroughly enough to have a good idea of where the rules are.

Be careful about three problems generally associated with Bluebook use. First, although expectations of what a citation should communicate are fairly uniform throughout the country, some jurisdictions and publishers follow slightly different citation patterns. You can see from cases excerpted within your casebooks that not every state's citation rules are precisely the same as those in the Bluebook. And some publishers of reporters, digests, and annotation and looseleaf services have developed their own citation styles, which differ in a few small ways from Bluebook rules. But because the Bluebook's rules coincide with state and federal rules much more often than not, and because it is the most complete citation code, it is used nationally by law reviews and in legal writing courses. And as long as you are required to follow Bluebook rules—which will be at least throughout law school and probably afterward—you assume a risk whenever you copy a citation out of a library book without asking yourself whether you have first converted it into Bluebook form. The experienced reader will quickly spot a nonconforming citation and can often tell which publication led the writer astray.

The second problem may arise if you later practice in a state where courts require a citation format different from Bluebook rules. When, in a clinical

§13.1   1. Read this chapter with a Bluebook close at hand. You will understand this material much better if you read each Bluebook rule as it is mentioned here. (The rule references in this chapter are to the 14th edition of the Bluebook.)
   2. Look through the Bluebook's table of contents to follow the organization explained here.

program or after graduation, you first begin preparing documents to be filed in a real court, you would be wise to discover the extent, if any, to which local requirements differ from Bluebook form.

The third problem concerns typefaces. The Bluebook was designed primarily for use by law reviews, which put all citations in footnotes, and most examples in the Bluebook are thus in typefaces appropriate to footnotes. In brief and memo writing, however, different typeface conventions prevail, and some law review footnote practices, such as large and small capitals, cannot be produced with a standard typewriter. Rules 1 and 1.1 explain how to adapt Bluebook rules and examples to citations in briefs and memoranda.

The rest of this "tour" explains some rules that are not entirely clear in the Bluebook. As mere commentary, these explanations are, of course, only secondary authority, the Bluebook itself being the primary authority.

§13.2   Citation to Various Types of Authority

Citations to cases are controlled by rule 10; constitutions by rule 11; statutes by rule 12; and administrative regulations by rule 14. Rule 13 explains how to cite to legislative histories; rule 15 to books; rule 16 to articles in law reviews and other periodicals; rule 17 to newspapers; and rule 18 to looseleaf services. Restatements are covered by rule 12.8.5, and the Code of Professional Responsibility by rule 12.8.6.

You will cite most often to cases and statutes, and those citations are a bit more complicated than others.

§13.2.1   Citation to Cases

Aside from a signal (rule 2.2) or any explanatory parenthetical (rule 10.7), a case citation has six components, which must appear in the following order:

1. the *case name* (rule 10.2)
2. the *official reporter* (rule 10.3)
3. an *unofficial reporter,* if required (rule 10.3)
4. the *court,* if its identity is not "conveyed unambiguously" by the name of the official reporter (rule 10.4)
5. the *date* of the decision (rule 10.5)
6. the *subsequent history,* if any (rule 10.7).

For example, this citation

People v. Onofre, 51 N.Y.2d 476, 415 N.E.2d 936, 434 N.Y.S.2d 947 (1980), *cert. denied,* 451 U.S. 987 (1981).

221

is made up of the following parts:

1.	case name	*People v. Onofre*
2.	official reporter	51 N.Y.2d 476
3.	unofficial reporter (two for this court)	415 N.E.2d 936 434 N.Y.S.2d 947
4.	court	[not specified because N.Y.2d reports only cases from the New York Court of Appeals]
5.	date	(1980)
6.	subsequent history	*cert. denied,* 451 U.S. 987 (1981) [in 1981, the United States Supreme Court denied a petition for a writ of certiorari]

If you have interpolated the cite into a sentence of your own composition, the complete cite is followed by a comma unless the cite ends the sentence.

Not every citation will have all six components. For instance, there is no subsequent history if, after the decision cited to, no further appeal was taken (see rule 10.7). As in the example above, the court need not be specified if the official reporter is included and if it publishes the decisions of only one court (see rule 10.4). In federal cases, citations to unofficial reporters do not appear unless the official citation is not yet available (see rule 10.3.1). California and New York have two unofficial reporters each, and decisions that appear in both unofficial reporters must be cited to both (see the California and New York entries in the Bluebook tables). A citation to the official reporter would not appear where the official reporter has not yet published the opinion (see rule 10.3.1), or where the state has abandoned its official reporter (see the state's entry in the Bluebook tables to find out).

Three aspects of rule 10.4 sometimes prove troublesome for beginners. First, because the reader needs to know exactly which court rendered the decision, it is not enough merely to name the *type* of court: the *specific* court itself must be identified. Thus, "U.S. Ct. App." does not tell the reader which of the thirteen circuits was responsible for the decision. One of the approved abbreviations (such as "8th Cir.") must be used instead. Similarly, "U.S. Dist. Ct." is not sufficient for the United States District Court for the Eastern District of Pennsylvania; "E.D. Pa." tells the reader exactly which court made the decision.

Second, although rules 10.4 and 10.5 do not explicitly allow it, you can omit the court or the date from the citation where the same information is included in the preceding text:

> The Seventh Circuit has held that . . . . *Goldberg v. Hoffman,* 225 F.2d 463 (1955).

> As early as 1897, the New York Court of Appeals held that . . . . *People v. Conroy,* 151 N.Y. 543, 45 N.E. 946.

You can thus stress a case's weight, if that depends on the identity of the court or the date, and you can avoid constant, unspecific, and tedious references to "the court" every time a case is introduced.

Third, although rule 10.4(b) prohibits identification of the subdivision of an intermediate state court except where that is "of particular relevance," the geographic subdivision is often "of particular relevance" in states where the intermediate appellate court is segmented geographically, such as New York and California, because the subdivision can affect the authoritative value of the decision. For example, in New York the intermediate appellate court is the Appellate Division of the state's Supreme Court, which is divided into four Departments. Even where an Appellate Division decision is cited as persuasive authority outside New York State, the identity of the Department can be of "particular relevance." In a defamation case being litigated in Colorado, for instance, an opinion from the First Department (which includes Manhattan) may have added weight because the concentration of publishers and broadcasting media in New York City has given the First Department a fair amount of experience and expertise in the field. This problem does not, of course, arise in states, such as Pennsylvania and Maryland, where the jurisdiction of the intermediate appellate court is not geographically segmented.

Rule 10.2.1 regulates, in a somewhat complex way, the manner in which case names appear in citations. Although the rule is not simple, the Bluebook explanation of it is straightforward.

The subsequent history of a decision is set out according to rule 10.7. The subsequent history includes only the result of appeals from the decision cited to. (The prior history is cited to only in the circumstances described in the second paragraph of rule 10.7.) Where there is a subsequent history — and there often is not — the years of both lower and appellate decisions are included if they are different (as they were in *Onofre*). If both decisions were made in the same year, that year is listed only at the end of the citation and not elsewhere. Rule 10.7.2 governs the situation where the case name changed during the appeal.

§13.2.2 Citation to Statutes

Aside from the signal and any explanatory parenthetical, a citation to a statute currently in force has four components:

1. the *name* of the statute as it was originally enacted, if the statute is still known by that name;
2. the *section* being cited to, as *originally numbered* when enacted — if the statute is still known by its enacted name;
3. a reference to the *current codification,* providing title, article, chapter, and section numbers, to the extent required by rule 12.3 and using information provided in the Bluebook tables; and
4. the *date* (and supplement, if any), as determined under rule 12.3.1.

For example, this citation

    Wilderness Act, § 2(b), 16 U.S.C. § 1131(b) (1982).

is made up of the following parts:

1. statute name   Wilderness Act

2. section in   § 2(b)
   original
   enactment

3. current   16 U.S.C. § 1131(b)
   codification

4. date   (1982)

Generally speaking, the third component is the most important; the rest of the citation is built around it.

Most statutes are no longer known by the names under which they were originally enacted. Sometimes, that is because the statute has been recodified so many times that its enacted name has been forgotten. Just as often, the statute was a routine enactment in the first place and never had a name, or at least not one worth remembering. Where the section being cited to in the code is thus no longer identified with the session law in which it was originally enacted, the citation consists only of the third and fourth components:

    18 U.S.C. § 4 (1982).

In some instances, additional material is required; the last paragraph of rule 12.1 contains an outline of the rules governing those situations. As with cases, any signal and explanatory parenthetical appear, respectively, at the beginning and end of the citation. Forms for textual references to statutes are suggested in rule 4.3(b).

Rules 3.4 and 6.2(b) regulate citation to specific sections of a statute. Rules 12.2 and 12.4 exhaustively explain the differences between citations to codifications and citations to session laws, as well as the uses of each. Rule 12.2.1 governs citation to statutes no longer in force, and rule

12.2.1(c) describes how to cite both a statute and its amendments where they are not published in the same place.

Under rules 3.4 and 6.2(b), a section symbol ("§") is used in long- and short-form citations and sometimes in textual references; "section" is used in textual references if "§" would look awkward; "Section" is used at the beginning of textual sentences; "sec." is used only in very specialized circumstances; and "sect." is never used. Readers will expect to see the "§" symbol even if your typewriter has no such key.[1]

§13.3 Rules Governing All Citations

Authority can be referred to in three different ways: a full citation ("*Terry v. Ohio*, 392 U.S. 1 (1968)"), a short-form citation ("*Id.* at 14"), or a textual reference ("In *Terry*, the Supreme Court ruled . . . .").

A full citation should be used whenever you first mention an authority and wherever clarity would be promoted by communicating all the information found in a full citation. Generally, the worst place for a full citation is near the beginning of a sentence:

> In *Curley v. United States*, 160 F.2d 229, 233-34 (1947), the D.C. Circuit held that a trial judge should grant a motion for a directed verdict of acquittal where the evidence would necessarily cause reasonable jurors to entertain a reasonable doubt about the defendant's guilt.

Here you have to climb over the citation just to find out what the rest of the sentence is about. Either of the following would be better:

state the rule for which the authority stands and then follow with a citation	A trial judge should grant a motion for a directed verdict of acquittal where the evidence would necessarily cause reasonable jurors to entertain a reasonable doubt about the defendant's guilt. *Curley v. United States*, 160 F.2d 229, 233-34 (D.C. Cir. 1947).
if the source of the authority should be emphasized, it	The D.C. Circuit has held that a trial judge should grant a motion for a directed verdict of acquittal where the evidence would necessarily cause reasonable jurors to entertain a reasonable doubt

§13.2 1. You can solve this problem in either of two ways. The first is to type a lowercase *s* and then type another *s* about a third of a line directly above the first, so that the upper loop of the first interlocks with the lower loop of the second. (This is approximately how the symbol was created in the first place.) The other solution is to leave space while typing so that you can add the "§" in pen while proofreading.

can be re-ferred to in the sentence preceding the citation	about the defendant's guilt. *Curley v. United States,* 160 F.2d 229, 233-34 (1947).

Full citations to cases (rule 10) and statutes (rule 12) have been explained in the preceding pages. The Bluebook has elaborate rules in its specific part governing full citations to every other kind of authority (rules 11 and 13 through 19).

Short-form citations, governed by Bluebook rule 4, may be used at any time after authority has been introduced with a complete citation, except where a short form would cause confusion. Confusion would occur, for example, if a short-form citation were to appear many pages after the full citation.

Beginners often encounter two problems with short-form citations. One arises from the once permitted but now prohibited practice of using "*supra*" with primary authority (see rule 4.2). Since so much previously published material follows the old rule, the second sentence of rule 4.2 is sometimes overlooked by students.

The other problem is that rules 4.1 and 4.3 are often misunderstood. Taken together, rules 4.1 and 4.3 amount to the following for citation of cases in briefs and legal memoranda: short-form citations to cases include the name of the first party only, or, if the first party is a frequent litigant— such as "United States," "California," or "State"—the name of the second party instead. If the citation should refer to a specific page in the decision, the following information is added: volume number, name of reporter, and the page referred to (the last preceded by "at"). The first page number of the decision does not appear in a short-form citation. In this example, both official and unofficial reporters are cited to:

> *Beshada,* 90 N.J. at 200, 447 A.2d at 544.

Just to show you what is missing in a short-form cite, the following would be the corresponding full citation:

> *Beshada v. Johns-Manville Products Corp.,* 90 N.J. 191, 200, 447 A.2d 539, 544 (1982).

If the immediately preceding citation is to the same case, "*Id.*" should be used in a short-form cite instead of the name of the first party, even if the preceding citation is also in short form. Be careful to "[i]ndicate any particular" (rule 4.1) in which the second citation is meant to differ from the first. Thus, where "*Id.* at 414" is followed by "*Id.,*" the reader has in both instances been referred to page 414. Where "*Id.*" is used and a page number inside the case is to be indicated, the name and volume number of the official reporter are omitted, but that is not true where a party's name is used. Thus,

> *Id.* at 200, 447 A.2d at 544.

but

> *Beshada,* 90 N.J. at 200, 447 A.2d at 544.

There is no logical reason for the distinction, but it is clearly made in the examples for rules 4.1 and 4.3.

A textual reference is the mention of authority in text without the formalities of either a long- or short-form Bluebook citation. There are two textual references in the following sentence, one to a case and the other to a statute:

> In *Sanders,* the Supreme Court held that section 10 of the Administrative Procedure Act does not provide . . . .

A textual reference is not the integration of a Bluebook citation into a sentence. The following includes a full citation and no textual reference:

> Since 5 U.S.C. §§ 701-706 (1982) does not so provide, jurisdiction depends instead on . . . .

A textual reference, if written unambiguously, is an appropriate device where discussing authority previously cited in full. But many students do not realize that because, although some Bluebook rules, such as 4.3(b) and 6.2(b), are based on the use of textual references, no rule overtly regulates them.

Citations, whether full or short form, are arranged in citation sentences and clauses according to rule 2.1. Where an authority supports an entire sentence of your text, you must put the citation in a citation sentence:

> A defamation defendant enjoys an absolute privilege for expressions of mere opinion. *Gertz v. Robert Welsh, Inc.,* 418 U.S. 323 (1974).

On the other hand, where an authority supports only part of a sentence, the citation is interpolated into the textual sentence as a citation clause:

> A defamation defendant enjoys an absolute privilege for expressions of mere opinion, *Gertz v. Robert Welch, Inc.,* 418 U.S. 323, 339-40 (1974), and it is a question of law, to be determined by the court and not the jury, whether a statement at issue is one of fact or of opinion, *Information Control Corp. v. Genesis One Computer Corp.,* 611 F.2d 781, 783 (9th Cir. 1980).

This is a densely packed sentence, full of citation clutter, but it is one that many lawyers would write. You probably found it a bit hard to climb over the

Gertz cite so you could get to the rest of the sentence. The following is a little better:

> A defamation defendant enjoys an absolute privilege for expressions of mere opinion. *Gertz v. Robert Welch, Inc.*, 418 U.S. 323, 339-40 (1974). And it is a question of law, to be determined by the court and not the jury, whether a statement at issue is one of fact or of opinion. *Information Control Corp. v. Genesis One Computer Corp.*, 611 F.2d 781, 783 (9th Cir. 1980).

Where several authorities are cited for the same point, the order in which they appear in citation sentences and clauses is governed by rule 2.4.

Depending in part on whether you are doing practical or academic writing, your purpose in citing an authority could be communicated either through your own discussion of the authority or through signals (rules 2.2 and 2.3) at the beginning of the citation. Although signals are essential to the massive compression in law review footnotes and in other kinds of academic writing, they cannot communicate the type of precise information needed by the reader of a brief or memorandum. In those documents, your purpose must be communicated through your own explanations of the authorities. Thus, although the Bluebook has much to say about signals, the only signal that should appear frequently in practical writing is the invisible one: under rule 2.2(a), the *absence* of a signal at the beginning of a citation is itself a signal telling the reader that the authority "(i) states the proposition, (ii) identifies the source of a quotation, or (iii) identifies an authority referred to in text."

Rule 3 governs citation to pages, sections, volumes, and other subdivisions of an authority. Rule 3.3 explains how to direct a reader to a specific page in an authority in what is called a "pinpoint cite" or a "jump cite." But rule 3.3 does not tell you when that must be done. A quotation *must* be cited to a specific page. Where you refer to only part of a long opinion—even without quoting—a reader is entitled to know the pages you have in mind. "Long" means four pages or more in a West reporter or the equivalent amount of text in another publication.

Three provisions of Rule 6 (abbreviations and symbols) might seem perplexing in the beginning. First, under rule 6.1(a), no space appears between initials or between initials and numbers, although a space must appear between "longer abbreviations" and anything else. Thus: "S.W.2d," but "Cal. 3d" and "F. Supp." Second, under rule 6.1(b), where an abbreviation is formed by deleting part of the middle of a word and leaving part of the beginning and end, an apostrophe is inserted where the deletion was made. "Aff'd" and "Dep't" are correct, but "affd." and "Dept." are not. Finally, examples throughout the Bluebook use "2d" and "3d"—and *not* "2nd" and "3rd."

There are two kinds of parentheticals in legal citations. The first is an integral part of the citation and provides required information, such as the court and year for a case (Bluebook rules 10.4 and 10.5), the code year for a statute (rule 12.3.1), the edition and publication year for a book (rule 15.4), and any notation about alterations in the quotation (rule 5.2).

The second kind is an explanatory parenthetical that provides information that could be expressed in the writer's text but for economy might instead be compressed into the citation. (See rules 10.6 for cases and 12.7 for statutes.) Some of this information is a technical comment on the authority and is usually better placed in the citation unless you want it emphasized in the text:

in citation: *Carey v. Population Services Int'l,* 431 U.S. 678, 691-99 (1977) (plurality opinion).

emphasized in text: Although a majority of seven justices struck down that portion of the statute which prohibited distribution of nonprescription contraceptives to persons under the age of 16, only four justices supported the rationale now urged in this court. *See Carey v. Population Services Int'l,* 431 U.S. 678, 691-99, 702-03, 707-08, 713-16 (1977).

You will run into trouble, however, if you go overboard trying to express the *substance* of an authority in explanatory parentheticals:

Carey v. Population Services Int'l, 431 U.S. 678, 691-99 (1977) (state statute prohibiting distribution of nonprescription contraceptives to persons under 16 years old is unconstitutional because sexual activity may not be constitutionally deterred by increasing its hazards).

Not only is the explanatory parenthetical here awkward and hard to read, but it oversimplifies and inevitably misrepresents the material in order to pack it into parenthetical form.

If the material is complicated and important to the issue, explain it in text. Use an explanatory parenthetical only for information that is simple and not an important part of your discussion or argument. And resist the temptation to use explanatory parentheticals to avoid the hard work of explaining complicated and important authority.

§13.4 *Bluebook Rules on Quotation Format*

Beginners have many more problems with quotations than they think they will. This section explains the complex Bluebook rules on quotation format. Section 13.5 explains the additional faults of over-quoting, unnecessarily long quotations, quoting out of context, failing to place quotation marks around and give credit to the words of others, inaccurate quotations, sloppy placement of quotation marks, and quoting from headnotes.

Bluebook rule 5 governs the format of quotations. The provisions on quotation alterations and omissions (rules 5.2 and 5.3) are not as clearly set out in the Bluebook as they might be. These are the most essential requirements:

You must use brackets to enclose additions and substitutions that you place inside quotation marks, including the transformation of a lowercase letter into a capital or vice versa (rule 5.2). Parentheses and brackets convey different messages, and one cannot substitute for the other. If your typewriter will not make brackets, leave space and pen them in while proofreading.

If you incorporate a quote with capitalized words into a sentence of your own, the capital letter must be reduced to a lowercase letter unless the capital denotes a proper name. For example:

wrong: The court *held* "*Un*conscionability includes an absence of meaningful choice."

wrong: The court *held,* "*Un*conscionability includes an absence of meaningful choice." [1]

right: The court *held that* "*[u]n*conscionability includes an absence of meaningful choice."

If you omit citations from a quote, or if you add or delete italics or underlining, you must express that in a parenthetical following the citation (rule 5.2). The following is an example in the correct format:

In order to obtain the names of a defamation defendant's confidential sources, a plaintiff must prove that he or she has "*independently* attempted to obtain the information elsewhere and has been unsuccessful." *Silkwood v. Kerr-McGee Corp.,* 563 F.2d 433, 438 (10th Cir. 1977) (emphasis supplied).

Under rule 5.3, if you delete words (other than a citation) from a quote, you must indicate that by an ellipsis (". . .").[2] There are two exceptions. First, where you incorporate a quotation into a sentence of your own composition—as in the unconscionability and *Silkwood* examples above—do not place an ellipsis at the beginning or the end of the quotation. The incorporation itself suggests the possibility that something might have been omitted. Second, do not place an ellipsis at the beginning of a quotation, even if you intend the quote to stand on its own as a complete sentence. If the quote is not incorporated into a sentence you have written and if the first

---

§13.4   1. This form works for dialogue in a novel, but not when analyzing the words of a court.

2. When the final words of a sentence are omitted, the sentence ends with *four* periods—three for the ellipsis and one to stop the sentence (rule 5.3(iii)).

letter of the quote was not capitalized in the original, capitalize that letter and place it in brackets to indicate an alteration.

A quotation of 50 words or more belongs in a single-spaced, indented quotation block (rule 5.1). The citation for such a quotation goes at the beginning of the next line of the writer's own text, not at the end of the quotation block (rule 5.1(a)), and quotation marks are not used to set off block quotes because the indentation alone will do that. The following is wrong on both counts:

> Although in *Roth* the Supreme Court held that a government could, without satisfying the traditional clear-and-present-danger test, restrict public distribution of obscene material, it came to the opposite conclusion when faced with a statute that punished private possession of obscene materials in one's own home:
>
> > "It is true that in *Roth* this Court rejected the necessity of proving that exposure to obscene material would create a clear and present danger of antisocial conduct or would probably induce its recipients to such conduct. . . . But that case dealt with public distribution of obscene materials and such distribution is subject to different objections. For example, there is always the danger that obscene material might fall into the hands of children . . . or that it might intrude upon the sensibilities or privacy of the general public." *Stanley v. Georgia*, 394 U.S. 557, 567 (1969).
>
> A number of the Court's later right-to-privacy rulings have been based in part on *Stanley*.

The block quote should not begin and end with quotation marks, and the citation to *Stanley* should be in the writer's text and not in the block:

> . . . there is always the danger that obscene material might . . . intrude upon the sensibilities or privacy of the general public.

Stanley v. Georgia, 394 U.S. 557, 567 (1969). A number of the Court's later right-to-privacy rulings have been based in part on *Stanley*.

But, more fundamentally, this big block quotation should not exist in the first place because it is so bulky that most readers will ignore it. See question 13-A in §13.5.

§13.5 How to Scrutinize Your Writing for Effective Use of Quotations

During rewriting, ask yourself the following questions:[1]

---

§13.5 1. Your teacher may mark your work in part by referring to some of these questions by the number-letter codes used here.

13-A Have you edited quotations down to the essential words? The block quotation from *Stanley* on the preceding page would have been much more readable if the writer had edited it down to its essence and incorporated it into the writer's own text:

> Although in *Roth* the Supreme Court held that a government could, without satisfying the traditional clear-and-present-danger test, restrict public distribution of obscene material, it came to the opposite conclusion when faced with a statute that punished private possession of obscene materials in one's own home. In *Stanley v. Georgia*, 394 U.S. 557 (1969), the Court struck down such a statute and distinguished *Roth* because publicly distributed pornography "might fall into the hands of children" or "intrude upon the sensibilities or privacy of the general public." *Id.* at 567. A number of the court's later right-to-privacy rulings have been based in part on *Stanley*.

This version is shorter, flows better, and makes the writer's meaning much more clear. The essential words are still quoted and the rest are paraphrased.[2] In fact, the edited version takes the reader's attention straight to the critical words because those words are integrated into the writer's own text.

Why should a reader have to plow through a big block quotation just to find the 17 words quoted in the edited version? Your readers will refuse to do that. A busy reader tends to skim over or even skip large quotations because the perceived value of the quotation rarely seems to outweigh the tedious business of finding the juicy words hidden within it. The best you can usually hope for with a block quotation is that the reader will actually read the first sentence, skim the second, and skip the rest unless the first two sentences are gripping. (This should not seem so odd: you probably read newspaper stories the same way.) The more block quotations you use, the more quickly a reader will refuse to read any of them. And judges and supervising attorneys view large quotations as evidence of a writer's laziness: your job is to find the essential words, isolate them, and concisely paraphrase the rest. When you throw a big block quotation at a reader, you are asking the reader to do some of your work.

Generally speaking, quoted words should not appear in your work unless they fit into one of the following categories:

1. words that must be *interpreted* in order to resolve the issue;
2. words that are so closely identified with the topic under discussion that they are *inseparable* from it;
3. words that, *with remarkable economy,* put the reader in touch with the thinking of a court, legislature, or expert in the field; or

---

2. The author of the second version is not a better writer than the Supreme Court justice who wrote *Stanley*. The two simply had different purposes. The justice had the monumental task of justifying a significant decision of constitutional law, but the author of the third example was only trying to explain, as concisely as possible, the difference between *Roth* and *Stanley*.

4. words that are the most eloquent and succinct *conceivable* expression of an important idea.

Beginners are much too quick to think that words, merely because printed in a book, can satisfy the third or fourth criteria. It is that kind of awe that causes a student to write a sentence like the following:

> The court relied on "[w]ell-established jurisprudence of our sister states . . . holding that baseball is a strenuous game involving danger to . . . players . . . and that one who, with full knowledge of this danger, attends . . . and places himself in a position of danger, assumes the risks inherent in the game."[3]

The writer of this sentence did some editing, but the quoted words are really worth no more than the following:

> Relying on "[w]ell-established" precedent in other states holding baseball to be a dangerous game, the court concluded that anyone who knows of that danger and nevertheless plays baseball "assumes the risks inherent in the game."

The most convincing descriptions of precedent are almost entirely in the writer's own words, punctuated with very few and very short quotations that convey the essence of the court's approach.

Have you avoided snippet quotations? The problem here is too many quotations, rather than quotations that are too long, | 13-B | although the effect on the reader is similar. At its most extreme, snippetizing takes the form of a quote from and cite to case A, followed by a quote from and cite to case B, followed by a quote from and cite to case C, and so on, without substantial discussion of the cases or of the ideas expressed in the quotes. When reading something like this, one imagines the person who submitted it plucking bright feathers from random sources, throwing them into a heap on the page, and hoping that the result will be seen as proof of a conclusion of law. It never is. With rare exceptions, quoted words from authority are not magical incantations. If anything, strings of snippet quotations give the reader the feeling of sliding over the surface of complex ideas that the writer refuses to explain. A writer whose quotations are too long and too many is sometimes called a "cut-and-paste artist" because the product is not really writing at all. Little thought goes into it, and readers have no confidence in it because what they want is your analysis, which comes only with hard work — not scissors and glue. Quoted words belong in your writing only if they satisfy one or more of the criteria in 13-A.

---

3. Quoting from *Gaspard v. Grain Dealers Mut. Ins. Co.*, 131 So. 2d 831, 834 (La. Ct. App. 1961).

| 13-C | **Have you been careful not to quote out of context?** Readers of legal writing are professional skeptics who often verify context. "Sentences out of context rarely mean what they seem to say, and nobody in the whole world knows that better than the appellate judge. He has learned it by the torturing experience of hearing his own sentences read back to him." [4]

| 13-D | **Have you quoted and cited when using the words of others?** Whether done out of sloppiness or out of an intent to deceive, this is treated as plagiarism. One attorney was professionally disciplined because he plagiarized large portions of a thesis he submitted while enrolled in a law school's post-graduate degree program. The court held that the plagiarism constituted "conduct involving dishonesty, fraud, deceit or misrepresentation" in violation of DR 1-102(A)(4) of the Code of Professional Responsibility.[5] The court was unpersuaded by the attorney's defense that his plagiarism was unintentional, "the result of academic laziness and . . . not . . . an intentional effort to deceive his thesis examiners." [6] A disciplinary hearing board found — and the court agreed — that "it is inconceivable . . . that a person who has completed undergraduate school and law school would not know that representing extensively copied material as one's own work constitutes plagiarism." [7]

| 13-E | **Have you quoted accurately?** Reading a case, a student spots language that may be quotable. The student starts to copy it out, and — although the student does not realize it at the time — some of the words written down are not the same as those that appear in the case. But the words written down are the ones that eventually appear in the student's memorandum or brief. You will be surprised at how easily supervisors, judges, and teachers can spot this, and it usually causes them to lose some confidence in the writer. You may also be surprised at how easily you can make this sort of mistake. Although the cause might be inexcusable sloppiness, more often it is the natural tendency to recompose unconsciously in one's own style while copying. The best prevention is to proofread your notes while you still have the original source in front of you.

| 13-F | **Have you placed quotation marks exactly where they belong?** The most common problems are (1) omission of the quotation marks that close a quotation, even though the opening quotation marks are included ("Where does the quote end?" writes the teacher in the margin); (2) omission of the quotation marks that open a quotation, even though the closing marks are present ("Where does the quote begin?" writes the teacher); and (3) where there is a quote within a quote, failure to change the double quotation marks of the original to single marks.

---

4. Prettyman, *Some Observations Concerning Appellate Advocacy*, 39 Va. L. Rev. 285, 295 (1953).
   5. *In re Lamberis*, 93 Ill. 2d 222, 443 N.E.2d 549 (1982).
   6. *Id.* at 225-26, 443 N.E.2d at 550.
   7. *Id.* at 226, 443 N.E.2d at 551.

Have you been careful not to quote from a headnote? A court's opinion is limited to the text appearing in the reporter *after* the name of the judge who wrote it. The one- or two-sentence headnotes that appear between the case's name and the opinion itself are supplied by the publisher and are not written by the court. Those headnotes may be useful in research, but they are not part of the opinion and have no authoritative value, even if they resemble parts of the opinion. Moreover, the headnotes are written in a distinct style, instantly recognizable by the experienced reader. For example, a publisher's headnote might read as follows:

> That portion of award of double costs and attorney fees imposed upon counsel would be imposed upon counsel personally, even though client was responsible for pursuing litigation, where client received bad legal advice.[8]

This is typical of headnote style. Every "the," "a," and "an" has been omitted. More important, the sentence is so terse that a reader has only the barest idea of what the court might actually have written.

Compare the headnote with the heart of the passage it is meant to summarize:

> In sum, this appeal rests on a serious misstatement of state law. It is hard to imagine that a lawyer could advise a client to defy an outstanding judgment on the ground that an application for a stay had been filed but had not been granted, or that a lawyer could inform us — without a shred of authority — that in Illinois an application for a stay has the effect of a stay itself. . . . [A]n advocate must represent his client within the existing structure of the law, and not some imagined version of it. . . .
>
> Rule 11 requires counsel to study the law before representing its contents to a federal court. An empty head but a pure heart is no defense. . . . Counsel who puts the burden of study and illumination on the defendants or the court must expect to pay attorneys' fees under the Rule. . . .
>
> . . . Ordinarily we impose attorneys' fees on the party, leaving party and lawyer to settle accounts. But we do not suppose that the representations about state law were approved by [this lawyer's client] personally; . . . she has received bad legal advice. We therefore impose part of the award on counsel personally.[9]

Between the headnote and the opinion itself, the difference in style — and even substance — is unmistakable. The reader will instantly spot it, feel cheated of a direct description of the case, and think the writer lazy and unreliable.

The solution is not to quote the entire longer passage from the opinion. Instead, explain the case in your own words, quoting from the court only to the extent necessary according to the criteria set out in 13-A.

---

8. Publisher's headnote to *Thorton v. Wahl,* 787 F.2d 1151, 1152 (7th Cir. 1986).
9. *Thorton v. Wahl,* 787 F.2d 1151, 1154 (7th Cir. 1986) (text of court's opinion).

Exercise I.   The First Amendment (Quotations)

1. You are in the midst of writing a memorandum involving the right-of-assembly clause and no other part of the First Amendment, and you intend to reproduce for the reader the words to be interpreted. This is the text of the entire amendment:

> Congress shall make no law respecting an establishment of religion, or prohibiting the free exercise thereof; of abridging the freedom of speech, or of the press; or the right of the people peaceably to assemble, and to petition the Government for a redress of grievances.

Finish writing the following sentence: "The First Amendment provides . . . ."
2. Do the same for a memorandum involving the freedom-of-speech clause.

Exercise II.   The Separation of Powers (Citations and Quotations)

Correct the following passage for incorrect use of quotations and citations. Correct every error you can find, adding and subtracting to the citations as necessary. If a Bluebook rule requires a change, write the rule's number in the margin.

The constitutional doctrine of separation-of-powers precludes judicial review of prosecutorial discretion. *Pugach v. Klein,* 193 F. Supp. 630 (U.S. Dist. Ct.); *Powell v. Katzenbach,* 359 F.2d 234 (D.C.Cir. 1965), certiorari denied 384 US 906 (1965) reh. den 384 US 967 (1966); *Inmates of Attica Correctional Facility, et al. v. Rockefeller,* 477 F. 2nd 375 (U.S.Ct.App. 1973). These decisions are based on the ideas that "(t)he discretion of the Attorney General in choosing whether to prosecute or not to prosecute, or to abandon a prosecution already started, is absolute," Smith v. United States, 375 F.2d at 247, cert. denied 389 U.S. 841 (1967), and that "it is not the function of the judiciary to review the exercise of executive discretion." Newman v. U.S., 382 F.2d 479, p. 482 (U.S.Ct. App. 1967. Nevertheless, it has been clear since *Yick Woo v. Hopkins,* 118 U.S. 356, 6 S.Ct. 1064, 30 L. Ed. 220 (1886) (discriminatory enforcement violates equal protection) that prosecutorial discretion is not absolute. The United States Supreme Court has, however, spoken approvingly of plea bargaining while not taking any position on whether the separation of powers precludes judicial review.

Generally, prosecutorial discretion is not supervised by state courts. "District Attorney has broad discretion in determining when and in what manner to prosecute a suspected offender." *People v. DiFalco,* 406 N.Y.S.2d 279, 44 N.Y. 482, 377 N. E. 2nd 732. "Prosecutor is allowed broad discretion in law enforcement and is not obliged to treat two similarly situated defendants alike. *Ward v. State,* (Del. 1980) 414 A.2d 499, 500.

Consequently,

"prosecutors are not insulated against ulterior influence. . . . They are free to avoid investigating any case, and they are free to refuse to act on evidence found when they do investigate. They are never required to state findings of fact, . . . never required to follow their own precedents or to explain departures from them, and are never required to discuss publicly their policy positions." 2 DAVIS ADMINISTRATIVE LAW TREATISE 224 (1979 2d ed.)

NOTE: The passage below appears on page 224, volume 2, of Kenneth Culp Davis's *Administrative Law Treatise:*

Over nearly two centuries, both legislators and executives have generally ignored the manner in which prosecutors have exercised their discretion, and the judicial doors have been generally closed to those who want to assert that discretion has been abused. Unlike judges, prosecutors are not insulated against ulterior influence. Their discretion is unguided by statutory standards, and it is unguided by rules which the prosecutors themselves might make. They are free not to investigate in any case, and they are free to refuse to act on the evidence found when they do investigate. They are never required to state findings of fact, never required to explain decisions made on questions of law, never required to follow their own precedents or to explain departures from them, and never required to discuss publicly their policy positions. They are free, if they choose, to accept a plea of guilty in return for charging a lesser crime, no matter how easily they can prove the serious crime. They are not required to act openly, and many of their most important decisions are kept secret. The victim of a crime typically has no remedy even if he can prove that failure to prosecute is an abuse of discretion.

IV
THE SHIFT TO ARGUMENT

14 Creating Strategies and Theories

§14.1 Inside the Process of Creation

The process of creation will usually go through five stages:[1]

1. *recognition:* first, you identify a problem that you must solve, or a decision that you must make, or some other situation in which you must choose between or among alternatives;
2. *preparation:* then you analyze the problem and gather information in a fairly open-ended manner;
3. *option-generation:* you think up the largest reasonable number of potential solutions;
4. *option-evaluation:* you test potential solutions to see how well they would work; and
5. *decision:* you compare the evaluated options and choose the most effective one.

Frequently, different stages—particularly option-generation and option-evaluation—become intertwined, and at least some parts of them occur unconsciously, which led Graham Wallas to use the terms *incubation, illumination,* and *verification* instead:[2]

§14.1 1. Researchers in this field have formulated and described these stages in slightly different ways. *See, e.g.,* T. Amabile, *The Social Psychology of Creativity* 79-81 (1983); S. Arieti, *Creativity: The Magic Synthesis* 15-18 (1976); J. Dewey, *How We Think* 12-15 (1933).
2. *The Art of Thought* 80 (1926).

In the daily stream of thought these . . . stages constantly overlap each other as we explore different problems. An economist reading a Blue Book, a physiologist watching an experiment, or a business man going through his morning letters, may at the same time be "incubating" on a problem which he proposed to himself a few days ago, be accumulating knowledge in "preparation" for a second problem, and be "verifying" his conclusions on a third problem. Even in exploring the same problem, the mind may be unconsciously incubating on one aspect of it, while it is consciously employed in preparing for or verifying another aspect.[3]

You already have some experience doing this kind of thing in the structured thinking evoked by the study of authority and facts and by the making of predictive judgments. When you analyze authority or facts, you notice ambiguity or a gap (the stage of *recognition*); you read further, looking for raw information that might explain the ambiguity or help fill the gap (*preparation*); you try to think up the largest reasonable number of competing explanations (*option-generation*); you assess each option for how well it explains the ambiguity or fills the gap (*option-evaluation*); and you choose the most accurate explanation (*decision*). When you make a predictive judgment, you notice a need to know the future behavior of courts or of people (*recognition*), gather raw information relevant to the future (*preparation*), postulate the largest reasonable number of competing predictions (*option-generation*), test each prediction for its probability (*option-evaluation*), and select the most likely prediction (*decision*).

You are about to start learning yet another level of lawyerly analysis: strategizing. And the process here follows a similar pattern. When you create a strategy, you will notice a need to control a particular event (*recognition*), gather raw information about the assets available to you and the impediments you must overcome (*preparation*), think up the largest reasonable number of competing methods for controlling the event (*option-generation*), assess each method for its effectiveness (*option-evaluation*), and choose the most effective method (*decision*).

These sequences of thought all rest on habits of *disciplined curiosity*. Recognition, for example, requires the ability to spot quickly what John Dewey called a "forked-road situation . . . that is ambiguous, that presents a dilemma, that proposes alternatives"[4] — a place, in other words, where your thinking can make a difference and cause things to happen. Recognition is the opposite of passivity, which always sends you down the easier or more obvious road without considering the one less often taken. To be good at preparation, you must be able to judge relevance, to see patterns and interrelationships among ideas and facts, and to use the practical tools of lawyering (such as the library). The decisional stage naturally requires the assertiveness necessary to make a choice for which you will be answerable professionally.

But option-generation and option-evaluation pose the greatest challenges for students, in part because they require contrary skills. To think up

3. *Id.* at 81-82.
4. *How We Think* 15 (1933).

the largest number of reasonable alternatives for option-generation—in other words, to look below the surface of the facts and law for deeper possibilities and meaning—you must be able to do what psychologists call "shifting perceptual set" or what Robert Heidt has called "recasting":[5]

Mr. Projectionist, roll the film please:

Fade In

> *Five people walk into an open and uncrowded public park in the afternoon. One sets a stepstool on a pathway, ascends the stepstool, and begins to criticize U.S. foreign policy and to urge listeners to resist that policy. A small crowd gathers. Shouts hostile to the person on the stepstool emerge from the crowd. Shouts hostile to those shouts emerge from others in the crowd. A policeman on the scene arrests the person on the stepstool, directs her to a police car, and drives her away.*

Dissolve.

What did we just see? How do we describe what the person on the stepstool did?

To her attorney, she merely exercised her constitutionally protected right to free speech. All she did was talk. She didn't hit, touch, or threaten. . . . If any crimes or civil violations occurred, they were the illegal arrest committed by the police who should have protected, rather than arrested her, and the assaults and emotional distress torts committed by anyone in the crowd who threatened or outrageously insulted her.

To the prosecutors, she breached the peace, incited to riot, and engaged in disorderly conduct. . . . She may also have obstructed a public right of way, committed a public nuisance, and participated in an unlawful assembly. Because she came in a group, she probably also violated the separate laws against conspiring to commit these offenses. . . .

A passerby accidentally injured when the crowd dispersed, or when the crowd's presence blocked the pathway, would describe what she did differently. To the passerby, she negligently caused physical injury. After all, by foreseeably gathering the crowd, she increased the risk that the passerby would suffer the injury he did. Likewise, a listener intentionally injured by a member of the crowd might describe her conduct as negligent use of language which foreseeably angered the one who struck him. . . . A listener indirectly referred to and criticized by her remarks might describe her behavior as slander or, failing that, intentional infliction of emotional distress.

These examples barely scratch the surface of the possible descriptions of what the woman in the park did. If she was profane, she may be guilty of obscenity. If she called for a strike, she may have committed an unfair labor practice. If she called for a boycott, she may have conspired to restrain trade. If she spoke loudly, she may have violated a noise ordinance. If she or her friends handed out leaflets, we may describe what she did as littering. . . . Had this not been a largely unregulated public park, she might also have violated a host of permit laws as well as other laws regulating the time, place and manner of such expression.

5. *Recasting Behavior: An Essay for Beginning Law Students,* 49 U. Pitt. L. Rev. 1065 (1988).

[Because we are still in option-generation, and have not yet gotten to the stage of option-evaluation, the goal for the moment] is not to discuss whether these various claims would necessarily succeed but to awaken you to the many different ways a lawyer can recast, that is, describe, phenomena. Our language and our law are wonderfully rich for this purpose. As an aspiring lawyer, you want to cultivate your capacity to recast phenomena in as many different ways as possible. You cannot rely on your client for this. It is part of your job. The client may bring you the phenomena. The client may, in effect, show you the film excerpt we've just seen. But it is up to you, the lawyer, to conceive the different recastings, the different descriptions of phenomena, the different stories that can be told. . . .[6]

The biggest impediment to this kind of thinking is "the false assumption that phenomena are phenomena, facts are facts, and that they can be, or ought to be, described in just a couple of ways." [7] That assumption will lock you into the first credible idea that comes into your mind, and it will blind you to all the other possibilities. Among other things, good option-generation means refusing to guess, assume, or be satisfied with appearances.

Option-generation depends on an uninhibited flow of association, during which judgment is suspended and ideas that later evaluation might show to be sound arrive mixed together with ideas that eventually turn out to be wrong or even silly. The poet Schiller wrote that option-generation is meager

if the intellect examines too closely the ideas already pouring in, as it were, at the gates. Regarded in isolation, an idea may be insignificant, and venturesome in the extreme, but it may acquire importance from an idea which follows it; perhaps, in a certain collation with other ideas, which may seem equally absurd, it may be capable of furnishing a very serviceable link. The intellect cannot judge all these ideas unless it can retain them until [all can be seen together. When many alternatives are being collected,] the intellect has withdrawn its watchers from the gates, and the ideas rush in pell-mell, and only then does it review and inspect the multitude. [People who are ineffective at option-generation] reject too soon. . . .[8]

The key is to avoid premature judgment, to defer evaluation until after you have developed an array of alternatives. Your ability to come up with the widest range of possibilities can be constricted by snap evaluation of ideas as soon as they are expressed, by any verbal aggression you might have, by other people's verbal aggression, by a desire to conform, or by what Kenney Hegland calls the "fear of making a fool of yourself." [9] Lon Fuller, the great contracts scholar, wrote that option-generation does not easily happen

---

6. *Id.* at 1065-67.

7. *Id.* at 1067-68.

8. Quoted at Stein, *Creativity as Intra- and Inter-Personal Process,* in *The Creative Encounter* 21-22 (Holsinger, Jordan & Levenson eds. 1971). Wallas wrote that "the final 'flash,' or 'click' . . . is the culmination of a successful train of association, which may have lasted for an appreciable time, and which has probably been preceded by a series of tentative and unsuccessful trains." G. Wallas, *The Art of Thought* 93-105 (1926).

9. *Trial and Practice Skills* 181 (1978).

when you ask yourself "anxiously at every turn that most inhibitive of questions, *What will other people think?*'" [10]

Paradoxically, option-evaluation requires the very qualities that would impoverish option-generation: a ruthless skepticism, a pragmatic sense of the realistic, a precise ability to calculate risk, and a fear that an idea might truly be foolish. The trick is to turn those qualities off while thinking up options and then to turn them back on once you have assembled a full range of options from which to choose. During option-generation, you will do best if you think with an artist's intellectual freedom and tolerance for chaos, but during option-evaluation you must become a completely different kind of person, viewing things with the cold-blooded realism of a person who must take responsibility for success or failure. The critical thinking on which option-evaluation depends is taught aggressively throughout the law school curriculum. But because option-generation and option-evaluation depend on contrary qualities, you must be careful not to let that critical skepticism —of which we teach so much—overwhelm your ability to imagine the widest range of possibilities.

Recognition, preparation, and decision can pose certain problems for beginners, but you will have—and are probably already having—more difficulty with option-generation and option-evaluation. Only rarely does a person come to law school already skilled at both generation and evaluation. Most law students need substantial improvement in both, although— because those two stages require such contrary states of mind—you might start off with more ability at one than the other. But there are many effective ways of generating and evaluating options. As you become a professional, you will need to develop styles of generating and styles of evaluating that best make use of the person you are, taking advantage of your strengths while controlling your weaknesses.

§14.2   Strategic Thinking

There are 55 reasons why I shouldn't have pitched him, but 56 why I should.

> —*Casey Stengel, New York Yankees manager, on why he started Ed Lopat in the final game of the 1952 World Series*

My main objection to Lou was that he managed by hunch and desperation. You ask Casey Stengel why he made a certain move and he will tell you about a roommate he had in 1919 who demonstrated some principle Casey was now putting into effect. You ask Lou and he will say, 'The way we're going, we had to do *something*.' If there is a better formula for making a bad situation worse, I have never heard it.

> —*Bill Veeck, owner of the Cleveland Indians, on why he wanted to fire manager Lou Boudreau and hire Casey Stengel in 1946*

10. *On Teaching Law*, 3 Stan. L. Rev. 43 (1950) (emphasis in original).

A strategy is a plan for causing a particular result. The desired result is called a goal.

In litigation and in war, the process of strategizing is pretty much the same. The strategist makes a complete list of all the things that must be done in order to win. These are immediate goals, the ultimate goal being final victory itself. Then, for each immediate goal, the strategist makes another list of the various available strategic options. After weighing the predicted effectiveness and riskiness of each option, the strategist selects the best one for each immediate goal and then organizes them into the sequence of actions most likely to lead to the ultimate goal. Finally, the strategist executes this web of interlocking strategies. Lawyers and generals are relied on for their skill at controlling events through strategies systematically built in this way.

In some situations, like a baseball game, the events the strategist is trying to control are so spontaneous that only part of the strategizing can be thought out beforehand; the rest must be done as events unfold. Other types of conflict, such as a lawsuit, are so drawn out that only generalized strategies can be developed at the beginning, with the understanding that they will become more detailed in light of events to come. In both situations, however, a good strategist anticipates events in advance and prepares contingency strategies long before they are needed.

It will be a while, though, before you are assigned tasks that require either spontaneous strategizing or grand strategy. For the moment, let us focus on the kind of strategic thinking that would go into a written argument that a lawyer plans to submit to a court in the form of an appellate brief or a memorandum in support of or in opposition to a motion. There your goal is to cause a specific result in the reader's mind, and *all* the strategizing and execution occurs long before the reader begins to read. That means, first, that you can be expected to have fully strategized every aspect of the document before submitting it, and, second, that you should be able to explain the entire strategic sequence, its origin, and its execution to a teacher and, later in your career, to a supervisor or colleague.

In postmortems of your work, you should expect that a teacher or supervisor may ask a litany of questions about strategy:

What was your goal?

What was your strategy?

What other options did you consider and reject?

For each rejected option, why was it inferior to the strategy you did choose?

What led you to believe that the selected option would in fact achieve the ultimate goal?

Did you do all the things necessary to execute the strategy you chose?

Did you do anything that impeded that strategy?

If the goal was not achieved, why not?

Supervisors and teachers ask these questions because a lawyer's task is *to cause desired things to happen.* When you are critiqued on writing in which you have attempted to persuade, you should be prepared to answer questions like these in order to identify *exactly* how you succeeded — or did not succeed — in causing the desired result. "It seemed like a good idea at the time" and similar answers are not explanations of strategic thinking. The supervisor or teacher will be trying to make sure that your planning is free of the kinds of thought that can prevent good strategy, such as overlooking opportunities to influence events, relying on unrealistic assumptions, and engaging in wishful thinking and other forms of self-deception.

The first sophisticated strategic judgment that you will have to make in legal work is the development of a theory that will persuade a court to rule in your client's favor.

§14.3 Theories: Of the Case, of the Motion, of the Appeal

To make their decisions, judges need more than raw information about the law. They need a melding of law and fact into a concept — or a small number of related concepts — on which the decision can be based. Think back to the last major decision you had to make — perhaps the choice of a career, the selection of a law school, a decision about where to live, or the purchase of a car or an appliance. If your decision-making was conscious and deliberative — as judges hope their decisions are — you can probably recall an idea — or a small number of related ideas — that caused you to choose one career over another, one law school over another, and so forth. And if your decision-making was conscious and deliberative, there was probably a moment when you first identified and appreciated this idea (or small group of ideas). At that moment, you probably also realized that one of the alternatives had become inevitable. Some people who specialize in sales work call this moment the "selling point" because the decision to buy becomes inevitable once the selling idea is fully appreciated by the buyer.

Persuading is selling, and judges have accurately been described as "professional buyers of ideas." [1] Judges have their selling points, and both lawyers and judges use the word *theory* to refer to the collection of ideas that, in a given case, a lawyer offers for purchase. At trial, each lawyer propounds a *theory of the case.* Where the court is to decide a motion or an appeal, the phrases *theory of the motion* or *theory of the appeal* might be used instead. Each lawyer proposes a theory, and the court chooses between them, or — if neither theory is satisfactory — the court may fashion one of its own, often causing unhappiness to both sides.

A theory is a view of the facts and law — intertwined together — that can justify a decision in the client's favor. If Welty is prosecuted for burglarizing

§14.3 1. Peck, *Strategy of the Brief,* Litigation, Winter 1984, at 26, 27.

Lutz's apartment,[2] for example, the prosecution's theory of common law burglary might be that Lutz's actions did not imply permission to break the threshold and enter the apartment, while Welty's actions show beyond a reasonable doubt that when she stepped into the apartment, she had already formed an intent to assault Lutz.[3] To prove the element of a breaking, for example, the prosecutor might point to four facts: (1) Lutz opened the door only six inches, (2) he never told Welty she could enter, (3) his only reason for stepping away from the door was to turn down the volume on his stereo so that he could hear what Welty was already saying while she was outside the apartment, and (4) as soon as Lutz discovered that Welty had entered the apartment, he ordered her to leave. To prove the element of "intent to commit a felony therein," the prosecutor might focus—in a way you have already explored in Chapter 12—on Welty's rage at the time she entered the apartment.

On the other hand, Welty's attorney's theory might be that the prosecution's evidence itself necessarily creates reasonable doubt about whether she broke through a threshold to get into Lutz's apartment and about whether, at the instant she walked through the door, she intended to strike him. To substantiate this theory, Welty's attorney might argue that there was nothing to break once the door was open; that Lutz's actions could reasonably have been understood by Welty to have implied permission to enter and continue the conversation inside the apartment; and that Welty's actions before she was ordered to leave are consistent with an innocent intent to persuade Lutz to behave in a more neighborly fashion. If believed, this theory should cause an acquittal on the charge of burglary.[4]

Although both theories address the facts in terms of the law of burglary and of the prosecution's burden of persuasion, one theory favors the prosecution and the other favors the defendant. You might see something of how hard adjudicating is by putting yourself in the position of the judge and jury in this case, and by considering the consequences if you make a mistake: either an innocent person could be punished or a person could go free despite evidence of guilt beyond a reasonable doubt.[5] You might also understand some of the difficulties of advocacy by putting yourself in the

2. See pages 205 and 207.

3. The other elements of common law burglary would not be hard to prove: Welty did, in the nighttime, enter the dwelling of another. See §§6.3-6.4.

4. For the separate charge of assault, the lawyer might have to ask some questions to develop a further theory: for example, if Welty struck Lutz because she thought he had become so angry that he might strike her, she might—to the charge of assault (but not burglary)—argue self-defense.

5. Notice that the law does not necessarily consider it wrong for a guilty person to go free. For centuries under the common law, the rule has been that a guilty person *must* be left unpunished if the prosecution cannot prove guilt beyond a reasonable doubt. That is because our culture considers it far more horrible to punish the innocent than to free the guilty, and our law therefore imposes on the prosecution a burden of persuasion heavy enough to create confidence that innocent people are not being punished. Thus, a prosecution theory must do more than show the likelihood of guilt: if it does not also exclude every reasonable explanation of innocence, the prosecution will have ignored its own burden of persuasion. And a criminal defense theory is not necessarily a theory that the defendant is innocent: if the evidence of guilt is clear but not overwhelming, the defense theory would have to be that the evidence does not exclude every reasonable possibility of innocence.

position of each of the lawyers and asking yourself how you would go about persuading the decision-makers to adopt your theory *and to reject the other one,* both on the facts and on the law.

A theory's success is measured by whether it is adopted by the adjudicator. A theory is worth arguing if it stands a substantial chance of being adopted by a fair-minded and reasonable person who must make the adjudicator's decision. George Vetter[6] has formulated six "bench marks" through which the marketability of a theory can be predicted:

> First, the theory must have a firm foundation in strong facts and the fair inferences to be drawn from the facts.

And it must also have a firm foundation in law. A foundation can be firm even though the law is not yet settled through mandatory authority: what is needed is the likelihood that the law will, in the end, favor the theory.

> Second, if possible, the theory should be built around the so-called "high cards" of litigation, incontestable or virtually incontestable facts, such as self-certifying documents, patently undoctored pictures, admissions against interest, the testimony of independent witnesses, clear scientific facts, and so on.

You use the "high cards" as a foundation because that is exactly what the adjudicator—whether judge or jury—will do: in court, ambiguous evidence and debatable inferences are usually resolved in whatever way is most consistent with the evidence that is incontrovertible. When the time for decision arrives, the adjudicator's natural tendency is to say, "Let's start with what we *do* know."

> Third, and as a corollary of the second bench mark, the theory should not be inconsistent with, or fly in the face of, incontestable facts.
> Fourth, the theory should explain away in a plausible manner as many unfavorable facts as it can. . . .
> Fifth, the theory should be down to earth and have a common-sense appeal. . . .

A theory has a commonsense appeal if its internal logic is consistent, if it is plausible and relatively simple, if its explanations are consistent with the adjudicator's experiences in life, and if it reflects the adjudicator's values and morality and the values and morality of the community to which the adjudicator feels answerable.

> Sixth, the theory cannot be based on wishful thinking about any phase of the case.

A judge looks for reliability in a theory, in its supporting arguments, and in the lawyer who is trying to sell the whole package. Like any other kind of

---

6. *Successful Civil Litigation* 30-31 (1977).

consumer, a judge buys only when struck with a feeling of confidence that the purchase will turn out well, without causing injustice or embarrassment on appeal or before the public. Like most people who have had much opportunity to observe human nature, judges become fairly astute at surmising how various kinds of people behave under given circumstances. And like most people with substantial responsibilities, judges see the world as a place that works only when people are reasonable, rather than extreme, and judges feel safer when they can make narrow decisions, rather than earth-shaking ones, because earth-shaking decisions provide more ample room for error. Thus, the most easily sold theories are those that are based on reasonable and believable interpretations of the evidence and the authorities; that would lead to reasonable results; that do not ask a judge to believe that people have behaved in improbable ways; and that do not ask the judge to change the law more than absolutely necessary.

A theory that sells in an appellate court necessarily has a flavor different from one that sells easily in a trial court. That is because trial judges and appellate judges do not see the world in precisely the same way. A trial court is a place of routine, and trial judges want to make decisions the way they are usually made and not in ways that would greatly disturb the world. Although trial judges sometimes try to avoid the full impact of appellate authority, the rulings of the courts to which a trial judge's decision could be appealed are like orders from a superior, and the trial judge needs and wants to know, through those rulings, what the supervising courts expect. By contrast, appellate judges are conscious of their responsibility to see the bigger picture and to keep the law fair and reasonable, even if that requires modifying the common law now and then to fit changes in society. Judicial circumspection and the doctrine of stare decisis keep these changes in direction to a minimum, however, and appellate courts generally presume the decision below to be correct, reversing only if deeply troubled by what happened in the lower court.

Exercise I. Goslin's House

Read the persuasive memorandum in Appendix D. What theory did Goslin's attorney choose? Write it out in one — or at most two — sentences. Can you think of any other theories that Goslin's attorney could have considered and rejected? Do you believe that the best theory was used? Why or why not?

§14.4 Designing a Theory

Before the memorandum in Appendix D was written, Goslin undoubtedly showed his lawyer a deed that, on its surface, seemed to give the nephew every right to have Goslin and his belongings removed. A lawyer who lacks the skill of theory design might say to such a client something like this: "Well, Mr. Goslin, you made a mistake. In future, don't give a deed without securing some rights for yourself, either by making a collateral contract or by taking payment for your equity. In the meantime, I think you'll have to move out." Another—and better—lawyer might look under the surface for possibilities: at the time of the deed, did Goslin believe he was giving up all his property rights? Did he think he was going to continue to live in the house? Had the nephew said or done anything that could show that the nephew thought Goslin was making a gift or was going to move out? Is there anything in the history of this uncle and this nephew on which some sort of reliance theory might be based? Since people do not tend to negotiate with their relatives at arm's-length or with written contracts, and since people turn on each other even in family relationships, might some part of the law go so far as to enforce understandings between relatives, even if those understandings have never been spoken or written down? Notice the technique: first, open doors to factual possibilities; then discover how the law treats those possibilities and find out whether there is evidence to prove them.

Unlike Athena, a theory does not spring forth in final form from the forehead of an attorney Zeus. Instead, a germ first occurs and then grows as new information is learned and more law researched. Although research guides the growth of the theory, the theory also guides the course of the research, each filling in the gaps of the other. Sometimes, this is rapid progress; at other times, it may be painfully slow. George Vetter[1] has described a sequence of steps in the development of a theory of the case:

> First, isolate the legal and factual issues in the case. Be sure about the nodes on which the case will turn. . . .
> Next, take an objective look at the proof pro and con on these issues.
> Third, pin-point the critical areas. This means assessing and weighing the results of the analysis on the first two points. . . . At this stage, you must begin to think about how to exploit your strong points and your opponent's weak points, and how to shore up your weak points and attack your opponent's strong points.

So far, you have prepared and you have begun to generate options. Vetter's fourth step is a transition between option-generation and option-evaluation.

> Fourth, come up with a tentative theory and check it against the . . . bench marks. If it falls way below the marks, scrap it. If it partially passes muster, set about strengthening it. . . .

The best way to make an objective assessment is to pretend to be the adjudicator and to ask yourself how persuaded you would be by the theory you are considering. Forget that it is your own theory you are judging, and be as skeptical, impatient, and pragmatic as the typical judge can be.

§14.4 1. *Successful Civil Litigation* 32-33 (1977).

Fifth, as you strengthen and develop the theory, keep checking it against the bench marks.

Now you are moving back and forth between option-generation and option-evaluation. As evaluation reveals problems, generation is used to find solutions.

Finally, from the time you begin to develop a theory, try it out on a colleague. It is too easy to miss the forest for the trees deep in the preparation of a case.

This process of theory development is the most important — and perhaps the most satisfying — form of creativity in a litigator's work.

Exercise II.   Goslin's Nephew's House

Return to the persuasive memorandum in Appendix D, and assume that you represent the nephew. Your client tells you that he never had any intention of making a gift to his uncle of $11,500 in mortgage payments, that he never wondered why Goslin gave him the deed ("my uncle gets an idea in his head and then does it — asking him why just causes a confrontation and unpleasant words"), and that otherwise events occurred as Goslin has described them. What theories are available to the nephew? Which is most likely to persuade a court to rule against Goslin on the motion before the court? Why?

15

Argumentation Strategy

§15.1   What Judges Expect from Attorneys

You already know that in our system of litigation the lawyers — and not the judge — are responsible for framing the issues, developing the theories and arguments, and adducing the evidence. You also know that judges are busy people who must view lawyers' assertions skeptically and who must make large numbers of decisions within very limited periods of time. From that, you have undoubtedly realized that judges need complete but concise arguments that can be quickly understood.

In addition, the volume of litigation has grown so much in the past three decades that courts — both trial and appellate — are utterly dependent on written arguments submitted by attorneys. In the last century, an appellate court might listen to oral argument in a single case for hours or even days at a time, but the parties' written briefs were usually so sketchy that modern lawyers can barely recognize them as genuine. Now that situation is reversed. Many appeals today are decided without oral argument and without any other personal contact between attorneys and judges. Where there is oral argument, the common practice is to restrict each attorney to fifteen or twenty minutes. Understandably, on appeal the brief now bears most and often all of the burden of persuading the court. A similar evolution has occurred in trial courts, and it is not unusual today for a judge to complete a case without a trial, without a hearing, without an oral argument, without a conference in chambers, and solely on the basis of the attorneys' written submissions in connection with a motion to dismiss or a motion for summary judgment.

Judges are evaluated on their skill at the art of judging, not on whether they know all the law. Although judges know a great deal about rules of procedure (which they use constantly), they often know less about individual rules of substantive law (which come up less often). And judges cannot specialize in particular areas of substantive law: they must decide any case you bring before them. Unless a case turns on parts of the law about which a judge has thought deeply lately, the judge depends on the attorneys to show what the law is today and how it governs the case. And a judge knows nothing at all about the facts of a case except for what can be learned through the attorneys and their evidence.

Judges will want you to *teach* them your case. That is why you should think of a brief or memorandum as a *manual* that a judge can use to learn how to make the decision at hand. Because important decisions are hard to make and can worry the decision-maker, a lawyer who can show the court how the decision should be made, laying out all the steps of logic, stands a better chance of influencing the result. If done in a respectful tone, this is not as presumptuous as you might think. If you have prepared properly, you will know much more about the decision than the judge will. But you must teach the court without insulting its intelligence, and you must do so in the clearest and most concise manner possible. Judges will find it hard to rule in your favor if you are condescending or if you waste their time.

§15.2   Argumentation Techniques

> Luck is the residue of design.
>
> —*Branch Rickey*

This section explains the techniques of using argumentation to persuade:

1. Design a compelling theory and back it up with compelling arguments.
2. Limit your contentions to those that have a reasonable chance of persuading the court.
3. Give the court a clear statement of the rule or rules on which the case turns.
4. Rely on an appropriate amount of authority with appropriate amounts of explanation.
5. Show the court how to make the decision by explaining exactly and in detail how the law governs the facts.
6. To the extent they advance the theory, make the facts and people involved come alive on the written page.
7. Show the judge how you should prevail from a policy standpoint.
8. Organize to emphasize the ideas that are most likely to persuade.
9. Make your organization obvious.
10. Reinforce the theory with carefully chosen wording.

11. Enhance your own credibility through careful rewriting and editing.
12. Make it easy for the judge to rule in your favor.

You will find this material easier to understand if you read the memorandum in Appendix D before continuing here.

1. Design a compelling theory and back it up with compelling arguments.

Until you provide proof, a judge will not believe anything you say. In litigation writing, proof is a well-argued theory that leads to no result other than victory for your client. You can develop a theory through the process described in §14.4. And the quality of your theory can be measured by the criteria set out in §14.3. But even a good theory does not sell unless it is argued.

An argument is a demonstration that the logic of a situation requires the result proposed by the arguer.[1] A good argument affects its audience because it causes the decision the audience makes. An argument is much more than a random collection of stray comments that sound good for the arguer's client and bad for the opposing party. Those kinds of comments might be useful raw materials, but they become an argument only when they coalesce into a coherent presentation that *influences* the audience. When you design an argument, your first question should be "What will make the reader want to agree with me?"

A persuasive argument is neither extravagant nor belligerent. To a judge, extreme statements sound unreliable. Because judges are experienced, professional skeptics, they are rarely fooled by inaccurate or farfetched statements, and when they find such a statement in an argument, in their view a dust of untrustworthiness settles over the whole argument, the theory, and the lawyer involved. A judge tends to have what Hemingway, in another context, called "a built-in, shock-proof, shit detector."[2] Because you cannot afford to be seen as unreliable, you need to be similarly equipped so that you can examine — with a judge's skepticism — each statement you contemplate making. In addition to the skills explained in the preceding chapters, it helps to have a mature and thorough understanding of human nature (some of which can be acquired in law school, even if it is not listed in the catalog).

It is not enough that everything you say is believable. You can be so reasonable that you cannot win because — although the judge might believe all you say — your individual statements, even when taken together, do not add up to proof that your client is entitled to what you have asked for. A good theory and good arguments are reasonable and accurate, appear reliable, and make your client's victory appear *inevitable* — either because the higher courts will reverse any other result, or because it is the only right thing to do, or both. The feeling of inevitability is a judge's selling point. It is

---

§15.2   1. When "Argument" is capitalized, it instead means the largest portion of a persuasive memorandum or brief. There may be many arguments in an Argument.

2. *Writers At Work: The Paris Review Interviews, Second Series* 239 (G. Plimpton ed. 1965).

reached by laying out for the judge every step of logic so that the advocate's conclusion becomes more and more irresistible as the argument proceeds. A judge knows when the selling point approaches, because the job of deciding seems to grow easier.

The selection of a theory and the selection of arguments are strategic choices that you should be prepared to explain in terms of the litany of strategy questions that appears in §14.2.

2. Limit your contentions to those that have a reasonable chance of persuading the court. You may be tempted to throw into an argument every flattering thing you can say about your theory and everything that might disparage your adversary's theory, assuming that they cannot hurt and might help. But such "shotgun" writing does hurt and hardly ever helps. The best approach is to develop fully the strong contentions and leave out the weak ones. Paradoxically, the result is usually a document that—although more compact—more deeply explores the ideas on which the decision will be based.

The technique is, first, to subdue the judge's skepticism into a general feeling of *confidence* that your theory can be relied on if the judge wants to rely on it, and then, on the foundation of confidence, to build a feeling that your client is the *inevitable* winner. You cannot build the feeling of inevitability without preliminarily laying a foundation of confidence. And weak contentions—even if placed near strong ones—excite skepticism, rather than quiet it. If a judge believes that you have indiscriminately mixed unreliable contentions with seemingly attractive ones, the judge's natural temptation is to dismiss the whole lot as not worthy of confidence, for the same reason that a person considering the purchase of a house justifiably suspects the integrity of the entire structure after cracked beams are found in the attic. Just as it is the builder's job to select only sturdy materials, so it is the lawyer's job—and not the judge's—to separate out the weak ideas before the memorandum or brief is submitted. A judge has neither the time nor the inclination to delete all the suspect material and then reassemble the remainder into something sturdier.

When you determine whether a contention has a reasonable chance to persuade, you are, of course, making a predictive judgment. A "reasonable chance" does not mean certainty and might not even mean probability. To be worth making, however, a contention should have the capacity to seem tempting and attractive to a judge.

The decision to include or omit an argument is a strategic choice, which you should be prepared to explain in terms of the litany of strategy questions that appears in §14.2.

3. Give the court a clear statement of the rule or rules on which the case turns. Unless you have authority directly on point, that rule might not be exactly as stated in the cases to which you cite, and you may need to devote careful thought to its phrasing. A court needs what Karl Llewellyn called the advocate's "own clean phrasing of the rule," together with "a passage which so clearly and rightly states and crystallizes the background and the result that it is *recognized* on sight as doing the needed work and as practically demanding to be lifted into the opinion."[3] Particularly in appellate courts, judges know that they will have to write an opinion justifying their decision, and that the opinion should be as convincing as possible to the parties, to the bar, to the public, and to any still higher court to which the decision could be appealed. That is a hard task where a gap in the law must be filled. The judge who asks in oral argument in a gap-filling case, "Counselor, what rule would you have us enforce?" really wants to know—assuming the lawyer ultimately prevails—how the court should word the second component of the paradigm when it writes the opinion.

You already know that, for any given rule, the available authority will usually support several different formulations on a continuum from broad to narrow. The selection of one formulation over another is a strategic choice that you should be prepared to explain in terms of the litany of strategy questions that appears in §14.2. Your decision should be based on a balancing of two separate factors. First, out of any given set of authority, some formulations are more likely than others to be accepted by a court. Second, regardless of their acceptability to a court, some formulations more logically support the client's position.

4. Rely on an appropriate amount of authority with appropriate amounts of explanation. To rule in your favor, a court would need to believe that you have provided sufficient authority, although the typical judge is unwilling to tolerate an exhaustive explanation of every case you cite. How do you steer a middle course between under-citing and over-citing and between under-explaining and over-explaining?

Begin by predicting the amount of citation and explanation a skeptical but busy judge will need. Then carefully study the available authorities. Place in a "major authority" category those that are likely to *influence* the court and in a peripheral category those that are merely somewhat related to the issue. Think in terms of cause and effect: if you had to make the judge's decision, which authorities would be most likely to have an effect on you, *even an effect adverse to your clients' position?* Those are the authorities you must discuss, and many of them will best be discussed at length. Except where necessary to fill holes in your argument not settled by the major authorities, peripheral authorities should eventually be discarded.

The quantity of authority and the volume of explanation will depend on how much is needed to clarify the issue involved, how disputed that issue will be, and how important that issue is to your theory. At one extreme, an idea may be so complex, so disputed, and so critical that it must be supported by a synthesis of many cases, comprehensively explained over many pages. If one case happens to satisfy all of the most important criteria—on point, from the highest court in the jurisdiction, well-reasoned, clearly expressed, recent—that one case may be enough (although, to the extent something is lacking, a second or third case might be selected and discussed briefly to supply the missing ingredient). Rarely, however, does one author-

---

3. *The Common Law Tradition: Deciding Appeals* 241 (1960) (emphasis in original).

ity dispose of so much. If the question is complex, disputed, and critical—and if there is no recent, well-reasoned, and clearly expressed decision on point from the highest court in the jurisdiction—it would probably be sufficient to discuss in detail the two or three most useful cases, aiming to give the court confidence without tiring its patience.

At the other extreme, if the court is apt to be satisfied with a mere conclusory explanation, you should limit citation to one or at the very most two cases. If an idea is undisputed and routine, such as an uncontested procedural test,[4] it should be enough to cite, with little or no explanation, to the most recent decision from the highest court in the jurisdiction that has invoked the test.

If the court must fill a significant gap in local precedent, many cases may be needed to create an adequate synthesis. The court will generally want to know the extent of the gap, which can be defined only by explaining what local law does and does not settle. Typically, the court will also want to know how other jurisdictions solve the problem. If many jurisdictions have ruled on the question, the court will need to know which is the majority or plurality rule and which rule is favored by the recent trend of decisions. This can be supported only by a precise statement of the score: the number of jurisdictions that have adopted the majority or plurality rule; the number of jurisdictions that have adopted other rules; and the number of jurisdictions that have switched since a date that you have selected in order to define the trend. Unfortunately, the score must in turn be supported by a citation for each jurisdiction. This is one of the very few situations where a string citation or a footnote (or both) are acceptable.[5] The point is to show jurisdictions, not decisions, and one case per jurisdiction is usually sufficient. It is not enough to try to prove the score through citation to indirect authority, such as a law review article. Not only must the law be proved through direct authority from each jurisdiction, but it is extremely unlikely that indirect authority, once it is printed, accurately represents the *current* state of the law.

Finally, notice in the memorandum in Appendix D how the more advantageous aspects of the weight of authority are made more clear by direct references to the courts that have decided the cases relied on. Certainly, the identity of the courts can be learned from the citations, but, when a sentence begins by referring to the highest court in the jurisdiction ("The Court of Appeals has held"), the reader knows from the beginning that whatever follows is more settled in the law than it otherwise would be.

The selection of authority is another strategic choice, which you should

4. Notice, for example, how the test for a preliminary injunction is proved in the memorandum in Appendix D.

5. Except where needed to "prove the score" of jurisdictions, string citations are usually ignored by judges because in nearly every other instance a string cite demonstrates nothing. And a "score-proving" string cite is often so long that it belongs in a footnote to avoid breaking up the discussion in the text. With that exception, footnotes do not belong in memoranda and briefs. Footnotes were invented to store material that would otherwise break up the flow of text. Material that is collateral enough to be dropped into a footnote is not likely to help a decision-maker and should usually be eliminated from a document on which a decision is to be based.

be prepared to explain in terms of the litany of strategy questions set out in §14.2.

5. Show the court how to make the decision by explaining exactly and in detail how the law governs the facts. A court rules for one party over another not merely because the law is abstractly favorable, but, more importantly, because the law and facts *combine* favorably. The judge often reaches the selling point only where the law and facts are finally combined — woven together — to show that what the writer wants is inevitable. Beginners sometimes devote so much attention to the law that they overlook the final step of arguing the facts — weaving the law into the facts to show the court precisely how the decision should be made. After all the work of explaining the law, a beginner might assume that the application to the facts is obvious, but it hardly ever is. Do not assume that merely mentioning the facts is enough: *show* the court exactly how the determinative facts require the decision you seek.

In the memorandum in Appendix D, are the law and facts woven together wherever that can logically be done? If so, is it done within the framework of a paradigm structure? If not, what is missing and where?

6. To the extent they advance the theory, make the facts and people involved come alive on the written page. This may be the most valuable technique because it usually has the most effect in causing the judge to want to rule in your favor.

A plot is more than a story. A story is merely "a narrative of events arranged in their time-sequence," [6] but a plot reveals character and causality. The standard illustration of the difference is in E. M. Forster's classic lectures on fiction: " 'The king died, and then the queen died' is a story. 'The king died, and then the queen died of grief' is a plot." [7] When most of us read "The king died, and then the queen died," we see in the mind's eye either no image or at best an image of stick-like figures without personality. But when we read "The king died, and then the queen died of grief," we see instead an image of at least one real human being: she may be wearing fairy-tale-like clothing, but she is genuinely suffering as real people do.

When a judge, reading an argument, visualizes stick figures or no image at all, the case seems boring and unimportant, and the judge is not motivated to rule in your favor. But the judge begins to take sides if he or she can visualize real people doing real things to each other. When you read the argument in the memorandum in Appendix D, you probably took sides at some point. Start reading the argument from the beginning until you find the place at which you began to favor either Goslin or his nephew. What was it that got to you? Was it the *picture* of a 74-year-old man in the home he had lived in for 24 years being treated harshly by young people — ingrates — who had moved in and were trying to throw him out? If this or similar scenes were to appear in a judge's mind, they would have extraordinary power over

6. E. M. Forster, *Aspects of the Novel* 86 (1927).
7. *Id.*

the disposition of Goslin's motion because they show who deserves to win and who deserves to lose. In the memorandum in Appendix D, how are mental images created? Find the passages that put them into your mind. What did the writer do to help you see them?

Before you begin to write, make a list on scratch paper of the determinative facts. You will have to discuss those facts to make your argument, and that is where your opportunities occur. For each fact, ask yourself what the fact illustrates about the *people* involved: does it show who is an innocent victim, who is predatory, who is inexcusably foolish, and so forth. For each fact, ask yourself further what the fact illustrates about *what happened:* does it show the events to have been accidental, caused by one person's carelessness, the result of another's greed and cunning, and so on. Only by knowing what each fact reveals can you turn a story into a plot.

When you describe these facts in your writing, do not characterize them with emotion-laden verbiage. Although a fact is determinative because the law coldly makes it so, a judge is capable of forming a human reaction to it. That is not merely because the judge is human, but also because the judge prefers to make decisions that are fundamentally fair. On the other hand, a judge's professional self-image is naturally offended by an argument that reads like political oratory or a story in a tabloid newspaper. *Vividness,* which causes the effect in Goslin's memorandum, is not the same as luridness, which demeans an argument and the judge who reads it. If a fact will seem compelling to a court, that fact will speak for itself. All you will need is a calm description of the fact, in simple words and with enough detail to make the picture vivid. When reading Goslin's Argument, you may have thought that his nephew was deceitful, irresponsible, selfish, and cruel, but the writer never called him any of those things. Instead, the writer simply described what happened in such a way that *you* formed those opinions. (Forster did not say, either, that the queen loved the king: he only told you why she died.)

Your decisions about which facts to use in this way and how to use them are strategic choices, and you should be prepared to explain them in terms of the litany of strategy questions set out in §14.2.

7. Show the judge how you should prevail from a policy standpoint. Not only must you show the court that your client deserves individually to win, but you also must demonstrate that what you want makes sense in other cases as well. In a system of precedent where rules are to be applied even-handedly, judges want confidence that society will be protected if other like cases are decided as you want your client's case resolved. If a court must choose between competing rules, for example, you should spend more than a little effort showing that the rule you urge is better than others. Even where the rule is settled and the issue is how it should be applied, a court is still less likely to rule in your favor if it is not confident that what you want is, in a very general sense, a good idea.

Policy must be proved with authority. Some policy is openly announced in decisions and statutes, but more often it is implied. Some policy considerations can be found in every era in every American jurisdiction. For example, courts everywhere like solutions that are easily enforceable, promote clarity in the law, are not needlessly complex, and do not allow true wrong-doers to profit from illegal acts. Other policy considerations may differ from state to state. In states such as Arizona, for example, public policy strongly disfavors solutions that interfere with land development, while in states like Vermont policy prefers agriculture, conservation, and the environment. Some states favor providing tort remedies even at some risk to judicial efficiency, although in others the reverse is true. Still other policy consider-ations differ from era to era. Some activities once greatly favored in the law — such as the building and operation of railroads in the last century — now enjoy no special treatment, while other things — such as a woman's reproductive control over her own body — are now protected in a way they once were not.

Lawyers tend to introduce policy-based arguments with phrasings like the following:

> This court should reject the rule urged by the defendant because it would cause . . .

> Automobile rental companies [or some other category of litigants] should bear the risk of loss because . . .

> Not only is the order requested by the plaintiff not sanctioned by this state's case law, but such an order would violate public policy be-cause . . .

Remember, however, that policy arguments are used to reinforce argument from authority. Only where authority is unusually sparse should policy arguments play the predominant role in a theory. The selection of arguments — policy-based and otherwise — is a strategic choice that you should be prepared to explain in terms of the litany of strategy questions that appears in §14.2.

8. Organize to emphasize the ideas that are most likely to persuade. In general, the most effective sequence is to present first the issues on which you are most likely to win; within issues, to make your strongest arguments first; and, within arguments, to make your strongest contentions and use your best authority first. Michael Fontham has said that the "best strategy is to strike quickly, establish momentum, and maintain the advantage through a forceful presentation of contentions selected for their persuasive effect." [8] You can use paradigm structures to accomplish all of this. The overall effect should be to focus the reader's thoughts on the ideas that can cause you to win.

First impressions tend to color how later material is read, and, like most people, a judge reads most carefully at the beginning. Moreover, because judges are so busy, they expect the strongest material first. If they find themselves reading weak material early, judges either begin to form an

---

8. *Written and Oral Advocacy* 108 (1985).

adverse opinion or—worse—stop reading altogether.[9] Judges expect law-yers to get immediately to the point. A judge quickly becomes impatient with long prefatory passages of historical background because that kind of material is rarely useful in making a decision. Even in a constitutional case where the issue is the drafters' intent one or two centuries ago, the historical material is part of the argument, not a preface to it. An argument—and even a predictive memorandum—written in the style of a law review article is considered especially offensive because law review writing aims to be densely encyclopedic and is not focused to assist decision-making.

But sometimes the logic of the dispute requires that the strongest mate-rial be delayed to avoid confusing the court. Some arguments are simply hard to understand unless preceded by less punchy material. In these situa-tions, you must weigh your need for clarity against your need to show merit from the start.

9. Make your organization obvious. Because a theory is not a collection of stray thoughts, you cannot afford to let the judge grope for understanding about how your contentions are related to each other. In-stead, use the techniques of forceful writing[10] to help the judge see your focus. Very soon after you begin to discuss each issue, tell the judge exactly what your theory is. (Is that done in the memorandum in Appendix D? If so, where?) Use a thesis sentence to state each contention before you begin to prove it. And use transitional words and phrases to show how your conten-tions are cumulative:

> There are three reasons why . . . . First, ... Second, ... And finally, ...

> Not only has the defendant violated . . . , but she has also . . . .

10. Reinforce the theory with carefully chosen wording. Word choice is a valuable part of a persuasive strategy. The careful use of words can advance the ideas that make up your theory. For example, in the memo-randum in Appendix D, the transaction between Goslin and his nephew is referred to as a "transfer" infrequently, and then only because it is abso-lutely necessary in satisfying the third element of the test for a constructive trust. Otherwise, "deed" is used because the writer's theory is that Goslin continues to hold certain property rights to his home, the deed being only partial evidence of what really happened. The continual use of "deed" reminds the judge of the writer's limited interpretation of the transaction:

---

9. You read a newspaper the same way: you expect the most important or most entertaining material near the beginning of a newspaper story, and when you have had enough, you stop reading and go on to a different page. Newspaper editors know that, and newspaper stories are written with the least valuable material at the end, so that readers can reasonably decide how much of a story to read. Just as your method of reading a newspaper would be thrown off if the most valuable material were strewn randomly throughout the story, so a judge's method of reading a memorandum or a brief would become muddled if the strongest arguments might appear anywhere.

10. See §4.3.

Goslin gave his nephew a piece of paper that transferred legal but not equitable ownership. If used often, "transfer" would have implied a concession psychologically, and perhaps intellectually as well.

Notice also that, although the writer says the nephew has "not yet reciprocated" the tuition help he received from Goslin, the writer does not argue that the nephew has failed to "repay." If money has not been "repaid," it is borrowed money, and there is no evidence that the tuition money was a loan. The writer's theory is instead that the nephew's moral obligation to help a relative was heightened by the earlier tuition assistance, and that Goslin reasonably thought "at the time of the deed" that his nephew was trying to help him keep — rather than lose — his property. To call it "repayment" would only arouse the court's skepticism. The idea of "reciprocation" does the same job without running that risk. Do you begin to see how carefully you must choose words to advance your theory precisely and not to confuse it?

Within limits, you can even advance the theory through the way you refer to the parties. Whenever the reader meets the plaintiff in the memorandum in Appendix D, the latter appears with dignity as "Mr. Goslin." Even though his neighbors might know him to treat humans and pets vilely and to have vicious opinions that offend decent-minded people, he is a sympathetic figure in litigation as long as the court knows him to be "Mr. Goslin," the elderly widower who only wants to live out his last days in his own home. Herbert Skeffington, however, is always "the nephew" or "the defendant," with no dignity other than his role as nephew and with no personality other than what he reveals about himself through the way he treats his uncle. While he is only the shadowy "nephew," it is easier to think him capable of deceit, greed, and cold-bloodedness. But if the judge were to think of him as Mr. Skeffington — and to think of the other interlopers as Mr. Skeffington's wife Amelia and their children Wendy and Tom, aged respectively eight and four — it is a little harder to think ill of them.[11]

Simple, concrete words can paint the pictures on which your theory is based. In the memorandum in Appendix D, notice how facts are described almost entirely in short, everyday words with very specific meanings. That is so not only of Goslin's facts, but also of the facts of the precedents on which the argument is based. When you read there about *Sinclair,* for example, you might have imagined any number of things: a man working amid mounds

---

11. There are some conventions about how parties are referred to in persuasive writing. In criminal cases, the prosecution usually refers to the other party as "the defendant," or — if there are more than one — "defendant Brooks" and "defendant Martini." The defendant's attorney, on the other hand, will generally use the defendant's name: "Mr. Brooks" or "Mrs. Martini." In civil cases, an attorney will try to humanize the client with a name while depersonalizing the opposing party by referring instead to that party's status in court ("the plaintiff"), or out of court ("the airline"), or both ("the defendant insurance company"). If an opposing party already has a well-defined identity, the lawyer might refer to both parties by name ("Pennzoil has sued Texaco because . . . "). Appellate courts, however, will be confused if you refer to the parties as "the appellant" or "the appellee," and many prohibit it, preferring instead references to the parties' statuses in the trial court ("plaintiff," "defendant") or to the identities on which the dispute is based ("the city," "the employee"). *See, e.g.,* Rule 28(d) of the Federal Rules of Appellate Procedure. Virtually all courts — trial and appellate — will allow an attorney to refer to the attorney's own client by name.

of paper in a busy clerk's office, people continually saying to him, "Please do it, just this once" — or instead sitting at home in his parlor with his sister nearby. If you saw scenes like these, you did so because of the natural human tendency to picture the characters moving through the plot.

But readers see scenes only where writers have given some concrete descriptions to build on: the clerk's office, the sister, and so on. The knack is, first, to isolate the very few facts that are determinative under the law and therefore essential to the scene, and then to describe those facts in words that are simple and concrete enough for the desired image to come quickly into the reader's mind. This is simple and concrete:

> The two had seen each other at least monthly since the nephew was a boy.

This is not:

> The two had occasion to come together for social and family purposes on a periodic and regular basis of at least once each month since the nephew's extreme youth.

Did you see an image when you read the first example? Maybe a front door opened; people greeted each other as they do at family gatherings; and so on. Did you see an equally vivid image when you read the second example?

You can do harm with words that claim too much. The first example is actually less persuasive than the second:

> It is obvious, therefore, that the defendant understood the consequences of his acts.

> Therefore, the defendant understood the consequences of his acts.

The additional words in the first example supply no extra meaning but instead divert the reader's attention from the message of the sentence. And if you claim that a proposition is obvious, you ask to be excused from the obligation to supply proof. That kind of implied request stimulates the healthy suspicions of a reader whose experience has taught that little is obvious in litigation.

11. Enhance your own credibility through careful rewriting and editing. If your theory is to sell as readily as you would like, you must help the judge trust you. Understandably, judges do not trust easily. Their decisions are important ones, and you will always face at least one competing attorney with another theory to sell. Edit out inaccuracies, imprecision, incorrectly used terms of art, and other forms of intellectual sloppiness; sloppiness with citations and other matters of format and layout; sloppiness with the English language, its spelling, its punctuation, and other matters of grammar and syntax; typographical errors; invective and unnecessary personal statements about parties, attorneys, or judges; and empty remarks that do not advance the argument (such as rhetorical questions and irrelevant histories of the law). Any of these suggest a lawyer who cannot be relied on—and judges will be quick to draw that inference. Most of these faults will also confuse or distract the judge or waste judicial time. (And rhetorical questions dissipate the force of the argument, rather than advancing it.) Other things being equal, a document can be more persuasive if its appearance is flawless. Not only does that kind of perfection make the document ingratiatingly easy to read, but it also tells the judge that the writer is careful about everything, especially the ideas involved.

12. Make it easy for the judge to rule in your favor. Submit a memorandum or brief that is easy to use. Think about the problems a judge would have with the document, and solve them before submission. Not only should the writing be clear, concise, and focused sharply on the issue at hand, but the type should be easy to read; margins should be large enough that each page does not look oppressively dense; and headings should look like headings (and not like part of the text). Remember how you have felt when you have bought an appliance and been saddled with an owner's manual that was hard to use and understand.

§15.3   Argumentation Ethics

Advocacy is not a free-for-all. The rules of professional ethics[1] place limits on what a lawyer is permitted to do in argument.

First and most basically, a lawyer is forbidden to "[k]nowingly make a false statement of law or fact" to a court.[2] The whole system of adjudication would break down if lawyers did not speak honestly to courts.

Second, a lawyer is required to inform a court of "legal authority *in the controlling jurisdiction* known to the lawyer to be *directly adverse* to the position of the [lawyer's] client and not disclosed by opposing counsel."[3]

---

§15.3   1. To regulate the behavior of lawyers, nearly every state has adopted, as its rules of professional ethics, one or the other of two model codes drafted by the American Bar Association. The older of the two is the Model Code of Professional Responsibility, which dates from 1969. The newer code is the 1983 Model Rules of Professional Conduct. Although some states have adopted the Model Rules, others have continued to use the Model Code. The usual method of adoption is by incorporation into the state's court rules. Some states have adopted a code without making any changes at all in the original ABA draft. Others have made small changes, and a few states have substantially altered whichever code they have adopted. California has rejected both ABA codes and written its own set of rules. Each state has a system of professional discipline that punishes lawyers for violation of the state's ethics code. The available punishments include censure, suspension of the lawyer's license to practice, and disbarment. A state's code of professional ethics is statute-like, with a body of interpretive case law.

2. Model Code of Professional Responsibility, DR 7-102(A)(5). The same prohibition, in virtually the same words, appears in Rule 3.3(a)(1) of the Model Rules of Professional Conduct.

3. Model Rules of Professional Conduct, Rule 3.3(a)(3) (emphasis added). The same requirement, in virtually the same words, appears in Disciplinary Rule 7-106(B)(1) of the Model Code of Professional Responsibility.

The system of adjudication would suffer immeasurably if courts could not depend on lawyers to give a full account of controlling law. (In §15.4, we will explore the ways in which you can comply with this requirement while least damaging your case.)

Third, a lawyer is not permitted to advance a theory or argument that is "frivolous"[4] or "unwarranted under existing law,"[5] except that a lawyer may make a "good faith argument for an extension, modification or reversal of existing law."[6] In a legal system like ours, where "the law is not always clear and never is static," the rules of ethics permit a lawyer to advance theories and arguments that take advantage "of the law's ambiguities and potential for change."[7] But a frivolous theory or argument—one that stands little chance of being adopted by a court—is unfair to courts and to opposing parties because it wastes their time, effort, and resources.

Separate court rules—procedural, rather than ethical in nature—also punish lawyers who make frivolous arguments. In federal courts, for example, "[e]very pleading, motion, and other paper"—including memoranda and briefs—must be signed by an attorney, whose signature "constitutes a certificate . . . that to the best of the signer's knowledge, information, and belief formed after reasonable inquiry [the document] is well grounded in fact and is warranted by existing law or a good faith argument for the extension, modification, or reversal of existing law."[8] If an attorney signs a memorandum or brief that does not satisfy that standard, the court has the power to order the attorney, the attorney's client, or both to reimburse the opposing party for expenses—including attorney's fees—incurred in arguing against the offending document.[9]

§15.4 What to Do About Adverse Authority and Arguments

Adverse authority will not go away just because you ignore it: if the court does not find it, opposing counsel probably will. There are, in fact, a number of reasons for you to address adverse authority. First, as you have just read, the ethical rules require it. Second, a lawyer who ignores adverse authority is seen by courts as unreliable and unpersuasive, while a lawyer who speaks with candor is more easily trusted and respected by the bench. Third, a lawyer who ignores adverse authority throws away the opportunity—often the only opportunity—to give the court reasons for not following it. The first reason applies only to authority within "the controlling jurisdiction,"

4. Model Rules of Professional Conduct, Rule 3.1.
5. Model Code of Professional Responsibility, DR 7-102(A)(2).
6. These words appear in both codes. Model Rules of Professional Conduct, Rule 3.1; Model Code of Professional Responsibility, DR 7-102(A)(2).
7. Drafters' comment to Model Rules of Professional Conduct, Rule 3.1.
8. Fed. R. Civ. P. 11.
9. *Id.*

but the others apply to any adverse authority that can be predicted to influence the court, even precedent from other jurisdictions.

If the authority is a statute, court rule, or administrative regulation, you must show that the provision was not intended to govern the controversy, or that it was intended to govern it but favorably to your client, or that the provision itself is not law. The last is the least often successful. Although it may seem tempting to argue, for example, that a statute you do not like is unconstitutional, courts rarely sustain such attacks. In fact, if a statute or similar provision is susceptible to more than one meaning, courts are obliged to choose one that would not violate a controlling constitution. You should frontally attack a statute only if there is significant doubt — shared by respected lawyers — about its validity.

If the adverse authority is precedent, consider distinguishing it, focusing on significant — and not merely coincidental — differences between the precedent and your case. Be careful. The differences on which you rely should be important enough to impress a skeptical judge who is looking for the basis of a decision, and hyper-technical discrepancies and minor factual variations are not persuasive. Another approach might be to reconcile the precedent with your case, showing that — although the precedent seems superficially adverse — its underlying policy would actually be furthered by the ruling you want from the court. Still another approach is to attack the precedent head-on, challenging its validity on the grounds that it is poorly reasoned or that changes in society or in public policy have made it unworkable. Although the doctrine of stare decisis does not absolutely forbid the overruling of precedent, a frontal attack on mandatory case law is nearly always an uphill fight, to be attempted only when there is very serious doubt — again shared by at least some respected lawyers — about the precedent's viability. In general, do not ask a court to overrule mandatory authority if you can win through distinguishing, reconciliation, or some other skill of precedent analysis. Judges simply prefer distinguishing and reconciling precedent to overruling it. But things are different where local law has a gap and where the challenged authority is not mandatory: if a judge must choose between competing out-of-state rules, he or she will not be able to decide without rejecting at least some precedent as ill-founded.

With both precedent and statutes, you might consider taking more than one approach, arguing in the alternative — but only if neither alternative would weaken the persuasive force of the other. It is not illogical, for example, to argue, first, that a statute was not intended to govern the facts before the court and, alternatively, that, if the statute is interpreted otherwise, it should be held unconstitutional.[1] It is illogical, however, to argue, first, that the statute was not intended to govern the facts and, alternatively, that it should be construed to provide a benefit and not a detriment to the client.

You should attack opposing arguments, as well as adverse authority, because, if you do not, the court will assume that you have no defense to them. But make your own arguments first. Your theory will be more easily

§15.4 1. For an example of exactly these alternative arguments, see the brief in Appendix E.

understood if you argue it before you attack opposing arguments. Generally, you can win more easily if the court's dominant impression is that you deserve to win, rather than that your adversary deserves to lose. And a defensive tone can undermine an otherwise worthwhile argument.

If you are responding to a memorandum or brief that your adversary has already propounded,[2] you have been put on notice of most of the arguments that threaten you because they will appear in the document to which you are responding. In addition, the court itself might uncover arguments not mentioned by your adversary. Even if an argument has not been mentioned by your adversary, you should attack it if it has a reasonable chance of occurring to and persuading the court. In nonresponsive writing you must think up all the possible threatening arguments and then predict which have a reasonable chance of being put before—and persuading—the court, attacking every argument that fits that description.

How much emphasis should you give to an attack on an adverse argument or authority? Give it as much emphasis as necessary to convince the judge not to rule against you. Little treatment is necessary if the point is minor and if the argument or authority is easily rebutted. You will, of course, need to say more if the point is more significant or if your counter-analysis is more complex. You cannot reduce the force of adverse arguments and authorities by giving them minimal treatment in your own writing: they have lives and voices of their own.

Beginners often have difficulty writing the thesis and transition sentences that introduce attacks on opposing arguments. In responsive writing, it is enough to refer to what opposing counsel has said and then to get on with the counter-argument:

> The plaintiff misconstrues section 401(d)(1). Four other circuits have already decided that section 401(d)(1) provides for X and not, as the plaintiff contends, for Y. [*Follow with an analysis of the circuit cases.*]
>
> No appellate court has held to the contrary, and the few district court decisions cited to by the plaintiff are all distinguishable. [*Follow with an analysis of the district court cases.*]
>
> The legislative history also demonstrates that Congress intended to provide for X and not for Y. [*Follow with an analysis of the legislative history.*]

Here the opening sentences are written so that opposing counsel's contention is surrounded by the writer's counter-contention and the beginning of the counter-contention's proof. And the thesis sentences that follow argue

---

2. In practice, the attorney going forward—the movant in a trial court or the appellant on appeal—serves a memorandum or brief on the opposing attorney and files one or more copies with the court. Then the opposing attorney serves and files an answering memorandum or brief. And the first attorney may complete the exchange with a reply memorandum or brief. The writing done in this situation is called *responsive* because the answering and reply documents each respond to the document that preceded. In some situations—usually in trial courts—the attorneys serve and file their documents at the same time, each without having seen the other's writing. Most law school persuasive writing assignments are similarly *non*responsive.

affirmatively and not defensively. The effect is much more forceful than a sentence that begins like this:

> The plaintiff has argued that section 401(d)(1) provides for Y, but . . . .

In nonresponsive situations — where you can predict but do not actually know which arguments your adversary will make — begin simply by denying the contention while emphasizing your counter-contention:

> Section 401(d)(1) provides for X and not for Y.

The following sounds defensive and almost silly:

> Opposing counsel might argue that section 401(d)(1) provides for Y, but . . . .

Opposing counsel might never argue it, but it may occur to the judge or to the judge's law clerk.

Both in responsive and in nonresponsive writing, a dependent clause can be useful in thesis and transition sentences:

> Although the House Judiciary Committee report states that its bill would have provided for Y, section 401(d)(1) more closely tracks the bill drafted in the Senate Judiciary Committee. Both that committee's report and the conference committee report flatly state that section 401(d)(1) provides for X.

Be careful, however, not to use a dependent clause to make a relatively minor problem look like a major one. For example, compare

> Although a few district courts have held that section 401(d)(1) provides for Y, every circuit that has faced the question has held the contrary.

with

> Every circuit that has faced the question has held that section 401(d)(1) provides for X. [*Analysis of circuit cases.*] The few district court cases to the contrary are distinguishable.

§15.5   *Writing in a Procedural Posture*[1]

Because most of a legal education is spent studying the substantive law of torts, property, and so on, students tend to view issues in the abstract

§15.5   1. If you are confused about procedural postures, review §12.5.

("should the plaintiff win?"). But because of the system of motions and the procedural rules attached to them, judges instead see issues in terms of the motion context in which they are raised. If, for example, a defendant moves for summary judgment, you are wrong if you define the issue as whether the defendant should win. The issues the judge will see are whether there is a material dispute of fact and whether, on the material and indisputable facts, the defendant is entitled to judgment as a matter of law. The judge's view is the correct and more precisely focused one because a summary judgment can be granted only if the answer to both these questions is yes. Similarly, on appeal the question is not whether the appellant should have won in the trial court, but instead whether the trial court's ruling was error as defined by the applicable standard of review.[2]

The procedural posture and the rules governing it control the way the judge makes the decision. If you want to influence that decision, you must show the judge how to make it within the procedural rules he or she must follow. And if you want to predict that decision accurately, you must take those same rules into account. How can you do that in writing?

First, remember that in a motion or appeal the threshold rule is *not* the rule of substantive law that provides the remedy sued for. The threshold rules are procedural: in a trial court, the rules that govern how the motion is to be decided or, on appeal, the rules that govern the trial court's decision, together with the rule that defines the appellate court's standard of review. For example, the memorandum in Appendix D has been submitted in support of a motion for a preliminary injunction in a suit to enforce a constructive trust. To prevent things from getting worse before the court can render a judgment, Goslin has moved for an order enjoining his nephew preliminarily (while the suit is pending) from assaulting him, endangering his health, conveying the property to someone else, or otherwise impeding Goslin's use of the dwelling. In deciding the motion, the court will evaluate the record in terms of the elements of the test for a preliminary injunction: likelihood of success on the merits, threatened irreparable harm, and a balancing of the equities. And, quite properly, Goslin's Argument begins with that test.

Second, recall that *some* procedural tests contain an element that incorporates the underlying substantive rules on which the litigation as a whole is based. In the test for a preliminary injunction, that happens through the element requiring likelihood of success on the merits. In the test for a summary judgment, it is done through the element requiring entitlement to judgment as a matter of law.[3] Those elements incorporate the entirety of one or more substantive rules. In the memorandum in Appendix D, for example, Goslin can demonstrate likelihood of success on the merits only by showing that the record before the court contains all the elements of the test for a constructive trust—and that concern occupies the largest part of Goslin's Argument.

Be careful about these incorporation elements: they can include *all* the substantive rules that will determine the ultimate judgment in the case at

2. Standards of review are explained in §§12.5.4 and 20.5.
3. See §12.5.2.

hand. For example, if the nephew had raised the affirmative defense of unclean hands, Goslin would be able to demonstrate likelihood of success on the merits only by showing *both* that the record contains all the elements of a constructive trust (his cause of action) *and* that the record lacks at least one element of the test for unclean hands (the nephew's affirmative defense). (Not every procedural test, however, incorporates a substantive test.)

Third, organize your paradigm variations around the procedural test. If the procedural test incorporates a substantive test, the substantive test operates as a sub-rule. To see how that is done, study Goslin's Argument, which includes several paradigmed proofs inside the organization of an umbrella paradigm. The umbrella structure—through which the entire Argument is organized—is built on the test for a preliminary injunction. Each element of the test is proved through a distinct paradigmed proof:

> *Umbrella Paradigm:* proof—supplied element-by-element (below)—that Goslin is entitled to a preliminary injunction

A. paradigmed proof that Goslin is likely to succeed on the merits (i.e., that he will eventually be able to prove a constructive trust)

   1. paradigmed proof of a confidential relationship

   2. paradigmed proof of an implied promise

   3. paradigmed proof of a transfer

   4. paradigmed proof of unjust enrichment

B. paradigmed proof that Goslin is threatened with irreparable harm

C. paradigmed proof that equity favors an injunction

Because the first element (likelihood of success on the merits) incorporates a rule of substantive law (the test for a constructive trust), it includes paradigmed proofs (one for each element of the test for a constructive trust) inside a larger paradigmed proof (likelihood of success on the merits), which is in turn inside yet another paradigmed proof (the test for a preliminary injunction).

Although that may all sound complicated, it is the precise sequence of logic that a judge would need to go through in order to decide whether Goslin should be granted a preliminary injunction. The judge would have to decide whether Goslin has carried his burden of persuasion as to each of the elements of the test for a preliminary injunction, including all the elements of the constructive trust test, which is incorporated into the element of likelihood of success on the merits. An argument carefully organized in this way can systematically demolish a judge's skepticism because it demonstrates, element by element, how a party has carried — or, if you are arguing the other side, failed to carry — a burden of persuasion.

Finally, do not go overboard in citing to authority for the procedural test. Procedural tests are routine rules that judges use constantly and generally know by heart. A conclusory explanation[4] is usually sufficient for rule proof.[5] You should provide more only in two situations. The first is where authority will help you guide the court in rule application.[6] And the second is where the parties disagree about the proper formulation of the procedural rule. The second situation occurs very infrequently.

§15.6   Researching to Account for Your Case's Procedural Posture

In the library, you are looking for two kinds of rules:

First, you are searching for the rules that govern the *substance* of the controversy. This is by far the larger research task in nearly all cases. The most common examples of substantive rules are definitions of causes of action, crimes, affirmative defenses, and other formulas through which a court could substantively grant or deny relief. You have studied many of them already in the courses on torts, property, contracts, and criminal law, and you have undoubtedly done some of this kind of research already.

Second, the task that will be new to you is to find the *procedural* rules that govern how the court's decision is to be made. Some examples are

1. rules setting out the tests for granting various motions ("Summary judgment is appropriate if there is no genuine issue of material fact and if the moving party is entitled to judgment as a matter of law");
2. rules controlling how the court must evaluate the record before it on the motion to be decided ("In deciding a motion for summary judg-

---

4. See §7.1.2.
5. And that is all that was needed at the beginning of Goslin's Argument. See Appendix D.
6. That is done at certain points in Goslin's Argument. See Appendix D.

ment, the court views the evidence in the light most favorable to the party opposing the motion");

3. if an appeal has been taken, the rule defining the standard of review in the appellate court ("On appeal, a grant of summary judgment is reviewed de novo").

A court evaluates the record differently for different types of motions. And the standard of review differs from one kind of appeal to another. Much time will be saved in the library if you first identify the type of motion involved and then look in the procedural statutes and court rules and in the digests for procedural rules that govern the motion's disposition. For any given motion, you will probably find part of the procedural law in a statute or court rule and the rest in interpretive case law.

Before you start researching, ask yourself some questions: If the matter is in a trial court, what is the procedural posture? If it is on appeal, from what type of order has the appeal been taken? On what "facts" will the court now rule? For a motion to dismiss a complaint, for example, the facts are the allegations in the complaint. For a motion for summary judgment, the facts are the evidence submitted in support of and in opposition to the motion (usually through affidavits, exhibits, answers to interrogatories, and deposition transcripts). For a motion for a directed verdict or a motion for judgment notwithstanding the verdict, the facts are the testimony and exhibits that became evidence during the trial.

If you find the procedural rules in a procedural statute or court rule, the language you find may be subtle, but it will not be terribly hard to recognize. The section heading alone will usually announce that you have arrived at the correct place. In case law, when a court mentions the rules governing how a motion is to be decided, it usually does so immediately after reciting the facts and immediately before beginning the legal analysis (just as it was done in Goslin's memorandum[1]). That is because the procedural rules are a threshold through which the court must pass in order to begin the analysis. This is typical of the kind of language you will find:

> A complaint should not be dismissed for failure to state a claim unless it appears beyond a doubt that plaintiffs can prove no set of facts in support of their claim which would entitle them to relief. [Citations omitted.] The allegations of plaintiffs' complaint must be assumed to be true, and further, must be construed in [the plaintiffs'] favor. [Citations omitted.] The issue is not whether plaintiffs will ultimately prevail, but rather whether they are entitled to offer evidence in support of their claims. [Citation omitted.][2]

The first sentence is the test that must be satisfied before the motion can be granted. The rest are some of the rules that govern how the court is to evaluate the record before it on this particular type of motion.

---

§15.6 1. See Appendix D.
2. *United States v. Aceto Agric. Chems. Corp.*, 872 F.2d 1373, 1376 (8th Cir. 1989).

V

MEMORANDA AND BRIEFS: BUILDING A COMPLETE DOCUMENT

16 Writing Memoranda

Form follows function.

—*motto of the Bauhaus school of architecture*

§16.1 Introduction

You learned in Chapter 3 that memoranda and briefs are variations on a common structure, the major component of which is the Discussion in an office memorandum or the Argument in a persuasive memorandum or appellate brief. Chapters 6 through 13 have explained how to write a Discussion, and Chapters 14 and 15 have explained additional skills needed to write an Argument. This chapter outlines the other components in memoranda, both predictive and pursuasive. (The same thing is done for briefs in Chapter 21.) Chapters 17 through 19 explain how to write the components that—after the Discussion and the Argument—are the most difficult: fact statements, questions presented, and (in persuasive documents) point headings.

§16.2 Office Memorandum Format

An office memorandum might be read many times over a period of months or years by several different attorneys, including the writer, who may use it as a resource long after it is drafted. A memorandum might be written, for example, after a client has asked whether a lawsuit would be worth commencing. It would be used most immediately for advice to the client. If the result is a suit, some parts of the memorandum might be read again when the complaint is drafted. The memorandum might be consulted a third time when the attorney responds to a motion to dismiss; a fourth time while drafting interrogatories; a fifth time before making a motion for summary judgment; a sixth time before trial; and a seventh time in preparing an appeal.

Although the details of format may vary from law office to law office and from case to case, a thorough office memorandum usually includes the following:

1.   a memorandum heading
2.   a Question Presented
3.   a Brief Answer
4.   a Statement of Facts
5.   a Discussion
6.   a Conclusion
7.   the author's signature

(See the sample office memorandum in Appendix C.)

The *memorandum heading* simply identifies the writer, the immediately intended reader (who is often the writer's supervisor and is usually the person who requested the memorandum), the date on which the memorandum was completed, and the subject matter.

The *Question Presented* defines the issue that the memorandum is intended to resolve. (Questions Presented are explained in Chapter 18.)

The *Brief Answer* summarizes the prediction with at least an allusion to the determinative facts and rules, both of which are more fully analyzed in the discussion. For the reader in a hurry, the Brief Answer should set out the bottom-line response in the most accessible way. Compare two Brief Answers, both of which respond to the following Question Presented:

QUESTION PRESENTED

Did the District Attorney act unethically in announcing an indictment at a press conference where the defendant's criminal record was recited, where an alleged tape-recorded confession was played, where ballistics tests on an alleged murder weapon were described, and where the defendant was produced for photographers without the knowledge or consent of her attorney?

BRIEF ANSWER

Under DR 7-107(B) of the Code of Professional Responsibility, it is unethical for a prosecutor before trial to publicize, among other things, any criminal record the defendant might have, any confession she might allegedly have made, or the results of any tests the government might have undertaken. Under DR 1-102(A)(5), it is also unethical to engage in conduct "prejudicial to the administration of justice." That has occurred here if the press conference — and particularly the presentation of the defendant for photographers—created so much pretrial publicity that the jury pool has been prejudiced. Therefore, the District Attorney violated DR 7-107(B) and may have violated DR 1-102(A)(5).

BRIEF ANSWER

Yes. Except for the production of the defendant for photographers, all the actions listed in the Question Presented are pretrial publicity specifically prohibited by DR 7-107(B) of the Code of Professional Responsibility. In addition, if the jury pool has been tainted, even production of the defendant for photographers was unethical under DR 1-102(A)(5), which prohibits conduct "prejudicial to the administration of justice."

The first example is closer to the way you might think through the Brief Answer. But to make it useful to the reader you would have to rewrite it into a form that—like the second example—could be more quickly read and understood.

The *Statement of Facts* sets out the facts on which the prediction is based. (Fact statements are explained in Chapter 17.)

The *Discussion* usually takes up more than half of the memorandum. It proves the conclusion set out in the Brief Answer. If the discussion is highly detailed or analyzes several issues, it can be broken up with sub-headings to help the reader locate the portions that might be needed at any given time.

Some lawyers tend to write the Discussion before writing anything else; their reason is that the other components of the memorandum will be shaped in part by insights gained while putting the Discussion together. Other lawyers start by writing the Statement of Facts because the facts seem easier to describe. (Lawyers who write the Discussion first would say that they cannot begin by writing the fact statement because, until they have worked out the Discussion, they do not know enough about the facts, particularly which facts to emphasize as determinative and which to exclude as insignificant.) Another group of lawyers are flexible. They start with whatever component begins to "jell" first, and they often draft two or more components simultaneously.

The *Conclusion* summarizes the discussion in a bit more detail than the Brief Answer does. The Brief Answer is designed to inform the reader who needs to know the bottom line but has no time to read more. The Conclusion is for the reader who needs and has time for more detail, but not as much as the Discussion offers. The Conclusion or Brief Answer can also provide an overview for the reader about to plunge into the discussion. Although the Brief Answer is limited to answering the Question Presented, the Conclusion is an appropriate place to suggest alternatives or to recommend among the various options under consideration. If the Conclusion or Brief Answer is to be qualified or conditioned, specify the condition ("if the jury pool has been tainted . . .") or qualification ("although the courts of this state have not interpreted DR 1-102(A)(5) in the context of pretrial publicity . . .").

The *signature* appears under the typed words "Respectfully submitted."

§16.3 *Persuasive Memorandum Format*

When a motion is made, each side has the opportunity to submit a memo-randum. A plaintiff moving for a preliminary injunction, for example, will submit a document that might be titled "Memorandum in Support of Plain-tiff's Motion for a Preliminary Injunction," and the opposing party's docu-ment might be titled "Memorandum in Opposition to Plaintiff's Motion for a Preliminary Injunction."

Like the reader of an office memorandum, the judge (and the judge's law clerk) may look at each memorandum more than once. Depending on the judge's work habits and on the nature of the motion, at least some part of the memorandum might be read once for an understanding of the issues in-volved, a second time in preparation for a hearing or oral argument on the motion, a third time while deciding the motion, and a fourth time while writing an opinion.

Although conventions differ from jurisdiction to jurisdiction, generally the components of a memorandum of law are the following:

1. a cover page
2. a Table of Contents
3. a Table of Authorities
4. a Preliminary Statement
5. a Question Presented
6. a Statement of the Case
7. an Argument, broken up by point headings
8. a Conclusion
9. an indorsement (and, in some courts, the attorney's signature)

(See the sample persuasive memorandum in Appendix D.)

If local rules permit, the format might vary according to the attorney's own assessment of the complexity of the motion and the most persuasive way to present the attorney's theory. As with an office memorandum, each component is set off with a heading, and the writer cannot assume that the components will be read in sequence or at one sitting.

The *cover page* includes a caption and title, which correspond to the memorandum heading at the beginning of an office memorandum. The caption identifies the court and the parties, specifying their procedural designations (plaintiff, defendant, etc.). In a criminal case, the prosecution is called, depending on the jurisdiction, "State," "Commonwealth," "Peo-ple," or "United States," and no procedural designation follows those terms in the caption. The title identifies the memorandum and the purpose of its submission ("Memorandum in Opposition to Defendant's Motion to Dis-miss").

The *Table of Contents* begins on the page after the cover page, and the *Table of Authorities* appears on the first page after the Table of Contents.

The tables are put together and paginated just as they would be in an appellate brief.[1]

The *Preliminary Statement* briefly sets out the case's procedural posture by identifying the parties (to the extent that is necessary), listing the relevant procedural events, and describing the motion before the court and the relief sought. If it can be done very concisely, the Preliminary Statement might also summarize the parties' contentions. The point is to tell the judge why the matter is before the court and to specify the type of decision the judge will have to make. That can usually be done in less than a page.

Although a persuasive *Question Presented* is at least superficially similar to the Question Presented in an office memorandum, here the Question should persuade as well as inform. A convincing Question Presented is— for the small number of words involved—one of the most difficult drafting tasks in legal writing. The skill is explained in Chapter 18.

The *Statement of the Case* corresponds to the Statement of Facts in an office memorandum, but, again, there are differences in substance and in drafting technique, all of which are explained in Chapter 17.

The *Argument* corresponds to the Discussion in an office memorandum, but, here again, the goal is not merely to explain, but also to persuade. The Argument is the most complex component of a persuasive memorandum, but you have already learned all but one of the skills required. The exception is the skill of constructing *points* and *point headings*. An Argument is organized into *points*, each of which is a single, complete, and independent ground for relief. Each point has a heading and may have sub-headings, all of which are reproduced verbatim in the table of contents. Points and point headings are explained in Chapter 19. As with office memoranda, lawyers differ about which part of a persuasive memorandum they draft first. But with persuasive memoranda, the better practice may be to write the first draft of the point headings and sub-headings while outlining the Argument. In fact, the headings and sub-headings *are* an outline of the Argument.

In a persuasive memorandum, the *Conclusion* is intended only to remind the reader of what the writer seeks (or opposes), with an allusion to the writer's theory, if that can be compressed into one or two sentences. Although a Conclusion in a persuasive document is shorter than a Conclusion in an office memorandum, it cannot persuade if it is cut to the bone. Compare the following:

CONCLUSION

For all these reasons, this court should preliminarily enjoin construction of the logging roads here at issue.

CONCLUSION

Thus, the Forest Service's authorization of these logging roads violates the National Environmental Policy Act, the Administrative Pro-

---

§16.3 1. See §21.1. The tables are explained in Chapter 21 (on appellate brief writing) because they are sometimes omitted from law school memorandum assignments.

cedure Act, and the enabling legislation of the Forest Service. The harm would be irreparable, and an injunction would promote the public interest. This court should therefore grant an order preliminarily enjoining the Forest Service from building the roads.

The goal is to remind the court, in just a few sentences, of precisely what the lawyer wants done and why it should be done.

The *indorsement*, like the signature in an office memorandum, appears under a line reading "Respectfully submitted." The indorsement, however, is entirely typewritten and includes the attorney's name, a notation of the party the attorney represents, and the attorney's office address and telephone number. In some jurisdictions, the attorney also signs the memorandum.[2]

2. *See, e.g.,* Rule 11 of the Federal Rules of Civil Procedure.

17 Fact Statements: Objective and Persuasive

§17.1   Fact Statements Generally[1]

> There is nothing more horrible than the murder of a beautiful theory
> by a brutal gang of facts.
>
> —*La Rochefoucald*

A reader looks to the Statement of Facts in an office memorandum or the Statement of the Case in a persuasive memorandum or brief to learn the factual basis for the issues. That means that all facts analyzed elsewhere in the document should be recited in the fact statement. And no analysis, argument, or other discussion of the law appears in the fact statement, which is strictly a record of the material facts. The genre is called a fact *statement* because the facts are stated there and analyzed elsewhere.

Unless litigation has begun, a Statement of Facts in an office memorandum describes facts in a nonprocedural manner: a narrative, for example, of what has happened to the client, with careful notations as to the sources of various items of information. But if an office memorandum is written during litigation, the Statement of Facts is often drafted on two different levels:

---

§17.1   1. In this chapter, the uncapitalized term *fact statements* refers generically both to Statements of Facts in office memoranda and to Statements of the Case in persuasive memoranda and briefs. The capitalized term *Statement of Facts* means only an objective fact recitation in an office memorandum. And the capitalized term *Statement of the Case* means a fact recitation in a persuasive memorandum or in an appellate brief. You will understand this chapter more easily if, before continuing here, you read the Statement of Facts in the office memorandum in Appendix C, the Statement of the Case in the persuasive memorandum in Appendix D, and the Statements of the Case in Appendices E and F.

procedural facts are mixed together with nonprocedural facts[2] that might become the basis for future procedural events. For example:

> Although the defendant testified at her deposition that she purchased the stock with an inheritance, a bartender recalls serving the defendant and being told by her that she bought securities in her own name with funds from her insolvent business.

The deposition testimony is a procedural fact. The conversation in the bar is not. If the bartender later testifies about the conversation, that testimony will be a procedural fact, but the conversation itself will forever remain nonprocedural.

On the other hand, a Statement of the Case in a persuasive memorandum or an appellate brief describes only procedural facts: allegations in pleadings, testimony, other evidence, and so forth. A Statement of the Case might include a sentence like this:

> Although the defendant testified that she purchased the stock with an inheritance, Marvin Kalmar, a bartender, testified that, while drinking in his bar, she instead told him that the real source of funds for this purchase was the insolvent business that is the subject of this litigation.

Unlike the first quotation, which describes testimony and a contrasting conversation, this sentence describes only testimony. In Statements of the Case, nonprocedural facts must be excluded, a process called *limiting the statement to the record*. Judges react very harshly when they find, in a Statement of the Case, discussion of facts not in the record.

Judges also react harshly when a Statement of the Case contains interpretations or characterizations[3] of the record, which should appear only in the Argument because that is what they are. If you have trouble distinguishing between a fact and the type of factual inference that cannot be made in a fact statement, ask yourself whether an opposing attorney would dispute what you say. Although even an inference can be treated as a fact if it is undisputed, a disputable statement about the facts is more than purely factual because dispute itself involves argument and analysis. Judges are offended by a Statement of the Case that is not free of argument, and they distrust the rest of the document and the lawyer who wrote it. The most effective Statements of the Case persuade entirely through organization that emphasizes helpful facts and through word choice that is favorable but cannot be disputed by an adversary.

In any kind of fact statement, sources of information should be noted. The reason ought to be clear by now. To a lawyer, a nonprocedural event is not independent: it withers away and dies unless attached either to someone

---

2. If you are unsure about the difference between procedural and nonprocedural facts, see §12.1.

3. See §12.1.

who can testify to it or to some object (such as a document) that can become nontestimonial evidence of it. In Wintu, an Indian language in northern California, the verb forms encourage, if not require, a speaker to state the source of knowledge for every remark. For example:

> *pi k'upabe* = "I saw him chopping wood"
> *pi k'upanthe* = "I heard him chopping wood"
> *pi l'upake* = "I have been told he is chopping wood"
> *pi k'upa'el* = "I assume he is chopping wood" [4]

The verb forms seem to make it hard to say merely "he is chopping wood": certainly to a lawyer (and perhaps to a Wintu) such a naked statement would appear to be either complacent or a claim to omniscience. No one seems to know how the Wintu language developed such precision.[5] But because English lacks it, careful lawyers discipline themselves to recite the source of knowledge for a fact, not only in fact statements, but also in written and oral argument and often in simple conversation. Because truth is so hard to ascertain, every "fact" is qualified by its source.

The first task in organizing a fact statement, whether objective or persuasive, is to make a list of the determinative facts.[6] A fact statement should emphasize the determinative facts and explain them in detail. It should use explanatory facts only as glue to hold the determinative facts together, and it should omit the coincidental facts.[7]

The second step is to outline a statement that would set out the determinative and explanatory facts in a sequence that a reader would find easy to understand. In some cases, the most effective sequence is chronological, with occasional departures from chronological order to focus on determinative facts. But more often, a topical organization works better because you can use structure to imply logical relationships among facts.[8] How are the

4. Chafe, *About Language: A Richness of Words, A Babel of Tongues* in *The World of the American Indian* 150, 152 (1979).

5. Although the English language is a wonderful professional tool, it certainly has weaknesses. Some effort is needed, for example, to overcome the sexism in English. And, unlike Wintu, English does not demand that you state the source of factual knowledge: you will have to develop that habit yourself. Wintu, by the way, is not the only Native American language to reach levels of precision not common in English. Because the Hopi language, for example, does not separate time from space, it projects the kind of "continuous 'fabric' of time and space" inherent in theoretical physics, and Hopi may be better adapted than English to precise discussions of quantum mechanics and the theory of relativity. B. Lopez, *Arctic Dreams: Imagination and Desire in a Northern Landscape* 246 (1987).

6. See §12.2.

7. A date should appear in a fact statement only if it is truly relevant to the issues. Beginners often include every available date because dates are the easiest of all facts to state. But irrelevant dates cause two problems. First, they clutter and thus obscure the truly important facts. Second, they mislead the reader by implying that time is an issue. For example, where a fact statement begins

> The summons and complaint were served on February 1, 1988, . . .

the reader is given the impression that the controversy is about a statute of limitations or some other issue involving time.

8. A particularly long or complex fact statement can be made more accessible by breaking it up with sub-headings that are reprinted verbatim in the table of contents.

fact statements in Appendices C, D, E, and F organized? For each, is the organization effective or ineffective? Why?

Regardless of the method of organization, a fact statement begins with a paragraph that orients the reader. In an office memorandum, this paragraph would identify the most important people involved and the transaction out of which the issues grow. In a persuasive memorandum or an appellate brief, that might already have happened in the Preliminary Statement,[9] which identifies the parties, describes the nature of the litigation, and specifies the procedural posture and perhaps the grounds for the motion or appeal. The first paragraph of the Statement of the Case completes the introduction by summarizing the most compelling facts that are the heart of the writer's theory. (Later in the Statement of the Case, those facts are developed more fully.)

Depending on the case and on the lawyer's work habits, a fact statement might be written after, during, or before the rest of the document. Many lawyers write an objective fact statement before writing the rest of an office memorandum. With briefs and persuasive memoranda, some lawyers write the Statement of the Case after finishing the Argument because the process of theory development is over only when the Argument is complete. Some lawyers write the Argument and the Statement of the Case simultaneously, using separate pads. Others outline the Statement of the Case while writing the Argument. But virtually every lawyer modifies his or her habits somewhat from document to document, simply because a practice that works well in one instance might not work well in another.

Exercise I.   What Is a Fact? (Reprise)

Of the nine events listed on pages 201-04, which can be mentioned in a Statement of the Case?

---

§17.2   Techniques for Persuasively Stating Facts

> If you want to win a case, paint the Judge a *picture* and keep it simple.
>
> —*John W. Davis*

"It may sound paradoxical," wrote Justice Jackson, "but most contentions of law are won or lost on the facts."[1] But if you cannot argue, characterize, or state inferences in a Statement of the Case, how can you persuade

---

9. See §§16.3 and 21.1.
§17.2 1. *Advocacy Before the Supreme Court: Suggestions for Effective Case Presentations*, 37 A.B.A.J. 801, 803 (1951).

there? The accepted techniques all involve careful selection of facts and the suggestion of inferences through wording and organization:

1. Reflect your theory throughout the Statement.
2. Breathe life into the facts by telling a revealing story about people.
3. Without mentioning the elements of the controlling rule or rules, focus on the facts that would satisfy or negate those elements.
4. Emphasize favorable facts.
5. Neutralize the unfavorable facts that must be reported.
6. Start with a punch.
7. Humanize your client.

1. Reflect your theory throughout the Statement.   Tightly focus the Statement of the Case on facts that advance your theory. If the Statement wanders aimlessly and indiscriminately through the facts, the reader will not understand your theory and may not even grasp the story.

Every word should be selected to make the theory more clear. In the Statement in Appendix E, you learn that the defendant "suffers from gender dysphoria syndrome," while the prosecution's Statement in Appendix F instead says the defendant "planned to undergo surgery" that would alter gender. Do these phrasings advance the theories? How? When referring to the defendant, the prosecution's Statement uses the words "he," "him," and "her." The defendant's Statement, on the other hand, uses feminine pronouns and calls the defendant "Ms. Bresnahan." Is any of that unethical?[2] Would the court be misled? Has either attorney risked credibility? Or do these phrasings reflect legitimate differences in the parties' theories?

Throughout the Statement, the reader should be conscious—from the way the facts are cast—of whom you represent. If the reader wonders about that, even for a few sentences, you have probably not written a persuasive Statement.

2. Breathe life into the facts by telling a revealing story about people.   Even with value-neutral words and without fact interpretation, you can make the plot come alive by setting out the facts that show who has behaved properly and who has not, letting the facts themselves make the case. For example, *Hatahley v. United States*[3]

> involved, on its face, cold jurisdictional and legal problems: Were rights under the Taylor Grazing Act, a federal law, affected by a state law regulating abandoned horses? Had there in any event been compliance with the state statute's terms? Did the Federal Torts Claims Act cover intentional trespasses within the scope of federal agents' authority? The injuries for which redress were sought were the carrying off of horses and mules belonging to the plaintiffs, who were Navaho Indians.

2. See §§15.3, 17.3.
3. 351 U.S. 173 (1956).

. . . Here is how the facts were set forth in [the plaintiffs'] brief:

> The animals were rounded up on the range and were either driven or hauled in trucks to a Government-owned or controlled corral 45 miles away. Horses which could not be so handled were shot and killed by the Government's agents on the spot. . . . [T]he horses were so jammed together in the trucks that some died as a result, and, in one instance, the leg of a horse that inconveniently protruded through the truck body was sawed off by a federal employee. . . . (Fdg. 23, 25; R. 33-34.) Later, the animals were taken in trucks to Provo, Utah, a distance of 350 miles, where they were sold to a glue factory and horse meat plant for about $1,700—at about 3 cents a pound (R. 93, 293)—no part of which was received by petitioners (Fdg. 24; R. 34).[4]

The Supreme Court held that "[t]hese acts were wrongful trespasses not involving discretion on the part of the agents, and they do give rise to a claim compensable under the Federal Tort Claims Act."[5] Certainly, much legal analysis went into the decision, but, on this fact statement, does the result surprise you?

After reading the Statement of the Case for the movant in a trial court or for the appellant on appeal, the judge should be left with the feeling that something is unacceptably wrong with what has happened. The movant or the appellant, after all, wants the judge to *do* something about the facts. But after reading the Statement of the Case of an appellee or a party opposing a motion, the judge should instead believe the facts are fair and just—or at least that they are not so unjust as to call for judicial intervention. One way to arouse those feelings is to show how the facts are vividly, even interestingly just or unjust. Can you still see in your mind trucks, horses, a corral, a saw? Does that scene sum up what *Hatahley* was all about?

3. *Without mentioning the elements of the controlling rule or rules, focus on the facts that would satisfy or negate those elements.* If you must carry a burden of pleading, production, or persuasion, you can emphasize in the Statement of the Case the facts that you will later use in the Argument to show that you have discharged the burden. If any of those facts are undisputed, you can point that out:

> Dr. Charbonneau testified without contradiction that Ms. Leyland's injuries could have been caused only by a blow from a long, thin object "about the size and shape of a nightstick." (T. at 97.)

Regardless of which party has a burden, you can also point to inconsistencies in the evidence and things that are missing from the record:

> Although Officer Joyner testified that Ms. Leyland was assaulted by another prisoner in her cell (T. at 178), he could not name or describe that prisoner (T. at 187), and there is no evidence anywhere in the

---

4. Wiener, *Briefing and Arguing Federal Appeals* 58-59 (1967). (The references to "Fdg." and to "R." are citations to the record. You will see similar citations in other examples in this chapter. Section 17.4 explains what a record is and how to cite to it.)

5. *Hatahley,* 351 U.S. at 181.

record that another prisoner was at any point assigned to or given access to her cell. Moreover, although the warden of the county jail testified that arresting officers are not normally permitted in cell blocks (T. at 245), Officer Joyner was the sole witness who claimed to have seen an assault in Ms. Leyland's cell.

Who do you think beat up Leyland? Every word in this passage is value-neutral, and none of the evidence is interpreted or characterized. Although it persuades, the passage sounds clinically objective. The writer has merely brought together facts that had been scattered about in the record.[6] And the writer has refrained from stating inferences—such as "Officer Joyner should not be believed"—that should be left for the Argument.

4. Emphasize favorable facts. That can be done through organization: readers tend to be most attentive at the beginning, less attentive at the end, and least attentive in the middle. It can also be done by describing favorable facts in detail and by omitting unnecessary facts that cloud the picture you want the reader to see. Notice, for example, that the name of the warden is missing from the example above: the essential fact is the warden's official position, and the name would have no effect on the court. Specifics about dates, times, and places can be seductively concrete when you are writing, but to a reader they can also obscure what really happened. Compare the following:

> At 2:10 A.M., on Tuesday, September 2, 1986, Officer Joyner was told by his dispatcher to investigate a disturbance on the fourth floor of the building at 642 Sutherland Street. (T. at 162.) There he took a complaint from Kenneth Novak, a tenant in apartment 4-C, and, as a result, arrested Ms. Leyland, who lives in apartment 4-E. (T. at 163-65.) Officer Joyner was not able to leave the building with Ms. Leyland until 2:45 because she had been asleep and needed to dress. (T. at 166-67.) Ms. Leyland testified that she was so tired that she fell asleep in the police car during the drive to the precinct station. (T. at 14.) Cynthia Scollard, a police booking clerk, testified that she was on duty at about 3:05 A.M. on September 2, when she heard a commotion in the precinct parking lot. (T. at 145.) Ms. Scollard further testified that she noticed Ms. Leyland's injuries as soon as Officer Joyner turned Ms. Leyland over to her, and that Ms. Leyland appeared to be very tired at the time. (T. at 147-49.)

with this:

> Ms. Leyland was awakened and arrested by Officer Joyner at her apartment shortly after 2 A.M. on the day she was beaten. (T. at 162-67.) A police booking clerk testified that she heard "a man yelling

---

6. "Merely" describes the appearance, not the work needed to create it. Finding the raw materials in the record is a large task.

in the parking lot" just before Officer Joyner brought Ms. Leyland into the precinct station. (T. at 145.) The booking clerk also testified that she immediately noticed bleeding from Ms. Leyland's lip and from the side of her head (T. at 147-48), and that Ms. Leyland's face began to swell during booking (T. at 148-49).

In the first passage, the date, the address, the precise times, the booking clerk's name, and the details about Leyland's tired state are all clutter. The second passage omits the unnecessary, opening up room to dwell on the details that are truly essential. And the carefully edited quotation in the second example brings the story to life (as does the edited quotation in the example near the bottom of page 288).

    5. Neutralize the unfavorable facts that must be reported. The most effective method is to juxtapose an unfavorable fact with other facts that explain, counter-balance, or justify it:

> Even though the booking clerk testified that Ms. Leyland did not complain to her that she had been beaten by Officer Joyner, the booking clerk also testified that Officer Joyner stood next to Ms. Leyland throughout the booking procedure. (T. at 166-69.) Ms. Leyland testified that she had no memory of being booked (T. at 32), and Dr. Charbonneau testified that persons who suffer a head injury like Ms. Leyland's are often "stunned and impassive" immediately afterward. (T. at 104.)

The most effective juxtapositions are often found in sentences structured around an "even though" contrast—as the first sentence in this paragraph is. A far less effective method is to de-emphasize an unfavorable fact by tucking it into an obscure part of the Statement of the Case and summarizing it without much detail. Hiding an unfavorable fact will not make it go away. And if you seem to be trying to ignore the fact, you will not be viewed as credible and reliable. If you do not try to neutralize it, you forfeit an opportunity to persuade.

    6. Start with a punch. Express the essence of your theory at the very beginning of the Statement. Do not start with neutral facts, unfavorable facts, or unimportant facts. In the briefs in Appendices E and F, notice how each Statement begins with strong allusions to the writer's theory. The defendant's Statement in Appendix E opens by describing the defendant's medical condition and the experts who testified to it. The prosecution's Statement in Appendix F begins by describing the clothing the defendant was wearing when arrested, together with the undisputed testimony that the defendant's genitalia at the time were male.

    7. Humanize your client. Be careful how you refer to the parties. In an appellate brief, you only cause confusion if you refer to them continually as "appellant" and "appellee": in many courts those designations are not allowed in the Statement and Argument because they tell the reader nothing more than who lost below.[7] The procedural designations from the trial court are more clear: "the plaintiff" and "the defendant" in a civil case or, in a criminal case, "the defendant" and "the State" (or "the People," "the Government," or "the Commonwealth"). More still can be conveyed by using some generic factual designation related to the issues: "the buyer" and "the seller" in a commercial dispute or "the employer" and "the employee" in a discrimination case. But, unless it would be confusing, your client's real name is often the best tactical choice. The passages on pages 288-290 would lose much of their liveliness if "Ms. Leyland" were reduced to "the plaintiff." The same thing would happen if Officer Joyner were to gain anonymity as "the arresting officer," although in many other cases a depersonalized opposing party would seem easier to dislike ("the insurance company," "the union," "the hospital").

§17.3 Fact Ethics

You recall that a lawyer is forbidden to "[k]nowingly make a false statement of law or fact" to a court.[1] In §15.3, we explored the consequences of a false statement of law. Courts react just as harshly to false statements of fact. One court announced, for example, that "transgressions in this field must meet with severe disciplinary action, if the courts and bar alike are to perform their duties to litigants and the public."[2]

There are three quick ways in a fact statement to incur the fury of a court. One is by straight-out misrepresentation: making a statement about a fact that is inconsistent with the actual record. The second is misrepresentation by omission: presenting a version of the record that ignores facts favoring the opposing party.[3] The third is misrepresentation by describing inferences as though they were facts. Even in the Argument, a lawyer

> may assert any inferences from the facts of the case that seem to him arguable, but he cannot present his inferences from the facts as if they were the very facts themselves. When he is indulging, as he has every right to do, in inferences or reasoning from the facts, he must say so—there are many words in the English language fitted to express this process of inference—and to be effective he should state the facts in the record from which he is making his inferences.[4]

7. *See, e.g.,* Rule 28(d) of the Federal Rules of Appellate Procedure.

§17.3 1. Model Code of Professional Responsibility, DR 7-102(A)(5). The same prohibition, in virtually the same words, appears in Rule 3.3(a)(1) of the Model Rules of Professional Conduct.

2. *In re Greenberg,* 15 N.J. 132, 138, 104 A.2d 46, 49 (1954).

3. "[T]he 'summary of the material facts' required by rule 13, Rules of Appeal, means something more than just the facts favorable to the appellant. While possibly it is too much to hope that an appellant's summary will be completely objective, the court is not impressed by a statement of facts which completely ignores the evidence produced by the other side." *Manteca Veal Co. v. Corbari,* 116 Cal. App. 2d 896, 898, 254 P.2d 884, 885 (1st Dist. 1953).

4. *In re Greenberg,* 15 N.J. 132, 135, 104 A.2d 46, 47-48 (1954).

Even if it were not unethical, factual misrepresentation never fools a court and hurts only the misrepresenting lawyer and that lawyer's client. Misrepresentations are quickly spotted by opposing attorneys, and once a misrepresentation is pointed out to a court, the entire memorandum or brief is treated with suspicion.

§17.4   The Record

Let's look at the record.

—Al Smith

There is yet another way to incur judicial wrath over a fact statement. It does not involve a question of ethics, but judges will be furious just the same — and in most cases they can in one way or another penalize the offending lawyer. Virtually everywhere in the country, court rules require that each assertion of fact in a memorandum or brief be cited to a specific page in the record.[1] That is so not only when you recite a fact in the Statement of the Case, but also when you analyze the fact in the Argument — even though the reader would be able to find the cite by a search through the Statement of the Case.

The record might include any or all of the following: (1) the pleadings;[2] (2) transcripts of testimony for hearings, depositions, and trial, if any of these have occurred; (3) affidavits, if any were submitted in support of or in opposition to a motion; (4) exhibits introduced into evidence at a trial or hearing or attached to affidavits; and (5) any relevant prior court orders in the same case and, on appeal, the judgment below, together with any judicial opinions written to explain a relevant order or judgment.

The Statement must make clear through citation the source of each fact described. Not only is this required by court rules in every jurisdiction, but citations have a persuasive effect of their own. Meticulously complete citations communicate that every fact recited in the Statement is fully supported in the record, while spotty or absent citations arouse a court's skepticism. Remember that in legal writing generally a citation proves no

---

§17.4 1. *See, e.g.,* Rules 28(a)(3) and (e) of the Federal Rules of Appellate Procedure.

2. Remember that pleadings are not evidence. If the issue before the court is whether a burden of pleading has been carried, the pleadings are the only source of "facts," and the "facts" must be described as allegations. On a motion to dismiss a complaint in a wrongful death action, it is wrong to write "The deceased was run over by the defendant's truck." Because no evidence has been submitted, the only accurate statement is that the complaint alleges that the deceased was run over by the defendant's truck. You do not, however, have to begin every factual sentence with "The complaint alleges." It is enough to begin the fact statement with a sentence like this: "The complaint alleges the following." But if the issue is whether a burden of production or persuasion has been carried, the source of facts must be evidentiary (not pleadings) because the burden at issue is an evidentiary one. Depending on the motion before the court, evidence could appear in the form of testimony or affidavits, either of which might be supplemented with exhibits. See §§12.5.1-12.5.3.

more than the sentence that precedes it and, if the citation is placed inside a sentence, the citation proves only the portion of the sentence that precedes it. When you refer to a fact in the Argument, you must cite again to the record, even if you have already done so in the Statement of the Case. A judge who wants to check the record should not have to search the Statement of the Case for the citation.

The Bluebook has no adequate rules for citing to the record, and every jurisdiction has rules and customs of its own.[3] On appeal, one merely cites to the record as a whole ("R. at 393.") or to the joint appendix[4] as a whole ("JA at 99."). In a persuasive memorandum submitted to a trial court, one cites to specific documents within the record, such as "Compl. ¶ 22" (complaint at paragraph 22), "T. at 98" (transcript at page 98), or "Myers Reply Aff. ¶ 12" (Myers reply affidavit at paragraph 12). In any event, the citation is placed in a parenthetical:

> The plaintiff alleged only that the goods were not delivered on time. (Compl. ¶ 22.)

> Although Officer Joyner wrote on an incident report that Ms. Leyland was injured when she resisted arrest (R. at 98), he testified at trial that she was injured when assaulted by another prisoner in her cell (R. at 178).

Notice that the citation ends with a period if it stands alone as a citation sentence, but not if it is interpolated into a textual sentence.

Exercise II. Bank Robbery (Statements of the Case)

1. Chester Gordon is being tried under the federal bank robbery statute.[1] The prosecution has rested its case, and Gordon's attorney has moved for judgment of acquittal, arguing that the prosecution has failed to make out a prima facie case. Gordon's attorney has submitted a memorandum in support of the motion, and the prosecution has submitted a memorandum in opposition. The Statements of the Case are reproduced below. Go through each Statement and decide, fact by fact, whether the writer has done an effective job.

For the prosecution:

> Ms. Vaughn, the bank teller, testified that the defendant entered the bank at 10:30 A.M. on December 19. (T. at 29) She further testified that he walked up to her window and gave her a note that read "please give me money — I don't know how to do a hold-up." (T. at 33.) Additionally, she testified as to the weight, height, ap-

---

3. Local rules and custom sometimes allow latitude in the abbreviations used in citations to the record. If you use abbreviations that may be unfamiliar to the court, include a footnote near the beginning of the Statement of the Case, explaining what the abbreviations mean.
4. The joint appendix is an abbreviated form of the record on appeal. See §20.2.
1. See pages 81-82.

proximate age, demeanor, and appearance of the defendant. (T. at 31-32.) She estimated his height at six feet and his weight at 160 pounds. (*Id.*) She herself is five feet, six inches tall, and she weighs 126 pounds. (T. at 32.) Ms. Vaughn testified that she scooped up all the cash at her window — in her estimation, about ten thousand dollars — put it in an envelope, and gave it to the defendant. (T. at 34.) He began to put it in his pocket, and she hit him. (T. at 37.) While she delayed his escape, a security guard rushed over and wrestled the defendant to the ground. On redirect examination, she testified that she felt "shaken up" at that time. (T. at 79.) Ms. Vaughn also testified that the bank instructs tellers to give money to anyone who announces that a robbery is in progress.

For Chester Gordon:

The only witness to the incident at issue was the bank's teller, who testified that Mr. Gordon smiled through the incident and was wearing a suit (T. 31, 53). She admitted that he never displayed a weapon, made a threatening gesture, or even said anything to her (T. 51). Instead, he walked up to her window and handed her a note that read, in its entirety, "please give me money — I don't know how to do a hold-up" (T. 33). The teller testified that she believed that under bank policy she was compelled to give Mr. Gordon money, which she did — in an envelope. As Mr. Gordon looked down to put the envelope in his suit-coat pocket, she reached over the counter, grabbed his tie, jerked him forward, and punched him in the face twice, knocking him backward, where a security guard wrestled him to the floor. On redirect examination, she testified that she felt "shaken up" by all this (T. 79).

2. Now rewrite each Statement.

Exercise III.   Persuasive Fact Statements

Draft two persuasive fact statements — one favoring each party — using the facts and authority either from an exercise of your teacher's choice in either of Chapter 10 or Chapter 11 or from a writing assignment that you have previously completed in this course.

18 Questions Presented: Objective and Persuasive

§18.1 The Roles and Structure of a Question Presented[1]

In predictive writing, the Question Presented defines the issue that an office memorandum is meant to answer:

> Is a prisoner guilty of escape where he was beaten by a group of inmates who threatened to attack him as long as he remained in the same prison; where prison authorities did nothing to protect him; where he scaled the prison wall immediately after a second beating; but where he then hid from police for sixteen months and was finally captured trying to leave the country?

The determinative facts define the issue so that, as a matter of legal inquiry, it becomes the question "presented" by the situation. "Is a prisoner guilty of escape?" may be a question, but it is not a Question Presented.

In objective writing, the Question Presented itemizes the facts that the writer predicts to be determinative. In persuasive writing, a Question Presented has two functions. First, the court expects it to define the type of decision that the court is asked to make. And second, within limits described later in this chapter, you can use the Question to persuade by marshalling the facts at the core of your theory. Given the relatively few words involved, a persuasive Question Presented can be one of the most

§18.1 1. You will understand this material more easily if you read the Questions Presented in the office memorandum in Appendix C; in the persuasive memorandum in Appendix D; and in the briefs in Appendices F and G.

difficult drafting jobs in legal writing. If the Question defines the decision with pure objectivity, it does not perform the second function of a persuasive Question Presented. And if it argues the case, it does not fulfill the first. The solution is to persuade through juxtaposition—as you do in a Statement of the Case—but much more concisely.

Whether objective or persuasive, a Question Presented is a list of determinative facts attached to an inquiry. Usually—but not always—the most reliable format is to begin the Question with the inquiry and to start listing the determinative facts only after the inquiry is complete. The inquiry should at least allude to the rule or rules that would govern the result. The determinative facts are usually listed in a series of clauses, each beginning with "where" (or "when"):

> **inquiry:**   Is a prisoner guilty of escape
>
> **facts:**   *where* he was beaten by a group of inmates who threatened to attack him as long as he remained in the same prison; *where* prison authorities did nothing to protect him; *where* he scaled the prison wall immediately after a second beating; *but where* he then hid from police for sixteen months and was finally captured trying to leave the country?

Here the governing rules alluded to are those that define the crime of escape and its defenses. This Question is, of course, an objective one. The first three facts suggest the possibility of an acquittal, but the answer will depend on whether they are a sufficient defense under local law and whether they are overcome by the last fact, which is terrible for the defendant's case.

Beginners are sometimes tempted to use other formulas that only confuse and annoy readers. For example, the following are easy to write but hard to read:

> **facts before inquiry:**   Where a prisoner was beaten by a group of inmates who threatened to attack him as long as he remained in the same prison, where prison authorities did nothing to protect him, where he scaled the prison wall immediately after a second beating, but where he then hid from police for sixteen months and was finally captured trying to leave the country, is he guilty of escape?
>
> **facts and inquiry intermingled:**   Is a prisoner, who was beaten by a group of inmates threatening to attack him as long as he remained in the same prison and who received no protection from prison authorities, guilty of escape where he scaled the wall only after a second beating but where he then hid from police for sixteen months and was finally captured trying to leave the country?

Can you understand either of these questions on the first reading? On the second? The words are virtually the same as those in the Question Presented on page 295; only the order is different. The inquiry is best placed first because none of the determinative facts makes any sense until the reader knows the inquiry to which those facts are relevant.

The inquiry can begin with whatever verb is most appropriate to the issue:

Is a prisoner guilty . . . ?

Did the Circuit Court err . . . ?

Does the First Amendment prevent . . . ?

Should a manufacturer be enjoined . . . ?

Or the inquiry can instead begin with the word *whether*, even though the result is not a grammatically complete sentence:

Whether a prisoner is guilty . . .

Whether the police violated . . .

Whether the First Amendment prevents . . .

Whether a manufacturer should be enjoined . . .

But "whether" Questions often seem weaker and more tedious than Questions that begin with a verb.

In some cases, the list of determinative facts is so complex that a reader would drown in a series of "where" clauses. This is especially so where the same set of determinative facts raises several distinct and independent issues, and where the facts themselves are difficult to describe concisely. In such cases, lawyers sometimes use a different format, expressing the determinative facts in an introductory paragraph, and then posing the Question or Questions. An example is the Question Presented in the brief in Appendix E.

In a persuasive Question Presented, the least confusing way to refer to the parties is generically: "a prisoner," "a malpractice insurer," "an employee," and so forth. It is very confusing to call the parties "appellant" or "appellee." "Plaintiff" and "defendant" can also be confusing, unless the Question itself makes clear what kind of plaintiff and what kind of defendant are involved ("Does a complaint state a cause of action for personal injuries where the defendant is alleged . . . ?"). Obviously, in a criminal case it is never confusing to refer to one party as the defendant: the only other party is the government. And a procedural designation might add clarity in a civil case if the issue itself is so procedural that the parties' procedural identities are essential.[2] And although a busy judge can be confused when the parties

2. Some examples: "Has a defendant been properly served where the summons was handed to him in a plain manila envelope?" "May a plaintiff serve an amended complaint, without leave of court, before the defendant's time to answer has expired?"

are referred to by name only, it may be tactically wise to try to personalize a party beset by some institutional opponent, if the context will make clear who is who.[3]

A Question Presented is drafted in three stages. First, write out a narrow statement of the inquiry ("Is a prisoner guilty of escape?") and a separate list of the facts that you believe to be determinative, omitting facts that are merely explanatory or coincidental.[4] Second, tinker with the list, perhaps while writing and rewriting the other components of the memorandum or brief. Add or subtract facts as you come to understand the issue better, and refine the list's wording as you learn the possibilities and limitations of each fact. Third, work out a final phrasing of the list and join it to the inquiry in a single sentence. The Question Presented is often the last part of a document to reach its final form.

§18.2   How a Persuasive Question Presented Persuades

A *picture* held us captive.

— *Wittgenstein*

Consider a case in which a stockbroker gets tired of his work and decides to do something meaningful. He retains a partnership interest in his brokerage firm but persuades a gourmet bakery to take him on as an apprentice baker. The bakery has perfected a method — which it keeps secret — of imparting a citrus taste to croissants. As a precaution, the bakery requires its employees to sign a covenant not to compete with the bakery for three years in either of the two urban counties in an otherwise rural state. After a short time, the stockbroker quits and forms his own company to bake and sell gourmet baked goods. The bakery sues for an injunction to prohibit competition from the apprentice. The trial court grants the injunction, and the apprentice appeals. In the jurisdiction where this arises, a covenant not to compete is enforceable if the prohibition on competition is "reasonably limited" in duration and geographic area, if it "does not exceed that reasonably necessary for protection of the employer's business," if it "is not unreasonably restrictive" of the employee's rights, and if it does not violate public policy.[1]

For a Question Presented, the apprentice's attorney might draft something like this:

> Did the Superior Court err in enjoining an apprentice baker from working "in any baking capacity" for three years in all of the state's

---

3. *See, e.g.,* the Question Presented in the brief in Appendix E.
4. See §12.2.
§18.2 1. *Am. Credit Bureau v. Carter,* 462 P.2d 838, 840 (Ariz. Ct. App. 1960).

cities, with three-quarters of the state's population, where the plaintiff's only claim of potential injury is that, in starting his own business, the apprentice might use a croissant recipe?

The bakery's attorney, on the other hand, might write a very different Question:

> Did the Superior Court properly enjoin the violation of a three-year covenant not to compete in the baking business, where the enjoined "apprentice baker" is actually a successful stockbroker who was trained as a baker entirely by the plaintiff, who had access to the hitherto secret recipe for the plaintiff's biggest-selling product, and who has now set himself up in business as the plaintiff's only competitor in a specialized two-county gourmet baked goods market?

Notice several things. First, this would be a difficult case to decide. A judge inclined to reverse the trial court's injunction, for example, must pause at the prospect of a former employee, especially this one, profiting from doing that which he had expressly promised not to do. On the other hand, a judge inclined to affirm should be troubled by the idea of a person being prohibited — in such a heavily populated area and for three years — from working in a field he seems to enjoy. But if a case deserves to be hotly litigated, it is bound to have problems in it for both sides.

Second, each Question sets out the attorney's theory of the case without arguing it. Even if you do not know much about the legal rules involved in this appeal, you can predict from the Questions alone a great deal of what will be argued later in the brief. The apprentice's attorney is certain to argue that the covenant is unreasonable in time (three years), substance ("in any baking capacity"), and area (three-quarters of the state's population). The bakery's attorney is equally certain to argue that the covenant's geographic area is reasonable because of the nature of the market, that its duration is reasonable because of the nature of the product, and that the court should view the apprentice as a stockbroker and businessman and not as a person who really makes his living with bread dough in his hands. The knack is to state the Question in such a way as to suggest its solution.[2]

Third, the Questions persuade by listing facts the opposing attorney cannot claim to be untrue or missing from the record, and by describing those facts in words the opposing attorney cannot reasonably claim to be inaccurate. The apprentice's attorney cannot deny that the apprentice is a successful stockbroker, that he received all his bakery training from the plaintiff, that he has the plaintiff's "hitherto secret" recipe, or that he "has now set himself up in business as the plaintiff's only competitor." And the bakery's attorney cannot deny that the covenant prohibits the apprentice from working as a baker in an area with three-quarters of the state's popula-

---

2. "Chief Justice White was happily endowed with the gift of finding the answer to problems by merely stating them." Frankfurter, *Some Reflections on the Reading of Statutes,* 47 Colum. L. Rev. 527, 530 (1947).

tion, or that the bakery has claimed no other potential injury than that "the apprentice might use a croissant recipe." The bakery's attorney would have reached too far if the bakery's Question had posited that "the injunction covers *only* two counties" because those two counties include three-quarters of the state's population and cannot reasonably be dismissed as "only." The Question Presented persuades only if based on undeniable descriptions of facts.

Fourth, neither attorney has pretended that the other side's strongest facts do not exist. The Questions are two intellectual constructs between which the court must choose, and a court is not likely to choose one that ignores a significant and troubling aspect of the controversy. Thus, the apprentice's attorney must concede that his client suddenly created a company to compete, but he does so in words that suggest that the bakery will not suffer much as a result ("the plaintiff's only claim of potential injury is that, in starting his own business, the apprentice might use a croissant recipe"). The bakery's attorney can hardly ignore the fact that the state's population is concentrated in the two counties covered by the covenant, but she mentions that in a phrase showing why the covenant ought to address that area ("a specialized two-county gourmet baked goods market"). As in a Statement of the Case, the key here is juxtaposition.

Fifth, neither Question posits a conclusion of law as though it were a fact. A court is neither informed nor persuaded when a question merely asks whether a set of black-letter elements equal the satisfaction of a test ("Is a covenant not to compete enforceable if it is reasonably limited in duration and geographic area, if its prohibitions are reasonably necessary to protect the employer's business, if it does not unreasonably restrict the employee's rights, and if it does not violate public policy?"). Although the answer to such a Question is affirmative, the Question has no persuasive effect because it is not grounded in the facts of the case before the court. To define the decision the court must make, you must recite the facts that you believe should determine the result. And a conclusion cannot be posited as a factual given: it must be *argued* in the Argument.

Sixth, words in these Questions are carefully chosen to create a picture through nuance. In the bakery's Question, the apprentice is "actually a successful stockbroker." That has two purposes. One is to show that he is not really being cut off from a livelihood. The other is to draw an image of a dilettante who has dabbled in a fancy and has now decided to make a fast profit at the expense of the person who trained him ("has now set himself up in business"). His own attorney, not eager to make that plain, writes more neutrally of an "apprentice."

Seventh, although the two lists of determinative facts are complex, they are expressed so concisely that each question can be understood on the first reading. This takes much writing and rewriting. It is partly a process of finding the most concise phrasing and partly a process of finding the most meaningful level of abstraction or compression. In an earlier draft of the bakery's Question, the phrase "was trained as a baker *entirely* by the plaintiff" might have been "was trained as a baker by the plaintiff *and has never received any other instruction or experience in the field.*" Do you see how much clout a single, carefully chosen word ("entirely") can carry? Finding the right level of abstraction or compression is not easy. An overly specific formulation of a fact is too detailed to imply the fact's relevance and usually so verbose as to confuse the reader. An overly general formulation often oversimplifies and is too rarefied to open up the picture that you want the reader to see — the picture that captures the decision-maker.

Eighth, the facts set out in these two Questions are expressed in clauses that describe the evidence precisely but in nouns and verbs that emphasize some things and de-emphasize others. The bakery's attorney, for example, writes that the apprentice "has now set himself up in business." That has much more of a derogatory punch than the apprentice's attorney's corresponding words — "in starting his own business" — which do not so clearly show us a picture of an opportunist. And the alleged betrayal of the bakery is expressed mostly in verbs that put the spotlight on the apprentice ("who was trained as a baker entirely by the plaintiff, who had access to the [plaintiff's] hitherto secret recipe").

Ninth, each Question is drafted in a positive tone to invite the answer the writer seeks. The apprentice's attorney asks whether the Superior Court erred and then lists facts suggesting that it did. The bakery's attorney asks whether the Superior Court ruled correctly and then lists facts supporting an affirmative answer.

Finally, although the factual lists themselves look short, the case cannot possibly be so factually simple. An appeal of this kind might be based on a trial or hearing transcript hundreds of pages long, and an attorney writing a brief would need many hours to study it and the other documents that together are the record below. Somewhere in all the fire and smoke of direct and cross-examination are the relatively small number of facts that could determine the court's decision, and the attorney's task — as you know — is to find them and to design a theory around them. That is a precise art: you cannot afford to miss a fact the court would likely find determinative or to include one about which the court would not care much.

§18.3 How to Evaluate Your Questions Presented for Persuasiveness

Frank Cooper has suggested six standards[1] for judging the effectiveness of a Question Presented:

1. The issue must be stated in terms of the facts of the case [rather than in terms of assumed legal conclusions].
2. The statement must eliminate all unnecessary detail.
3. It must be readily comprehensible on first reading.
4. It must eschew self-evident conclusions.

§18.3   1. *Writing in Law Practice* 80 (1963).

5. It should be so stated that the opponent has no choice but to accept it as an accurate statement of the question.
6. It should be subtly persuasive. [Or: would a disinterested but skeptical reader think, "This attorney has the winning side"?]

We can add two more:

7. It should clearly define the decision the court has been asked to make.
8. It should set out your theory clearly and convincingly.

And we can list the ways in which a Question Presented can *fail* to communicate your theory:

First, a Question does not communicate a theory if it *lacks determinative facts:*

> Did the Superior Court properly enjoin the violation of a three-year covenant not to compete in the baking business in either of this state's two urban counties?

A question like this is so unpersuasive as to cause a reader to stop short and ask, "Whom does this writer represent?"

Second, a Question communicates an incomplete theory if its list of *determinative facts is incomplete:*

> Did the Superior Court properly enjoin the violation of a three-year covenant not to compete in the baking business, where the enjoined apprentice was trained as a baker entirely by the plaintiff?

If you did not know about the facts not mentioned here, would this Question persuade you?

Third, a Question communicates a misleading theory if *nondeterminative facts are listed:*

> Did the Superior Court properly enjoin the violation of a three-year covenant not to compete in the baking business, where the enjoined apprentice was trained as a baker entirely by the plaintiff, which sued the apprentice immediately after he went into business for himself . . . ?

This Question suggests that the apprentice has raised a laches issue, which has not actually happened.

Fourth, a Question communicates no theory if *it is unreadable:*

> Did the Superior Court properly enjoin the violation of a covenant not to compete, which applied only to the baking industry and included a prohibition on competition that lasted three years, where the defendant was a baking apprentice who has made and continues to

make a substantial income as a stockbroker, where he was trained as a baker by the plaintiff and has never received any other instruction or experience in the field, where he had access to the plaintiff's hitherto secret recipe, where he has now set himself up in business as the plaintiff's only competitor, and where the parties compete in a specialized gourmet baked goods market which extends over two counties?

Can you understand this at one reading? Can you tell immediately what facts are important? Compare it — phrase by phrase — with the Question on page 299. There is no difference in meaning. In fact, the only difference is that the Question above is verbose where it should be concise and detailed where it should be abstract and compressed. (Another way to make a Question unreadable is to use an obtuse sentence structure. See the two examples on page 296.)

Fifth, a Question communicates no theory or an incomplete theory if any of the "facts" are either (1) *subjective characterizations* —

> Did the Superior Court properly enjoin the violation of a three-year covenant not to compete in the baking business, where the enjoined apprentice is actually a successful stockbroker who deceived the plaintiff into disclosing its hitherto secret recipe, and who has now betrayed his former employer by setting himself up in business . . . ?

or (2) *conclusions of law* —

> Did the Superior Court properly enjoin the violation of a three-year covenant not to compete in the baking business, where the covenant's restraints are reasonable in duration and geographic area, where they are reasonably necessary to protect the employer's business . . . ?

Although both of these examples sound impressive, they mean nothing and will be ignored by a court. In a Question Presented, a judge needs to learn the most determinative facts, not the lawyer's characterizations and conclusions. If you find characterizations and conclusions in a Question you have written, cut them out and *replace them with the facts that would make them true.* Which facts, for example, make this restraint reasonably necessary to protect the bakery's business? Those facts belong in the Question, and the conclusion of law should come out.

Sixth, a Question communicates a confusing theory if written *on the assumption that the reader already knows the case:*

> Did the Superior Court properly enjoin the violation of a three-year covenant not to compete, where the defendant is actually a successful stockbroker who was trained entirely by the plaintiff, who had access to the plaintiff's hitherto secret recipe, and who has now set himself up in business as the plaintiff's only competitor?

Did the plaintiff train the defendant to be a stockbroker? Is this a suit to enjoin competition in the stock brokerage industry? What does a recipe have to do with this? Remember that the reader might not yet have read the Statement of the Case and has certainly not yet read the Argument. Many judges use the Question Presented as an introduction to other parts of the memorandum or brief.

Seventh, a Question communicates an unpersuasive theory if it *does not overcome a judge's natural tendency to ask "So what?" or "Is this really so bad that I should use the awesome power of the court to interfere?"*

> Did the Superior Court properly enjoin the violation of a three-year covenant not to compete in the baking business, where the enjoined apprentice, a stockbroker, was trained as a baker by the plaintiff, had access to a secret recipe, and has started a baking business?

Compare this Question — phrase by phrase — with the one on page 299. A judge might yawn at this one but not at the other. Why would that be so? The same facts are listed in both Questions. What does the Question on page 299 have that the one above lacks?

Eighth, Questions communicate no theory if *the reader's attention is diffused* through several Questions that really add up to only one (or a few):

> 1. Did the Superior Court properly enjoin the violation of a covenant not to compete, which was limited to a three-year period in a two-county area?
>
> 2. Did the Superior Court properly enjoin the violation of a covenant not to compete, where the enjoined former employee had access to the plaintiff's hitherto secret bakery recipe and has now set himself up as the plaintiff's only competitor?
>
> 3. Did the Superior Court properly enjoin the violation of a covenant not to compete, where the former employee is a successful stockbroker who does not depend on baking for his livelihood?

This is like trying to cut water with a knife.

Exercise I.   Bank Robbery (Questions Presented)

The following Questions were all drafted for appellate briefs in a case involving the federal bank robbery statute.[1] Using the criteria in §18.3, evaluate the effectiveness of each Question.

1.   Should the District Court have granted the defendant's motion for judgment of acquittal on a charge of committing robbery by intimidation in violation of 18 U.S.C. § 2113(a), where the defendant, although he did not show a weapon or threaten violence, gave a bank teller a note that would put a reasonable person in fear, where the teller did not

---

1. See pages 81-82 and 293-94.

hesitate to comply with his demand, although she courageously struck him after he took the money she surrendered, and where she testified afterward that she was "shaken up" by this stressful situation?

2. Whether the Government was entitled to put its case to a jury where a bank teller testified that the defendant—who was charged with bank robbery "by intimidation"—handed her a note announcing that he was conducting a "hold-up," where she gave him all the cash at her window, and where she felt "shaken up" after the defendant's capture, in which she assisted.

3. Whether the District Court should have granted the defendant's motion for judgment of acquittal on Count I of an indictment for bank robbery "by intimidation" where there was uncontroverted evidence that the defendant was pleasant and smiled throughout the alleged robbery; that he made no threatening gestures or statements and carried no visible weapon; and that the teller, after giving him cash, reached over the counter, grabbed him by the tie, and punched him twice in the face.

4. Has the Government failed to make out a prima facie case of bank robbery "by intimidation" where the sole evidence of intimidation is a note, handed to a teller, that read "please give me money—I don't know how to do a hold-up"?

Exercise II.   Drafting Persuasive Questions Presented

Draft two persuasive Questions Presented—one favoring each party—using the facts and authority either from an exercise of your teacher's choice in Chapter 10 or Chapter 11 or from a writing assignment that you have previously completed in this course.

19 Point Headings and Sub-Headings

§19.1 How Points and Headings Work

In a brief or persuasive memorandum, the Argument is divided into points. Each point is given a heading and may be divided by sub-headings.[1]

A point is an independent, complete, and free-standing ground for a ruling in your favor on a Question Presented. If only one ground would support a favorable ruling on the Question, you have only one point for that Question and only one point heading, although the point itself could be broken up into sub-headings to the extent that would help the reader. If, on the other hand, you have two or more favorable theories, each of which could stand alone as a *complete* and *independent* ground for relief, each theory is a separate point and is to be summarized in a separate heading.

How could you have more than one complete and independent reason for a ruling in your favor? Take an appeal from a dismissal at the commencement of an action. As they would appear in the Table of Contents, the appellee's point headings might read as follows:

    I.   THE DISTRICT COURT
         PROPERLY DISMISSED THE
         COMPLAINT FOR FAILURE
         TO STATE A CAUSE
            OF ACTION.

---

§19.1 1. You will understand this material more easily if, before reading this chapter, you study the point headings and sub-headings in the Tables of Contents of the memorandum in Appendix D and the briefs in Appendices E and F.

II.   THE DISTRICT COURT
      PROPERLY DISMISSED THE
      ACTION BECAUSE THE
      SUMMONS WAS IMPROP-
      ERLY SERVED ON THE
      DEFENDANT.

III. THE DISTRICT COURT
      PROPERLY DISMISSED THE
      ACTION ON THE GROUND
      OF RES JUDICATA.

IV.   THE DISTRICT COURT
      PROPERLY DISMISSED THE
      ACTION ON THE GROUND
      THAT THE PLAINTIFF'S TIME
      TO SUE HAS EXPIRED.

If true, any one of these should be sufficient for affirmance. A complaint that fails to set out a cause of action should be dismissed even if properly served and even if the action is not barred by res judicata or the statute of limitations. An action should be dismissed if the summons was not properly served, even if the complaint does state a cause of action—and so on.

Sub-headings can be used to develop a point heading:

I.   THE DISTRICT COURT PROP-
     ERLY DISMISSED THE COM-
     PLAINT FOR FAILURE TO
     STATE A CAUSE OF ACTION.

     A.   The plaintiff's claim is
          solely that the defendant
          School District did not
          "adequately" teach him.

     B.   Virtually every jurisdiction
          that has considered the
          question has refused to rec-
          ognize a tort of "educa-
          tional malpractice."

     C.   Because an education is
          the result of the efforts of
          both student and teachers,
          a failure to learn cannot be
          attributed solely to the
          school.

        D.   A tort of "educational
             malpractice" would disrupt
             the public schools.

            1.   Scarce educational
                 resources would be di-
                 verted to pay damages
                 or insurance premiums.

            2.   A litigious atmosphere
                 would interfere with
                 teaching and learning.

    II.   THE DISTRICT COURT PROP-
           ERLY DISMISSED THE AC-
           TION BECAUSE THE
           SUMMONS AND COMPLAINT
           WERE IMPROPERLY SERVED
           ON THE DEFENDANT.

The numbering and lettering sequence is the same as with an outline:

     I. [point heading]
         A. [sub-heading]
            1. [secondary
               sub-heading]
            2. [secondary
               sub-heading]
         B. [sub-heading]
    II. [point heading]

A solitary sub-heading is inappropriate: if you find yourself with an "A" but no "B," either create a "B" or, failing that, incorporate the substance of "A" into the point heading itself. On the other hand, a point heading is roman-numbered even if it is the only one you have.

In Appendices D, E, and F, you will notice that in many instances the first paragraph after a sub-heading lacks a thesis sentence. That is because a sub-heading often eliminates the need for a thesis sentence in the first paragraph that follows. Where that first paragraph in some way summarizes the material under the sub-heading, the paragraph's thesis is already expressed by the sub-heading itself. In fact, while you rewrite and reorganize an Argument you may at times find yourself promoting a thesis sentence into a sub-heading or demoting a sub-heading into a thesis sentence.

When you set up headings and sub-headings in a Table of Contents and in an Argument, study the examples in Appendices D, E, and F for format. Both in the Argument and in the Table of Contents (where they are printed verbatim), point headings appear entirely in capital letters. Sub-headings are underlined in the Argument but not in the Table of Contents. And in both places, all headings and sub-headings are single-spaced. In the Argument, headings and sub-headings are centered with large margins on both sides and white space above and below. Headings and sub-headings should be obvious to a reader who is skimming. That reader does not easily notice this:

I. THE DISTRICT COURT PROPERLY DISMISSED THE COMPLAINT
    FOR FAILURE TO STATE A CAUSE OF ACTION.

But a better layout on the page has a more arresting effect:

> I. THE DISTRICT COURT PROP-
>   ERLY DISMISSED THE COM-
>   PLAINT FOR FAILURE TO
>   STATE A CAUSE OF ACTION.

If you have only an inch or two left at the bottom of a page in the Argument, do not put a heading there; put it instead at the top of the next page. For the same reason that newspaper headlines do not appear at the bottom of a newspaper page, point headings and sub-headings look silly if they appear at the bottom of an Argument page without any text underneath.

Before you have completed your research, you can start to outline the Argument by rough-drafting the point headings and sub-headings. If you organize the authority for each point and sub-point, you will be able to identify the gaps that must be filled with further research.

§19.2 How to Evaluate Your Headings and Sub-Headings for Effectiveness

The effectiveness of your point headings and sub-headings can be judged by the following criteria:

1. When collected in the Table of Contents, the headings and sub-headings should lay out a complete and persuasive outline of your theory.
2. Each point should be an independent, complete, and free-standing ground for a ruling in your favor.
3. Headings and sub-headings should not assume information that a judge would lack when reading the Table of Contents.
4. The sub-headings should be neither too many nor too few.
5. Each heading and sub-heading should be a single sentence that can be immediately understood.
6. Each point heading should identify the ruling you want.
7. The controlling rules should be identified in the headings or sub-headings.

8. The one, two, or three most determinative facts should at least be alluded to in either the headings or sub-headings.
9. Headings and sub-headings should be forceful and argumentative.

1. When collected in the Table of Contents, the headings and sub-headings should lay out a complete and persuasive outline of your theory. Many judges read the point headings in the Table of Contents before reading any other part of the brief. The point headings are thus your opportunity to introduce and outline your theory. Although the reader would have to study the Argument to learn how the theory works, the headings—when read together in the Table of Contents—should lay out the significant steps of logic on which the theory is based, outlining a paradigm-structured argument, with rule proof and rule application and perhaps with policy arguments and counter-analyses. (Notice how that is done with the headings and sub-headings in §19.1.) If you draft the headings after you write the Argument, be sure that the headings and sub-headings present a complete and coherent picture of your theory when they are isolated in the Table of Contents. When you compile the headings and sub-headings in the Table of Contents, you may find that you have to redraft them because only then might you discover gaps or inconsistencies not apparent when the headings are scattered in the Argument.

Look at the Tables of Contents of the memorandum in Appendix D and in the briefs in Appendices E and F. Read the headings and sub-headings there as you believe a judge would on first opening each document. From the headings, can you understand each writer's theory? Why or why not?

2. Each point should be an independent, complete, and free-standing ground for a ruling in your favor. A careless beginner might write four or five "point" headings for material that will yield only one or two genuine points. This is caused by confusing a point with a contention. Check yourself in the following way: If you have several point headings, look at each one in isolation: if the court were to believe everything you say in and under that heading, but were to believe absolutely nothing else in the Argument, would you win? If the answer is no, the "point" cannot stand on its own, and you have fewer points than you thought you did. You have a real point only if the court can make some ruling in your favor based on what is in and under that heading alone.

Beginners sometimes make the opposite error of grouping several points under one heading. This happens most often where the writer's adversary is the one charged with a burden of pleading, production, or persuasion. If the adversary must carry a burden for several elements, the failure to support any element creates a complete and independent ground for a ruling against the adversary. For example, in the memorandum in Appendix D, Goslin is entitled to a preliminary injunction only if he can show (1) that he is likely to succeed ultimately on the merits, (2) that he would suffer irreparable harm without a preliminary injunction, and (3) that a balancing of the equities favors an injunction. Goslin has only one point because he must prove all those elements to win. But depending on the ways in which the law and the evidence might favor Skeffington (the nephew), he—as the party not charged with a burden—might have more than one point. If the nephew could show that Goslin is not likely to succeed on the merits, *and* that Goslin is not threatened with irreparable harm, *and* that the equities run against an injunction, the nephew would have three separate points because Goslin must carry all three of those burdens or lose.

3. Headings and sub-headings should not assume information that a judge would lack when reading the Table of Contents. Put yourself in the judge's position: when turning to the Table of Contents for the first time, the judge knows nothing of the case. How would you react to this heading?

> I. THE SUPERIOR COURT
>   PROPERLY DENIED THE MO-
>   TION TO QUASH BECAUSE
>   OF THE FIRST AMENDMENT.

Quash what? What does the First Amendment have to do with this? The following is better:

> I. THE SUPERIOR COURT
>   PROPERLY REFUSED TO
>   QUASH THE PLAINTIFF'S
>   SUBPOENA, WHICH DID NOT
>   VIOLATE THE JOURNALIST
>   WITNESS'S FIRST AMEND-
>   MENT RIGHT TO MAINTAIN
>   THE CONFIDENTIALITY OF
>   HIS SOURCES.

4. The sub-headings should be neither too many nor too few. For each point, the number of sub-headings should equal the number of *significant* steps of logic inherent in the argument. For example, the failure-to-state-a-cause-of-action point on pages 308-09 depends on the following steps of logic:

- The complaint alleges only educational malpractice: because the complaint cannot be interpreted to allege any other kind of claim, it can survive a motion to dismiss only if this state were to recognize a cause of action for educational malpractice.
- The idea of recovering for educational malpractice has been scorned by other courts.
- Such a tort is impractical because a court would not be able to determine how much of the fault was the student's and how much was the school's.

- Such a tort would damage schools by disrupting the educational process.

These are the very steps represented in the sub-headings on pages 308-09. More sub-headings would have fragmented the argument so much that the reader would not quickly see how it fits together. Fewer sub-headings would have hidden the logic.

5. Each heading and sub-heading should be a single sentence that can be immediately understood. What does this heading mean?

    I.   BECAUSE THIS STATE'S
SHIELD LAW PROVIDES NO
EXPLICIT PROTECTION FOR
THE MEDIA AGAINST RE-
VEALING NONCONFIDENTIAL
INFORMATION OR SOURCES
AND BECAUSE THE LEGISLA-
TIVE HISTORY IS SILENT, THE
SCOPE OF ART. 9, § 765 IS
LIMITED TO PROTECTING
ONLY CONFIDENTIAL INFOR-
MATION OR SOURCES, AND
THE SUPERIOR COURT
THEREFORE ERRED IN
QUASHING A SUBPOENA
THAT SOUGHT INFORMATION
THAT THE APPELLANT, A
NEWSPAPER REPORTER, HAD
OBTAINED THROUGH CON-
VERSATIONS IN WHICH HE
HAD NOT PROMISED TO KEEP
HIS INFORMANTS' IDENTITIES
IN CONFIDENCE.

A monster like this has two parents. One is the urge to put everything in the point heading and save nothing for the sub-headings. The other is simple verbosity: even more than elsewhere, conciseness is a real premium in a heading. Rewriting can produce something like this:

    I.   THE SUPERIOR COURT PROP-
ERLY REFUSED TO QUASH
THE SUBPOENA BECAUSE THE
EVIDENCE SOUGHT IS NOT
CONFIDENTIAL AND IS
THEREFORE NOT PROTECTED
BY THIS STATE'S MEDIA
SHIELD LAW.

    A.　Art. 9, § 765 permits a
       litigant to obtain informa-
       tion that the media has not
       treated as confidential.

    B.　The appellant journalist
       concedes that he did not
       promise confidentiality to
       his sources.

6. Each point heading should identify the ruling you want.　A point heading fails this criterion if it leaves a judge wondering "What do you want me to do?" In a trial court, you can tell the judge what you want by identifying the order or judgment that you argue should be granted or denied. On appeal, you can do the same thing by identifying the order or judgment appealed from and by calling it either correct or erroneous (which implies that you want it affirmed or reversed). To all of the following headings (from three different cases), a judge's reaction would be "What do you want from me?":

    Case A:　I.　THE PARTIES NEVER FORMED
               A CONTRACT TO MERGE.

    Case B:　I.　THE COMPLAINT DOES NOT
               STATE A CAUSE OF ACTION.

    Case C:　I.　THE EVIDENCE SOUGHT IS
               NOT PROTECTED BY A
               PRIVILEGE.

In a trial court, the following would at least tell the judge what you want:

    Case A:　I.　THE DEFENDANT'S MOTION
               FOR SUMMARY JUDGMENT
               SHOULD BE GRANTED BE-
               CAUSE THE PARTIES NEVER
               FORMED A CONTRACT TO
               MERGE.

    Case B:　I.　THE COMPLAINT SHOULD BE
               DISMISSED BECAUSE IT
               DOES NOT STATE A CAUSE
               OF ACTION.

    Case C:　I.　THE MOTION TO QUASH
               SHOULD BE DENIED BE-
               CAUSE THE EVIDENCE
               SOUGHT IS NOT PRO-
               TECTED BY A PRIVILEGE.

On appeal, the following would do the same job; notice how each heading identifies the ruling appealed from:

Appeal A: I. BECAUSE THE PARTIES NEVER FORMED A CON-TRACT TO MERGE, THE CIR-CUIT COURT SHOULD HAVE GRANTED THE DEFENDANT'S MOTION FOR SUMMARY JUDGMENT.

Appeal B: I. THE COMPLAINT STATES A CAUSE OF ACTION, AND THE DISTRICT COURT ERRED IN DISMISSING IT.

Appeal C: I. THE SUPERIOR COURT PROPERLY REFUSED TO QUASH A SUBPOENA FOR EVIDENCE NOT PROTECTED BY A PRIVILEGE.

Be careful about two things. First, this criterion applies only to *point* headings, not sub-headings. Second, the examples above satisfy this criterion *but not the next two.*

7. *The controlling rules should be identified in the headings or sub-headings.* A reader who must make a decision is not influenced until the governing rules are set out. Compare the last examples in the preceding criterion with the following:

Appeal A: I. BECAUSE THE PARTIES NEVER FORMED A CON-TRACT TO MERGE, THE CIR-CUIT COURT SHOULD HAVE GRANTED THE DEFENDANT'S MOTION FOR SUMMARY JUDGMENT.

　　　A. In an action for breach of contract, a defendant is entitled to summary judgment where the plaintiff is not able to produce evidence of the existence of a contract.

Appeal B: I.   THE COMPLAINT STATES A CAUSE OF ACTION, AND THE DISTRICT COURT ERRED IN DISMISSING IT.

     A.   This court has recognized the tort of wrongful discharge.

Appeal C: I.   THE SUPERIOR COURT PROPERLY REFUSED TO QUASH A SUBPOENA FOR EVIDENCE NOT PROTECTED BY THE FIRST AMENDMENT.

     A.   The First Amendment does not protect evidence in the possession of a journalist where the journalist did not obtain it under a promise of confidentiality and where the evidence cannot be obtained elsewhere.

Be careful: the examples above satisfy this criterion *but not the next one.*

8. *The one, two, or three most determinative facts should at least be alluded to in either the headings or sub-headings.* This is what pins down for the reader how the rules entitle you to what you want. Compare the examples in the preceding criterion with the following:

Appeal A: I.   BECAUSE THERE WAS NO EVIDENCE THAT THE PARTIES EVER FORMED A CONTRACT TO MERGE, THE CIRCUIT COURT SHOULD HAVE GRANTED THE DEFENDANT'S MOTION FOR SUMMARY JUDGMENT.

     A.   In an action for breach of contract, a defendant is entitled to summary judgment where the plaintiff is not able to produce evidence of the existence of a contract.

B.   The written contract was never signed, and there was no evidence of an oral understanding that could survive the Statute of Frauds.

Appeal B: I.   THE COMPLAINT STATES A CAUSE OF ACTION, AND THE DISTRICT COURT ERRED IN DISMISSING IT.

A.   This court has recognized the tort of wrongful discharge.

B.   The complaint alleges that the plaintiff was discharged solely because he questioned the defendant employer's corrupt contributions to political campaigns.

Appeal C: I.   THE SUPERIOR COURT PROPERLY REFUSED TO QUASH A SUBPOENA FOR EVIDENCE NOT PROTECTED BY THE FIRST AMENDMENT.

A.   The First Amendment does not protect evidence in the possession of a journalist where the journalist did not obtain it under a promise of confidentiality and where the evidence cannot be obtained elsewhere.

B.   This journalist did not promise his source confidentiality, and his source did not request it.

C.   The evidence sought cannot be obtained elsewhere because the journalist's source has died.

Each of the examples above reflects a paradigm-structured argument, with a conclusion, a rule, an implied rule proof, and an express rule application. (Rule proof can be implied because the reader will understand that where a rule is stated in a heading, the proof will appear in the Argument under that heading.)

9. Headings and sub-headings should be forceful and argumentative. Each heading and sub-heading should state an essential idea in an assertive way and show how that idea fits into the writer's theory. The two faults to avoid are topic headings and headings with a tone of weakness or neutrality. These headings are topical:

> Disruption in the public schools.
>
> Absence of a contract to merge.
>
> Wrongful discharge.
>
> Confidentiality.

And these have been rewritten to be argumentative:

> The public schools would be disrupted if this court were to recognize a tort of educational malpractice.
>
> The parties made no contract to merge.
>
> The complaint states a cause of action in wrongful discharge.
>
> The journalist neither promised confidentiality nor was asked for it.

This heading sounds weak and almost neutral:

> Arbitration was ordered by the Superior Court incorrectly, no agreement to arbitrate having been made.

This is more argumentative:

> Because the parties never agreed to arbitrate, the Superior Court should not have granted an order compelling arbitration.

Exercise.   Point Headings and Sub-Headings

Draft two sets of point headings and sub-headings — one favoring each party — using the facts and authority either from an exercise of your teacher's choice in Chapter 10 or Chapter 11 or from a writing assignment that you have previously completed in this course.

20 Appellate Practice

§20.1 Introduction to Appeals

A *judgment* (or, in equity, a decree) is the document a court makes to terminate a lawsuit and to record the court's final determination of the parties' rights. If either party has been awarded relief, the judgment may include commands or awards of money. A defendant may be required to pay damages, for example, or be permanently enjoined from doing prohibited acts, or—in a criminal case—be sentenced to a term of imprisonment.

An *order,* on the other hand, is a court's command during the lawsuit that something be done or not be done while the litigation is still in progress. In the course of a single lawsuit a court may make one or two orders, or a handful of orders, or dozens of orders, depending on the complexity of the case and how long it remains in litigation. Some orders may control the discovery process; others may manage the court's calendar or the trial itself; and still others may award parties provisional relief, such as preliminary injunctions. Some orders have very little effect on the ultimate outcome of a case; an example would be an order commanding that a deposition be held on a day preferred by the witness, rather than on the day specified in a notice of deposition. Other orders may have the practical effect of ending the case and declaring the winner; the leading example would be an order dismissing a complaint for failure to state a cause of action in a situation where the plaintiff is unable to produce an amended complaint that would do much better.

The document you have learned to call an opinion or a decision is neither a judgment nor an order. You have by now read hundreds of opinions, most of them in the casebooks you study for other courses, but you may never have seen an order or a judgment. The order or judgment is a court's *action*, and the opinion records the reasons for that action.

Subject to the limitations described in §20.4, a party aggrieved by a trial court's judgment or order can appeal to a higher court, where a group of judges will decide whether the trial court's judgment or order was correct or erroneous. The appellate process performs three functions. The most obvious is the correction of errors made by trial courts. A second function is to cause the law to be applied uniformly throughout the jurisdiction, to the extent that is practical. And the most intellectually challenging function is the formation and clarification of the law itself through appellate decisions that fill gaps in the common law and in statutory interpretation.

In those jurisdictions with two levels, or tiers, of appellate courts, the intermediate court tends to view its goal largely as error correction, although it must also necessarily cause some uniformity in application of the law and, to a lesser extent, engage in law formation and clarification. A court of last resort, on the other hand, generally believes that its task is primarily to form and clarify law. Such a court may be willing to perform the other two functions only where the intermediate court has not merely failed to do so, but failed badly. In the jurisdictions with only one appellate court, of course, that court is responsible for all three appellate functions equally.

Issues of state law can be appealed only once in a one-tiered state and no more than twice in a two-tiered state. For issues of federal law litigated in federal courts, there can be no more than two appeals because the federal courts are organized into a two-tiered appellate system. Where an issue of federal law arises in the courts of a state with two appellate tiers, however, three appeals are possible because the United States Supreme Court has jurisdiction to decide federal issues even if originally raised in a state court. Thus, if a defendant convicted in a California criminal trial believes that his conviction is defective because the trial court misinterpreted the state statute defining the crime (a state issue) and because the trial court erroneously admitted into evidence items seized in violation of the Fourth Amendment to the United States Constitution (a federal issue), the defendant can appeal both issues to the California Court of Appeal. If that court affirms, the defendant may be able to appeal both issues further to the California Supreme Court. If unsuccessful there, the defendant may be able to appeal to the United States Supreme Court, but only on the federal issue because the United States Supreme Court has no jurisdiction over issues of state law.

With some exceptions (explained in §20.4), the dissatisfied party generally has a right to seek review by the appellate court immediately above the trial court. That one appeal should be enough, in most instances, to perform the error-correcting function of the appellate process. In a state with a one-tiered appellate system, this appeal *as of right* will be to the state's supreme court, but in other states and in the federal system, it will be to an intermediate court of appeals.

Any appeal to a still higher court will be *discretionary* because it will not happen unless a court permits it. Although every litigant should be entitled to one appeal for error-correction purposes, the other two functions of the appellate process are performed best if the higher appellate courts in two-tiered jurisdictions can concentrate their efforts on those issues where law needs to be made or clarified. Thus, the higher appellate courts in two-tiered systems are invested with *discretionary appellate jurisdiction,* which means that they are empowered to choose the appeals they will hear and to turn others aside. A party unhappy with a judgment made by a United States District Court, for example, has a right to have that judgment reviewed by a United States Court of Appeal, but there can be no further appeal to the United States Supreme Court unless that court gives its permission by granting a would-be appellant[1] a writ of certiorari.

What kinds of issues are important enough to persuade a discretionary appellate court to exercise its jurisdiction? Generally, such a court may be inclined to grant leave to appeal or a writ of certiorari — the terminology differs from jurisdiction to jurisdiction — where the party seeking permission to appeal wants the court to fill a troubling gap in the jurisdiction's law. A gap tends to be troubling where lower courts have published opinions coming to opposite results on analogous facts or where a significant part of society needs clarification of the law. Some gaps are large. An example occurs where a court is asked to recognize a cause of action that some states have adopted and others have rejected. But even relatively small gaps can be troubling: a court that has recently recognized a particular cause of action, for example, may need to decide several further appeals until all the elements are clearly defined. If, however, local law is settled, clear, and consistently applied, a discretionary appellate court is likely to give permission to appeal only in two instances. The first is where the intermediate appellate court appears to have made an error that would represent an intolerable failure of the intermediate court's error-correction function. And the second is the unusual situation where the discretionary appellate court is receptive to changing the law.

In the Supreme Court of the United States and in the highest court of every state, all the judges meet together to hear and decide appeals. In some intermediate appellate courts, appeals are heard by panels, rather than by the full court. In the United States Courts of Appeals, for example, decisions are made by panels of three judges; only in rare cases can a party who has lost before a panel persuade the full court en banc to review the panel's decision. Ultimately, of course, the losing party can petition — usually unsuccessfully — for review by the United States Supreme Court.

---

§20.1 1. In practice, the parties might be given any of a variety of procedural designations on appeal. Depending on the appellate court and on the type of appeal, the party who initiates the appeal is called either "the appellant" or "the petitioner," and the other party is "the appellee" or "the respondent." If the appealing party is "the appellant," the other party is generally "the appellee," although a very few courts call the other party the "respondent" instead. If the appealing party is "the petitioner," the other party is always "the respondent" (and never "the appellee"). An appellant or petitioner who cross-appeals may, depending on the court, be called a "cross-appellant" or "cross-petitioner" or even something as convoluted as a "respondent/cross-petitioner." For convenience, in this text "appellant" refers to a party who has commenced an appeal, and "appellee" designates the opposite party. Before writing a brief, check whether, in the court where the brief will be filed and in the type of appeal involved, "petitioner" and "respondent" are used instead. Local court rules can usually resolve this question. If you cannot find the answer that way, see how the parties are referred to in a reported appeal that *procedurally* most closely resembles your own.

§20.2   The Life Cycle of an Appeal

In §1.3, you learned something of the life cycle of a lawsuit up to the point of appeal. Although practice varies from court to court, the life cycle during appeal continues in more or less the following way:

First, the appellant *serves and files whatever document*[1] *is required by law to commence the appeal.* If the appeal is as of right, the document is a notice of appeal, an uncomplicated paper that is no longer than a page and need not specify grounds for the appeal. If leave to appeal is required, the appellant must petition for it, specifying errors and arguing their importance. The notice of appeal is short and simple because it is a mere declaration that the appellant is doing what he or she has a right to do, but the petition for discretionary review *asks* for something and is therefore far more complex. Because the denial of such a petition forecloses appeal, its contents are critical and must be drafted persuasively. The notice or petition must be served and filed within the time required by law, and the time limits can vary from jurisdiction to jurisdiction. A notice of appeal is filed with the clerk of the court being appealed *from,* rather than the clerk of the court being appealed to, but the contrary is true of a petition for leave to appeal.

The second step in the appeal is the *transmittal of the record* from the court below to the court above. Although one might imagine this to be an easy matter of the clerk of one court locating a file and sending it to the clerk of another court, it happens that way only in cases where the record is very simple. A record can be simple, for example, where the appeal is from an order dismissing a complaint for failure to state a cause of action. There the record might not include much more than the complaint, the papers submitted by both parties in connection with the defendant's motion to dismiss, and the court's order.

Most appeals, however, arise only later in the litigation, and in those cases the preparation and transmittal of the record can delay matters for months and add thousands of dollars to the cost of the appeal. Wherever the trial court has held a hearing or trial, one or more court reporters will have to type up a transcript from stenographic notes, a time-consuming process that can produce literally volumes of material. Appellate courts have tried to reduce the delay and expense in several ways. Many jurisdictions encourage

---

§20.2   1. Except for the notice of appeal, which is directed to the court being appealed from, all papers filed in the appeal begin with a caption different from the one used in the court below. The name of a different court, of course, appears at the top of the caption, and the docket number is the one assigned in the court being appealed to. The party designations in the caption also change. Depending on the applicable court rules—which vary considerably from jurisdiction to jurisdiction—a plaintiff who appeals, for example, might in the appellate caption become an appellant, a plaintiff-appellant, a plaintiff-petitioner, or some other designation.

the parties to agree that the court reporter will transcribe only relevant portions of the proceedings. And many jurisdictions charge the appealing party with the responsibility for ensuring that the record is forwarded within a specified period of time, with a penalty if that is not done.

The third step — required in some jurisdictions and optional in others — is the assembling of an abbreviated version of the record called the *joint appendix* or the *record appendix*.[2] At the appealing party's expense, it is printed in sufficient quantity that a copy can be given to each judge who will hear the appeal. The appellate judges need the joint appendix because the full record can be gargantuan, and the appellate court will have only one copy of it. Even if all the judges hearing an appeal were to work in the same building, it would be impractical to ask them to share a single copy, which may be bound into several bulky volumes. Moreover, in many appellate courts the judges do not do all of their work in the same building: they have additional chambers near their homes, which may be scattered about a state, a district, or a circuit, and they gather only when scheduled to hear oral arguments and to deliberate. Whether chambers are scattered or located centrally, the judges can work most efficiently if each has a copy of the most important parts of the record, and if the full record is available in the clerk's office as a reserve. In some jurisdictions where the appendix is optional, appealing parties are excused from providing a full record if the appendix is sufficient.

Although rules vary from jurisdiction to jurisdiction, there are generally two methods of assembling the appendix. The parties can simply agree on a joint appendix, but that does not happen often. More commonly, the appellant designates those portions of the record that he or she wants in the appendix; the appellee counter-designates portions to be added; and the portions are combined and printed in the same sequence in which they appear in the full record.

The fourth step is the *drafting of briefs*, which each attorney files with the appellate court and serves on opposing counsel. For the attorneys, this is the most intellectually challenging part of appellate work, and it is the subject of Chapter 21.

In a court without discretionary jurisdiction, the fifth step — and the first in which the appellate court becomes actively involved — is *screening*. Until relatively recently, most appeals were given a full adjudication that included oral argument and a formal opinion, whether or not published. Because of geometrically increasing appellate caseloads, that time is gone forever. Now, in most appellate courts, the appellant must struggle to get a full adjudication, and a wise appellee fights to prevent it. If the appeal is not given full treatment, it is shunted onto a summary adjudication track, where

2. Do not confuse the joint appendix with either of two parts of an appellate brief: the Statement of the Case or an appendix that a party might choose to add to the brief to set out in full those statutes that a court might be asked to construe. The Statement of the Case is the attorney's summary of the record, while the joint appendix is an abbreviated version of the record itself. The Statement of the Case and a statutory appendix are each only a few pages long, and both are printed as part of the brief. The joint appendix is often larger than the brief, and it is printed separately.

there may be no oral argument or formal opinion, where the judges might not even meet to discuss the appeal, and where the result is usually affirmance. Courts that do not have discretionary jurisdiction use screening to ensure that their error-correction function is performed economically while they concentrate on the most important appeals, which are still given full adjudicatory treatment. The factors that motivate a court without discretionary jurisdiction to give an appeal full adjudicatory treatment are not very different from the factors that would cause a discretionary court to accept an appeal that it is not obligated to decide. Screening is done by one or more specially assigned judges, who may be assisted by attorneys employed by the court to study the briefs and the record. In some courts, every appeal is screened, while in others screening occurs only when a party — usually the appellee — requests it. Some courts require the attorneys to meet with a judge in a pre-briefing or pre-argument conference, which is used partly for screening, partly to clarify and limit the issues, and partly to encourage negotiation between the parties. A few courts without discretionary jurisdiction — most notably the United States Court of Appeals for the Second Circuit — refuse to screen (except perhaps in pre-argument conferences) and require oral argument in every case on the theory that the judicial effort conserved by screening is not greater than the effort consumed by the screening itself.

In virtually all appeals in a discretionary court and in fully adjudicated appeals in a court without discretionary jurisdiction, the next step is *oral argument.* Each attorney is allotted a predetermined period, such as fifteen minutes, to speak in open court with the judges, who may ask a number of questions. Although brief-writing is the most challenging work in appellate practice, oral argument is often the most satisfying because it is the attorney's only chance to persuade while speaking directly with the judges about the problems and issues raised by the appeal. Where the judges and the attorney are perceptive and well-prepared, oral argument can be the most scholarly type of conversation known in the practice of law,[3] and it is the subject of Chapter 22.

After oral argument, the judges confer and discuss the merits of the appeal. In some courts, this conference occurs on the same day as argument; in others, it may happen several days later. One judge is selected to write the court's opinion. In some courts, the assignment is made by chance rotation, but in others it is made by the presiding judge. In the United States Supreme Court, the assignment is made by the most senior judge among the

---

3. "I can see the Chief Justice as he looked at that moment. . . . [B]efore counsel began to argue, the Chief Justice would nib his pen; and then, when everything was ready, pulling up the sleeves of his gown, he would nod to the counsel who was to address him, as much as to say 'I am ready; now you may go on.' I think I never experienced more intellectual pleasure than in arguing that novel question to a great man who could appreciate it, and take it in; and he did take it in, as a baby takes in its mother's milk." This is how Daniel Webster recalled his oral argument to the Supreme Court, led by Chief Justice John Marshall, in *Gibbons v. Ogden,* 22 U.S. (9 Wheat.) 1 (1824), one of the leading cases interpreting the commerce clause of the Constitution. (The quote is from 1 C. Warren, *The Supreme Court in United States History* 603 (1935).) Although pens have not been "nibbed" since they were made from feathers, modern appellate litigators know every other sensation Webster described.

majority. The assigned judge drafts an opinion and circulates it to the other judges, who might suggest changes or might draft and circulate concurring or dissenting opinions of their own. In routine appeals, the draft majority opinion is often quickly approved, and concurrences and dissents may be held to a minimum. But in more complex and troubling cases, views can change, and an opinion originally written as a dissent may become transformed into the court's opinion, while the original majority draft is demoted into a dissent.

If the losing party can appeal further, the whole process may begin again, with a new notice of appeal or petition for some sort of leave to appeal—more likely the latter, as one moves up the appellate ladder.

§20.3   The Roles of the Brief and of Oral Argument

Modern lawyers, who think of the brief as the centerpiece of the appeal, are often shocked when they learn that two centuries ago oral argument in a single appeal might go on for a dozen hours or more, spread over two or three days, and that briefs were originally two- or three-page outlines that were optional. The flavor of appellate practice then is captured by the wording of the rule through which the United States Supreme Court, in 1795, first required appellate lawyers to state their positions in writing: "The Court gave notice to the gentlemen of the bar that hereafter they will expect to be furnished with a statement of the material points of the case from the counsel on each side of a cause." [1] The "statement of the material points" was really nothing more than a list of the one-sentence propositions on which an argument is built. In a modern brief, the list survives as the collection of point headings found in the Table of Contents of a brief. [2]

As court calendars became more and more congested, the time allotted for oral argument shrank and shrank still further, while the size of briefs expanded until today in the United States Supreme Court each side may file a brief not exceeding 50 closely printed pages but may argue orally for no more than 30 minutes. This does not mean that the brief is now everything, while oral argument is an afterthought. Each is critical, but in a different way. To understand how, you must be able to visualize the effect of the dramatic increases in appeals on the work of appellate judges. [3]

Depending on the court, an appellate judge might in a month hear oral arguments and confer with colleagues on several dozen appeals, and in many courts substantially more than a hundred appeals. For each appeal,

§20.3   1. Rule VIII, Feb. Term, 5 U.S. (1 Cranch) xvi (1795).

2. See Chapter 19.

3. A court's caseload is measured in appeals filed in a given year. The explosion of filings in the United States Court of Appeal for the District of Columbia Circuit is typical of what has happened to many other appellate courts. In 1965, that court had 797 filings; in 1975, 1,275 filings; and in 1985, 2,087 filings. Imagine the increase in a court's workload when its cases nearly triple in twenty years.

the judge will have to read at least two briefs[4] and in multiparty cases or public-interest cases[5] a half-dozen briefs or more, together with portions of the record. The judge will have to write majority opinions in a proportion of the appeals not summarily disposed of; on a five-judge court, for example, each judge is assigned one-fifth of the majority opinions. In addition, the judge may feel obligated to write several concurring or dissenting opinions. The judge will also have to read opinions drafted by other judges and at times will write memoranda to colleagues suggesting changes in those opinions. The judge will spend a fair amount of time reading some of the cases and statutes cited to in all these briefs and draft opinions. And the judge may have screening and other administrative responsibilities. With all this work, the typical appellate judge would find it a luxury to spend as much as an hour reading the average brief, and the time available is often no more than half an hour per brief. That is why briefs, although large, must be carefully crafted to reveal their logic while demanding the least possible time and effort from the reader. More time is spent, of course, on briefs where the appeal raises deeply troubling issues than on briefs in more routine cases. And a judge who writes an opinion may consult portions of the briefs throughout the drafting of that opinion.

In a work environment like this, the brief and oral argument are asked to perform different functions. The brief can best lay out the theory of the appeal by explaining in persuasive detail the authorities and evidence on which a favorable decision should be based. A successful brief not only persuades the judge that the brief writer ought to win, but it can also be used as a manual explaining exactly how to make the decision and how to justify it. A judge may use the brief for initial screening, to prepare for oral argument, to prepare for the conference with other judges, and for guidance in writing an opinion.

The oral argument, on the other hand, can do two things better than the brief can. First, in oral argument the attorney can more immediately motivate the court by focusing on the most important ideas—the few facts, rules, and policies—that most make the attorney's theory of the appeal compelling. Although the brief should show both the forest and the trees, the oral argument can be a bit more powerful at illuminating the forest, and conversely it is a horrible medium through which to examine the trees. Second, in oral argument the attorney can try to discover, through the bench's questions, each judge's doubts, and the attorney can on the spot explain exactly why those doubts should not prevent a ruling in the attorney's favor. Oral argument, in fact, is the attorney's only opportunity to learn directly from the judges the precise problems they have with the attorney's theory. Oral argument's greater efficiency at these two things is not a reason to skimp on trying to accomplish them through the brief as well. Oral argument lasts only a few minutes, and memories of it can fade. The

4. The appellant files an opening or main brief; the appellee responds with an answering brief; and the appellant may rejoin with a reply brief but is not required to do so.
5. In cases that would affect groups that are not parties, the court may grant permission for nonparties to file briefs as amicus curiae (friends of the court).

brief, on the other hand, has permanence: it is always among the judge's working materials, and it "speaks from the time it is filed and continues through oral argument, conference, and opinion writing." [6]

Briefs and oral argument have evolved as they have less by design and more out of a gradual recognition by the courts of how different kinds of information can most efficiently be conveyed. Detail is communicated best in writing, which can be studied. Conversation, on the other hand, both encourages spontaneous dialogue and lends itself to the broad sweep of underlying ideas.

§20.4   Limitations on Appellate Review

You have already learned of one limitation on the scope of appeals: many courts have *discretionary appellate jurisdiction* and use it to avoid deciding large numbers of cases.[1]

In addition, appellate courts will disturb an order or judgment only if it is based on *reversible error*. Although a troubling result below will certainly make an appellate court receptive to an appellant's theory of error, an appellate court will nevertheless affirm unless the appellant can point to a specific error by the trial court that the law considers ground for reversal. Be careful of two kinds of situations, neither of which will lead to a reversal. In the first, the result below seems not to have been preferable, but no error by the court below can be identified. In the absence of reversible error, an appellate court will not substitute its preferences for the result below. That is because an appeal is not an open-ended reconsideration of what happened in the trial court: an appeal is only a review for the kind of mistake the law categorizes as error. In the second situation, error can be identified, but it did not lead to the order or judgment appealed from. Even if the result below was not preferable, and even if the court below committed error, an appellate court will reverse only if the result below is traceable to the error. Error that affected the result below is called *material* or *prejudicial*. Error without such an effect is called *harmless*.

To identify error, and to figure out whether it was material or harmless, look to the procedural posture in the trial court. For example, assume that the plaintiff has requested a particular jury instruction; that the trial court denied the request and instead gave another instruction; that the jury returned a verdict for the defendant; and that, on the basis of the verdict, the trial judge entered a judgment for the defendant. The issue on appeal cannot be whether the plaintiff should have won; rather, it is whether the trial court so erroneously instructed the jury that the entire case should be tried again to a jury properly instructed. If the instruction was error, but if the record

6. Goodrich, *A Case on Appeal—A Judge's View*, in *A Case on Appeal* 10-1 (ALI-ABA 1967).

§20.4   1. See §20.2.

shows that the error was not so material as to lead the jury astray, the error was harmless and will not be reversed. The more outrageous the jury's verdict, the more motivated an appellate court will be to find material error, but, if material error cannot be found, the judgment will nonetheless be affirmed.

Appellate review is also limited, for the most part, to *issues of law*. A jury's verdict is a purely factual determination and thus not generally reviewable on appeal.[2] Where a case is tried to a judge without a jury, the judge makes findings of fact that correspond to a jury's verdict. Are judicial findings of fact reviewable on appeal? In some appellate courts, they are not. In the appellate opinions you have read for other courses, you may have noticed the stock phrasing used in such courts to introduce a factual finding over which one party is unhappy: "The trial court found as a fact, not reviewable by us on appeal, that . . . ." In other appellate courts, judicial fact finding is reversible, but only if it is "clearly erroneous."[3] This standard is harder on appellants than that applied to a trial judge's conclusions of law, which can be reversed if merely "erroneous."

Appellate review is further limited to *issues preserved below*. An issue is preserved below only if the appellant raised it and the court below decided it. Because an appeal is a review for error, an appellate court will not concern itself with matters the lower court could have—but did not—decide. Unless the appellant raises the issue and seeks a decision below, the matter is deemed waived. Be careful: it is often not enough merely to raise an issue below. If the court below makes no decision, and if the appellant does not press for one, the waiver can still be implied, although in certain situations an appellate court may remand a case so that the lower court can make the decision not made previously.

There are two exceptions to the requirement that error be preserved. The more rigid exception concerns subject matter jurisdiction,[4] defects in which can never be waived because a court should on its own motion refuse to adjudicate a case outside its competence. The more flexible exception concerns "plain error," which is error so fundamental to the process of justice that it cries out to be corrected even if the appellant seemed unconcerned about it when it happened.[5] Be careful here too: "plain error" is not a concept that can be invoked whenever an appellant has been careless

---

2. As you may have realized by now, a dissatisfied party attacks a jury's verdict by challenging judicial conduct that permitted or caused the jury to return the verdict. The dissatisfied party might argue that the judge improperly instructed the jury or that the judge should have granted a motion for a directed verdict or a motion for judgment notwithstanding the verdict.

3. *See, e.g.,* Rule 52(a) of the Federal Rules of Civil Procedure.

4. Subject matter jurisdiction is a court's competence, or its power, as defined in the law, to decide various *categories of disputes.* You already know, for example, that federal courts lack subject matter jurisdiction to decide claims under state law, with certain narrowly defined exceptions such as diversity actions. Personal jurisdiction—which is waivable—is an entirely different concept and one with which you may already be familiar from the course in civil procedure. Personal jurisdiction is a court's power to adjudicate the rights and liabilities *of a particular party.* A state court has personal jurisdiction over a defendant where the defendant has been properly served with a summons and where the defendant has the constitutionally required contacts with the state involved.

5. *See, e.g.,* Rule 52(b) of the Federal Rules of Criminal Procedure.

below. Only in the rarest of circumstances is an appellate court so shocked that it will save an appellant who, in the court below, did not even try to save himself.

What happens where, in the trial court, a party advanced several different grounds, all in support of the same relief, and where the court granted the relief on one ground and ignored the rest? The ignored grounds are not waived because it would have been pointless to press for a decision on them. In fact, if an appellate court rejects the ground adopted by the lower court, the appellate court can still affirm, if it chooses to do so, on one of the grounds ignored by the lower court. A correct result is affirmable even if the lower court went about it for the wrong reason.

Appellate review is still further limited to issues that are actually *raised on appeal*. An appellate court does not survey the record below looking for error: in the adversary system, that is the job of the appellant's attorney. If the appellate court has discretionary appellate jurisdiction, an issue is waived unless raised in the petition seeking leave to appeal. In any appellate court, an issue is waived unless raised in the brief.[6] Only very rarely does an appellate court overlook this limitation and itself raise an issue not asserted by a party. This happens most strikingly when the appellant's attorney has not realized that some of the judges are interested in changing legal rules that the parties have taken for granted.

Appellate courts will review only *final* orders and judgments. Although finality generally occurs when the court below has nothing left to adjudicate, in many jurisdictions the law hedges the concept often. One reason is that finality itself is not always easy to recognize. Sometimes an order may plainly be one that does not terminate litigation on a particular issue, but it may so alter the positions of the parties that the effect would be final if not reviewed. Another reason is that it is hard to accomplish the purpose of the final order rule — economizing everyone's effort and speeding the real end of a lawsuit by reviewing on appeal only the trial court's finished product — without at the same time precluding review of some types of interlocutory orders that ought not be immune from appellate scrutiny. As a result, most jurisdictions have developed, through statutes and case law, a number of exceptions to the final order rule.[7] And one jurisdiction dispenses with the rule entirely for civil cases in its intermediate appellate court,[8] although not

---

6. Issues are not waived merely because they are omitted from oral argument. There are two reasons. The first is that one of the goals in oral argument is to focus on the heart of the case, leaving many of the details for the brief. The second is that, even if an attorney wanted to mention in oral argument every ground asserted in the brief, an appellate court's questioning is often so thorough that the attorney would not have an opportunity to do so. However, courts often ask in argument whether an attorney abandons a particular ground raised in the brief, and an affirmative answer is an explicit waiver.

7. For example, under 28 U.S.C. §§ 1291 and 1292, federal appellate courts are authorized to review a variety of interlocutory orders, including certain discovery orders and orders granting or denying preliminary injunctions. And the Supreme Court has developed a collateral order doctrine "whose reach is limited to trial court orders affecting rights that will be irretrievably lost in the absence of an immediate appeal." *Richardson-Merrell, Inc. v. Koller,* 472 U.S. 424, 430-31 (1985).

8. See N.Y. Civ. Prac. Law § 5701(a)(1).

in its highest appellate court.[9] More than any other limitation on appellate review, the final order rule requires a detailed knowledge of local law.

And, with two exceptions, appellate courts will not consider facts that do not appear in the *record below*.[10] One exception involves the doctrine of judicial notice, through which a court—trial or appellate—will, without evidence, accept as proven certain facts that are beyond dispute.[11] Do not make more of this than it really is. The following are examples of the kinds of indisputable facts of which courts will take judicial notice: a meter equals 39.37 inches; Cleveland is in Cuyahoga County, Ohio; January 22, 1990, was a Monday.

The other exception is for what are called "legislative facts," a type of generalized information, largely empirical, that guides a court in the development of law—as opposed to the "case facts" or "adjudicatory facts" or "historical facts," all of which refer to the specific events that transpired between the parties. Legislative facts can include empirical data on the detrimental effects of racial segregation, or on the national deterioration of groundwater quality, or on the ways consumers use videocassette recorders. Although the adversary system is not very efficient at collecting legislative facts,[12] appellate courts need them when making or changing law. And although legislative facts can be placed in the trial record, an attorney called in to handle an appeal sometimes finds a need to put before the appellate court legislative facts not developed in the record below. The appellate attorney might include in the brief carefully selected and amply documented empirical research that complements but does not crowd out the legal analysis that is the core of argument.[13] Empirical material added on appeal is not set out in the Statement of the Case, because it is not part of the record below. Rather, it appears, with citations, in the Argument, most often in support of policy contentions.

9. See N.Y. Const. art. VI, § 3(1), (2), (4).

10. You can determine whether a fact is truly in the record by thinking in terms of the procedural posture below. If the order appealed from is one dismissing a complaint for failure to state a cause of action, a fact is in the record if it is alleged in the complaint. That is because of the rule that, for the purpose of deciding a motion to dismiss a complaint, all facts properly pleaded are treated as though they could be proven. (And, of course, on such a motion the only factual record before the trial court is the complaint itself.) But the situation is different where the motion below challenged a party's evidence, rather than allegations (see §§12.5.1 and 12.5.2). For example, assume that the appeal is from a summary judgment. If a fact appears as an allegation in a pleading but does not appear in any evidentiary form, it is not "a fact in the record" because the motion below tested evidence and not allegations.

11. The federal formulation of the rule is typical: "A judicially noticed fact must be one not subject to reasonable dispute in that it is either (1) generally known within the territorial jurisdiction of the trial court or (2) capable of accurate and ready determination by resort to sources whose accuracy cannot reasonably be questioned." Fed. R. Evid. 201(b).

12. Legislatures are far more efficient at using the knowledge of experts, collecting and studying empirical research, and weighing conflicting scientific analyses. Courts must rely on individual attorneys, who are rarely able to match the resources of legislative staffs.

13. A brief that uses a fair amount of empirical material is called a "Brandeis brief," after the successful one submitted by Louis D. Brandeis in *Muller v. Oregon,* 208 U.S. 412 (1908).

§20.5   Standards of Review

A standard of review is a "measuring stick"[1] with which the appellate court gauges whether the trial court has committed reversible error. For both legal and practical reasons, a party seeking reversal assumes the burden of showing that the decision below violates the standard of review. The legal reason is that in most jurisdictions an order or judgment is presumed correct on appeal until the appellant demonstrates that the standard of review has been violated. The practical reason is that appellate courts are temperamentally "affirmance-prone": unless deeply troubled by what happened below, an appellate judge will not be motivated to change it.[2] A wise appellee puts much effort into showing that the standard of review has not been violated.

How much error does it take to cause reversal? That depends on the jurisdiction, the issue, and the procedural posture below. The jurisdiction matters because the standards of review differ somewhat from state to state and between the states and federal government. The issue and the procedural posture matter because, even within the same jurisdiction, different standards are applied to different rulings by the court below.

Many rulings of law—such as orders dismissing pleadings, summary judgments, directed verdicts, jury instructions, and judgments notwithstanding the verdict—are evaluated on appeal "de novo."[3] For these rulings, the appellate court measures error simply by asking itself whether it would have done what the trial court did. The appellate court can do that because all of these rulings present pure questions *of law*. If the jurisdiction permits a judge's findings *of fact* to be challenged on appeal, the appellate court will apply a higher standard. In federal appeals, for example, a judge's fact-finding will be reversed only if it is "clearly erroneous."[4] And on an issue where the lower court has *discretion,* the result below will be reversed only for an "abuse of discretion." A trial court has a wide range of discretion on issues of equity and on issues concerning management of the progress of the litigation. Examples of the latter include rulings on discovery motions and on the conduct of the trial. A de novo standard is neutral, like a pane of clear glass through which light passes without distortion, but the other standards are like filters and lenses that modify the image.

---

§20.5   1. Godbold, *Twenty Pages and Twenty Minutes — Effective Advocacy on Appeal,* 30 Sw. L.J. 801, 810 (1976).

2. Judges become understandably annoyed with attorneys who write and speak as though there were no standards of review. A typical judicial admonishment is the following: "The one certain thing is that the advocate who believes that these rules will disappear if he ignores them jeopardizes his case. You should remember that appellate judges live day in and day out with these procedural rules. . . . If you forget them, you may be sure that we will remind you of them and perhaps with some impatience." Kaufman, *Appellate Advocacy in the Federal Courts,* 79 F.R.D. 165, 168 (1978).

3. "De novo" is the term used in federal courts for this type of standard. Many states use other but synonymous phrases, such as "independent and nondeferential review."

4. *See, e.g.,* Rule 52(a) of the Federal Rules of Civil Procedure.

21 Writing the Appellate Brief

§21.1 Appellate Brief Format

You learned in §3.3 that the structure of a brief tracks—in amplified form—the structure of a memorandum. Although rules on format differ from court to court, the required structure might commonly include the following:[1]

1. a cover page containing a caption and other information that might be required by local rules;
2. a Table of Contents (sometimes called an Index);
3. a Table of Authorities;
4. where the appeal rests on the interpretation of a constitutional provision, statute, administrative regulation, or court rule, a re-printing of the relevant material;
5. a Question Presented or Questions Presented;
6. a Statement of the Case, which might be preceded by a separate Preliminary Statement;
7. a Summary of the Argument;
8. an Argument, broken up with point headings;
9. a Conclusion; and
10. an indorsement.

---

§21.1 1. Some courts require additional material, such as a statement specifying how the court acquired jurisdiction over the appeal in question. And some courts restrict the material that may appear in an appendix to a brief. You should add an appendix to a law school brief only in the infrequent situation where the relevant portion of a constitutional provision, statute, court rule, or regulation is too bulky to print in the text of the brief.

As you read the description below of each of these components, compare the sample briefs in Appendices E and F.

The *cover page* includes the caption, followed by the document's title (such as "BRIEF FOR APPELLANT") and the name, address, and telephone number of the attorney submitting the brief. The caption includes the name of the appellate court, the appellate court's docket number, and the names of the parties and their procedural designations (appellant, appellee, etc.) in the appellate court. Many courts require that the caption also include the parties' procedural designations in the trial court.[2] In federal appellate courts, the appellant is listed first in the caption, but in most state appellate courts the parties appear in the same order in which their names appeared in captions in the trial court. The cover page is unnumbered.

The *Table of Contents* begins on the page after the cover page. It lists all of the components of the brief (except the cover page and the Table of Contents itself); reproduces the point headings and sub-headings from the Argument; and sets out the page on which each component, point, or sub-point begins. Because the point headings and sub-headings are reproduced verbatim in the Table of Contents, a reader can look there for an outline of the argument and for a quick grasp of the attorney's theory of the appeal. When read together in the Table of Contents, the point headings and sub-headings should express the theory persuasively and coherently.

The *Table of Authorities* appears on the first page after the Table of Contents. It indexes the cases, statutes, constitutional provisions, court rules, administrative regulations, treatises, and law review articles cited in the argument, together with references to the pages in the brief where each authority is cited. In the Table, every authority is listed in a complete citation conforming to Bluebook rules, and an asterisk is placed to the left of those citations that form the core of the writer's theory. A footnote identifies those citations as "authorities chiefly relied on" or similar words to the same effect.

The Table of Authorities is broken down into three sections headed "Cases," "Statutes," and "Miscellaneous." Cases are listed in alphabetical order. If constitutional provisions, court rules, or administrative regulations are cited, they are listed with statutes, and the heading is enlarged to accommodate them. (In a brief where all of these materials are cited, the heading would read "Constitutional Provisions, Statutes, Court Rules, and Administrative Regulations.") Under the heading, the citations appear in the following order: federal constitutional provisions, state constitutional provisions, federal statutes, state statutes, court rules, federal administrative regulations, state administrative regulations. "Miscellaneous" is reserved for sec-

---

2. In a criminal case, the prosecution's *trial court* procedural designation is always implied and never expressed. For the accused, the trial court procedural designation is, of course, "defendant"—as in "Merritt Bresnahan, defendant." But it would seem silly to write "People of the State of New York, Prosecution." That is because phrases like "State v. Bresnahan," "People v. Bresnahan," "Commonwealth v. Bresnahan," and "United States v. Bresnahan" unambiguously communicate that Bresnahan is being prosecuted by whatever government customarily uses the designation that precedes the "v." And that is why the captions on the cover pages to the briefs in Appendices E and F look asymmetric: Merritt Bresnahan is the "Defendant-Appellant," but The People of the State of New York are only the "Appellee."

ondary authority, such as restatements, treatises, and law review articles, and they are listed there in that order.

Both the Table of Contents and the Table of Authorities should be set up on the page so that they are easy to use. In the Table of Authorities, for example, the authorities and the page numbers should be separated so that the difference is immediately obvious. Imagine a Table filled with entries like this:

S. Burlington County NAACP v. Township of Mt. Laurel, 67 N.J. 151, 336 A.2d 713, cert. denied, 423 U.S. 808 (1975) 9, 12

Tidewater Oil Co. v. Mayor of Carteret, 44 N.J. 338, 209 A.2d 105 (1965) 10, 15

Village of Euclid v. Ambler Realty Co., 272 U.S. 365 (1926) 8, 14

As a reader, you would probably find the following a bit easier on the eye:

S. Burlington County NAACP v. Township of Mt. Laurel, 67 N.J. 151, 336 A.2d 713, cert. denied, 423 U.S. 808 (1975) 9, 12

Tidewater Oil Co. v. Mayor of Carteret, 44 N.J. 338, 209 A.2d 105 (1965) 10, 15

Village of Euclid v. Ambler Realty Co., 272 U.S. 365 (1926) 8, 14

For pagination purposes, a brief is broken down into two parts. The two Tables (sometimes called the "front matter") are paginated together in lowercase roman numerals. The rest of the brief (the "body") is paginated separately in arabic numbers, beginning with "1," on the first page after the Tables. Although this may seem odd, it has a very practical purpose. Because the Tables must include page references to the body, the body is typed first. And because you cannot know how many pages the Tables will occupy until they are typed, the body must begin on page 1. The only efficient solution is to use two separate paginations: lowercase roman for the Tables and arabic for the body.

The *Constitutional Provisions, Statutes, Regulations, and Court Rules Involved* is the easiest part of the brief to draft. It is a place where the court can learn two things. The first is a list of the codified or promulgated law (as opposed to precedent) that is *critical* to the decision the court is asked to make.[3] The second is either the precise wording of those relevant portions or—if the relevant portions are extensive—an indication that they are reproduced in an appendix to the brief.[4] If the material is complicated enough to warrant an appendix, the reference to it could read something like this:

> The following statutes and court rules are set out in the Appendix: Sections 362 and 363 of title I of the Bankruptcy Reform Act of 1978, *as amended*, 11 U.S.C. §§ 362, 363 (Supp. II 1984), together with Bankruptcy Rules 1002 and 1003.

On the other hand, if the provisions are short, this portion of the brief might be written in a manner somewhat like the following:

> The First Amendment to the United States Constitution provides, in pertinent part, as follows:
>
> > Congress shall make no law . . . abridging the freedom of speech or of the press; or the right of the people . . . to petition the Government for a redress of grievances.[5]

Phrase the heading of this section of the brief to fit its content. The bankruptcy example above would appear under the heading, "Statutes and Court Rules Involved," while the heading over the First Amendment would read "Constitutional Provisions Involved."

A persuasive *Question Presented,* one of the most difficult tasks in legal writing, is explained in Chapter 18.

The *Preliminary Statement* briefly sets out the appeal's procedural posture by identifying the parties (if that is necessary), listing the relevant procedural events, and describing the order or judgment appealed from. If it can be done very concisely, the Preliminary Statement might also describe

---

3. A provision is critical to the decision if the parties disagree about its meaning and if the court cannot dispose of the appeal without resolving the disagreement. *A court rule that merely provides for the type of motion made below is not critical to the decision* unless the issue before the court is itself procedural, requiring the court to choose between two contradictory interpretations of the court rule. Although custom requires the use of the misleading word "Involved" in the heading to this portion of the brief, the only provisions printed under the heading are those that are *at the heart* of the issues before the court. They are much more than "Involved."

4. In law school brief-writing assignments, this is usually the only type of appendix permitted.

5. A court is aided by a reasonable editing of the relevant provisions. For example, in an appeal challenging the dismissal of a city employee for writing a letter to the editor criticizing the mayor, the example above is a reasonable editing of the First Amendment. With the excised portions stricken through, this is the full text of the Amendment: "Congress shall make no law ~~respecting an establishment of religion, or prohibiting the free exercise thereof; or~~ abridging the freedom of speech, or of the press; or the right of the people ~~peaceably to assemble, and~~ to petition the Government for a redress of grievances." Since the case poses no issue concerning the establishment clause, the free exercise clause, or the peaceable assembly clause, nothing is lost by excising them.

the reasoning of the court below and identify the grounds on which the decision below is challenged on appeal. The point is to tell the court why the matter is before it and to specify the type of decision the court will have to make. That can usually be done in less than a page. This portion of the brief goes by different names in different courts. Where it is not titled "Preliminary Statement," the heading might read "Proceedings Below," "Nature of the Proceedings," or the like.[6] In some courts, it must be set out separately from the Statement of the Case. In other courts, it is often merged into and becomes the first passage within the Statement of the Case.[7] Still other courts allow the attorney to decide whether to join or to separate the two.

The *Statement of the Case* is explained in Chapter 17.

A *Summary of the Argument* is what its name implies. The point headings and sub-headings, as they appear in the Table of Contents, *outline* the argument. The Summary does more: it *condenses* the argument into a few paragraphs — usually one paragraph per issue — with more meat in them than can be put into headings. The Summary should not repeat the point headings.

In a complex appeal, the *Argument* will be divided into points, each of which is a separate and integral theory that, standing alone, would be enough to support a ruling in the client's favor on a question presented. It is unusual in law school briefs for either side to have more than two points, and the appeals assigned often lend themselves to only one point. Points and point headings are explained in Chapter 19.

Although some lawyers use the *Conclusion* to reargue and resummarize the theory of the appeal, the better practice is to limit the conclusion to a one-sentence reiteration of the relief desired, together with an unamplified identification of the ground on which the relief would be based. For example:

> For all the foregoing reasons, the order of the Circuit Court for Albemarle County should be affirmed on the ground that the complaint does not state a cause of action.

A judge who needs to know immediately what the writer wants should be able to find that precisely stated in the Conclusion. This is particularly important where there are cross-appeals —

> For the foregoing reasons, the District Court's order should be affirmed insofar as it enjoins enforcement of Glendale Ordinance 88-162, and in all other respects the District Court's order should be reversed.

or where an appellant seeks alternative relief —

---

6. In some courts, the Preliminary Statement is called the "Statement of the Case," and the Statement of the Case (as that term is used in this book) is called a "Statement of Facts."

7. *See, e.g.,* Rule 28(a)(3) of the Federal Rules of Appellate Procedure.

> For the forgoing reasons, Mr. Merkle's conviction should be reversed because the Superior Court admitted into evidence a "confession" coerced in violation of his Fifth Amendment rights, or, in the alternative, this matter should be remanded to the Superior Court for resentencing because the original sentence exceeds the statutory maximum.

The *indorsement* is similar to the indorsement in a persuasive memorandum.[8]

In every court — trial or appellate — the contents of briefs and other submitted documents are controlled by rules designed to make submissions useful to judges.[9] Because an inadequate brief makes adjudication even harder for judges who already have heavy caseloads, judges become exasperated when court rules are ignored. And even the most fair-minded judge is less likely to rule in favor of a party whose attorney has made the job of deciding more difficult. Particularly egregious violations of court rules can result in the court's striking the brief, in financial penalties imposed on the attorney, and even in dismissal of the appeal.[10]

§21.2   How Judges Read Briefs

How does a judge read a brief? The answer may vary considerably from judge to judge, but the following is not unusual:

> So far as I am concerned, before the oral argument I read over the briefs and some material parts of the records, in somewhat cursory fashion, enough to

8. See §16.2.

9. These rules typically set out the kinds of material that each brief must contain; the maximum permitted length; required margins; permitted forms of reproduction; the number of copies to be filed and served; schedules for filing and service; and the permitted manner of service. *See, e.g.,* Rules 28, 31, and 32 of the Federal Rules of Appellate Procedure. Some rules can be surprisingly specific, and, although their purpose might not be immediately apparent to you, they generally make a great deal of sense. For example, Rule 28(d) of the Federal Rules of Appellate Procedure requires that counsel "keep to a minimum references to the parties as 'appellant' and 'appellee.'" Although that is exactly what the parties are, the terms themselves can be confusing in a brief because they indicate nothing more than who is unhappy with the result in the court below. For better ways of referring to the parties, see pages 263 and 291. (In captions, of course, "appellant" and "appellee" must appear.)

10. For example, in *Huffman v. Pursue, Ltd.,* 419 U.S. 892 (1974), the Supreme Court issued the following order:

> Brief for appellants does not comply with this Court's Rules 39 and 40 with respect to conciseness, statement of questions without unnecessary detail, and printing of appendices thereto. Accordingly, as provided in paragraph 5 of Rule 40, brief of appellants is hereby stricken. Counsel for appellants may file a brief complying with the Rules within 20 days of the date of this order. Oral argument will be allowed only by counsel who have filed briefs that conform to the Rules.

Although this must be a humiliating experience for an attorney, it is one of the least onerous things a court will do with a nonconforming brief.

know what the points in the case are and what the positions of the opposing parties are. When the oral argument is over, the answer to the controversy is sometimes indisputably clear. But in most cases it is not and a real study is in order. Usually I first read both parties' statements of the questions presented; then I read the appellant's statement of the general nature of the controversy. Then I look at his outline of argument to see what points he makes. Then I look at the appellee's outline of argument to see what he is going to do in reply. Then I go to the joint appendix to see what the trial court or the administrative agency did. Then I read the appellant's statement of the facts and the appellee's statement. Thereafter I examine the two briefs one point at a time, first the appellant's and then the appellee's, on the first point; then both briefs on the second point, etc. If the point is an obvious one, or if one side or the other seems to be wholly without strength on it, I do not spend too much time on that point in my first study. On the really contested points I study both sides, read the cases, and, if facts are critical, check the record references. The briefs on the critical points are often reread and reread.[1]

Other judges might read the various parts of a brief in a different sequence — perhaps reading the point headings before anything else — and a particular judge might vary the sequence from case to case. But the following observations generally describe the use to which a brief is put:

First, you must write for several different readers. The smallest appellate panel is three judges; nearly all appeals to the United States Courts of Appeals are decided by panels of this size. The largest regularly sitting appellate panel — the United States Supreme Court — is nine judges.[2] State supreme courts include five or seven judges. And on every court, briefs are also read by law clerks or research attorneys who assist the judges by studying the briefs and recommending decisions.

Second, a brief is not read like an essay, from beginning to end at a single sitting. It is read in chunks, at different times, depending on the needs of the reader. You read an appliance or automobile owner's manual in pretty much the same way, and a brief is most basically a manual that should show the court how to make the decision and how to write the opinion that will justify and explain it. If a poorly thought-out owner's manual has caused you annoyance and frustration, you can imagine what a judge experiences with a brief that ignores the judge's needs.

Third, a brief is read for differing reasons, depending on who is reading and when, and the brief must be constructed to satisfy all of these uses without frustrating the reader. If screening[3] is done after briefs are filed, that is the first purpose to which a brief will be put. The judges will also either scan or study the brief in preparation for oral argument, and afterward they will read it again to decide how to vote. One judge will be assigned to write the court's opinion, and while writing that opinion, he or she will reread various portions of the brief several times, looking for the detail

§21.2 1. Prettyman, *Some Observations Concerning Appellate Advocacy,* 39 Va. L. Rev. 285, 296 (1953).

2. Larger panels occur in the unusual instance where a United States Court of Appeals hears a matter en banc.

3. See §20.2.

needed to justify and explain the decision. And all along the way, the judges will be assisted by law clerks who check up on the details of the brief while the judges focus on the broader principles. Each segment of the brief must be written to satisfy all of these purposes.[4]

Fourth, a brief must include several different places where a judge can "enter" the brief by learning what the appeal is all about. A judge will go first to a part of the brief that reveals the fundamental issues in the appeal and the brief writer's theory on each issue. A judge ought to be able to find that material plainly set out in four different places: the point headings and sub-headings (collected in the Table of Contents); the Questions Presented; the Summary of Argument; and the Statement of the Case. Each judge has a favorite starting place. Not only do you have no way of knowing when you write the brief where a given judge prefers to begin, but you are writing for several judges and must accommodate them all. Thus, you must draft these four components so that each can separately be a self-sufficient and self-explanatory entry point for any predictable reader.

Fifth, your readers are already overburdened by so many appeals that you must assume a certain amount of fatigue. Imagine going through over a hundred briefs a week yourself. How attentive would you be after examining half of them? After a while, a brief will be able to penetrate your thinking only if it is easy or even a pleasure to read; if it clearly and concisely explains the material; if it individualizes the appeal by bringing the parties and arguments to life; and if its appearance is both professional and inviting.[5] Otherwise, the brief's impact is bound to be limited.

Finally, courts will penalize attorneys who bring frivolous appeals or submit papers that include frivolous assertions.[6] Although judges deeply

---

4. You can give the writing judge needed detail while not overburdening other readers if you structure each segment in the Argument to focus on the decisive material first, supplying supportive detail afterward. There are two keys to this. First, progress from decisive material (rules, facts, or policy) to supporting detail so that the reader in a hurry can start skimming when detail becomes abundant. Do so in large discussions (a point), medium-sized ones (a sub-point), and small ones (an explanation of a given precedent). Second, mark off the beginning of even small discussions with effective transition or thesis sentences so that the skimming reader is alerted to slow down. (Large and medium discussions should be marked off, naturally, with headings and sub-headings.) If you indiscriminately mix up decisive material with supportive detail, you are asking for more attention than the non-writing reader can give you, and you will even frustrate the writing judge, who expects your organization to identify the important material. The paradigm explained in Chapter 7 will help you in this respect. And if the skimming reader cannot tell where a new discussion begins, that reader will continue skimming and miss decisive material. The paragraphing concepts described in Chapter 5 will help you avoid this problem.

5. A professional-looking document is so flawless in all the details — cite form, conformity with court rules, punctuation, and so on — that it inspires trust in the author. In any form of selling, a potential buyer can buy only by making a certain leap of faith in the seller's reliability and integrity, and a professional-looking document is itself evidence that the author is a meticulous lawyer who can be relied on. A visually inviting document is laid out on the page so that reading becomes comfortable and the reader easily *sees* (as well as reads) what the writer is up to: headings are distinct and blocked into the center of the page; print is easy to read; margins are reasonable; and there is generally enough white space that the reader does not experience the claustrophobia that you have undoubtedly felt while trying to read an insurance policy or a lease. All other things being equal, a visually inviting document is more likely to be read with care.

6. *See, e.g.,* Fed. R. App. P. 38 and Fed. R. Civ. P. 11.

appreciate a brief that makes reasonable and clearly expressed arguments,[7] frivolous arguments and appeals clog up courts by requiring judges to make unnecessary decisions, and the judges involved understandably react harshly.[8]

§21.3 Developing a Theory of the Appeal

In Chapter 14, you learned that a theory is attractive only if it is solidly built on the record and the law, explains away unfavorable facts, is framed in terms of basic fairness to the parties, and appeals to logic and common sense. An effective appellate theory, however, has some additional qualities.

First, a persuasive theory of the appeal is grounded on the procedural posture below and the standard of review in ways described in §21.4. For the attorney urging reversal, the theory is one of *error*, while for the attorney defending the result below, the theory is one of *absence of error*. And neither error nor its absence can be explained without taking into account the procedural posture below and the standard of review.

Second, a persuasive appellate theory goes beyond a technical analysis and addresses the judges' concern about a fair and just result. An appellant must show both error and injustice: "If you can convince the appellate judges that the court below is wrong as an intellectual matter, but leave them with the impression that no worthwhile damage was done, the prior result will be affirmed."[1] Although an appellee might succeed by showing either an absence of error or an absence of harm, the wiser strategy is to try to show both, if that can credibly be argued.

Third, a persuasive appellate theory does not ignore any of the limitations on appellate review described in §20.4. An appellate court must necessarily reject a theory that asks the court to violate restrictions on the court's own power to act.

Fourth, a persuasive appellate theory asks the court to make no more law than is necessary to the attorney's goal. Most judges do not believe that their purpose on the bench is to change society in fundamental ways, and you will

---

7. "A carefully prepared, carefully stated, lawyer-like written argument is a work of art and a joy forever." Prettyman, *Some Observations Concerning Appellate Advocacy*, 39 Va. L. Rev. 285, 296 (1953).

8. For example, after holding that an appellant's brief advanced "an argument to recover the Property that is insufficient even to give it standing to challenge the forfeiture, challenged as vague a statute that clearly covers its situation and argued that it was denied due process in the face of decisive Supreme Court authority to the contrary," a court required the appellant to pay an amount equal to twice the court costs of the appeal, plus the appellee's attorney's fees, and it remanded the case so that the trial court could determine whether to tax sanctions against the appellant's attorney as well. *United States v. A Single Family Residence*, 803 F.2d 625, 632 (11th Cir. 1986).

§21.3 1. Lampon, *Observations on Appellate Advocacy*, 14 N.H.B.J. (No. 3) at 105, 106 (Winter 1973).

have a better chance to win if your theory asks only for those changes truly necessary to the result you want.

Fifth, a persuasive appellate theory is soundly grounded in public policy. Judges engaged in law formation or clarification are understandably sensitive to policy concerns. Some policy is inferable from or explicitly stated in the jurisdiction's case law and statutes. In a more general sense, policy arguments can be constructed by showing that if the court were to rule against you, the resulting precedent would be impractical or would otherwise cause more harm than good.

Finally, a persuasive *appellant's* theory raises no more than two, three, or at most four claims of error. A theory is damaged, not strengthened, by adding additional but weaker grounds to the two or three best ones available. The weaker grounds by their mere assertion cheapen the stronger ones and take up room in the brief that is better used to more fully develop the grounds most likely to cause reversal. Good theory development requires the good judgment to choose the strongest grounds; the self-discipline to focus the court's attention on them alone; and the courage to ignore other grounds that may seem tempting but, in the end, are unlikely to persuade.

§21.4   Handling the Standard of Review and the Procedural Posture Below

The only way to find out which standard controls a given appellate issue[1] is to research local law in the same manner that you would research rules governing the procedural posture in a trial court.[2] Look for authority that tells you not only what the standard is, but also what it means and how it works. As with procedural postures, the authority may turn out to be a procedural statute or court rule, or case law, or a statute or rule with interpretive case law. And, as with procedural postures, the critical language may be easier to spot in a statute or court rule than in a case. Where a court mentions the standard of review in a decision, it usually does so immediately after reciting the facts and immediately before beginning the legal analysis. This is an example of the type of language you will find:

> A dismissal for failure to state a claim pursuant to Fed. R. Civ. P. 12 is a ruling on a question of law and as such is reviewed de novo. [Citation omitted.] Review is limited to the contents of the complaint.[3]

Here we learn what the standard is ("de novo") and a little — but certainly not everything — about how it operates ("Review is limited to the contents

§21.4 1. "Unless counsel is familiar with the standard of review *for each issue,* he may find himself trying to run for a touchdown when basketball rules are in effect." Godbold, *Twenty Pages and Twenty Minutes — Effective Advocacy on Appeal,* 30 Sw. L.J. 801, 811 (1976) (emphasis added).

2. See §15.6.

3. *Kruso v. Int'l Telephone & Telegraph Corp.,* 872 F.2d 1416, 1421 (9th Cir. 1989).

of the complaint"). Occasionally, a court will tell you much more about how the standard is used:

> "In reviewing the [National Labor Relations] Board's decision, we must scrutinize the entire record, 'including the evidence opposed to the Board's view from which conflicting inferences reasonably could be drawn.'" [Citation omitted.] Nevertheless, this court will defer to the Board's judgment and the Board's factual findings shall be conclusive if supported by substantial evidence on the record considered as a whole. [Citation omitted.] This "court may not substitute its judgment for that of the Board when the choice is 'between two fairly conflicting views, even though the court would justifiably have made a different choice had the matter been before it *de novo.*'" [Citation omitted.] We shall also defer to the Board's inferences in areas where the Board is considered to have "specialized evidence and expertise." [Citation omitted.][4]

And the court might explain in the same passage both the standard of review and the rules governing the procedural posture in the trial court:

> The grant or denial of a motion for preliminary injunction is a decision within the discretion of the trial court. [Citation omitted.] Appellate review . . . is very narrow. [Citation omitted.] Accordingly, a district court's decision will be reversed only where there is a clear abuse of discretion. [Citation omitted.] That discretion is guided by four requirements for preliminary injunctive relief: (1) a substantial likelihood that the movants will ultimately prevail on the merits; (2) that they will suffer irreparable injury if the injunction is not issued; (3) that the threatened injury to the movants outweighs the potential harm to the opposing party and (4) that the injunction, if issued, will not be adverse to the public interest. [Citation omitted.][5]

Occasionally, you will come across an issue that is subject to a bifurcated or even (as here) a trifurcated standard of review:

> Our standard of review on the laches issue has various components. We review factual findings such as length of delay and prejudice under the clearly erroneous standard; we review the district court's balancing of the equities for abuse of discretion; and our review of legal precepts applied by the district court in determining that the delay was excusable is plenary. [Citation omitted.][6]

How do you handle the standard of review in a brief? If on appeal the issue is considered de novo, you need not mention the standard unless you have a special reason for doing so.[7] But be careful: although you need not

---

4. *NLRB v. Emsing's Supermarket, Inc.,* 872 F.2d 1279, 1283-84 (7th Cir. 1989).
5. *Haitian Refugee Center, Inc. v. Nelson,* 872 F.2d 1555, 1561-62 (11th Cir. 1989).
6. *Bermuda Express, N.V. v. M/V Litsa,* 872 F.2d 554, 557 (3d Cir. 1989).
7. If the ruling below is not of the kind that appellate judges scrutinize every day, the appellant might have a special reason for pointing out that review is de novo, because the other standards make reversal harder. But every appellate judge knows that the following are pure rulings of law and are therefore reviewed de novo: orders dismissing pleadings, summary judgments, rulings on motions for directed verdicts, jury instructions, and rulings on motions for judgment notwithstanding the verdict. Two of these rulings are at issue in the briefs in Appendices E and F, and that is why the standard of review is not mentioned there.

refer to a de novo standard, you must invoke and use the procedural test that governed the trial court.[8] If, for example, the appeal is from a summary judgment, remind the court, near the beginning of your Argument, that summary judgment requires that no material fact be in dispute and that the party awarded judgment be entitled to it as a matter of law.[9] Although you would need to cite to local authority to prove such a rule, a conclusory proof is usually sufficient because the rule is a routine procedural one with which the court is predictably familiar. It is not enough merely to state the rule and then ignore it for the rest of the Argument. Instead, use it and corollary rules wherever they are relevant, weaving the substantive and procedural law together to show either error (if you seek reversal) or the absence of it (if you urge affirmance).

If, however, the standard is not de novo, you must deal with the standard, as well as with the procedural test used below. State both near the beginning of each issue's argument and cite to local authority. (Unless the law is unclear, a conclusory proof of the standard is generally enough.) Then use both wherever relevant throughout the Argument. Again, it is not enough merely to set out the standard at the beginning and ignore it thereafter: weave the standard and the substantive law together to show the court exactly how the standard was violated (if you seek reversal) or how it was not violated (if you are arguing for an affirmance).

If you are unsure of how to go about all this, take a look at several opinions in which the court for which you are writing the brief has used both the standard of review and the trial court procedural rules appropriate to your case. Chances are that you will see them invoked near the beginning of the opinion and used at logically appropriate spots thereafter. Look for a definition of the standard, and try to learn its relationship to other procedural rules and get a feel for the court's expectations about how the standard should be used.

§21.5   The Process of Writing a Brief

Before starting to write, you must digest the record, do a significant amount — but *not all* — of the research, and develop the basic shape of your theory. Digesting the record is more than merely reading it: study the record to identify potential reversible error[1] by the trial court and to find every fact that could be used to prove error or to defend what the trial court did. Look for both kinds of facts regardless of whether you represent the appellant or the appellee. Facts favorable to your position will, of course, become ammu-

---

8. See the Appendix E and F briefs.
9. See §12.5.2.
§21.5   1. Unless error is material to a final order or judgment, is preserved in the trial court, is not already waived on appeal, and can be shown to be reversible from facts already in the record, an appellee will have a good argument for an affirmance. See §20.4.

nition. But your theory must also show the appellate court why and how the facts that run against you should not become determinative.

Before you begin to write, do enough research to have all the ingredients for your theory. That includes both authorities that help you and authorities that hurt you (and therefore will have to be explained away). It includes all the major authorities on each issue, as well as enough of the lesser authorities for you to have a good handle on relevant policy, on the procedural posture that governed the decision below, and on the standard of review in the appellate court. It also includes enough Shepardization for you to know that all the authorities you have are still good law. And, if a gap in the law must be filled, it includes enough authority for you to know which of the competing rules enjoys majority or plurality status in other jurisdictions and which rule benefits from the recent trend of decisions. But you do not need to find everything in the library on your issue before you begin to write. In fact, if you try to find everything before beginning to write, your brief will probably suffer. That is a natural consequence of the inseparability of writing and thinking: an attempt at writing will show you more precisely what the issues are and what kinds of raw materials your argument will need to fill out the Argument. Conversely, you will never be able to focus on the most important authority if you collect such a huge mass of material that its size alone becomes a block.

Because the act of writing helps flesh out your theory, you cannot avoid having to return to the library after you have begun to write. You must allow time for that by beginning to write as soon as you have the core authorities and enough lesser authority to start filling in areas not disposed of by the core authorities. Three things lead students to overinvest in the library and underinvest in the work of writing. First, research is just not as hard or as painful as writing can be, and some students use research to avoid writing until it is too late to do a good writing job. Second, anxiety can cause a student to be afraid to stop researching until fully "protected" with authority ("I can't write—I don't have enough"). And third, until you have written a substantial part of a first-draft Argument, you cannot know how much more authority you will eventually need. The act of writing will show exactly how much and what kind of authority you lack.

Just as a judge does not read a brief from front to back, neither does a lawyer write it from beginning to end. The Table of Contents and Table of Authorities are always done last, after the rest of the brief has already been typed.[2] The order in which the other parts are written differs from lawyer to lawyer and from appeal to appeal because one lawyer's work habits are not necessarily effective for someone else and because an effective lawyer adapts to the peculiarities of the individual task at hand. Eventually, you will settle into a range of work habits that are effective for you, but your first brief is an opportunity to begin to define yourself professionally.

To help you start, consider two very different methods of writing a brief.

_____
2. See §21.1.

Order in Which a First Draft Might Be Written	
Model I	*Model II*
1. point headings	1. Questions Presented
2. Argument	2. Statement of the Case
3. Statement of the Case	3. point headings
4. Questions Presented	4. Argument
5. rest of brief	5. rest of brief

A lawyer who uses Model I outlines the Argument by composing the point headings and sub-headings and by listing under each heading the material to be covered there when the Argument is written. The logical next step is drafting the Argument itself. This lawyer might draft the Statement of the Case after the Argument on the ground that the relevance of various facts is not fully understood until after the Argument is written. The Questions Presented would be written afterward because the lawyer identifies the most determinative facts — the ones recited in the Questions — while working out the Argument and the Statement of the Case.

Conversely, a lawyer using Model II would begin the first draft by writing the Questions Presented on the theory that the other parts of the brief will be more focused if the issues are first precisely defined. A lawyer who uses this model writes the Statement of the Case next, using it to work out the details of the theory of the appeal (which the Model I lawyer does while writing the Argument). Both lawyers draft the point headings before the Argument because the Argument is easier to write in the segments created by the headings.

A lawyer with flexible work habits might use Model I in an appeal where the authority and issues are difficult and complex and Model II in a more fact-sensitive appeal. Some lawyers write the Question Presented and the Statement of the Case (and sometimes even the Argument) simultaneously, moving back and forth from one pad to another (or from one word processing disk file to another).

Before writing each subsequent draft, work on something else for a while or take a break to put the brief out of your thoughts. Come back to it in a frame of mind that enables you to put yourself in the judge's position: If you were a skeptical judge, would you be persuaded? Is the brief clear and easy to read? Does it teach you the appeal and show you how to make the decision? Reverting to your role as writer, would you be able to explain to someone else how you have organized the Argument around some variation of the paradigm explained in Chapter 7? Do you begin applying a rule to the facts before you have finished proving it (a sure sign that your organization is out of control)? At the other extreme, have you invested so much energy in proving a rule that you have forgotten to show the court how the rule governs the facts of your appeal? If a particular rule is not clearly expressed in the authorities, have you stated it yourself and then proved it with a synthesis? Where a gap in the law must be filled, have you defined the gap and explained the extent of local law before you begin to rely on persuasive authority? Is the argument framed in terms of the procedural posture below and the standard of review on appeal? Have you used argument techniques (§15.2) and fact description tactics (§17.3)? Do your Questions Presented and Point Headings satisfy the criteria in §§18.3 and 19.2? Throughout the brief, do you see ways to reduce verbiage and solve other problems?

It is a good idea, even before you begin research, to set up a schedule with a series of deadlines. Start from the date on which the brief is due, and figure out how many days it will take to have the final draft typed, proofread, and photocopied. Then set a deadline on which those tasks will begin and all revising and rewriting must stop. Figure out how long it will take to turn a second or third draft into a final draft and so on, working your way backward in time to deadlines where each draft must be finished and, for the first draft, where each component must be done. Writing a brief is a big job, and writing it in the time available requires self-discipline from you.

Parenthetically, students and lawyers tend to report that the following are the five hardest tasks in writing a brief: (1) organizing the extended analysis of the Argument; (2) developing a compelling theory of the appeal and articulating it persuasively; (3) in the Statement of the Case, persuasively describing the record below; (4) writing persuasive Questions Presented; and (5) writing clear and complete point headings and subheadings.

§21.6   Ethics on Appeal

You recall from the discussion of argumentation ethics in §15.3 that a lawyer is forbidden to "[k]nowingly make a false statement of law or fact" to a court.[1] Richard Uviller evaluates three statements that are meaningful and useful if accurate, but otherwise are deceptions:

1. *"This is a case of first impression."* For various reasons, counsel on appeal may feel he can do better by persuading the court that it is writing on a clean slate, unhampered by murky or generally unfavorable prior judicial grapplings. He may wish to stress broad social policy or the equities in the case before the court. To allow his argument freer rein, he simply ignores decisions which, while not controlling, bear on the point in issue and might be influential against his cause. Although the statement lacks precision, it may be taken as a term of art to mean that the point in context has never been addressed. If there is no governing precedent, the statement may pass for true, strictly speaking. But when it is made with the conscious purpose of concealing pertinent language elsewhere, an element of deception is perceptible.

---

§21.6 1. Model Code of Professional Responsibility, DR 7-102(A)(5). The same prohibition, in virtually the same words, appears in Rule 3.3(a)(1) of the Model Rules of Professional Conduct.

2. *"Authorities are in conflict on the point."* Such a declaration has much the same slate-wiping function as the previous one. It should be used to begin or conclude a discussion of the authorities said to conflict. But just as pertinence is often a matter of judgment, so conflict is not always so clear-cut. Since all cases are different in some respects from all others, and since few judicial opinions are unqualified or unrelated to the factual context of the issue, a discussion of precedent may usually be framed in a way to heighten uncertainty or inconsistency. Thus—particularly in a well-litigated area—counsel can usually juxtapose holdings or quotations in such a way as to make the unfavorable appear to be balanced or modified by another case which draws out some of its sting. Often this is the essence of appellate advocacy, and, insofar as counsel's analysis is probing and imaginative, it must be regarded as useful to the development of the law. But there comes a point at which the exercise is perverted: introducing false stress between cases, burying the strong elements of consistency, picking and trimming quotations to serve partisan purposes—in a word, intentionally robbing the literature of such meaning as it can justly claim—this must be counted among the ways that the law can be misrepresented.

3. *"The cases hold X."* This statement might be deemed false in any of several situations: (a) In fact, no cases hold *X*, and perhaps some hold *non-X.* . . . (b) The cases hold something close to *X* or a significantly qualified *X*. This is the art of the paraphrase, a common device of the zealous advocate trying to get a bit more mileage out of a helpful precedent than it is fairly good for. Since courts often enlarge on prior holdings, counsel may claim to be simply pointing the way. But, of course, it is one thing for a court to set new precedent (by disregarding the qualifier, for example) and quite another for counsel to tell the court that it has already established the precedent he seeks. (c) The cases contain the proposition *X* in dictum, but not in their "holdings." The distinction between holding and dictum . . . is not always apparent and sometimes unduly formalistic. But it is not so empty of meaning that counsel may freely stretch any useful fragment of language into precedent. (d) Some cases indeed hold *X* but others, which counsel ignores, conflict in significant respects.[2]

In addition, knowingly false statements of fact and frivolous arguments are as unethical in an appellate court as in any other kind of tribunal.[3]

---

2. Uviller, *Zeal and Frivolity: The Ethical Duty of the Appellate Advocate to Tell the Truth About the Law,* 6 Hofstra L. Rev. 729, 731-32 (1978).

3. See §15.3.

VI
INTO THE COURTROOM

22 Oral Argument

The power of clear statement is the great power at the bar.

—*Daniel Webster*[1]

§22.1 Your Three Goals at Oral Argument

First, you want to engage the judges' attention by getting them *interested* in your case and *motivated* to rule in your favor. They will hear many other arguments on the same day, and they will read many other briefs in the week they read yours. They will forget your theory of the appeal unless you touch their natural desire to do the right thing.

Second, you want to focus the judges' attention on *the few aspects of your case that are most determinative:* the one or two issues that are fundamental, the facts that are most prominent in your theory, the rule or rules for which a decision in your favor would become precedent, and the policy considerations that most compel the result for which you argue. Justice Brennan has written that "often my whole notion of what a case is about crystallizes at oral argument."[1] Judges expect oral argument to help them find the heart of the dispute. That is because, as you have already learned,[2] oral argument works best when it concentrates on the few large ideas that are most relevant, while details are best left to the briefs.

Third, you want *access to the court's thinking.* Ideally, you want to discover each doubt the judges have about your theory and every confusion

---

1. The same words have also been attributed to Rufus Choate, Judah P. Benjamin, and perhaps others.

§22.1 1. Harv. L. Sch. Occasional Pamph. No. 9, at 22-23 (1967).

2. See §20.3.

they entertain about any part of your case — all so you can satisfy doubt and clear up confusion. And you want to learn which issues the judges think are most important: if those are profitable issues for you, you can concentrate on them, and if they are the wrong issues, you can try to persuade the court of that. The only way you can get access to the court's thinking is through the questions you are asked when the judges interrupt you. In fact, you will go to court *for the express purpose of being interrupted* because the most effective thing you can do in oral argument is to persuade through your answers to the judges' questions. And when the judges interrupt, they are usually not trying to debate with you. For the most part, they are telling you what troubles them and asking you to help them make the decision.[3]

§22.2   The Structure of an Oral Argument

The appellant typically begins by reminding the court of the nature of the case, the facts most essential to the appellant's theory, the procedural history, and the issue before the court. This is a reasonably effective opening:

> Your Honors, I am Clyde Farnsworth, representing Merritt Bresnahan, the appellant here and the defendant below. This is an appeal from a criminal conviction.

An alternative start would be "May it please the court. I am . . . ." Usually, it would help to name the crime, but the attorney defers that so he can define his client first.

3. *Bender v. Williamsport Area School Dist.*, 475 U.S. 534 (1986), illustrates the risks of ignoring a judge's concerns as revealed by questions from the bench. After some initial litigation, a public school had permitted a student club to hold prayer meetings on school property during regular school hours. The United States Court of Appeals held that the school's actions violated the establishment clause of the First Amendment, and the students appealed to the Supreme Court. Charles Fried, the United States Solicitor General at the time, argued as an amicus curiae, seeking a ruling significantly redefining the relationship between government and religion. At oral argument, Justice Stevens asked him whether one of the parties had had standing to appeal to the Court of Appeals in the first place. (If that party had lacked standing in the Court of Appeals, the Supreme Court would not have jurisdiction to decide the First Amendment issue.) Fried brushed the Justice's questions aside: "On the jurisdictional point, Justice Stevens, we do discuss that on page five of our brief." The Justice later returned to the jurisdictional issue: "But at the time the appeal was taken, what was the controversy? Who was fighting with whom? Was there any allegation that any . . . child was offended by these meetings?" — all questions important to establish standing. Fried's answers could not have satisfied a skeptical judge:

Fried: "Mr. Youngman, I believe, at that time was claiming on his behalf as a parent."
Stevens: "Where in the record do you find that?"
Fried: "I cannot point you to the section of the record."

By a five-to-four vote — and in an opinion written by Justice Stevens — the Supreme Court held that it lacked jurisdiction and could not decide the constitutional question. What influence do you think oral argument had on the Court's decision? (The argument is quoted in L. Caplan, *The Tenth Justice: The Solicitor General and the Rule of Law* 236-37 (1987).

Ms. Bresnahan suffers from a medical condition known as gender dysphoria syndrome. A person with this condition is psychologically of one gender but was born with the reproductive organs of the other gender. Psychotherapy has been shown to have no effect on this disorder. But the suffering it causes is so profound that clinics at leading hospitals must resort to sex reassignment surgery to alleviate the condition. And wise medical practice requires that before so radical a step, the patient must dress and live as a person of the psychological gender for a long period.

This recitation is pared to the bone, but it brings out all the facts that are most determinative for a decision in the attorney's favor. The attorney has a duty to point out the most adverse facts as well. That can be done through juxtaposition, as in a written fact statement. Here it is done through implication: has the surgery yet been performed? What does that mean about the defendant's physical state?

On her doctor's orders, Ms. Bresnahan was so dressed when she was arrested for violating section 240.35 of the Penal Law, which punishes anyone who — in the words of the statute — is "in any way disguised by unusual or unnatural attire" and "loiters, remains, or congregates in a public place" with others similarly attired. When arrested, Ms. Bresnahan was walking to lunch in the financial district of Manhattan with two other people who suffer from the same disease.

This is one of the few situations where words should be quoted in an oral argument: they are the very words that court must interpret.

By appropriate motions in the trial court, Ms. Bresnahan sought dismissal of the charge on the grounds that her conduct could not violate the statute, and that, if it did, the statute would invade, among other things, her constitutional right to privacy. Even though the People concede that Ms. Bresnahan was following her doctor's orders according to accepted medical treatment, the trial court denied the motions and convicted her.

This is the procedural posture below. The appellate court needs to know it because it determines the standard of review.

Notice how the facts are used once again to set up the theory.

The questions before this court are whether the legislature really meant to punish people like Ms. Bresnahan, and, if the legislature did, whether her constitutional right to privacy nevertheless pro-

The statement of the issues leads into the argument that follows.

tects her freedom to choose her own
clothing.

> The legislature did not intend . . .

The sequence need not be as it is here. For example, it might be more effective in another case to state the procedural history or the issue, or both, before the facts. But the facts are what make this opening compelling, and they usually provide the energy in a compelling start. One of the leading appellate advocates of this century said that "in an appellate court the statement of the facts is not merely a part of the argument, it is more often than not the argument itself. A case well stated is a case far more than half argued." [1]

If you represent the appellee, your opening should be designed to show the court vividly how your theory differs from the appellant's:

> If the court please, I am Allan Kuusinen, for the People.
>
> The defendant concedes that he is and was anatomically male but had dressed up as a woman to disguise that fact. When arrested, he was walking down the street with two other men who were similarly disguised. They could have committed any of a number of crimes and left their victims utterly unable to identify them.
>
> That is exactly the danger the legislature meant to prevent. And because the legislature's goal is reasonable, section 240.35 does not violate the defendant's constitutional right to privacy.

Usually, the body of the argument begins most effectively with a statement of the rule or rules on which your conclusion rests. If two or more separate conclusions are being urged, the transition from one to another should be clear to the listener:

> . . . Thus, section 240.35 was never intended to punish a patient for complying with an accepted medical treatment.
>
> The second question before the Court is whether section 240.35, if it has the meaning urged by the People, violates Ms. Bresnahan's constitutional right to privacy. . . .

Except in the opening, an appellee's argument does not differ much structurally from an appellant's. Although some of what an appellee says grows out of notes taken while the appellant argues, most of an appellee's argument can be planned in advance. From the appellant's brief, the appellee knows before argument the theory the appellant will advance.

§22.2 1. Davis, *The Argument of an Appeal*, 26 A.B.A.J. 895, 896 (1940). Some courts study the briefs so carefully before argument that they consider a fact recitation to be a waste of time, and in those courts attorneys are discouraged — either informally or through the courts' rules — from opening with the facts.

Unless the bench is "cold,"[2] the judges' questions may so occupy you that you are surprised to find that your time is about to or already has run out. (When the chief or presiding judge, in a firm tone, says "Thank you," your time is finished.) If your time has expired, conclude with a sentence in which you specify the relief you seek ("Therefore, the judgment below should be affirmed because . . ."). But if you are in the midst of answering a question when your time runs out, quickly finish that first. On the other hand, if you still have a little time, summarize your argument in a few sentences and conclude in the same sentence you would have used if your time had run out. If you complete your argument before your time expires, conclude anyway, pause to see whether you will be asked further questions, and, if not, sit down. If, on the other hand, the judges continue to ask you questions after your time expires, answer them fully: the court has impliedly enlarged your time. Whatever the situation, you can signal your intent to finish by using an introductory phrase such as "In conclusion, ..."

If the appellant has reserved one or two minutes for rebuttal,[3] the appellant can use that time, after the appellee's argument, in order to reply. A court considers its time wasted if an appellant uses rebuttal to reiterate arguments already made or to raise new arguments for the first time. Rebuttal should be used instead to correct significantly inaccurate or misleadingly incomplete statements made by the appellee, and preferably not more than one or two of those. If the appellee's misstatements are trivial, an appellant looks petty correcting them. If it turns out that there is no need for rebuttal, an appellant appears confident waiving it. A rebuttal ends with a sentence reminding the court of the relief sought.

§22.3   Questions from the Bench

Some questions are neutral requests for information about the record, the law, the procedural posture, or the theory of the appeal. Some are challenges, asking you how you would overcome an adverse policy or equity argument or a contrary interpretation of authority or the record. Some are expressed as concerns: the judge asks how a particular problem in the case can be resolved. Some questions are openly friendly, usually asking the attorney to focus on an aspect of the case that the judge believes to be particularly persuasive. And some questions are neutral prompts, suggesting that whatever the attorney is discussing at the time can be dispensed with in favor of more relevant material. Some questions are asked because the answer is crucial to the judge's thinking. Others grow out of the sponta-

2. A "hot" bench is one that erupts with questions, and a "cold" bench is one that listens impassively.
3. The time reserved is subtracted from the time allowed for the appellant's main argument. You can reserve time by telling the court after you introduce yourself in the opening to your main argument.

neity of the moment, and the answer may have little or no impact on the decision.

When you hear a question, listen to it carefully, and do not be afraid to pause for a moment to think before answering. (Never interrupt a question.) Try to figure out the question's purpose and exactly what is troubling the judge. Then craft your answer to satisfy the skepticism or curiosity implied by the question. In the answer, do not give too little or too much. It is a mistake to give a one-sentence reply to a question that a judge plainly considers to be the crux of the case, but it is also a mistake to spend three minutes resolving a straightforward request for simple information.

If you are not sure what the judge is asking about, signal that in your answer so that the judge can help you out in case you have missed the gist of the question:

> If Your Honor is asking about the possibility that the issue has not been preserved for review — and please correct me if I've misunderstood — trial counsel made a timely objection and moved for . . .

If you do not understand the question, ask for clarification:

> I'm sorry, Your Honor; are you asking about whether the order appealed from is final?

This is one of the very few kinds of questions that *you* might ask during an oral argument.[1]

Do not leap to large assumptions about a judge's predispositions from the questions the judge asks. A neutral judge might ask challenging questions just to see whether your theory will hold up. A friendly judge might ask challenging questions to cause you to argue matters that the judge believes might persuade others on the bench. And an adverse judge might ask friendly or neutral questions out of politeness and a sense of fairness.

In any event, answer the question on the spot. Do not promise to get back to it later at a place in your outline where you had already planned to discuss the subject: other questions may prevent you from getting that far, and the

---

§22.3 1. If a judge poses a hypothetical and if you would need additional facts to answer the question, it is appropriate to ask whether those facts are in the hypothetical:

> Would the police be aware that the suspect has the mental retardation you mentioned?

But it is also appropriate not to ask and to give two answers, one with the supplemental facts and one without:

> If, hypothetically, the police do not know that the suspect is retarded, perhaps the evidence should not be suppressed, but if they do know, the cases require that it be suppressed. And in this appeal, the police did know about the analogous fact that the suspect was still stunned because of the concussion.

If a judge asks about a case or a statute about which you have forgotten something, it is appropriate to ask for help:

> I'm sorry, Your Honor, but did *Mansfield* precede the holding in *Soares*?

answer will be most persuasive immediately after the question is asked. Even if a question asks you to discuss an entire issue earlier than you had planned, do it and rearrange the order of your presentation to accommodate the judge's needs. Later, when you reach the spot where you had intended to discuss the issue, simply skip what you have already covered.[2]

In answering, state your conclusion first and your reasoning second. As you have seen in so many ways, the law-trained mind most easily understands discourse that lays out a conclusion before proving it. If you get wrapped up in a lot of preliminary material before producing a conclusion, the conclusion can be obscured or even lost, and you will create the appearance of being unhelpful or even evasive.

Answer the question you are asked, not one you would rather have been asked. The only way you can persuade is by facing directly the problems raised by the question and by showing the judge why those problems should not prevent a decision in your favor. *In every fully litigated case, each side has points of weakness.* If your side of your case did not have them, your adversary would have given up long ago. Where a judge has truly identified a point of weakness, face it and give a realistic counter-argument. Here are three different samples:

> I agree, Your Honor, that in that hypothetical the police would have had probable cause, but the facts of the hypothetical are not the facts of this case. . . .

> Yes, *Soares* did so hold, but later rulings of this court have impliedly undermined *Soares.* . . .

> Certainly, the record does reflect two isolated events that might be construed as evidence of good faith by the defendant, but the record also includes many, many events, stretching over several years, that show exactly the opposite. . . .

Not only are hedging and lack of candor ways of avoiding the job at hand, but they harm your credibility with the court. If, on the other hand, you can surround yourself with an aura of honesty and reliability, your arguments will be all the more persuasive.

If you are asked a question to which you do not know the answer, the best thing to say is exactly that. Judges are skilled interrogators, and you will quickly be found out if you try to fake your way through an answer. If you once knew the answer, you might feel a little better saying something like "I'm sorry, Your Honor, but I don't recall." But judges know that you are

---

2. In some schools, students are assigned to coauthor briefs, usually in teams of two, and to split the oral argument. If your school follows this practice, you may be asked questions about material that your colleague intends to argue. Do not respond by saying that your colleague will answer the question. Judges resent that, and you should know enough of the other student's material to be able to give at least a summary answer. If you are arguing first, your colleague can, during his or her allotted time, elaborate on your summary. Courts, by the way, discourage lawyers from splitting arguments, in part because of this problem.

human, and, unless the point you do not know is a big one, you gain credibility by admitting that you cannot answer.[3]

During the answer, build a bridge to the rest of your argument. If the question causes you to make part of your planned argument out of order, you can return to your argument at a point that is logically related to the answer. If the answer covers material that you had not planned to speak about, use the answer to lead back to your planned argument. If this is done smoothly, it may be hard for a listener to tell where the answer has ended and the planned presentation has picked up again. Bridge-building helps you redirect the argument back to your theory of the appeal so you can show the court how your theory, as a coherent whole, satisfies each concern raised from the bench. It is, after all, the theory that you are selling.

You will be better able to manage questions if you develop what one judge calls "controlled flexibility": "a relaxed resilience allowing one to respond to a judge's question, coupled with an internal gyro compass enabling one to return gracefully to a charted course."[4] This requires a "pair of talents — yielding to the sometimes centrifugal force of a judge's query and returning as soon as possible to one's own centripetal force."[5]

§22.4   Delivery, Affect, and Style

The most effective way to present arguments is in a tone of what has been called "respectful intellectual equality":[1]

> [I]f the lawyer approaches a court with an appreciation so great that it amounts to awe, perhaps verging on fear, he will not be able effectively to stand up to the court's questioning. . . . It is just as important, however, not to talk down to a court, no matter how much the individual advocate may be more generously endowed with quick perception. . . . The only proper attitude is that of a respectful intellectual equality. The "respectful" part approximates the quantum and type of respect that a younger [person] should show when speaking to an older one. . . . It is not inconsistent with this element of respect, however, for the advocate to argue an appeal on the basis that it is a discussion among equals. . . . Counsel must stand up to the judges quite as he would stand up to the senior members of his own firm. If he permits himself to be overawed . . . , then he — and his case — are well on their way to being lost.[2]

---

3. In practice, a lawyer might offer to file a supplemental brief or memorandum if he or she is afraid that the unanswered question might be crucial to the decision. These offers are usually refused, and that is a signal that the point is not critical after all.

4. F. Coffin, *The Ways of a Judge* 131 (1980).

5. *Id.*

§22.4   1. Wiener, *Oral Advocacy,* 62 Harv. L. Rev. 56, 72-74 (1948).

2. *Id.*

Although the judges' power is their authority to decide your case, it is their *need* to decide the case that — paradoxically — causes them to look to you for intellectual leadership.

What works best in this situation is not a speech, but a *conversation* in which you take the initiative, talking *with* the judges — not at them. It is a peculiar species of conversation, limited by the formalities of the occasion and by a focus on the decision the bench must make, but it is a conversation nonetheless. If you do the following, you can create for yourself a persuasive presence that helps you reach and engage the bench:

Look straight at the judges — preferably with eye contact — throughout the argument. Look at your notes only to remind yourself of the next subject for discussion, and even then get your eyes off your notes and back to the bench as quickly as possible. Whenever you look away from the judges, their attention can wander to other thoughts, partially tuning you out. And judges become annoyed with lawyers who read their arguments to the court.[3]

Stand up straight and do not distract the court with restless or anxious movement. Do not play with a pen, shuffle your papers around frequently, put your hands in your pockets, or sway forward and back. Limit your gestures to those that naturally punctuate your argument. A visually busy lawyer radiates nervousness, rather than the confidence needed to establish psychological leadership. Every lawyer — even the most experienced — is nervous before making an oral argument, but that anxiety tends to disappear once the attorney becomes engaged in the conversation. (For beginners, the moment of engagement — when you are so caught up in the work that you forget to be nervous — might not come for several minutes into the argument. But with each succeeding performance that moment will move closer and closer toward the opening, until eventually it coincides with the words "May it please the court" or "Your Honors, I am . . . .")

Speak loudly enough that the judges do not have to strain to hear you. If you are soft-spoken by nature, breathe in deeply before you begin and exhale while speaking your first words. Do this again whenever your voice falters. Make your lungs do the work, not your throat muscles. You will be surprised at how well your voice can carry. (If you already have a powerful voice, do not get carried away: nobody likes to listen to shouting.)

Use the tone and volume of your voice to emphasize the more important things you say. A monotone becomes monotonous. Pause before or after your most important remarks.

Communicate tenacity and what one judge has called "disciplined earnestness": "a communicated sense of conviction that pushes a case to the limits of its strength but not beyond. One somehow brings together one's words and body language, facial expression and eye contact, to radiate a sense of conviction without making every point a life-and-death issue."[4]

Unless asked, avoid multitudes of detail in discussing authority. Be-

3. See U.S. Sup. Ct. R. 44(1) (". . . The court looks with disfavor on any argument that is read from a prepared text") and Fed. R. App. P. 34(c) (". . . Counsel will not be permitted to read at length from briefs, records, or authority").
4. F. Coffin, *The Ways of a Judge* 132 (1980).

cause oral argument works best when focused on the big ideas in the appeal, you are better off concentrating on rules of law, policy arguments, and broad descriptions of authority. Citations and the minutiae of authority are very hard to follow when delivered orally, and they ought to be in your brief anyway. If your case is built on a synthesis of authority, describe it generally ("the majority of jurisdictions," "the recent trend of cases in other states," "seven of the federal circuits," "this court has previously held"). But if there is controlling authority, that itself is a big idea and deserves attention, especially where you are asking a court to construe an unsettled statute or to overrule precedent. But even then, do not give the full citation: the name and the year of a case are enough. And if you must quote—as you might with a crucial statute or holding—limit yourself to the half-dozen or so essential words that the court must interpret.

Know your record thoroughly, use it to its full advantage, and do not discuss "facts" outside the record. And, as with authority, do not supply unnecessary detail unless asked for it. Concentrate on the few facts that are most determinative, and mention along the way one or two facts that most bring the story to life. Some facts do not logically have legal significance, but they help the judges "see" the story and put the case into a realistic perspective. For example, in the appellant's opening in §22.2, it is certainly not determinative that, when arrested, the defendant "was walking to lunch in the financial district of Manhattan with two other people who suffer from the same disease," but it helps the court visualize the defendant's theory that the conviction appealed from represents a preposterous application of a statute.

§22.5   Formalities and Customs of the Courtroom

Dress not merely for business, but in conservative clothing that conveys the impression that you are a careful and reliable professional.

Stand at the lectern throughout your argument. Do not stroll out from behind it unless you must go to your materials in order to answer a question.

In court, lawyers do not speak to each other. They speak only to the bench and—when the bench gives permission—to witnesses and juries. And because there are no witnesses or juries in appellate courts, you will speak only to the judges.

The dignity of the occasion will be demeaned if you speak in slang, in emotional rhetoric, or in terms that unnecessarily personalize the attorneys or judges. Even when discussing your adversary's arguments, refer to them as the party's, rather than as the lawyer's. There is a world of tonal difference between "The plaintiff mistakenly relies . . ." and "Mr. Maggione has mistakenly told you . . . ." Similarly, do not speak to the bench in flattering language. Judges are satisfied with respect; they are offended by obsequiousness.

While your adversary argues, listen attentively and without facial expressions that convey your opinion of what is transpiring. Take whatever notes you will need to help you respond in your own argument, if you are the appellee, or in rebuttal, if you are the appellant. Under no circumstances should you interrupt your adversary's argument.

§22.6   Preparation for Oral Argument

Prepare two versions of the same presentation. One version should include the material that you *must* argue — in other words, the core of your case — and, when delivered without interruption, it should fill no more than 30 or 35 percent of the time you are allowed. The other version is an expanded development of the first. It includes the first version, as well as supplemental material that makes the core of your case more persuasive, and, without interruption, it should fill about 80 or 90 percent of the available time. You will know within the first three or four minutes of the argument whether the bench is hot or cold. If it is hot, you can deliver the core presentation and work the supplemental material into your answers. If the bench is cold, you can deliver the expanded argument.

There are a number of ways to prepare notes for you to use at the lectern. After many arguments, you will eventually discover the type and style of notes that work best for you, but the consensus of experienced advocates is that you are better off with the fewest notes because you will need them only to remind you of the subjects you intend to cover and of a few key phrases that you intend to use.[1] In fact, if you are well prepared, you will know your case so well that a single page on a legal-size pad is probably sufficient. (Take each brief to the podium as well, in case you are asked about either of them.) You can outline both versions of your argument on a single page divided by a vertical line. For example, the lawyer who wrote the appellant's brief in Appendix E might be able to make an oral argument from a very condensed page of notes like the one on page 366. Some advocates find it helpful to take to the lectern notecards with synopses of the record and of the major relevant cases. You might or might not find such synopses helpful. If you already know your case thoroughly, the cards will only get in your way.

Plan your argument by weaving together policy, the facts, and the controlling rules of law into a seamless theory. Show how policy and the facts compel your conclusion, while the technical law can be used to justify it. If the standard of review and the procedural posture below place burdens on you, be sure to show the court how you have carried those burdens. If the burdens rest on your adversary, show instead how he or she has failed to

---

§22.6   1. If, in preparing the argument, you come up with an excellent phrasing for a difficult concept, you might write down those few words to remind yourself to use them. Otherwise, your notes should be only a list of subjects to cover.

core	_suppl_
facts 　disease 　treatment (no psythrpy) 　how arrested 　motions below	
issues 　1. "wh'r leg're really meant to 　　　punish people like B" 　2. if yes, rt to priv	
statutory issue 　1. not disguised "med prof'n 　　　considers her clothing to 　　　be an accurate communi- 　　　cation of the state of her 　　　gender"	how gender determined "no magic moment" when 　becomes fem
2. modern med treatment	hosps & clinics accepted trtmt kind of pain
3. history	farm revolt sim statutes gap in auth
rt to priv issue 　1. scope of rt	clothing cases
2. no comp'g st int	fund rt st's crime cont theory
3. even if comp'g, ovrbrd	lesser restrict
4. not "rat'l basis" summary	no cause/effect

carry them. Remember that you cannot cover every argument in the brief: focus on the most important material.

Make a ruthless list of every weakness in your case and every question that you would therefore ask if you were a judge, and prepare an answer to each of those questions. The judges will care a great deal about policy concerns: if they do as you ask, how, for example, will the law in the future treat cases that are similar to—but not exactly the same as—yours? You are not just trying to win a case; you are helping the judges make law. How can the bench craft a holding in your favor so that, as precedent, it does not subsequently cause injustice?

Try also to predict which concessions you will be asked to make. Figure out which concessions you cannot afford to make and which you will have to make in order to protect the reasonability of the rest of your case. If you think about this for the first time when you are actually asked to make the concession, a very large part of your case could easily disappear in a snap misjudgment.

Practice making your argument to a person who will ask you tough questions but who knows little about your theory of the appeal. If the person mooting you knows too much about your theory, you will not be able to practice teaching your case. (Oral argument is a respectful form of teaching: you will teach the court how to view the appeal through your theory.)

Finally, spend a little time in the library. A month or more — in real appeals, several months — might have passed since you researched the brief. Check the *Shepard's* supplements to see whether controlling statutes have been amended or repealed, whether one of the key cases has been overruled, and whether any of the recent precedents has been reversed or affirmed. You need not check every citation in your brief, but you do not want to discover in the courtroom that some important texture of the law has changed.

§22.7   State v. Dobbs and Zachrisson: *An Oral Argument Dissected*

To help you understand how oral argument influences judicial decision-making, this chapter concludes with a dissection of the arguments in a real appeal,[1] comparing them to the decision subsequently made by the court to whom the arguments were addressed.

In the city where this case arose, Dobbs operated an illegal book-making business in one neighborhood, and Zachrisson ran a similar enterprise in another neighborhood. Dobbs and Zachrisson were each indicted on 16 counts of bribery and one count of conspiracy to bribe. (They were not indicted for illegal gambling, perhaps because the police lacked the evidence required by the gambling statute.) At trial, a police officer named Porfier testified that Zachrisson had given her money on the understanding that she would refrain from enforcing the law against him and Dobbs and would instead arrest their competitors. The prosecution also introduced tape recordings of conversations between Porfier and the defendants. Dobbs and Zachrisson testified in their own defense, but a jury convicted on all 34 counts.

---

§22.7   1. The names of everyone involved in this appeal — including the judges and the attorneys — have been changed. The citations to local authority have all been changed, and the wording of the local statutes has been altered slightly to make them easier for you to understand. To make the story easier to follow, many of the facts have been simplified, but not in ways that are relevant to the court's analysis. Some of the people described here are composites from a larger cast of characters in the original appeal.

Porfier testified that initially she approached Zachrisson in an attempt to recruit him and perhaps other bookies as informants. She suggested that Zachrisson set up a meeting with any other bookies he thought might be interested. Zachrisson suggested Dobbs. A meeting of the three of them was arranged, but Dobbs did not show up. At this and other meetings, Porfier wore a "body wire" (a hidden microphone that transmits to a nearby tape recorder). Zachrisson told Porfier that he needed police protection from aggressive bookies with mob connections who were moving into his territory. The jury heard a tape recording of Zachrisson telling Porfier that if she made it easier for him to make a profit, he could "send some money [her] way." Porfier told him that she would have to think it over, and that he should find out whether Dobbs wanted to make the same arrangement.

A week or so later, Zachrisson and Porfier met again. Porfier told Zachrisson that she would accept money from Zachrisson and Dobbs, that she would not arrest them or their employees, and that she would arrest their competitors. Zachrisson told her that Dobbs was "interested." Zachrisson began making periodic payments to Porfier of $100 to $200 (all of which she turned over to the police department). Zachrisson and Dobbs continued their operations without police interference, and some of their competitors were arrested.

A few months after this arrangement began, Zachrisson told Porfier that he and Dobbs—whom Porfier had still not yet met—wanted to expand their gambling enterprises and were willing to bring in Porfier as a silent partner. Zachrisson told Porfier that she would receive a percentage of the profits in exchange for police protection. Subsequently, Porfier met with Zachrisson and—for the first and only time —Dobbs. During that meeting, Dobbs stated that he was in accord with Zachrisson's goals, but Porfier did not start receiving a share of the profits until a few weeks later.

At trial, Zachrisson and Dobbs each asserted the defenses of entrapment and coercion, which are separately defined in the state's Criminal Code:

§ 32. Defense of entrapment

In a prosecution for any crime, it is an affirmative defense that the defendant engaged in the prohibited conduct because he was induced or encouraged to do so by a public servant, or by a person acting under a public servant's direction, where the public servant or the person acting under his direction acted for the purpose of obtaining evidence against the defendant for the purpose of a criminal prosecution, and where the methods used to obtain that evidence created a substantial risk that the crime would be committed by a person not otherwise disposed to commit it. Conduct that merely provides a defendant with an opportunity to commit a crime is not entrapment.

§ 963. Bribery; defense of coercion

(a) In a prosecution for bribery, it is a defense that the defendant conferred the prohibited benefit on a public servant as a result of that public servant's coercion of the defendant.

(b) For the purposes of this section, a public servant coerces a defendant when he or she instills in the defendant a fear that, if the defendant does not comply with the public servant's wishes, the public servant will cause physical injury to the defendant or another, cause damage to property of the defendant or another, cause criminal charges to be brought against the defendant or another, or otherwise abuse the public servant's power as an official of the government.

At trial, Zachrisson testified that he paid Porfier because he was afraid that he would be arrested if he did not, and he presented evidence that during the time these payments were being made he had complained to others that he was being shaken down by Porfier. Dobbs testified that Porfier had threatened to put him out of business if he did not agree to pay her off. Both defendants moved for directed verdicts of acquittal on the grounds that the evidence of coercion and entrapment was so clear that those issues had ceased to be questions of fact for the jury and that the defendants were therefore entitled to acquittals as a matter of law. (If this confuses you, see §12.5.2.) The trial court denied the motions. On appeal to the state's supreme court, both defendants argued in their briefs that their convictions should be reversed because the motions should have been granted.

In his appellate brief, Dobbs asserted two additional grounds for reversal. First, Dobbs argued that the trial court committed reversible error in instructing the jury that if they convicted him of conspiracy, they could also convict him of bribery because of the acts of a co-conspirator. There was no evidence that Dobbs gave any money to Porfier directly, but the trial court instructed the jury that Dobbs could be found guilty of bribery for the payments made by Zachrisson if the jury concluded beyond a reasonable doubt that Dobbs and Zachrisson had conspired to bribe Porfier.

Second, Dobbs argued that his rights to a speedy trial had been violated because the trial did not occur until 18 months after indictment. There are two separate rights to a speedy trial. One is provided by the Sixth Amendment to the United States Constitution ("an accused shall enjoy the right to a speedy and public trial"), which applies to state prosecutions as a result of the due process clause of the Fourteenth Amendment. The other right is provided by § 27 of the state's Criminal Procedure Code, which provides that an indictment must be dismissed if the prosecution is not ready for trial within six months after the indictment. (The constitutional test lacks such a clear deadline and in general is much more elastic.) Delay in coming to trial might arise from prosecutorial tardiness, from tardiness on the defense side of the case, from court congestion, or from some combination of these sources. When a defendant moves to dismiss an indictment for lack of a speedy trial, the trial court tries to determine the sources of delay. Delay due to defense tardiness is ignored as "excludable time." (Otherwise, defendants would profit from procrastination by their own attorneys.) Delay caused by prosecutorial tardiness is "chargeable time" because prosecutors are expected to take the initiative in moving cases to trial. You will see in a few moments whether this state treats court congestion delay as excludable or chargeable time. An appellate court will not automatically reverse a conviction where the trial court erroneously denied a speedy trial motion. You learned in §20.4 that reversals occur only for trial court errors that are material or prejudicial. As you read the oral arguments and the state supreme court's decision, pay close attention to how the attorneys and the court address the question of whether Dobbs was prejudiced by the delay in his case.

The following is a condensation of the transcript of the oral arguments in the state supreme court.[2] Immediately after the transcript, you will read a synopsis of the court's decision.

THE CHIEF JUDGE: Mr. Womack?

WOMACK [for Zachrisson]: May it please the court. I will argue the issues of coercion and entrapment. My brief sets out the statutory definition of coercion in a bribery case. The evidence at trial was that Zachrisson, after he had made one or two payments, went to a friend of his and reported, in the friend's words, that he was being "shaken down." The friend then went to a judge in a neighboring county and reported that Zachrisson was being shaken down by the police, that over a period of months the police had been intimidating Zachrisson and asking him for money in exchange for favors. You can't read the summary of the meetings here and not be convinced that the police were the principal participants, instigators and initiators of all the activity that lead up to the money changing hands. I think there is a question of law as to whether this was voluntary.

What do you think of this opening? Does it suggest immediately that what happened in the trial court should make us uncomfortable? How would you have improved it?

JUDGE BECENTI: The police denied it, didn't they?

WOMACK: Yes.

2. The portions of the oral arguments that are most closely related to the state supreme court's decision are reproduced here, and the rest are omitted. For the most part, the words in the transcript are the words actually spoken by the attorneys and the judges, but some phrasing has been altered slightly to help you understand what happened and to smooth over transitions from one part of the argument to another. The issues presented in this appeal are not easy, and the briefs explained in much greater detail the complex law involved. When you compare the oral arguments to the synopsis of the court's decision at the end of this chapter, try to understand the cause-and-effect relationship: how do the arguments seem to have influenced what the court did? Without actually interviewing the judges themselves and reading the court's internal memoranda and the briefs submitted by the parties, we cannot reconstruct with certainty the process through which the court reached its decision, but some tentative conclusions are revealed by comparing the oral argument to the court's decision.

JUDGE BECENTI: Doesn't that make it a question of fact, to be resolved by a jury?

WOMACK: No, I think entrapment can be decided on the undisputed, undeniable facts here.

JUDGE BECENTI: As a matter of law?

WOMACK: As a matter of law. Porfier has known the defendants for approximately six years, knew that they were small-time gamblers, knew that they were involved with after-hours bars, having dealings with them over a year and a half period. Those are misdemeanors, but bribery is a felony. The testimony was that everybody knew the defendants were gamblers. Yet the police spent all that time, seeing them on a regular basis and never arrested them for any gambling offenses.

JUDGE BECENTI: They investigated organized crime and gambling, didn't they — an ongoing thing?

WOMACK: If they were investigating organized crime, what came of it? Why did it take them almost two years to get the defendants for bribery?

JUDGE STEIN: Doesn't that argument cut both ways because if it took that long the coercion wasn't very effective?

WOMACK: I disagree. Porfier exacted promises of a hundred dollars a week from these defendants. Porfier manufactured a crime. She got very little money from Zachrisson and then pressured him to introduce her to Dobbs. And that in itself was improper conduct.

JUDGE BECENTI: You'd have to argue that that's entrapment as a matter of law, wouldn't you? The facts were decided against you in the trial court, and we're bound by that.

WOMACK: Yes, I would argue that it was entrapment as a matter of law and that coercion was proved. Porfier engaged in improper conduct because she decided that

The state supreme court can reach the questions of coercion and entrapment only if there are issues of law and not of fact (see §20.4). In a trial court, what might seem to be a fact issue can at times be converted into a law issue through one of the motions described in §12.5.2. That is what these defendants tried to do through their motions for directed verdicts. Trial and appellate judges are inclined to let juries decide matters like these as fact issues unless there is a good reason not to. Here, is the court being given a good reason?

Generally, rhetorical questions do not persuade. It is more effective to lay out each step of the argument.

Is this the most compelling way to describe what happened? Can you think of something better?

Do you find this theory persuasive? If you do not, is

she wanted to get the defendants for a higher crime than gambling. And in this way Zachrisson's reluctance to commit the crime was overcome by persistence. I believe in this case that's obvious. Zachrisson resisted making payments, and the payments did not begin until long after the demands had started. Porfier just kept going because she wasn't satisfied with arresting the defendants on petty gambling charges.

JUDGE STEIN: Is there anything wrong about that, as long as it doesn't amount to entrapment? If something is going on, is there any reason why police can't wait before arresting until they accumulate more evidence?

WOMACK: No, Your Honor, if it's indeed going on, but in this case it wasn't going on when Porfier first got involved. I see my time is up. Thank you.

THE CHIEF JUDGE: Ms. Underwood?

UNDERWOOD [for Dobbs]: Your Honors, Johnny Dobbs met with this police officer only once, and that was after the officer demanded that Dobbs be there. He came only after she made five separate demands that he meet with her. Dobbs met with the officer on one occasion and never saw her again. There was no evidence in this trial that he had anything else to do with Officer Porfier. And at that one meeting, he said only one thing of any substance. When the officer suggested that she should arrest some competing gamblers to shake them down, Dobbs said, "Do we really have to arrest people? I don't want that to happen." He disagreed with the plan proposed. And when somebody said, "Johnny, you're not saying much," he replied, "You don't learn anything by talking." These are not words of joining a conspiracy. These are not words of attempting to bribe anyone. And if this is the only evidence in the case, he cannot be considered to have joined a conspiracy. He certainly didn't do it through his own words. The law is clear and

that because the theory is faulty or because it is not being adequately supported by the facts and law at the attorney's disposal?

Notice how this attorney starts off with her best facts to undermine the bench's confidence that whatever happened in the trial court was probably not unjust. (Remember that appellants have the burden of demonstrating error and that appellate courts are affirmance-prone.) This presentation paints a vivid picture with a few, very carefully selected facts. As you read the synopsis of the state supreme court's decision, try to figure out what effect that picture had on the bench.

settled that the words of somebody else cannot bind a defendant to a conspiracy. There was no evidence that he ever committed any other act in this whole scheme. On this kind of record, the jury should not have been instructed that they could convict Dobbs of bribery.

In fact, Porfier tried five times to get Dobbs to meet with her. And when he finally did meet with her—and this leads into the issues of coercion and entrapment—the first thing she said was "I can put you out of business; I can go into your neighborhood tomorrow and arrest your people and close you down." These words are coercive as a matter of law. And it is also entrapment as a matter of law because the police officer forced the meeting where she made these coercive statements. Here, the police officer created the crime of bribery . . .

This transition is smooth but also clearly announced so that the bench can follow the attorney's organization.

JUDGE ORTIZ [interrupting]: You haven't mentioned your speedy trial issue, which you argue in your brief. You still press it?

UNDERWOOD: Yes, absolutely, every point in the brief. In the trial court we tried to demonstrate—and the court wouldn't permit us—that other cases that had been indicted after Dobbs were tried before him, even though those other defendants were not in jail.

Notice how the attorney picks up the question and uses it as a springboard for argument.

JUDGE ORTIZ: You consistently answered ready?

UNDERWOOD: Every time.

JUDGE ORTIZ: There was an 18-month delay?

UNDERWOOD: Yes, Your Honor.

JUDGE ORTIZ: The only excuse given in the trial court was calendar congestion?

UNDERWOOD: Yes.

JUDGE ORTIZ: And you sought no continuances or adjournments during this period?

Are Judge Ortiz's questions hostile? Or does he seem to be helping the attorney make clear that the delay was not caused by the defense and that the question has been properly preserved for appellate review?

UNDERWOOD: Not one.

JUDGE ORTIZ: When you made your motion for speedy trial relief, you claimed both a constitutional violation and a violation of our speedy trial statute?

UNDERWOOD: Yes, both issues raised below . . .

JUDGE BECENTI [interrupting]: Were there extensive plea bargaining negotiations?

This exchange seems to have sparked the interest of Judges Becenti and Stein. What do you think Judge Ortiz was trying to accomplish?

UNDERWOOD: Not one minute of it, Your Honor.

JUDGE STEIN: Has there been any showing of prejudice?

This is the tough question. And in answering, the attorney tries to put the best appearance on a fact that she must admit.

UNDERWOOD: Yes, in the human sense, but not in the sense that we couldn't find any evidence.

JUDGE BECENTI: Any lost witnesses, anything like that?

Any equivocation by the attorney on these matters would be quickly discovered and cause the court to lose confidence in the attorney's candor. These are not facts that are open to reasonable interpretations. Either Dobbs was in jail, for example, or he was not.

UNDERWOOD: No.

JUDGE STEIN: Were the defendants in jail during this time or were they out on bail?

UNDERWOOD: No, Dobbs was not in jail.

JUDGE STEIN: Have you read our opinion in *Weatherby*?

UNDERWOOD: Yes, Your Honor, I know . . .

JUDGE STEIN [interrupting]: That must not have disappointed you.

Weatherby seems at least superficially to favor Dobbs. If Judges Stein and Ortiz had to make a decision on this issue right now, how do you think they would rule? Why do you think so? As you read the argument for the State and the synopsis of the court's decision, remember the prediction you made here.

UNDERWOOD: Well, . . .

JUDGE ORTIZ [interrupting]: You say this was 18 months?

UNDERWOOD: Yes.

JUDGE ORTIZ: *Weatherby* was 18 and a half months.

UNDERWOOD: Yes, I know, Your Honor.

JUDGE ORTIZ: And Weatherby is now at home.

UNDERWOOD: If the court please, I chose to concentrate today on the other grounds for reversal because I know Your Honors were aware of that, and I feel that that was an argument I didn't need to press any further. I think I've taken all my time. Thank you very much.

As you read the synopsis of the state supreme court's decision, ask yourself whether this might be a diplomatic way of explaining a strategy decision. If so, why would the explanation need to be diplomatic?

THE CHIEF JUDGE: Mr. Lysander?

LYSANDER [for the State]: May it please the cou . . .

JUDGE STEIN [interrupting]: What about *Weatherby*, Mr. Lysander, isn't that dispositive of the speedy trial issue?

Judge Stein has gotten *very* interested in the speedy trial aspect of the case.

LYSANDER: Your Honor, in this case, the speedy trial motion was made orally and not in writing. It was made on the eve of trial and without any prior notice to the prosecution. *Weatherby* is distinguishable because there the issue was raised in the trial court in a way that permitted the prosecution to find out the reason for every delay and to put that reason in the trial court record. That didn't happen here.

Do you think this attorney was prepared to answer questions on the speedy trial issue?

JUDGE STEIN: In this appeal, did the prosecution oppose the motion in the trial court on the ground that it needed an opportunity to prove that each delay was justified?

LYSANDER: I'm not sure, Your Honor.

JUDGE STEIN: Perhaps the motion should have been made in writing and with prior notice to the prosecution, but if it were not and if the prosecution didn't object to that, I would think that your procedural objection would have been waived.

LYSANDER: Your Honor, this was a pre-*Bachman* case. Before your holding in *State v. Bachman*, both the prosecution and defense were presenting their arguments in trial courts under somewhat lax procedural standards. However, . . .

JUDGE STEIN [interrupting]: But the defendant shouldn't be prejudiced then by that fact, if there were relaxed standards.

LYSANDER: That's correct, Your Honor, but I'm simply saying that the prosecution would be prejudiced in that we were never given the opportunity to have a hearing to develop a complete factual record for the reasons for each delay.

JUDGE STEIN: But wasn't the only excuse advanced trial court congestion?

LYSANDER: The prosecution answered ready for trial for the first time only three months after the indictment, and there was difficulty getting a free courtroom on that date.

JUDGE STEIN: And we held in *Weatherby* that courtroom congestion is no excuse.

LYSANDER: But you also held in *Greenfield* that the trial court's inability to schedule a trial was an excuse. And there has never been an allegation of prejudice to Dobbs because of the delay, and Dobbs was the only defendant to raise this issue in the trial court.

Read coldly in a transcript, this answer might seem flippant. But if it is spoken in the proper tone of voice it becomes exactly the "respectful intellectual equality" that persuades. We can never know how much the court was influenced by this answer (or by the prosecution's brief), but compare the answer to the court's decision on this issue.

JUDGE ORTIZ: But the question is now before us, and it was raised below — although you say it was raised orally instead of on papers —

LYSANDER: That's correct.

JUDGE ORTIZ: The only excuse the prosecution offered is calendar congestion, is that correct?

Has this attorney had any effect at all on Judges Ortiz and Stein? When you read the synopsis of the court's decision, notice how they vote.

LYSANDER: That is the only excuse I am aware of, but we never had an opportunity for a hearing, so I do not know what would have developed had there been a hearing.

JUDGE ORTIZ: At the time the motion was made, there was no excuse given other than that?

LYSANDER: No, but as a practical matter, when a motion like that is made on the eve of trial all of a sudden — just before a three-

and-a-half-week trial that everybody has been preparing for—on the eve of trial when the defendant suddenly claims his speedy trial rights have been violated, the prosecutor would have to do an investigation in order to be able to account for each and every continuance that happened in the past.

JUDGE STEIN: Was there any request by the prosecutor for additional time to answer the motion—so the prosecutor could develop the record that you're now suggesting could have been developed?

LYSANDER: I don't believe that there was, Your Honor, but if there had been, that would have defeated the ends of getting the trial completed as soon as possible. [pauses] Concerning the question of whether the defendants were entrapped by the police . . . .

(The remainder of the State's argument is omitted.)

State v. Dobbs and Zachrisson

BECENTI, J. Dobbs's bribery convictions are reversed, his conspiracy conviction is affirmed, and all of Zachrisson's convictions are affirmed.

Dobbs's bribery convictions are reversed because the trial court erroneously instructed the jury that they could convict him of bribery for the payments made by Zachrisson. Because there was no evidence that Dobbs actually made any bribe payments, there must be a reversal of the convictions for bribery and a dismissal of the indictment as to those counts. Liability for a substantive offense like bribery may not be predicated solely on a defendant's participation in an underlying conspiracy.

A conspirator is not necessarily an accessory to a crime committed in furtherance of the conspiracy. Under section 129 of the Criminal Code a person is criminally responsible, as an accessory, for the act of another if he or she "solicits, requests, commands, importunes, or intentionally aids" the other person to engage in that offense. Conspicuously absent from the statute is reference to one who conspires to commit an offense. That omission cannot be supplied by construction. It may be true that in some instances a conspirator's conduct will suffice to establish liability as an accessory, but the concepts are, in reality, analytically distinct. To permit mere guilt of conspiracy to establish the defendant's guilt of the substantive crime without any evidence of further action on the part of the defendant would be to expand the basis of accessory liability beyond the legislative design. In interpreting our own state's Criminal Code, we decline to follow the rule followed in federal prosecutions. [Citation omitted.]

But we reject Dobbs's further claim that his statutory and constitutional rights to a speedy trial were violated by the delay between his indictment and his trial. Dobbs does not claim to have been prejudiced by the delay in coming to trial. He was not incarcerated, and he does not assert that any of his witnesses have disappeared or suffered a fading of memory. *State v. Weatherby* is therefore distinguishable from this appeal. Moreover, when Dobbs moved in the trial court to dismiss for lack of a speedy trial, court congestion was assigned as the reason for the delay, and the prosecution was ready for trial within three months of the indictment. Thus, Dobbs is not entitled to dismissal pursuant to our speedy trial statute, which requires that the prosecution be ready on time but places no corresponding obligation on the trial court. See *State v. Greenfield*.

Finally, defendants urge that the prosecution failed to disprove the bribery defense of coercion beyond a reasonable doubt and that the evidence establishes the affirmative defense of entrapment as a matter of law. The record does not support these contentions. The defendants' motions were correctly denied, and the issues were properly submitted to the jury.

The record before us presents a conflict between the prosecution's version of events and that of the defendants. The defendants asserted that the police officers induced their participation in the bribery scheme and employed coercive tactics to ensure compliance. Although the record does reveal some evidence of conduct that might be construed as harassment, there is also evidence of mutual co-operation. Hence, resolution of the issues was a purely factual matter within the province of the jury.

[There were no dissents.]

APPENDICES

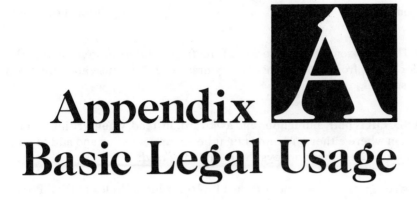

Appendix A
Basic Legal Usage

Beginners sometimes have trouble with the following words and phrases:

AFFIRM: Precedent can be followed or overruled — but never affirmed. An appellate court "affirms" only when it refuses to reverse the ruling of a lower court *in the same litigation.* See *OVERRULE.*

AND is a weak vehicle for showing causation, although it is otherwise a perfectly good conjunction. Compare these sentences:

> The arresting officers reasonably believed that the defendant would need protective clothing on such a cold night, and they did not violate his Fourth Amendment rights by searching his jacket before handing it to him.

> The arresting officers did not violate the defendant's Fourth Amendment rights by searching his jacket before handing it to him, since they reasonably believed that he would need protective clothing on such a cold night.

> Because the arresting officers reasonably believed that the defendant would need protective clothing on such a cold night, they did not violate his Fourth Amendment rights by searching his jacket before handing it to him.

The first sentence communicates the cause-and-effect relationship in the least forceful way. The second sentence is better because the effect is stated

379

first. The third sentence is also more forceful, but for a different reason: the reader knows from the sentence's very first word that cause-and-effect will be described.

AND/OR is both ambiguous and awkward. Instead, when writing about a situation where either *and* or *or* might be accurate, use *or* and add to your list an extra item that conveys the meaning of *and*:

wrong: Under Rule 11 of the Federal Rules of Civil Proce-
                    dure, sanctions can be imposed on the attorney
                    and/or on the client.

right: Under Rule 11 of the Federal Rules of Civil Proce-
                    dure, sanctions can be imposed on the attorney, on
                    the client, or on both.

APPEAL: The past tense is spelled *appealed*.

APPLY is nearly incapable of communicating a precise relationship be-tween a subject and an object:

The Freedom of Information Act *applies* to this case.

Does the Act require that the document at issue be published in the *Federal Register*? Does the Act require that the document be given to anyone who asks for a copy? Does the Act require that the document be available for photocopying, but not at government expense? Or does the Act give the government a justification for refusing to do any of these things? The quoted sentence would be much more helpful if *applies* were replaced with a verb or a verbal phrase that communicates exactly what the Act does. *INVOLVE* and *DEAL WITH* are equally imprecise.

ARGUE: Lawyers argue, but courts do not. Argument is discourse in-tended to persuade others. One argues when one lacks the power to decide, and one argues to those who have that power. A court therefore is said to have "decided," "held," "found," "ruled," "concluded," etc. Judges "argue" only in dissent.

AS is a bad substitute for the more forceful *because* and *since*. Not only is *as* a weaker word, but it can confuse the reader, who sees it much more often used to join contemporaneous events ("the driver accelerated *as* the child ran into the street").

BUT is sometimes not the best way to show argumentative contrast. Compare these sentences:

The Court of Appeal has held that the objection is waived if not made at trial, but it has also held that, even without an objection, a conviction should be reversed where a prosecutor's conduct was an inflammatory as it was here.

Although the Court of Appeal has held that the objection is waived if not made at trial, it has also held that, even without an objection, a conviction should be reversed where a prosecutor's conduct was as inflammatory as it was here.

In the second example, *Although* tells the reader from the very beginning of the sentence that the first clause, however damning, will be shown — before the sentence is over — not to matter. *But* works perfectly well, however, as an ordinary conjunction in sentences not based on argumentative contrast.

COUNSEL: Other forms are spelled *counselor*, *counseling*, and *counseled*.

COURT refers to an institution and not a group of people. The word is therefore used with singular verbs and pronouns.

wrong:	The court have held . . .
	They reversed . . .
right:	The court has held . . .
	It reversed . . .

DEAL WITH is nearly incapable of communicating a precise relationship between a subject and an object:

State v. Torvaldsen deals with common law larceny.

What does *Torvaldsen* do to larceny? Define it? Define only one of the elements? Clarify the difference between larceny and false pretenses? Or decide that there is no longer an offense by that name because the legislature has replaced it with the statutory crime of theft? Instead, use a verb that tells the reader precisely what happened. *APPLY* and *INVOLVE* are equally imprecise.

DICTUM is the singular, and **DICTA** the plural. Do not use a singular verb with *dicta* or a plural verb with *dictum*.

FIND and **FOUND:** When a court "holds," it decides a question of law, but when a court "finds," it determines, on the basis of evidence, what the facts are. Conclusions of law are not "found."

FOR is a poor substitute for the more forceful *because* and *since*. Not only is *for* a weaker word, but it can confuse the reader, who sees it more often used as a preposition ("the plaintiff has sued both *for* damages and *for* an injunction").

HOLD: See *FIND* and *SAY.*

I: Pronouns identifying the writer are frowned on, except for the use of *we* in judicial opinions. Your goal is to emphasize the ideas under discussion, rather than your own role. "I believe," "we submit," "in our case," and the like are distracting clutter.

IF and *whether* are sometimes confused. *If* introduces a condition, while *whether* prefaces an alternative. A job applicant receives a letter containing the following sentence:

> Please call and let me know *whether* you anticipate any other offers before our hiring committee can meet next week.

This literally means that the applicant should telephone the writer regardless of whether other offers are anticipated: the writer wants to be told one way or the other. A writer who wants to be informed only in the event of an anticipated offer from another employer should instead say the following:

> Please call and let me know *if* you anticipate any other offers before our hiring committee can meet next week.

INNOCENT: "Innocence" has little meaning in criminal law, which cares instead about whether guilt can be proved. A defendant does not escape punishment because he is "innocent": if he escapes punishment, it is because the prosecution has not proved his guilt beyond a reasonable doubt. Despite what you hear on the evening news, defendants do not plead "innocent," and juries do not find them "innocent." A defendant instead pleads "not guilty" and in so doing does not claim to be innocent: that plea is a demand that the government prove the defendant's guilt. And, if acquitted, the defendant will be found "not guilty" because the government has not proved his guilt beyond a reasonable doubt; the jury takes no position on the defendant's "innocence."

INVOLVE is nearly incapable of communicating a precise relationship between a subject and an object:

> Section 452(a) *involves* the Rule Against Perpetuities.

Here *involves* communicates only that § 452(a) has some connection with the Rule Against Perpetuities. Has § 452(a) codified the Rule? Modified it? Abolished it? Use a verb that tells the reader precisely what happened. *APPLY, DEAL WITH,* and *involve* are the triplets of imprecise verbs.

IT, when used as a referent, can cause vagueness. See *THIS.*

IT IS is a grammatical expletive. (The problem here is not with the sort of words that should not appear in a family newspaper; those are *anatomical* expletives.) See *THERE ARE.*

JUDGMENT: In legal writing, *judgment* is *always* spelled with only one *e.*

LAW and *statute* are not synonymous. A lay person might write that the legislature should "pass a law," but a lawyer would use "enact a statute" instead. That is because lawyers understand the "law" to be the sum of statutes and precedent. (In a few jurisdictions, however, the names of individual statutes include the word *Law,* rather than *Act* or *Code.* An example is the New York Penal Law, cited to in the briefs in Appendices E and F.)

MOTION, in the procedural sense, is a noun, not a verb. A motion is a request for a court order or a judgment. To get an order or a judgment, a lawyer "moves" or "makes a motion." (Like everybody else, a lawyer "motions" only by making a physical gesture, such as when hailing a taxi or a waiter.) The object of the verb *to move* is not "the court." A lawyer "moves for an order" or "moves that the court order X to do Y." A lawyer does not "move the court for an order." Moving the court would take the strength of Hercules.

OUR: See *I.*

OVERRULE and *reverse* mean different things. On appeal, the judgment or order of the court below in the same case can be "reversed," but a court "overrules" precedent created in a prior case. In addition, for reasons explained in §8.3, a court cannot overrule the precedent of a higher court, a court of equal rank, or a court in another jurisdiction. (In another context, *overrule* has an entirely different meaning: when a trial judge rejects an attorney's objection to something the opposing attorney has done, the objection is "overruled.")

REVERSE: See *AFFIRM* and *OVERRULE.*

SAY: Statutes do not "say" things, and courts "say" only in dicta. When a court "holds," it is doing and not merely talking, just as a legislature does when it en*acts* a statute. (In statutes, legislatures "provide," "create," "abolish," "prohibit," "penalize," "define," and so forth.) The verb *to hold* has synonyms — *to conclude, to determine, to decide, to reason, to define,* etc. — but *to say* is not one of them. On the other hand, a judge writing a concurrence or dissent does not act for the court, and therefore can accurately be considered to "say" things.

SINCE is an acceptable synonym for *because*, especially in passages where one word or the other must be used several times. But *since* is the weaker of the two, and it causes confusion if the reader does not know immediately from the context whether it refers to causation or to time. For that reason, *because* is the better word to start a dependent clause at the beginning of a sentence discussing causation:

> Because the corporation declared a large dividend last year, it lacks funds to invest in equipment.

If this had begun with *since*, you would not have known until near the end of the sentence whether the dependent clause introduced causation or marked a point in time ("Since the corporation declared . . ."). In fact, with this example, *since* could cause perplexity anywhere in the sentence because it could confuse time with causation:

> The corporation lacks funds to invest in equipment since it declared a large dividend last year.

SO, although useful in many ways, is not an effective vehicle for showing causation. Compare these two sentences:

> The magistrate who issued the arrest warrant was able to evaluate the reasonableness of Det. Bloom's conclusion that the defendant was hiding in his friend's home, so the arrest warrant was sufficient authority, under the rule of *Commonwealth v. Sadowski*, for the police to search that home.

> Because the magistrate who issued the arrest warrant was able to evaluate the reasonableness of Det. Bloom's conclusion that the defendant was hiding in his friend's home, the arrest warrant was sufficient authority, under the rule of *Commonwealth v. Sadowski*, for the police to search that home.

Although the second sentence is much more clear and forceful than the first, the only difference between them is that in the second sentence *so* has been deleted and replaced (at the beginning of the sentence) by the stronger word *because*. The limp, little word *so*, which is so often used for other purposes, cannot catch the reader's attention as well as *because* does. Depending on the writer's purpose, the second example above might be improved still further by stating the effect before the cause:

> The arrest warrant was sufficient authority, under the rule of *Commonwealth v. Sadowski*, for the police to search the home of the defendant's friend because the magistrate who issued the warrant was able to evaluate the reasonableness of Det. Bloom's conclusion that the defendant was hiding there.

STIPULATE is a term of art and means an agreement (or part of one), usually between the parties to a lawsuit. Judicial opinions cannot "stipulate" (although they might refer to stipulations made by the parties). Nor can statutes or lawyers' briefs "stipulate."

THAT, when used as a referent, can cause vagueness. See *THIS*.

THE is sometimes omitted by lawyers, but only before the following party designations: *plaintiff, defendant, appellant, appellee, petitioner*, and *respondent*. Other omissions of *the* make the writer sound illiterate. And much of the time you will appear more literate if you retain *the* even before party designations. It is fine to title a document "Memorandum of Law in Support of Defendant's Motion for Summary Judgment," but inside the memorandum you are better off writing "The defendant is entitled to summary judgment because the plaintiff has adduced no evidence that could show . . . ."

THE COURT: In some students' writing, "the court ruled in *Johanneson* . . ." will be followed by "the court ruled in *Di Prete* . . . ," even if *Johanneson* was decided by the United States Supreme Court and *Di Prete* by the Oregon Court of Appeals. Because opinions are printed in law school casebooks and discussed in law school classrooms without any differentiation within the hierarchy of authority (see §8.3), students are sometimes led into the sloppy habit of writing as though there were only one court in the entire common law world. The patience of a judge or supervisor is severely strained where "the court's" true identity can be learned only by inspecting a citation that might occur several lines after the writer has begun to discuss the case. You can begin by writing "The Oregon Court of Appeals ruled in *Di Prete* . . ." and thereafter use the phrase "the court."

THERE IS, THERE ARE, and **IT IS:** These grammatical expletives are sometimes appropriate, although less often than you might think. Sometimes grammatical expletives are helpful or even unavoidable ("there are four reasons why the plaintiff will not be able to recover . . ."). At other times, however, they obscure the writer's message in a fog of pretentious verbiage. Compare these passages:

> There was a breaking and an entry of the dwelling of another in the nighttime, but there was no intent to commit a felony therein. Therefore, the defendant is not guilty of burglary.

> The defendant is not guilty of burglary because, although she broke and entered the dwelling of another in the nighttime, she did not do so intending to commit a felony therein.

The first example may be typical of a rough draft, but in a final draft the passage should have evolved into something like the second example, which is more direct and easier to understand.

THIS and other referents (*IT, THAT, WHICH*) are vague unless the objects or ideas they refer to are immediately clear to the reader. For example:

> On September 9, the supplier threatened to withhold deliveries to the manufacturer, which, due to desperate need, purchased elsewhere at higher cost. The supplier then notified the manufacturer's own customers of the situation. *This* caused the damages for which the manufacturer now seeks recovery.

To what does "this" refer? The communication to the customers? The threat? The timing of the threat? The entire pattern of behavior? How could the meaning be made more clear?

VERBAL is not a synonym for *oral. Verbal* means "having to do with words"—either spoken or written. A "verbal communication" is one not made through shrieks and gestures. An "oral communication" is a spoken one, rather than one made in writing.

WE: See *I.*

WHEN and **WHERE** are not used to set out definitions.

wrong:	Burglary is *where* [or *when*] the defendant breaks and enters the dwelling of another, in the nighttime, to commit a felony therein.
right:	Burglary is the breaking and entering of the dwelling of another, in the nighttime, with intent to commit a felony therein.

WHETHER: See *IF,* with which *whether* is sometimes confused.

WHICH, when used as a referent, can cause vagueness. See *THIS.*

Appendix B
24 Rules of Punctuation

In any language, it is a struggle to make a sentence say exactly what you mean.

—Arthur Koestler

Your teacher may mark your work in part by referring to some of the paragraphs in this appendix.

Commas

Never place a comma between a subject and its verb or between a verb and its object. | **B-1**

wrong: The argument that the defendant committed arson by holding a lighted cigarette to a wall of the Astrodome, is not supported by the case law.

Here the writer seems to have added a comma because the reader will be out of breath after reading the gargantuan subject of this sentence. The solution is not just to eliminate the offending comma, but to recast the whole sentence:

right: The case law does not support the argument that the defendant committed arson by holding a lighted cigarette to a wall of the Astrodome.

B-2 Generally, do not use a comma as a substitute for an omitted word. Commas are most often asked to substitute for the word *that*. In nearly every instance, *that* belongs in the sentence and the comma does not:

> **wrong:** The court held, Antwerp Forwarders are liable for loss of the piano.
>
> **right:** The court held that Antwerp Forwarders are liable for the loss of the piano.

B-3 Do not place a comma between the parts of a double subject. And — with two exceptions — do not place a comma between the parts of a double predicate or a double object. A comma does not belong inside this double subject:

> **wrong:** *The Supreme Court of Pennsylvania, and the Supreme Judicial Court of Massachusetts* have adopted the same rule.
>
> **right:** The Supreme Court of Pennsylvania and the Supreme Judicial Court of Massachusetts have adopted the same rule.

Nor does it belong inside this double predicate:

> **wrong:** The plaintiff *served a request for admissions, and awaited the result.*
>
> **right:** The plaintiff served a request for admissions and awaited the result.

or this double object:

> **wrong:** The jury convicted *Malone, and the Grutz brothers.*
>
> **right:** The jury convicted Malone and the Grutz brothers.

Essentially, each of these examples is a list of two items, and generally the items in a list of two are separated only by a conjunction. There are two exceptions. The first is where the second item in the list is to be emphasized:

> **right:** The plaintiff's motion is supported by sixteen exhibits, but not one affidavit from a person with first-hand knowledge.

The other exception is where the list is so complicated that a comma is needed to help the reader know where the first item ends:

right: The plaintiff argues that Gripstra defrauded him of his life savings, and that the bank did nothing to stop it.

Use a comma to separate two or more adjectives modifying, in series, the same noun: **B-4**

right: The plaintiff's attorney made a long, impassioned summation.

But delete the comma if the adjectives are separated by a conjunction.

right: The plaintiff's attorney made a long and impassioned summation.

right: The plaintiff's attorney made a long but ineffectual summation.

Use commas to set off nonrestrictive words, phrases, and clauses, but not to set off restrictive words, phrases, and clauses. **B-5** A restrictive word, phrase, or clause is one that cannot be deleted from the sentence without destroying the basic sense of the sentence. The phrase in the middle of this sentence should be surrounded by commas because it is *non*restrictive:

wrong: The Court of Special Appeals the second highest court in the state was created only a few decades ago.

right: The Court of Special Appeals, the second highest court in the state, was created only a few decades ago.

If "the second highest court in the state" were deleted, some meaning would be lost, but the basic sense of the sentence would be intact. ("The Court of Special Appeals was created only a few decades ago.") But if the phrase is left in, the sentence is unreadable without the commas (as you can see from the "wrong" example above).

The clause in the middle of the sentence below is restrictive:

wrong: A prisoner, who is granted parole, will be released.

right: A prisoner who is granted parole will be released.

Here, would it make sense to say "A prisoner will be released"? If not, the "who" clause is restrictive. The sense of the sentence would be destroyed without it.

The two examples that follow are punctuated differently. Although the words in the examples are identical, the punctuation changes the meaning completely.

nonrestrictive clause:	The defendant, who has expressed remorse before being sentenced to prison, is well on the way to rehabilitation.

This is a sentence about a particular defendant whom we might as well call Smith. Smith stood before a judge and said he was sorry, and the judge then sentenced Smith to prison. The writer of the sentence knows what Smith said and where Smith has been sent. The sentence records the writer's optimism that Smith will become a right-thinking and law-abiding member of society. The subject of the sentence is "The defendant." The clause that comes afterward ("who has expressed remorse before being sentenced to prison") is nonrestrictive because it *describes* Smith but does not *define* him by telling us how he is different from all other defendants.

restrictive clause:	The defendant who has expressed remorse before being sentenced to prison is well on the way to rehabilitation.

This is a sentence about *all* defendants who have said they are sorry in these circumstances. The writer is not speaking about any particular defendant, and the writer may never have heard of Smith. The sentence records the writer's optimism that all such defendants will become right-thinking and law-abiding members of society. The subject of the sentence is "The defendant who has expressed remorse before being sentenced to prison." The clause that is part of that subject ("who has expressed remorse before being sentenced to prison") is restrictive because it *defines* the category of defendants about whom the writer has something to say.

The writers of these two examples might have similar views of human nature, but—because of the way they have punctuated their sentences—they have said two entirely different things.

B-6 Use a comma to set off an independent clause from a preceding dependent clause.

right:	After the plaintiff's microwave oven blew up, she sued the manufacturer.
also right:	The plaintiff sued the manufacturer after her microwave oven blew up.
wrong:	The plaintiff sued the manufacturer, after her microwave oven blew up.

B-7 Similarly, use a comma to set off all but the shortest prefatory phrase from the rest of the sentence.

wrong:	Because of the appeal execution of the judgment has been stayed.

right:	Because of the appeal, execution of the judgment has been stayed.
right:	At trial, the disputed evidence was admitted.
also right:	At trial the disputed evidence was admitted.

Use commas to set off a word, phrase, or clause that has been inserted into a sentence as an appositive or an aside. `B-8`

right:	Wiley, the plaintiff, appealed.
right:	The motion will, on those grounds, be denied.

If an aside is less closely related to the structure of the rest of the sentence, use parentheses or dashes instead:

right:	The complaint was served on December 11 (nine days after the stipulation).
right:	The legislature decided—regardless of the effect on court backlogs—not to increase the number of judges in the state.

If a transitional word precedes a clause, set it off with a comma. If it occurs in the middle of a clause, set it off with commas if it `B-9` **amounts to an aside.** Some of the most commonly used transitional words are *accordingly, consequently, furthermore, hence, however, moreover, similarly, therefore,* and *thus.*

right:	Furthermore, this appeal is frivolous.
also right:	This appeal is frivolous; however, sanctions should be imposed on the attorney alone.
also right:	We therefore impose on the attorney a fine of five hundred dollars.
also right:	We are not unmindful, however, of the appellant's responsibility here.

Use commas appropriately when referring to places and dates. When specifying both a locality (city or county) and the `B-10` larger geographic entity within which it is found (county, state, or nation), set off the latter with commas.

wrong:	The novel is set in Klamath County, Oregon even though she was living in Paris, Texas when she wrote it.
right:	The novel is set in Klamath County, Oregon, even though she was living in Paris, Texas, when she wrote it.

Similarly, when expressing a precise date (month, day, year), set off the year with commas.

> **wrong:**   The court relied on the June 16, 1904 manuscript.
>
> **right:**   The court relied on the June 16, 1904, manuscript.

But in dates made up only of the month and year, place no comma between the month and year.

> **wrong:**   The month was October, 1983.
>
> **right:**   The month was October 1983.

B-11   When a word, phrase, or clause should be "set off" by commas, that means one comma preceding and a second comma following. If you carelessly omit one of the commas, the reader must struggle to figure out what you are trying to say.

> **wrong:**   The Court of Special Appeals, the second highest court in the state was created only a few decades ago.
>
> **right:**   The Court of Special Appeals, the second highest court in the state, was created only a few decades ago.
>
> **wrong:**   Joe who has been granted parole, will be released.
>
> **right:**   Joe, who has been granted parole, will be released.

Obviously, the preceding comma is omitted if the set-off word, phrase, or clause begins the sentence.

> **right:**   Because of the appeal, execution of the judgment has been stayed.

And the comma that follows is omitted if the set-off word, phrase, or clause ends the sentence.

> **right:**   The defendant is Anaheim Liquidators, a California corporation.

Commas and Semicolons

B-12   In a list of three or more, separate the listed items with commas unless they are so complicated that semicolons would help the reader.

right:	The plaintiff sued, went to trial, and lost.
right:	The court ordered the corporation dissolved; placed the property under the control of a receiver; and enjoined the defendants from conducting business by interstate telephone, wire, or delivery service.

If two independent clauses are joined by a conjunction in the same sentence, place a comma before the conjunction. **B-13**

wrong:	The wholesaler contracted to buy pipe but the manufacturer breached.
right:	The wholesaler contracted to buy pipe, but the manufacturer breached.

If two independent clauses are joined in the same sentence but are not separated by a conjunction (such as *and* or *but*), separate them with a semicolon. **B-14**

wrong:	The wholesaler contracted to buy pipe, however, the manufacturer breached.

The word *however* is *not* a conjunction.

right:	The wholesaler contracted to buy pipe; however, the manufacturer breached.

A *comma splice* is the incorrect use of a comma to separate independent clauses not joined by a conjunction.

Law students seem particularly tempted to use a comma instead of a semicolon where the second clause begins with a conjunctive adverb such as *however, moreover, accordingly, hence, consequently, nevertheless, otherwise, thus,* or *therefore*. There are three ways of curing a comma splice. The first is to exchange the comma for a semicolon. The second is to retain the comma but add a conjunction. (But this usually will not work if the second clause begins with an adverb: in the incorrect example above, try inserting *and* or *but* before *however*.) The third is to convert the comma into a period and to turn the second clause into a separate sentence. (But where the clauses are short and are surrounded by short sentences, this cure may produce sing-song sentences.) The cure you select should depend on the context and your goals in the passage where the comma splice occurs.

Hyphens

If two or more words are combined into a single adjective, hyphenate them. **B-15**

wrong: a forty page brief

right: a forty-page brief

wrong: an off the record conference at the bench

right: an off-the-record conference at the bench

But an adverb and adjective are not hyphenated.

wrong: legally-sufficient grounds

right: legally sufficient grounds

B-16 When hyphenating a word between lines, break up the word only between syllables. A syllable of only one or two letters is not broken off at all.

wrong: A large proportion of the sanct-
                ions ordered under Rule 11
                have occurred in the Southern
                District of New York and the
                Eastern District of Illinois.

right: A large proportion of the sanc-
                tions ordered under Rule 11
                have occurred in . . . .

If you are not absolutely certain of a word's syllable breaks, consult a dictionary. To an experienced reader, hyphenation in the middle of a syllable looks illiterate.

Dashes

B-17 Use a dash only to set off an aside that either deserves emphasis or is not closely related to the structure of the rest of the sentence. The dash is not an all-purpose piece of punctuation.

wrong: The Supreme Court affirmed—it held that Con-
                gress had intended to create an immunity in cases
                like these.

right: We reverse, and—because this is not the first time
                we have so held—we point out to the District
                Courts that the wisest practice is to use the exact
                wording of the pattern jury instructions.

right: The legislature decided—regardless of the effect
                          on court backlogs— not to increase the number of
                          judges in the state.

On a typewriter, construct a dash by joining two hyphens, | **B-18**
and insert a space before the dash and another space after it. |

wrong: The legislature decided - regardless of the effect on
                          court backlogs--not to increase the number of
                          judges in the state.

right: The legislature decided -- regardless of the effect
                          on court backlogs -- not to increase the number of
                          judges in the state.

Colons

Use a colon to introduce material that satisfies an expecta- | **B-19**
tion raised by the words preceding the colon. Typical uses of |
a colon are to introduce an example, a list, or an explanation that clarifies
the first part of the sentence.

right: The Supreme Court has restated this principle nu-
                          merous times: in *Griswold,* in *Stanley,* in *Eisen-*
                          stadt, and in other cases.

Do not use a colon in any of the following situations: **B-20**

a. between a preposition and its object:

wrong: The corporation does business in: Sri Lanka, Tan-
                          zania, Nigeria, and Malta.

right: The corporation does business in Sri Lanka, Tan-
                          zania, Nigeria, and Malta.

b. between a verb and its object:

wrong: The area codes he calls most often are: 202, 212,
                          213, 215, 312, 415, and 913.

right: The area codes he calls most often are 202, 212,
                          213, 215, 312, 415, and 913.

395

c. after the following words and phrases:

such as
for instance/for example
that is
namely

Parentheses and Brackets

| **B-21** | Use brackets — not parentheses — to enclose alterations in quotations. |

    wrong: The court reasoned that "(t)he policy of protecting individual liberties would be eroded if . . . ."

    right: the court reasoned that "[t]he policy . . . ."

If your typewriter does not make brackets, add them in ink. Brackets and parentheses convey entirely different messages to the reader.

| **B-22** | Where numbers are used in text to denote items in a list, enclose each number completely in parentheses. |

    wrong: At common law, a person was guilty of burglary if he or she 1) broke and 2) entered . . . .

    right: At common law, a person was guilty of burglary if he or she (1) broke and (2) entered . . . .

Quotation Marks with Other Punctuation

| **B-23** | Be careful about punctuation at the beginning and the end of a quotation. |

Where you add quoted material to a sentence of your own composition, placement of punctuation might get tricky at the beginning or end of the quotation. These are the rules: *A comma or a period goes INSIDE the quotation marks*, even if it is your comma or period and did not appear in the original quotation. *But a colon, semicolon, or dash goes OUTSIDE the quotation marks.*

Apostrophes

Use apostrophes properly. A judge or supervising attorney will view inability to use apostrophes as a sign of semiliteracy on your part. Compare the following: | **B-24**

> *It's* means "it is."
>
>> *but*
>
> *Its* is the possessive of *it.*
>
> *Who's* means "who is" or "who has."
>
>> *but*
>
> *Whose* is the possessive of *who.*
>
> *You're* means "you are."
>
>> *but*
>
> *Your* is the possessive of *you.*
>
> *Parties* is the plural of *party.*
>
>> *but*
>
> *Party's* is the possessive of *party.*
>
>> *and*
>
> *Parties'* is the plural possessive of *party.*

Each of the following will strike the typical reader as a form of verbal atrocity:

> These meetings were always conducted at the *informers* whim.
>
> The courts have limited this precedent to *it's* facts.
>
> Both the legislature and the *court's* have refused to modify the rule.

The rules on apostrophes are not hard to learn:

a. To make a noun plural, in most cases add an *s* without an apostrophe. Of course, some nouns take special forms. Where the noun ends in *y*, the *y* is usually converted to *ie*. There are other exceptions—with words like *sheep* and *dictum*—but you already know them.

b. To make most nouns possessive, add an apostrophe and an *s*. (Again, there are exceptions.)

c. Pronouns have their own possessive and plural forms. There are only a few pronouns, and you learned their possessive and plural forms long ago. If you have forgotten, the examples here should jog your memory.

   d. Words often contracted cause trouble. The ones you should watch out for are *who, you,* and—most especially—*it.* Since the contraction is formed with an apostrophe, the corresponding possessive cannot be. Fortunately, these words *do not add an* s *when they become plural.* Therefore, unlike other words, those most often contracted form the possessive by adding an *s* without an apostrophe:

   contraction: *it's* ("it is")

   possessive: *its*

   contraction: *you're* ("you are")

   possessive: *your*

   contraction: *who's* ("who is")

   possessive: *whose*

Of course, in your legal writing, contractions should appear only when you are quoting someone else. See 4-P.

Appendix C
Sample Office Memorandum

This appendix contains an office memorandum of the type described in §16.2. An office memorandum records an attorney's objective prediction of the way an issue would be decided if that issue were presented to a court.

(In Appendix D, you will find a persuasive memorandum of the type described in §16.3. The Appendix D memorandum was written later in the same case to persuade the court to rule in the client's favor.)

TO: Clyde Farnsworth

FROM: Julie Barnett

DATE: March 10, 1990

RE: Eli Goslin; constructive trust

QUESTION PRESENTED

Will Goslin, who is 74 years old, be able to impose a constructive trust on the title to his home, which he deeded over to his nephew after the latter, to prevent foreclosure, promised to make three years of payments remaining on the mortgage, where the nephew gave nothing else for Goslin's equity, where Goslin has no other assets and no other place to live, and where Goslin made no statement at the time of the deed that would reveal his reasons for giving it?

BRIEF ANSWER

A court is likely to impose a constructive trust, in Goslin's favor, on the nephew's title to the house. Goslin is able to prove each of the four elements of the New York test for a constructive trust: a confidential or fiduciary relation between Goslin and his nephew; a promise, implied by the nephew to hold title while allowing and helping Goslin to live in the house; Goslin's transfer of title to the nephew in reliance on that promise; and unjust enrichment if the promise is broken. (This memorandum does not consider an action to set aside the deed on the grounds of fraud, undue influence, or impaired capacity -- all of which have already been researched and rejected.)

STATEMENT OF FACTS

Last year, Goslin found himself unable to pay the mortgage on the house where he has lived for the past 24 years. Herbert Skeffington, a nephew, offered to make the mortgage payments. Goslin deeded the house to Skeffington, who has since moved his family into the house, ordered Goslin to leave, and twice struck Goslin.

Goslin is a 74-year-old arthritic widower who has been retired for nine years. His only income is from

-1-

social security. Until last year, he also had income
from an investment, but he became unable to meet the
mortgage payments on his house when the business went
bankrupt. The house was Goslin's only asset, and the
mortgage had only three more years to run. He has been
married twice, and both wives are deceased. His son is
dead, and his daughter lives in Singapore. He has no
place other than the house in which to live.

When Goslin found that he could no longer pay the
mortgage, Skeffington offered to make the remaining
$11,500 in payments as they became due. Within a few
days afterward, Goslin, without stating his purpose to
anyone, gave a deed to the property to Skeffington and
got the bank to agree to transfer the mortgage to him.
At the time, the house was worth approximately $95,000
and was unencumbered except for the mortgage that
Skeffington had offered to pay. Aside from the promise
to make mortgage payments, Skeffington gave no value
connected to the deed.

Goslin has told us that he made the deed for the
following reason: ''At the time, it seemed like the
right thing to do. He was going to pay the mortgage,
and after a certain point -- maybe after I'm gone --
the place would become his. I didn't think it would
end up like this.'' Skeffington had not asked for a
deed, and Goslin arranged for the deed before telling
the nephew about it. Goslin knew at the time that
Skeffington would not need a deed to make the mortgage
payments: the bank would have been willing to accept
Skeffington's check if it were accompanied by Goslin's
payment stub, or, alternatively, Skeffington could
simply have given the money to Goslin, who could in
turn have paid the bank. As far as Goslin knows,
Skeffington has made the payments as they have become
due.

At the time of the deed, neither Goslin nor his
nephew said anything about changing the living ar-
rangements in the house. Goslin continued to live
alone in the house until a few weeks ago, when Skeffington's rental apartment was burned out and he
moved, along with his wife and two children, into the
house. Goslin neither consented to nor protested this.
A few days later, Skeffington ordered Goslin to move
out, which Goslin has refused to do. Since then Skeffington has, at the top of his voice, frequently
repeated the demand. While yelling at Goslin, Skeffington has twice, with the heels of his palms, suddenly shoved him in the chest and sent him staggering.
Skeffington has threatened to strike Goslin again and
to pack up Goslin's belongings and leave them and
Goslin on the sidewalk. Skeffington takes the position

-2-

that his family has no other place to go, and that the
house is the only thing he owns.

Skeffington is 36 years old, and throughout Skeffington's life he and Goslin have seen each other at
least monthly at family get-togethers, including each
other's weddings. Seventeen years ago, Goslin contributed $3,200 to Skeffington's college tuition. The two
of them have never discussed whether this was to be
treated as a gift or a loan, and Goslin does not
recall which he intended or even whether he had an
intent at the time. He says that he considered both
the tuition money and his nephew's offer to pay the
mortgage to be ''the sort of thing people in a family
do for each other.'' In any event, except for the
mortgage payments, the nephew has never given Goslin
money directly or indirectly, and he has not announced
an intention to compensate Goslin for the tuition
money.

DISCUSSION

The Court of Appeals has held that a constructive
trust arises where the record shows ''(1) a confidential or fiduciary relation, (2) a promise, (3) a
transfer in reliance thereon, and (4) unjust enrichment.'' McGrath v. Hilding, 41 N.Y.2d 625, 629, 363
N.E.2d 328, 330, 394 N.Y.S.2d 603, 606 (1977) (citations omitted).

The courts are likely to hold that Goslin's relation
with his nephew is confidential. The Appellate Division, First Department, has held that a relationship
between an aunt and a niece is a confidential one for
the purpose of a constructive trust action. Tebin
v. Moldock, 19 A.D.2d 275, 284-85, 241 N.Y.S.2d 629,
637-39 (1963), modified on other grounds, 14 N.Y.2d
807, 200 N.E.2d 216, 251 N.Y.S.2d 36 (1964). The Court
of Appeals has held that such a relationship can exist
even between an unsuccessful suitor and the woman who
has refused to marry him. Sharp v. Kosmalski, 40
N.Y.2d 119, 121-22, 351 N.E.2d 721, 723, 386 N.Y.S.2d
72, 75 (1976).

Although a confidential relation might not exist
between an uncle and a nephew if contact has been rare
and if both viewed the relationship as merely technical, that is not true here. Goslin and his nephew have
seen each other at least monthly since the nephew was
a boy; they attended each other's weddings, frequent
family social activities, and other events; and Goslin
paid part of the nephew's college tuition.

-3-

The courts are also likely to find here a promise
-- even if not stated in words -- by the nephew to
hold title in name only for Goslin's benefit while
doing nothing that might prevent Goslin from continuing to live in his home. The Court of Appeals has held
several times that a writing is not required in these
cases, and that the Statute of Frauds will not prevent
a constructive trust. Sharp, 40 N.Y.2d at 122, 351
N.E.2d at 723-24, 386 N.Y.S.2d at 75; Pattison v.
Pattison, 301 N.Y. 65, 92 N.E.2d 890 (1950); Foreman
v. Foreman, 251 N.Y. 237, 167 N.E. 428 (1929). ''Equity
in this area has always reached beyond the facade of
formal documents, absolute transfers, and even limiting statutes on the law side.'' Tebin, 19 A.D.2d at
284-85, 241 N.Y.S.2d at 638.

Not only is a written promise unnecessary to a
constructive trust, but the Court of Appeals has held
that the promise need not even be orally stated where
it ''may be implied or inferred from the very transaction itself.'' Sharp, 40 N.Y.2d at 122, 351 N.E.2d at
723, 386 N.Y.S.2d at 75. In Sharp, a 56-year-old
farmer conveyed his farm to a 40-year-old woman who
had declined his offer of marriage. After the transfer,
the woman ordered the farmer off the property. Although
the record contained no evidence of a promise in
words, the Court of Appeals held that an understood
promise was inherent in the actions of both parties
because

> it is inconceivable that plaintiff would convey
> all of his interest in property which was not only
> his abode but the very means of his livelihood
> without at least tacit consent upon the part of
> the defendant that she would permit him to continue
> to live on and operate the farm.

Id. at 122, 351 N.E.2d at 724, 386 N.Y.S.2d at 75.

In family relationships, New York courts have been
extremely reluctant to accept a transferee's claim,
under suspect circumstances, that a transfer was an
absolute gift. For example, in Sinclair v. Purdy, 235
N.Y. 245, 139 N.E. 255 (1923), a brother, who was
employed as a court clerk and was continually asked to
pledge his property for other people's bail, deeded it
over to his sister, receiving nothing in return. The
Court of Appeals held that the circumstances implied a
promise, and Judge Cardozo wrote for the court that

-4-

[h]ere was a man transferring to his sister the
only property he had in the world. . . . Even if
we were to accept her statement that there was no
distinct promise to hold it for his benefit, the
exaction of such a promise, in view of the relation, might well have seemed to be superfluous.

Id. at 254, 139 N.E. at 258.

The courts are likely to consider Goslin's circumstances to be at least comparable to those of the
farmer in Sharp and the brother in Sinclair. Goslin
owned nothing of substance other than his home. At the
time of the transfer, he had been retired for nine
years, and his only income was from social security.
His income had just been reduced because of the bankruptcy of a small business in which he had had an
interest. The house itself was worth approximately
$95,000 at the time of the transfer, and the three
years of mortgage payments remaining totalled $11,500.
Even Skeffington's promise to make the mortgage payments cannot be considered a payment to Goslin because,
if Skeffington really took clear title, the mortgage
payments would benefit him and not Goslin. In addition,
seventeen years ago, the nephew had received $3,200
from Goslin for college tuition, and he had not returned any of it. Although the parties have never
talked with each other about whether the tuition money
was a gift or a loan, the courts are likely to consider
the label unimportant and instead focus on mutual
family responsibilities. Accordingly, the courts are
not likely to conclude that Goslin intended to make an
absolute gift of his house. Instead, they will more
probably hold that Goslin and his nephew had an unstated understanding that the nephew's mortgage payments were to reciprocate Goslin's contributions to
the nephew's college tuition.

The courts will probably so hold even though the
nephew could have made the mortgage payments without
having received a deed. Of all the facts here, the one
most damaging to Goslin's case is the absence of any
need to deed the house over to the nephew. For example,
the bank would have accepted the nephew's check, as
long as it was accompanied by a stub from Goslin's
payment book, and the stub could have been filled out
by Goslin or his nephew. Or the nephew could have
simply given Goslin the money and let him make the
payments.

Under the case law, however, the absence of a need
for a transfer is irrelevant. The farmer in Sharp, for
example, seems to have given a deed for purely senti-

-5-

mental reasons, but the Court of Appeals considered it to be subject to a constructive trust anyway. <u>Sharp</u> can reasonably be interpreted to stand for the proposition that, no matter how quixotic a transferor's purpose may have been, a promise of some kind will be implied where the parties have a family or other emotionally charged relationship and where the property transferred is the bulk of the transferor's assets. Although Goslin did not have the same practical need to make a transfer that the court clerk had in <u>Sinclair</u>, the Court of Appeals did not treat the court clerk's need as essential to its decision.

The third element of the test for a constructive trust is a transfer in reliance on the promise. The transfer itself is not in dispute here, and, for the reasons described above, Goslin should be able to prove that he granted the deed in reliance on his nephew's promise.

Goslin should also be able to establish the fourth element, which has been described variously as ''unjust enrichment under cover of the relation of confidence,'' <u>Sinclair</u>, 235 N.Y. at 253, 139 N.E. at 258; as a situation where ''property has been acquired in such circumstances that the holder of the legal title may not in good conscience retain the beneficial interest,'' <u>Sharp</u>, 40 N.Y.2d at 121, 351 N.E.2d at 723, 386 N.Y.S.2d at 74; and as circumstances where ''discernible promises, made in a confidential relationship, have been broken or repudiated, and the trusted one will be unjustly enriched by reason of the breaches,'' <u>Tebin</u>, 19 A.D.2d at 280, 241 N.Y.S.2d at 634. The courts held in <u>Sharp</u> and in <u>Tebin</u> that a plaintiff need not prove that the party who accepted the transfer did so with a fraudulent intent. ''A constructive trust may be imposed even though the transferee fully intended to perform his promise at the time of the conveyance.'' <u>Ferrano v. Stephanelli</u>, 7 A.D.2d 420, 424, 183 N.Y.S.2d 707, 711 (1st Dep't 1959). It is enough to show that the entrusted party has breached the promise on which the grantor relied.

Here, the nephew took a deed upon promising to make three years of mortgage payments and without paying anything for Goslin's sizeable equity. On these facts, the courts are likely to decide that the nephew has tried to pervert his assumption of a family responsibility into a windfall. (Although it is not necessary to a ruling in Goslin's favor, the nephew's offer could have been seen by both parties as reciprocation for Goslin's help in putting the nephew through college.)

-6-

CONCLUSION

Goslin can demonstrate all the elements of a constructive trust. He had a relationship of confidence
with Skeffington because they are uncle and nephew and
have acted that way for years. The most reasonable
interpretation of the facts is that both parties
understood an implied agreement that Skeffington would
take title in name only and for the purpose of protecting the house for Goslin's use. The deed was a
transfer of Goslin's home and only asset and could
have been made only in reliance on that promise. And
without a constructive trust, Skeffington would be
unjustly enriched because he would have clear title to
a $95,000 asset in exchange for $11,500 in mortgage
payments.

                              Respectfully Submitted,

                              Julie Barnett
                              Julie Barnett

Appendix **D**
Sample Persuasive Memorandum

This appendix contains a persuasive memorandum of the type described in §16.3. The memorandum was written to persuade a court to grant a client's motion for a preliminary injunction.

(In Appendix C, you will find a predictive memorandum of the type described in §16.2. The Appendix C memorandum was written earlier in the same case to record an objective prediction of the court's eventual decision.)

```
SUPREME COURT OF THE STATE OF
NEW YORK, IROQUOIS COUNTY
```

```
ELI GOSLIN,

                    Plaintiff

          -against-                    No. 2109/90

HERBERT SKEFFINGTON,

                    Defendant
```

```
         MEMORANDUM IN SUPPORT OF
         PLAINTIFF'S MOTION FOR A
         PRELIMINARY INJUNCTION
```

```
                        Clyde Farnsworth, Esq.
                        Attorney for Plaintiff
                        32 Fontanka Street
                        Bedford Falls, NY 14218
                        (900) 555-1111
```

TABLE OF CONTENTS

TABLE OF AUTHORITIES

-ii-

PRELIMINARY STATEMENT

Eli Goslin, the plaintiff, is a 74-year-old retired widower living on social security. The defendant, Herbert Skeffington, is Mr. Goslin's nephew. Last year, Mr. Goslin became unable to continue to pay the mortgage to the home in which he has lived for 24 years. The nephew offered to make those payments for him, and Mr. Goslin gave the nephew a deed. The nephew does not deny that Mr. Goslin never stated an intention to make, through this deed, an absolute gift of Mr. Goslin's sole asset. Nor does the nephew deny that he has moved into Mr. Goslin's home without permission; that he has ordered Mr. Goslin to move out; that he has struck Mr. Goslin on at least two occasions; and that Mr. Goslin has no other place to live.

Mr. Goslin has sued to impose a constructive trust on the nephew's deed, and he has simultaneously moved for an order that would preliminarily enjoin the nephew from assaulting him, endangering his health, conveying any interest in the property, or in any way impeding Mr. Goslin's use of his home. This memorandum is submitted in support of that motion.

QUESTION PRESENTED

In an action to impose a constructive trust, should a nephew be preliminarily enjoined from assaulting his 74-year-old uncle and from preventing the uncle from living in the latter's home of 24 years, where the nephew received a deed from his uncle after promising to prevent foreclosure by making only three years of mortgage payments; where the uncle has no other assets and no other place to live; and where the nephew has moved into the house without the uncle's permission, struck the uncle at least twice, and repeatedly ordered the uncle to move out?

STATEMENT OF THE CASE

Mr. Goslin has lived in his home for 24 years and has been retired for nine years. (Goslin Aff. ¶ 1). At the time of the deed at issue, his mortgage would have been amortized in three additional years. (Id. at ¶ 2.) Because of a business reversal and bankruptcy last year, Mr. Goslin lost all income other than social security and became unable to pay his mortgage. (Id.) Seventeen years ago, Mr. Goslin had helped to

pay the college expenses of the defendant, who is Mr.
Goslin's nephew, and in the intervening years the
nephew never returned this money or reciprocated in
any other way. (<u>Id</u>. at ¶ 11.) To prevent foreclosure,
however, the nephew finally did offer to pay the
remainder of Mr. Goslin's mortgage payments as they
became due. (<u>Id</u>. at ¶ 2-3; Skeffington Aff. ¶ 11.)

Mr. Goslin made out a deed to his nephew. (Goslin
Aff. ¶ 2.) He did so as part of what he believed to be
a mutual effort in which he thought that his nephew
''was trying to help me keep -- rather than lose -- my
home.'' (<u>Id</u>. at ¶ 3.) Mr. Goslin states that he had no
intention to make, through this deed, an absolute gift
of his home and only asset. (<u>Id</u>. ¶ 4.) And the nephew
has submitted no evidence that Mr. Goslin has ever
expressed an intent to make such a gift.

The nephew admits that he received the deed only
after he offered to make mortgage payments totalling
$11,500. (Skeffington Aff. ¶ 12.) The nephew does not
deny that at the time the house was worth approximately
$95,000; that his uncle's equity was worth approxi-
mately $83,500; and that the nephew paid nothing for
his uncle's equity. (See Goslin Aff. ¶¶ 7-8.) Although
the amount Mr. Goslin had contributed to the nephew's
college tuition was $3,200, that money would have
grown substantially over the intervening seventeen
years if Mr. Goslin had invested it instead. (<u>Id</u>. at
¶ 11.)

Eight months after receiving the deed, the nephew
moved his family into Mr. Goslin's home without Mr.
Goslin's permission, and he ordered his uncle to move
out. (<u>Id</u>. ¶¶ 1-3.) The nephew does not deny that at
least twice in the last few weeks he has struck his
uncle, and that he has continued to order his uncle to
leave, often yelling at the top of his voice. (See <u>Id</u>.
¶¶ 1, 3, 5-6). Nor does the nephew deny that he has
threatened to strike Mr. Goslin again and to pack up
Mr. Goslin's belongings and leave them and Mr. Goslin
on the sidewalk. (See <u>Id</u>.)

Mr. Goslin is arthritic and 74 years old, and the
nephew is 36. (<u>Id</u>. ¶¶ 1-2.) Mr. Goslin's wife and son
are both dead, and his daughter lives in Asia. (<u>Id</u>.)
Except for this house, he has no place in which to
live. (<u>Id</u>.)

Although, when he made the deed, Mr. Goslin understood that the nephew would be able to tender the
mortgage payments to the bank without having title to
the house, Mr. Goslin thought a deed appropriate
because he expected that ''after a certain point --
<u>maybe after I'm gone</u> -- the place would become'' the

-2-

nephew's. (<u>Id</u>. at ¶ 9 (emphasis added).) Mr. Goslin
and the nephew have seen each other at least monthly
at family get-togethers throughout the nephew's life
and had attended each other's weddings. (<u>Id</u>. ¶ 15) Mr.
Goslin believed that the nephew's offer to make the
mortgage payments to be ''the sort of thing people in
a family do for each other'' -- and in no way different
from Mr. Goslin's payment of some of the nephew's
college expenses (<u>Id</u>. ¶¶ 9-10, 14.) And Mr. Goslin
says that he offered the deed in the same spirit. (<u>Id</u>.
¶ 9.)

<u>ARGUMENT</u>

I.   THE DEFENDANT SHOULD BE PRELIMINARILY
     ENJOINED FROM ASSAULTING MR. GOSLIN,
     ENDANGERING HIS HEALTH, CONVEYING
     TITLE TO MR. GOSLIN'S HOME, OR IN
     ANY OTHER WAY IMPEDING MR. GOSLIN'S
               USE OF HIS HOME.

A party should be granted a preliminary injunction
if he can demonstrate (1) that he is likely to succeed
on the merits; (2) that, absent a preliminary injunction, he is likely to suffer irreparable harm concerning the subject of the action; and (3) that a balancing
of the equities favors a preliminary injunction. <u>Town
of Porter v. Chem-Trol Pollution Services, Inc.</u>, 60
A.D.2d 987, 988, 401 N.Y.S.2d 646, 647 (4th Dep't
1978). The record before the court contains ample
evidence of all of these elements.

A.   <u>Mr. Goslin is likely to succeed on
     the merits in the underlying action
     to impress a constructive trust on
     the title to his home, which is held
                by the defendant.</u>

The facts here fit the classic pattern of abuse of
family trust and confidence in which New York courts
have traditionally impressed a constructive trust. Mr.
Goslin -- an elderly man in such financial difficulty
that he might lose his home, his only asset -- deeded
it over to a trusted nephew, the defendant, whom Mr.
Goslin once helped put through college. (Goslin Aff.
¶¶ 2-3, 11.) Mr. Goslin made out the deed only after
the nephew offered to prevent foreclosure by paying

-3-

the $11,500 remaining due on the mortgage. (Id. at
¶¶ 2-3.) The nephew paid nothing for Mr. Goslin's
equity, which was approximately $83,500 at the time of
the deed. (Id. at 7-8.) Since obtaining the deed, the
nephew has assaulted and harassed Mr. Goslin, trying
to intimidate him into leaving the home that the
nephew promised to save and in which Mr. Goslin has
lived for 24 years. (Id. at 1, 3, 5-6.) In these
circumstances, the nephew's claim of an absolute gift
is inherently incredible.

The Court of Appeals has held that it is reversible
error not to impress a constructive trust where the
record shows ''(1) a confidential or fiduciary relation, (2) a promise, (3) a transfer in reliance
thereon, and (4) unjust enrichment.'' McGrath v.
Hilding, 41 N.Y.2d 625, 629, 363 N.E.2d 328, 330, 394
N.Y.S.2d 603, 606 (1977) (citations omitted). On a
motion for a preliminary injunction, the movant is
required to make only a prima facie showing and need
not provide the full quantum of evidence that would be
needed to prove the underlying cause of action at
trial. Tucker v. Toia, 54 A.D.2d 322, 326, 388 N.Y.S.2d
475, 478 (4th Dep't 1976).

> 1.   The defendant is Mr. Goslin's nephew,
>   and the relationship between them is
>   by definition confidential.

The Appellate Division, First Department, has held
that the relationship between an aunt and a niece is a
confidential one for the purposes of a constructive
trust action. Tebin v. Moldock, 19 A.D.2d 275, 284-85,
241 N.Y.S.2d 629, 637-39 (1963), modified on other
grounds, 14 N.Y.2d 807, 200 N.E.2d 216, 251 N.Y.S.2d
36 (1964). The Court of Appeals has further held that
such a relationship can exist even between an unsuccessful suitor and the woman who has refused to marry
him. Sharp v. Kosmalski, 40 N.Y.2d 119, 121-22, 351
N.E.2d 721, 723, 386 N.Y.S.2d 72, 75 (1976).

Here, Mr. Goslin and his nephew had, at the time of
the deed, a trusting family relationship on which a
person in Mr. Goslin's position could naturally hope
to rely. Seventeen years ago, Mr. Goslin had given the
nephew $3,200 for college tuition, and the nephew had
not yet reciprocated. (Goslin Aff. ¶ 11.) The two had
seen each other at least monthly since the nephew was
a boy and had attended each others' weddings and a
number of other family functions. (Id. at ¶ 15.)

-4-

> ## 2. The record shows an unstated promise by the defendant nephew to hold title in name only and for Mr. Goslin's benefit and to do nothing that might prevent Mr. Goslin from living in his own home.

The Court of Appeals has several times held that a written instrument is not needed to prove such a promise, and that the Statute of Frauds will not prevent a constructive trust. Sharp, 40 N.Y.2d at 122, 351 N.E.2d at 723-24, 386 N.Y.S.2d at 75; Pattison v. Pattison, 301 N.Y. 65, 92 N.E.2d 890 (1950); Foreman v. Foreman, 251 N.Y. 237, 167 N.E. 428 (1929). ''Equity in this area has always reached beyond the facade of formal documents, absolute transfers, and even limiting statutes on the law side.'' Tebin, 19 A.D.2d at 284-85, 241 N.Y.S.2d at 638.

Not only is a written promise unnecessary to a constructive trust, but the Court of Appeals has held that the promise need not even be orally stated where it ''may be implied or inferred from the very transaction itself.'' Sharp, 40 N.Y.2d at 122, 351 N.E.2d at 723, 386 N.Y.S.2d at 75. In Sharp, a 56-year-old farmer conveyed his farm to a 40-year-old woman who had declined his offer of marriage. After the transfer, the woman ordered the farmer off the property. Although the record contained no evidence of a promise in words, the Court of Appeals held that an understood promise was inherent in the actions of both parties because

> it is inconceivable that plaintiff would convey all of his interest in property which was not only his abode but the very means of his livelihood without at least tacit consent upon the part of the defendant that she would permit him to continue to live on and operate the farm.

Id. at 122, 351 N.E.2d at 724, 386 N.Y.S.2d at 75.

In family relationships, New York courts have been extremely reluctant to accept a transferee's claim, under suspect circumstances, that a transfer was an absolute gift. For example, in Sinclair v. Purdy, 235 N.Y. 245, 139 N.E. 255 (1923), a brother, who was employed as a court clerk and was continually asked to pledge his property for other people's bail, deeded it over to his sister, receiving nothing in return. The Court of Appeals held that the circumstances implied a promise, and Judge Cardozo wrote for the court that

> [h]ere was a man transferring to his sister the
> only property he had in the world. . . . Even if
> we were to accept her statement that there was no
> distinct promise to hold it for his benefit, the
> exaction of such a promise, in view of the rela-
> tion, might well have seemed superfluous.

Id. at 154, 139 N.E. at 258.

Mr. Goslin was just as unlikely to have given away
his home. He owned nothing else of substance. (Goslin
Aff. ¶ 4.) At the time of the deed, he had been retired
for nine years, and his only income was from social
security. (Id. at ¶ 2.) His income had just been reduced because of the bankruptcy of a small business in
which he had had an interest. (Id.) The house itself
was worth approximately $95,000 at the time, and the
three years of mortgage payments remaining totalled
$11,500. (Id. at ¶¶ 7-8.) (Even the nephew's promise
to make the mortgage payments cannot be considered a
payment to Goslin because, if the nephew really took
clear title, the mortgage payments would benefit him
and not Goslin.) Seventeen years ago, the nephew had
received $3,200 for college tuition and had not yet
reciprocated. (Id. at ¶ 11.) At the time of the deed,
Mr. Goslin was 74 years old, arthritic, and without
any other place to live. (Id. at ¶¶ 1-2.) On these
facts, it can hardly be believed that Mr. Goslin would
have made an unconditional gift of all the equity in
his home. The more plausible explanation is that he
and his nephew had an unexpressed understanding that
the nephew's mortgage payments were to reciprocate Mr.
Goslin's assistance with the nephew's college education.

That is so even though the nephew did not need a
deed in order to make Mr. Goslin's mortgage payments.
Under the case law, the absence of a need for a deed
is irrelevant. The farmer in Sharp, for example, seems
to have given a deed for purely sentimental reasons,
but the Court of Appeals considered it to be subject
to a constructive trust anyway. Sharp can reasonably
be interpreted to stand for the proposition that -- no
matter how quixotic a transferor's purpose may have
been -- a promise of some kind will be implied where
the parties have a family or other emotionally charged
relationship and where the property transferred is the
bulk of the transferor's assets. Although Goslin did
not have the same practical need to make a transfer
that the court clerk had in Sinclair, the Court of
Appeals did not treat the court clerk's need as essential to its decision.

-6-

3. The nephew himself contends that the deed was a transfer.

As to the third element of the test for a constructive trust -- a transfer in reliance on the promise -- the nephew himself contends that the deed was a transfer. For the reasons set out above, the record shows that Mr. Goslin granted the deed in reliance on the nephew's promise.

4. Without a constructive trust, the nephew will be unjustly enriched.

The final element of the test for a constructive trust has been described variously as ''unjust enrichment under cover of the relation of confidence,'' Sinclair, 235 N.Y. at 253, 139 N.E. at 258; as a situation where ''property has been acquired in such circumstances that the holder of the legal title may not in good conscience retain the beneficial interest,'' Sharp, 40 N.Y.2d at 121, 351 N.E.2d at 723, 386 N.Y.S.2d at 74; and as circumstances where ''discernible promises, made in a confidential relationship, have been broken or repudiated, and the trusted one will be unjustly enriched by reason of the breaches,'' Tebin, 19 A.D.2d at 280, 241 N.Y.S.2d at 634. The courts held in Sharp and in Tebin that a plaintiff need not prove that the party who accepted the transfer did so with a fraudulent intent. ''A constructive trust may be imposed even though the transferee fully intended to perform his promise at the time of the conveyance.'' Ferrano v. Stephanelli, 7 A.D.2d 420, 424, 183 N.Y.S.2d 707, 711 (1st Dep't 1959). It is enough to show that the entrusted party has breached the promise on which the grantor relied.

Here, the nephew took a deed upon promising to make three years of mortgage payments and without paying anything for Mr. Goslin's equity of approximately $83,500. (Goslin Aff. ¶¶ 2-3, 7-8.) The nephew took the deed from an elderly man who desperately needed to stay in his own home because he had no other place to go -- and continues now to have no other place to go. (Id. at ¶¶ 1-2.) The nephew took the deed at a time when Mr. Goslin had made mortgage payments for 24 years and needed to do so for only three more years to be able to live there for the rest of his life without making any mortgage payments at all. (Id. at ¶ 1.) And the nephew's offer to make mortgage payments is most

-7-

reasonably seen as reciprocation for Mr. Goslin's help
in putting the nephew through college. Here, the
nephew has tried to pervert into a windfall his assumption of a family obligation.

      B.   Without an injunction, Mr. Goslin is
           threatened with irreparable harm in
           the form of assault and the loss of
               his own home.

    A movant is threatened with irreparable harm when
the opposing party creates a risk of injury that a
final judgment could not sufficiently remedy.
Schlosser v. United Presbyterian Home, 56 N.Y.2d 615,
615, 391 N.Y.S.2d 880, 881 (2d Dep't 1977). By definition, that is true where a defendant's conduct
would leave a plaintiff with ''no alternative residence . . . during the pendency of the action.'' Id.
at 615, 391 N.Y.S.2d at 881. In Schlosser, a defendant
landlord was preliminarily enjoined from imposing
disputed rent increases that the plaintiff senior
citizens would have been unable to afford. In the
matter now before this court, the defendant nephew has
assaulted Mr. Goslin, who is 74 years old and arthritic. (Goslin Aff. ¶ 1-3, 5-6.) He has also threatened to assault him again and to pack up his belongings
and leave them and him on the street, even though he
has no other place to go. (Id.) Although a preliminary injunction is discretionary, City of Buffalo v.
Mangan, 49 A.D.2d 697, 697, 370 N.Y.S.2d 771, 772
(4th Dep't 1975), and ''a drastic remedy to be sparingly used,'' Town of Porter v. Chem-Trol, 60 A.D.2d
at 988, 401 N.Y.S.2d at 647, an injunction should be
granted where necessary to preserve a deteriorating
status quo until the court can make a judgment on the
merits, Tucker, 54 A.D.2d at 325, 388 N.Y.S.2d at 478.
This court should exercise its discretion and provide
even a drastic remedy where an elderly man in frail
health is threatened with assault and the loss of his
only available place to live.

      C.   This injunction would not burden any
           legitimate conduct by the nephew,
           and the equities are therefore
               favorably balanced.

    A balance of the equities favors a preliminary
injunction where the threatened irreparable injury

-8-

would be ''more burdensome'' to the movant than any
harm the opposing party might experience because of an
injunction. <u>Metropolitan Package Store Ass'n, Inc. v.
Koch</u>, 80 A.D.2d 940, 941, 437 N.Y.S.2d 760, 761 (3d
Dep't 1981). Even where the facts are in dispute, a
preliminary injunction should be granted where necessary to preserve the status quo and where the injunction will not cause the enjoined party ''great
hardship.'' <u>City Store Gates Mfg. v. United Steel
Products</u>, 79 A.D.2d 671, 671, 433 N.Y.S.2d 876, 877
(2d Dep't 1980). Here, Mr. Goslin would suffer far
more hardship if he were locked out or assaulted, or
if his health were otherwise endangered, than the
defendant would suffer if none of these things were to
happen.

CONCLUSION

Therefore, this court should grant an order preliminarily enjoining the defendant nephew from assaulting
Mr. Goslin, endangering his health, conveying any
interest in the property, or in any way impeding Mr.
Goslin's use of his home. Mr. Goslin is likely to
succeed on the merits of the underlying action for a
constructive trust. He is threatened with irreparable
harm in the form of violence and the loss of his only
available place to live. And the defendant would
suffer no harm if enjoined.

                              Respectfully Submitted,

                              Clyde Farnsworth, Esq.
                              Attorney for Plaintiff
                              32 Fontanka Street
                              Bedford Falls, NY 14218
                              (900) 555-1111

-9-

Appendix E
Sample
Appellant's Brief

This Appendix contains the appellant's brief from a hypothetical appeal. (Appendix F contains the appellee's brief from the same appeal.) To economize your reading, each brief has been limited to only two of the issues that could have been raised on these facts.[1] The material that remains is substantial enough to give you realistic examples of how various tasks might be handled in a brief you would be assigned to write.

Consider two caveats. First, do not imitate something in these briefs without understanding why it was done here and without determining whether it would be effective in an appeal for which you are writing a brief. If, for example, you find that you like the style of the Questions Presented in one of these briefs, contemplate the possibility that that style might not work as well with your theory and with the facts and law of your appeal. In the course for which you are using this book, one of your most important goals is to learn how to make your own writing decisions so that you can begin to develop professional self-sufficiency. That goal is defeated if you imitate unquestioningly the appearance of a sample brief.

The second caveat has to do with differences in brief format from jurisdiction to jurisdiction. This brief and the brief in Appendix F follow a format that homogenizes the rules of many jurisdictions. Every jurisdiction's rules have at least a few local idiosyncrasies that would seem quirky elsewhere. Although these briefs were written for a hypothetical appeal set in New York, the idiosyncrasies of New York format have been eliminated from

---

1. In addition to the grounds asserted in the brief in this appendix, a defendant in a similar case might also choose to argue that the statute involved is unconstitutionally vague, that it violates First Amendment rights to freedom of expression and to freedom of assembly and association, and that it violates the Fourteenth Amendment right to equal protection.

421

what you will read here.[2] That is because sample briefs ought to illustrate those brief-writing practices that are most common nationally. If, however, you are asked to follow local format rules with which these briefs would be inconsistent—and your teacher will tell you if that is so—be careful to observe those rules in spite of what you see here.

2. For example, in New York, the non-appealing party is called the "respondent," even though the appealing party is the "appellant." (See N.Y. Civ. Prac. L. § 5511.) The common practice elsewhere, however, is that the non-appealing party is a "respondent" only when the appealing party is a "petitioner," and an "appellant" is always opposed by an "appellee." The briefs in these appendices follow national and not New York practice in this and in several other respects.

COURT OF APPEALS OF THE STATE OF NEW YORK

THE PEOPLE OF THE STATE OF NEW YORK,

                              Appellee

           -against-   No. 90-341

MERRITT BRESNAHAN,

                       Defendant-Appellant

BRIEF FOR DEFENDANT-APPELLANT

                    Clyde Farnsworth, Esq.
                    Attorney for Defendant-Appellant
                    32 Fontanka Street
                    Bedford Falls, N.Y. 14218
                    (900) 555-1111

TABLE OF CONTENTS

-i-

-ii-

TABLE OF AUTHORITIES

CASES

* Authorities chiefly relied upon are marked with an
asterisk.

-iii-

CONSTITUTIONAL PROVISIONS AND STATUTES

-v-

STATUTE INVOLVED

Section 240.35(4) of the New York Penal Law provides as follows:

> A person is guilty of loitering when he . . .
>   4. Being masked or in any manner disguised by unusual or unnatural attire or facial alteration, loiters, remains or congregates in a public place with other persons so masked or disguised, or knowingly permits or aids persons so masked or disguised to congregate in a public place; except that such conduct is not unlawful when it occurs in connection with a masquerade party or like entertainment if, when such entertainment is held in a city which has promulgated regulations in connection with such affairs, permission is first obtained from the police or other appropriate authorities; . . . .
>   Loitering is a violation.

PRELIMINARY STATEMENT

Merritt Bresnahan appeals from a conviction for loitering under section 240.35(4) of the Penal law (N.Y. County inf. no. 9437/88). Before trial, she moved, pursuant to sections 170.30(1)(a) and 170.35(1)(c) of the Criminal Procedure Law, to dismiss the information on the ground that § 240.35(4) violates her right to privacy under the United States Constitution. The Criminal Court of New York City and County reserved decision until the end of trial. After the close of the evidence at trial, Ms. Bresnahan additionally moved for a trial order of dismissal pursuant to §§ 290.10 and 320.20 of the Criminal Procedure Law on the ground that the People had not introduced legally sufficient evidence that she had been -- as a conviction under § 240.35(4) would require -- ''masked or in any manner disguised by unusual or unnatural attire or facial alteration.'' The Criminal Court, Judge Celeste Remay, denied both motions, convicted Ms. Bresnahan of violating § 240.35(4), and sentenced her to a fine of two hundred dollars. Ms. Bresnahan appealed the denial of each motion; Appellate Term affirmed; and this appeal followed.

-1-

QUESTIONS PRESENTED

Merritt Bresnahan suffers from gender dysphoria
syndrome, a chronic and potentially disabling disorder
in which the patient experiences unremitting anguish
from a belief that his or her reproductive organs do
not represent the patient's true gender. Psychotherapy
has no effect on this syndrome, also known as transsexualism, and the only medically accepted treatment
is sex reassignment surgery, preceded by a long period
of hormonal injections. Responsible medical practice
includes requiring such a patient to dress, during the
hormonal, pre-operative phase of treatment, in the
clothing of the gender that matches the patient's
belief. Ms. Bresnahan was so dressed, as required by
her doctors, at the time she was arrested for loitering
under Penal Law § 240.35(4). She was charged with no
other offense. The issues presented on appeal are the
following:

1. Whether the trial court should have granted Ms.
Bresnahan's motion for a trial order of dismissal,
where the sole evidence that she was ''masked
or . . . disguised'' showed that she was dressed
exactly as her doctors had prescribed.

2. Whether the trial court should have granted Ms.
Bresnahan's motion to dismiss the information on the
ground that § 240.35(4) violates her right to privacy
under the United States Constitution.

STATEMENT OF THE CASE

At trial, the court heard testimony about Ms.
Bresnahan's medical condition from her physician and
her psychotherapist, both of the Gender Identity
Clinic at Murray Hill Hospital. There was uncontradicted evidence from both doctors and from Ms. Bresnahan herself that she suffers from gender dysphoria
syndrome and has for that reason been compelled to
enter a long-term treatment program at the Clinic (R.
at 81-96, 388-406, 409-44).

Dr. Gustav Marquard, Ms. Bresnahan's psychotherapist, testified that he had treated her since the
spring of 1983 (R. at 387), had himself been in psychiatric practice for 24 years, and had been associated
at various times with the gender identity clinics at a
number of hospitals (R. at 385-86). He further testified to the consensus of psychiatric opinion concerning gender dysphoria syndrome, also known as

-2-

transsexualism. It is a chronic disorder in which the
patient suffers from ''an unrelenting and uncontrolla-
ble feeling that he or she is not the gender that
matched the reproductive organs assigned at birth''
(R. at 389). Transsexuals find their reproductive
organs to be ''repugnant'' (R. at 391); often are
unable to maintain normal social relationships (R. at
390); suffer from ''drastic depressions precipitated
by loathing their own bodies'' (R. at 392); and, in
some cases, become at risk to suicide or mutilation of
their own bodies (id.). The cause of the disorder is
unknown (R. at 398), and psychotherapy cannot provide
effective treatment (R. at 396). A transsexual is not
a homosexual or a transvestite (R. at 400). The syndrome becomes apparent in early childhood, often at
about four years of age, and the child's gestures and
play habits are uniformly of the opposite gender (R.
at 401-02). As a result, the child ''suffers merciless
teasing and rejection, which continues in more sophisticated form throughout adulthood'' (R. at 402).
Because a transsexual ''despises his or her own body
and is in turn found disgusting by others, such a
person is among the most unhappy patients a psychotherapist can treat'' (R. at 403).

   Dr. Amelia Levin, Ms. Bresnahan's treating physician at the Gender Identity Clinic at Murray Hill
Hospital, testified that she is aware of the treatment
programs at nine such clinics in North America and
Europe (R. at 419), and that each such clinic pre-
scribes treatment along the following pattern: First,
the patient is given ''an exhaustive psychological
workup to confirm the diagnosis'' (R. at 419). Then,
over a period of six months to two years, the patient
is given hormonal injections which alter the body's
appearance (id.). During this period, a clinic typically requires the patient to ''live and dress as the
gender the patient believes him- or herself to be,''
and, if the patient does not satisfy this requirement,
treatment is stopped ''because sex reassignment surgery would not then be indicated as a permanent change
in the patient's life'' (R. at 419-20). At an appropriate point, the patient is provided with sex reassignment surgery, in which the original sexual organs
are replaced with those that are consistent with the
patient's ''psychological gender'' (R. at 422). After
such surgery, a transsexual who was, for example, born
with male reproductive organs would have ''an internal
sexual structure like that of a woman who has undergone
a total hysterectomy and ovariectomy, which is not
unusual in naturally born women after a certain age''

-3-

(R. at 423-24). Medically, such a transsexual would at this point be considered a female (R. at 423), although there may be later procedures and continued hormonal treatment (R. at 425-26). Sex reassignment surgery is only one of ''several stages in a sex role assimilation, and it must be preceded by a complete psychological and social assimilation'' (R. at 427). The surgery is thus ''not viewed medically as a sex change operation'' because a substantial amount of gender has already been transformed before the surgery takes place (R. at 426).

Dr. Marquard testified that after completion of treatment the typical patient ''lives a far happier life'' as a result of the elimination of the patient's inner conflict and of the elimination of conflict between the patient and others unable to tolerate the disorder (R. at 406).

Both Dr. Marquard and Dr. Levin testified that it is ''irresponsible'' medical practice to provide physical treatment without at the same time requiring ''cross-dressing'' because of the need to ensure that the patient is able to live the life to which surgery will irreversibly commit her (R. at 326, 399). Both doctors also testified that there are two additional benefits: to prepare the patient for surgery (R. at 341-43, 432-36) and to relieve some of the patient's suffering until hormonal therapy has made surgery possible (R. at 347-49, 401-04). Both doctors also testified that the weight of medical opinion is that at the time Ms. Bresnahan was arrested female clothing was appropriate to her state of gender because gender is determined by hormonal composition and psychological condition, as well as by reproductive organs and chromosomes (R. at 344, 405-06, 443). Both doctors further testified that they had informed her of this fact and prescribed cross-dressing for her (R. at 349, 405-06, 440-42), and Ms. Bresnahan confirmed that she had been so informed and was cross-dressing ''under doctor's orders'' (R. at 176-80).

Ms. Bresnahan testified that she was 29 years old at the time she was arrested (R. at 171), was employed as a financial analyst for a stock brokerage firm (R. at 170), and had dressed exclusively in female clothing and lived as a woman since the age of 16 (R. at 173) because of a belief, held since her earliest childhood memories, that she was born female (R. at 178-79). Ms. Bresnahan described in detail her childhood play with dolls and several years of conflict with parents, other children, and school authorities ''because of my femininity'' (R. at 182-96). Ms. Bresnahan testified

-4-

that her office colleagues accepted her as a woman (R.
at 199) and that, at the time she was arrested, she
was on her way to lunch, accompanied by two other
transsexuals who also work in the financial district
of Manhattan (R. at 203).

Ms. Bresnahan testified in detail about the humiliation she experienced as a result of being arrested on
the street one block from her office, strip-searched
at a police station, and compelled to explain to her
supervisor the reason why she had not returned from
lunch on the afternoon she was arrested (R. at 202-07).
Dr. Marquard confirmed that Ms. Bresnahan had experienced a ''profound'' depression after the arrest, and
that her treatment plan had to be extended approximately six months as a result (R. at 407-09). Ms.
Bresnahan testified that for several days after the
arrest she felt unable to return to her office (R. at
208) and that she no longer felt safe in public (R. at
210-11).

The People submitted no evidence of any pattern of
crimes committed by groups of people disguising their
gender.

At the close of the evidence, the trial judge ruled
from the bench on both of Ms. Bresnahan's motions. He
held that § 240.35(4) can constitutionally penalize
cross-dressing by a transsexual, and he therefore
denied her motion to dismiss the information (R. at
468). He also denied her motion for a trial order of
dismissal, holding that a person is ''masked
or . . . disguised'' within the meaning of § 240.35(4)
when that person ''is wearing the clothing of one
gender but has the reproductive organs of the other''
(R. at 470). The Appellate Term affirmed without
opinion (R. at 481).

                    SUMMARY OF ARGUMENT

The People did not produce evidence legally sufficient to demonstrate a violation of Penal Law
§ 240.35(4), and the Criminal Court therefore erred in
denying Ms. Bresnahan's motion for a trial order of
dismissal. The Criminal Court heard extensive and
uncontradicted expert testimony that Ms. Bresnahan
suffers from a disease that requires her to dress as
she did when arrested. An examination of the statute's
history and that of similar statutes elsewhere shows
that the Legislature's real purpose was to deter
political violence by groups of masked or disguised
individuals. Moreover, a cross-dressing transsexual is

-5-

not disguised at all because the weight of scientific opinion, recognized in the case law, is that cross-dressing accurately informs the bystander of the patient's state of gender. No reported decision any-where in the United States has held that a statute like § 240.35(4) can be enforced against a cross-dressing transsexual. Whenever courts in other juris-dictions have been asked to use similar statutes to punish persons with gender dysphoria syndrome, the courts have either declared the statutes unconstitu-tional or have held that they do not apply to trans-sexuals.

In addition, the Criminal Court should have granted Ms. Bresnahan's motion to dismiss the information on the ground that § 240.35(4) violates her constitu-tional right to privacy. The right to privacy can be invaded only (1) where the People can demonstrate a compelling state interest and (2) where the invasion is no larger than necessary to accomplish that inter-est. Here, the only interests advanced by the People are a desire to prevent the use of disguises in crimes committed by gangs and an interest in preventing groups of disguised males from gaining access to women's washrooms. These interests are not compelling, and even if they were, they support no intrusion greater than a statute that limits its punishment to persons who appear together in public disguised <u>for a criminal purpose</u>. Section 240.35(4) instead punishes all persons who appear together in public with their identities obscured, no matter how innocent the pur-pose.

Even if a compelling state interest were not re-quired, § 240.35(4) cannot be sustained under the lesser ''rational basis'' test. The People have not introduced any evidence that § 240.35(4) is connected to any verifiable danger to the public. Although § 240.35(4) is claimed to be justifiable as a crime control measure, even under the rational basis stan-dard there is no basis for an assumption that people who cross-dress for medical reasons will also do so to commit crimes.

In the only case on point with this appeal, the Illinois Supreme Court has ruled that an ordinance similar to § 240.35(4) cannot constitutionally be enforced against transsexuals. The only cases that have permitted governmental regulation of an adult's appearance have involved prison inmates, nude bathing, massage parlor employees, and public employees.

-6-

ARGUMENT

I.   THE CRIMINAL COURT SHOULD HAVE
     GRANTED MS. BRESNAHAN'S MOTION FOR A
     TRIAL ORDER OF DISMISSAL BECAUSE THE
     PEOPLE FAILED TO INTRODUCE LEGALLY
     SUFFICIENT EVIDENCE THAT SHE HAD
     BEEN ''MASKED OR . . . DISGUISED''
     IN THE SENSE REQUIRED BY PENAL LAW
                   § 240.25(4).

There was uncontroverted evidence that Ms. Bresnahan suffers from gender dysphoria syndrome and that
she was arrested while dressed exactly as medically
prescribed for her (R. at 368). At the close of the
evidence, she moved for a trial order of dismissal on
the ground that the People had not introduced legally
sufficient evidence that she had been -- as a conviction under § 240.35(4) would require -- ''masked or in
any manner disguised by unusual or unnatural attire or
facial alteration.'' The trial court denied the motion, ruling that § 240.35(4) is satisfied by evidence
establishing, among other things, that ''a defendant
is wearing the clothing of one gender but has the
reproductive organs of the other'' (R. at 470). This
Court has routinely held that, ''[i]n analyzing a
statute or rule, courts look to their spirit or purpose, and the objectives of the enactors must be kept
in mind.'' Albano v. Kirby, 36 N.Y.2d 526, 530-31, 330
N.E.2d 615, 619, 369 N.Y.S.2d 655, 659 (1975); Williams
v. Williams, 23 N.Y.2d 592, 599, 246 N.E.2d 333, 337,
298 N.Y.S.2d 473, 479 (1969). The history of
§ 240.35(4) and of like statutes in other states
demonstrates that the Legislature did not intend that
people wearing clothing considered medically appropriate for them should be deemed ''masked or . . . disguised'' and therefore punished.

     A.   Section 240.35(4) is derived from
          legislation designed to protect the
          public from violent criminals in
                      disguise.

Section 240.35(4) is descended from a statute
enacted in 1845 in response to an insurrection that
had broken out among male Hudson Valley tenant farmers
who were unable to pay their rents and had begun to
disguise themselves as Indians and women for the
purpose of murdering officials serving them with

-7-

writs. See <u>People v. Simmons</u>, 79 Misc. 2d 249, 253,
357 N.Y.S.2d 362, 366 (Crim. Ct., Kings County 1974)
(dicta). The original legislation was entitled ''An
Act to Prevent Persons Appearing Disguised <u>and Armed</u>''
(emphasis supplied), and, among other things, it
provided that

> Every person who, having his face painted,
> discolored or concealed or being otherwise dis-
> guised in a manner calculated to prevent him from
> being identified, shall appear in any road or
> public highway, or in any field, lot, wood or
> enclosure, may be pursued and arrested . . . .

1845 N.Y. Laws, ch. 3 § 1.
    In 1881, this provision was codified as section
887(7) of the former Code of Criminal Procedure, which
defined a vagrant as ''[a] person who, having his face
painted, discolored, covered or concealed, or being
otherwise disguised, in a manner calculated to prevent
his being identified, appears in a road or public
highway, or in a field, lot, wood, or enclosure.''
N.Y. Code Crim. Proc. § 887(7) (McKinney 1958). A
parallel provision, more closely resembling the section at issue in this appeal, appeared later in the
former Penal Law. See N.Y. Penal Law §§ 710, 711
(McKinney 1944). Section 240.35(4) appeared in its
present form when the current Penal Law was enacted.
1965 N.Y. Laws, ch. 1030. Section 887(7) of the prior
Code of Criminal Procedure was deleted shortly thereafter. 1967 N.Y. Laws, ch. 681.
    No reported opinion interprets § 240.35(4), and
only three reported cases interpret any of the predecessor statutes. In the earliest, the Erie County
Court concluded that § 887(7) of the former Code of
Criminal Procedure was not violated by a man who stood
in front of a theater, advertising the entertainment
within while wearing a dress, wig, slippers, and
makeup. <u>People v. Luechini</u>, 75 Misc. 614, 136 N.Y.S.
319 (1912). The court noted that, if this behavior
were considered criminal,

> there is no reason why the disguised circus
> ''barker,'' the midway ''ballyhoo,'' or even the
> masquerader at the ball could not be convicted of
> vagrancy under this statute, . . . and such a
> conviction, although perhaps it might be deemed
> righteous by many, would be going far beyond
> anything conceived by the legislature.

-8-

<u>Id</u>. at 616, 136 N.Y.S. at 320-21.

   Both of the other two cases are distinguishable from this appeal. In <u>People v. Gillespi</u>, 15 N.Y.2d 529, 202 N.E.2d 565, 254 N.Y.S.2d 121, <u>amended</u>, 15 N.Y.2d 675, 204 N.E.2d 211, 255 N.Y.S.2d 884 (1964), and <u>People v. Archibald</u>, 27 N.Y.2d 504, 260 N.E.2d 871, 312 N.Y.S.2d 678 (1970), this Court, without opinion, affirmed convictions, under § 887(7) of the former Code of Criminal Procedure, of defendants who appeared in public in female clothing even though there was no evidence that they were anything other than unequivocally male. In neither case was there even a shred of evidence that the defendant, at the time of the offense, was wearing clothing considered by the weight of scientific opinion to be appropriate to that defendant's gender. Instead, the evidence in both cases established that the defendants had con-cealed their true identities by disguising their true genders. In contrast, Ms. Bresnahan provided the trial court with abundant and uncontroverted evidence that she has for some years worn female clothing at all times, that the weight of scientific opinion considers female clothing to be appropriate to the medically determined state of her gender at the time of her arrest, that she had been informed of that fact by both a physician and a psychotherapist, and that both doctors had prescribed the wearing of female clothing at all times as part of a pre-operative treatment plan (R. at 318-52, 395-406, 418-44).

   A few other states have at times maintained statutes similar to § 240.35(4). Although no reported decision determines whether any of these statutes can be vio-lated by a transsexual's wearing of medically pre-scribed clothing, the context in which all of them were enacted plainly shows that they were meant to punish people who used disguises to facilitate politi-cal violence. In that way, they are remarkably similar to the antecedents of Penal Law § 240.35(4). For example, the former Texas Penal Code provided that

      If any person shall go into or near any public place masked or disguised in such manner as to hide his identity or render same difficult to determine, he or she shall be guilty of a misde-meanor, . . . provided this article shall not apply to private or public functions, festivals or events not fostered or presented by <u>any secret society or organization.</u>

-9-

Tex. Penal Code § 454a, repealed by 1973 Tex. Gen. Laws, ch. 399 (emphasis supplied). This section was enacted in 1925, at a peak of Ku Klux Klan violence, together with other sections entitled ''Masked individuals parading on public highway'' (§ 454f), ''Masked person entering church'' (§ 454d), ''Masked person entering house'' (§ 454c), and ''Masked persons assaulting . . . '' (§ 454e). 1925 Tex. Gen. Laws, ch. 63.

A similar statute in Oklahoma provides that

> It shall be unlawful for any person in this state to wear a mask, hood or covering, which conceals the identity of the wearer; provided this act shall not apply to the pranks of children on Halloween, to those going to, or from, or participating in masquerade parties, to those participating in any public parade or exhibition of an educational, religious or historical character, to those participating in any meeting of any organization within any building or enclosure wholly within and under the control of said organization, and to those participating in the parades or exhibitions of minstrel troupes, circuses or other amusements or dramatic shows. . . .

Okla. Stat. tit. 21, § 1301 (1983). This section was enacted just before -- and apparently for the same reason as -- former section 454a of the Texas Penal Code, 1923-24 Okla. Sess. Laws, ch. 2. When enacting § 1301, the Oklahoma legislature also made it criminal for a masked or disguised person to demand entry to a house, Okla. Stat. tit. 21, § 1302 (1983), and made it an aggravated offense to commit assault while masked or disguised, § 1302.

A California statute more generally provides that

> It shall be unlawful for any person to wear any mask, false whiskers, or any personal disguise (whether complete or partial) for the purpose of:
> One -- Evading or escaping discovery, recognition, or identification in the commission of any public offense.
> Two -- Concealment, flight, or escape, when charged with, arrested for, or convicted of, any public offense. . . .

Cal. Penal Code § 185 (West 1970). It may or may not be a coincidence that this statute was enacted during

-10-

another period of widespread Ku Klux Klan violence,
1873-74 Cal. Stat., ch. 614.

A few municipalities have enacted ordinances prohibiting persons from appearing in public in clothing
customarily worn by the other gender. Only three
reported cases have construed ordinances of this type
on facts comparable to this appeal. In one such case,
the Illinois Supreme Court ruled -- for reasons set
out in Point II of this brief -- that an ordinance
penalizing ''[a]ny person who shall appear in a public
place . . . in a dress not belonging to his or her
sex, with intent to conceal his or her sex'' could not
constitutionally be enforced against transsexuals.
City of Chicago v. Wilson, 75 Ill. 2d 525, 389 N.E.2d
522, 523 (1978) (quoting Chi. Mun. Code § 192-8). In
another such case, a similar Cincinnati ordinance was
declared unconstitutional for violating First Amendment rights. City of Cincinnati v. Adams, 42 Ohio
Misc. 48, 330 N.E.2d 463 (Hamilton County Mun. Ct.
1974). In the remaining decision, the trial court
declined to hold the ordinance unconstitutional but
instead decided that a transsexual lacks the capacity
to develop the mens rea required for a violation. City
of Columbus v. Zanders, 25 Ohio Misc. 144, 266 N.E.2d
602 (Franklin County Mun. Ct. 1970).

B.   A necessary and lawful medical
      treatment would become impossible in
      this State if a transsexual, dressing
      as medically prescribed, can be held
      to have violated § 240.35(4).

This Court has held that where there is doubt as to
a statute's meaning ''and a choice between two constructions is afforded, results become important, for,
although 'Consequences cannot alter statutes
. . . [they] may help to fix their meaning.''' Town
of Smithtown v. Moore, 11 N.Y.2d 238, 244, 183 N.E.2d
66, 69, 228 N.Y.S.2d 657, 661 (1962) (citations omitted). This Court has also held that ''[i]t is the duty
of the courts to construe statutes reasonably and so
as not to deprive citizens of important rights.''
Pansa v. Damiano, 14 N.Y.2d 356, 360, 200 N.E.2d 563,
565, 251 N.Y.S.2d 665, 668 (1964).

In this state and in others, the law has recognized
and endorsed sex reassignment surgery as a necessary
treatment for persons who, like Ms. Bresnahan, suffer
from gender dysphoria syndrome. In this state, a
health insurer cannot escape liability for the costs

-11-

of sex reassignment surgery on the ground that it is
merely ''cosmetic'' and not a needed medical procedure. Davidson v. Aetna Life & Casualty Ins. Co., 101
Misc. 2d 1, 420 N.Y.S.2d 450 (Sup. Ct., N.Y. County
1979). The Seventh Circuit has even required a prison
to provide treatment for prisoners suffering from
gender dysphoria syndrome. Meriwether v. Faulkner, 821
F.2d 408 (7th Cir.), cert. denied, 108 S. Ct. 311
(1987). In this state, a professional sports organization that discriminates against a transsexual athlete
can be held liable under the New York Human Rights
Law, N.Y. Exec. Law §§ 290-301. (McKinney 1982).
Richards v. United States Tennis Ass'n, 93 Misc. 2d
713, 400 N.Y.S.2d 267 (Sup. Ct., N.Y. County 1977).
Under § 207 of the New York City Health Code, a birth
certificate can be amended reflecting a court-ordered
change of name following ''convertive surgery.'' See
Anonymous v. Mellon, 91 Misc. 2d 375, 398 N.Y.S.2d 99
(Sup. Ct., N.Y. County 1977). A number of other states
have similarly provided for the amendment of a birth
certificate after sex reassignment surgery. See, for
example, Ariz. Rev. Stat. Ann. § 36-326 (Supp. 1985);
Cal. Health & Safety Code §§ 10475-79 (West Supp.
1985); Hawaii Rev. Stat. § 338-17.7 (Supp. 1984); Ill.
Rev. Stat., ch. 111.5, § 73-17 (1977); La. Rev. Stat.
Ann. § 40.61 (West Supp. 1985); Mass. Ann. Laws ch.
46, § 13 (Michie/Law. Coop. Supp. 1985); N.J. Rev.
Stat. § 26:8-40.12 (Supp. 1985); N.M. Stat. Ann.
§ 24-14-25 (1978); Tenn. Code Ann. § 68-3-203 (Supp.
1985).

The Criminal Court heard extensive and uncontradicted expert testimony to the effect that sex reassignment surgery is the only successful treatment for
gender dysphoria syndrome, but that such surgery must
be preceded by an extended period in which the patient
dresses according to her psychological sex (R. at
318-52, 395-406, 418-44). The same view is also reflected in the case law and in the medical literature
considered by other courts. See, for example, City of
Chicago v. Wilson, 75 Ill. 2d 525, 389 N.E.2d 522,
524-25 (1978); City of Columbus v. Zanders, 25 Ohio
Misc. 144, 266 N.E.2d 602, 604-06 (1970). In Davidson
v. Aetna Life & Casualty, the court noted that

> The overall process of sex-reassignment surgery
> is both long and arduous. . . . Among the require-
> ments [for treatment at the Johns Hopkins Hospital
> Gender Identity] Clinic is that the patient has
> lived in the female role for a minimum of one
> year, proving to her own satisfaction and to

-12-

441

others her ability to be rehabilitated gainfully
in society as a female and to function satisfacto-
rily emotionally, vocationally and socially as a
female without a vagina although possibly hormon-
ally estrogenized. . . . The Clinic further states
that the operation cannot be looked upon as a sex
change operation; rather it is simply the final
anatomical step in a gender role assimilation of
which the psychological and social steps have
already been carried out.

As the Criminal Court was informed through expert
medical testimony, the practice of pre-operative
''cross-dressing'' is necessary for three reasons. The
first is to test the patient's determination and
ability to live fully as her psychological gender
before surgery irreversibly commits her to it (R. at
326, 399). The second is to prepare her for the drastic
and final step of surgery (R. at 341-43, 423-26). The
third is simply to relieve some of the patient's
suffering until hormone therapy has made surgery
possible (R. at 347-49, 401-04).

      <u>C</u>. <u>Because Ms. Bresnahan wore clothing</u>
          <u>that was medically appropriate for</u>
          <u>her and did so under medical advice,</u>
          <u>she was not ''masked or . . . dis-</u>
                    <u>guised.''</u>

A cross-dressing transsexual is not disguised. The
weight of scientific opinion, recognized in the case
law, is that cross-dressing accurately informs the
bystander of a transsexual's gender. This is not a
case where a defendant who lives daily life as a man
had at the time of arrest concealed his identity by
dressing as a woman. Ms. Bresnahan's identity <u>is</u> that
of a woman. Her friends, neighbors, and colleagues
know her as a woman. Medicine considers her primarily
to be a woman. And at the time of arrest she was
dressed as a woman.
No reported decision anywhere in the United States
has held that a statute like § 240.35(4) can be enforced against a cross-dressing transsexual. And the
law has established a policy -- through the amendment
of birth certificates and through interpretation of
health insurance contracts -- of assisting persons
afflicted with gender dysphoria syndrome to obtain
treatment through sex reassignment surgery. That
policy would be subverted if § 240.35(4) were inter-

-13-

preted to prohibit the necessary and inoffensive
pre-operative procedure of cross-dressing.

This Court has more than once noted that it ''will
not blindly apply the words of a statute to arrive at
an unreasonable or absurd result. If the statute is so
broadly drawn as to include the case before the court,
yet reason and statutory purpose show it was obviously
not intended to include that case, the court is justified in making an exception through implication.''
Williams v. Williams, 23 N.Y.2d 592, 599, 246 N.E.2d
333, 337, 298 N.Y.S.2d 473, 479 (1969) (citations
omitted). ''It is, moreover, always presumed that no
unjust or unreasonable result was intended and the
statute must be construed consonant with that presumption.'' Zappone v. Home Ins. Co., 55 N.Y.2d 131, 137,
432 N.E.2d 783, 786, 447 N.Y.S.2d 911, 914 (1982).

Thus, even viewing the evidence in the light most
favorable to the prosecution, the People failed to
make out a prima facie case that Ms. Bresnahan was
''masked or in any manner disguised,'' and the Criminal
Court therefore committed reversible error in denying
her motion for a trial order of dismissal.

> II. THE CRIMINAL COURT SHOULD HAVE
>   GRANTED MS. BRESNAHAN'S MOTION TO
>   DISMISS THE INFORMATION BECAUSE
>   PENAL LAW § 240.35(4) VIOLATES HER
>   RIGHT TO PRIVACY UNDER THE UNITED
>   STATES CONSTITUTION.

> A. The constitutional right to privacy
>   includes the right to choose one's
>   own clothing.

This Court has observed that the right to privacy

> is not, as a literal reading of the phrase might
> suggest, the right to maintain secrecy with re-
> spect to one's affairs or personal behavior;
> rather, it is a right of independence in making
> certain kinds of important decisions . . . unde-
> terred by governmental restraint -- what we re-
> ferred to in People v. Rice (41 N.Y.2d 1018, 1019)
> as ''freedom of conduct.'' . . . [T]he Supreme
> Court took pains in Carey v. Population Services
> Int'l (431 U.S. 678, 684-85) to observe that ''the
> outer limits'' of the decision-making aspect of
> the right to privacy ''have not been marked by the
> Court.'' . . .

-14-

People v. Onofre, 51 N.Y.2d 476, 485-86, 415 N.E.2d
936, 939, 434 N.Y.S.2d 947, 949-50 (1980), cert.
denied, 451 U.S. 987 (1981). The right to privacy
grows out of the First Amendment guarantees of freedom
of speech and association, the Fourth Amendment right
to freedom from unreasonable governmental searches and
seizures, the Ninth Amendment's reservation to the
people of powers not expressly granted to government,
the Fourteenth Amendment's equal protection clause,
the concept of liberty inherent in the Fourteenth
Amendment due process clause, and the penumbras of
history and logic surrounding the Bill of Rights as a
whole. Onofre, 51 N.Y.2d at 485-86, 415 N.E.2d at 939,
434 N.Y.S.2d at 949.

   Pointing to Stanley v. Georgia, 394 U.S. 557 (1969),
and Eisenstadt v. Baird, 405 U.S. 438 (1972), this
Court has further concluded that the United States
Supreme Court has not limited the right to privacy to
situations of ''marital intimacy'' or ''procreative
choice.'' Onofre, 51 N.Y.2d at 487, 415 N.E.2d at
939-40, 434 N.Y.S.2d at 950. In Stanley, the Supreme
Court held that the right to privacy is violated by a
statute that criminalizes the possession of obscene
materials in one's own home. In both Stanley, 394 U.S.
at 564, and Eisenstadt, 405 U.S. at 453-54 n.10, the
Court quoted with approval Justice Brandeis's dissent
in Olmstead v. United States, 277 U.S. 438 (1928),
where he noted that ''[t]he makers of our Constitution . . . conferred, as against the Government, the
right to be let alone -- the most comprehensive of
rights and the right most valued by civilized man''
(emphasis supplied).

   This Court has held that the right to privacy was
violated by § 240.35(3) of the Penal Law, another
subdivision of the same loitering statute at issue in
the present appeal. Section 240.35(3) had penalized
loitering ''in a public place for the purpose of
engaging, or soliciting another person to engage, in
deviate sexual intercourse or other sexual behavior of
a deviate nature,'' and this Court ruled that the
state cannot constitutionally punish loitering which
neither is done for a criminal purpose nor is ''offensive or annoying to others.'' People v. Uplinger, 58
N.Y.2d 936, 938, 447 N.E.2d 62, 63, 460 N.Y.S.2d 514,
515 (1983), cert. dismissed, 467 U.S. 246 (1984).

   The Supreme Court has assumed that the constitutional right to privacy includes ''matters of personal
appearance.'' Kelley v. Johnson, 425 U.S. 238, 244
(1976). The issue in Kelley was whether a police
department could establish hair-grooming regulations

-15-

for its officers. In holding that the department had
demonstrated a sufficiently strong governmental interest to overcome the officers' assumed privacy rights,
the Court noted that it perceived a ''highly significant'' distinction between the privacy rights of
police officers to an appearance of their own choosing,
on one hand, and, on the other, privacy rights of
persons not employed by a uniformed police department.
Id. at 245. Relying on Kelley, the Illinois Supreme
Court has ruled that an ordinance punishing any person
appearing in public ''in a dress not belonging to his
or her sex, with intent to conceal his or her sex''
cannot constitutionally be enforced against transsexuals. City of Chicago v. Wilson, 75 Ill. 2d 525, 389
N.E.2d 522, 523 (1978) (quoting Chi. Mun. Code
§ 192-8). The defendants in Wilson were -- like Ms.
Bresnahan -- transsexuals, and (as explained more
fully below) the issues presented to the Illinois
Supreme Court were the same right-to-privacy issues
raised in this appeal.

As long ago as 1958, the United States Supreme
Court noted in passing the existence of a constitutional right to wear clothing of one's own, rather
than of the government's, selection. In Kent v. Dulles,
357 U.S. 116, the court concluded that a citizen
cannot constitutionally be deprived of the right to
travel abroad on the ground that the choice of where
to journey ''may be as close to the heart of the
individual as the choice of what he eats, or wears, or
reads.'' Id. at 126 (emphasis supplied). The right to
autonomy in one's personal appearance is connected to
what the Supreme Court has called the historically
recognized right of ''every individual to the possession and control of his own person,'' Union Pacific
Ry. Co. v. Botsford, 141 U.S. 250, 251 (1891). Through
the Fourteenth Amendment, the right to privacy is
protected from state, as well as federal, interference. Roe v. Wade, 410 U.S. 113 (1973).

None of this analysis is altered by the Supreme
Court's decision in Bowers v. Hardwick, 478 U.S. 186
(1986). There, the Court decided that the Constitution
has not granted a fundamental right to engage in sex
with a person of one's own gender. The Court held that
an activity that has been criminalized in most states
throughout the nation's history cannot be considered
to be ''implicit in the concept of ordered liberty.''
Id. at 191-94 (quoting Palko v. Connecticut, 302 U.S.
319, 325 (1937)). In contrast, as explained throughout
this brief, the law in many states has for several
years taken steps to protect the medical treatment of

-16-

transsexuals; no reported decision anywhere in the
United States has ever held that a statute like
§ 240.35(4) can be enforced against transsexuals; and
the Supreme Court itself observed in Kent that the
liberty to wear what one pleases is one of those
liberties natural to a free society.

> B. The right to privacy is a fundamental
> right and can be invaded only where
> the People can demonstrate a compel-
> ling state interest and only where
> the invasion is no larger than
> necessary to accomplish that
> interest.

It is settled law that the right to privacy is a
fundamental right. Carey v. Population Services Int'l,
431 U.S. 678, 684-86 (1977); Roe, 410 U.S. at 147-64;
Griswold v. Connecticut, 381 U.S. 479, 485 (1965). The
Supreme Court has repeatedly held that a state can
invade the right to privacy, or any other fundamental
right, only where it can demonstrate a compelling
state interest requiring such an invasion. Carey, 431
U.S. at 685-86; Roe, 410 U.S. at 147-65; Griswold, 381
U.S. at 485. Even where a state can show a compelling
interest that could justify some limitation on the
right to privacy or another fundamental right, any
such limitation must ''be narrowly drawn to express
only those interests.'' Carey, 431 U.S. at 686.
     In Carey, for example, the Supreme Court struck
down § 6811(8) of the New York Education Law, which
made it criminal, among other things, to advertise the
sale of contraceptives and to distribute even non-pre-
scription contraceptives without first obtaining a
pharmacist's license. The state argued that the prohibition on advertising was justified because contraceptive advertisements would offend and embarrass large
portions of the public and would encourage sexual
activity among young people, but the Court held instead
that neither of these considerations could be considered compelling in the face of First Amendment rights
and the right to privacy. Id. at 700-02. The state
argued further that the prohibition on distribution of
contraceptives by non-pharmacists was justified by the
state's interests in promoting quality control, protecting the health of the user, and preventing minors
from selling contraceptives, but the Court held these
concerns were neither compelling nor (excepting the
last) even likely to be achieved by the state's invasion of contraceptive users' right to privacy. Id. at
686-91.

-17-

C. Section 240.35(4) is not supported
    by a compelling state interest.

Here, the only interests advanced by the People
are, first, a desire to prevent the use of gender and
other disguises in crimes committed by groups of
people and, second, an interest in preventing groups
of disguised males from gaining access to women's
washrooms and other areas where women may be vulnerable. There is no evidence anywhere in the record to
suggest that at any time in this century police anywhere in New York State have encountered difficulties
apprehending groups of criminals who have disguised
themselves in clothing of the opposite gender. Nor is
there any evidence in the record of even a single
crime in this state committed by a group of men who
got into a women's washroom or the like disguised as
women.

These same interests were cited by the city of
Chicago in an unsuccessful attempt to justify an
ordinance similar to § 240.35(4), but the Illinois
Supreme Court held them to be so insubstantial that
they could not even meet the lesser standard of providing a rational basis for the city's invasion of
constitutional privacy rights. City of Chicago v.
Wilson, 75 Ill. 2d at 533, 389 N.E.2d at 523-25. In
Wilson, transsexuals had been arrested, even though
their pre-operative treatment called for them to
cross-dress. The court found the record there as
barren as the record here of evidence that could
substantiate even a rational basis, much less a compelling state interest, and -- in the only reported
decision on the privacy issue posed by the present
appeal -- the Illinois Supreme Court held that, ''as
applied to the defendants here,'' the Chicago ordinance created an ''unconstitutional infringement of
their liberty interest,'' id. at 534, 389 N.E.2d at
525.

D. Even if one of the interests advanced
    by the People were deemed compelling,
    § 240.35(4) nevertheless invades
    privacy rights more than necessary
    to satisfy such an interest.

Even if a government's interest is compelling, it
must choose the least restrictive means to accomplish
it. In deciding right to privacy cases, the courts

-18-

have often looked for guidance to decisions applying
First Amendment and other fundamental rights. For
instance, in <u>Griswold</u>, 381 U.S. at 485, where it
determined that Connecticut's complete prohibition on
the use of contraceptives violated the right to privacy
because it could not be supported by a compelling
state interest, the Supreme Court quoted with approval
<u>NAACP v. Alabama</u>, 377 U.S. 288, 307 (1964), a First
Amendment freedom of association case, for the principle that a ''governmental purpose to control or prevent
activities constitutionally subject to state regulation may not be achieved by means which sweep unnecessarily broadly and thereby invade the area of protected
freedoms.'' In <u>United Mine Workers v. Illinois State
Bar Ass'n</u>, 389 U.S. 217, 222 (1967), another freedom
of association case, the Court noted that it has
''repeatedly held that laws which actually affect the
exercise of these vital rights cannot be sustained
merely because they were enacted for the purpose of
dealing with some evil within the State's legislative
competence, or even because the laws do in fact provide
a <u>helpful</u> means of dealing with such an evil'' (emphasis supplied).

Section 240.35(4) is not the least restrictive
alternative to achieve either of the purposes advanced
by the People, and the statute is therefore defectively
overbroad. Even if this Court were to conclude that
the state has a compelling interest in preventing the
use of gender disguises in crimes committed by groups
of people, that conclusion could sustain only a statute
that limits its punishment to persons who appear
together in public disguised <u>for a criminal purpose</u>,
and § 240.35(4) is not so limited. Instead, it punishes
<u>all</u> persons who appear in public with their identities
obscured, no matter how innocent the purpose. Here,
there was ample and uncontradicted evidence that Ms.
Bresnahan dressed as she did as a result of the requirements of a widely recognized medical treatment
program. As set out more fully in Point I of this
brief, the law in New York and elsewhere has made
adjustments to further the objectives of this kind of
treatment by amending birth certificates and requiring
reimbursement under properly drawn health insurance
contracts where persons suffering from gender dysphoria syndrome are forced to go through the same type
of medical treatment that led to Ms. Bresnahan's
arrest. No valid governmental purpose is advanced by
restricting a transsexual's choice of attire, and the
statute could have been drafted to avoid such an
imposition on her liberty.

-19-

E. Even if a compelling state interest
were not required, § 240.35(4)
cannot survive scrutiny under the
lesser ''rational basis'' test.

As explained more fully above, the Illinois Supreme
Court has ruled that an ordinance similar to the
statute here at issue cannot constitutionally be
enforced against transsexuals. In City of Chicago v.
Wilson, 75 Ill. 2d 525, 389 N.E.2d 522 (1978), the
city claimed both of the purposes asserted by the
People in the present appeal, together with two others:
''to protect citizens from being misled or defrauded''
and ''to prevent inherently antisocial conduct which
is contrary to the accepted norms.'' Id. at 532, 389
N.E.2d at 524. The Illinois court determined that none
of these rationales could meet even the lesser rational
basis test applicable where a constitutionally protected right is not deemed fundamental or, in equal
protection cases, where discrimination is not based on
a suspect classification.
    A governmental purpose satisfies the rational basis
or rational connection test where ''there is an evil
at hand for correction, and . . . it might be thought
that the particular legislative measure was a rational
way to correct it.'' Williamson v. Lee Optical Co.,
348 U.S. 483, 488 (1955). But here the People have not
introduced any evidence that § 240.35(4) is connected
to any verifiable danger to the public. Although
§ 240.35(4) is claimed to be justifiable as a crime
control measure, the Illinois Supreme Court concluded
that even under the rational basis standard ''we
cannot assume that individuals who cross-dress for
purposes of therapy are prone to commit crimes.'' City
of Chicago v. Wilson, 389 N.E.2d at 525.
    Nor can § 240.35(4) be justified by a desire to
promote a particular standard of sexual morality. Not
only was such a purpose unpersuasive in City of Chicago
v. Wilson, but it would be inconsistent with the law's
policy, described in Point I of this brief, of encour-
aging treatment of gender dysphoria syndrome through
sex reassignment therapy. And this Court expressly
rejected just such a purpose in People v. Onofre, 51
N.Y.2d at 489, 415 N.E.2d at 942, 434 N.Y.S.2d at 952.
    Finally, in Kelley v. Johnson, 425 U.S. 238, 245
(1976), the Supreme Court permitted a police department to regulate the appearance of its officers but
noted that there is a ''highly significant'' difference between the broad rights of ''the citizenry in
general'' and the narrower rights of public employees.

-20-

Since Kelley, the only cases that have permitted governmental regulation of an adult's appearance have involved prison inmates, e.g., Hill v. Estelle, 537 F.2d 214 (5th Cir. 1976); nude bathing, e.g., Williams v. Kleppe, 539 F.2d 803 (1st Cir. 1976); massage parlor employees, e.g., Harper v. Lindsay, 616 F.2d 849 (5th Cir. 1980); public employees, e.g., Ball v. Board of Trustees of the Kerrville, Ind., School Dist., 584 F.2d 684 (5th Cir. 1978), cert. denied, 440 U.S. 972 (1979); and prohibitions on nudity and semi-nudity, e.g., South Florida Free Beaches, Inc. v. City of Miami, 734 F.2d 608 (11th Cir. 1984). (Goldman v. Weinberger, 475 U.S. 503 (1986), was not a right-to-privacy case; it held instead that armed services personnel do not have a free-exercise-of-religion right under the First Amendment to wear yarmulkes indoors while on duty.)

F. Section 240.35(4) violates Ms. Bresnahan's constitutional right to privacy.

For the reasons set out above, the purposes advanced by the People do not arise to a compelling state interest. Even if they did, under the cases described above, § 240.35(4) nevertheless cannot be enforced against transsexuals because it does not accomplish those purposes in the least restrictive manner. The required ''[p]recision of regulation,'' NAACP v. Button, 371 U.S. 415, 438 (1963), could be achieved only by a statute that would punish appearing in public in prohibited attire for a criminal purpose. Moreover, enforcement of § 240.35(4) against transsexuals cannot survive scrutiny even under the lesser rational basis test.

For three reasons, the right-to-privacy question in this appeal is not governed by this Court's decisions in People v. Gillespi, 15 N.Y.2d 529, 202 N.E.2d 565, 254 N.Y.S.2d 121, amended, 15 N.Y.2d 675, 204 N.E.2d 211, 255 N.Y.S.2d 884 (1964), and People v. Archibald, 27 N.Y.2d 504, 260 N.E.2d 871, 312 N.Y.S.2d 678 (1970), where constitutional challenges to a predecessor statute of § 240.35(4) were turned aside. First, in neither case did a defendant challenge the statute for violating the constitutional right to privacy. In Gillespi, this court was asked to decide only whether the statute was unconstitutionally vague and an unreasonable and arbitrary exercise of police power. In Archibald, the appeal was based only on due process

-21-

and First Amendment grounds. Second, even if those defendants had raised some type of privacy issue, they could not have raised the question presently before the court. In neither case was there any evidence that a defendant suffered from gender dysphoria syndrome or any other medical condition that would have required attire that might be deemed to violate the statute. Third, even if <u>Archibald</u> and <u>Gillespi</u> had determined precisely the privacy issues presently before the court, those cases would have been impliedly overruled by this Court's later decisions in <u>People v. Onofre</u>, setting out this Court's perception of the right to privacy, and <u>People v. Uplinger</u>, striking down, on the basis of that perception, another subdivision of the same loitering statute at issue in this appeal.

Thus, the Criminal Court should have granted Ms. Bresnahan's motion to dismiss the information on the ground that § 240.35(4) violates her constitutional right to privacy.

<u>CONCLUSION</u>

For all the foregoing reasons, Ms. Bresnahan's conviction should be reversed, and the information should be dismissed.

> Clyde Farnsworth, Esq.
> Attorney for Defendant-Appellant
> 32 Fontanka Street
> Bedford Falls, N.Y. 14218
> (900) 555-1111

Appendix F
Sample Appellee's Brief

This brief responds to the appellant's brief that appears in Appendix E. (See the introductory note at the beginning of Appendix E.)

COURT OF APPEALS OF THE STATE OF NEW YORK

THE PEOPLE OF THE STATE OF NEW YORK,

                    Appellee

        -against-   No. 90-341

MERRITT BRESNAHAN,

                    Defendant-Appellant

BRIEF FOR APPELLEE

                              Hon. Martha Bosley
                              District Attorney
                              New York County
                              BY: Allan Kuusinen, Esq.
                              Asst. District Attorney
                              1 Hogan Place
                              New York, N.Y. 10013
                              (212) 555-1111

TABLE OF CONTENTS

TABLE OF AUTHORITIES

CASES

* Authorities primarily relied on are marked with an
asterisk.

-iv-

STATUTES

MISCELLANEOUS

<u>STATUTE INVOLVED</u>

Section 240.35(4) of the New York Penal Law provides as follows:

> A person is guilty of loitering when he . . .
> 4. Being masked or in any manner disguised by unusual or unnatural attire or facial alteration, loiters, remains or congregates in a public place with other persons so masked or disguised, or knowingly permits or aids persons so masked or disguised to congregate in a public place; except that such conduct is not unlawful when it occurs in connection with a masquerade party or like entertainment if, when such entertainment is held in a city which has promulgated regulations in connection with such affairs, permission is first obtained from the police or other appropriate authorities; . . . .
> Loitering is a violation.

<u>PRELIMINARY STATEMENT</u>

The defendant was convicted in New York City Criminal Court, New York County, Judge Celeste Remay, of loitering in violation of Penal Law § 240.35(4) (New York County inf. no. 9437/88). Before trial, the defendant moved, pursuant to Criminal Procedure Law §§ 170.30(1)(a) and 170.35(1)(c), for an order dismissing the information on the ground that Penal Law § 240.35(4) violates his right to privacy under the United States Constitution, and the Criminal Court reserved decision on this motion until the end of trial. After the close of evidence at trial, the defendant moved for a trial order of dismissal, pursuant to Criminal Procedure Law §§ 290.10 and 320.20, alleging an absence of legally sufficient evidence that he had been ''masked or in any manner disguised by unusual or unnatural attire'' in the sense prohibited by § 240.35(4). Ruling from the bench, the Criminal Court denied both motions, convicted the defendant, and sentenced him to a fine of two hundred dollars. The Appellate Term affirmed without opinion, and this appeal followed.

<u>QUESTIONS PRESENTED</u>

Is a man ''masked or in any manner disguised by unusual or unnatural attire,'' within the meaning of

-1-

Penal Law § 240.35(4), when he assumes a female voice and gestures and wears a skirt, blouse, high-heeled shoes, and stockings for the admitted purpose of causing others to believe he is a woman?

Does the constitutional right to privacy permit a state to penalize congregating in public by three or more men dressing as and imitating women on the grounds that men so disguised could gain entrance to women's washrooms and similar places and that a victim of a crime committed by such a group could mistakenly identify them to police as women?

STATEMENT OF THE CASE

Both the defendant and the arresting officer testified that when arrested the defendant was wearing a blouse, a skirt, high-heeled shoes, stockings, and women's undergarments (R. at 109, 187), and that when arrested the defendant was standing on a street corner in the company of two other men similarly attired (R. at 108-10, 114, 193-94).

The arresting officer, the defendant, the defendant's physician, and the defendant's psychiatrist all testified that when arrested the defendant had a penis, testicles, and a scrotum (R. at 110, 189, 373, 449). The defendant's doctors further testified that at the time of trial the defendant still had these organs (R. at 373, 449); that he had never had a vagina, uterus, or ovaries (id.); and that, regardless of any medical treatment that may be performed on him in the future, he would never have ovaries or a uterus and would have male sex chromosomes for the rest of his life (R. at 374-75, 448). The arresting officer testified that each of the defendant's companions had a penis, testicles, and a scrotum and did not have a vagina (R. at 114-15). The defendant's companions were also arrested for violating Penal Law § 240.35(4). They both pleaded guilty at arraignment and are not parties to this appeal.

The defendant's testimony conceded that when arrested he was not travelling to or from a masquerade party authorized by the police department (R. at 209). The arresting officer testified that he at first believed the defendant and his companions to be women (R. at 101), and the defendant testified that his purpose in dressing as he did was to create exactly this impression (R. at 213). The arresting officer testified that the defendant and his companions ''would have succeeded in fooling me'' if the officer

-2-

461

had not overheard one of them make a remark the substance of which was not testified to because of a
defense objection (R. at 98, 103). The officer testified without contradiction that all three convincingly
affected feminine voices, inflections, gestures, and
walks (R. at 98-101).

The defendant testified that he planned to undergo
surgery to remove his penis, testicles, and scrotum
and replace them with an artificially constructed
vagina (R. at 197), but he and his doctors all testified that such an operation had not yet occurred (R.
at 189, 197, 373, 449). The defendant's physician
further testified that even after such surgery the
defendant would not have ovaries, a uterus, or female
sex chromosomes and would not be able to bear children
(R. at 448-52). Although both doctors testified that
they had advised the defendant to wear female clothing
before surgery (R. at 349, 405-06, 440-42), they and
the defendant all admitted that each had been aware
before the defendant's arrest that such conduct could
lead to legal difficulties (R. 179-80, 406, 442). The
doctors also admitted that their pre-operative treatment plan would not be ''significantly'' disturbed if
a patient like the defendant were to refrain, before
surgery, from appearing in public with two or more
other such men in female dress (R. at 408, 449).

The Criminal Court found as a fact that the defendant was ''anatomically a man'' both at the time of
arrest and at the time of trial (R. at 467). The court
denied the defendant's motion for a trial order of
dismissal, holding that a defendant is ''masked or in
any manner disguised by unusual or unnatural attire''
within the meaning of § 240.35(4) when that defendant
''is wearing clothing of one gender but has the reproductive organs of the other'' (R. at 470). Discovering
no constitutional infirmity in the statute, the court
also denied the defendant's motion to dismiss the
information (R. at 468). The defendant was convicted
(R. at 471-72), and the Appellate Term affirmed (R. at
478).

SUMMARY OF ARGUMENT

The Criminal Court properly denied the defendant's
motion for a trial order of dismissal. The only element
in dispute involved the question of whether the defendant was ''in any manner disguised by unusual or
unnatural attire.'' Here, the defendant and his co-
defendants dressed as women, and the arresting officer

-3-

testified that he at first believed them to be women.
The defendant's own experts testified that his reproductive organs were male. Nothing in the statute
requires the People to prove that a defendant had
disguised himself in order to commit some unlawful or
antisocial act. In fact, this Court has twice held
that § 240.35(4)'s predecessor statutes did not require
the People to prove a malicious intent, and that even
the most innocent of reasons will not excuse going out
in public disguised in unnatural attire among a group
similarly disguised.

Section 240.35(4) does not interfere with the
defendant's medical treatment because it does not
prohibit an individual male from appearing in public
dressed in female clothing. The statute instead prohibits three or more persons from appearing in public
disguised and in concert, and it does so because in a
crime-ridden society groups of disguised people can be
dangerous. A disguise such as the one used by the
defendant can be so convincing that a victim may
firmly believe that he or she has been robbed by women
even though the criminals were in fact men. Not only
does the disguise prevent identification of criminals,
but a group disguised in the way these defendants were
can gain admission to confined areas, such as
washrooms, where women are particularly vulnerable to
attack.

Section 240.35(4) does not violate the defendant's
constitutional right to privacy, and the Criminal
Court properly denied his motion to dismiss the information. The United States Supreme Court has held that
a state can regulate attire without offending the
constitutional right to privacy unless the party
challenging the regulation can show that there is no
rational connection between that regulation and some
form of public good. Only in matters of marriage,
procreation, contraception, abortion, child rearing,
education, and family relationships must a state
demonstrate a compelling state interest, and none of
those categories include any sort of right for a group
of men to disguise themselves as women.

The defendant has not shown that § 240.35(4) lacks
a rational relationship to a public need. Under the
rational connection or rational basis test, a statute
is constitutional even if not perfectly consistent
with the Legislature's goals. This Court has affirmed
convictions under § 240.35(4)'s predecessor statute,
and those convictions were attacked on the same constitutional grounds asserted by the defendant here.
Even if the men in this appeal were not disguised in

- 4 -

order to commit crimes, the Legislature is entitled
under the Constitution to regulate together both the
truly dangerous and the apparently dangerous, particularly where even the apparently dangerous strikes the
public as immoral.

ARGUMENT

I. THE CRIMINAL COURT PROPERLY DENIED
    THE DEFENDANT'S MOTION FOR A TRIAL
    ORDER OF DISMISSAL BECAUSE THERE WAS
    LEGALLY SUFFICIENT EVIDENCE SUBSTAN-
    TIATING EACH ELEMENT OF LOITERING,
    AS DEFINED BY PENAL LAW § 240.35(4).

A. The only element in dispute raised
    the question of whether the defendant
    was ''in any manner disguised by
    unusual or unnatural attire.''

Under § 240.35(4), a defendant is guilty of loitering if he (1) is ''in any manner disguised by unusual
or unnatural attire,'' (2) ''loiters, remains or
congregates in a public place,'' and (3) does so
''with other persons so . . . disguised.'' Nothing in
the statute requires the People to prove that a defendant disguised himself for the purpose of committing some unlawful or antisocial act. As explained
more fully below, this Court has twice held that under
§ 240.35(4)'s predecessor statutes the People need not
prove a malicious intent. People v. Archibald, 27
N.Y.2d 504, 260 N.E.2d 871, 312 N.Y.S.2d 678 (1970);
People v. Gillespi, 15 N.Y.2d 529, 202 N.E.2d 565, 254
N.Y.S.2d 121, amended, 15 N.Y.2d 675, 204 N.E.2d 211,
255 N.Y.S.2d 884 (1964). Section 240.35(4) provides an
exception where permission has been obtained from
''the police or other appropriate authorities'' for a
''masquerade party or other like entertainment.''
    The defendant concedes every element of the offense
but one. The defendant's expert medical witnesses
conceded that, both at the time of trial and of the
offense, he had a penis, testicles, and a scrotum and
did not have a vagina or ovaries (R. at 373, 449).
After denying the defendant's motion for a trial order
of dismissal, the trial judge found as a fact that the
defendant was, at the time of the offense, a male (R.
at 459). The defendant concedes that when arrested the
defendant was wearing a blouse, a skirt, high-heeled

-5-

shoes, stockings, and women's undergarments (R. at 109, 187); that when arrested he was standing on a street corner (R. at 108, 193); that the two persons with him when he was arrested have the same kinds of sexual organs he does (R. at 114, 198) and were wearing clothing similar to his (R. at 109-10, 198). The defendant does not maintain that he was so dressed in connection with an officially sanctioned masquerade party ''or like entertainment.'' Instead, he claims that he was not ''disguised by unusual or unnatural attire'' because at the time of his arrest he had plans to have a sex change operation and become a woman at some date in the future.

    B.   Under this Court's precedents, a defendant is ''disguised by unusual or unnatural attire'' when wearing clothing that misleads the public about the defendant's true gender.

This Court held in <u>Archibald</u> and in <u>Gillespi</u> that even the most innocent of reasons will not excuse disguising one's self with attire normally used by the opposite gender and going about in public with others similarly clothed. The defendant in <u>Archibald</u> was arrested on a subway platform while returning home from a masquerade party and wearing a dress, a wig, high-heeled shoes, makeup, and women's undergarments. He was convicted under § 887(7) of the prior Code of Criminal Procedure (since repealed, 1967 N.Y. Laws, ch. 681), which made no exception for masquerade parties and which provided that a person could be sentenced as a vagrant if he appeared in public ''disguised, in a manner calculated to prevent his being identified,'' N.Y. Code Crim. Proc. § 887(7) (McKinney 1958). Relying on the straightforward wording of the statute, the Appellate Term rejected the defendant's contention that ''the People must prove a specific intention of employing the disguise to commit some illegal act.'' <u>People v. Archibald</u>, 58 Misc. 2d 862, 863, 296 N.Y.S.2d 834, 836 (1968). This Court affirmed, without opinion but citing to <u>Gillespi</u>.

The defendants in <u>Gillespi</u> were also convicted under former Code of Criminal Procedure § 887(7) for dressing like the defendant in this case. They argued on appeal that the statute was unconstitutional, that evidence that a man wore a woman's clothing is not sufficient proof that he was ''disguised,'' and that such a conviction could not be sustained without

-6-

evidence of intent to mislead for a criminal purpose. This court nevertheless affirmed.

The only other reported New York case on this question is an Erie County Court decision from 1912, People v. Luechini, 75 Misc. 614, 136 N.Y.S. 319, which held for the defendant but which has certainly been overruled in substance by this Court's later decisions in Archibald and Gillespi. Only one other court in the United States, a municipal court in Ohio, has issued a reported decision adopting a position similar to the one urged by the defendant on this question, and that decision -- City of Columbus v. Zander, 25 Ohio Misc. 144, 266 N.E.2d 602 (Franklin County Mun. Ct. 1970) -- was based on a theory of diminished mental capacity that is not recognized in New York law. See N.Y. Penal Law §§ 15.00-15.25 (McKinney 1975).

Moreover, the Legislature could have placed words in § 240.35(4) requiring proof of a criminal purpose or creating an exception for disguises used by trans-sexuals, but it did neither of those things. This Court has held that ''where as here the statute de-scribes the particular situation in which it is to apply, 'an irrefutable inference must be drawn that what is omitted or not included was intended to be omitted or excluded.''' Patrolmen's Benevolent Ass'n v. City of New York, 41 N.Y.2d 205, 208-09, 359 N.E.2d 1338, 1341, 391 N.Y.S.2d 544, 546 (1976) (quoting Cons. Laws of N.Y., Book 1, Statutes, § 240 (McKinney 1971)). Section 240.35(4) unambiguously penalizes the act of appearing in public ''disguised by . . . unnat-ural attire'' with others ''so . . . disguised.'' This Court has held that, ''where the statutory language is clear and unambiguous, the court should construe it so as to give effect to the plain meaning of the words used.'' Patrolmen's Benevolent Ass'n, 41 N.Y.2d at 208, 359 N.E.2d at 1340, 391 N.Y.S.2d at 546. This Court has also ruled that, although the consequences of a particular interpretation may be important where a statute lends itself to two different meanings, ''[i]f the construction to be accorded a statute is clearly indicated, it is to be adopted by the courts regardless of consequences.'' Town of Smithtown v. Moore, 11 N.Y.2d 238, 244, 183 N.E.2d 66, 69, 228 N.Y.S.2d 657, 661 (1962). The plain meaning of § 240.35(4) is ''clearly indicated'' by the words the Legislature did use, and, although no legislative committee reports or similar documents explain the purpose of § 240.35(4), there are good reasons for drafting the statute as the Legislature did.

-7-

Section 240.35(4) is a necessary and reasonable regulation of public behavior. It does not prohibit an individual male from dressing up in female clothing and then appearing in public -- as shocking as that behavior might be to a very large proportion of the population. It does not even forbid several males from doing that at the same time, as long as the clothing does not create an illusion so complete as to obscure their true identities. The statute instead prohibits three or more persons from appearing in public disguised and in concert, and it does so because of the serious danger such behavior poses for others.

The difficulties of law enforcement would be magnified if a crime-ridden society were to permit the appearance in public of groups of people who cannot readily be identified, and for that reason legislatures in other states have enacted statutes similar to § 240.35(4). See Cal. Penal Code § 185 (West 1970); Okla. Stat. tit. 21 § 1301 (1983). In this state and elsewhere, the law of conspiracy is based on the concept that a greater public danger is created when criminals act together than where they act individually. The danger is multiplied where a disguise not only prevents identification of criminals after a robbery or other crime, but where the illusion created by the disguise is so convincing that a victim may firmly believe that he or she has been robbed by women although in fact the criminals were men. Moreover, where the disguise misleads the observer as to the true gender of a group of males, that group can gain admission to confined areas, such as washrooms, where women are particularly vulnerable to attack. If the defendant's interpretation of § 240.35(4) were to prevail in this Court, any three people who can demonstrate an interest in a sex change operation would be licensed to disguise their true identities and put the public at risk.

    C.   The People presented legally suffi-
        cient evidence that this defendant
        was ''disguised by unusual or unnat-
            ural attire.''

In reviewing trial evidence for legal sufficiency, the evidence must be viewed in the light most favorable to the People. People v. Malizia, 62 N.Y.2d 755, 465 N.E.2d 364, 476 N.Y.S.2d 825, cert. denied, 469 U.S. 932 (1984). Here, the defendant was disguised. He and

-8-

his co-defendants dressed as women, and the arresting
officer testified that he at first believed them to be
women (R. at 101). The defendant's own experts testified that his reproductive organs were male (R. at
373, 449). Although the defendant's doctors testified
that medical science sympathizes with his psychological confusion, the New Jersey Superior Court, Appellate Division, has noted that ''most experts would be
satisfied'' that a pre-operative transsexual, such as
the defendant, ''should be classified according to the
biological criteria,'' M.T. v. J.T., 140 N.J. Super.
77, 86, 355 A.2d 204, 209 (1976) (dicta) (emphasis
supplied). In M.T., a post-operative transsexual had
married and subsequently sued for support and mainte-
nance. The husband argued that the marriage was void
because the transsexual had always been male. In a
thorough opinion, the New Jersey Appellate Division
carefully considered the medical literature and legal
authority and concluded that, although a pre-operative
transsexual is a male, a sex change operation could
render one female.

Even as to post-operative transsexuals, New York
authority is not very confident that a man can ever
become a woman. One trial court has held that a health
insurer can be made to pay for a sex change operation
if it is not explicitly excluded in the insurance
policy, Davidson v. Aetna Life & Casualty Ins. Co.,
101 Misc. 2d 1, 420 N.Y.S.2d 450 (Sup. Ct., N.Y.
County 1979), but that court held only that the operation could alleviate psychological suffering, not that
it could produce a woman. Another trial court did hold
that for practical purposes a post-operative transsexual could be considered the equivalent of a woman,
Richards v. United States Tennis Ass'n, 93 Misc. 2d
713, 400 N.Y.S.2d 267 (Sup. Ct., N.Y. County 1977),
but that decision remains the opinion of a single
trial court unreviewed on appeal and joined only by
dicta in an isolated change-of-name case, In re Anonymous, 57 Misc. 2d 813, 293 N.Y.S.2d 834 (Sup. Ct.,
N.Y. County 1968). Another change-of-name decision
specifically refused to consider the question of
whether a post-operative transsexual had acquired the
opposite gender. In re Anonymous, 64 Misc. 2d 309, 314
N.Y.S.2d 668 (Sup. Ct., N.Y. County 1970).

Even Richards, a trial court decision, does not
accurately represent the law generally. All of the
reported cases that have considered that matter have
held that pre-surgery transsexuals are not considered
women under the various federal and state statutes
that prohibit sex discrimination in employment. See,

-9-

for example, <u>Sommers v. Budget Marketing, Inc.</u>, 667
F.2d 748 (8th Cir. 1982); <u>Kirkpatrick v. Seligman &</u>
<u>Latz, Inc.</u>, 636 F.2d 1047 (5th Cir. 1981); <u>Holloway v.</u>
<u>Arthur Andersen & Co.</u>, 566 F.2d 659 (9th Cir. 1977);
<u>Sommers v. Iowa Civil Rights Comm'n</u>, 337 N.W.2d 470
(Ia. 1983). In each of these decisions, a pre-surgery
transsexual's cross-dressing disguise caused so much
difficulty with restrooms and other aspects of the
work place that the courts held it justifiable to fire
the transsexual. Even post-surgery transsexuals have
not been protected by the same statutes. <u>Ulane v.</u>
<u>Eastern Airlines, Inc.</u>, 742 F.2d 1081 (7th Cir. 1984),
<u>cert. denied</u>, 471 U.S. 1017 (1985); <u>In re Grossman</u>,
127 N.J. Super 13, 316 A.2d 39 (1974).

Moreover, although the New York City Board of
Health will issue an amended birth certificate to a
post-operative transsexual, deleting any reference to
gender and incorporating a court-ordered change of
name, courts have repeatedly refused to compel the
Board to issue birth certificates that call transsexuals women, even after surgery. <u>Anonymous v. Mellon</u>,
91 Misc. 2d 375, 398 N.Y.S.2d 99 (Sup. Ct., N.Y.
County 1977); <u>Hartin v. Director of Bureau of Records</u>
<u>& Statistics</u>, 75 Misc. 2d 229, 347 N.Y.S.2d 515 (Sup.
Ct., N.Y. County 1973); <u>Anonymous v. Weiner</u>, 50 Misc.
2d 380, 270 N.Y.S.2d 319 (Sup. Ct., N.Y. County 1966).
These courts have acquiesced in the Board of Health's
adoption of a report by the New York Academy of
Science, which found that, even after surgery, ''male-
to-female transsexuals are still chromosomally males
while ostensibly females,'' and which warned that a
post-operative transsexual's desire for ''concealment
of a change of sex . . . is outweighed by the public
interest for protection against fraud.'' <u>Weiner</u>, 50
Misc. 2d at 382-83, 270 N.Y.S.2d at 322 (quoting the
Academy report). For these and other reasons, New York
has moved with caution where the aspirations of transsexuals have led them to seek special benefits. For
example, this Court has affirmed the denial by the
Commissioner of Social Services of financial assistance to pay for a sex change operation desired by an
indigent transsexual. <u>Denise R. v. Lavine</u>, 39 N.Y.2d
279, 347 N.E.2d 893, 383 N.Y.S.2d 568 (1976).

Thus, there was legally sufficient evidence before
that court substantiating every element of the offense
defined by § 240.35(4), and the Criminal Court therefore properly denied the defendant's motion for a
trial order of dismissal.

-10-

II.   THE CRIMINAL COURT PROPERLY DENIED
      THE DEFENDANT'S MOTION TO DISMISS
      THE INFORMATION BECAUSE PENAL LAW
      § 240.35(4) DOES NOT VIOLATE THE
      UNITED STATES CONSTITUTIONAL RIGHT
      TO PRIVACY.

A.   Section 240.35(4) would violate the
     constitutional right to privacy only
     if the defendant could demonstrate
     that it is not rationally connected
     to any need for public protection.

The United States Supreme Court has held that a
state can regulate attire without offending the constitutional right to privacy so long as there is a
rational connection between that regulation and some
form of protection provided to the public. In the
leading decision on the question, the Court distinguished an interest in controlling one's own appearance from the more well-established right to control
one's body, and it concluded that the Constitution
allows a government more freedom to regulate appearance than ''certain basic matters of procreation,
marriage, and family life.'' Kelley v. Johnson, 425
U.S. 238, 244 (1976). Under Griswold v. Connecticut,
381 U.S. 479 (1965), Roe v. Wade, 410 U.S. 113 (1973),
and their progeny, a state can regulate an individual's
decisions concerning procreation and allied questions
only if the state can demonstrate that it has a compelling interest in doing so and that its means of
regulation are the least restrictive manner of satisfying that interest.
     But in Kelley, the Court ruled that a state has the
power to regulate an individual's appearance unless
that individual can demonstrate that the state's
regulation ''is so irrational that it may be branded
'arbitrary' and therefore a deprivation of [the individual's] 'liberty' interest in freedom to choose his
own'' appearance. Id. at 248. And in Bowers v. Hardwick, 478 U.S. 186, 190 (1986), where the Court determined that a homosexual's right to privacy was not
violated by a state sodomy statute, the Court interpreted its right-to-privacy precedents to require a
compelling state interest only in matters of marriage,
procreation, contraception, abortion, child rearing,
education, and family relationships. In the only
reported decision to consider whether a statute like
§ 240.35(4) violates the constitutional right to

-11-

privacy, the Illinois Supreme Court did not require a
compelling state interest and instead applied the
rational connection test. City of Chicago v. Wilson,
75 Ill. 2d 525, 389 N.E.2d 522 (1978).

   A compelling state interest is not required here
because the right to dress as one pleases -- if it is
a right at all -- is not one of the fundamental rights
at the core of constitutional freedoms. In Bowers, the
Supreme Court held that ''[n]o connection between
family, marriage, or procreation on the one hand and
homosexual activity on the other has been demonstrated.'' Id. at 191. Nor is there any connection
between family, marriage, or procreation and men
disguising themselves as women. In Kelley, the Court
even declined to determine whether the Fourteenth
Amendment -- and presumably the right to privacy
inherent therein -- actually provides a right to wear
whatever one wants. Id. at 244. Instead, the Court
merely assumed the existence of such a right because
the regulation there at issue was so plainly supported
by a rational connection to the public interest that
the more difficult question of whether such a right
exists at all could be deferred to another day. Id.
Where a fundamental right has been found in a case
involving personal appearance, the matter of appearance has been merely incidental to a First Amendment
issue of freedom of speech, not a right to privacy.
See Cohen v. California, 403 U.S. 15 (1971) (antiwar
slogan on jacket); Tinker v. Des Moines Indep. Community School Dist., 393 U.S. 503 (1969) (antiwar arm-
bands). Since Kelley, abundant precedent has permitted
governmental regulation of appearance because individuals challenging the regulation of appearance were
unable to demonstrate that it lacked a rational connection with a need to protect the public in some way.
See, for example, South Fla. Free Beaches, Inc. v.
City of Miami, 734 F.2d 608 (11th Cir. 1984) (ordinance
prohibiting shirtless jogging); Harper v. Lindsay, 616
F.2d 849 (5th Cir. 1980) (ordinance regulating attire
of massage parlor employees); Williams v. Kleppe, 539
F.2d 803 (1st Cir. 1976) (prohibition on nude bathing).

         B.   The defendant has not shown that
              § 240.35(4) lacks a rational
              connection to some need for
              public protection.

   Under the rational connection or rational basis
test, a ''law need not be in every respect logically

-12-

consistent with its aims to be constitutional. It is
enough that there is an evil at hand for correction,
and that it might be thought that the particular
legislative measure was a rational way to correct
it.'' <u>Williamson v. Lee Optical, Inc.</u>, 348 U.S. 483,
487-88 (1955). In <u>Williamson</u>, the Court held that an
Oklahoma statute was constitutional because none of
the rights asserted against it were fundamental and
because it had a rational connection to an identifiable
risk to the public. Among other things, the statute
prohibited opticians (who grind lenses and fit frames)
from selling eyeglasses except on a prescription
written by an optometrist or an ophthalmologist, both
of whom have at least diagnostic training and the
latter medical training as well. Although the Court
recognized that the Oklahoma statute ''may exact a
needless, wasteful requirement in many cases,'' it
found a rational connection, sufficient to justify the
statute, because ''in <u>some</u> cases the directions contained in the prescription are essential'' and the
''legislature <u>might</u> have concluded'' that wastefulness
on many occasions is balanced by what is essential on
others. <u>Id</u>. at 487 (emphasis supplied). Thus, the
essence of the test is deference to the legislature,
as ''it is for the legislature, not the courts, to
balance the advantages and disadvantages'' of a statute that need be supported only by a rational connection to a public need.

So, too, in <u>Kelley</u>, the Court upheld a police
department's regulation of its officers' hair groom-
ing. The Court pointed to the public's interest in
being served by police officers neatly and uniformly
attired and groomed, and it concluded that governmental decisions of this kind are ''entitled to the same
sort of presumption of legislative validity as are
state choices designed to promote other aims'' within
the state's general authority. <u>Id</u>. at 247. The Court
held it to be reversible error to evaluate such a
challenge on the basis of ''whether the State can
'establish' a 'genuine public need' for the specific
regulation'' because the true test is whether the
party challenging the regulation ''can demonstrate
that there is no rational connection between the
regulation . . . and the promotion of safety of persons and property.'' <u>Id</u>. In <u>Bowers</u>, the Supreme Court
went even further and held that a legislature can have
a rational basis to proscribe conduct simply because
the public perceives it to be ''immoral and unacceptable.''

The defendant has not carried such a burden in this

-13-

appeal. This Court has affirmed convictions under
§ 240.35(4)'s predecessor statute, People v. Archibald,
27 N.Y.2d 504, 260 N.E.2d 871, 312 N.Y.S.2d 678 (1970);
People v. Gillespi, 15 N.Y.2d 529, 202 N.E. 2d 565,
254 N.Y.S.2d 121, amended, 15 N.Y.2d 675, 204 N.E.2d
211, 255 N.Y.S.2d 884 (1964), and other states have
similar enactments, Cal. Penal Code § 185 (West 1970);
Okla. Stat. tit. 21, § 1301 (1983) -- all because of
the danger that would be created if groups of people
were permitted to disguise their identities in public
without any supervision by the police and because of
the deeply held public belief that it is immoral for a
person to disguise his or her true gender. Even Professor Tribe notes that governments throughout the
world have traditionally felt it within their competence to regulate attire for the public good. L.
Tribe, American Constitutional Law, 960-61 (1978). In
a modern society that is more mobile and anonymous
than ever before, it would be cause for insecurity
among public and police if potential crime victims
could not be confident that groups of strangers met on
the street and elsewhere are in fact who and what they
appear to be.

The type of disguise chosen by the defendant in
this appeal is a particular cause for governmental
concern. It is immediately clear that people who
disguise themselves with ski masks or the like are
involved in something suspicious, even if those people
are not identifiable. Here, however, the defendant and
his companions so convincingly dressed themselves up
as women that the arresting officer did not at first
recognize them to be men (R. at 101). They could have
gained entrance to a women's washroom, to the dressing
rooms in apparel stores, and to other areas where
women would be vulnerable to harassment or attack.
They could also have committed a crime while deceiving
the victim into believing that the perpetrators were
women and not men. Even if these particular men were
not disguised in order to commit crimes, the Legislature is entitled -- under the rule articulated in
Williamson and like cases -- to ''balance the advantages and disadvantages'' and to regulate together
both the truly dangerous and the apparently dangerous
where the Legislature deems that necessary to protect
the public and particularly where even the apparently
dangerous strikes the public as immoral.

For even lesser reasons, regulation of the attire
of massage parlor employees has been permitted, even
though many employees might inadvertently violate the
regulations for perfectly innocent reasons. See, for

-14-

example, <u>Harper v. Lindsay</u>, 616 F.2d 849 (5th Cir.
1980). Prohibitions on nude bathing, <u>Williams v.
Kleppe</u>, 539 F.2d 803 (1st Cir. 1976), and even shirtless jogging, <u>South Fla. Free Beaches, Inc. v. City of
Miami</u>, 734 F.2d 608 (11th Cir. 1984), have been upheld,
although the public interest they protect is only
aesthetic.

Although the Illinois Supreme Court, in <u>City of
Chicago v. Wilson</u>, 75 Ill. 2d 525, 389 N.E.2d 522
(1978), held that an ordinance similar to § 240.35(4)
could not be enforced against transsexuals, there are
two reasons why that holding should not be persuasive
in the instant appeal. The first is that, although the
<u>City of Chicago</u> court applied a rational connection
test to the challenged statute, it incorrectly placed
the burden of proof on the government, rather than on
the party challenging the ordinance. The court reasoned that ''the State is not relieved from showing
some justification for its intrusion,'' <u>id</u>. at 532,
389 N.E.2d at 524, and it concluded that ''[i]nasmuch
as the city has offered no evidence to substantiate
its reasons for infringing on the defendants' choice
of dress . . . we do find that section 192-8 as applied
to the defendants is an unconstitutional infringement
of their liberty interest,'' <u>id</u>. at 534, 389 N.E.2d at
525. In <u>Kelley</u>, the Supreme Court held this to be
error, and it there reversed a lower court that had
done the same thing. The second reason is that the
statute at issue in <u>City of Chicago</u> was a far more
drastic one than § 240.35(4). Section 192-8 of the
Chicago Municipal Code punished any person who appeared in public ''in a dress not belonging to his or
her sex,'' even when that person was alone. Section
240.35(4) does not do that: its scope is limited to
the more dangerous situation in which people appear in
public both disguised <u>and</u> in groups.

Not only is § 240.35(4) narrowly drawn, but a
conviction under it does not create a criminal record
because the offense it defines is a violation and not
a crime. N.Y. Penal Law §§ 10.00(1), (3), (6) (McKinney
1983); N.Y. Crim. Proc. Law § 160.60 (McKinney 1971).
Moreover, the impact of § 240.35(4) on the defendant
in this appeal is not very substantial. The statute
does not prohibit him from dressing as a woman before
he has a sex change operation. It punishes him only
for so dressing in public with two or more other men
who are doing the same thing. Both the defendant's
physician and the defendant's psychiatrist testified
that if he were to refrain before his surgery from
going out in public with other men dressed as women,

-15-

there would be no ''significant'' detrimental effect
on his pre-operative therapy (R. at 408, 449).

The defendant mistakenly relies on <u>People v.
Onofre</u>, 51 N.Y.2d 476, 415 N.E.2d 936, 434 N.Y.S.2d
947 (1980), <u>cert. denied</u>, 451 U.S. 987 (1981). <u>Onofre</u>
was impliedly overruled by the Supreme Court in <u>Bowers</u>
because the New York sodomy statute struck down in
<u>Onofre</u> was in every substantive way identical to the
Georgia sodomy statute upheld by the Supreme Court in
<u>Bowers</u>. Moreover, <u>Onofre</u> was not premised on any
provision of the New York State Constitution, and the
ever-expanding federal right-to-privacy theory enunci-
ated in <u>Onofre</u> is condemned in <u>Bowers</u>, 478 U.S. at
194-95.

Thus, § 240.35(4) does not violate the defendant's
right to privacy under the United States Constitution,
and the Criminal Court properly denied his motion to
dismiss the information.

<u>CONCLUSION</u>

For all the foregoing reasons, the defendant's
conviction should be affirmed.

Hon. Martha Bosley
District Attorney
New York County
BY: Allan Kuusinen, Esq.
Asst. District Attorney
1 Hogan Place
New York, N.Y. 10013
(212) 555-1111

-16-

475

Index

Index

Index